Transport Policy and Planning in Great Britain

How can we manage transport in the 21st century? Peter Headicar makes sense of this large and complex field with explanations of the nature and origin of current policy and planning in Britain as well as the instruments available to national and local governments for tackling problems and fostering sustainable development. The decisions taken about policies and priorities are explored alongside the mechanisms through which choices about the future are conceived and evaluated. In particular, this book addresses the links between transport and spatial planning which are often poorly appreciated.

Designed as an essential text for transport planning students and as a source of reference for planning practitioners, it also furthers understanding of related fields such as urban and regional planning, environmental studies and public policy. Based on the postgraduate course the author developed at Oxford Brookes University, this indispensable text draws on a lifetime of professional experience in the field.

Peter Headicar is Reader in Transport Planning at Oxford Brookes where he leads the postgraduate teaching programme in transport.

The Natural and Built Environment Series
Editor: Professor John Glasson
Oxford Brookes University

Transport Policy and Planning in Great Britain
Peter Headicar

Introduction to Rural Planning
Nick Gallent, Meri Juntti, Sue Kidd and Dave Shaw

Regional Planning
John Glasson and Tim Marshall

Strategic Planning for Regional Development
Harry T. Dimitriou and Robin Thompson

Introduction to Environmental Impact Assessment
John Glasson, Riki Therivel and Andrew Chadwick

Methods of Environmental Impact Assessment
Peter Morris and Riki Therivel

Public Transport
Peter White

Urban Planning and Real Estate Development
John Ratcliffe and Michael Stubbs

Landscape Planning and Environmental Impact Design
Tom Turner

Controlling Development
Philip Booth

Partnership Agencies in British Urban Policy
Nicholas Bailey, Alison Barker and Kelvin MacDonald

Development Control
Keith Thomas

Expert Systems and Geographic Information Systems for Impact Assessment
Agustin Rodriguez-Bachiller and John Glasson

Transport Policy and Planning in Great Britain

Peter Headicar

Routledge
Taylor & Francis Group

LONDON AND NEW YORK

First published 2009
by Routledge
2 Park Square, Milton Park, Abingdon, Oxon OX14 4RN

Simultaneously published in the USA and Canada
by Routledge
270 Madison Avenue, New York, NY 10016, USA

Routledge is an imprint of the Taylor & Francis Group, an informa business

© 2009 Peter Headicar

Typeset in Goudy by
HWA Text and Data Management, London
Printed and bound in Great Britain by
CPI Antony Rowe, Chippenham, Wiltshire

British Library Cataloguing in Publication Data
A catalogue record for this book is available from the British Library

Library of Congress Cataloging-in-Publication Data
Headicar, Peter.
    Transport policy and planning in Great Britain / Peter Headicar.
        p. cm. – (The natural and built environment series)
    Includes bibliographical references and index.
    1. Transportation and state – Great Britain. 2. Transportation – Great
    Britain – Planning. I. Title.
    HE243.H43 2009
    388.0941–dc22   2008035192

ISBN 10: 0–415–46986–4 (hbk)
ISBN 10: 0–415–46987–2 (pbk)
ISBN 10: 0–203–89446–4 (ebk)

ISBN13: 978–0–415–46986–9 (hbk)
ISBN13: 978–0–415–46987–6 (pbk)
ISBN13: 978–0–203–89446–0 (ebk)

Contents

Illustrations	xii
Preface	xvii
Abbreviations	xix
Introduction	1

PART I
The nature of transport   5

1 **Transport and economic development**   9
  1.1 Introduction   9
  1.2 Transport and the economy   9
  1.3 Transport supply   13
  1.4 Transport costs   18
  1.5 Car ownership, licence-holding and car availability   22

2 **Population, land use and travel**   26
  2.1 Introduction   26
  2.2 Population and settlement   26
  2.3 Age structure   28
  2.4 Household composition, size and income   29
  2.5 Economic activity and employment   30
  2.6 Land use patterns   33
  2.7 Personal activity and use of time   36
  2.8 Personal travel by mode and trip purpose   39
  2.9 Variations in travel by settlement size and socio-economic group   42

3 **Traffic, its impacts and public attitudes**   45
  3.1 Introduction   45
  3.2 Traffic volume, composition and distribution   46
  3.3 Casualties   49
  3.4 Perceived danger and insecurity   52

3.5 Noise	53
3.6 Local air pollution	55
3.7 Visual intrusion	57
3.8 Fuel consumption, CO_2 emissions and climate change	58
3.9 Public attitudes	59

PART II
The evolution of transport policy and planning — 65

4 Before mass motorisation: the period to 1955 — 67
4.1 Introduction	67
4.2 Early improvements to roads and waterways	68
4.3 The development of the railway network	69
4.4 Coping with the motor vehicle	71
4.5 Regulating urban passenger transport	73
4.6 Developing a national road network	75
4.7 Nationalised transport	76
4.8 Controlling development	77

5 The motorway age (1955–79) — 79
5.1 Introduction	79
5.2 The inter-urban motorway programme	79
5.3 The Reshaping of British Railways	82
5.4 Post-war town planning: new towns and green belts	84
5.5 Traffic in Towns	86
5.6 Urban transport planning	88
5.7 'Homes before Roads' – the demise of urban motorways	90
5.8 Maintaining socially necessary services	92
5.9 'The party's over' – adjusting to resource constraints	93

6 The Conservatives after 1979: 'rolling back the state' — 96
6.1 Introduction: the return of ideology	96
6.2 Testing the water: deregulation, commercialisation and privatisation	97
6.3 The assault on local government	98
6.4 Bus deregulation	99
6.5 Rail privatisation	100
6.6 New rail developments	102
6.7 The re-making of development planning	104
6.8 Inner cities and urban development corporations	105
6.9 'Roads for Prosperity'	106

**7 The 1990s paradigm shift: new realism and sustainable
    development**   109
7.1 Introduction   109
7.2 Climb-down over the National Roads Programme   110
7.3 The new realism   111
7.4 'Sustainable development'   113
7.5 PPG13 – 'Reducing the need to travel'   115
7.6 Environmental assessment   117
7.7 The 'Great Debate'   118
7.8 The revival of planning   120
7.9 Local transport planning   121

8 A new deal for transport?: New Labour 1997–2004   123
8.1 Introduction   123
8.2 'A consensus for radical change'   123
8.3 The content of the 1998 White Paper   125
8.4 Changes to local and regional government   128
8.5 The Ten-Year Transport Plan   129
*8.6 Blown off course: the road hauliers' blockade and the
     Hatfield rail crash*   132
8.7 Breaking the Logjam – urban road user charging   134
8.8 'Sustainable Communities Plan'   135
8.9 Clearing the decks – the 2004 White Paper   137

**PART III
Ends and means**   141

9 The State and its role   143
9.1 Introduction   143
9.2 The nature of 'the State'   144
9.3 The role of the State   146
9.4 Sources of market failure   147
9.5 The treatment of equity   152
9.6 Conclusion on State action   156

10 Institutional arrangements   157
10.1 Introduction   157
10.2 The structuring of Central Government   158
10.3 Devolved government and regional administration   164
10.4 Public and private ownerships   166
10.5 Executive agencies and other public bodies   168
10.6 Local government   169

11 Policy aims: issues, objectives and targets   176
  11.1 Introduction   176
  11.2 Issues   176
  11.3 The role of objectives   182
  11.4 Objectives set nationally   183
  11.5 The role of targets   186
  11.6 Targets set nationally   189

12 Policy instruments (1): infrastructure investment   192
  12.1 Introduction   192
  12.2 The nature of investment   193
  12.3 The rationale for public investment   194
  12.4 The financing of public investment   197
  12.5 Recent government policy towards transport investment   200
  12.6 Investment appraisal and cost-benefit analysis   203

**13 Policy instruments (2): the regulation of vehicles, operators
     and services**   207
  13.1 Introduction   207
  13.2 The licensing of motor vehicles, drivers and operators   208
  13.3 Competition in the transport industries   210
  13.4 Rail regulation   213
  13.5 Regulation of bus and coach services   214
  13.6 Taxis and other demand-responsive transport   220
  13.7 Community transport   221

**14 Policy Instruments (3): the regulation of traffic
     and development**   223
  14.1 Introduction   223
  14.2 The changing role of traffic management   224
  14.3 Traffic management: responsibilities and powers   225
  14.4 Network management   228
  14.5 Control of on-street parking   229
  14.6 Speed limits   231
  14.7 Traffic calming and street management   233
  14.8 Air quality management   235
  14.9 Control of development (including private off-street parking)   237

15 Policy instruments (4): fiscal measures   242
  15.1 Introduction   242
  15.2 Motoring taxation   243
  15.3 Parking charges   245
  15.4 Road user charging   247

15.5 Rail passenger service subsidies and fare regulation   249
15.6 Bus service subsidies   251
15.7 Concessionary fares   253
15.8 School transport   256

16 Behavioural change measures ('Smarter Choices')   258
16.1 Introduction   258
16.2 Car dependency   259
16.3 The stance of central government   262
16.4 Overview of 'Smarter Choices'   263
16.5 Travel plans   266
16.6 Marketing and the 'Sustainable Towns' initiative   271

PART IV
Strategies, plans and planning procedures   275

17 National planning   277
17.1 Introduction   277
17.2 The nature of planning   277
17.3 The pattern of plans   280
17.4 The meaning of 'national planning'   282
17.5 National planning in England   283
17.6 National planning in Wales   286
17.7 National planning in Scotland   288
17.8 Sub-national planning: an overview   290

18 Regional strategies   293
18.1 Introduction   293
18.2 Strategic planning in the English regions   293
18.3 Regional Spatial Strategies   296
18.4 Regional Transport Strategies   300
18.5 Changes consequent on the Sub-National Review   302
18.6 Strategic planning in London   304
18.7 Regional Transport Strategies in Wales   305
18.8 Regional Transport Strategies in Scotland   308

19 Local development frameworks, community strategies and area agreements   311
19.1 Introduction   311
19.2 Distinctive features of the development planning system   312
19.3 The role of local development plans   313
19.4 Local Development Frameworks   315
19.5 The form and content of development plan documents   319

19.6 *Local development planning in Wales and Scotland*   322
19.7 *Sustainable Community Strategies*   323
19.8 *The new local performance framework and Local
    Area Agreements*   325

20 **Local transport plans**   330
20.1 *Introduction*   330
20.2 *The role of Local Transport Plans*   330
20.3 *Procedures for preparing LTPs*   332
20.4 *The funding context for LTPs*   335
20.5 *The form and content of LTPs*   338
20.6 *Objectives and priorities*   339
20.7 *Performance indicators and targets*   341
20.8 *The treatment of major schemes*   343
20.9 *Local Transport Planning in London, Wales and Scotland*   344

21 **Project appraisal**   348
21.1 *Introduction*   348
21.2 *The common appraisal process and its significance*   348
21.3 *The Appraisal Summary Table (AST)*   349
21.4 *Forecasts and modelling*   351
21.5 *'Value for money'*   353
21.6 *The generation of proposals*   361
21.7 *Supplementary analyses*   363
21.8 *Sustainability Appraisal (SEA)*   366

22 **The approval of plans and projects**   367
22.1 *Introduction*   367
22.2 *Regional Spatial Strategies and Development Plan Documents*   367
22.3 *Individual development proposals*   370
22.4 *Public inquiries*   372
22.5 *The Infrastructure Planning Commission*   374
22.6 *Regional Funding Allocation*   377
22.7 *Funding approval for major transport schemes*   380

PART V
The contemporary policy agenda   385

23 **The immediate agenda**   387
23.1 *Introduction*   387
23.2 *The National Roads Programme*   387
23.3 *National road user charging*   390
23.4 *The Transport Innovation Fund*   392

23.5 A strategy for National Rail   394
23.6 Putting Passengers First   397
23.7 Transport governance in city regions   400
23.8 Growth Points, Eco-towns and the Community Infrastructure
      Levy   402
23.9 The DfT's current 'vision' and targets   405

24 **Future scenarios and strategic choices**   408
24.1 Introduction   408
24.2 Thinking about the future   409
24.3 The Stern Review and the Climate Change Programme   411
24.4 Further scenarios for reducing CO_2 emissions from transport   413
24.5 The Eddington Report   418
24.6 Roads and Reality   421
24.7 Towards a Sustainable Transport System   425
24.8 Goals, challenges and the NATA refresh   428

25 **Postscript: thinking afresh**   433
25.1 Introduction   433
25.2 A holistic view: behavioural change not business as usual   434
25.3 Priority objectives: reducing traffic growth and
      protecting accessibility   437
25.4 Lessening individual car ownership   438
25.5 Rethinking inter-urban travel   442
25.6 Better use of inter-urban roads   444
25.7 Conclusion   448

Bibliography   449
Government publications   456
Index   461

Illustrations

Figures

1.1	Growth in passenger and freight transport compared with GDP 1958–98	12
1.2	The national road network	14
1.3	The national rail passenger network	17
1.4	Bus mileage operated by area 1985/86–2006/07	18
1.5	Punctuality and reliability of national rail services 1997/98– 006/07	21
1.6	Changes in real income and transport costs by mode 1980–2006	22
1.7	Households with regular use of cars	23
1.8	Household car ownership by area type	24
1.9	Car availability amongst adults 1975/76–2006	25
2.1	Households by household type 1971–2001	30
2.2	Personal accessibility to facilities on foot or by public transport	35
2.3	Trips in progress by hour of day	37
2.4	Trips by age by purpose	39
2.5	Travel by car and all other mechanised modes 1952–2006	40
2.6	Travel by non-car modes 1952–2006	40
2.7	Distance travelled per person per week as a car driver	42
2.8	Travel per person by age group and by mode	43
2.9	Walking difficulty by age group	43
2.10	Travel per person by car availability and by mode	44
3.1	Road traffic 1950–2006	47
3.2	Road traffic by category 1950–2006	47
3.3	Change in traffic volume by road type 1976–2006	48
3.4	Distribution of traffic between road classes by vehicle type 1986 and 2006	49
3.5	Fatalities per year on the highway network 1950–2006 by user group	50
3.6	Road casualties and casualty rates 1950–2006	50
3.7	Change from 1986 in road casualty rates by user group	51
3.8	Transport as a source of air pollution in UK 2005	56
3.9	Change in pollutant emissions from transport and other end users UK 1990–2005	56

3.10   Fuel consumption by transport and other uses UK 1980–2006   58
3.11   CO$_2$ emissions from domestic transport and non transport sources
       UK 1980–2006   59
3.12   Opinion ratings of road-related issues listed by priority for action   61
3.13   Hierarchy of transport needs   62
10.1   The pattern of devolved administration   158
10.2   The main divisions of sub-national government in England   172
12.1   Indexed comparison of GDP and transport expenditure 1991–2011   201
12.2   Public and private investment 1991–2001 and planned 2001–2011   202
13.1   Bus passenger journeys in London and other areas 1982–2005   217
15.1   Petrol price and its components 1992–2006   244
15.2   Rail subsidy and patronage 1980–2005   249
15.3   Local authority support for local bus services by area
       1996/97–2006/07   253
15.4   Concessionary fare reimbursement by area 1984/85–2005/06   255
17.1   Planning and plans in the wider context of governance   278
17.2   The hierarchy of plans 'translating aspiration into action'   280
17.3   The relationship of the National Transport Strategy to other
       planning instruments in Scotland   288
17.4   The pattern of plans for England (outside London), London,
       Wales and Scotland   290
18.1   The relationship of Regional Spatial Strategies to other planning
       processes   295
18.2   The 'streamlined process' proposed for Integrated
       Regional Strategies   304
18.3   Regional Transport Consortia in Wales   306
18.4   Scottish Regional Transport Partnerships   309
19.1   The local development framework   316
19.2   The development plan document (DPD) process   318
19.3   The New Local Government Performance Framework   327
19.4   New Local Area Agreements   328
21.1   Illustration of variable demand forecasting   353
21.2   The overall study process   362
22.1   DfT contribution to local authority major scheme costs   382
24.1   UK MARKAL-Macro model emissions reduction pathways   414
24.2   Effects of additional capacity and pricing on flows and speeds
       on the strategic network in 2041   424
24.3   Eddington's suggested long-term decision-making cycle   426
24.4   Indicative timetable for preparation of 2012 forward
       transport plans   427
24.5   Strategic transport corridors   428
24.6   Initial assessment of challenges underlying transport goals   432

Tables

1.1   Average length of passenger journeys and freight haul
      1976 and 2006   12

1.2	Proportion of households within specified walking times of nearest railway station and bus stop	15
2.1	Population, density and cars per household by settlement size	28
2.2	Number of trips and average trip time by trip purpose in 2006 and change from 1995/97	38
2.3	Trips and miles per person and average trip length by main mode in 2006 and change from 1995/97	41
2.4	Miles per person, average trip length and speed by purpose in 2006 and change from 1995/97	41
3.1	Sources of noise and levels of response	54
3.2	Proportion of respondents viewing a range of traffic impacts as 'very serious for them' in 1995	60
3.3	Opinion ratings of bus and train-related issues, listed by priority for action	62
10.1	Overview of public bodies and powers in relation to transport and land use	160
10.2	The structuring of Central Government in relation to transport, planning and the environment 1997–2008	162
10.3	Owners and operators of light rail and metro systems in the UK	167
10.4	Local government in England outside London (by geographical county)	175
11.1	Objectives and sub-objectives in the NATA framework	185
11.2	Objectives and PSA targets published in 2004	190
13.1	Rail passenger franchises	215
14.1	Recommended speed limits for single-carriageway roads in rural areas	233
15.1	Sources of bus service support in England 2007/08	251
16.1	Car reliance: percentage of drivers for whom it would not be practicable to use other modes to undertake selected activities	260
16.2	Impact of soft factors on future traffic levels	265
16.3	Impact (car travel reduction) of different types of soft measure	265
19.1	Former ring-fenced transport-related grants transferred to the single Area-Based Grant from 2008/09	329
20.1	The formula-based element of LTP2 funding for 'integrated transport'	336
20.2	Changes arising from use of the formula approach to integrated block funding	337
20.3	Mandatory indicators for LTP2 (to 2008/09)	343
21.1	The public accounts worksheet	355
21.2	The transport economic efficiency worksheet	357
21.3	Values of time	358
21.4	VfM categories	359
21.5	Outline of affordability and financial sustainability worksheet	365
23.1	Authorities awarded Congestion TIF 'pump-priming' funding	393
23.2	Forecast rail passenger revenue and application of Government funding 2009/10–2013/14	396

24.1   Expected carbon savings from transport measures included
       in the Climate Change Programme [MtC a year against 1990 base]   413
24.2   Potential carbon reduction from policy packages and
       selected measures   416
24.3   Better use measures   420
25.1   Promoting travel choices for motorway journeys utilising new
       interchanges   446

Boxes

2.1   Local geography and spatial polarisation   32
3.1   Nature and effects of pollutants from transport   55
7.1   Principles of the New Realism   112
8.1   Principal outputs expected to be delivered by the Ten-Year
       Plan (to 2010)   131
10.1   Executive agencies and non-departmental public bodies
       sponsored by the Department for Transport (select list)   169
11.1   An illustrative list of transport-related issues   178
11.2   'The New Deal for Transport'   184
11.3   Roads: 'Where we want to be'   186
11.4   PSA targets relating to road traffic congestion   191
12.1   Monetised items included in DfT's cost-benefit analysis   206
13.1   Changes relevant to provision of bus services within the
       Transport Act 2000   218
14.1   Purposes for which a Traffic Regulation Order may be introduced   226
14.2   The Content of Air Quality Action Plans   236
14.3   Transport Assessments of development proposals   240
15.1   Proposed simplified national rail fare structure   251
16.1   Segmentation of the population into attitudinal types   261
16.2   Types of soft measure   264
16.3   Policy initiatives important in fulfilling the potential of Smart
       Choices   266
17.1   Stages in an idealised planning process   278
17.2   The role of land use planning in relation to transport   284
18.1   Requirements of a Regional Spatial Strategy   298
18.1   Requirements of a Regional Transport Strategy   301
19.1   The nature of local spatial planning   315
19.2   Integration of transport and land use policies   320
19.3   Guidance on local development planning relevant to transport   321
19.4   Objectives of a Community Strategy   325
20.1   Features of the 2008 LTP2 Progress Reports   335
20.2   Performance management and direct engagement   342
21.1   DfT comparison of options for linking the A303 to the M5   360
22.1   Tests of soundness applied to Regional Spatial Strategies   369
22.2   Statutory consultees on development applications   371
22.3   The content of national policy statements   377
22.4   Criteria for regional funding allocation advice   378

22.5	Components of a major scheme business case	381
23.1	The Highways Agency's management system replacing the Targeted Programme of Improvements	389
23.2	Rail enhancements identified in the High Level Output Specification for Control Period 4 (2009–2014)	397
23.3	Changes to bus service regulation	399
23.4	Possible functions for sub-regional alliances	401
23.5	Proposals for delivering 2 million new homes by 2016	403
23.6	Indicators included in PSA5 (for 2008/09–2010/11)	406
24.1	Public attitudes to climate change and transport	418
24.2	The impact of transport on economic performance	419
24.3	Eddington's recommended objectives-led approach to planning	426
24.4	Future policy goals	430

Preface

The main reason for writing this book was the thoroughly unoriginal one that, in attempting to teach the subject at Oxford Brookes University, I found that there was nothing published which dealt with the subject in the way I thought it ought to be. As a lecturer this made life difficult – though challenging and ultimately rewarding. From the students' perspective it also meant that there was no easy way of bridging the gap between what they heard in the classroom and wading through a list of references a mile long.

The reasons for taking such an individualistic standpoint probably have to do with my own educational and professional background. I was fortunate enough to take degrees in land use planning, transport and public policy – a combination which has left me forever committed to the view that transport planning is about people, places and politics rather than vehicles, infrastructure and modelling. I also spent the first half of my professional career working in planning practice and have continued to think that this is an appropriate focus of interest even whilst working within the cloisters of academe. Unfortunately, as any glance at the academic transport journals will testify, this is not a perspective which appeals to many career researchers.

So a further reason for writing this book was to try and bridge a different sort of gap – the one noted by George Bernard Shaw when he said that 'those who can, do and those who can't, teach'. People who come to learn how planning and governance 'work' through experience at the highest professional levels do not normally have the time or inclination to write books. Equally those who are paid to write (literally in the performance-monitored industry of higher education) do not have a very good idea – it seems to me – of what planning in the real world is actually like. This book is not a manual for 'doing' transport planning or even a close study of 'what is being done' in a grass-roots sense but it is a view of the subject which I hope will be relevant and interesting to those who are working, or are setting out to work, in transport planning practice.

Anyone teaching or studying the subject is faced with the dilemma that, like the universe of which we are part, it seems to be expanding at something approaching the speed of light! Certainly the volume of material available via the web has these properties. Any course – any book – which attempts to chart something approaching the totality can therefore be but the merest glimpse. Hopefully, having tested it out on successive cohorts of students, the picture which is presented here will enable people working in particular fields to 'see where they are' and – equally important – see what others are doing and why and to make the connections between them.

The fact that this book has a single author hopefully means that it has a coherent structure and offers a reasonably comprehensive and integrated treatment of the subject. The downside is that there is a limit to what any one person – this one at least – can get their mind around and put into print if the book is ever to see the light of day. Inevitably therefore the span of topics and their treatment presented here is somewhat idiosyncratic. From an academic perspective I am also conscious that the book gives inadequate recognition of the work of those whose insights are secreted away in the many research journals. (Rectifying this would have delayed publication several more years!)

As far as students and other readers are concerned however I hope that sufficient references are given to provide 'leads' into the literature which people can pursue as they wish. The texts written by Stephen Glaister and others (2006) and by David Banister (2001 and 2005) provide valuable overviews with their own distinctive properties and are recommended as the first port of call before plunging into more specialised material. Iain Docherty and Jon Shaw's edited book *Traffic Jam* (2008) provides a timely analysis of the substance of transport policy in Britain under ten years of New Labour. Geoff Vigar's book (2002) reports on policy during a slightly earlier period but deserves special mention because it is so rare in attempting to bridge the theory–practice gap.

Space and time have prevented me from including even a taster of what the field of policy studies has to offer. However Michael Hill's text (2005) – originally trialled on me and others whilst a student at Bristol University – should be a definite follow-up for anyone interested in understanding the various dimensions of power and why things ultimately happen, or not, the way they do.

Special acknowledgement needs to be made of *Local Transport Today* – the unofficial 'house journal' of professional transport planners – and thanks offered to publisher Peter Stonham and editor Andrew Forster. It is unimaginable how we could all function without it, or how a book like this dealing with contemporary policy and practice could ever be written. In the later parts of the book there are many references to particular issue numbers (e.g. *LTT 450*) which are not listed in the bibliography. LTT offer an online database of all issues since 2004 and, if you don't already have it, you are strongly recommended to get access to it!

On a personal note I would like to thank John Glasson and Steve Ward for their initial encouragement to publish. My immediate colleagues at Oxford Brookes, Stephen Brown and Tim Jones, and successive cohorts of graduate students have given their interest and support which have made the running of the course and the 'project' of writing of this book seem worthwhile. In a different way the domestic support and forbearance of my partner Jill Loveday – confronted with someone apparently 'staring at a screen' for days and months on end – has been equally invaluable.

Ultimately, though, the book is dedicated to future students who I trust will want to engage with the complex, fascinating and vitally important subject that is transport planning. This book cannot resolve the complexity but will hopefully make it seem less bewildering – and thereby empower people who want to work in the field to go out and make their own, more effective contribution.

Abbreviations

AA	Automobile Association
ACORP	Association of Community Rail Partnerships
AONB	Area of Outstanding Natural Beauty
APR	Annual Progress Report (of Local Transport Plans)
AQMA	Air Quality Management Area
ASC	Approved Scheme Cost
AST	Appraisal Summary Table
ATCO	Association of Transport Coordinating Officers
ATM	Active Traffic Management (of motorways)
BAA	British Airports Authority
BCR	benefit/cost ratio
BERR	Department of Business, Enterprise and Regulatory Reform (successor to DTI since 2007)
BR	British Rail (1962–97)
BSA	British Social Attitudes
BSOG	Bus Service Operators Grant (formerly Fuel Duty Rebate)
BTC	British Transport Commission (1947–62)
CBA	cost benefit analysis
CBI	Confederation of British Industry
CCP	Climate Change Programme
CfIT	Commission for Integrated Transport
CIF	Community Infrastructure Fund
CIL	Community Infrastructure Levy
CP4	Control Period 4 (Rail 2009/10–2013/14)
CPA	Comprehensive Performance Assessment (of local authorities)
CPRE	Campaign for the Protection of Rural England
CPZ	controlled parking zone
CSR	Comprehensive Spending Review
CTA	Community Transport Association
CTRL	Channel Tunnel Rail Link
CVS	Council for Voluntary Service
dB(a)	A-weighted decibels (noise measurement)
DCLG	Department of Communities and Local Government (since 2006)
DCSF	Department for Children, Schools and Families (since 2007)
DECC	Department of Energy and Climate Change
Defra	Department of the Environment, Food and Rural Affairs (from 2001)

DETR	Department of Environment, Transport and the Regions (1997–2001)
DfES	Department for Education and Skills (to 2007)
DfT	Department for Transport (since 2002)
DG	Director General
DIUS	Department for Innovation, Universities and Skills (since 2007)
DIY	do-it-yourself
DOE	Department of the Environment (1970–97)
DPD	Development Plan Document (within LDFs)
DRT	Demand Responsive Transport
DTI	Department for Trade and Industry (to 2007)
DTLR	Department of Transport, Local Government and the Regions (2001–02)
DTp	Department of Transport (1977–97)
DVLA	Driver and Vehicle Licensing Agency
EIA	Environmental Impact Assessment
EIP	Examination in Public
EIS	Environmental Impact Statement
EU	European Union
EWS	English, Welsh, Scottish (privatised rail freight company)
GAF	Growth Area Funding
GDP	gross domestic product
GLA	Greater London Authority (since 1999)
GLC	Greater London Council (1965–86)
GLDP	Greater London Development Plan (pre-1986)
GOMMMS	Guidance on Methodology for Multi-Modal Studies
GOR	Government Offices for the Regions (later further abbreviated to GO, as in GOSE etc.)
HA	Highways Agency
HGV	heavy goods vehicle
HLOS	High Level Output Specification (national rail)
HOV	high occupancy vehicle (as in HOV lanes)
HQ	headquarters
HST	high speed train; see also IC125
IC125	Inter-city 125 (high-speed diesel train introduced in 1970s); also referred to as HST
ICI	Imperial Chemical Industries
ICT	information and communications technology
IHT	Institution of Highways and Transportation
IPC	Infrastructure Planning Commission
IPPR	Institute for Public Policy Research
IRS	Integrated Regional Strategy (proposed replacement in England for RSS/RTS and RES)
ITA	Integrated Transport Authority (proposed replacement of PTAs)
KSI	killed and seriously injured
LAA	Local Area Agreement
LDF	Local Development Framework (England)
LEA	Local Education Authority
LIP	Local Implementation Plan (variant of LTP used in London)
LSP	Local Strategic Partnership

LT	London Transport (to 1999)
LTP	Local Transport Plan
LTT	Local Transport Today (fortnightly publication)
MAA	Multi-Area Agreement
MCC	Metropolitan County Council (1974–86)
MHLG	Ministry of Housing and Local Government (pre-1970)
MMS	multi-modal study
MOT	Ministry of Transport (pre-1970)
MOV	multi-occupied vehicles (as in MOV lanes)
MP	Member of Parliament
MSA	motorway service area
MtC	megatonnes of carbon
NAO	National Audit Office
NATA	New Approach to Transport Appraisal
NBC	National Bus Company
NDPB	non-departmental public body
NHS	National Health Service
NPPG	National Planning Policy Guideline (Scotland)
NPV	net present value
NRTF	National Road Traffic Forecasts
NTM	National Transport Model
NTS	National Travel Survey
ODPM	Office of the Deputy Prime Minister (forerunner of DCLG during Prescott's period as Secretary of State 2002–06)
OFT	Office of Fair Trading
ONS	Office of National Statistics
OPRAF	Office of Passenger Rail Franchising (1993–2000)
ORR	Office of the Rail Regulator
PCV	passenger carrying vehicle
PGS	Planning Gain Supplement (proposal replaced by CIL)
PHV	private hire vehicles
PNR	private non-residential (parking space)
PPG	Planning Policy Guidance
PPP	Public Private Partnership
PPS	Planning Policy Statement
PRT	Personal Rapid Transit
PSA	Public Service Agreement
PSBR	Public Sector Borrowing Requirement
PSI	Policy Studies Institute
PSO	Public Service Obligation Grant (for provision of rail passenger services 1974–97)
PTA	Passenger Transport Authority
PTE	Passenger Transport Executive
PTEG	Passenger Transport Executive Group
PTP	Personalised Travel Plan
QC	(Bus) Quality Contract
QP	(Bus) Quality Partnership
QRA	Quantified Risk Assessment
RAC	Royal Automobile Club

RBC	Rural Bus Challenge
RBSG	Rural Bus Services Grant
RCEP	Royal Commission on Environmental Pollution
RDA	Regional Development Agency
RES	Regional Economic Strategy (England)
ROSCO	(Rail) Rolling Stock Company
RPB	Regional Planning Body (England)
RPG	Regional Planning Guidance (to 2004)
RSS	Regional Spatial Strategy (England; superceded RPG from 2004)
RTP	Regional Transport Partnership (Scotland)
RTP	Regional Transport Plan (Wales)
RTP	Residential Travel Plan
RTPI	Royal Town Planning Institute
RTS	Regional Transport Strategy (Scotland and England)
SACTRA	Standing Advisory Committee on Trunk Road Assessment
SCI	Statement of Community Involvement
SDS	Spatial Development Strategy (London)
SEA	Strategic Environmental Assessment
SNR	Sub-National Review (in England)
SoFA	Statement of Funds Available (national rail)
SoS	Secretary of State
SPZ	special parking zone
SRA	Strategic Rail Authority (1997–2005)
SSSI	Site of Special Scientific Interest
STAG	Scottish Transport Appraisal Guidance
STP	School Travel Plan
SUV	sports utility vehicle
TA	Transport Assessment
TAG	Transport Appraisal Guidance (England)
TCPA	Town and Country Planning Association
TfL	Transport for London (since 1999)
TIA	Traffic Impact Assessment
TIF	Transport Innovation Fund
TOC	train operating company
TPI	Targeted Programme of Improvements (Highways Agency)
TPP	Transport Policies and Programme (1974–99)
TPS	Transport Planning Society
TRL	Transport Research Laboratory
TRO	Traffic Regulation Order
TSG	Transport Supplementary Grant
TSGB	Transport Statistics in Great Britain (annual publication)
TSO	The Stationery Office (publisher of Government documents)
UDC	Urban Development Corporation
UK	United Kingdom
UTSG	Universities Transport Studies Group
VAT	value added tax
VED	Vehicle Excise Duty (annual road vehicle licence)
VfM	Value for Money
VOSA	Vehicle and Operators Services Agency

WAG	Welsh Assembly Government
WCML	West Coast Main Line
WelTAG	Welsh Transport and Planning Appraisal Guidance
WPL	Workplace Parking Levy
WSP	Wales Spatial Plan (but NB there is also a transport consultancy with the same initials)
WTP	Workplace Travel Plan

Introduction

Transport is a vital part of everyday life. It enables people to make their regular journeys from home to work, school and shop and provides the essential means of access to health care and other welfare services. It makes possible increasingly diverse and discriminating patterns of social and leisure activity. Businesses rely on transport to bring employees and customers to their premises and to convey the goods and services essential to their functioning. For all these purposes transport does not simply cater for existing requirements – it opens up (or constrains) opportunities individually and collectively.

Ideally transport would be a trouble-free, even pleasurable, activity. In a very large number of situations it is – probably more so than transport planners recognise (since inevitably their work tends to concentrate on problem areas). Even if not entirely trouble-free the benefits from transport in general, and the convenience of the private car in particular, means that there is a seemingly insatiable demand as incomes rise.

But of course transport and travel are *not* trouble-free – increasingly so as we seek to cram more of them into finite amounts of space and time. For many individuals the problems do not rise above the level of minor inconvenience or irritation – the delay of the occasional traffic queue, the bus or train which is late, or the difficulty in finding a parking space. But for others the consequences of transport inefficiency are more profound – commuters whose daily journey is a source of stress and fatigue, parents who are afraid to let children out on their own, people who feel marooned by inadequate public transport, householders whose lives are plagued by the noise and pollution of heavy traffic, businesses whose operations are undermined by congestion and unreliability. In aggregate the economic, social and environmental costs are colossal.

Faced with such poor and deteriorating conditions the ordinary person is likely to claim that 'they' (meaning some unspecified God-like agency who is watching over such things) should be doing something about it. However because of the scale and extent of problems – and the apparent inability of governments to tackle them successfully in the past – there is no great expectation that improvements will materialise. Rather a sense of inevitability prevails. Arguably traffic and transport have taken over the role previously occupied by the weather in the national psyche – a seeming force of Nature about which we can share common complaint but actually do nothing.

But of course, as a society, we *can* and are doing things about transport. However, exactly who does what, and how these actions contribute to the conditions we experience at any particular place and time is enormously complex. How and why are conditions the way they are? Who is responsible for doing something about them?

What determines whether they take action or not? What are the options available and what are their implications?

These are the kinds of question this book sets out to answer. They are applied to inland surface transport in general and personal travel and accessibility in particular. The focus of attention is on the behaviour of *public bodies* both in relation to matters over which they have direct control and those in which they seek to influence the behaviour of others – be they transport operators, other businesses or private individuals. The nature of the technical evidence used to inform or 'justify' public decisions on transport proposals is a particularly important feature. However the book is *not* a manual detailing the techniques of forecasting, design or assessment (activities which, somewhat confusingly, are often presented as 'transport planning' in themselves).

Anyone looking to the transport planning process as a means of bringing about improvements is likely to be confronted by a series of obstacles of the 'I wouldn't start from here' variety. The context in which planning is undertaken for the future is inextricably tied to the legacy inherited from the past. Understanding the complexity of the present 'operating environment' is the pre-requisite for effective planning and is the raison d'etre for writing this book.

To help develop this understanding the book is organised in five main parts:

- Part 1 'The nature of transport' – describes the characteristics of travel and transport provision, and the perceptions people have of them, in the context of trends over the last 50 years.
- Part 2 'The evolution of transport policy and planning' – reviews the main features of public decision-making in the fields of transport and land use planning to date. This is in broadly chronological order, organised around a series of themes which characterise the nature or intention of policies being pursued during particular periods. Their collective outcome is the legacy within which travel and transport planning are undertaken today.
- Part 3 'Ends and means' – considers the main dimensions of public choice surrounding transport, viz:

  - whether to 'intervene' at all (given that transport and travel can and do exist independently of any action by the State)
  - which objectives to aim for (i.e. the 'ends' to be pursued)
  - which instruments to employ (i.e. the 'means' for achieving these ends).

  In each case the contemporary situation is examined in relation to arguments of principle and to practical possibilities which have either been adopted in the past or might be adopted in future.
- Part 4 'Strategies, plans and planning procedures' – examines the formal mechanisms which exist for translating national policies into plans and programmes at regional and local levels. The opportunities available for people to raise and challenge options and the criteria by which these are judged are critical in determining eventual outcomes. Hence the rules governing planning procedures and the approval of plans and projects are themselves a key area of policy choice.
- Part 5 'The contemporary policy agenda' – reviews recent Government initiatives which define the current official policy agenda. It also explores longer-term scenarios and reports on work under way in planning for the period after 2014. Finally a personal reflection is offered on the innovations which need

to be pursued if transport is to play its part in an overall strategy of sustainable development.

A brief introduction is included at the beginning of each part to give a fuller explanation of its contents.

Part I

The nature of transport

Transport is such a pervasive feature of contemporary life that it may seem unnecessary to spend much time studying the nature of it. Many people seem to think they understand it well enough already. Given half a chance in casual conversation they will not only give you their opinion on the causes of present transport problems but identify the solutions as well!

However a few minutes thought or discussion – particularly with people outside your own immediate circle – should demonstrate that what each of us thinks of as 'transport' is likely to depend on which modes of transport we use ourselves and the context in which we use them (e.g. in town or country, or for business, commuting, shopping or leisure). There are plainly different requirements for example between people and freight and between motorised and non-motorised modes.

There is also a distinction to be made between the vehicles and the infrastructure which together comprise a transport system. All transport involves the movement of some person or object (usually in a specially designed vehicle) and a purpose-built track or other adapted space over which it can be moved. The two are obviously functionally inter-dependent, but not always in balance. Can there in fact be such a thing as an 'unsafe' road which needs to be improved, or are what we call 'accidents' the result of inappropriate driver behaviour?

Another way of viewing transport is in terms of the interactions between users of a particular mode. The speed I am able to drive along a road, or the comfort I have when travelling on a train, will depend on the number of other people who decide to travel the same way at the same time. So it is not just the nature of the transport system itself which determines the conditions I experience; the way other people use it affects me too (and me them).

This applies even more to the interaction *between* modes, particularly where (as with roads) they make use of the same space. The needs of buses, vans and lorries could be met much better if there weren't also cars to cater for (both moving and parked). Pedestrians and cyclists would have a much easier time if all motorists could be banned. (Motorists might well return the compliment!)

Then we need to consider the way transport systems and their users taken together interact with everything else. Traffic flows down a street may be welcomed by frontage shopkeepers who benefit from passing trade, but cursed by other residents because of the threat they pose to safety and the local environment. Increasing traffic levels on scenic rural roads may represent improved access to countryside recreation for some but reduced enjoyment for others.

Understanding what transport represents at a particular place and time for all the different users and non-users is thus much more complex than might first appear. But for planning purposes making sense of a situation in 'snapshot' mode alone is not enough. Planning is essentially concerned with change – anticipating it and seeking to influence it. So recognising where current conditions 'sit' in a trajectory of change – and identifying the factors which determine this trajectory – are critical.

Transport improvements – particularly individuals' acquisition of a private car – can themselves be an important impetus to people changing their travel behaviour. So the link between travel and transport provision is not merely in that one direction. The two interact.

The social and economic forces promoting change or acting as a brake on it are deep-seated and relatively slow-moving. To understand the source of present conditions and to identify the main drivers and constraints on change we have to review trends over a long period. In this first part of the book we set out to portray the current nature of transport and travel in Great Britain in the context of changes which have taken place over the last half century.

Although fifty years seems like a convenient round number the mid-1950s is not an arbitrary starting date. It marks the time when the country began to resume normality after the Second World War. 1953 was the year when the use of public transport reached its peak. Travel by car exceeded travel by public transport for the first time in 1959. Freight haulage by road overtook the volume carried by rail in 1955.

The 1950s thus mark the beginning of the modern transport era characterised by the dominance of the motor vehicle. It was in the 1950s that the ownership of private cars began to change quite rapidly from a luxury affordable only by the well-off to the commonplace household item it is today. The transformation to a fully motorised society represents the seismic shift whose consequences we are still grappling with. It is a transformation which is still far from complete – we are little more than halfway to a notional scenario in which every adult has their own private car.

In reviewing trends we look first at the relationship between transport and economic development (Chapter 1) and then at changes in population, land use and travel behaviour which are to a large extent linked to the underlying economic changes (Chapter 2). Their combined effect will then be presented in terms of the trends in traffic growth and its various impacts (Chapter 3). Increasingly it is public attitudes towards these impacts as much as the demands for transport itself which are conditioning transport policy and hence a commentary on attitudinal trends is included as well.

Unless stated otherwise all the figures quoted come from the annual compendium of Transport Statistics for Great Britain (TSGB) – with most information presented for England, Scotland and Wales together or the associated commentary on Transport Trends prepared by the Government Statistical Service. Fuller information on personal travel is derived from the National Travel Survey (NTS), itself now reported on annually. These can be accessed via the DfT website (www.dft.gov.uk/statistics) whilst the full extent of official statistics can be accessed at www.statistics.gov.uk. For non-transport data, use is made of the compendium published as Social Trends.

Many of the indicators which we now regard as important for transport planning were not surveyed in the past. In particular, information on travel (i.e. people) as distinct from transport (vehicles) only began to be collected in 1965 and at intervals thereafter. The recording of certain types of impact and public attitudes to them is more recent still. In many cases it is therefore only possible to present trends for recent periods and between specific survey dates.

Because we are concerned mainly with 'national' policy the characteristics of transport and travel are generally presented as aggregate or average figures in order to give the overall picture. (Sometimes, depending on the statistical source, figures for Wales and/or Scotland have to be excluded.) Where characteristics vary within the national population we try and show their range as well.

In particular the *spatial* dimension of variation is highlighted. This is because our personal understanding of transport is likely to be strongly conditioned by the nature of the areas we happen to know well. In fact there are wide variations both within and between regions and these are becoming more pronounced over time. Whatever you think transport is like in Great Britain the reality is almost certainly different!

1   Transport and economic development

1.1 Introduction

It is currently fashionable, in certain social circles at least, to discuss people's travel behaviour as a matter of lifestyle choice, in much the same way as whether they buy organic food. Of course individuals can make quite radical changes to enhance their own well-being and/or to support some altruistic principle. (We will be exploring later – in Chapter 16 – the scope which exists for such changes in behaviour.) But there is a danger of extrapolating from this and imagining that transport policy in the round can be presented as *primarily* a matter of personal choice.

For a start, not all transport is personal in nature. Just under a fifth of all road vehicle miles is represented by freight movements which deliver the goods and support the services which are central to our lives. Of the remaining (mostly car) mileage about 40% is made up of personal travel for commuting or business purposes, and a further 30% is for education (including escort), shopping or personal business reasons. Although there may be some scope for people to alter the *means* of travel involved in these journeys, their overall volume and pattern is essentially determined by the spatial organisation of economic activity in their home area. Leisure journeys which utilise sports or entertainment facilities are constrained similarly. Many social journeys involve the maintenance of links with friends and family who have become physically separated as a result of moving to take up opportunities offered by different job, housing or education markets.

To begin with we therefore review the fundamental relationship between transport and economic development and how this has evolved to create the patterns of travel on which we now depend to sustain our present living standards and social networks (1.2). We then look at trends in transport supply and transport costs (1.3 and 1.4) and at changes surrounding car ownership and licence holding which are central to the private car becoming the dominant travel mode (1.5).

1.2 Transport and the economy

Before the era of mechanised transport, trade and travel was limited to what could be accomplished on foot or horseback or by wagon, barge or sail. The settlement pattern of villages, market and coastal towns across most of the country reflects this. Even when mechanised transport was developed, its use for regular personal travel was inhibited by cost. The density and form of present-day towns derives from the fact that walking was and still is used for a large proportion of everyday journeys.

Transport investment, including exploitation of the opportunities created by mechanical invention, depended on the surplus generated from economic development. Economic development itself is facilitated by transport improvements – both the capability of vehicles and the standards of the infrastructure on which they operate. Together these reduce the time and cost involved in overcoming distance and thus enhance the opportunities for trade, specialisation of production and economies of scale. A classic example of this is provided by the brewing industry which has evolved from small, independent local firms serving their tied houses by horse and drey to national and even international conglomerates with transport forming a massive logistical component in their operation.

The accompanying growth in personal incomes has facilitated the purchase of passenger transport, initially in its cheaper public or 'mass' form – trams, trains and buses – but increasingly via the acquisition of private, individualised modes – bicycles, motor-cycles and cars. Mechanised transport not merely reduces the time and effort involved in accessing facilities used previously, it also opens up a wider range of opportunities which can be utilised given the ability to make longer journeys.

Because the volume of transport today is on such an enormous scale it is tempting to imagine that travel itself is the product of the mechanised era. Yet centuries before the invention of either the steam, internal combustion or jet engines, merchants, diplomats, scholars and artists moved across the known world exchanging ideas and goods, imposing religious and secular orders in shifting networks that represent the very core of our civilisation. Meanwhile the mass of ordinary people lived, worked and died near where they were born. Even today, in a society seemingly preoccupied with mobility, many people still live within a few miles of their birthplace. But it is the transformation in the daily lives of these ordinary people which has produced the enormous growth in travel and traffic that is the object of attention of today's transport planners and the focus of this book.

Successive periods of economic development, often coupled with technological advances in transport and communication, have altered the organisation and location of industry. In itself this has generated enormous increases in freight movement and business travel which can be regarded as the 'baseload' of contemporary transport demand. But it has also altered the economic poles around which ordinary people sustain their lives. Nationally there have been migrations over successive generations to the more prosperous areas – first from villages to the towns and cities of the industrial revolution, then to London and other cities with more modern industries, more recently to southern England as a whole which is dominated by the growth of 'London' as a metropolis of world-wide significance. Locally the focus of urban activity has also shifted – firstly from religious centres and agricultural markets to concentrations of heavy industry and mass manufacture; more recently to today's regional office complexes, shopping centres, universities and mega-hospitals.

But there have also been fundamental changes in the living habits of people themselves associated with economic advancement in general and transport improvement in particular. In the 18th and 19th centuries only a tiny minority of aristocrats or successful entrepreneurs was able to enjoy the benefits of both town and country by having residences in both and moving seasonally between them. Subsequently the mechanisation of transport – train, tram, bus, then car – facilitated suburbanisation, giving the mass of the population the benefits of more spacious housing and better living environments whilst retaining a degree of everyday access to both town and country, albeit at the price of ever greater dependence on transport.

Today, in relation to London particularly, 'suburbanisation' amongst wealthier groups takes the form of weekly commuting to second homes in the country or by the sea, sometimes outside Britain altogether.

Transport improvements also provided operators with the opportunity to market leisure experiences to appeal to the growing time and money available to city dwellers. These included the seaside resorts promoted by the Victorian railway companies, the outings into the countryside by charabanc (motor coach) during the inter-war period, and the overseas package holidays by charter air firms later in the 20th century. As the private car came to dominate domestic travel so the marketing initiative shifted to today's sports, entertainment and heritage sites, even humble garden centres, to woo the mobile family into literally 'spending' their leisure time.

The significance of economic growth for personal travel is greater than the performance of the national economy alone would suggest because transport has the characteristics of a 'superior good', i.e. people consume proportionally more of it as they become more affluent. In the thirty years to 1998 the share of average UK household expenditure on transport increased from 13% to 17%, mostly because of the spread of two-car ownership. In absolute terms, expressed in 1998/99 prices, this represented an increase from £32 to £55 a week (Aldous 2000).

Service industries have responded to this greater personal mobility by restructuring their operations into fewer outlets offering a greater range of goods or services at lower cost. This is most evident in the restructuring of retailing (from small 'high street' shops into supermarkets, DIY warehouses and the like) but also in a range of public services such as doctors' surgeries, general hospitals, schools, libraries and post offices. A consequence of this is an increase in the average length of journeys, with the additional monetary costs accounting for part of the increased household expenditure on transport.

In effect some of the higher costs of production or distribution previously associated with services organised in smaller, more dispersed units have been transferred to the transport costs of the consumer. Whilst this is normally seen as economically beneficial in aggregate it does prompt questions about ancillary impacts (e.g. on safety, the environment and fuel consumption) which the additional transport has created. It also masks large shifts in the relative accessibility, and hence welfare, of different groups within the population depending on where they happen to live and whether or not they have use of a car.

Viewed in terms of both economic organisation and personal lifestyles the scope for growth in travel through further exploitation of the opportunities presented by greater mobility seems almost infinite. Certainly throughout most of the second half of the 20th century there was an almost direct relationship between growth in the national economy and the increase in freight movement and personal travel (Figure 1.1).

It is important to emphasise that the growth in transport derives not so much from an increase in the volume of goods being carried or the number of journeys being made but in the average *length* of haul or journey. This reflects the spatial restructuring of both business operations and personal lives which greater mobility makes possible. Over the last thirty years the average length of personal journeys has increased by a third, and the average freight haul by more than two-fifths (Table 1.1).

However this growth in length does not derive from uniform increases in the average distance of all journeys. For person journeys there has been a marked decrease in short journeys (under 1 mile) linked with a decline in walking as a mode. Meanwhile there has been a 'surge' in the proportion of journeys in the 5–10 and 10–25 mile

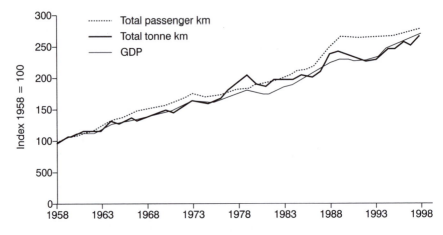

Figure 1.1   Growth in passenger and freight transport compared with GDP 1958–98 (source: Chart 3a Transport 2010 DETR 2000f)

Table 1.1   Average length of passenger journeys and freight haul 1976 and 2006

	1976	2006	% change
Journeys: Number per person per year	935	1,037	+11%
Average journey length (miles)	5.2	6.9	+33%
Freight: Goods lifted (m. tonnes)	1,857	2,203	+19%
Average length of haul (kms)	82.4	118.5	+44%

distance categories (Potter 1996). Significantly these are distances which are typical of journeys to, around or between towns rather than within them. The 10–25 mile band is also the one which has the highest proportion by car (85%).

This link between transport and economic development can be viewed as operating negatively as well as positively. Capacity limits on transport networks and worsening congestion are commonly held to inhibit economic growth and are thus used as an argument for greater investment to rectify an 'infrastructure deficit'. This raises the question of whether the observed relationship between growth in the economy and in transport is a necessary one or whether it is possible to 'decouple' them. (The issue is critical to the possibility of sustainable development over the longer term which we discuss in Part 5.)

At this point we may simply note that there is some evidence of this decoupling in recent years. Since the early 1990s the overall amounts of passenger and goods traffic have risen more slowly than the national economy even though, by historical standards, this period has been characterised by an exceptionally long period of continuous growth. In the decade to 1996 GDP increased by 21% whilst goods movement and passenger travel, following their traditional close association, increased by 21% and 19% respectively. In the decade to 2006 however GDP increased by 32% but the equivalent increases in transport were only 9% and 11%. (For further consideration of this important change see Headicar 2008.)

1.3 Transport supply

The quality of transport supply acts to facilitate or constrain the growth in travel. By quality we mean not merely the speed and safety offered by individual sections of route or the services operating over them but their configuration as a network relative to the patterns of demand generated by land use activity in an area. By reducing travel time the same connections can be made at less cost or better connections made for the same cost.

The patterning of accessibility created by transport networks influences travel choices and hence the resulting patterns of demand. It also has an effect on decisions by firms and households over where to locate and hence, over time, contributes to the evolution of settlements and, more locally, to patterns of land use and built form.

The development of the nation's highway network to accommodate the motor vehicle differs from the earlier development of the railway network in that ownership of the infrastructure has been separate from ownership of the vehicles running on it. In addition the infrastructure remains predominantly publicly owned whilst the vehicles are mostly private. The extent to which firms and households can gain advantage from the vehicles they have acquired has thus depended on public decisions about the standard of the road network.

The policy issues surrounding this are considered in Part 2. Suffice it to say that the 1950s represent a landmark in the evolution of transport policy in that official approval was given to the radical restructuring of the national road network in order to realise the capabilities of the motor vehicle. In a period of just twenty years (from 1960 to 1980) a motorway network of almost 1,600 miles was built which had symbolic as well as functional significance in marking a transition to a new era. In the 25 years since only 600 miles has been added to it. Instead, during this time, the length of dual carriageway 'A' roads has increased by nearly 2,000 miles (to 4,900 miles).

The current form of Britain's national road network is shown in Figure 1.2. From this it can be seen that motorways and dual carriageways are concentrated in the more central and southern parts of England. This reflects the pattern of urbanisation and hence the density of traffic movements. However it is important to note that these types of road as well as providing greater physical capacity also make possible higher traffic speeds. The *relative* accessibility of parts of the country not served by these types of road therefore tends to worsen, with potentially deleterious economic consequences. This explains the long-standing campaigns for dual carriageway improvements to serve remoter, lightly populated areas – for example the A11 to Norwich, the A30 through Cornwall or the A1 north of Newcastle.

Even within particular cities and sub-regions the configuration of the main road network and the standard of its component sections often leaves much to be desired even after a century of purposeful investment. This is partly because of the inevitable 'lumpiness' of highway schemes and the fact that the network remains in a state of continuing improvement. (For example if bypasses or dual carriageway sections have been introduced along some parts of a route then the shortcomings of the unimproved sections tend to become even more conspicuous.) In some cases highway authorities' practice of 'leaving the most difficult bit until last' may result in a desired standard of improvement never being achieved along the length of a route. This could – and arguably should – have happened with the M3 at Twyford Down near Winchester and currently threatens to occur at the unimproved section of the A303 trunk road at Stonehenge.

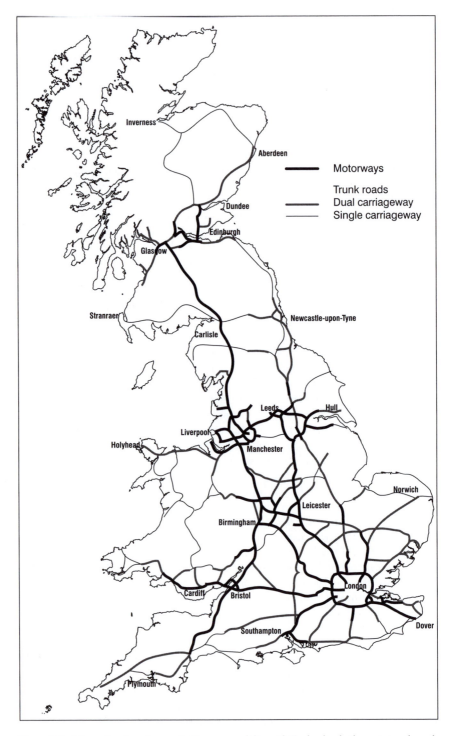

Figure 1.2   The national road network (For comparability with England only the main trunk roads are shown in Scotland and Wales. For a full map of these countries see the Transport Scotland and Transport Wales web-sites.)

The railway network also has its gaps and discontinuities though these have arisen for different reasons. The present national network comprises a series of lines originally built by separate railway companies, sometimes in competition with one another. A process of company amalgamation and then nationalisation allowed for more consistent development of trunk routes but the rationalisation which was initiated in the 1960s was never completed as intended. As a result the present 'network' contains lines and stations which have survived against all the odds, rather like prehistoric life-forms from another age. Meanwhile others which would have had a much better claim to be operating today have disappeared.

Even in the heyday of railways topographical features meant that stations were often located at some distance from the settlements they served. In rural areas the combination of line and station closures reduced accessibility to stations still further whilst in urban areas (except in London and a few other cities where suburban services were developed) the outward spread of development reduced accessibility to stations originally built to serve their Victorian core.

In the last quarter of the 20th century there were some reversals of these trends. British Rail developed a number of inter-city 'Parkway' Stations on the edge of cities designed to attract motorists living in outer areas – Bristol Parkway being probably the most successful. In the provincial conurbations Passenger Transport Authorities opened or re-opened more than a hundred stations serving housing areas and small towns, boosting patronage on the local services for which they were responsible. In addition there are now 34 stations on the Docklands Light Railway in this redeveloped area of East London and over 220 stations or stops on new metro or tram systems in provincial cities. Nevertheless in built-up metropolitan areas and other large urban areas today 80% of the population live more than 1 km – a convenient walking distance – from a railway station (Table 1.2).

The proportion of the rail network which has been electrified has increased steadily during the last 80 years and now represents about a third of the total. However much

Table 1.2 Proportion of households within specified walking times of nearest railway station and bus stop by area type (source: National Travel Survey)

Area type	Time to railway station (1996/98)			Time to bus stop* (2006)		
	< 7 mins	7–13 mins	14+ mins	< 7 mins	7–13 mins	14+ mins
London	26%	34%	40%	88%	10%	1%
Metropolitan built-up areas	7%	10%	82%	91%	7%	1%
Large urban areas (over 250k pop'n)	7%	12%	81%	90%	8%	1%
Medium urban areas (25–250k)	6%	12%	82%	90%	9%	2%
Small/medium urban (10–25k)	4%	8%	87%	85%	12%	3%
Small urban (3–10k)				82%	13%	3%
Rural (less than 3k)	3%	4%	93%	72%	12%	15%
All	8%	13%	80%	86%	10%	4%

* with daytime service at least once an hour

of this is concentrated in South-East England on London commuter routes (Figure 1.3). Key national investments have been the electrification of the West Coast Main Line (from London Euston to Birmingham, Manchester and Glasgow) in the 1960s and 70s and the East Coast Main Line (London Kings Cross to Leeds, Newcastle and Edinburgh) in the 1980s.

As important as the spread of electrification has been the improvements in track and signalling on principal routes. These permit the running of trains at over 100 mph, and particularly enable utilisation of the high speed (125 mph) diesel train introduced in the 1970s. Recent major enhancements to the national rail network have been the upgrade of the West Coast Main Line (to permit use of tilting 'Pendolino' trains at up to 140 mph) and the completion of the first High Speed Line from the Channel Tunnel to London St Pancras as part of the Eurostar network operating at 186 mph.

As with the national road network so the national rail passenger network results in accessibility disadvantages for the more peripheral parts of Britain. In fact the route network alone disguises these differences since on many of the remoter lines only a relatively slow and limited service is operated. Even in more urbanised regions, because of the way investment and through services have been concentrated on lines connecting major cities, the relative position of cities and large towns located off these routes, such as Hull, Bradford and Blackpool, has deteriorated.

Except for the link to the Channel Tunnel the physical extent of the network has remained virtually the same for the last 30 years but the intensity of services operated over it (or more accurately on its main urban and inter-urban elements) has altered quite dramatically. From a low point of around 185m loaded train miles a year in 1982 operations increased under British Rail to 225m in 1990/91. This resulted from a more commercial policy in the use of resources and exploitation of the opportunities presented by a new generation of diesel-multiple units. After rail privatisation and in the context of another period of economic growth operations have increased again to a current level of 288m in 2006/7.

Figures for the extent of bus and coach networks are not available, partly because the networks themselves are subject to frequent change. Some indication of trends in service levels can be gauged nevertheless from the vehicle mileage operated (Figure 1.4). From the post-war peak this fell by a fifth to 1977. The use of public subsidy halted this trend until the deregulation of services outside London in the mid-1980s, whereupon a major increase in supply ensued in the larger urban areas. This was partly due to the greater use of minibuses and other smaller single-deck vehicles which made it practicable to operate higher density services (in terms of both network and frequency) more suited to a competitive environment.

The initial increases in bus mileage nevertheless give a misleading impression of the extent of improvement in service levels. This is because, in pursuit of commercial objectives, a greater proportion of total mileage was operated on the most heavily used routes, often in direct competition. In the metropolitan areas particularly the lack of co-ordination in services and ticketing, coupled with uncertainty over changes in bus routes, meant that for many passengers no overall improvement was perceived. Since the mid-1990s however the converse applies – because of company amalgamations and less 'on the road' competition there has been greater opportunity for operators to deliver a more effective service for a given mileage, so the decline in service level is probably not as great as the absolute reduction in mileage would imply. Overall mileage in the metropolitan areas has now returned to much the same level as operated prior

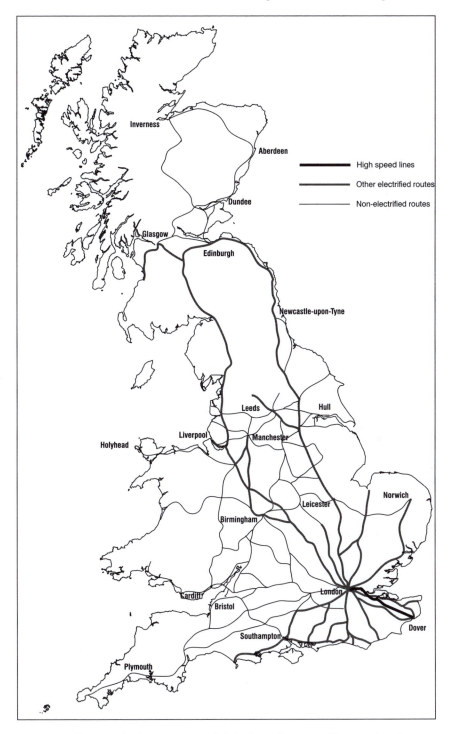

Figure 1.3   The national rail passenger network (suburban and minor rural lines not shown)

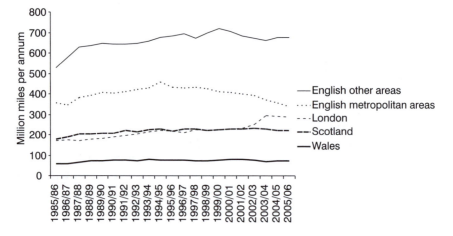

Figure 1.4   Bus mileage operated by area 1985/86–2006/07

to deregulation whilst in the English shire counties, Scotland and Wales it remains some 25% higher. As will be explained later (13.5), events in London have followed a completely different path and, remarkably, bus mileage here is some 70% greater than it was 20 years ago.

Figures from the National Travel Survey provide insight into changes in bus service levels in different types of area (see Table 1.2 previously). Between 1975/76 and 1996/98 the proportion of households living within 7 minutes (500 metres) of a bus stop with a daytime service at least once an hour increased by four percentage points (to 87%). Since then the situation in most urban areas is unchanged but a grant regime established by the Government has contributed to a stabilisation (and some improvement) of conditions in smaller towns and rural areas. Only in villages (settlements less than 3,000 population) do a significant minority of households not have access to an hourly bus service – 2 in 7 households live more than 500 metres from such a service and 1 in 7 more than 1 kilometre.

1.4 Transport costs

The cost of transport is a product of three main factors – the time and distance involved in making a journey and the unit cost of transport itself (per passenger or tonne kilometre). The time and distance elements are influenced by the innate standards of the transport systems available (link speeds and network connectivity) but also by their relationship to the pattern of demand generated by the distribution of land use.

For commercial transport purposes travel time converts into a component of monetary cost because of the need to pay a driver (and possibly a marginal additional requirement in fleet size) whilst for business travel it typically represents a cost in terms of lost working time.

For private travel the amount of non-working time taken up in travel will have a deterrent effect similar to monetary cost although in our everyday lives we do not calculate what this is. However we recognise that there are situations where, even if we can afford to make a journey the time involved makes it not worthwhile (in effect that the overall cost of the journey is greater than the value of the activity forgone).

Strangely, given the enormous amount of public expenditure on transport over the last 50 years, there is no official process which has monitored what overall improvement has been derived in savings in travel time and/or distance. (Individual schemes may demonstrate improvement to gain initial approval, but their value over the longer term is influenced by action or inaction on other parts of the network and how the pattern of travel demand evolves.)

On the nation's road network there have clearly been very large time savings along the main inter-urban corridors where motorways and other dual carriageways have been built. Many 'A' roads forming part of the primary route network connecting principal towns (those marked by green-backed road signs) have also had their alignments improved permitting higher speeds and greater opportunities for overtaking. Journeys not directly served by these routes have not experienced any *absolute* disadvantage (because the traditional routes remain and may even have benefited from some displacement of traffic). But equally it is not clear, taking into account the additional expense involved in making 'detours' to use the improved routes, what proportion of these other journeys have benefited and by how much. Even without the effect of consequential changes in land use, areas of the country away from the main corridors will have experienced *relative* disadvantage in seeing little improvement in travel times from highway investment for journeys, say, of less than 25 miles.

For rail passenger journeys a similar pattern of change has taken place through improvements in track, signalling and motive power but with the added dimension of higher frequencies (as well as higher speeds) on the trunk routes. Hence journeys which are no longer catered for by through services incur the penalty of one or more interchanges as well as possibly a more indirect route. These disbenefits may or may not be offset by the gains of greater speed on the trunk route – the length of trip is likely to be a determining factor. However the change in conditions across the country is more polarised than with road travel because whilst trunk services have been improved greatly many smaller towns have lost their rail services altogether. For people without a car living in such places (or in rural areas more generally) merely gaining access to the network can be problematic as there is no coherent system of connecting bus or coach services. At the other extreme however the development of high speed trains has given special advantage to cities which can command limited stop services. In travelling by car from London to Newcastle for example there is no gain in average speed to be had from driving all the way along the A1 than to any of the towns in between. That is not the case with rail travel.

As well as noting the changes in travel times on the national road and rail networks separately we can also observe changes in their *relative* position. Historically railways were built to serve the centres of towns. Motorways and trunk roads by contrast have mostly only been built to provide connections at or near the edge of towns as they evolved some 120 or more years later. The standard of main roads connecting the centres of towns to their periphery are very variable and are often affected by congestion. Hence in considering the relative speed of inter-urban travel measured 'door to door' it is critical whether the origin and destination of trips is close to the centres of towns or to their outer edge. (The same consideration applies in comparing rail and air services between the principal cities over about 150 miles.) Over the last half century the significance of this has grown enormously with the decentralisation of much business and retail activity (attracted by the vastly improved opportunities for road and air travel) as well as by the continued preference of higher income groups for homes in outer suburban and dormitory rural areas.

For local travel to or within urban areas there have been improvements in rail networks and services serving the main centres in the provincial conurbations. The Tyne and Wear Metro was the most significant example of its kind when it opened in the early 1980s but has nevertheless struggled since to retain patronage in the face of radical physical and economic restructuring within the conurbation (Gillespie et al. 1998). This includes the effects of new motorways threaded between the former separate towns which have transformed the opportunities for car travel between suburban locations. Similar transformations on an even larger scale have occurred in the other conurbations. In a league of its own is the enormous 118 mile long 'beltway' created by the M25 which encircles the continuously built-up area of London and now functions as a sort of 'inner ring road' to the expanding megalopolis across much of southern England.

In urban areas as a whole the traditional mainstay of public transport – the bus – has been unable to offer anything in the way of improvements to rival the private car. Except where the availability or cost of non-residential parking has acted as an impediment the attributes of car travel are superior on almost every count. (The typical urban bus journey involves time and monetary costs three times greater than those borne by motorists.)

Across urban regions the increasingly dispersed pattern of trip origins and destinations has meant that the logical response of road-based public transport to lengthening journeys – the development of coach services – has generally not transpired. Services to airports – because of their scale and concentration of trips – are an important exception.

Bus services have not usually been able to take advantage of major road developments. In fact the design of these and of new residential areas have often had an adverse effect on bus services by forcing them to adopt slow and/or tortuous routes in order to continue to access developed areas. The introduction of one-person operation on buses in the 1970s and 80s (i.e. doing away with conductors) lengthened journey times because of the delay involved in cash transactions with the driver. The effects of this have since been lessened by the development of pre-payment systems, most impressively in London.

Most serious of all, urban bus services have suffered from worsening traffic congestion. This has not only lengthened journey times still further but caused service irregularity and bunching, sometimes to a catastrophic degree. Significantly there is no national monitoring of bus punctuality (only 'reliability' which refers to the percentage of scheduled mileage actually operated). Congestion presents bus operators with the unwelcome choice of accepting service deterioration or of assigning additional buses into operating cycles in order to maintain reliability – adding to their costs simply to forestall patronage losses.

The introduction of congestion charging (as in Central London) or comprehensive bus priority measures elsewhere is helping to reverse this spiral. The latter have the unusual benefit of giving the bus a visible advantage over the car (i.e. a higher speed along the route concerned), but can only be introduced where the highway layout permits. However the very notion of giving buses 'priority' over cars is politically controversial and this has acted to limit the introduction of such schemes and even provoke their abandonment in some places.

In recent years attention has come to be focused more on congestion and other sources of unreliability in transport operations since the *predictability* of travel times has been found to influence people's perception of journey opportunities as well as the nominal times and costs involved. The monitoring of conditions has begun, though typically for only a few years.

Since 1999 the Department of Transport has been collecting traffic speed data on major roads in the 18 largest urban areas in England. These show that average traffic speeds have fallen by an average of 4% at peak times and 8% at off-peak times over the last seven years. On motorways and trunk roads traffic conditions are being monitored on sections of the network with the slowest journeys (11.6); over an initial two years average journey times have increased by 2.9%.

The reliability of rail passenger services has been monitored for ten years. The running of all scheduled services is recorded and measured against the timetable. They are classed as being 'on time' if they arrive at their final destination within 10 minutes of the scheduled time in the case of long distance services and 5 minutes for other services. Initially the 'on time' performance of all operators averaged just under 90% but plummeted by more than 10 points following the Hatfield rail crash in October 2000 (8.6). Overall performance has since improved and is now better than pre-Hatfield levels (Figure 1.5). These figures deserve to be seen in the context of the increasingly intensive operations described in the previous section – a situation which rapidly compounds the effect of any disruption in service.

As far as the unit costs of transport are concerned these are strongly influenced by the loadings which can be achieved. For example over the last 50 years road freight transport has benefited not only from the time savings arising from investment in the national road network but also from the increased loads it has been practicable (and legal) to carry. Bus operators by contrast have had to face the conundrum of a long-term decline in passenger loadings. Before deregulation their response was to reduce mileage operated, although at a slower rate than the decline in passengers, resulting in a drop in average loadings. Since deregulation bus mileage has been increased considerably and an overall stabilisation of patronage achieved (due also to changes in concessionary fares policies) but at the price of a further drop in average loading. In 1955 buses carried an average of 22 people per mile. By 1980 this was barely 15 and is currently less than 10.

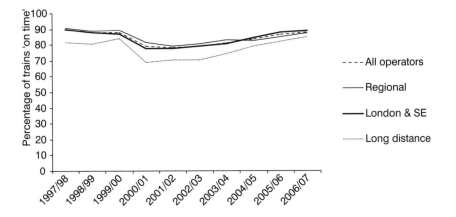

Figure 1.5   Punctuality and reliability of national rail services 1997/98–2006/07

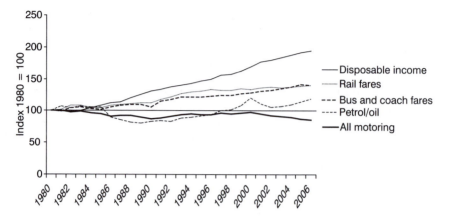

Figure 1.6   Changes in real income and transport costs by mode 1980–2006

As we have seen, train mileage has also increased over the last 25 years but in the context of rising demand. Although average loadings per train have risen this is less significant than the fact that the infrastructure on which the trains operate now carries two-thirds more travel. Unlike buses the efficient utilisation of track as well as vehicles forms a critical part of the economics of the rail industry.

The policies followed by train and bus operators (the former subject to Government policy) have involved a steady increase in real fare levels (Figure 1.6). Although these increases generate almost ritual outrage in the media they are in fact well below the rate at which disposable incomes have increased, meaning that, in aggregate, travel by either mode is becoming more affordable. However in terms of overall transport repercussions it is much more significant that the overall cost of car ownership and use has not increased at all over the last 25 years. The progressive decline in cost relative to disposable incomes underlies the protracted growth in private car travel that we have already noted.

In terms of 'modal choice', costs are normally on the basis 'out-of pocket' expenses only, which for the private car only involves fuel (plus parking charges on some journeys). Fuel costs have been subject to more fluctuation because of changes in the market price of petrol or diesel and because of the effects of changes in Government policy towards fuel duty (15.2). However the overall rate of increase has remained below that of rail and bus fares so that in relative terms a shift *away* from public transport has been encouraged.

Finally we should note that not all motorists experience costs in the manner depicted above. Those with company cars will have the fixed costs paid for cars used for private purposes and in some cases fuel costs too. About 5% of all household cars are company owned. This minority is significant because, as we will see, they account for a disproportionate share of overall car mileage.

1.5 Car ownership, licence-holding and car availability

As far as household car ownership is concerned the second half of the 20th century marks a period of profound change. In the early 1950s only 1 in 7 households had regular use of one or more cars. Today only 1 in 4 do *not*. (Note that strictly the term

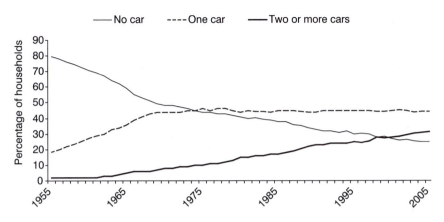

Figure 1.7 Households with regular use of cars

'regular use' rather than 'ownership' is used in order to overcome the complications arising from company owned vehicles being used as private cars.)

Until 1970 the growth in car ownership was almost entirely reflected in the increase in households with a single car (see Figure 1.7). This was linked, both in cause and effect, with the small proportion of women who were able to drive. Since then the most prominent feature has been the growth in households with two or more cars. However their numbers have been almost exactly matched by a continued shift from the 0 to 1 car owning category. As a result the proportion of households owning one car has remained almost constant nationally for the last thirty-five years at around 45%.

Over the last decade the proportion of 1-car households has increased most in the former industrial areas of North West and North-East England and Scotland – places where non-car-ownership was previously highest. Elsewhere 1-car households are more likely to comprise lone adults (in a similar way that 2- and 3-car households represent multi-adult households). In other words, amongst households with working adults especially, car ownership is becoming more an *individual* phenomenon with the numbers of cars owned by a household a product of the number of adults within it.

Whilst income has been a major factor in the growth of car ownership amongst the population as a whole it is also a factor which continues to differentiate groups within it. At present amongst households in the lowest quintile (fifth) of incomes 34% have use of one car and 7% two or more (2002/03). Amongst the highest quintile the equivalent figures are 40% and 52%. There are of course many more single-adult households (especially elderly people and lone parents) in the lowest quintile and vice versa.

Household car ownership varies between different types of area, but not solely as a product of composition and/or income. The proportion of households with 2 or more cars is twice as large in rural areas as it is in London and the metropolitan areas. For households without a car the position is reversed and the difference even more extreme (Figure 1.8). The effect of socio-economic differences between these areas is compounded by the fact that, for a given household type, the level of car ownership in rural areas is higher – in other words the inaccessibility otherwise experienced without use of a car makes owning and running them a greater priority within the household budget (Cullinane and Stokes 1998). By contrast the changing transport conditions

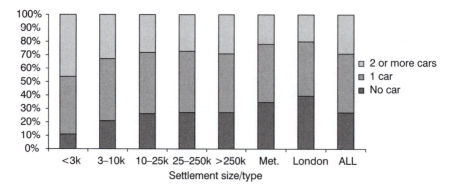

Figure 1.8   Household car ownership by area type (source: National Travel Survey 2006)

in London are having the reverse effect. Uniquely the proportion of households in the capital with two or more cars actually *fell* in the decade to 2001.

Car ownership within households normally depends on at least one of its members being able to drive. Amongst older people especially this is not necessarily the case. In the 60–69 age group for example 14% of men and 42% of women do not have a licence, mostly because they never learnt to drive. Over time the significance of this factor is lessening as more people have learnt to drive when they were young and these cohorts are working their way through the population. Inability to drive remains higher amongst women in all age cohorts although amongst adults in their twenties today there is now only a 12-point difference between men and women.

Over the last ten years however there has been a surprising reversal in the trend towards greater licence-holding amongst young people. The proportion of 17–20 year olds with a licence has *fallen* from 43% to 34%. Possible reasons for this include the increasing costs of insurance and driving lessons, fewer people applying for a driving test (there has been a sustained drop since a theory element was added in 1996) and a larger proportion of young people entering higher education and taking on debts. Even if these are unwelcome constraints amongst a group that would otherwise prefer to drive, the fact that a greater proportion are learning to live as adults *without* driving could have longer term effects on their travel behaviour and attitudes when they (mostly) do eventually obtain a licence.

Household car ownership is an item included in the Census of Population. This enables information to be generated at different spatial levels for all parts of the country and it is common therefore for planners to use car ownership as a proxy for car availability. However because of variations in household composition and in licence holding by age and gender this can be misleading. For example because non-car-ownership is more common amongst lone adult households the proportion of *people* living in such households is lower than the household figures imply (19% as compared with 25%). However the presence of one or more cars in a household does not automatically convey 'availability' on its members. Children of course can only enjoy availability as passengers at best. But even amongst adults availability will depend on licence holding and on the relationship between the number of cars and the number of drivers in their household.

Since 1975 the National Travel Survey has categorised adults in car-owning households according to whether they are a 'main driver' (i.e. people who use one

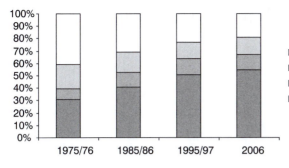

Figure 1.9 Car availability amongst adults 1975/76–2006

of the household cars most), another driver or non-driver. During this period the proportion of main drivers has increased from 31% to 55% (Figure 1.9). However because of changes in licence-holding noted previously, the increase has been much more marked amongst women than men (13 to 47% compared with 51 to 63%). It is also worth noting that the rate of increase in 'main drivers' (or – possibly more significant – the decrease in people without this level of availability) has slowed significantly in the last decade.

The growth in the number of households where all adults are main drivers (i.e. each has their 'own' car) not only transforms the mobility and independence of the individuals concerned, it also feeds through into decisions on location and travel by the household as a whole which are predicated on this attribute. We explore the nature and significance of 'car dependence' when considering the potential for behavioural change (Chapter 16).

2 Population, land use and travel

2.1 Introduction

In the previous chapter we described the changes in mobility arising from economic growth in general and from investment in transport infrastructure and private car ownership in particular. Because of the scale and pervasiveness of these changes it is easy to overlook the significance of other factors which affect travel. In this chapter we look at changes in these other factors – in the characteristics of the population, in the spatial patterning of land use and in the mix of human activities and their patterning in time. We explain and report on each of these before finally examining their overall outcome as reflected in trends in personal travel,

We begin by considering changes in overall population numbers and their spatial distribution (2.2). We then look at the socio-economic characteristics of the population in terms of age structure (2.3), household composition (2.4) and economic activity (2.5). (In practice these are inter-related.)

People's choices of activity outside their home are conditioned by the pattern of land use development and its relationship to the networks of different transport modes. The pattern which has evolved over the last fifty years is the product of social and economic forces on the one hand and public policy in the field of town planning on the other. We identify the main trends and their transport implications in section 2.6.

In section 2.7 we look at changing patterns of personal activity as reflected in the number, purpose and timing of trips. This feeds into final sections on travel itself which first identify overall changes in the distance people travel by purpose and mode (2.8) and then explore variations in travel amongst groups within the population (2.9).

2.2 Population and settlement

For planning purposes two aspects of population are fundamental – overall numbers and how these are distributed spatially in the pattern of settlement.

Between 1951 and 1991 the population of Great Britain grew fairly slowly from 49.2 to 55.9 million. Since 1991 however the population of England has increased quite sharply (from 47.9 to 50.1 million). By contrast it has increased only marginally in Wales (to 3.0 million) and declined marginally in Scotland (to 5.1 million).

The rate of overall population change is the product of two separate factors – net natural change (itself the difference between the number of births and deaths) and net migration (the difference between the number of people leaving and entering the country). The 1960s and 70s were characterised by net out-migration and the overall increase in population was the result of natural increase more than offsetting its effects. Today the situation is quite different with net in-migration accounting for two-thirds of the population increase.

More important for planning purposes are local variations in the rates of population change, principally the product of migration amongst different age groups. A key feature of the last fifty years has been the phenomenon of 'counter-urbanisation' – a general shift of population from conurbations and larger cities to freestanding towns and rural areas (Breheny 1995). When analysed by local authority area most large towns and cities continue to show population losses for this reason. Exceptions are Cardiff, Leicester, Leeds/Wakefield and Aberdeen plus Edinburgh and Greater London which have reversed the trend altogether.

In many parts of the country however this counter-urbanisation process takes the form of a spreading out of cities from within their traditional boundaries into dormitory areas beyond. Rather than an overall loss of population the change is therefore better represented as a local redistribution within a wider area. If analysis is conducted using 'functional regions' (based on Travel to Work Areas rather than individual local authorities) the pattern becomes clearer (Champion and Dorling 1994). There are some places (notably Glasgow, Tyne and Wear and much of Merseyside and Greater Manchester) where major losses from the cores of cities have not been offset by gains in surrounding areas, resulting in overall decline. On the other hand there are places such as the West Midlands and Bristol where losses within the core have been countered by significant growth in at least some of the surrounding districts.

There is also a large area of south-eastern Britain where almost no part has experienced significant population loss and in many places there have been substantial gains. Over the last 15 years or so this has included Greater London itself. Intriguingly the boundary of this area almost exactly follows the line of Fosse Way – the Roman road running north-east/south-west from Lincoln via Leicester and Bath to Exeter. It is to this south-eastern half of the country that the bulk of migration, from both within and outside Britain, is taking place. The only other urbanised region characterised by significant growth in both the core city and its environs is Edinburgh, although on a much smaller scale.

Shifts in the distribution of the population gradually alter local densities. Population density is of fundamental importance to transport as areas with higher densities have more opportunities closer at hand and thus tend to offer better accessibility and generate shorter trips. They also imply more intensive travel demand within a given area. This suggests greater potential for public transport on the one hand (because it benefits from economies of scale) and greater probability of traffic congestion on the other. Conversely low density areas tend to be associated with poorer accessibility, longer trips, limited scope for public transport and greater opportunity for the unconstrained use of the private car. As discussed later (2.6) these density effects are compounded – for better or worse – by patterns of land use and urban form.

The overall pattern of settlement – i.e. the spatial distribution of the population – has been shaped by mobility constraints in the era before motorisation and by town planning policy since. The result in most areas is a quite a sharp distinction between urban (predominantly built-up) and non-urban (predominantly rural) areas. Most of urbanised Britain has overall densities of between 20 and 40 persons per hectare (by local authority area). Only Inner London is more densely occupied than this. Small towns have densities at the lower end of this range but since a higher proportion of

Table 2.1   Population, density and cars per household by settlement size (source: England and Wales 2001 Census)

Settlement size	All persons (m)	% of total pop'n	Persons per h'hld	Persons per hectare	Cars per h'hld	% of 0-car h'hlds
Total population	52.3					
All in settlements >1.5k	46.8	89%	2.35	39.1	1.05	29%
500k +	17.9	34%	2.36	44.6	0.93	35%
200–499k	6.9	13%	2.35	40.1	1.05	28%
50–199k	9.0	17%	2.34	38.1	1.07	27%
10–49k	7.8	15%	2.35	35.6	1.16	23%
1.5–9.9k	5.3	10%	2.36	31.2	1.29	19%

their trips involve travel to places other than the 'home town' the (low) density of the surrounding rural areas takes on greater significance. Large parts of the country which are predominantly rural – most of Scotland and Wales, northern and eastern England especially – have overall densities of less than 1 person per hectare.

For urban areas there is a correlation between density and settlement size and both have an influence on travel behaviour (ECOTEC 1993; Banister 2005). Larger settlements are associated with less travel per head because there is a greater probability of people being able to fulfil their travel requirements within their 'home' settlement (although distances increase in the very largest cities).

Overall 34% of the population in England and Wales live in the largest settlements (cities of more than 500,000 population) and 10% in the smallest (villages with less than 1,500). Average household size is virtually the same in all areas but the average number of cars per household decreases with settlement size and the proportion of households without cars increases (Table 2.1). Counter-urban shifts in population therefore imply higher levels of car ownership which, as we will see, are in turn reflected in higher car use.

2.3 Age structure

In addition to changes in the total population nationally and locally there have been important changes in its composition by age and the way in which these characteristics are distributed within the country.

Children are forming a smaller proportion of the total population and people over retirement age a larger one. This is due to declining birth rates on the one hand (a combination of later first births and fewer children amongst women of child-bearing age) and better health and life-expectancy amongst older people on the other. In 1951 24% of the population were under 16 and fewer than 14% over 60(F)/65(M). In 2004 the shares were almost identical (at 19%).

There are now 5 million people aged 65–74 and 4.5 million – mostly women – aged 75 and over. These numbers are projected to increase by about a third in the years to 2021 alone. This has particular significance for transport because of the combination of physical mobility difficulties and low car availability which characterises people in these upper age bands (Mitchell 2000).

Across the country the proportion of children in the population varies according to the socio-economic characteristics of the adult population and differences in local housing markets. (Families with young children seeking private housing tend to be 'forced out' of pressurised housing areas.) Areas with particularly high proportions of children include East London, the West Midlands and former industrial towns in the north of England on either side of the Pennines. Areas with particularly low proportions of children include Central London (including the Boroughs of Camden and Wandsworth), Oxford, Cambridge and Edinburgh, plus – for rather different reasons – Brighton and Bournemouth.

Variations in the proportion of old people derive not from the indigenous characteristics of local populations but from the effects of migration associated with rural and coastal areas – both young people moving out and retired people moving in. As a result there is a concentration of elderly people virtually throughout the coastal margins of England and their rural hinterland plus almost the whole of Wales, northern England and Scotland outside their main urbanised areas. By contrast there is a relatively low and declining proportion of older people within an area of about 40 miles of Central London – a product of youthful in-migration plus the incentive amongst the elderly to escape (or capitalise upon) a much-inflated housing market.

2.4 Household composition, size and income

The way in which people come together into households of various types and sizes is also of fundamental importance to transport planning. This is because of the resultant demand for separate dwellings, because of the income shared between household members, and because car ownership and many personal activities are organised on a household basis. The presence of dependent children is also important because of their distinctive travel requirements. With younger children especially their needs for supervision and escort place constraints on the economic activity and travel behaviour of adults within their household.

Most households can be categorised on the basis of whether they contain a single adult or a couple and whether they have dependent children. Over the last thirty years there have been pronounced changes in household composition with a larger proportion of single-person households (18% to 29%) and a smaller proportion of households with children (50% to 39% – see Figure 2.1). The growing lone-parent category includes both women (overwhelmingly) who have never married or formed a similar relationship and former couples who have separated or divorced.

An important consequence of these changes has been a reduction in average size of households – from 2.9 to 2.4 persons since 1971, continuing a long-term trend. Falling household size contributes to traffic growth by reducing car occupancy. (There are fewer journeys undertaken as a household which involve two or more people.) It also increases the number of cars which are likely to be owned per adult, thereby increasing car availability and car use.

Falling household size also means that a larger number of dwellings and potentially a larger area of development is needed to house a given population. Coupled with the growing demand for amenity and space which comes with higher incomes (including the ability to store and use cars) this has contributed to the reduced population density of built-up areas. In fact, rather paradoxically, the growing tendency for people to 'live apart' can add to the demand for housing space to enable others to come and stay from time to time. This can arise with parents and their grown-up children, with divorced

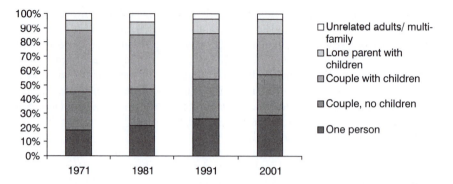

Figure 2.1   Households by household type 1971–2001

couples each retaining a 'home' for their children, for couples who live apart during the week to come together at weekends and so on.

In fact these examples, plus the complications of second homes and weekly commuting, highlight the oversimplification which is endemic to the recording of household characteristics in the Census. It reports where and how people are 'normally' resident but because of people's increasingly mobile circumstances the picture it presents is inevitably at odds with what is actually going on at any one time.

Household size and composition affects household income and – as we noted in the previous chapter – household car ownership. Partly because of this link household income has a strong influence on the volume and mode of travel by household members (2.9 below).

Household income varies greatly by area. The proportion of 'rich' households (estimated at more than £60,000 a year in 2001) varies from 1% to 8% by local authority area with the higher bands almost entirely concentrated in the 'Outer South-East' in a wide arc from Mid-Sussex via Hampshire, Oxfordshire and Hertfordshire to Cambridge (Dorling and Thomas 2004). More significant in terms of absolute numbers is the variation in 'poor' households. Using a relative measure of poverty the proportion of poor households increased nationally in the decade to 2001 (to 24%). Proportions above 40% by local authority area are very sharply concentrated in East Central London and in Glasgow whilst proportions above 30% are concentrated in East London, Leicester, Nottingham, Hull, East Manchester, Liverpool, North Lanarkshire and Dundee.

2.5 Economic activity and employment

For transport planning purposes rates of economic activity are important because of their effect on incomes and, in most cases, because of the resulting demands for commuting journeys. Conversely low levels of employment amongst people who might otherwise be available for work raise issues of accessibility and the cost of travel. The connections between non-employment, low income, low car availability and dependence on local opportunities are profoundly important in tackling social exclusion (Social Exclusion Unit 2003).

Overall the number of employed people is a function of two factors – the proportion of the population who are economically active (that is in or seeking work) and the proportion of these who actually obtain employment. The number of people who are technically defined as unemployed is quite small – about 1.5 million in the UK in 2001 or 2.5% of the population. Hence it is the definition of 'economically active' which is critical. In the Census children and people over 75 are excluded automatically. Within a nominal working range of 16–74 other non-economically active categories are students in full-time education (5.2%), people who have retired (9.8%) and those of pre-retirement age who claim benefit on grounds of permanent sickness or disability (4.2%). There is then an 'other' category (7%) consisting mainly of people who are caring for children unpaid full-time. The proportions of students, retired and permanently sick have been rising; those of full-time carers falling.

Excluding the economically inactive and the unemployed leaves little more than 2 in 5 of the population currently in work. In 2001 only 29% of the population were full-time employees and 8% – mostly women – part-time (less than 30 hours a week). Six per cent were 'self-employed' – a category which includes those running their own small businesses or working freelance (often from home) as well as agency workers who are in effect casual employees. This contrasts markedly with the situation in the past. In 1961 for example (when the numbers of students and old people were very much fewer) 3 out of 5 were in work and 30% of the population were categorised as 'housewives and others'.

From a low point during the recession of the early 1980s the total number of people in work has increased, due to greater economic activity by women, reducing rates of unemployment and international immigration. Changes in the structure of the economy from manufacturing to services over successive decades are a further factor in the increased participation of women. Since 1971 (using statistics from the Labour Force Survey) the employment of men below pensionable age has fallen from 92% to 79% whilst for women it has risen from 56% to 70%. Hence there is now only an overall difference of 9 percentage points between the sexes.

However these rates vary considerably according to whether a person's household has dependent children (i.e. under 16s plus 16–18 year olds in full time education) and whether it contains a couple or a lone parent. Married or cohabiting fathers with dependent children have an employment rate of 91% (2004); mothers in this situation 71%. Lone mothers with dependent children have an employment rate of 53%.

Women have also figured disproportionately in the growth in higher education. (In the 1960s the ratio of students was almost 2:1 male to female; today there are 20% more women in higher education than men.) This is but the 'tip of the iceberg' marking the changed status of women more generally. In our sphere of interest this has had major implications for the day-to-day running of households, for household decision making and for child-bearing, car ownership and licence-holding and patterns of travel to work and school.

Amongst university students as a whole the experience of living away from home, the creation of new social networks, and the pursuit of good employment opportunities has an effect on where these better educated people live subsequently. Their migration to the larger cities – especially London – (and their depletion from other areas) is one of the most pronounced examples of the trend to greater spatial polarisation over recent decades (Box 2.1).

At the other end of the educational scale people without any formal qualifications have a much lower employment rate. This, together with the effects of household composition accounts for differences in employment rates within regions which are much greater than between them. Within Greater London for example there is a 25-point difference (54–79%) in the employment rate of people of working age

---

Box 2.1 Local geography and spatial polarisation

The UK has become a country where local geography has structured society more than at any point in its recent past. In the 1950s and 1960s almost all areas of the country had more similar populations.

Fifty years ago older people lived alongside young people. Men and women were more equitably distributed in each local area. In each area were found similar proportions of people who were rich and poor, who had received a good education or almost no education at all, who were living in comfortable housing or who were dealing with very poor housing conditions.

There were variations, but most of the variations were to be found within local areas rather than between them. Particular industries did dominate particular areas but there was near full employment of men everywhere and everywhere required the services of professionals to very similar degrees, who tended to live locally.

That country is now no more. It was no utopia but it was a place where local geography mattered less. Ironically it is the increased movement between places that has led to places now mattering more. Rapid road-building and growth in car ownership has allowed people who can to live much further from their workplace than before. Long distance migration has become more common, breaking up families and creating places which cater more specifically for people of different ages than was the case in the past ...

People's choices over where to live are constrained and made increasingly by changing markets. Individually we may feel that we made the choices we thought we had. Collectively we are acting in ways that the censuses reveal to be the product of wider underlying influences and which are leading to a country more divided by its geography than ever before.

Source: Dorling and Thomas 2004

---

between the inner eastern borough of Tower Hamlets and the suburban borough of Bromley.

A critical factor influencing personal travel and accessibility is the way these employment rates are translated into the characteristics of households. Since 1992 increasing employment has resulted in there being 2 million additional households in which all members of working age are in work. (Currently 57% of all households containing at least one person of working age are in this category.) However the number of wholly workless households (that is households with at least one person of working age but no one in work) has not fallen to the same extent. Sixteen per cent of all working age households – 3 million in total – fall into this category. The concentration of such households in many poorer inner city areas is a recognised social and economic problem. More easily overlooked is the plight of individual disadvantaged households in other types of area (particularly rural ones) where the norm is affluence and extensive car-based mobility.

2.6 Land use patterns

All travel has origins or destinations at land uses (with or without built development) at particular places – so-called 'trip ends'. Hence the spatial distribution of land uses (homes, workplaces, schools, parks and so on) has a constraining effect on the pattern of travel. No one travels 'nowhere'. However because people exercise choice between possible destinations, the extent to which the land use pattern does or could influence the overall amount and mode of travel is more debatable (Stead 2001; Simmonds and Coombe 2000).

Most trips have people's homes as either their origin or destination. Hence the pattern of residential development is of fundamental importance to transport planning and is the aspect we consider here first. However equally important is the location of other uses since these are the places people need to get to on a day-to-day basis. It is the *spatial relationship* between these two main types of land use which affects the length and cost of journeys and which conditions people's accessibility. How well the links are catered for by different transport modes will also influence people's travel choice – fostering car use on the one hand or offering opportunities for non-car travel on the other.

We have already made reference to the location of residential development in commenting on the pattern of settlement. The defining feature of British planning policy since the Second World War has been the principle of 'urban containment' (Hall et al. 1973). This has been interpreted as literally halting the outward physical growth of some of the larger cities, especially London, and managing the selective and controlled peripheral expansion of other towns. The combination of city restriction, Green Belt designation of surrounding country areas, and diversion of residential expansion to freestanding towns further afield is one of the factors which has contributed to the process of counter-urbanisation referred to earlier (Headicar 2000).

The outer areas of larger towns and cities were once characterised by relatively low density, 'up-market' housing. By contrast planning policy in the post-war decades resulted in mainly overspill public housing at relatively high densities in the post-war period and – where urban extensions have been permitted – in large 'mass market' private estates since. Higher income groups have migrated instead to new individual properties in smaller towns or rural areas, or 'gentrified' former agricultural cottages, converted disused barns etc.

Allied to the limits placed on peripheral expansion, the value of developable land has risen sharply. Much new development has therefore been encouraged to take place on small 'infill' sites within the boundaries of settlements, large and small. In general only limited growth has taken place in villages (mostly those within easy reach of a main town) – normally in the form of 'rounding off' what are seen as natural boundaries. However the fact that there are numerically so many more of these settlements means that a large proportion of all residential development has taken place *outside* towns even though it is the latter which have typically been earmarked for 'expansion' (in areas where expansion was needed).

The combination of in-filling plus redevelopment at higher building densities (criticised by some as 'town cramming') has had the effect of limiting the decline of population density within most urban areas notwithstanding the drop in average household size. Hence remarkably during a half-century characterised by the growth in private car ownership and use (which by itself would have generated unimaginable sprawl) towns have become more rather than less 'built-up' (Headicar 2003). In theory therefore it is – or should be – possible to make trips on foot, by bike or by bus in much the same way as it was 50 years ago. This was not the objective of containment policy but it is of enormous importance today. It would be very much more difficult now to pursue sustainable travel policies otherwise.

From another perspective however the policy of urban containment has had less fortunate outcomes. The physically freestanding towns to which much new housing has been allocated – including the deliberately planned 'New Towns' – do not function in the predominantly self-contained way they did fifty or even thirty years ago (Breheny et al. 1993). Increased incomes and mobility have greatly enhanced the opportunities which people seek to fulfil, the choices they exercise, and the volume of travel they make accordingly.

Much inter-urban commuting derives from variations in local housing markets with better-off people in some areas choosing to live at a distance from their workplace and less well-off people being forced to in others. However the counter-urban shift in residential location has not been due solely to the effects of planning policy or housing markets on people who remain tied to employment in main urban areas. Major changes have taken place also in the geography of workplaces linked to changes in the nature of employment itself (Gillespie 1999).

The consequences of de-industrialisation experienced in the 1970s and 80s were felt most severely in the conurbations where traditional manufacturing and distribution activities were concentrated. (Many such areas have since been regenerated for residential purposes, contributing to their turn-round in population over the last 10–15 years.) More significantly the expansion of service employment, particularly in the private sector, took place predominantly in freestanding towns and rural areas. Of the 2.9 million net new jobs of this type created between 1981 and 1996, 70% were located in such areas.

As with population trends however such statistics can be misleading since developments near the edge of cities may be located within the administrative area of the adjoining 'rural' district or freestanding town. Many of the new breed of business parks located close to motorway junctions fall into this category. It would be wrong therefore to infer that there has been a general dispersal of new employment. Rather there has been a combination of trends with decentralisation in and around individual towns and cities coupled with increasing concentration at relatively few places within regions. Locally however the scattering of employment development, often unrelated to traditional centres or public transport nodes, has left a legacy of car-dominated commuting which is extremely difficult to counter.

Evidence of office development completions in England and Wales between 1995 and 2003 indicates that these are now highly clustered regionally and sub-regionally (WSP and Arup 2005). Most development has taken place in London and in about half a dozen major cities including Leeds, Manchester and Birmingham at the centres of their respective conurbations (although not necessarily in the centres of the cities themselves). Remoter freestanding cities such as Plymouth, Norwich and Hull, although they are important sub-regional centres, have seen very little such development. Meanwhile there has been significant growth in certain motorway corridors outside, but linked to, major cities – in the M11 and M3/M4 corridors to the north and west of London, in the M42 corridor to the east of Birmingham and the M6 west of Manchester. Significantly all of these have good access to international airports.

Similar trends are evident in the pattern of retail development although the degree of concentration regionally is less pronounced. Over the last decade or so there has also been greater success through planning policy in reversing the previous exodus of investment from traditional centres. The few very large regional centres previously permitted 'out of town' (e.g. MetroCentre near Gateshead or Merry Hill near Dudley in the West Midlands) nevertheless represent a huge legacy of car journeys drawn from wide areas. The same is true to a lesser extent of regional facilities such as hospitals and universities which have been newly developed in similar locations. These places are typically more accessible by car (including the opportunity to park) and less accessible by public transport relative to more traditional central locations, especially from their wider sub-regional catchments.

Within individual urban areas a suburbanising process has characterised the relocation of offices and public buildings, the development of supermarkets and other bulk goods retailers, and the provision of leisure facilities such as multi-screen cinemas and sports complexes. Ironically it is the process of *functional* centralisation (i.e. the replacement of a number of older, smaller facilities with one large new, better-equipped one) which has often prompted this *physical* dispersal (i.e. because of the need for a large single site). For facilities which do not serve an entire urban area the move to a suburban location may reduce average travel distances. However developments outside *centres* (city or suburban) are likely to suffer from poor public transport accessibility and generate little public transport use.

The role retained by traditional centres coupled with new facilities being developed at a limited number of locations has typically left major areas of new residential development with few facilities close at hand (schools, doctors' surgeries, post offices, general stores and the like). This lessens personal accessibility and may present difficulties for some groups in fulfilling their travel needs but its significance for actual travel behaviour can be exaggerated. Although the provision of local facilities of this kind offers the *opportunity* to make short journeys by non-car modes the evidence is that in the main people with the choice do not do so (Farthing et al. 1996). Accessibility to local facilities on foot or by public transport (from all household locations) is an item which has recently been added to the National Travel Survey, reflecting DfT's interest in accessibility indicators (Figure 2.2), and will therefore enable this important attribute to be monitored over time.

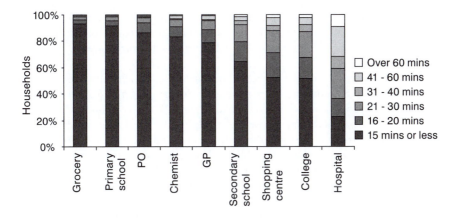

Figure 2.2 Personal accessibility to facilities on foot or by public transport (source: National Travel Survey 2006, Table 5.9)

2.7 Personal activity and use of time

The population and land use characteristics described in this chapter thus far and the transport system characteristics described in the previous one all create an envelope of potential for travel (opportunity or constraint). But travel itself depends fundamentally on what people choose to do with their time. This embraces

*   what activities they wish to engage in (including forms of travel which are enjoyed for their own sake)
*   whether these can be undertaken at home (either intrinsically or by utilising some form of telecommunication, e.g. telephone, TV, email or internet)
*   whether direct contact is preferred, and what degree of choice they want to exercise between places with the requisite facility.

Although historically it has been possible to expand the degree of choice available through expenditure on transport, we are not able as individuals to expand the amount of time at our disposal. This raises the intriguing question of what proportion of our 24-hour day or 365-day year we want to spend travelling (treating this as the necessary means of engaging directly in a non-home activity) rather than in the activities themselves, whether at home or away.

Over the last thirty years and more one might have expected the revolution in telecommunication and information technology to have greatly reduced the demand for travel. Equally the spread of car availability and improvement in transport systems should have reduced the average time needed to fulfil a particular trip requirement. And yet the number of trips undertaken per person and the amount of time spent travelling have both altered only a little. Trips currently number 1,037 a year on average (i.e. 20 per week) whilst travel time occupies 383 hours (i.e. just over an hour a day). Over the last ten years the average number of trips per year has fallen by 5% whilst the time spent travelling has increased by 4%.

Note that the NTS defines a trip as a one-way course of travel having a single main purpose. Outward and return halves of a return trip are treated as two separate trips. A single course of travel – popularly referred to as a journey – which involves a change of purpose along the way is subdivided into two trips. Incidental purposes such as stopping to buy a newspaper are disregarded, but not purposes such as taking or collecting a child from school ('escort education') in the course of another trip. Walking and cycling trips are included but only insofar as they take place on the public highway.

Trip-making is concentrated between the hours of 7am and 6pm on weekdays but more narrowly on Saturdays and even more so on Sundays (Figure 2.3). Overall there are 5% fewer trips on Saturdays than on weekdays and 27% fewer on Sundays. However within the 'busy' part of the day, trips are relatively evenly spread at weekends whereas during the week there are peaks in the early morning and late afternoon linked with the beginning and end of the conventional school and working days. The afternoon peak is rather lower and more broadly spread because of the difference in finish times. (When manufacturing, with its traditional earlier start times, was more common there was a similar spread in the morning.)

The way in which school-times remain fixed and concentrated within a very narrow band is a distinctive feature which has major implications for transport planning. One of the main reasons why the 'school-run' receives so much public comment is that it

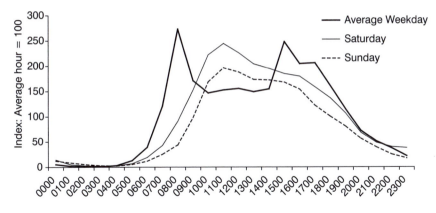

Figure 2.3   Trips in progress by hour of day (source: National Travel Survey 2006 Chart 6.2)

is thought to contribute disproportionately to traffic congestion in the morning peak hour. In fact 12% of traffic in urban areas at this time during term is accounted for by trips to school and 18% at the peak school travel time of 8.50am. (The proportions will of course be much higher in the vicinity of schools themselves.) The significance of the journey to school is compounded by the fact that so much *adult* activity has to be organised in time and place around it. (One in five 'school-run' trips in the morning are followed directly by a trip to work.) However the difference in traffic conditions which people notice in the school holidays is only partly due to the absence of escort education journeys (Bradshaw *et al.* 2000). It is also due to adults having more flexibility in the timing and routeing of their own journeys, including the greater probability of taking leave from work altogether.

The 'peakiness' of school travel is also more conspicuous today due to changes in commuting behaviour arising from the nature and organisation of work. A generation ago many more people were employed on similar fixed shifts or working days with the result that traffic conditions were more marked by weekday peaks and lower volumes at weekends. A combination of factors have altered this – the shift to service industries, the extension of shopping hours over more of the day and week, the growth in part-time employment, the introduction of flexi-time in offices and the increase in working at or from home.

Although much social and leisure activity is not formally organised in the same way, there are distinctive temporal patterns nevertheless which have important transport repercussions. For example the growth in students and other young adults travelling home or visiting friends at weekends creates exceptional peaks of overcrowding for train operators where these coincide with daily commuting flows. Likewise some of the worst traffic conditions on the nation's inter-urban roads are experienced in the run-up to public holidays as people make a mass exodus from cities, and on early Sunday evenings as people return from combinations of shopping excursions, days out in the country, afternoon sporting events, weekends away visiting friends and relations etc.

The individual purposes by which trips are coded in the NTS can be grouped into six main categories (Table 2.2). Shopping and personal business (including escort trips other than escort education) are the two largest categories. (Personal business includes trips to doctors, banks, hairdressers etc. plus eating and drinking except where the purpose was social or entertainment.) Visiting friends and entertainment/leisure trips together comprise almost a third of all trips. Over the last ten years the personal

Table 2.2   Number of trips and average trip time by trip purpose in 2006 and change from 1995/97
(source: National Travel Survey 2006 Table 2.1)

	Trips per person per year 2006	Share of total trips 2006 (rank)	Change in trips from 1995/97	Average trip time (mins) 2006	Share of total travel time 2006 (rank)	Change in average trip time from 1995/97
Commuting and business	195	0.19 (3)	−8%	29	0.25 (1)	+12%
Education and escort education	106	0.10 (6)	−8%	17	0.08 (6)	+16%
Shopping	219	0.21 (1)	−7%	18	0.17 (4)	+4%
Personal business/ other escort	202	0.20 (2)	+4%	17	0.15 (5)	+9%
Visiting friends	168	0.16 (4)	−12%	23	0.17 (3)	+15%
Entertainment/leisure	148	0.14 (5)	+8%	29	0.19 (2)	−2%
All purposes	1,037		−5%	22.2		+9%

business and entertainment/leisure categories have increased in both absolute and
relative terms. The others, particularly visiting friends, have declined.

The trip-duration characteristic of each of the main categories varies. Trips to and
from UK holiday destinations and day trips for leisure purposes are relatively long
and these account for the high average time of the entertainment/leisure category.
Likewise personal trips undertaken for business purposes raise the average time of
the commuting/business category. (Note that trips which are undertaken during the
course of business are excluded.) Overall a quarter of all travel time is spent travelling
for commuting or business purposes.

The total number of trips made by people of different ages does not vary greatly,
except that it is fewest amongst the most elderly, largely for mobility reasons. Women
under 60 make rather more trips than men, particularly in the 30–39 age group.

The mix of purposes however varies distinctively by age including of course the
absence of work-related journeys in the youngest and oldest groups (Figure 2.4).
In general, with increasing age participation in education declines whilst shopping
assumes greater importance. As one would expect, escort trips feature particularly
amongst the 30–39 and 40–49 age groups, social and leisure trips amongst young
adults, and those in their 60s and personal business trips amongst the over-70s.

Overall the mix of purposes does not vary very much between men and women
although evidence of the traditional gender stereotypes is present. Men make 42%
more work-related trips whilst women make 26% more shopping trips. Much the
biggest difference however is in escorting children to and from school. Amongst adults
in the 21–49 age groups women make more than four times as many such trips as men
(119 a year compared with 28). The rapid growth in this type of trip was something of
a social phenomenon, increasing by more than a half in the decade to the mid-1990s
(Dickson 2000) and prompted concern on much wider grounds than simply its travel
implications (Hillman *et al.* 1990). Equally remarkably however it appears to have
stabilised and even declined a little since.

Trip-making also does not vary greatly according to the income of a person's
household except at lower incomes where the linked attributes of non-car-ownership

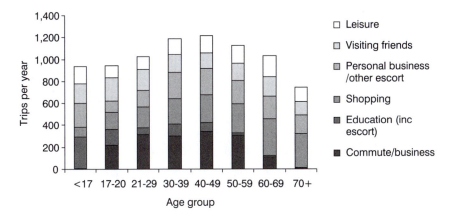

Figure 2.4 Trips by age by purpose (source: National Travel Survey 2006, Table 4.3)

and old age have their effect. Overall the number of trips per person ranges from 1,158 to 882 a year amongst members of households in the highest and lowest income quintiles and between 1,096 and 775 for those with and without cars. Car availability and licence-holding *within* car-owning households generate a further differential. People who are main drivers make 19% more trips than the all-person average and spend 17% more time travelling.

2.8 Personal travel by mode and trip purpose

In the previous section we noted that the volume of trip-making and the time spent travelling have changed very little and for the most part do not differ greatly between sections of the population. The same is not true of distance travelled or mode share and it is changes in these factors which underlie the long-term growth in travel generally and car travel in particular.

Because of the contemporary scale of car use it is not practicable to show the historical trends for all modes of travel in a single graph. Figure 2.5 therefore shows the split between car and all other mechanised modes. (Walking is not included in this data source.) Figure 2.6 shows the split between the individual non-car modes. Note that the vertical scale of the second figure is much enlarged and that the contribution of each mode is shown cumulatively.

Between the early 1950s and the mid-1960s car use grew at a rapid rate and increased its share from a quarter to two-thirds of all passenger travel. During the same period bus use and pedal cycling plummeted in absolute and relative terms. Thereafter although overall travel continued to grow, these particular trends slowed. By 1980 car use had grown to 80% of the total.

The steadiness of long-term trends was upset in the late 1980s and early 1990s by the economic 'boom and bust' of the time. However the previous pattern never re-established itself as the economy returned to normal and 1994 marks a watershed. Since this date travel by car has increased more slowly than hitherto and travel by other modes has undergone a striking turnround. In the period to 2006 total travel increased by 15%, car travel by 13% and other modes by 34%. As a result the share of all domestic travel undertaken by car has actually *declined* – from 87% to 85%.

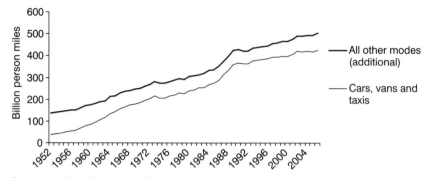

Figure 2.5   Travel by car and all other mechanised modes 1952–2006 (source: TSGB Table 1.1)

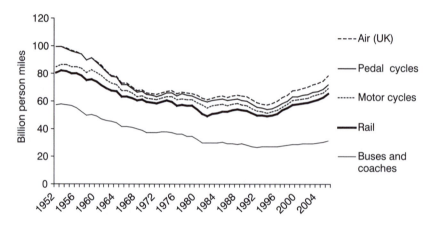

Figure 2.6   Travel by non-car modes (excluding walking) 1952–2006. Note that volumes are shown cumulatively (source TSGB Table 1.1)

Amongst the other modes rail has grown by 57%, bus nationally by 15%, motorcycling by 39% and domestic air travel by 81%.

Trends in walking, and its relationship to other modes, can be gleaned from NTS data (Table 2.3). Note however that the NTS generally presents data in terms of travel *per person* so this can lead to some discrepancy with the aggregate figures quoted above. On a per person basis the number of walking trips has fallen by 15% over the last decade but still represents 24% of the total. In distance terms however the amount of walking has not altered, although it represents less than 3% of all travel. Average trip lengths have increased for all modes (by 7% overall) *except* for car drivers. Remarkably, according to this data source, travel per person by car (taking drivers and passengers together) was no greater in 2006 than it was a decade previously.

Average figures about the use of individual modes other than the car or motorcycle (i.e. those which in theory are available to everyone) mask very large differences within the population. Local buses are used at least once a week by 27% of people but 44% use them less than once a year or never. Similar proportions never use rail or taxis. Almost 70% never cycle.

In terms of distance travelled differences between the main trip purposes are more marked than their share of trips would imply (Table 2.4). Trips for work and business

Table 2.3 Trips and miles per person and average trip length by main mode in 2006 and change from 1995/97 (source: NTS Tables 3.1 and 3.2)

	Trips per person per year 2006	Change from 1995/97	Miles per person per year 2006	Change from 1995/97	Average trip length miles	Change from 1995/97
Walk	249	−15%	201	0	0.7	+17%
Bicycle	16	−12%	39	−9%	2.4	+3%
Taxi/minicab	10	−9%	52	+13%	4.6	+22%
Local bus (exc. London)	49	−8%	233	+3%	4.8	+11%
Car/van driver	430	+1%	3660	+1%	8.5	0
Car/van passenger	228	+5%	2033	−2%	9.9	+2%
Motorcycle	3	−23%	34	−1%	11.3	+28%
National rail	16	+40%	466	+45%	31.8	+3%
All	1037	−5%	7113	+2%	6.9	+7%

Note: Other modes including modes unique to London are not shown

Table 2.4 Miles per person, average trip length and speed by purpose in 2006 and change from 1995/97 (source: NTS Tables 4.1 and 4.2)

	Miles per person per year 2006	Share of total 2006	Change from 1995/97	Average trip length miles	Change from 1995/97	Average trip speed mph	Change from 1995/97
Commuting and business	2,073	0.29	−4%	10.6	+5%	21.9	−6%
Education and escort education	306	0.04	+9%	2.9	+19%	9.9	+3%
Shopping	926	0.13	+1%	4.2	+9%	14.5	+5%
Personal business and other escort	976	0.14	+11%	4.8	+6%	17.0	−3%
Visiting friends	1,414	0.20	0	8.4	+17%	21.7	+1%
Entertainment/ leisure	1,438	0.20	+7%	9.7	−6%	20.3	−4%
All purposes	7,133		+2%	6.9	+7%	18.6	−2%

Note: In contrast to the preceding table this shows all travel

purposes are relatively long and average speeds relatively high. As a consequence they contribute almost 30% of overall passenger travel. Conversely trips connected with education are particularly short and slow. As a result they contribute only 4% of all travel although they comprise 10% of all trips (Table 2.2).

Overall during the last decade the general pattern is of fewer but longer trips resulting in little change in total distance travelled. The combination of longer trips but little change in average speed (except for slower commuting) produces longer average trip times. However the effect of this is offset by fewer trips so that there is little net change in total time spent travelling. All these figures, it should be emphasised, are on a *per person* basis.

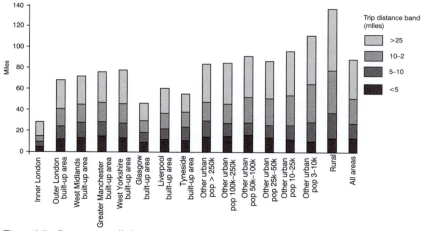

Figure 2.7   Distance travelled per person per week as a car driver by area type of residence, adults aged 17+ (source: NTS 2002-2006)

2.9 Variations in travel by settlement size and socio-economic group

As one would expect, average trip length and use of transport modes vary by settlement size. Residents of smaller settlements make longer trips and a greater proportion by car. Together these two factors mean that total travel by car is considerably higher (Figure 2.7). Compared with the average adult figure of of 89 miles a week made as a car driver, residents of small towns (3,000-10,000 population) make an additional 23 miles and residents of rural areas (settlements less than 3,000) an extra 49 miles. In both cases all the difference is accounted for by more travel over distances greater than 5 miles. Similar figures were derived from analysis of a body of NTS data collected between 1988 and 2001 (WSP and Arup 2005). This demonstrated that some of the difference is attributable to variation in the socio-economic characteristics of the population (especially the low values in Glasgow, Liverpool and Tyneside) but elsewhere this accounts for only between 1 and 7 miles a week between the area-types.

We showed previously the variation between age and gender groups in the number of trips made for different purposes (Figure 2.4). Characteristic differences in the trip length of these purposes also contribute to the volume of travel undertaken by these groups, as do differences in their use of transport modes consequent upon age, income and car availability.

Figure 2.8 shows the variation in total travel by age group and the amount undertaken by each of the main categories of transport mode. People in the 30–59 age groups travel about twice the distance of the youngest and oldest groups.

Distance travelled by public transport is greatest amongst young adults and then declines steadily with age. There is remarkably little travel by modes other than the car amongst children (given that those aged 11+ will travel relatively more within this group and are capable of walking, cycling or using public transport independently). The use made of public transport is also perhaps lower than might be expected amongst people aged 60+, given that (in 2006) all were entitled to free bus travel within their local authority area and could utilise discounted rail travel.

Travel amongst older age groups is strongly conditioned by their declining physical mobility (Figure 2.9). Below the age of 50 fewer than 5% of people have difficulty

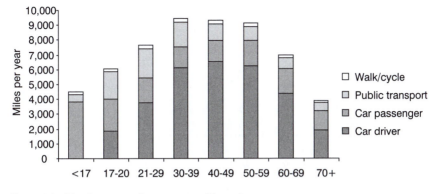

Figure 2.8   Travel per person by age group and by mode

walking. At age 70–74, 27% of men and 32% of women have difficulty walking. Beyond the age of 80 more than 1 in 6 men and 1 in 4 women do not go out on foot at all. The significance of these figures is compounded by the lower availability of cars to older people noted in the previous chapter. Together they have important implications for physical and emotional well-being as well as practically and financially in obtaining even basic goods and services.

Traditional differences in the use of transport modes between the sexes remain apparent. Men and women make a similar number of trips by car but 74% of men's trips are made as drivers compared with only 58% of women's. In using public transport men make proportionately more use of trains; women of buses. In particular women aged 17–20 and over 70 make about 1 in 6 of all their trips by bus. Men make more trips by bike than women. Women make more trips on foot in all age groups even though their mobility difficulties amongst the over 60s are greater.

Children's travel to school has aroused public concern and the attention of policy-makers. Current behaviour is in fact little different from the mid-1990s. Amongst children aged 5–10 the proportion walking and being taken by car is 52% and 41% respectively compared with 53% and 38% a decade ago. Amongst children aged 11–16 the current figures are 41% and 20%, virtually unchanged during this period. (These figures do however contrast with a decline in walking during the previous decade.) Two out of five children in the older group travel to school alone but, glaringly, fewer than 1 in 30 cycle.

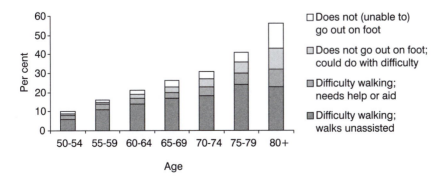

Figure 2.9   Walking difficulty by age group (amongst people over 50) (source: Noble (2000) from NTS 1992/98)

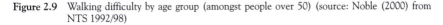

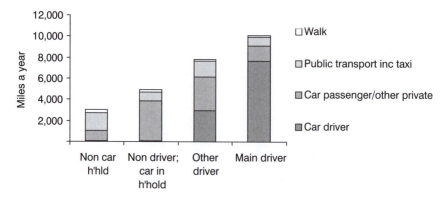

Figure 2.10 Travel per person by car availability and by mode (source: National Travel Survey 2006 Table 5.2)

Income is the biggest single factor differentiating the population in terms of distance travelled but not in the proportion by car. Members of households in the highest income quintile travel over 11,500 miles a year on average of which 80% is by car. Members of the lowest quintile travel about 4,100 miles a year of which nearly 70% is by car. Car mileage will also be influenced by whether the cars available to a household are company owned. The average mileage of company cars is 2.3 times that of privately owned cars. Significantly this ratio applies not just to total mileage but to commuting mileage as well.

Car availability has a greater influence on distance travelled than via trip-making alone. People who are main drivers in households with cars travel 10,100 miles a year whilst at the other extreme people in households without cars travel only 3,000 miles. On average men travel 1,600 miles a year further than women, mainly arising from differences amongst drivers in car-owning households. Although, as one would expect, there is a wide variation in the distance travelled by car depending on people's car availability, there is comparatively little in the absolute distance by public transport. In particular 'other drivers' in car-owning households travel almost as much by public transport as members of non-car-owning households (Figure 2.10).

3   Traffic, its impacts and public attitudes

3.1 Introduction

In the previous chapter we considered social and economic trends and their outcome as reflected in people's travel. In this chapter we look at trends in the volume and composition of traffic – that is in vehicle movement arising from the use of mechanised transport – and its impacts. As well as movements associated with personal travel there are those deriving from commercial journeys (in light vans) and from the conveyance of freight.

Strictly the term 'traffic' embraces all mechanised modes and, when we come to look at air pollution for example, their overall impact will be reported. However, in many contexts we will be confining attention to road-based modes, i.e. to the way the term is used in common parlance. In this chapter therefore, unless otherwise stated, 'traffic' refers to road traffic. Even here it is sometimes necessary to distinguish between mechanised and motorised traffic (the latter excluding cycling).

As a manifestation of motorised mobility traffic can be considered to have positive and negative impacts. Many of these have been referred to in the first two chapters. Ironically the attractions of greater mobility can rebound upon travellers themselves as people find their journeys taking longer, and becoming more unreliable and unpleasant through increasing congestion and overcrowding.

In this chapter however we focus on the impacts of motorised traffic and its associated road infrastructure upon people other than those making the journeys concerned. These impacts centre principally upon road safety and the environment. In a direct sense they are wholly negative in character although individual highway and traffic management schemes, whilst typically having negative impacts themselves, are often designed to bring about safety and environmental improvements elsewhere.

We begin by describing trends in the volume and composition of traffic and its distribution amongst different elements of the highway network (3.2). This is a relatively straightforward matter as comprehensive statistics have been maintained for several decades. The same is true (courtesy of police records) of traffic accidents and the casualties arising (3.3). Other forms of impact however are much more difficult to report on. This is partly because of the absence of comprehensive monitoring which in turn can be linked to difficulties in measurement and the costs of data collection.

The sense of danger experienced by people using the transport system is a case in point. There is no automatic correlation between measured objective conditions (the probability of being involved in an accident) and individuals' perceptions of danger. Some attitudinal data generated nationally can nevertheless provide insights into the significance of this issue and into the related matter of personal security whilst walking and using public transport (3.4).

With other types of impact there may be some monitoring of physical conditions but the significance attached to them for policy purposes depends on the application of more subjective norms – on the numbers of people affected and the context in which the impacts are experienced. We explore these considerations in relation to noise, air pollution and visual intrusion (3.5 to 3.7).

We then consider the related matters of fuel consumption and the emission of carbon dioxide and other greenhouse gases (3.8). Finally we devote a single section to reviewing evidence of public attitudes to traffic and transport viewed as a whole (3.9).

3.2 Traffic volume, composition and distribution

Even in relation to personal travel there is not a straightforward conversion of distance by mode into traffic volume. There are three additional considerations we need to be mindful of – population numbers, vehicle occupancy and multi-stage trips.

The trends in personal travel reported in the previous chapter were largely expressed in terms of travel per person. The increases in total population (2.2) will however mean that there is an increase in travel and hence traffic independent of any increase in per-person movement, all other things being equal.

Trends in vehicle occupancy also affect the rate of conversion from travel into traffic. Overall car occupancy rates have been declining although, as with several other aspects of car use, long-term trends have slowed or ceased during the last decade. The rate of single-car occupancy for example (60%) has not changed in this time. Average car occupancy is now 1.58.

Occupancy rates vary between trip purposes so the changing proportions of distance by purpose will impact upon traffic volumes. It is particularly important that in the case of commuting and business trips (which are relatively long and concentrated during weekday peak periods) car occupancy is low (1.2 persons per car). It is also important that occupancy rates for day-trips and trips to holiday destinations (which are higher than for other purposes) have been declining. As noted earlier, bus occupancy has declined markedly over the long term. All these factors have the effect of increasing the volume of traffic relative to overall distance travelled.

The results reported in the NTS derive from the coding of multi-stage trips (i.e. trips involving the use of more than one mode) according to main mode by distance. Hence the traffic associated with car or taxi stages to or from rail stations for example is additional to that represented by the number or length of trips by these modes. (Equally the overall volume of walking is under-represented in trip-based reporting, because of its common role as an ancillary mode.)

In depicting the long-term trends in road traffic by mode it is necessary, as with travel previously, to utilise two graphs (Figures 3.1 and 3.2). Because of the dominance of car traffic Figure 3.1 distinguishes between car traffic and all other vehicle types combined. Figure 3.2 shows the split between the non-car categories.

At first sight the graph for all traffic (Figure 3.1) appears to resemble that for all travel shown in the previous chapter (Figure 2.5). However this is misleading because of differences in their vertical scales. The volume of travel by mechanised modes is 3.7 times greater than it was at the beginning of the 1950s but the volume of traffic is 7 times greater. This is due overwhelmingly to car traffic increasing nearly 16-fold.

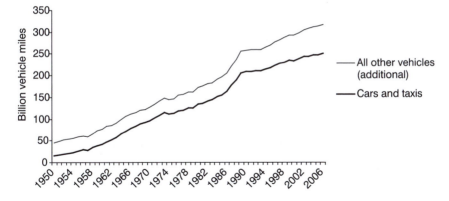

Figure 3.1   Road traffic (cars and other vehicles) 1950–2006 (source: TSGB Table 2.1)

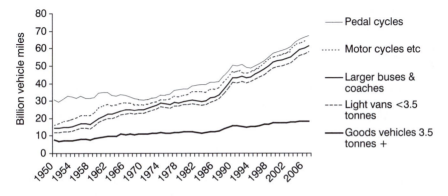

Figure 3.2   Road traffic by category (excl. cars and taxis) 1950–2006 (source: TSGB Table 7.1)

The shift to car use (and reduced car occupancy) means that much more traffic is now generated than the growth in personal travel would imply.

Amongst non-car traffic (Figure 3.2) the most striking features are the decline in cycling in the 1950s and 60s and the disproportionate growth of light vans which have doubled since the mid-1980s. Also since the mid-1980s bus and coach traffic has increased by almost a half.

A feature not evident in the graph is the increasing size of vehicles within the goods vehicle category and greater use of the largest, articulated variety with a maximum gross weight of 38 tonnes permitted in 1982. This has been the principal factor in the volume of goods vehicle traffic increasing at a slower rate than the volume of freight moved by road. In 1980 vehicles of this kind accounted for just over a quarter of heavy goods vehicle traffic. Since that time the volume of freight moved by road has increased by 80% but the volume of heavy goods traffic has increased by only 33%. However nearly a half of this traffic now consists of articulated vehicles whose mileage is 2.4 times greater than it was 25 years ago.

As a proportion of all freight moved within Great Britain, road haulage currently accounts for 63%, coastal shipping and canal 24%, rail 9% and pipeline 4%. Waterborne freight increased threefold until the 1980s but has been broadly stable since then. Freight carried by rail declined in absolute as well as relative terms to a third of its post-

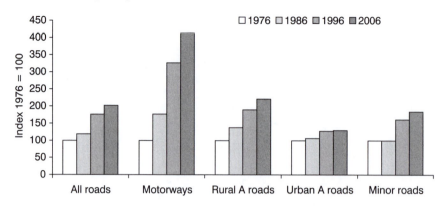

Figure 3.3   Change in traffic volume by road type 1976–2006

war volume by 1995. Since that date (which coincides with privatisation) a remarkable turn-round has been achieved with an increase of nearly 70%.

The increase in road traffic has not occurred uniformly across the road network; rather it has taken place predominantly on motorways and 'rural' A roads. The latter are defined as roads outside built-up areas of 10,000 population or more. As well as linking small/medium towns in rural areas these provide the only opportunity for inter-urban movement outside the motorways corridors. As illustrated in Figure 3.3, traffic on all roads has doubled over the last 30 years but on motorways it has quadrupled. Conversely traffic on A roads within urban areas has increased by only 30% and growth has almost ceased within the last ten years. Amongst minor roads traffic is growing more slowly on urban roads than on rural roads.

A combination of factors has contributed to these trends. The motorway network itself continued to be extended during the 1970s and 80s. This accounts for a large part of the exceptional growth in motorway traffic during the first half of the thirty-year period, but not more recently.

The higher rates of traffic growth generally outside urban areas reflect the counter-urban trends in residential population noted previously and the associated higher per capita rates of car use. The growth in car and business traffic on motorways and higher standard A roads has been fuelled by the redistribution of land use activity to locations served by these routes and by the longer trip lengths they foster. In addition, as new and improved roads have been built, the configuration of networks and associated direction signing have been revised with the aim of removing through traffic from towns. In larger urban areas increasing congestion plus the effect of local traffic management schemes geared to environmental improvements has also meant that a proportion of intra-urban (suburb to suburb) trips are now made more quickly via sections of *inter-urban* routes.

A further factor in the disproportionate growth of traffic on motorways and A roads outside urban areas is changes in the pattern of road freight movements. Businesses generally and the distribution industry in particular have been able to reorganise on the basis of fewer outlets and longer hauls (Table 1.1) taking advantage of the higher speeds available on these much-improved roads. The effect of this and associated land use changes can be seen in the shifts which have taken place in the distribution of traffic between the various classes of road by vehicle type (Figure 3.4). (Note that in this case only changes since 1986 are shown so the significance of increased motorway length as a contributory factor is much reduced.) Heavy goods vehicles in general

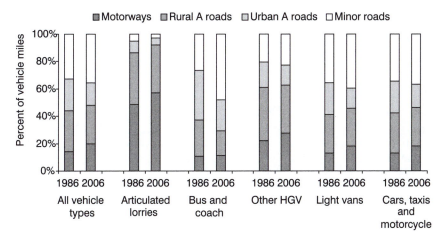

Figure 3.4   Distribution of traffic between road classes by vehicle type 1986 and 2006

and the largest (articulated) lorries in particular have always made greater use of inter-urban roads, but this feature has become even more pronounced. All but 8% of articulated lorry traffic now takes place on motorways or A roads outside towns.

The present distribution of all types of traffic also merits comment. The principle of a hierarchy is applied to the planning of the road network, to the standards of design used in its component levels and to the pattern of movement promoted through direction signing. This is so that investment can be concentrated on a limited mileage of heavily used roads, thus securing the greatest benefits of speed and safety and least environmental impact (per vehicle mile). As a result nearly two-thirds of all traffic is now on motorways and A class roads even though these only comprise one-eighth of the total road network.

The hierarchy principle is carried further with motorways. These have particularly high benefits (and costs) arising from the absence of frontage development, grade junctions and pedestrian movements built into their design. Thirty-one per cent of traffic operates on these special roads although they comprise only 7% of the main road network.

3.3 Casualties

Motorised transport is inherently hazardous, especially in situations where pedestrians and cyclists are also present. Over the last fifty years much of the investment in the transport system, including vehicle design, has been directed to improving safety performance. The number of fatalities on the highway network during this period are illustrated in Figure 3.5. (Note that the graph is 'stacked', i.e. the contribution of each user group is shown cumulatively.)

By comparison with contemporary standards accidents and casualty rates on the network in the early days of motoring were appallingly high. In the immediate post-war period when road traffic was a tenth of its present level more than 3,000 non-motorists and 2,000 motorcyclists and other motorists were killed each year. From one perspective the rate of improvement achieved since then during the transition to mass car use has been momentous. From another perspective the absolute level of carnage which continues to be sustained represents a staggeringly high price in personal and

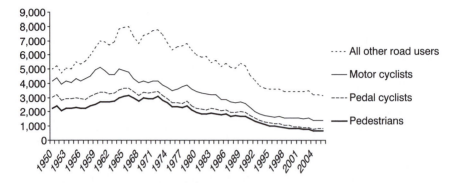

Figure 3.5 Fatalities per year on the highway network 1950–2006 by user group

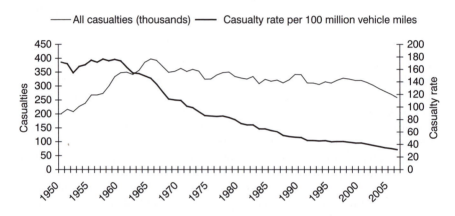

Figure 3.6 Road casualties and casualty rates 1950–2006

economic terms which as a nation we seem willing to pay in return for our enhanced mobility. Currently there are still some 3,000 people a year killed on the roads.

Almost 80 people are killed or seriously injured on the roads every day. Individually these tragic incidents are so commonplace that they are barely reported even in the local media. By contrast rail crashes, when they occur, are the source of national headlines. Over the last decade an average of six people *a year* have been killed in train crashes and about double this number killed accidentally through train movements. Probably less well recognised is the fact that, for vehicle occupants, the fatality rate of travel by bus and coach is one-eighth of travel by car.

For all types of road casualty – KSI (killed or seriously injured) and other – the overall picture since 1950 in terms of total numbers and rates per passenger mile is shown in Figure 3.6. This demonstrates that until the 1960s when the main road-building programme got under way, casualty rates remained much the same so that, with the rapid increase in traffic, the number of casualties grew steeply. The peak year was 1965. Thereafter improvements in the casualty rate kept just ahead of the increase in traffic so the number of casualties declined slightly. Since the late 1990s a targeted policy initiative has achieved a further improvement in the casualty rate and this coupled with a slowing of traffic growth has resulted in a drop of one-fifth in casualties in just the six years since 2000–2006.

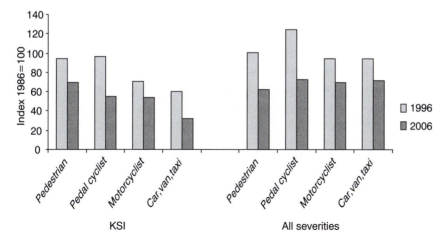

Figure 3.7   Change from 1986 in road casualty rates by user group

One of the main sources of improvement in casualty rates between the mid-1960s and mid-1990s was the redistribution of traffic between the main road types that we noted in the previous section. Motorways and A roads outside urban areas on which an increasing proportion of all traffic has taken place currently have casualty rates one-eighth and one-third respectively of roads in urban areas.

In the decade 1986–96 there was little improvement in overall casualty rates and the rate of casualties amongst pedal cyclists actually worsened by 25% (Figure 3.7). However the situation during the last decade has changed quite dramatically, reflecting amongst other things reduced speed limits on many rural A roads and the widespread introduction of speed cameras in both rural and urban areas at accident blackspots (14.5). Not only have casualty rates improved by around 30% amongst all user groups but KSI rates amongst pedestrians and cyclists have improved disproportionately. On a passenger mile basis however there remain enormous differences between the user groups. Pedestrians have KSI rates around 20 times worse, pedal cyclists 30 times and motor cyclists 60 times worse than car occupants.

In the case of pedestrians and cyclists however, expressing casualty rates per passenger mile may be considered an inappropriate basis of comparison. (Because of their slower speed they are exposed to the risk of accidents for a longer period of time per mile travelled.) On a time basis their rates would therefore be lower. On the other hand changes are taking place in the nature of these trips which means that, whatever unit of measurement is used, the trends in casualty rates are not strictly comparable. With cycling in particular there is a risk that improvements in casualty rates are being achieved by effectively consigning it to recreational use or other 'legitimised' situations.

As road accidents are reduced through better design and management of vehicles and infrastructure, the casualty rates which persist are increasingly attributable to human behaviour. Detailed analysis demonstrates that there are particular categories of user which remain high risk (DfT 2007k). For example drink-drive deaths *increased* from 460 to 580 in the five years to 2004. Excessive speed and failure to wear seat-belts also remain significant contributory factors. Motorcyclists, young drivers and those who drive for work are higher risk categories. As the Government's Review notes, these issues overlap. This is a good example of the more general point that contemporary transport policy is having to become more focused on seeking to influence individual behaviour and on the social – hence political – constraints which surround this.

3.4 Perceived danger and insecurity

The danger from traffic as perceived by pedestrians can be considered in three main contexts. The first is conditions generally on minor streets within residential areas where the main threat is from individual speeding cars. With estates built since about 1965 this threat has been much reduced by the widespread use of loop and cul-de-sac layouts, although at the price of introducing distributor roads which can create an unfriendly pedestrian environment at the neighbourhood level. Over the last decade the effects of 'rat-running' traffic through older estates and pre-1914 housing built along grid patterns have begun to be addressed through the use of traffic-calming measures (14.7).

The second context is on main roads within settlements where a complex mix of factors will affect pedestrians' perceptions. In addition to traffic volume and highway geometry (including pavement widths and the presence of refuges) these will include the speed and arrival pattern of vehicles, the intimidation presented by large buses and HGVs, and the obstruction or distractions caused by parked vehicles and turning movements. The introduction of signalised crossing points does not dispel anxiety from these sources especially amongst people with limited vision or physical mobility.

Traffic on main roads has two further impacts on pedestrian movement. The first is on the ability to move reasonably freely within and across the street itself and hence to utilise it as a 'place'. This can be critical in the functioning of the centres of small towns and in local urban centres. The second is a broader concern for severance, whether this applies to a whole village or neighbourhood community divided by a main road or to particular individuals in being able easily to access facilities which involve crossing the road. Measures which 'force' pedestrians to divert to signalised crossing points or to subways or overbridges may reduce danger and improve safety but risk aggravating severance. The possibility of redesigning and managing roads in these situations so as to achieve a better balance between the interests of motorists and other road users is only beginning to be explored (14.7).

The third context is the centres of towns where some combination of road-building, redevelopment and traffic management measures have typically led to the creation of pedestrianised areas. These offer the freedom from anxiety and intimidation of motorised traffic but there can be difficulties at their boundaries if this involves a sudden transition to the 'normal' regime of traffic priority. Unfortunately the price of achieving many pedestrianised centres has often been the creation of 'inner ring roads' dominated by fast-moving traffic which have the effect of denying local neighbourhoods safe and pleasant access to and from the centre on foot or bicycle.

Some evidence of perceptions of conditions for pedestrians in residential areas exists within the National Travel Survey which asks parents whether they allow children to cross roads on their own. Amongst 7–10 year olds 49% are not allowed to cross any roads on their own whilst amongst 11–13 year olds 32% are not allowed to cross any roads or only minor ones. Both these percentages are up 8 points in just the four years from 2002 to 2006 – a period during which child pedestrian casualties actually fell by nearly 30%!

Evidence about adults' perceptions and responses to conditions in influencing their own behaviour is contained in the ONS Omnibus Survey. Thirty-seven per cent of respondents stated that they would reduce their car use if there were safer walking routes and 31% if there were more cycle tracks away from roads. The desirability of promoting walking and cycling is acknowledged by the overwhelming majority; 73% agreed that pedestrians should be given more priority relative to traffic; 68% in the case of cyclists. Sixty-one per cent of men and 85% of women stated that they were frightened by the idea of cycling on busy roads.

Attitudes to walking are influenced by conditions other than just danger from traffic, notably by perceptions of personal security. Transport Trends, commenting on the ONS data, notes that more than 70% of respondents feel safe walking in local streets and that their local area is a pleasant place to walk in. It is salutary nevertheless that about 1 in 6 respondents do *not* feel this way.

Conditions for pedestrians are also important as the context in which people access public transport. Amongst regular bus users (unfortunately a self-selecting sub-group) only around 40% of women report feeling 'very safe' in walking to and from the bus stop and waiting at the stop. The figures for men are some 7% higher. About 50% of both genders feel this level of safety when travelling on the bus although the percentage varies with age – the youngest adults feeling least safe. Amongst public transport users the possibility of crime when making a journey generated some level of concern amongst almost two-thirds of those surveyed (69% women and 57% men).

Growing fears for personal security when walking and using public transport is bound up with broader concerns about street crime and anti-social behaviour more generally. The escorting of children for example is motivated even more by parental concerns about 'stranger danger' than about traffic (Sissons Joshi and Maclean 1995). Insecurity on public transport is more likely to derive from a perceived lack of social control (evidenced in graffiti, rowdiness, unwillingness of staff or fellow passengers to intervene etc.) than from witnessing actual personal attacks (Jones, M. 2007).

Trends in travel and transport operation nevertheless have a contributory role. More mobile populations and lifestyles reduce the degree of personal familiarity and informal 'policing' in local neighbourhoods. More people using cars, and more developments designed around car use, result in fewer used footways and bus stops leaving individuals feeling isolated and more vulnerable. Economies in public transport operation have led to the withdrawal of staff at railway stations, particularly in the evenings when fears about personal security are greater anyway.

3.5 Noise

'Noise' is not merely sound – the term itself highlights the fact that it is people's *response* to levels and types of sound which is the object of concern. This response depends on the source and variability of the sound as well as its intensity and upon the context in which it is experienced.

Transport is only one of a variety of sources which collectively contribute to the noise environment at a particular place. Overall however it is by far the most pervasive and the one most likely to contribute to disturbance or annoyance. Table 3.1 illustrates that transport sources occupy three out of the top four places in a league table of culprits. Noise from road traffic is the worst individual source with 84% of the population reporting hearing it (outside their homes) and 30% being moderately, very or extremely bothered, disturbed or annoyed by it. Almost 1 in 5 of the population report having their sleep disturbed by traffic noise and a similar proportion that it interferes with being able to have the windows or doors of their homes open.

Table 3.1   Sources of noise and levels of response (source: Defra from BRE National Noise Incidence Survey 2000 (England and Wales))

Source	Per cent respondents reporting hearing	Per cent respondents bothered, annoyed or disturbed		
		To some extent	Moderate	Very or extremely
Road traffic	84	40	22	8
Aircraft	71	20	7	2
Neighbours/other people nearby	81	37	19	2
Trains or railways	36	6	2	1
Building construction or road works	49	15	7	2
Sports events	34	4	1	0

Between 1990 and 1999 the proportion of the population hearing traffic noise increased by 6 points but the proportion said to be adversely affected by it at some level decreased by a similar amount. This is in line with the more general finding from the National Noise Incidence Survey which reports that noise levels on most indicators have undergone a small reduction except background noise at night-time. Nevertheless 54% of the UK population are estimated to experience average noise levels which exceed the World Health Organisation's recommended daytime level of 55 dB(a). Eight per cent exceed the qualifying level at which remedial measures are required by law if they arise from the development of a new road.

The population affected by aircraft noise in the vicinity of major airports is subject to specific monitoring (reported in TSGB). At London Heathrow the number subjected to levels causing disturbance has fallen by more than a half since 1990 (to 313,000) despite a 28% increase in air transport movements. Within this the number experiencing higher levels of disturbance has fallen more sharply still. Similar trends have taken place at the other major airports although the absolute numbers of people affected is much smaller.

Noise experienced by pedestrians in the vicinity of main trafficked streets is not a subject which has been monitored. Over time, despite the general increase in traffic, the combination of improvements in vehicle technology, the redistribution of traffic (especially HGVs) away from urban areas in general and town centres in particular will have improved the noise environment in many places where pedestrians are concentrated. However sudden high levels of noise experienced on pavements arising from the passage of large and/or fast-moving vehicles, together with accompanying air turbulence, will add significantly to the perceptions of danger noted in the previous section.

The redistribution of heavy traffic out of urban areas and its concentration into fast-moving flows on motorways and the like is not however an unalloyed blessing from an environmental point of view. The extensive envelopes of high noise levels which surround them not only affect properties in the areas concerned but also blight large tracts of countryside, greatly reducing their recreational value. In this context rather than merely noting areas subject to traffic noise (the procedure followed when assessing individual road developments) it may be more important to register their effect in diminishing areas which retain the attribute of 'tranquility' which can be considered a finite environmental resource (CPRE 2006). The extent and intensity of street lighting, especially on main roads in rural areas, is an associated phenomenon which is eroding the remaining areas from which it is possible to see a dark night sky.

3.6 Local air pollution

Transport is the source of a number of air pollutants (Box 3.1). Mostly these are of concern because of their damage to health. However nitrogen oxides and sulphur dioxide also contribute to the formation of ozone which is a harmful secondary pollutant and a greenhouse gas. Concentrations of pollutants from motor vehicles are also perceived as smell and smoke which are particularly unpleasant when experienced at close quarters by pedestrians and cyclists.

The significance of transport as a share of emissions from all sources and in terms of volume is depicted in Figure 3.8. Transport is the main source of 1,3-butadiene but carbon monoxide, nitrogen oxides and particulates are currently the most significant in terms of volume.

Dramatic reductions have been achieved in the volume of emissions since 1990 through a series of progressively tighter standards set under EU regulation. The requirement to install three-way catalytic converters in all new petrol-engined cars from 1993 represented a reduction of 90% or more in emissions of carbon monoxide, hydrocarbons and oxides of nitrogen from these vehicles. At the same time the installation of traps on diesel-engined cars and vans reduced their emission of particulates by about two-thirds. Progress with buses and HGVs (which have much higher emission levels of particulates and oxides of nitrogen) has been slower but the Euro III standards applied in 2002–05 represent a reduction of between a half and a third compared with pre-1993 levels.

Box 3.1 Nature and effects of pollutants from transport

- 1.3-butadiene: Mainly from combustion of petrol. Carcinogenic.
- Carbon monoxide: Formed from incomplete combustion of carbon-containing fuels. Reduces capacity of blood to carry oxygen to body cells; people with existing diseases affecting delivery of oxygen to heart or brain (e.g. angina) particularly at risk.
- Oxides of nitrogen: Produced by combustion in air. NO2 enhances the response to allergens in sensitive individuals; at high levels causes inflammation of airways. Contributes to formation of secondary particles and ground level ozone; damages vegetation.
- Particulates: Particles derived from engine emissions, tyre and brake wear. Exposure associated with respiratory and cardiovascular illness and mortality.
- Benzene: Derives from combustion. Carcinogenic.
- Sulphur dioxide: Derives from combustion of fuels containing sulphur [now mainly coal and heavy oils]. Causes constriction of the airways of the lung; particularly affects people suffering from asthma and chronic lung disease.
- Lead: [Emissions now confined to the combustion of coal, iron and steel.] Exposure to high levels may result in toxic biochemical effects.

From Defra Air Quality Strategy 2007 Table 1

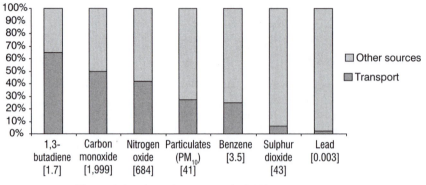

Figures in brackets show amount in 1,000 tonnes

Figure 3.8   Transport as a source of air pollution in UK 2005

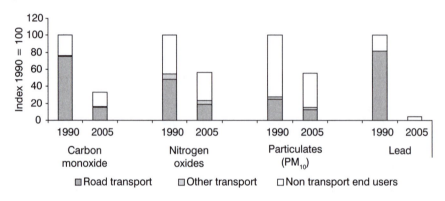

Figure 3.9   Change in pollutant emissions from transport and other end users UK 1990–2005

After successive reductions lead was finally eliminated from the content of petrol in 2000. At the same time the benzene and sulphur content of motor fuels was also much reduced. Figure 3.9 shows the proportionate reduction in emissions from all sources since 1990 (for the four pollutants for which published data is available from TSGB) and, within these, the amount generated from road and other forms of transport.

The significance of the emissions which remain depends on their distribution in time and space. Concentrations which occur where people are exposed to them are of particular concern. A system of local air quality management has been introduced under which local authorities are required to monitor local concentrations of pollutants and to designate air quality management areas (AQMAs) where target levels are likely to be exceeded (14.8). The latest national review notes that to date around 200 local authorities in the UK have designated parts or all of their districts as an AQMA (Defra 2007). The majority of these have been declared because of NO_2 and PM_{10} targets being exceeded, mainly due to road transport emissions.

3.7 Visual intrusion

For most people streams of traffic or seas of parked cars are not in themselves objects of beauty. Only rarely are highways or other transport engineering structures regarded as the source of visual satisfaction and a positive contribution to the urban scene. The paraphernalia of ancillary items associated with highway operation and traffic management (lighting columns, direction signs, traffic lights, bus passenger shelters etc.) to varying degrees almost always presents an unsightly clutter.

As with the other types of impact the significance of visual intrusion depends very much on its context, although in this case the damage inflicted is more aesthetic and affects well-being and 'quality of life' rather than physical health or safety. The main concerns are areas of town or country which have been designated for their architectural or historic value (i.e. as conservation areas or historic monuments) or for their landscape value (Areas of Outstanding Natural Beauty – AONBs – or National Parks). Here and elsewhere the sense of visual despoilation may be aggravated by noise and by the jarring speed of fast-moving or large vehicles.

The trend of redistributing main traffic flows, especially HGVs, has usually created opportunities to improve the visual environment of town and village centres without countervailing losses. However the Okehampton (A30) and Newbury (A34) bypasses were celebrated examples where the environmental damage caused to the neighbouring landscape was held by many to undermine the case for the scheme, notwithstanding the attempts of engineers and landscape architects to integrate the new structures.

In proposing alignments for new roads, attempts are made similarly to avoid ecological sites of special scientific interest (SSSIs). However, as with community severance in built-up areas, the insertion of barriers within the landscape inhibiting the movement of flora and fauna may weaken the viability of local habitats (although motorway and railway embankments may also flourish as unofficial linear nature reserves!). The physical subdivision of otherwise 'unspoiled' landscape also contributes to the loss of tranquil areas noted previously. These contextual features mean that the significance of highway development is much greater than the simple figure of loss of greenfield land would imply (9,000 hectares in the decade to 2004 as reported in *Transport Trends*).

Whilst public attention is focused on places where the impact of traffic or transport structures is especially damaging there is also a more general creeping destruction of urban quality, famously christened 'subtopia' (Nairn 1957). This arises not so much from the effects of traffic and highways in themselves as from the character of development they tend to spawn. Contemporary manifestations are large retail warehouses or scattered office blocks in 'business parks' surrounded by acres of surface car parking with little connection, visually or functionally, with their surrounding neighbourhoods. The design of many modern, higher density housing developments is also often dominated adversely by the requirement to provide extensive parking space within sight of individual dwellings. However these unfortunate trends have generated their own backlash and there have been important initiatives recently to reassert the value of urban quality even in 'mundane' situations such as the average high street or housing estate (14.7).

3.8 Fuel consumption, CO_2 emissions and climate change

The use of oil by transport modes (as petrol or diesel) is important in terms of the utilisation of this finite resource, and its combustion is the major source of carbon dioxide emissions from this sector of the economy. Figure 3.10 shows that since 1980 the nation's overall consumption has remained broadly constant but that transport has consumed a much increased share (from 41% to 66%).

Consumption by road transport increased by almost a half during the 1980s (roughly pro rata with traffic growth). Since 1990 however it has increased much more slowly due to a combination of increasing vehicle efficiency and a reduced rate of traffic growth. During this time vehicle miles per annum have increased by 23% but consumption has increased by less than half this. By contrast the fuel consumed by air transport (domestic and international, uplifted in the UK) has doubled and is the main source of the increasing consumption of the transport sector.

Improvements in the efficiency of cars are offset by the trend towards greater ownership of larger engined models, especially amongst company-owned cars. The proliferation of larger sports utility vehicles (SUVs) is a particular expression of this.

In connection with greenhouse gas emissions the Kyoto Protocol requires the monitoring of a 'basket' of emissions, weighted by their Global Warming Potential. The target has been set of a 12.5% reduction below 1990 levels by 2012. Carbon dioxide (CO_2) contributes about 85% of the UK total and almost all emissions from the transport sector are of this kind. As far as road transport is concerned CO_2 emissions are a product of engine size and efficiency, vehicle design, driver behaviour and traffic speeds (i.e. of overall fuel consumption) and of the composition of fuels.

Since 1980 emissions of CO_2 from all sources have declined slowly (Figure 3.11). In 2005 they were 5.3% lower than in 1990 but higher than the trajectory required to meet the UK Government's own target of a 20% reduction by 2010. However emissions from transport sources have increased by 11% during this period (to 129m tonnes) and now comprise 23% of the total. (If presented by end-user category, i.e.

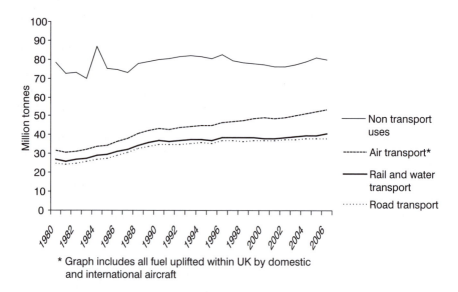

* Graph includes all fuel uplifted within UK by domestic
and international aircraft

Figure 3.10 Fuel consumption by transport and other uses UK 1980–2006

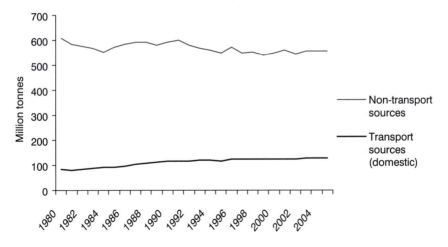

Figure 3.11 CO_2 emissions from domestic transport and non transport sources UK 1980–2006

including transport's share of emissions from power stations and other fuel-processing plants, this figure increases to 28%.)

In absolute terms the main contributors to transport's increase over the last decade have been light vans (up by 4.2m tonnes) and HGVs (4.6m tonnes). Emissions from cars peaked in 2002 and have since fallen back a little to the level of roughly a decade ago (70m tonnes). Emissions from domestic air transport have doubled during the decade but still only represent 2% of the transport total.

For comparison purposes CO_2 emissions arising from fuel supplied to international aviation at UK airports have increased 3.5-fold since 1980 (to 35m tonnes). Together with international shipping from UK ports these now represent a one-third addition to the domestic transport total. However they lie outside the Kyoto Agreement.

Although transport is not required to contribute pro rata to overall CO_2 reduction targets there are clearly grounds for concern that the trend in transport emissions is incompatible with the Government's declared intention of moving towards an overall 60% reduction by 2050. We return to this issue in the context of the contemporary policy agenda in Part 5.

3.9 Public attitudes

In this final section we review the available evidence about public attitudes to traffic and transport-related issues viewed as a whole. This not only enables the perceived condition and importance of the various issues to be compared; it also enables them to be placed within a broader context of public concerns more generally.

However some important caveats need to be registered about this type of evidence. Compared with many of the topics reported on previously, attitudinal research is more subject to variations arising from the particular methodology employed. Apparent discrepancies may therefore arise in results on particular topics where evidence is drawn from different sources. In addition, even where the same source is being used, fluctuations can occur over relatively short periods of time. This may reflect for example the degree of attention an issue has received in the national media. In this respect the British Social Attitudes Survey, which poses a similar set of questions on the same basis each year, is of particular value (accessible at www.britsocat.com).

BSA data from the 1980s revealed growing public concern about the environmental dangers of road traffic to the extent that new measurements had to be devised to capture the public mood (Taylor and Brooke 1998). However it was noted that this concern was 'relatively passive' such that, as candidates for public expenditure, roads and public transport barely featured at all as against 'core programmes' of health, education, pensions and law and order.

A question on 'threats to the countryside' saw 'motorways and road-building' rise from last to second place amongst seven during the decade to 1994 – both a source and a reflection of the growing controversy on this subject at that time (7.2). The seriousness with which a range of traffic-related issues was then viewed (in isolation) is shown in Table 3.2.

A pioneering piece of research on public attitudes to transport policy and the environment was commissioned in 1995 by the Government in the context of the 'Great Debate' initiated by the then Secretary of State for Transport Dr Mawhinney (7.7). A particularly interesting feature was its use of a methodology which enabled respondents' opinions to be recorded before and after being presented with factual information about transport conditions and about the likely cost and effectiveness of various policy options (Jones et al. 1996). This highlighted the important distinction to be made in utilising attitudinal data generally between identifying what members of the public currently think and what courses of action would address their real concerns in practice.

In this exercise air pollution and traffic congestion were regarded as very serious *national* problems, with road safety being of particular concern to people with young children. Fewer people regarded these problems as being very serious at the local level although on average a quarter to a third still placed traffic congestion and air quality in this category. When presented with traffic projections about a third of all respondents changed their opinion in regarding transport-related issues as more serious, but the proportion was higher amongst respondents living in smaller settlements less exposed to current traffic problems.

Research undertaken a few years later for CfIT (the Commission for Integrated Transport) found that transport issues headed the public's *local* concerns (MORI 2001). When asked to identify the main problems in their local area almost 40% spontaneously listed at least one transport-related issue, with traffic congestion (mentioned by 14%) being the highest single concern.

Table 3.2   Proportion of respondents viewing a range of traffic impacts as 'very serious for them' in 1995 (source: BSA Survey reported in Taylor and Brooke 1998)

	%
Exhaust fumes from traffic in towns and cities	63
Traffic congestion in towns and cities	50
Congestion on motorway	42
Noise from traffic in towns and cities	32
Congestion at popular places in the countryside	22
Increased traffic on country roads	21

The same survey asked what aspects of transport warranted the highest priority for addressing over the next few years and how these are currently rated. (These aspects included factors such as cost and reliability as well as some of the safety and environmental considerations noted in this chapter, but are included here as they provide important insights for policy makers on relative priorities.) The question was asked separately of issues relating to roads, buses and trains.

Unsurprisingly (since many more people are frequent car users) the most important issues identified related to cars and roads. The top *six* roads-related issues were viewed as priorities by between 30% and 47% of the population, outstripping the highest single issue relating to buses and trains (punctuality and reliability, viewed as a priority by around 25% of the population). This places in context the often-quoted observation (confirmed in the BSA survey) that *when asked in isolation* around two-thirds of the population consider it 'very important' that public transport should be improved.

People's rating of the current condition of each issue was registered on a four-point scale (very good to very poor) so that a net overall rating (negative minus positive percentages) could be derived. In general, ratings of current conditions were reflected in the priority attached to an issue for public action, but not entirely. Noticeably the issue which received the worst net rating – global warming through vehicle emissions (–64%) – came only fifth out of the seven issues offered as priorities for action related to roads.

Details of the ratings for roads-related issues, listed in priority order, are illustrated in Figure 3.12. The top two priority issues are the cost of car use and congestion in towns – nicely encapsulating the conundrum facing policy-makers when contemplating parking charges or road pricing as means of tackling urban traffic congestion!

The net opinion ratings for issues relating to bus and train services are shown in Table 3.3, listed according to the proportion of *users* who viewed them as a priority for public action.

Except for 'ease of crossing roads' the net opinion ratings of all the roads-related features is extremely negative. Rather surprisingly by comparison most features relating to buses and trains receive a net positive rating – the conspicuous exceptions being rail fares and overcrowding. However, embedded in this is one of the methodological difficulties referred to earlier. Opinion about crossing roads is derived from *all* people

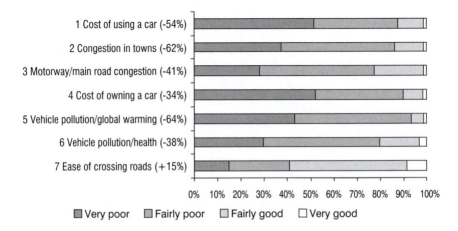

Figure 3.12 Opinion ratings of road-related issues listed by priority for action (source: MORI 2001 for CfIT)

Table 3.3   Opinion ratings of bus and train-related issues, listed by priority for action (source: MORI 2001)

Priority for action	Local bus issues	Net rating	Train issues (exc London Underground)	Net rating
1	Punctuality/reliability	+5%	Punctuality/reliability	–2%
2	Frequency	+5%	Level of fares	–40%
3	Level of fares	+4%	Overcrowding	–22%
4	Number of places accessed	+27%	Personal security	+7%
5	Personal security	+16%	Frequency	+16%
6	Overcrowding	+9%	Cleanliness	+12%
7	Cleanliness	+32%	Number of places accessed	+41%
8	Attitude of drivers	+33%	Journey time	+27%
9	Journey time	+31%	Attitude of staff at stations	+23%
10			Attitude of staff on trains	+35%

Note: Opinions of users only

(whether their daily travel involves much in the way of crossing trafficked roads or not) whereas opinion about public transport is only derived from users. Hence the many car drivers who never use buses and trains are omitted even though one can be sure that a large proportion would have poor opinions of them.

Recently, in connection with the DfT's review of its strategic goals (24.8), the Department has commissioned an 'On-line Citizens' Panel' of just over 600 people to elicit opinion in a structured manner. Although the panel is not representative of the population (of England and Wales) in a statistical sense it was established using quotas set by region, age, gender and urban/rural.

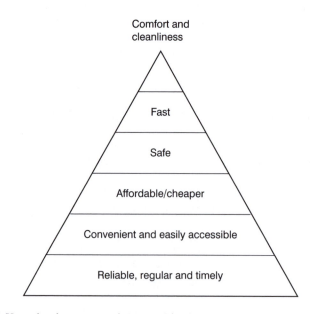

Figure 3.13 Hierarchy of transport needs (source: GfK 2008)

Panel members were asked to describe what they thought the most important things were which *they* wanted the transport system to do for them. The initial report (GfK Consumer Services 2008) comments that although members were not asked explicitly to reflect on whether the proposed goals were the right ones, 'reassuringly' the feedback does not suggest that the Department has missed anything which is uppermost in people's minds. In line with previous evidence the researchers note that the responses received indicated a 'hierarchy of transport needs' which can be represented in a pyramid consisting of six levels (a design based on Maslow's hierarchy of human needs proposed in his 1943 paper *A Theory of Human Needs*) (see Figure 3.13).

> The most basic need is shown at the bottom of the pyramid – a reliable, regular and timely transport system. The higher needs in the pyramid only come into focus when the lower needs are satisfied, so that once an individual has moved upwards to the next level, needs in the lower level will no longer be prioritised. However, if a lower set of needs is no longer being met, the individual will re-prioritise these needs by focusing attention again on the unfulfilled level.

Perhaps the most striking feature from all the evidence reviewed is the low priority given by the public to improving journey times (even on public transport, which is slower than car for most journeys). And yet, as we shall see, this is the attribute which assumes the most importance in the Government's assessments of investment in transport!

Part II

The evolution of transport policy and planning

The problems and opportunities which confront today's transport planners are not simply the product of the social and economic changes described in Part 1. They also reflect the decisions which national and local governments have taken in the past to influence these changes or to modify their outcomes.

In a developed country like Britain the 'resource' represented by our transport inheritance – physical, institutional and cultural – is enormous. Although this provides us with an immense advantage (in that we are not starting from scratch) it is also something of an obstacle. For practical reasons and in terms of winning public support the activities of present governments are inevitably concerned with making what are mostly marginal adjustments to the sum of what has been done in the past (although such measures will obviously be carefully targeted).

Here in Part 2 we consider the main policy measures which have been taken in the past, the results of which combine to form the setting for planning today. This inherited policy framework, it should be emphasised, is not the product of some coherent overall design. Rather it is better viewed as a patchwork quilt which has and continues to be worked on, with new pieces being added on some occasions, and old ones being renovated or replaced on others. The source of some of the pieces is very old indeed, much older than the last 50 years on which we concentrated in Part 1.

The evolution of transport policy is presented in broadly chronological order organised around particular initiatives or types of action characteristic of their time.

- Chapter 4 considers the period before 1955 during which some of the fundamental decisions were taken towards the treatment of the motor car and its impacts, but before the age of mass motorisation.
- Chapter 5 describes the events of the next 25 years (here labelled 'the motorway age') which were dominated by initiatives designed to address the requirements of this new era.
- Chapter 6 recounts the changes introduced by the post-1979 Conservative Government led by Margaret Thatcher and which, as in many other spheres, marked a radical departure from the political consensus which characterised the earlier post-war period.
- Chapter 7 deals with policy changes in the 1990s which reflected the arrival of 'sustainable development' on the political agenda and with challenges to the convention of 'predict and provide' in transport planning.
- Chapter 8 extends this into the period of the New Labour Government between 1997 and 2004 marked by the rise and fall of the aspirations set out initially in its 'New Deal' White Paper.

By following the evolution of transport and transport policy over several decades it is possible to see more clearly the degree of change over the longer term. This helps put our *present* situation in perspective and to recognise that it is neither inevitable nor immutable. Alternative types of behaviour, attitude and action have been adopted in the past and will inevitably arise in future.

Principal sources and further reading

For the details of the development of transport and transport policy generally before the era of mass motorisation see Bagwell and Lyth (2002) and Barker and Savage (2005). The social and political responses to the arrival of the motor car are examined in Plowden (1971), Barker (1987) and O'Connell (1998).

Evans (1992) contains a robust critique of the role of the Department of Transport from its inception. Starkie (1982) gives more focused treatment to roads policy during the motorway age.

Cherry (1972) contains sections on the role of transport in urban change. Hamilton and Potter (1985) focus on stages of transport development with particular reference to their effect on towns. Ward (1994) provides a definitive account of the evolution of the statutory planning system against the background of urban change.

From a public policy perspective Banister (2001), Glaister et al. (2006) and Vigar (2002) all contain overview chapters of transport policy since 1945. Vigar also examines the 1987–2001 period in detail in relation to the 'predict and provide' paradigm. Docherty and Shaw (2003) contains critical commentaries on various aspects of New Labour's 'New Deal'.

4   Before mass motorisation

The period to 1955

4.1 Introduction

As noted in Part 1, the 1950s marked the time when the motor car began to assume dominance as a form of transport and when public policy began to give serious consideration to the remodelling of the nation's transport networks and the redevelopment of urban areas to accommodate car use on a mass scale. It may therefore seem unnecessary to learn about the period before in order to understand our contemporary situation.

In fact the first half of the 20th century and earlier contributed to our present legacy in three main respects:

Physically

- The centres of most towns and cities and the patterning of inner urban areas derives from before the advent of the motor vehicle, even if many of the individual buildings have been redeveloped or added to since. Almost the whole of the railway network utilised and available to us today – that is the pattern of routes and the location of stations – is the product of the 19th century. Except for the national motorways and a relatively small length of other wholly new roads, the roads and settlements which form the core components of today's spatial structure are the product of the era before mass motorisation.

Institutionally

- Long before the motor vehicle, the State had had to address issues raised by the development of transport infrastructure and the operation of transport industries. The nature of the legislation that was passed and the institutions and procedures it brought into being are the foundation of many such features today. For example the idea that 'transport' should be institutionalised as an activity meriting a separate Government department derives from 1910 and – a veritable mixed blessing – is still with us a century later.

Culturally

- The historic notion of a 'public right of way' and the associated freedom of movement is of immense political and practical significance. It means that any measure – national or local – which potentially interferes with this freedom is subject to formal procedures which enable it to be challenged and scrutinised before a decision is made.

- Scarcely less important is the right to own and drive a motor vehicle on a public road network, much of which was not designed for this purpose. Public 'acceptance' of this was gained at the beginning of the 20th century when the motor car was little more than an expensive plaything enjoyed by a small social elite. The freedoms and status it conferred on its owners established it as an aspirational good which has underpinned its extraordinary development ever since. The inter-war years in particular witnessed momentous struggles between motorists and other groups concerning the regulations which should govern this potentially lethal and environmentally damaging vehicle. The clash between individual and collective interests is a source of almost unparalleled contentiousness which plagues deliberations over transport policy and planning to this day.

In this chapter we deal firstly with the development of transport networks before the advent of the motor car (4.2 and 4.3) and then with different types of measure introduced during the inter-war years to accommodate the rapidly developing new mode (4.4 to 4.6). In the final two sections (4.7 and 4.8) we report the radical initiatives in nationalisation taken by the post-war Labour Government in the fields of public transport (passenger and freight) and development rights – the latter itself partly prompted by the emerging effects of motorisation.

4.2 Early improvements to roads and waterways

The maze of roads that is the nation's highway system have been selectively improved over centuries and have been classified, managed and signed to form the unified network we use today. We have to make a very deliberate effort to recognise that it was not always like this. National roads and national policies are a comparatively recent phenomenon, excluding the few long-distance routes that have survived from the military occupation by the Romans. Roads and other forms of transport grew from very local beginnings.

State involvement in transport can be traced back to the Highways Act of 1555 which aimed to ensure the maintenance of roads in each parish in place of the previous manorial system. Every householder was required to provide four days a year unpaid labour for the repair of roads in his parish under the supervision of a local surveyor chosen from within the community. Later legislation allowed for those who could afford it to make a payment (with which to hire labour) in place of their own due – the forerunner of the modern system of local council taxes.

Use of the term 'road' invites misconceptions of modern engineered routes with waterproof surfaces. Until about 1750 roads were what they had always been – dirt tracks – whose use by wheeled carts, if possible at all, was very much dependent on the vagaries of local geology and recent weather. In order to prevent excessive damage Parliament had passed a succession of Acts to limit the weight of wagon loads and to prevent the use of narrow, rut-inducing wheels.

In the face of difficult overland travel, bulk goods were moved instead by coastal shipping supplemented by estuaries and navigable rivers penetrating inland. River improvements were made during the 17th and 18th centuries using Acts of Parliament to overcome objections from landowners fearful of incursions into their protected local markets. To these river improvements the construction of artificial waterways, i.e. canals, was a logical extension.

After the opening of the commercially successful Bridgwater Canal near Manchester in 1761 a rash of canal projects followed. Eventually these linked the Mersey, Trent, Severn and Thames and brought the benefits of cheap waterborne access to the rapidly industrialising towns of the Midlands. Local land owners and entrepreneurs who stood to gain from canal projects mostly took the initiative in promoting and raising the necessary capital, although there was a period of more widespread investment 'mania' in the early 1790s. A legacy from the system of local promotion was the different dimensions to which the canals and locks were built. This plus continued fragmented ownership and the absence of a central 'clearing house' system to facilitate the through conveyance of goods meant that Britain's canal network as a whole was never developed to challenge the railway as a bulk freight carrier.

With the growth of industry and internal trade in the second half of the 18th century the inherent deficiencies of the parish-based system of highway maintenance became highlighted. There was no incentive for local communities to invest in improvements which would primarily benefit longer distance travellers passing through. This problem was overcome by the creation of turnpike trusts – again often funded by local merchants or manufacturers who stood to gain from road improvement. By individual Acts of Parliament, authority was vested in a body of trustees to raise money for improvement works, to place gates across the road, and to charge tolls to road users for their passage. Such 'improvements' were often controversial and in places engendered riots. (Opposition to road user charging is nothing new!) By the beginning of the railway age in the 1830s there were some 1,100 turnpike trusts each administering about 20 miles of road on average and just over one-fifth of the country's road network in all.

The opportunity to recoup the cost of highway improvements facilitated a more serious and scientific approach to the construction of roads which in turn made possible very much greater continuous speeds. Passenger travel and the conveyance of mail over land was revolutionised with the rapid growth of the stagecoach network. Journeys measured in days in the 1750s were completed in hours in the early 1800s. Nevertheless travel by stagecoach – the forerunner of today's express coach – only appealed to the middle market. Richer people avoided the ignominy of public transport by using their own carriages and hiring post horses. Poorer people travelled more slowly and cheaply on wagons or by coastal shipping.

4.3 The development of the railway network

In their early years of development Britain's railways began similarly to the canals, with local companies securing Acts of Parliament to construct relatively short sections of line serving particular needs. Trunk routes, such as the London to Birmingham or the Great Western from London to Bristol were the exception. Even where railways joined, through-conveyance of goods was difficult until a clearing-house system was established in the 1840s which allowed for the apportionment of receipts between different companies.

In the middle of the 19th century Parliament was dedicated to the idea that consumers' interests were best served by competition, even though criticisms were voiced then and since about the waste of resources that this implied. Competition centred initially on winning sufficient backers to gain Parliamentary approval to construct a line, and then the private investment to fund it. Later, competition moved to the provision of services between urban centres where routes over the lines of two or more companies were possible. Competition was fuelled by the bravura tactics of individual railway entrepreneurs, and by successive waves of investment mania.

The procedure for companies to obtain Parliamentary authority for railway construction was enormously costly. The provisions of each Bill were extremely detailed and large amounts of time and money were spent countering, and ultimately buying off, opposition. This came not only from landowners and industrialists fearful of the environmental or local economic effects of a new railway, but also from promoters of rival schemes and from canal companies anxious to protect their revenues. Many schemes which would in practice have been mutually exclusive were promoted concurrently. Significantly the Private Bill procedures did not involve, and were not accessible to, the mass of the population. This may not seem all that remarkable in the social context of the mid-19th century but it may be more surprising to learn that this remained a route to approval for promoters of transport schemes up to the present day.

Quite apart from Acts authorising the construction of railways, Parliament was involved throughout the 19th century in a mass of legislation concerning various aspects of railway operation. But its attitude was essentially responsive – countering types of problem of a new scale and kind as they arose. Regulations were established covering the safety of construction and operation, rates and charges, and conditions for the carriage of goods. Much of the legislation was concerned with preventing abuse of the monopoly position which railways began to acquire in the field of transport generally and which individual companies enjoyed in particular parts of the country.

In an early example of public intervention in transport for social purposes an Act of 1846 required railway companies to provide at least one stopping train a day – the so-called Parliamentary Train – with third class carriages and fares of no more than one penny a mile. As with private motor cars a century later there was elitist resistance to the idea that this new mode of transport should be available generally to the mass of the population. The Act was therefore an important symbolic gesture although railway companies soon discovered that there was an enormous mass market waiting to be tapped, and third class travel rapidly outstripped the other two classes and became the norm. Interestingly of course the distinction between a minority of first class travellers and the remainder remains to this day.

The growing significance of railways was not simply due to the increasing geographical extent of the network but to the technical improvement in steam locomotives. This made possible very much faster journeys, generating growth in passenger travel at the expense of the stagecoaches, and much greater haulage capability, leading to the demise of the inland waterways.

Interesting examples of the social changes brought about by the railway were the adoption of Greenwich Mean Time as the standard time throughout the country, the growth of national daily newspapers for mass circulation produced and distributed from London, and the promotion of leisure excursions for mass travel to the seaside towns which developed as holiday resorts. Development of the railway also brought an end to the traditional practice of driving sheep, cattle and poultry long distances to market. Stagecoach services were abandoned except in remoter areas not served by railways whilst turnpike trusts, losing much of their revenue from passengers and goods, degenerated into bankruptcy. Horse-drawn transport generally reorganised itself as a feeder mode, collecting and delivering from railway stations, a pattern which continued well into the early decades of the 20th century. This feeder function remains an important element of today's taxi trade.

During the second half of the 19th century new railways continued to be developed – rural branch lines, duplicate trunk routes, and some city suburban lines. However, the attention of Parliament turned increasingly to the issue of 'amalgamation' of existing companies. For the companies themselves amalgamation had the advantage of securing larger operating territories, reaping economies of scale (including the benefits of through running of trains) and removing the need for costly new lines as a method of expansion. Parliament was initially sceptical of such proposals but as the logic of amalgamation began to show itself, the rate of proposals quickened. By the beginning of the 20th century the bulk of the railway network was controlled by about a dozen companies. As a corollary the system of controls placed on railways' commercial practices became more detailed, more universally applicable and more inflexible.

One element of increased control was the introduction of statutory workmen's fares by the Cheap Trains Act of 1883. These were designed to enable the working classes to engage in suburban commuting and thus help overcome the severe housing problems in the inner cities which the railways had themselves done much to create. As the scale of railway operation grew, so companies had enlarged their terminal stations, depots and goods yards, typically demolishing large areas of poor housing at the same time as greatly increasing the demand for labour.

The ending of the era of competition on the railways was hastened by the experience of the First World War during which the railway system was taken over by the Government and greater co-ordination imposed. After the War, nationalisation of the entire system was considered but the preferred solution was amalgamation into four large regional groupings – SR, GWR, LMS and LNER – which remained in private ownership. At the same time the regulation of freight charges was overhauled and a system of standard rates introduced based on 21 classes of merchandise. This system was expected to enable the railways to operate commercially. However a common scale of charges unrelated to the costs of provision plus the requirement not to discriminate against any business placed their way put the railways at a serious disadvantage in the face of competition from road hauliers which began to take place during the inter-war years.

4.4 Coping with the motor vehicle

The development of the internal combustion engine at the end of the 19th century was to create wholly new modes of passenger and freight transport. In the critical early years of its development however the motor vehicle enjoyed the enormous advantage that in both appearance and function it seemed to be little more than a 'horseless carriage' and was used in much the same way, requiring no new special facilities. Motoring in any case began more as a hobby amongst the privileged classes than as a serious mode of transport with potentially far-reaching consequences.

During the 19th century the growth of road transport using steam locomotion was deliberately stifled. Turnpike trusts imposed stringent tolls on the basis that these heavy vehicles damaged the road surface. Parliament passed the Red Flag Act of 1865 requiring road locomotives to travel at no more than 4 mph preceded by a man walking carrying a red flag. Following the introduction of the first motor vehicles into Britain in the early 1890s, legislation was altered to permit these lighter vehicles to travel at 12 mph (later 20 mph) and without attendant flag bearers.

For the bulk of the population the development at about the same time of the modern bicycle with pneumatic tyres was of far greater significance than the motor vehicle. The mobility offered by the bicycle changed social habits – for example extending the geographical range of courtship as reflected in the increased distances between the home parishes of rural couples getting married! Use of the bicycle by women was a conspicuous feature at a time marked by their campaigning for political emancipation. By contrast the development and marketing of the motor vehicle for many decades was conceived as a male prerogative.

Until industrialised production methods became more widespread in the 1920s, the number of commercial vehicles and indeed the number of motorcycles exceeded the number of private cars. For private travel horse-drawn traps remained the dominant mode until after World War I. In the early years of the 20th century, however, serious conflicts began to emerge between motorists and other road users, despite the very small number of vehicles by today's standards. One concern was the clouds of dust thrown up by fast-moving motor cars. This in turn related to the state of the roads themselves, an issue on which pedal cyclists through the Road Improvement Association had campaigned unsuccessfully during the previous 20 years. But road improvement raised the vexed question of funding.

The Royal Automobile Club put forward the proposal that motorists should pay an annual tax on their vehicles, the proceeds of which should go into a national fund to be distributed to local authorities for road maintenance and improvement. This seemingly generous offer was made in order to head off the greater evil (from the motorists' standpoint) of them being required to fund a new network of motor-roads altogether. The proposal for a Road Improvement Fund was adopted by the Liberal Government in 1907 with vehicle taxation based on engine horsepower and supplemented by a duty on petrol.

As vehicle ownership grew, so did the money in the road fund. This proved too tempting a revenue source for Chancellors of the Exchequer and the fund began to be raided for general public expenditure after 1926 and was wound up altogether as an earmarked source in 1937. Nevertheless the idea that the annual vehicle tax is or should be linked directly to expenditure on roads has proved remarkably enduring and continues to influence debates on motoring taxation and road pricing to the present day.

During the 1920s, public concern mounted at the rising toll of 'motor accidents'. Road deaths reached the appallingly high figure of 6,100 a year in 1928 at a time when there were fewer than two million vehicles on the road and the speed limit was still nominally 20 mph. Previous debates on a national speed limit had reached a stalemate between campaigners arguing that it was necessary in order to reduce casualties, and motoring organisations who saw this as a unacceptable limit on motorists' freedom and who maintained that it was reckless or dangerous driving which needed to be targeted instead.

Although similar views can be seen expressed in the popular press today, it is important to appreciate the very different social context in which debates over driving originally took place. Whilst car ownership increased dramatically during the inter-war years it remained almost exclusively within the province of the middle class – and at a time when this was a much narrower and more privileged group than 'white collar' occupations today. The very idea that leading members of local communities should be required to adapt their day-to-day behaviour (as potentially irresponsible motorists) was regarded as an affront. Such social niceties surrounding restrictions on driver behaviour persisted well into the era of mass car ownership – the comment that a motorist is 'unlucky' to have been 'caught' for speeding is still a familiar one; likewise the distinction that a traffic violation is not in the same category as other criminal offences.

A Royal Commission appointed to consider the issue of speed limits recommended that the general limit of 20 mph – long since ignored – should be abolished. This was enacted in the Road Traffic Act of 1930. At the same time penalties for dangerous driving were increased and compulsory third party insurance introduced. However these initiatives did not halt the escalating toll of road injuries and the Pedestrians Association in particular continued its lobbying campaign. In 1934 it secured legislative reward with the re-establishment of a speed limit within built-up areas (but raised to 30 mph), the introduction of a test for new drivers and provision for local authorities to install zebra crossings on which pedestrians would have priority. These innovations have proved remarkably long-lasting. Further and progressively more stringent regulations have been imposed on drivers and motor vehicles in the decades since, including in the mid-1960s a 70 mph speed limit on motorways, road-worthiness tests on motor vehicles, the fitting of seat-belts, and the creation of a new offence of driving in excess of defined blood alcohol levels.

Another long-lasting legacy of the 1930s has been the tension between cyclists and motorists over their respective 'rights' in the use of road space. Initially the two groups collaborated as members of the Road Improvement Association but differences in social class as much as in the requirements of the two transport modes resulted in increasing antipathy between them. Despite their much smaller number, motorists managed to assert the view that cyclists were a nuisance and deserved to be banished to segregated tracks. Cyclists then and since have campaigned against such treatment – not least because it renders them even more vulnerable at side crossings and main junctions where no special provision is made. Amazingly even in 2007 the Transport Minister was questioned over the wording of the Highway Code as to whether cyclists should use separate facilities where they existed on the basis that this could leave cyclists open to prosecution in the event of an accident where they had exercised discretion not to use them (LTT 469).

In the event only a few segregated cycle tracks were built alongside new arterial roads. In the postwar decades, despite the comprehensive replanning of many areas, provision of any kind for cyclists was omitted partly so as not to appear to encourage what was perceived to be a dangerous form of transport! Only in one or two new towns were wholly segregated networks created. More generally, as road layouts were enlarged and traffic volumes and speeds increased, the number of cyclists declined rendering those who remained an even more endangered species. Unsurprisingly, despite latter-day attempts at resuscitation in the interests of sustainability, cycling as a utility mode has become virtually extinct in many parts of the country.

4.5 Regulating urban passenger transport

Urban passenger transport has always been primarily road based. Even before the motor vehicle, towns were generally too compact, and journey distances therefore too short, for rail travel to be a worthwhile option. In the large conurbations there was however a flurry of suburban rail construction and electrification in the early decades of the 20th century, notably in London. Living and commuting by rail from the more pleasant rural environments at and beyond the urban edge was and remains a more expensive middle class prerogative.

The richest section of society never had to resort to public transport of any kind, utilising instead their own horse-drawn carriages, often kept in mews along the back of their terraced houses. Those who were better off but without their own transport could hire horse-drawn cabs – the forerunner of present day taxis – or travel in short-distance stagecoaches. Urban transport only came within reach of the bulk of the population with the introduction of trams – initially horse-drawn – which permitted larger 'omnibus' vehicles and lower fares.

Construction of tramways originally required their own individual Act of Parliament, but a general Tramway Act passed in 1870 made promotion much easier. In the 1890s acquisition by local authorities was often linked to their ownership of electricity production. Conversion from horse to electric traction extended the effective range of tram systems, especially in London. At the beginning of the 20th century trams enjoyed a period of great success and profitability in the main cities. Public authorities used them either as a source of revenue to supplement their rates or, as in the case of London, as a means of overcoming housing problems by holding down fares for longer distance journeys to new workers' housing estates being built at the city periphery.

In London itself, because of road congestion, a special Act was passed in 1872 which prevented tram development in the centre of the capital. This created the conditions in which sub-surface railway development became a commercial proposition. Routes which now form the Circle line of London Underground were first built on a 'cut-and-cover' basis using steam locomotion. The later introduction of electric traction made possible the development of the city's 'tube' system using deep-bored tunnels.

The substitution of motor for horse-drawn buses in the early years of the 20th century had a revolutionary effect. This was due not simply to their advantages as a transport mode (greater speed and range than horse-buses and freedom from the infrastructure costs and operating limitations of a tram track) but to their pattern of ownership. The low costs of entry into the industry meant that motor bus services were a highly competitive business from the outset.

Many local authorities sought to develop bus services of their own, either as extensions to, or as replacements for, their tram routes. (Electric trolley buses were also utilised in much the same way.) But authorities had no general powers for bus operation and had to secure individual Acts of Parliament which were hedged about with conditions and obligations. Private operators by contrast could set up business without such hindrances. This together with public concern at the aggressive and potentially dangerous tactics of competing operators on the roads, led to an entirely new licensing system being introduced under the 1930 Road Traffic Act. This regulated bus services for the next half-century, for much of which they were the dominant mode of urban transport.

The 1930 Act required new types of licence for the operators and drivers of bus services. Each route also required a Road Service Licence incorporating conditions relating to fares, stopping points, and times of operation. To prevent what was perceived as wasteful competition, licences were normally awarded to a single operator along a particular route with priority being given to the dominant or longest established operator along it. The failure of an operator to run services responsibly could lead to the withdrawal of his licence for a particular service or ultimately to disqualification from operation altogether.

A completely new system of administration was set up to consider licence applications. In place of the myriad of local authorities, traffic commissioners were appointed on a regional basis. (For operator licensing this system is retained to the present day.) In relation to services the role of the commissioners was essentially passive, i.e. responding to the applications submitted. Some desirable changes, e.g. to achieve better co-ordination of services, could be brought about by informal negotiation or by imposing conditions. Preference would also be given to applications which included an element of cross-subsidy, i.e. combining different sections of route, times of day or days of week which individually might be profitable or unprofitable in order to deliver a comprehensive service. However the commissioners had no duty to 'plan' services nor to promote agreement or amalgamation between companies to achieve greater efficiency.

An important exception at this time were the arrangements made in London. Chaotic traffic conditions in the capital had already led to the imposition of restrictions on bus operation in certain streets. There was recognition of the need to develop tube and suburban electrified railways to relieve road congestion, but also concern that investment might be inhibited whilst there was no protection from road-based competition.

To address this situation the 1933 London Passenger Transport Act was passed under which all bus, tram and underground railways in London were acquired or transferred to a new public authority – London Transport – established as a nationalised industry with a management board appointed by the Minister of Transport. In the capital therefore, except for conventional suburban railways, there was a monopoly of public transport operation throughout a wide area and not merely along particular routes. Uniquely, the principle of co-ordinated planning and of monopoly operation along individual routes has persisted in the capital to the present day.

4.6 Developing a national road network

The demise of the turnpike trusts in the railway age led to responsibility for highways falling back on to parish councils and their funding on to local rates. Amalgamation of parishes into highway districts was permitted in an *ad hoc* manner but it was not until local government was reorganised in 1888 and 1894 that a unified system was created, with county borough councils in the main towns and county councils elsewhere being the main highway authorities. Essentially this system has been retained to the present day, although with the superimposition of a higher tier of trunk roads and motorways which are the responsibility of Central Government, as described below.

After 1910 local authorities benefited from grants and loans paid by the Roads Board, set up to administer the Road Improvement Fund referred to earlier. A series of conferences was held between the Roads Board and local authorities during the period 1912–16 and these generated many of the improvement schemes which were undertaken in the subsequent inter-war period.

In 1919 the function of the Roads Board was transferred to the newly created Ministry of Transport. It was at this time that a national system of classifying roads was introduced, with rates of grant for improvement set at different levels depending on the class (i.e. importance) of road. In London the Ministry of Transport itself took responsibility for the building of a number of 'arterial' roads such as the Eastern and Western Avenues which were intended to take over the role of the traditional radial routes in these sectors.

Elsewhere especially high rates of grant were offered for the improvement of the most important inter-urban routes. However the initiative for bringing forward improvement proposals still rested with the county councils whose enthusiasm was inevitably conditioned by their share of the costs. Road interest groups therefore campaigned for the transfer of the most important roads to the Ministry of Transport in order to inject consistency and a national dimension into the planning and programming of improvements.

Under the Trunk Roads Act of 1936 the Ministry of Transport took over responsibility for 4,500 miles of the most important through routes. Sections of these routes passing through London and the county boroughs were excluded, although it was anticipated that in time bypasses would be constructed around the towns concerned thereby creating a continuous trunk road network. This division of responsibility has often left an important physical legacy as far as the form of the main road network is concerned around cities. In London for example the M1 and M4 motorways come to a noticeably abrupt end at the North Circular Road which marks the boundary of the former London County Council.

As a consequence of the Trunk Roads Act the Ministry of Transport acquired the unusual role for a central government department of a promoter and developer of schemes. Whereas previously its officials had spent their time inspecting the details of local authority proposals the new arrangements begged the question of who was to vet the Ministry's own schemes – an issue which assumed greater importance in later decades. The takeover also placed in doubt the credibility of the Ministry in being able to exercise impartially its policy formulation role in adjudicating between the claims of the various modes within transport as a whole.

4.7 Nationalised transport

During the first half of the 20th century the tide of opinion moved strongly towards the principle of national planning, co-ordination and eventually ownership of non-local freight and passenger transport services. The creation of the Ministry of Transport and of the trunk road network reported above were part of this trend.

Competition between longer distance road and rail passenger services was effectively nullified by the system of road service licensing introduced in 1930. However the Royal Commission advising on the reform of licensing had reported that: 'Without unification – however it may be accomplished – no attempt to bring about complete co-ordination would be successful.' A degree of co-ordination was nevertheless achieved independently by railway companies acquiring stakes in bus companies and to a lesser extent in road haulage which they used as feeders to rail depots.

As with road passenger transport more reckless developments in the road haulage industry were constrained by a licensing system introduced in 1933. Hauliers had to demonstrate their fitness as operators and comply with regulations governing drivers' hours and wages. Those engaged in public carriage (as opposed to firms' own business) also had to obtain Carriers' Licences. Existing businesses received licences automatically but subsequent applicants had to show that suitable transport facilities (road or rail) were not already in existence.

Despite the appeal of 'co-ordination' as a principle, little was actually done during the inter-war period to achieve it. The system of passenger service and freight carriers' licences was designed primarily to prevent wasteful competition, which is not the same thing.

After the war the election of a Labour Government on a strong socialist programme meant that the co-ordination issue would be addressed by greater administrative control rather than by allowing greater play for market forces as some advocated. The Transport Act of 1947 established the British Transport Commission (BTC) with a duty of 'providing or securing the provision of, an efficient, adequate, economical and properly integrated system of public inland transport and port facilities in Great Britain'. At the same time it was charged with paying its way, taking one year with another and also with consulting newly-created user consultative committees. Exactly how the Commission was to pursue and reconcile these potentially conflicting objectives was not identified, and indeed never resolved during the 15 years of its existence.

The 1947 Act also provided for the nationalisation of all railway and canal companies plus ancillary road haulage and passenger businesses (i.e. their compulsory acquisition by the State, with compensation being paid to their previous owners). Assets were transferred to the BTC and powers were given to it to acquire further road transport businesses. As from February 1950 private road hauliers were to be restricted to providing carriage services within 25 miles of their operating base, with the publicly owned group British Road Services thereafter assuming the monopoly of longer distance services.

The Road Haulage Association, acting on behalf of private road hauliers, mounted a strong campaign against the 1947 Act's provisions concerning road freight. The Conservative Party championed their cause, and promised to repeal these parts of the Act. Soon after the Party's re-election in 1951 the 25-mile limit was lifted and the denationalisation (or 'privatisation') of British Road Services began. At the same time – consistent with co-ordination through the market rather than administrative control – historic restrictions on the charging policies of railways were abolished in the 1953 Transport Act.

4.8 Controlling development

The growth of motor vehicles – buses and lorries as much as the private car – coupled with investment in inter-urban and arterial roads near the edges of towns facilitated rapid suburban development during the inter-war years. In London underground and suburban railways were deliberately extended with a view to promoting such development.

Critics of suburbia frequently described it as 'unplanned sprawl'. In fact many of the larger developments were carefully designed and formed part of 'town extension' schemes which local authorities had been given powers to prepare. They provided a stock of new accommodation built to good standards which enabled people living in crowded inner city slums to be re-housed. Nevertheless the threat to the countryside posed by isolated, sporadic development and by the outward march of towns prompted the establishment of the enduring campaigning group CPRE (originally the Council for the Preservation of Rural England).

From a public viewpoint there was particular concern about the unplanned 'ribbon development' which sprang up along main roads out of towns. The traffic generated by this development, including frontage access and turning movements off the main road, reduced safety and efficiency and undermined the benefit of highway improvements which were being made. This concern led to the passing of the Prevention of Ribbon Development Act of 1935 which banned all building within 220 feet of the centre line of a classified road without the consent of the Highway Authority. This was the precursor of a general obligation on local planning authorities to consult highway authorities about the impact of proposed developments on classified roads.

Control of development generally was provided for under the 1947 Town and Country Planning Act – another key piece of legislation of the post-war Labour Government. The essential – and highly controversial – feature of this Act was that it nationalised development rights. Thereafter property owners only had the right to continue to occupy land and use buildings as they had done previously. With certain minor exceptions any change of use, or new or extended buildings could only be undertaken with the permission of the local council designated as the planning authority. Although arrangements have fluctuated since for 'compensation' (i.e. for the loss of development rights) and for 'betterment' (the tax on enhanced property values arising from granting planning permission), the core system of comprehensive development control has remained to the present day.

Amongst many people there was – and remains – a view of development control as essentially a negative activity (i.e. preventing or limiting development, or making it subject to conditions). However this function has to be seen as complementary to statutory development planning – the other main component of the 1947 Act. In this context the overall objective is to secure development in accordance with 'the development plan'. County and borough councils were obliged to prepare plans for their areas, based on surveys of development needs followed by the identification of appropriate sites where these needs could be met. This in turn provided guidance to other council departments (e.g. schools and highways) and to utility companies who were responsible for provision of the infrastructure and services necessary for development to proceed.

The 1947 Act also strengthened local authorities' powers to acquire land compulsorily. This was particularly important in connection with areas designated for 'comprehensive development', notably town centres, where the fragmentation of land ownership would otherwise be a serious impediment.

From the perspective of the 21st century it is difficult to appreciate the extent to which the introduction of development plans was allied to development by local authorities and other public agencies (rather than the regulation of proposals from the private sector). In the early post-war years for example almost all housing development was public, i.e. local authority housing. In part this was a legacy of the centralised control necessary during the wartime period. It also reflected popular support for the notion of the 'Welfare State' as a means of ensuring adequate housing, education, healthcare, employment and social security.

Government action in the field of development planning needs to be seen as an adjunct to these broader goals. Nevertheless there was not a uniform political consensus, particularly where issues of property and private ownership were involved. The difference between the two main parties is neatly symbolised by the decision of the incoming Conservative Government in 1951 to exclude the word 'Planning' from the title of its Ministry of Housing and Local Government. It has been absent from the title of the government department responsible for planning ever since.

5 The motorway age (1955–79)

5.1 Introduction

The period 1955–79 does not neatly demarcate the building of motorways. The first section of motorway (the Preston bypass section of the M6) was opened in late 1958 and the last major new publicly-funded motorway – the M40 from Oxford to Birmingham – was opened in 1991. Widening of existing motorways and upgrading of all-purpose dual carriageways to motorway standard (such as much of the A1) has continued since. But the main period of motorway building symbolised the transition to a transport world dominated by mass car ownership that is recognisably similar to the one we inhabit today.

A similar boldness characterised the planning of towns during the same period. Extensive schemes for 'urban renewal' incorporated plans to restructure highway networks and to insert a new tier of roads geared to the requirements of motorised traffic. Enthusiasm was relatively short-lived however as the results started to appear on the ground and the social, environmental and financial costs of these grand designs came to be recognised.

More sophisticated and holistic arguments about transport came to be advanced at the same time as the economic fall-out from the oil price increases of the mid-1970s had to be addressed. The language of many official publications of this time has much more in common with the 'sustainable transport' rhetoric used today than the more confident but mechanistic arguments used at the beginning of the motorway age.

In this chapter we consider first the inter-urban road programme which was the hallmark of the new era (5.2) and then the rationalisation of the rail network which, in complementary fashion, marked the ending of the previous one (5.3). In the following sections we deal with aspects of urban planning – post-war town planning policy (5.4), the Traffic in Towns report and its aftermath (5.5), the emergence of more integrated 'urban transport planning' (5.6) and, within this, the demise of urban motorways (5.7). Section 5.8 deals with the measures taken in response to new social concerns in the transport field. We conclude with the onset of resource constraints in the mid-1970s which brought the long post-war period marked by steadily rising prosperity to a distinctive close (5.9).

5.2 The inter-urban motorway programme

Prior to World War II the Ministry of Transport had resisted calls for the building of purpose-built motorways on the basis of insufficient traffic. The development of the motor car industry in the UK was geared to the tastes of the middle class (a much smaller social group than today) and this explains the received wisdom of the time that car ownership would not extend to the mass of the population, with corresponding limits to prospective traffic growth.

After the war the official position changed and the case was accepted for the limited development of purpose-built motorways as an alternative to the improvement of existing routes. A proposal put forward previously by the County Surveyors' Society was used as the basis of an announcement by the (Labour) Transport Minister, Alfred Barnes, in 1946 to construct an 800-mile network. This formed the core of the motorway system developed subsequently. The powers to build such roads, excluding certain classes of traffic and without frontage access, were obtained in the Special Roads Act of 1949.

Post-war restrictions on public expenditure meant that motorway construction was delayed until after 1956. The first major route – the 75-mile section of M1 between Watford and Crick, near Rugby (replacing the traditional A5 route between London and Birmingham) – was opened in 1959. At its opening the Minister of Transport, Ernest Marples, commented:

> This motorway starts a new era in road travel. It is in keeping with the bold, exciting and scientific age in which we live.
>
> (quoted in Hamilton and Potter 1985 p. 52)

Over the next decade construction continued at a rate averaging 100 miles a year. Significantly this first phase proceeded without any of the vociferous campaigns from environmental groups which characterised later phases. Proposals for new roads and road improvements outside urban areas did not normally involve substantial property acquisition or environmental damage to local residents as route alignments could be chosen to minimise such effects. Difficulties could arise however where the quality of the natural environment over a wider area was inimicable to road building. Within the first phase of the national motorway programme the section of the M4 between Maidenhead, Reading and Swindon was notably delayed because of problems in agreeing the alignment which had the least environmental impact.

An innovative economic assessment was made of the use of the initial section of M1, comparing the time and cost savings of its users against the capital cost of construction (Coburn et al. 1960). This provided a demonstration of the economic value of the development and helped establish the motorway programme as a legitimate item of public expenditure in the eyes of the Treasury. These 'cost-benefit' techniques were developed subsequently to explore the relative merits of alternative versions of individual schemes and then to rank competing schemes as candidates for inclusion in the national road programme.

By the end of the 1960s the original plan for 1,000 miles of motorway was nearing completion. The Labour Government put forward proposals for the next stage of development in a consultation paper 'Roads for the Future' (MOT 1969). This emphasised the importance not merely of building individual motorways but of improving the standard of the nation's inter-urban network as a whole. In the following 1970 White Paper a target was set of a high quality 4,500-mile network of motorways and other dual carriageway roads to be completed over the following 15 to 20 years (MOT 1970). In essence this strategy was carried forward by the incoming Conservative Government a year or so later (DOE 1972b).

Although the substance of the inter-urban road programme did not change greatly, its presentation altered radically during the short period from 1969 to 1971 to give the appearance of responding to growing environmental concerns.

> Whereas the 1969 Green Paper had said nothing at all on environmental matters, the 1970 White Paper a year later saw the first appearance of the claim that 'new roads improve the total environment'. This claim has been continually restated ever since. By the time of (the) 1971 statement the public was encouraged to believe that environmental improvements were a prime determinant of the programme.
>
> (Evans 1992)

Peter Walker's designation as 'Secretary of State for Environment' combining the former Ministry of Housing and Local Government and the Ministry of Transport was a further example of this presentational change. The two departmental empires were bolted together at national and regional levels but genuine integration proved difficult and the two reverted to separate departments nationally in 1976.

Motorway building reached its peak in 1972 when 400 miles were opened in a single year. Thereafter the pace slowed considerably due to a combination of environmental objections, expenditure constraints and revised traffic forecasts. However the falling completion rates are misleading as an indicator of highway development since they reflect the progressive impact of the 1970 policy to give greater emphasis to upgrading existing roads. Such improvements were often planned and constructed in sections of five miles or so (typically incorporating a bypass of an existing settlement) even though in time they connected to form a continuous dual-carriageway route which for practical purposes is indistinguishable from a motorway. Examples are the A12 (London–Ipswich) and A38 (Birmingham–Derby–M1). Not surprisingly environmental campaigners viewed this as building 'motorways by stealth'.

During the 1970s the inter-urban road programme became the subject of increasingly vociferous opposition. This took place against the background of growing environmental concerns on a global scale highlighted in the influential 1972 Club of Rome report 'Limits to Growth'. The technique of economic cost-benefit analysis which the Department relied on to demonstrate the 'justification' for individual schemes had also received a public drubbing following its use by the Roskill Commission in evaluating possible sites for a third London airport. This had extended to putting a monetary value on a Norman parish church threatened with demolition – famously ridiculed as 'nonsense on stilts' (Hall 1980).

Doubts about long-term growth in the economy also came to the fore in 1973 when, as a result of the Arab–Israeli war, oil prices quadrupled and the availability of energy suddenly became recognised as a critical policy issue. A new dimension was added to debates about major roads concerning the 'need' for such schemes at all. The issue first became prominent at a public inquiry into the proposed M42 south of Birmingham. A coalition of national environmental groups sought to challenge the traffic forecasts upon which the scheme was based. The inquiry Inspector refused to allow the subject to be examined, the argument being that the principle of building the road was a matter of national policy confirmed by Parliament.

For a time the Government tried to hold the line established at the M42 inquiry and instructed its inspectors accordingly. Roads objectors, perceiving the inquiry process to be a farce, resorted to disruptive tactics instead (Tyme 1978). The administration and policing of roads inquiries in these circumstances became extremely difficult and politically embarrassing. Officials of the Department, not believing that a serious case could be mounted against inter-urban road building, concluded that disruptions were the product of political subversives who needed to be distinguished from 'genuine objectors'. An internal Departmental report of 1975 recommended that information officers should be appointed to counteract protest groups' propaganda and convince the 'silent majority' within the population of the advantages to be gained from road building.

In terms of expediting the roads programme, the attempt to confine planning and inquiry procedures was ineffective and even counter-productive. By the mid-1970s these initial stages of scheme implementation, originally scheduled for five years, had slipped to between 10 and 12 years. The situation was rapidly becoming unmanageable.

In response the Labour Government took three important initiatives:

1   to publish a White Paper on a regular basis which would set out the Government's policy on trunk roads as well as updating its current programme (DTp 1978a)
2   to establish a committee to review the Department's procedures for assessing trunk road proposals, with particular regard to traffic forecasting and economic evaluation techniques (DTp 1978b). (The Government accepted the committee's recommendations to allow for a *range* of estimates of traffic growth and for an appraisal framework which included environmental as well as economic factors.)
3   to undertake an internal review of highway inquiry procedures (DTp 1978c). (This resulted in the appointment of inspectors independently of the Department of Transport, the holding of a pre-inquiry meeting to identify relevant policy matters and to agree a procedural programme.)

A balance was also attempted on the vexed question of policy. Whilst retaining the principle that overall planning and methodology should be determined nationally the Department agreed to the examination of the way these were applied to local circumstances. Additional information was also to be provided to objectors, including alternative proposals considered by the Department in coming to their preferred version of the scheme.

These changes took a good deal of the heat out of inquiry proceedings, although objections to the narrowness of trunk roads planning remained. The scaling down of the roads programme and the shift in emphasis towards schemes addressing local problems also helped. The change was such that by 1980 Ministers were referring to 'the end of motorway building' being in sight.

5.3 *The Reshaping of British Railways*

The Reshaping of British Railways was the title of a very important report to the Government prepared by Dr Richard (later Lord) Beeching published in 1963 (MOT 1963). Beeching had no background in railway operations or management but was brought in by the Conservative Government from ICI to serve as Chairman of the British Transport Commission (BTC) and later of the British Railways Board. The deliberate introduction of someone with a commercial perspective and used to the disciplines of managing a large private company was a significant innovation.

The title of the report is indicative of an important policy thrust – to adapt railway operations to the era of the motor vehicle – but it is also somewhat misleading. The 'reshaping' involved the proposed closure of many parts of the railway network and it is this negative aspect of the report – the so-called 'Beeching cuts' – for which it is commonly remembered.

After World War II the railways were carrying their all-time maximum of freight and passenger traffic but the rail system itself was in a poor condition. In the initial post-war years borrowing for investment was limited but in 1955 – which happened to be the last year that railways made an operating surplus – the Government agreed to a Modernisation Plan prepared by the BTC. The Plan included the replacement of steam by diesel or electric traction and the improvement of track and signalling to permit higher speeds.

Although the need for modernisation had long been recognised, the Modernisation Plan itself is generally criticised for being under-researched and over-hastily implemented. The Plan was long-term in nature but the fact that railway finances began to deteriorate rapidly after 1955 was unfortunate given the competing claims for investment in the national road network being made at the same time. When Ernest Marples was appointed Transport Minister in 1959 he took the decision to scale down the Modernisation Plan.

In an attempt to solve the worsening financial problem Marples took two major initiatives. Firstly he dismantled what remained of transport integration and pursued the principles of competition instead. Under the 1962 Transport Act the BTC was abolished and in its place separate Boards were set up for railways, canals, docks and London Transport. The remaining publicly-owned elements of road transport businesses were placed under a transport holding company. Restrictions on the railway's ability to operate commercially were removed including for example allowing the use of surplus land for profitable property development. Much of the debt carried by BTC as a consequence of nationalisation in 1947 was written off, thus reducing the interest burden which railway incomes had to cover.

Marples' second initiative was to appoint Dr Beeching and to ask him to identify the changes which would be necessary to enable the railways to pay their way. Beeching's proposals were based on a survey of traffic and costs on the railway network. His report demonstrated much more forcibly than had previously been realised the huge variation in use and financial performance of different parts of the network and the extent to which elements such as rural branch lines, 'all stations' passenger services, and local goods yards had in practice already been superceded by road transport. One third of the railway's route miles carried only 1% of passenger traffic and 1.5% of freight.

Beeching proposed the closure of about one quarter of the 21,000-mile route network and the reduction of intermediate stations and goods yards on the remainder. At the same time he identified the profitable components represented by trainload freight and by intercity passenger services. In a further report published in 1965 he proposed concentration of investment on to a 3,000-mile trunk network on which development of these services would be promoted (MOT 1965).

The closure of small rural branch lines in favour of parallel bus services had been proceeding slowly for decades in response to the availability of a more convenient and economical alternative. However the scale and pace of closures began to change markedly at the beginning of the 1960s. Even where the economic logic appeared irrefutable, closure proposals generated very considerable local controversy.

British Railways had to go through a statutory procedure to gain ministerial approval to closing lines or stations. If there were public objections an inquiry would be held at which cases of hardship would be aired. (BR later learnt to adopt the tactic of gradually running down services before applying for closure proceedings so that the amount of residual hardship that could be demonstrated was minimal.) Usually the closure notice was accompanied by reference to alternative existing or proposed bus services. However no statutory protection surrounded these services and as subsequent research confirmed (Hillman and Whalley 1980), objectors were right to be sceptical about their adequacy and permanence.

Because of differences in the strength of local opposition actual implementation of Beeching's programme was patchy. As route closures of more than branch line status came to be considered it became more difficult to suggest reasonable alternatives and communities feared that a social and economic lifeline would be cut. Lines in remote areas such as Central Wales and in Scotland which were the most expensive to retain were also the most politically sensitive to close. Following the change of government in 1964 Labour Ministers began to refuse closure applications and indicated that the full implementation of the Beeching proposals would be unacceptable. Because of growing concerns about urban traffic congestion many passenger services in the provincial conurbations also benefited from a reprieve.

As far as freight is concerned Beeching noted that longer distance containerised transport was one of the potential growth markets for rail. However attempts by the redoubtable Labour Minister Barbara Castle to generate additional freight on the rail network as a whole proved a complete failure. Under the 1968 Transport Act the old system of carrier licensing (which protected the longer distance rail market) was abolished, with the intention of replacing it by a new quantity licensing system designed to favour rail for heavy goods journeys over 100 miles. To allow time for the development of 'Freightliner' container services a two-year delay was inserted before this provision was to come into force. In the event the government changed hands in 1970 and the proposal was abandoned.

The promotion of rail freight by the publicly owned National Freight Corporation set up under the Act also never developed in the way anticipated. Arguably this was because of the dominance of road haulage interests in its business but also because the increase in goods vehicles' dimensions and development of the inter-urban road network meant that the scope for economic haulage by rail was rapidly diminishing. In the ten years from 1967 to 1977 the amount of general freight carried by rail actually halved.

5.4 Post-war town planning: new towns and green belts

After World War II the idea of free-standing 'garden cities' was revived as a way of catering for the planned 'overspill' of housing requirements from the main cities. An Act passed in 1946 enabled the Government to designate areas for new towns and to establish 'New Town Corporations' to undertake the development and to organise the relocation of businesses and households from major cities. New Towns were created mainly around London in places such as Stevenage, Harlow, Basildon and Crawley with target populations of around 50,000 but smaller new towns were also designated in the vicinity of a few provincial industrial cities.

In many other areas however expansion continued in the form of peripheral housing estates, with councils often building up to the limits of their administrative boundaries. Usually further expansion was vehemently resisted by the 'rural' counties beyond. It was not just the physical effects they were objecting to. There were also strong underlying social and political motivations. Overspill council housing estates were inhabited by the predominantly Labour-voting working class. These were not welcome to the Conservative voters who traditionally dominated in country areas nor to the upwardly mobile urban migrants who bought into the privately owned housing which was increasingly being developed in the surrounding villages and small towns. In many areas therefore the 'historical accident' of city councils' administrative boundaries was, and continues to be, a dominant factor influencing the size and shape of their built-up areas.

Another garden city principle which found official endorsement in the post-war period was the designation of 'green belts'. Following a circular from Duncan Sandys, the Minister of Housing and Local Government in 1955, local planning authorities were invited to bring forward proposals in their development plans for areas of countryside encircling towns to be designated as green belts. These were intended to check the growth of large built-up areas, to prevent the coalescence of settlements and to preserve the character and setting of historic towns. They were also seen as offering the potential to cater conveniently for the countryside recreational needs of urban dwellers. The designated areas would enjoy lasting protection against development incompatible with their open character.

The concept of green belts enjoyed strong public support amongst residents near the urban fringe and continues to dominate discussion of planning issues in the areas concerned. Throughout their history however their appropriate purpose and application has been steeped in controversy (Elson 1986). In their original formulation green belts were but one element of an overall planned approach to urban development, inseparable from the creation of the garden cities needed to provide for new housing and population growth. In the minds of many however they were – and still are – viewed simply as a device for stopping urban growth.

Where green belts have been formally designated – principally around London and the other conurbations, but also around historic cities such as Oxford, Cambridge and York – their long-term effect has been to divert additional, mainly residential, development further afield. This 'leapfrogging' was facilitated by the improvement of the inter-urban road network, resulting in longer distance car commuting to the principal cities and associated increases in traffic. Conversely, for increasingly mobile city populations, recreational needs are sought in places much further afield than the 'countryside' immediately at hand, and the growth in average travel distances for these types of journey is even greater.

In the 1960s, when population projections were being revised sharply upwards, official enthusiasm for green belts cooled – recognising the dangers of permanently sanctifying large tracts of land from development needs. Meanwhile there was an important further round of new town designations – at Redditch and Telford for Birmingham, at Skelmersdale and Runcorn for Liverpool, at Warrington and Central Lancashire for Manchester, at Washington for Tyneside and at Livingston and Cumbernauld for Glasgow. In the South-East the target populations for the original 'Mark I' new towns were raised and there were further designations at Peterborough, Northampton and in North Buckinghamshire (named Milton Keynes). Significantly these later designations were for larger cities (around 200,000 population) located much further away from the capital, reflecting what was needed to approach the goal of 'self-containment' in a more mobile age.

5.5 *Traffic in Towns*

The problem of traffic in towns that dogged so much of the second half of the 20th century was not a prominent issue in the first half. Before the arrival of the motor vehicle many urban authorities had already taken powers to impose 'improvement lines' along main street frontages so that as redevelopment took place, buildings would be set back to create wide streets of a consistent standard. New roads built as part of the inter-war suburban expansion were typically constructed to much more generous standards from the outset, often incorporating verges and lay-bys and in some cases separate reservations for tram tracks. Traffic signals were introduced to resolve conflicts at the most important junctions from 1934. Such congestion as occurred in town centres was frequently attributed to 'through traffic' to which proposed bypasses were expected to offer a complete solution.

Town planning in the 1950s and 60s was characterised by 'urban renewal'. This set out to achieve the wholesale modernisation of town centres and inner residential areas, often involving widespread demolition and social upheaval. Today such action seems inconceivable but needs to be seen in the context of the destruction, delapidation and disruption which had already afflicted these areas during and after war-time bombing.

The rebuilding programme provided engineers and town planners with the opportunity to redesign individual streets and even the road layouts of whole districts. A manual published in 1946 by the Ministry of Transport encouraged the adoption of a hierarchical pattern of arterial and sub-arterial roads and the creation of residential and shopping 'precincts' (MOT 1946). Unfortunately, given the opportunities that were available, little progress was made. In cities such as Southampton, Sheffield and Plymouth whole shopping streets were rebuilt along traditional lines. Road patterns tended to follow geometric designs, with roundabouts at intersections which did not maximise capacity. Many of the conflicts between moving and access traffic, bus stops, pedestrians etc. remained. In Birmingham and Bradford new inner ring roads were built to relieve traffic from the city centres yet on these roads frontage development was still permitted.

By the end of the 1950s the Government's own programme of trunk road improvements was under way, catering primarily for longer distance commercial traffic. But in towns no programme of public highway investment preceded the rapid expansion in private motoring. In the twenty years after 1955 the number of cars owned increased from 3.6 to 13.4 million. The Government had not anticipated the scale and pace of such change nor the wider implications of mass motorisation. The result was that traffic and environmental conditions worsened rapidly, especially in London.

After the Conservatives' election victory of 1959, Ernest Marples responded to growing concern about urban traffic by taking two initiatives that were to have far-reaching consequences. The first was a series of measures aimed at 'getting the most out of existing streets'. The second was to commission a study on 'the long-term development of roads and traffic in urban areas and their influence on the urban environment'.

A specialist team – the London Traffic Management Unit – was established to explore ways of controlling traffic and parking in the capital so as to improve traffic circulation. The most important feature of the Unit's work was the idea of a comprehensive traffic management *scheme*, utilising a range of individual measures but applying them in a planned manner over a local area. Parking and loading restrictions were co-ordinated and extended along main roads to create a series of 'urban clearways'. The area covered by parking meters (a recent innovation) was also extended and enforcement was improved by the use of traffic wardens devoted solely to this task rather than police officers.

Implementation of these measures undoubtedly succeeded in improving the speed and throughput of traffic on major roads in Inner London. But many other road users found themselves seriously inconvenienced. Some local residents also discovered that their once quiet streets were commandeered almost overnight to form part of the main traffic network. Even motorists found that whilst travelling along main routes was quicker, actually getting to their destination and finding a place to park or unload was often more difficult. This kind of traffic management was in its own terms therefore only a temporary palliative and no long-term solution to the urban traffic problem.

The nature and scale of this problem, and appropriate ways of dealings with it, was explored in the Ministry's commissioned study published as *Traffic in Towns* (MOT and MHLG 1963). The study team was led by Colin Buchanan (and hence it is also known as the Buchanan Report). Buchanan was previously a Planning Inspector who had been singled out through having just written a book of his own on the subject entitled *Mixed Blessing* (Buchanan 1957). He recognised the huge attraction and advantages of the car to the individual but equally the scale of the challenge presented in accommodating widespread mobility if civilised qualities of the urban environment were to be protected.

Public debate at the time was full of imaginative (or alternatively far-fetched) ideas about possible solutions to the urban transport problem – everything from monorails, pneumatic tubes, and individual jet propulsion as well as comparatively mundane concepts such as urban motorways and decked cities (MOT 1967b; Richards 1966). By contrast the study team reflected that they were not dealing simply with a traffic problem (however daunting in itself) but with the future form and management of urban areas. In a remarkably prescient passage they commented:

> There could be no question of a simple 'solution' to the traffic problem. Indeed we found it desirable to avoid the term 'solution' altogether, for the traffic problem is not so much a problem waiting for a solution, as a social situation requiring to be dealt with by policies patiently applied over a period, and revised from time to time in the light of events. There is no straightforward or 'best' solution.
>
> (MOT and MHLG 1963 p. 8)

In defining the nature of the problem the Buchanan Report put forward the then novel idea that traffic was a function of land use. A number of important corollaries followed. Except for smaller towns and villages, bypasses did *not* offer a solution to traffic problems since the bulk of traffic had its origin, destination or both within the built-up area itself. However, by relating traffic flows to the land uses which generated them it was possible to study the volume and pattern of flows much more scientifically. Application of new computerised modelling planning techniques pioneered in the USA enabled the potential scale of future highway networks to be identified. These were used to demonstrate that it would be impracticable to cater for the full extent of potential car use in Britain's larger towns and cities at their prevailing land use densities. Hence restrictions on what was termed 'optional' car use would be necessary (notably commuting) and continued reliance on public transport 'unavoidable'.

However planning for future traffic was not just a matter of highway engineering. The principle of linking traffic with land use needed to be carried through into the design of access ways and buildings. As a general principle the study team maintained that the traditional pattern of all-purpose streets needed to be remodelled to create a new one consisting of a hierarchy of 'distributor roads' enclosing cells in which land use activities and access arrangements would predominate – so-called 'environmental areas'. In the centre of cities the density of land use activity was such that extensive redevelopment would be required, adopting new forms of 'traffic architecture' involving complex multi-level arrangements.

The report noted that it would not necessarily be appropriate to undertake such reconstruction in all areas. Indeed it was a matter for debate how far society would want to go in meeting the financial costs of catering for motorisation and accepting the physical consequences.

> The broad message of our report is that there are absolute limits to the amount of traffic that can be accepted in towns, depending upon their size and density, but up to those limits, provided a civilised environment is to be retained or created, the level of vehicular accessibility a town can have depends on its readiness to accept and pay for the physical changes required. The choice is society's. But it will not be sensible, nor indeed for long be possible, for society to go on investing currently unlimited sums in the purchase and running of motor vehicles without investing equivalent sums in the proper accommodation of the traffic that results.
>
> (ibid. para 444)

The *Traffic in Towns* report provided a much needed analysis of the urban traffic problem of remarkable clarity and comprehensiveness. The amount of public interest it generated was such that the report to the Government was reprinted in Penguin paperback form. However it was open to criticism that its estimates of the future traffic volumes, being derived from the very different circumstances of the United States, had been exaggerated (Beesley 1964). In any case with increasing car ownership and greater mobility, it was likely that there would be a natural decentralisation of activities. This would amount to a restructuring of functions *spatially* within a broader urban region rather than simply a physical restructuring within the confines of existing towns.

Seen in the context of today's environmental debates, the report was visionary in the way it placed environmental conditions at the centre of political choice and in its concept of 'environmental capacity'. However in policy terms the report was perhaps naive in imagining that the motoring public would readily accept limits on car use in order that environmental standards could be achieved. Governments in turn were always likely to try and avoid the expenditure and upheaval of redevelopment (or the inconvenience and unpopularity of car restraint). As experience since has shown, both were prepared to put up with poorer traffic and environmental conditions on traditional streets instead.

5.6 Urban transport planning

At the time *Traffic in Towns* was published 'urban transport planning' did not exist. Rather there were separate activities of highway engineering, traffic management, town planning and public transport operation. Parking control was in its infancy. Over the next ten years there was growing recognition that each of these had a contribution and indeed that the planning of all of them needed to be integrated within a broader view of urban transport and environment.

In 1963, with urban renewal still very much in the ascendant, the move towards integration centred first on bringing together highway and development planning. The Government's response to *Traffic in Towns* was to establish a joint urban planning group to offer advice to local authorities in the application of the report's principles (MOT and MHLG 1964). Over the subsequent ten years it also funded a series of 'land use/transportation studies' for most major towns and cities in the country. The methodology followed was extremely important in determining the way problems were identified, options selected, and possible solutions evaluated. Long after proposals from the original studies were abandoned, this technical 'transportation planning process' (the Americanisation is significant) continued to exert a powerful influence on urban transport policy and practice (Banister 2001). The need for integrated land use/transportation planning was a major factor in debates at the time about the re-organisation of local government and of the development planning system. Local authorities were amalgamated and their boundaries redrawn to reflect better contemporary settlement patterns, particularly in the conurbations (10.6).

As far as development planning is concerned a much enlarged Greater London Council (GLC) was charged with preparing a new style strategic plan – the Greater London Development Plan (or GLDP) – which would act as the policy framework for more detailed, site-specific plans prepared by individual boroughs. This was the forerunner of a two-tier system of structure and local plans introduced generally after 1968 and retained in much of the country for the rest of the 20th century. Policies covering 'the management of traffic' were included within the remit of Structure Plans for the first time. The new development planning system also contained the statutory requirement for public consultation in plan preparation – itself a reflection that public attitudes to development were beginning to alter.

Changes in local government and development planning were coupled with changes in local transport, particularly public transport in the provincial conurbations. Even though bus companies in these areas were all publicly owned, they operated independently. Unlike London there was no overall planning or co-ordination, nor was there any provision for government-supported subsidies or investment. Under the 1968 Transport Act therefore a Passenger Transport Authority (PTA) was established for each of seven conurbations (including Strathclyde in Scotland) whose members were drawn from local councils in the area. The PTA's responsibilities were administered through Passenger Transport Executives (PTEs) to whom were transferred the municipally owned bus companies in their area. These were then remodelled as single large undertakings operating as a monopoly over much of each conurbation – i.e. a similar arrangement as in London.

Unlike London the new bodies could also enter into agreement with British Rail to specify a fares and service pattern for conventional rail services in their area and to pay them for the net costs involved (so-called 'section 20' services). Powers to subsidise bus services – termed 'revenue support' – were also introduced. Funding for both was through a precept by the PTA on the rates of local councils. As far as investment was concerned the 1968 Act introduced a new system of 'section 56' grants from central government for local public transport, mirroring the pattern of grants to local authorities for classified roads.

Concern at deteriorating urban transport conditions prompted a committee of MPs to initiate an inquiry into urban transport planning. This proved extremely telling as evidence from a wide range of bodies pointed to a consensus on the need for a decisive shift in policy. The Committee challenged the then dominance in local authority programmes of major highway schemes:

> Firstly there should be a major and substantial effort to improve public transport … secondly, the use of private cars for the journey to work should be severely discouraged in areas where it impedes public transport.
>
> (House of Commons 1973 paras 26–28)

The report had significance at a local level in giving 'both credence and, at last, a measure of authority to the more articulate and well-considered opposition challenging local plans for urban motorways' (Starkie 1982 p. 88). Nationally it influenced government policy in developing a new system for local authority transport funding in place of previous arrangements whereby different types of expenditure received different levels of grant. From 1974 these were replaced by a single block grant referred to as a Transport Supplementary Grant (TSG). This covered a proportion of all expenditure on items accepted by the Government from within a local authority's programme submitted annually in a TPP (Transport Policies and Programme) document.

The legislative changes of the 1968–74 period had the effect of revolutionising the arrangements for land use and transport planning in the conurbations. New Metropolitan County Councils established in 1974 (and the Strathclyde Regional Council in Scotland) became the highway and traffic authority for their area, the strategic planning authority and the Passenger Transport Authority. They therefore had both functional responsibilities and geographical jurisdiction fit for the integrated approach which was seen to be needed. The GLC had a similar role. In principle at least, these authorities had the discretion to adopt a transport strategy involving any mix of capital investment and operating subsidies and any combination of modes, and would not stand to gain or lose government grants as a consequence.

5.7 'Homes before Roads' – the demise of urban motorways

During the 1960s the public mood had been characterised by optimism. Growing ownership and provision for cars was a very powerful symbol of new-found private prosperity. Urban renewal was also being tackled boldly with demands for new office accommodation increasingly the catalyst for development in central areas. Partnerships between local authorities and private developers were becoming the norm – the latter financed by the swelling coffers of private pension funds. Town planning generally and highway building in particular were approached with a long-term focus and degree of (over)confidence that would be unrecognisable to us today (Tetlow and Goss 1965).

In the late 1960s and early 1970s the climate of opinion surrounding urban planning began to change quite rapidly. However because of the lead time involved in major development schemes, action on the ground continued to reflect previous thinking. Housing redevelopment involving the bulldozing of large areas and the replacement of traditional streets by blocks of high-rise council flats and ill-cared-for public spaces became rapidly unfashionable. So too did many town centre schemes involving wind-swept precincts, multi-storey car parks and inconvenient 'walkways', their unfriendliness aggravated by brutal modernist designs and materials.

Both housing and town centre schemes typically involved major alterations in the road system and the building of new highways on a much larger scale. These incorporated unpleasant and sometimes downright threatening subways, burrows or bridges to circumvent traffic flows which themselves were of much greater volume and speed. The *process* of change – prolonged blight and physical upheaval – also came to be seen as destructive of local communities and a contributor to the economic and social decline of inner cities.

Large-scale highway projects which had been embarked on enthusiastically only a few years earlier began to run into serious opposition. Unlike more recent campaigns the basis of opposition did not centre so much on issues of long-term sustainability but more on the direct effects of individual schemes – land take, housing demolition, noise and air pollution, community severance and visual intrusion. Public disenchantment with comprehensive redevelopment effectively put paid to the overall restructuring of highways and access routes anticipated in the Buchanan report (Hills 1974).

Highway proposals nevertheless continued to be brought forward as individual schemes. Often these derived from lines drawn on maps many decades previously and had been incorporated in the networks tested in land use/transport studies. The most notorious example was the building of the elevated Westway motorway on the edge of Central London, linking White City and Euston Road. This formed part of an arterial road plan for London prepared in 1911, included in the London Transportation Study of the 1960s and opened in 1970. The design of the scheme was such that at one point residents in houses adjacent to the new road could almost reach out of their back bedroom windows and shake hands with people standing on the hard shoulder!

Whatever the arguments surrounding urban motorways in principle it was plainly unacceptable that people could have such environmental conditions imposed on them and without any compensation. Following investigation of the subject (DOE 1972a) the 1973 Land Compensation Act gave highway authorities the powers to purchase not merely the land and property required physically to construct the road, but to incorporate appropriate environmental mitigation measures as well. They were required to install insulation measures in all residential properties where as a result of new road construction or road widening, noise levels exceeded 68 dB(a). They were given discretion to pay for insulation against noise from road construction work and from traffic on *existing* altered roads. The Act greatly civilised urban road building procedures but its effect was more limited than anticipated since, by the mid-1970s, public opinion was already swinging against such schemes in principle.

In London the GLDP incorporated long-standing proposals for a series of new orbital routes – now of motorway standard and termed 'ringways'. Particularly contentious was the innermost Ringway 1 – the so-called 'motorway box' – whose planned alignment cut swathes through dense residential areas and which was estimated to require the demolition of homes belonging to 100,000 people.

The campaigns of local objectors against the ringway proposals were co-ordinated across the capital by an umbrella group, the London Amenity and Transport Association (Thomson 1969). But whilst the technical arguments were proceeding at the GLDP inquiry, raw politics took over in the shape of a decision by the London Labour Party to abandon support for the ringway proposals and to campaign in the 1973 GLC elections on a platform of 'Homes before Roads'. The Party won control and the ringway plans were abandoned before the report of the GLDP inquiry was published (Hall 1980).

Similar battles were being fought in cities elsewhere in the country. The return of local Labour administrations in 1973 was the scene of particularly dramatic policy shifts in Nottingham and Oxford. In both cases controversial road schemes were dropped and new strategies based on car restraint and public transport promotion were put forward as alternatives to road building.

5.8 Maintaining socially necessary services

Alongside the emergence of concern about the environmental impacts of transport was a growing recognition of its *social* significance. Initially questions of 'hardship' or 'social need' arose in the context of the withdrawal of bus and train services in rural areas. Soon however the debate widened to consider the role of public transport in catering for the needs of all those who did not have access to a car and for whom the road-building orientation of national and local policies offered nothing.

As far as railways were concerned the target of breaking even financially which had been set by the Conservatives in 1962 was abandoned. In its place Labour's 1968 Transport Act introduced a system of grants to pay for the retention of individual services, substituted a few years later by a single Public Service Obligation (PSO) grant in 1974. Payment was conditional on maintaining a pattern of services in broadly the form in which they were then operated. By the time the rail passenger network was stabilised in this way it had been reduced by about 40% from the one 20 years previously.

In relation to bus services the financial position of companies began to deteriorate in the 1960s as car ownership increased rapidly. Without expensive infrastructure to maintain, the response of operators was more incremental and less politically contentious than on the railways. Nevertheless rural areas were badly affected since services were sparse anyway and the reduction of bus frequencies often coincided with a loss of local facilities, thus compounding the accessibility problems of people without the use of cars.

Unlike rail services there was no public inquiry in the case of complete withdrawal of a bus service and no consideration of alternative facilities for people who would experience hardship. Service changes and fare increases required the approval of Traffic Commissioners but, whilst they and operators sought to minimise the effects of economy measures, the overall direction of change was unavoidable.

Following examination of the issue by the Jack Committee (MOT 1961) the 1968 Transport Act gave local authorities powers to make revenue support payments to operators for bus services in rural areas and government grants were available to assist with this. A more comprehensive treatment of the issue of socially necessary bus services outside London and the conurbations followed as part of local government re-organisation in 1974. County Councils were given responsibility for promoting the provision of a co-ordinated and efficient system of public passenger transport generally. Both capital investment and revenue support payments could be made to assist with these policies.

Local authorities' response to the possibility of supporting bus services was highly variable. Not only was there political resistance to the idea in some counties but professionally too the new responsibilities did not sit well within county surveyors' departments traditionally dominated by road building. (A separate 'sub-profession' – the Association of Transport Officers (ATCO) – was formed at this time by the officers involved.) The Government attempted to strengthen arrangements in 1978 by requiring county councils to prepare a five-year Public Transport Plan including an assessment of needs in rural areas. However solutions were intractable since in essence transport was being asked to make good 'deficiencies' in the availability of employment, shopping and other facilities over most of which local authorities had no control (Moseley et al. 1977).

Another innovation of social significance included in the 1968 Transport Act was the power given to local authorities to introduce concessionary fares for elderly and disabled passengers on local bus services. However take-up was again variable. The scale of concession offered to passengers and the time periods during which it was available remained a matter for local discretion until the New Labour Government legislated for a minimum half-fare concession thirty years later (15.7).

5.9 'The party's over' – adjusting to resource constraints

There is deep irony in the fact that, just as the overhaul of local government, planning and transport arrangements was being completed in line with the requirements of the motorised era, the economic assumptions on which it was based were blown apart by the oil crisis following the 1973–74 Arab/Israeli War. Public planning would never be the same again. As representatives from the International Monetary Fund laid down their requirements for baling out Britain's stricken finances in 1976, Anthony Crosland, Secretary of State responsible for local government, commented 'the party's over'.

Until that time transport and development plans had generally been prepared without serious regard as to whether the resources would be available to implement them (or to the blighting consequences of proposals if they were not). The approach of local authorities was typically to aim high and then to campaign long and hard to central government for the money necessary to turn vision into reality. The *Traffic in Towns* report did not diminish authorities' aspirations.

Pending the long-term aim of building new highway networks the Government pursued a number of avenues aimed at bridging the gap between the demand and supply of urban road space. In 1965 it set up a Traffic Advisory Unit to help local authorities adopt the techniques of large-scale traffic management schemes which had been pioneered in London. It also published new advice on car parking (MHLG 1965). Previously local planning authorities had been encouraged to set minimum standards for provision in new developments and to provide off-street car parks so as to ease the problems of parking on-street. Now it encouraged authorities to take a comprehensive view of parking policies and their possible contribution to limiting traffic congestion, including the setting of *maximum* rather than minimum requirements in new developments.

During the 1960s there was also extensive discussion of road pricing as a possible solution to the urban congestion problem. A specialist panel was appointed to investigate the technical possibilities (MOT 1964). As a policy option however more sensitive issues were at stake. The Ministry's own review of the subject was published in a report 'Better Use of Town Roads' (MOT 1967a) – a skilful title since it was essentially concerned with traffic *restraint*. Road pricing was acknowledged to be potentially the most efficient option, but not an immediately practicable one. In fact the report seemed to be written to justify the expedient conclusion that, since parking controls were already in existence, it would be easier to encourage local authorities to pursue these more vigorously than to embark on something entirely new and controversial.

When the Labour Government elected in 1974 began to undertake its review of transport policy the public expenditure situation was said to 'overshadow' all other developments. A 'ruthless examination' was undertaken of the various elements of transport spending to ensure that they were actually meeting overall aims – the results being published in a consultation document (DOE 1976). Its emphasis on an 'objectives-led' approach was an innovation.

The principle of a more 'targeted' approach to spending was proposed in the support of bus and train services. The consultation document was particularly damning of subsidies being used to limit fare increases – a practice that had started to take hold in London and the PTA areas in particular. Whilst recognising the need to cater for social needs, especially in rural areas, the document proposed an overall halving of support in the subsequent three years. However, in the White Paper which followed, the Government backed down on this particular proposal (DTp 1977).

Urban rail schemes which had been proposed in the conurbations were more vulnerable to cuts. Notable casualties were the so-called Picc–Vic line (an underground connection across Manchester City Centre between the two main railway stations) and a new tube line in Central London (originally the 'Fleet', later the 'Jubilee' line). However the Tyne and Wear Metro –a scheme involving the renewal of electrified suburban lines coupled with a new cross-centre tunnel in Newcastle and Gateshead – narrowly escaped abandonment. With its interchange stations fed by bus services from outlying areas plus a universal zonal ticketing scheme the Metro epitomised the sort of integrated public transport network which the 1968 Act had been intended to bring about.

As far as motorways and trunk roads were concerned the consultation document originally envisaged that a lower level of spending would imply some reduction in the 4,500-mile 'strategic network' proposed in 1970, and an extension (to the late 1980s) of the period during which it would be built. In the White Paper the concept itself was to be 'modified':

> The Government intends to adopt a more flexible approach … improving roads in phases, dealing with the worst stretches first, and varying the standard of a road throughout its length to reflect the different degree of use. It may lead to less tidy solutions and demand more of the lorry driver and motorist, but it is a necessary price to pay for putting resources where they are most needed.
>
> (ibid. paras 248–249)

The White Paper cited the example of the route from Manchester to Sheffield which had originally been planned as a motorway throughout. Instead it was decided that

> the solution which best met economic as well as environmental requirements was one comprising by-passes for the urban areas with only minor improvements to the existing road through the Peak District National Park.
>
> (ibid. para 250)

The significance of the Government's response to the financial crisis of the mid-1970s was not just that its spending plans were temporarily curtailed. Rather the whole trajectory of growth which had underpinned assumptions during the previous 20 years disappeared. An era which began confidently with local authorities preparing blueprints for the future ended with an air of resignation at seemingly forever having to 'muddle through'. Strategic planning in particular – the cutting-edge of planning practice in the early 1970s – fell back to earth with a bump almost before it had got off the ground.

Uncertainty surrounding the future price and availability of oil also prompted the Government to acknowledge that energy conservation should be a 'major national objective'. However it refuted the idea that conservation should be an 'over-riding objective, justifying sharp and profound changes throughout our way of life'. The Government expected a move towards more efficient engines as fuel prices rose – a 'natural' market response. Taxation was referred to as 'a valuable ally in promoting economy in the use of energy', but here, where the Government could actually make a positive contribution, no action was forthcoming.

Much the same was true in the area of land use planning and the promotion of non-motorised modes. The issues were recognised but no significant action taken:

> In the past, plans have often assumed an increasing supply of relatively cheap transport. Housing and employment have become increasingly separated. Larger hospitals, schools, offices and shops to serve wider areas have meant longer and often more difficult journeys...
>
> For the future ... we should aim to decrease our absolute dependence on transport and the length and number of some of our journeys; and to plan more consciously for those who walk as well as those who use mechanised transport...
>
> (ibid. paras 34–35)

For the first time, walking and cycling were identified as modes which might merit positive development. However the Department of Transport had very little direct experience of these subjects and in the 1977 White Paper they merited just three paragraphs (DTp 1977).

In relation to both transport and land use planning these new policy directions were perhaps too novel to find ready acceptance. As the threat of rising oil prices receded so the issue of energy conservation fell back down the policy agenda. In any case the whole thrust of the Labour Government's programme in the late 1970s became bogged down with trying to impose anti-inflation wage restraint on public sector industries whose unions represented the bed-rock of its political support. The 1979 'winter of discontent' was dominated by a succession of highly controversial strikes in these industries and ushered in the surprise election of a Conservative Government led by Margaret Thatcher. For the next 15 years transport policy took on a radically different tack.

6 The Conservatives after 1979

'Rolling back the state'

6.1 Introduction: the return of ideology

During the 18 years of Conservative rule from 1979 to 1997 the role of the State in relation to the ownership of Britain's transport industries and the provision of public transport services was transformed. The motivation for this had very little to do with transport itself; rather it was but one aspect of a much larger political agenda. The ideological enthusiasm which drove through the reforms was similar in kind (but opposite in direction) to the programme of the post-1945 Labour Government in establishing the Welfare State.

Between 1952 and 1979 there had been a large measure of consensus between the two main political parties on transport as on other sectors of government (Starkie 1982). Apart from skirmishes over the road haulage industry there had been notable continuity between one administration and the next regardless of political colour. The development of the inter-urban roads programme, the establishment of arrangements for integrated urban land use/transport planning and the gradual relaxation of controls to permit competition *between* the main transport industries all proceeded without dissent on matters of principle.

The conditions for radical political change were created by the economic upheavals of the mid-1970s. The Labour Governments of 1974–79 struggled to implement the financial strictures on public expenditure which the changed conditions required because they were contrary to the ethos on which the party's ideology was founded. This was that efficient and equitable development of the utilities and other socially important industries depended fundamentally on planned action (and expenditure) by the State.

This view was contradicted by advocates of liberalism in a new and 'extreme' form (Dunleavy and O'Leary 1987). They believed it was over-involvement by the State itself which was inhibiting progress. Monopoly ownership and/or State regulation meant that industries were being managed in ways which served the interests of bureaucrats and employees rather than consumers. The level of taxation necessary to fund State activities was crippling the rest of the economy and fuelling inflation. The answer was to scrap regulatory controls and to open up industries to the rigours of the free market. State-owned monopolies needed to be broken up and either sold or, if that was not possible, restructured to operate as commercial businesses.

In this chapter we look first at the tentative steps taken in the initial years of the Thatcher administration and the series of privatisations which followed (6.2). We then look at three particularly radical changes – the assault on local government, bus regulation and (delayed until the 1990s) rail privatisation (6.3 and 6.5). The Government's response to a revival of interest in rail developments is reported in section 6.6. This included urban light rail schemes which were conceived within a changing environment of more commercialised development planning and efforts to revitalise inner cities (6.7 and 6.8). We conclude with the 'Roads for Prosperity' White Paper published at the end of the 1980s which has the distinction of being the high water mark of unsustainable transport planning (6.9).

6.2 Testing the water: deregulation, commercialisation and privatisation

In their first term of office the Conservative's transport reforms were relatively mild. Under the 1980 Transport Act long-distance express coaches (services with a minimum passenger journey length of 15 miles) were exempted from service licensing. This not only enabled coach companies to compete with one another, but also to compete with rail. At the same time all bus fares were removed from regulatory control. A Civil Aviation Act in the same year made possible the introduction of competing air services against British Airways on domestic routes.

On the railways a 'Beeching mark II' report was commissioned to identify the scope for further closures in reducing the financial deficit. The Serpell Report (DTp 1983b) indicated that elimination of the deficit would require closure of 86% of the network. Not surprisingly, given that many of the rural constituencies which would have been worst affected by such cuts were Conservative held, these ideas were shelved prior to the 1983 election.

However the scope for efficiency savings identified in Serpell was taken up. British Rail was reorganised internally into 'business sectors', with groups of passenger services made financially accountable for their use of assets. Managers were encouraged to adopt a more commercial approach in developing markets and a number of improved cross-country services were introduced.

The Conservatives also began a programme of 'privatisation' (i.e. the selling of publicly-owned industries) which was accelerated after 1983. There were several strands to the argument in support of this. Private businesses were thought to operate more efficiently without potential political interference by Ministers in management decisions, and to be more responsive to the interests of their customers. The sale of companies generated much-needed revenues which helped the Government hold down the level of taxation – particularly useful at a time when social security expenditure (because of unemployment) was very high. The industries themselves were free to borrow money on the financial markets rather than be subject to Government restrictions and such loans no longer contributed to the Public Sector Borrowing Requirement (PSBR). By marketing the selling of shares to the general public the Government hoped that privatisation would increase interest in and allegiance to the workings of the private market as a whole. A similar attitude was fostered by the parallel decision to give tenants of council-owned housing 'the right to buy'.

The biggest and most newsworthy privatisations were of the former nationalised utilities – gas, water, electricity and telecommunications. In the transport field the main privatisations were as follows:

- National Freight Corporation (1982)
- British Airways (1987)

- British Airports Authority* (1987)
- National Bus Company (1987)
- Municipally owned bus companies (1987 onwards)
- London Transport Buses (1993)
- British Rail (1994–97)

[* BAA owns seven of the principal airports in Britain, including London Heathrow and Gatwick.]

6.3 The assault on local government

Public expenditure by local authorities in general was also an early target of the post-1979 Conservative Government. The system of government support for local authority spending generally was revised and based upon a standardised assessment of 'needs'. Spending above government-set thresholds was subject to penalities of grant reduction and later 'capped' altogether. The discretion which local authorities had previously possessed to determine the level of rates (i.e. local property tax) charged on businesses in their area was removed.

During the rest of the decade the Government struggled to find a way of reforming the system of domestic rates so that the costs arising from local authority policies were made more evident to individual voters. Eventually it opted for a tax based on a uniform charge to individual householders, officially referred to as the 'community charge' but universally dubbed the 'poll tax' after its mediaeval antecedent. The perceived inequity of the tax prompted widespread public demonstrations and, when implemented in 1989, campaigns of non-payment thereafter. Opponents of the tax however enjoyed unexpected compensation when Mrs Thatcher, who had converted it into a personal crusade, found herself forced out as leader by her own MPs shortly afterwards.

Expenditure by the GLC and Metropolitan County Councils (MCCs) on public transport revenue support was particularly objected to by the Conservative Government. After 1981 all these councils were Labour controlled and to varying degrees began to pursue policies of subsidised 'low fares' pioneered by South Yorkshire MCC. These raised very interesting questions of overall social cost-benefit and long-term impact on car ownership and travel behaviour. However such issues were drowned out in what became a public slanging match between the Prime Minister Margaret Thatcher and the Leader of the GLC, Ken Livingstone – in this earlier socialist incarnation dubbed 'Red Ken' in the popular press.

Following local elections in 1981 the GLC announced proposals for a system of low fares on London Transport services which the Labour Party had championed in its election campaign. Despite this mandate and acting within what were thought to be its powers to subsidise public transport as part of overall urban transport policy, the Conservative-controlled London Borough of Bromley mounted a legal challenge. The case was taken all the way to the Appeal judges in the House of Lords who – astonishingly – came down in favour of LB Bromley. Their judgment was based on a concept of 'fiduciary duty' which held that, whatever other provisions applied, a council needed to have regard to the interests of its ratepayers to use revenues wisely. The GLC was judged not to have investigated and demonstrated sufficiently the benefits of its proposed action. It was therefore forced to abandon its initial proposals although these were later reintroduced as part of a conurbation-wide zonal ticketing system that has since proved extremely successful.

Friction between the Government and local authorities continued during the 1980s. In 1983 the central government grant for transport expenditure (TSG) was confined to capital spending only (thus removing this element of national funding for the increased subsidy being paid to local bus services). On highway expenditure capital funding was also restricted to 'roads of more than local significance'. The discretion available to local authorities to determine their own mix of spending (a deliberate feature of the 1970s transport funding regime) was thereby eliminated. After the 1983 General Election the Government published a White Paper (DOE 1983) which proposed the ultimate solution of abolishing the GLC and the MCCs altogether. The arguments about the need for strategic planning which had prompted the setting up of the metropolitan counties only a decade earlier were dismissed as a 'passing fashion'.

Even before the proposals for abolition were translated into law the Government initiated a separate Act taking over immediate policy control of London Transport (LT) from the GLC. It then embarked on a policy of reducing subsidies by a combination of increased fares and savings in bus operating costs. London Transport Buses was reorganised into a number of subsidiary companies based on groupings of garages in different parts of the capital. A franchising system was progressively introduced for the licence to operate individual routes. LT subsidiaries (and other companies from outside the capital) competed for these franchises. In 1993 the LT bus companies were sold, but the franchising system retained.

The abolition of the GLC created a void as far as London-wide planning and co-ordination was concerned. To improve both the appearance and substance of overall co-ordination a separate Minister for London and a Cabinet sub-committee on the subject were created after the 1992 general election, but the Labour Party continued to campaign for the re-creation of a London-wide Authority.

In the other conurbations the Government was prepared to see most of the MCCs' former functions delegated to the 'lower tier' district or borough councils and did not take on any of the strategic functions itself. Somewhat surprisingly the conurbation-wide Passenger Transport Authorities were retained, although these reverted to their previous form of a Joint Board of representatives from the constituent local councils. Hence, whilst passenger transport planning continued to be undertaken for the whole conurbation, development planning, highways and traffic management were administered by the individual metropolitan councils.

6.4 Bus deregulation

Outside London the abolition of the metropolitan county councils coincided with radical change in the provision of local bus services. Under the 1980 Transport Act there had been a limited number of experiments in rural areas to test the effect of withdrawing the system of monopoly licensing on individual bus routes. However these were no guide to the potential effects of wholesale deregulation of bus services which the Government proposed (DTp 1984). There was no real evidence in Britain or elsewhere to go on and in this situation the authors of the White Paper had to rely on a mix of ideological assertion and academic theory.

Arguments centred on whether there was a 'contestable market' for bus service provision – i.e. whether, if the constraints of regulation were removed, the incumbent operators of routes would find themselves subject to competition. (If not, the intended benefits would not arise and the travelling public would be vulnerable to monopoly exploitation.) Particularly in the larger towns and cities it was also questioned whether, without public control, insufficient co-ordination of services, fares and ticketing would be achieved. On these the White Paper argued that:

This need not be the case because the commercial incentive will be there for operators to cater to the needs of such passengers. Informal measures of cooperation between operators will develop to ensure that their services connect …. Through-ticketing, which involves transaction costs, may be less common, but even in this arrangements can be expected to arise through the market where such are clearly to everyone's advantage.

(ibid. Annex 2 para 27)

There is a double irony in these blithe assertions. Not only did they vastly underestimate individual operators' preoccupation with their own interests (rather than the public transport market as a whole) but subsequent application of 'fair trading' rules condemned such cooperation as illegal anyway!

Bus deregulation outside London was legislated for in the 1985 Transport Act. (London was exempted because the process of internal competition between divisions of London Buses was already under way.) Under the Act the system of route licensing operating since 1930 was abolished and the post-1978 arrangement whereby councils subsidised *networks* of services run by particular operators was ended. Instead a clear distinction was created between commercial and subsidised services. One of the arguments advanced in the Buses White Paper was that development of profitable services had been inhibited because of the internal cross-subsidy which the previous licensing system had promoted. Under the new system subsidised services could only be considered after an initial 'registration' by operators of the services they intended to run commercially, with competitive tenders being invited by councils for other individual 'socially necessary' services. The 1985 Act also created the conditions for competition by requiring the sale of National Bus Company subsidiaries as well as the 'hiving off' to separate companies of the bus fleets owned by the PTEs.

In the provincial conurbations the combination of bus deregulation and the ending of fares subsidies represented a colossal upheaval. It was not simply that the ownership, organisation and funding of bus services was changed. In many areas the bus companies took the opportunity to recast the pattern and numbering of the services themselves. Anecdotal tales abounded of bus drivers as well as passengers not knowing where they were going! Congestion worsened on city centre streets as competing companies jockeyed for passengers and operators abandoned bus stations (for which they were liable to a commercial charge) in favour of using kerb-side stops as 'bus stands'. The chaos was compounded by the fact that after deregulation in October 1986 operators began to revise their registered services in an unco-ordinated manner in order to maintain profitability or to gain competitive advantage.

Deregulation had the intended effect of encouraging more operators to enter the market and for companies to experiment with new services, particularly using minibuses. The mileage operated increased and costs per vehicle mile fell. Annual public expenditure on supporting bus services was reduced by around 60% in the first three years. But in the conurbations particularly the combination of reduced subsidy, lack of network co-ordination and instability of service patterns had a disastrous effect with patronage falling by 26% in the first five years.

6.5 Rail privatisation

With rail services the Conservatives pondered long and hard on whether and how privatisation might be introduced. The central problem was that financially the industry was predominantly loss-making. The interaction of different parts of the operation were such that it was not possible simply to hive off profitable services from unprofitable ones as had been done with buses. The industry naturally enjoyed economies of scale and benefits from integration as the progressive amalgamation of private companies prior to nationalisation had shown. But selling the railways as a single company (as had been done with gas and telecommunications) or as a series of regional subsidiaries (as with water) raised problems of insufficient competition. If there was to be public commitment to retaining large parts of the network for social and economic reasons (but from which privatised companies were unable to extract commercial revenues) how could the taxpayer be protected from inefficient operation and excessive subsidy claims?

As with bus deregulation the eventual solution preferred by the Government was proposed and pursued with amazing single-mindedness – or, depending on one's point of view, with remarkable unwillingness to engage with public debate and professional advice. A White Paper was published in July 1992 and the Railways Act passed in 1993. The arrangements envisaged were hugely complicated and much of the detail had to be worked out over subsequent years as the Act's provisions were brought into being. There was no opportunity to examine the details in the round or to anticipate what the outcomes might be. The general public was overwhelmingly hostile to the idea and even Conservative MPs referred to the proposal as 'the poll tax on wheels'.

At the heart of the Government's scheme was the decision to split ownership and maintenance of railways assets – i.e. the infrastructure (track, stations and signalling) and trains – from the operation of services. This immediately eliminated the 'vertical integration' which had previously characterised the industry. However it opened the enticing possibility (to free-marketeers) of different operating companies competing to run services over the same track.

The infrastructure owned by British Rail was initially transferred to a separate company under a new accounting regime before being sold as a commercial undertaking (to RailTrack). The regime of access charges which this infrastructure company would be able to levy on train operators was set by an independent, but government-appointed Rail Regulator.

British Rail's passenger locomotives and rolling stock were divided into three and sold so as to create a market in leasing trains to operators. A similar subdivision and sale was originally undertaken for freight trains, but quickly the whole general rail freight operation was bought and run as a single company EWS (English, Welsh and Scottish). This was deemed acceptable given that freight services were to be run on a commercial basis, without public subsidy.

For passenger services the Government opted for a franchising model. British Rail's services were divided into about two dozen geographical groups. A government-appointed agency OPRAF (the Office of Passenger Rail Franchising) specified the minimum level of service to be operated and invited operating companies to bid competitively for the franchise to run on the routes concerned. The candidates typically included one company formed from the incumbent BR management and others from major bus companies such as Stagecoach and National Express.

Applications were judged on the basis of projected reductions in the subsidy requirement (or on some inter-city routes the payment of a surplus 'premium') and on companies' plans for improvements in trains or other facilities and for service enhancements over the required minimum. Unlike the 'free-for-all' which prevailed on local bus services many stipulations were included in the franchise specification concerning fares, through ticketing and provision of timetable information.

The process of selling British Rail's constituent businesses as separate companies and the specification and letting of so many passenger service franchises was extremely time-consuming. The Labour Party had registered its opposition to the proposals and the Conservative Government, fearful of losing office before the process could be completed, embarked on a timetable to finalise implementation before the 1997 general election. There were widespread criticisms that the nation's railway assets were undervalued in order to achieve a quick sale and thereby fulfil a political project. The whole of the nation's railway infrastructure was sold for £1.8bn – a figure even more derisory in the light of the billions of public money which had to be injected subsequently to salvage the industry after privatisation (15.5). Shares in both RailTrack and the rolling stock companies (ROSCOs) quickly rocketed to many times their initial offer price.

Despite the rhetoric of competition and market forces the privatised railway was in fact highly regulated. The principle of 'open access' which the Conservatives originally favoured had to be shelved in the face of opposition from the companies bidding for the passenger franchises. (In making fixed-sum bids to run services which were loss-making overall they did not want other companies being able to enter the market and 'cream off' profitable elements along their routes.)

The division of the railway industry into so many different private companies in order to generate competition meant that the actual business of running any part of it became extremely complex. Nevertheless, unlike bus deregulation, the transition to a privatised regime was comparatively smooth from the passengers' viewpoint. On the ground there was little change – in most places the same services continued to be run with the same trains, sometimes under the same management. There was not the instability of 'on the road' competition or frequent changes in services. Some of the changes which occurred during the first franchising period – for example on the Chiltern Line from London Marylebone to Birmingham, or on the Midland Main Line to Leicester and Nottingham – represented significant service enhancements. Railway user groups claimed that in the initial years after privatisation service reliability and punctuality declined, but the official figures showed very little overall change.

6.6 New rail developments

Separate from the mainstream of the national railway system the period of Conservative Government was also marked by several other important innovations in rail development and funding.

On a scale of its own was the Government's decision to sign a treaty with the French Government in 1986 agreeing to the construction of a rail-based Channel Tunnel. Scarcely less significant was Mrs Thatcher's view that a project of this magnitude, with exceptional scale and duration of attendant risks, should be undertaken and financed solely by the private sector. Planning debates surrounding the effects of the tunnel were contained by the Government's decision that a new high-speed rail link connecting the Channel Tunnel with London (CTRL) would not be needed for at least ten years. When the Channel Tunnel opened in 1994 and through 'Eurostar' services began operating between London and Paris/Brussels the negative British attitude to rail development contrasted unfavourably with the situation on the other side of the Channel where new high-speed lines were opened concurrently.

In the late 1980s a subsidiary company of British Rail was created to investigate routes for the CTRL, but on the strict condition that it too would not require public funding. It soon became clear however that the nature of the proposals consistent with this financial objective would be unacceptable environmentally. Michael Heseltine, as Secretary of State for the Environment, was instrumental in the bold decision to refuse initial proposals for the route through South London into the terminal being built for Eurostar services at London Waterloo and to opt instead for a more northerly route terminating at Kings Cross/St Pancras. This option killed two birds with one stone as it also opened up the prospect of revitalising the run-down area east of London (branded 'Thames Gateway') with intermediate stations at Ebbsfleet near Dartford and at Stratford.

The price for achieving the economic and environmental benefits of the revised route was relaxation in the previous stipulation about public funding. The Government maintained the letter of its original commitment however by arguing that its financial contribution to the project would be based on the benefits to passengers using *domestic* services which would result from the diversion off the existing lines of continental and Kent commuter services. In 1996 a 999-year lease to build and operate the new line was let to a private consortium (London and Continental Railways) with Government support worth £1.4bn.

In 1993 the Government also announced construction of an express rail link between London Paddington and Heathrow Airport as a joint commercial venture between the privatised British Airports Authority and British Rail. However for BAA this is essentially an ancillary feature to the operation of the airport, i.e. it is not a freestanding transport investment. This and other involvements in public transport ventures also has to be seen in the context of BAA's plans for construction of a fifth terminal at Heathrow ('T5'), whose potential traffic effects were one of the main issues considered at the planning inquiry begun in 1995.

Another major rail proposal which was made dependent in part on private funding was CrossRail – an east–west line under Central London connecting suburban services coming into Liverpool Street and Paddington. This was one of a series of proposals emerging from a Central London Rail Study published in 1989 aimed at relieving rail congestion, in this case principally on the London Underground. In 1993 the Government announced that the scheme was to be 're-examined' with the aim of securing the greatest possible involvement of the private sector. This was the prelude to interminable wranglings, not merely over the details of the scheme but over possible mechanisms whereby businesses and property owners who stood to gain from the development could be made to contribute to it financially. The scheme was finally approved in 2007 (with the colossal price-tag of £16bn) with the Government contributing about a third. The same period of delay afflicted the unfortunately titled Thameslink 2000 project (which increases capacity on a north–south axis across London but using an existing route) whose completion is now expected in 2015!

In 1982 the Government gave London Transport a cash-limited £77m in order to build a bargain-basement light rail scheme to serve the inaccessible Isle of Dogs part of the Docklands area designated for urban regeneration. The scheme used redundant former railway viaducts for much of its length, did not extend into Central London nor connect properly with the rest of the Underground network. When commercial development in the area generated rapid increases in patronage in the late 1980s the limitations of the system were quickly exposed. The stations had to be rebuilt to accommodate double-length trains and the line was extended in tunnel to terminate at Bank in the heart of the City.

When after 1984 the TSG paid to local authorities was confined to major highway schemes the possibility of capital spending on new urban rail schemes outside London was all but forgotten about. However the combination of rapid growth in road traffic volumes plus the association of the novel Docklands light rail system with successful urban regeneration prompted a number of authorities to consider the possibilities of light rail. At the head of the queue was Greater Manchester which had had to abandon its heavy rail Picc–Vic scheme. The PTA now came forward with a cheaper proposal known as 'Metrolink' which connected suburban lines to Bury and Altrincham on either side of the conurbation via new *on-street* tracks across the city centre. The system was in effect dual-mode, operating as a conventional train on the suburban lines, but as a tram through the city centre.

In the absence of TSG the possibility of a central government grant would have to be pursued by separate application for a grant under section 56 of the 1968 Transport Act which was still on the statute book. In 1989 the Government set out the terms under which applications would be considered (DTp 1989a). These represented a radical departure from anything contemplated previously. Instead of schemes being assessed and grant paid on the basis of the total social benefits relative to cost, only benefits to *non-users* of the system were to be included, i.e. reductions in traffic congestion, accidents etc. and any economic benefits that could not be captured directly through developer contributions. (Benefits to users were expected to be recouped through higher fares.) Furthermore, in the Manchester case, construction and operation for an initial 25 years was to be carried out under a concession to be bid for competitively on the basis of a company's contribution to the scheme's initial capital cost. (Actual services were to be run without subsidy.)

The rash of light rail schemes being considered by authorities elsewhere quickly diminished when the stringency of the Government's criteria became apparent and when it became clear that the total grant available even for acceptable schemes would be strictly rationed. Initial hopes for developer contributions also faded as the difficulty was recognised of actually securing them (given that established developments could enjoy a 'free ride' without contributing) and as the bubble of the 1980s property boom burst.

The cause of new light rail schemes was also not well served by the second proposal to be approved – the Sheffield Supertram – whose patronage and financial performance proved well below expectations. The go-ahead for two further schemes (Croydon Tramlink and Midland Metro between Wolverhampton and Birmingham) was given in 1994, but thereafter the Government indicated that approval of additional schemes was unlikely and urged local authorities to explore cheaper bus-based rapid transit solutions instead.

6.7 The re-making of development planning

Work on producing the new structure and local plans required by the 1968 Town and Country Planning Act sat uneasily alongside the fact that the planning system was increasingly unable to influence actual development outcomes (Brindley et al. 1989) since investment by the private sector was assuming increasing importance.

The zeal with which the public ownership and regulation of development was attacked post-1979 was no less than in the case of the transport industries noted above. However the process of reform was more patchy:

Planning was allowed to break down into a series of disjointed and pragmatic initiatives, operating in very different ways in different areas and policy settings. This was entirely consistent with other strands of Thatcherism. If there was 'no such thing as society', then it made no sense to plan as if there were.

(Ward 1994 p. 208)

Initially the Environment Secretary, Michael Heseltine, made a number of typically buccaneering claims that the planning process was stifling wealth-creation. In a series of ministerial circulars to planning authorities he made clear that a more 'positive' attitude (i.e. sympathetic to market forces) needed to be adopted.

In 1985 Heseltine's successor Nicholas Ridley notified authorities that there should be a presumption in favour of planning permission being granted unless objections could be sustained. A White Paper 'Lifting the Burden' (DOE 1985) stated that in future approved development plans would be but one of several material considerations to be taken account of in determining planning applications – in other words that planning policies could be over-ridden if other factors such as responding to business enterprise so indicated. Ridley was able to enforce these changes through major development applications which he was empowered to 'call in' for decision personally or which were referred to him on appeal. Several large-scale, out-of-town 'regional shopping centres' such as Cribbs Causeway near Bristol and Bluewater in Kent and their attendant massive traffic flows are Ridley's unfortunate personal legacy.

Whilst the Conservative Government wanted to relieve business and property developers from the burden of planning regulation they also had to have regard to the wishes of many Conservative voters who relied upon the planning system to protect their local amenity and property values. The virtues of individualism and self-reliance espoused by Mrs Thatcher found inconvenient but particularly virulent expression in the anti-development campaigns by well-heeled 'NIMBY' groups ('not in my back yard'). The political contradictions were well illustrated in the fate of several privately promoted 'new settlements' which were encouraged by the Conservative Government, but conceived independently of the statutory planning process. In the event public opposition was such that none of the proposed settlements won planning approval, although the outcome teetered for some time.

The development planning system was nevertheless substantially modified in the first half of the 1980s with the aim of speeding up the process. Structure plans were neatly obliterated in the conurbations as a consequence of the abolition of the GLC and the Metropolitan County Councils, thereby removing strategic planning from precisely those areas where it was most needed. A narrower form of 'unitary' development plan was introduced in the metropolitan districts instead.

6.8 Inner cities and urban development corporations

The Conservative Government could not detach itself from an obligation to address the profound economic, social and environmental problems of inner city areas which the private sector had effectively abandoned. The message was brought home to the population at large by a wave of riots in Liverpool and several other cities in the early 1980s.

Heseltine believed that the (Labour controlled) local authorities in the inner cities were incapable practically and politically of taking the action needed to generate the interest of the private sector. In a move of unabashed centralism the Government included in the 1980 Local Government, Planning and Land Act powers to create Urban Development Corporations (UDCs) and Enterprise Zones.

The UDCs had powers of land acquisition and development similar to the New Town Corporations set up by the post-war Labour Government. However the key differences were that UDC areas were designated within *existing* cities, were run by members appointed by the Secretary of State (excluding local authorities entirely), and had as their main objective the use of public funds to lever investment from the *private* sector. They were established initially in Merseyside and London Docklands, with further designations after 1987 in most of the country's other main cities. Enterprise Zones were smaller areas where simplified planning arrangements applied and where investors enjoyed tax exemptions for an initial ten years.

From a transport viewpoint the most significant consequence of these 'planning-free' areas was their exploitation by developers in promoting new kinds of large-scale 'out-of-town' shopping or leisure centres, often in direct competition with neighbouring city centres. These included the Metro Centre near Gateshead, Meadowhall near Sheffield and Merry Hill at Dudley within the West Midlands conurbation. Like the regional shopping centres referred to previously all of these drew car-borne visitors from wide catchment areas and in doing so relied fundamentally on motorways and trunk roads which had been planned (and publicly funded) with no such use in mind.

The ultimate symbol of the role of the private sector in urban regeneration (or alternatively of the private exploitation of public subsidies) was the proposal to develop a new office centre at Canary Wharf within the area of the London Docklands UDC. The project was literally on a monumental scale, designed to compete with the City of London at a time when financial services were expanding rapidly to capitalise on deregulation. Unfortunately the 'big bang' of 1987 turned to big bust shortly afterwards, the property market collapsed and the owners of Canary Wharf, Olympia and York, went into liquidation.

Regeneration of London's Docklands had always been hampered by poor accessibility and the Docklands Light Railway was inadequate in scale and scope if Canary Wharf was to succeed. In response the Government approved an extension of the underground Jubilee Line in 1993 which connected Canary Wharf with the main line terminals of London Bridge and Waterloo and with Central London. The authorisation was conditional on an initial £98m of an intended £400m contribution from the private sector as part of the refinancing of the Canary Wharf development. The decision was criticised on the basis that priority in public funding was being given to this expensive rail project over several others in the capital in order to bale out a flagship example of private enterprise. Resentment was compounded when construction of the line resulted in the escalation of costs from a planned £1.9bn to an eventual £3.6bn.

6.9 'Roads for Prosperity'

For much of the 1980s the development of the national road system proceeded comparatively uneventfully, in part because of the reduced length of completely new roads and because of improvements in road planning procedures. The most notable element in the programme was the construction of the orbital M25 around London, completed in 1986. Given political commitment to building the road, actual construction was greatly facilitated by a wide band of countryside encircling the capital which had conveniently been protected from other development during the previous 30 years by green belt designation!

From the day of its opening, traffic volumes on the M25 were much higher than planned and the resulting congested traffic conditions have entered the nation's folklore. Although planned as London's version of the 'bypass' for long-distance traffic promised when the trunk roads programme was launched before World War II, the road also functions as the outermost 'ringway' for the city itself, the inner rings never having been built.

Economic growth during the 1980s resulted in noticeably worse traffic conditions generally. (Road traffic increased nationally by a quarter in the five years from 1984 to 1989.) The Confederation for British Industry (CBI) and many other business organisations campaigned for increased transport investment in general and roads in particular. Crucially the CBI stressed the economic threat which congestion posed to the well-being of London and to the country as a whole in relation to its European competitors (CBI 1989). Its estimate that congestion was costing the nation £15 billion a year – more than £10 a week for every household – was a particularly effective campaigning weapon that was frequently quoted in policy debates for several years afterwards.

The economic link was acknowledged by the Government in the title of its White Paper 'Roads for Prosperity' published in 1989. The paper was prompted by an upward revision in national road traffic forecasts (NRTF) consequent on recent trends which pointed to an increase in traffic levels of between 83% and 142% by 2025 (DTp 1989b). The Government's response was to propose a doubling of national roads expenditure to produce what Ministers claimed would be 'the biggest road building programme since the Romans'.

Increasing traffic congestion was affecting all parts of the nation's road network. A notable feature of the White Paper therefore was the argument that different criteria applied to its inter-urban component:

> Much can be done in urban areas by using modern techniques of traffic management to ease congestion and delays; but people accept that the scope is limited. Road users do not expect, however, to endure stop-start conditions on ordinary journeys between cities.
>
> (DTp 1989d paras 8–9)

This of course overlooks the fact that many of the 'ordinary' journeys on the M25 and other motorways represent commuting and other journeys taking place *within* individual city regions.

The Government explained that it had considered various ways to eliminate unacceptable levels of congestion on inter-urban roads. The main alternatives to road-building were all swiftly dismissed in a few paragraphs – an interesting feature since little more than a decade later a completely opposite management-led approach came to be adopted instead (8.9).

When details of the programme were published they included widening most of the M1 and M25 as well sections of most other motorways leading to and around the main conurbations (DTp 1990). The emphasis on widening rather than on new routes is significant. Although it had the virtue of lessening overall environmental impact its key political advantage was that it could be implemented more easily. In most cases the widening could be accomplished within the land envelope of the existing road, thus avoiding the need for compulsory land purchase, and associated public inquiries and delays.

In the event the possibility of swift delivery proved unfounded. The onset of economic recession at the beginning of the 1990s coupled with changes in public opinion meant that the expanded programme barely got under way before it started to be cut back.

7 The 1990s paradigm shift

New realism and sustainable development

7.1 Introduction

The first half of the 1990s was marked by an unusual conjunction of events surrounding transport policy and planning. Their effect was not so much to bring about an immediate change in the nature of transport programmes but rather to change the terms of reference within which their underpinning policies were debated. The prevailing view of transport altered fundamentally and, dare one say it, permanently – a so-called 'paradigm shift'. The erstwhile dominant view of 'predict and provide' (Vigar 2002) did not simply swing to its opposite pole of 'predict and prevent' (Owens 1995) but there was no longer the implicit assumption that forecast traffic volumes should be catered for wherever possible. In many ways this transformation was but a more general application of the principle of demand management which had come to be accepted in urban transport planning in the 1970s – and for not dissimilar reasons.

In terms of intellectual argument there were two distinct but mutually reinforcing strands. Put simply, continuing as before was seen as neither practicable nor desirable. These two propositions arose from more complex sets of arguments advanced under the respective banners of 'the new realism' (in relation to transport specifically) and 'sustainable development' more generally

However, in a subject of such practical importance as transport, it is doubtful how far or how quickly intellectual arguments alone can bring about actual policy change. Arguably there has to be something more tangible, more visible to the ordinary person, which heightens awareness and provides a focus around which relatively esoteric issues can be seen to have concrete expression. In the 1990s this focus was provided by the inter-urban roads programme.

At the end of the 1980s, as the economy moved from 'boom' to 'bust', so the trend of traffic growth on which the expanded programme had been founded began to evaporate. Not only was there less pressing need to cater for growth, there were also fewer resources to fund it. Hence short-term political expediency in reducing public expenditure happened to coincide with the more abstract arguments of principle. The test of how genuinely these arguments had been absorbed would however have to wait until economic growth reasserted itself at the end of the 1990s.

Last but not least a defining political change at the end of the 1980s was the dramatic ousting of Margaret Thatcher. Under her successor, John Major, the Conservative Government took on a less evangelical, more conciliatory tone. Many of the transport policy options considered in the 1990s in response to an emerging 'new agenda' would have been unthinkable a decade earlier.

We begin this chapter by considering events following the 'Roads for Prosperity' White Paper (7.2) and then describe the nature and origin of 'new realism' and 'sustainable development' concepts (7.3 and 7.4). A remarkably swift official response was contained in the 1994 revision of PPG13 – the planning policy guidance note relating to the transport aspects of development planning (7.5). A more general response led by an EU directive was the formal introduction of environmental assessment procedures (7.6). The UK Government's review of the appropriate transport policy response was channelled through a consultation exercise presented as 'the Great Debate' (7.7).

Finally we report on the renaissance of interest in the planning process as reflected in the arenas of development and local transport planning (7.8 and 7.9).

7.2 Climb-down over the National Roads Programme

Publication of the 1989 National Road Traffic Forecasts (NRTF) provoked a storm of controversy. In public relations terms the DTp's use of headline figures for 35 years hence seriously backfired. Although the forecasts contained nothing particularly novel – merely carrying forward recent trends – they nevertheless imparted widespread shock. Rather than provide convincing evidence of the need for a greatly expanded roads programme they had the opposite effect of encouraging people to think whether this was the kind of future they wanted to plan for. The Conservative's own Secretary of State for the Environment after 1989, Chris Patten, gave public expression to this anxiety when he described the projected traffic increase as 'unacceptable' and emphasised that the NRTF figures were 'a forecast, not a target'.

For a while the Department of Transport pressed ahead with its planned expansion. In 1991 it announced a programme of rapid investment in the M25 in order to relieve congestion (just five years after its opening!). This involved widening 80% of its length to dual four lanes plus new dual carriageway 'collector–distributor' roads alongside the busiest sections to cater for local movements, thereby potentially creating a highway corridor containing an unprecedented 12 lanes of traffic. Ramp metering (access control) and variable message signing were also proposed. Surrey County Council mounted a legal challenge to the DTp's plans on the basis of the parallel link roads being presented as a series of separate schemes, thereby contravening the EC's 1985 directive on environmental assessment. In fact the Council's stand was a device for focusing opposition to the principle of increasing capacity, not least because of the consequences for traffic levels on its local roads which acted as links to and from the motorway.

The roads programme ran into increasing opposition. Individual schemes, as ever, were challenged by coalitions of local objectors and national environmental groups. NIMBYism remained prominent but objectors were increasingly framing arguments in terms of environmental issues more generally and the perception that road-building as a solution to the problems of traffic growth was to a degree self-defeating.

Wider public opinion was influenced by the campaigns which were mounted to try and prevent the construction of particularly controversial schemes at Solsbury Hill (Bath), Twyford Down (Winchester) and the Newbury Bypass. These featured a new breed of objectors who adopted tactics of direct action such as chaining themselves to diggers, burying themselves in tunnels or living in trees which were due to be felled along the route. The media naturally focused on these colourful elements and in particular on a roving campaigner nick-named 'Swampy' who became something of a folk-hero.

An element of the national roads programme which generated its own debate was the role played by 'bypasses'. (There were about 700 miles of such schemes.) The Department of Transport funded a series of projects designed to demonstrate how new traffic-calming measures could be used to improve conditions on former main roads once they were relieved of through traffic (DTp 1995a). Such action was needed in order that the environmental benefits claimed for bypass schemes were actually achieved and not lost to a general increase in traffic.

Although laudable in intent there was the suspicion that this initiative was being used as a public relations exercise for the roads programme as a whole (Potter 1993). Calls by local authorities to have responsibility for less important trunk roads transferred to them (so that they could be integrated better with local planning generally) were refused by the Conservative Government in its 1996 Green Paper (DTp 1996b) although accepted only two years later by New Labour.

Worsening public finances at the beginning of the 1990s forced the Government to forgo the increases in spending on national roads it had intended. But this did not necessarily represent any fundamental change in policy. It could be presented as simply deferring schemes and extending the programme over a longer timescale than originally planned, as had been done on similar occasions in the past. The real change began to be apparent when proposed schemes were dropped altogether. In 1993–94 these included the East London River Crossing, the M62 relief road west and north of Manchester and the M1–M62 link in West Yorkshire. In 1995 the M25's proposed parallel link roads were abandoned. The 1994 Trunk Roads Review scrapped 49 schemes altogether and a 1995 review reduced the size of the 1994 programme by a further two-thirds.

More significant than the deletion of schemes which never got beyond the stage of paper plans was the changing rhetoric used by the Government in support of the 1994 and 1995 Reviews. In 1994 the reduced programme was claimed to be 'less wasteful … and … compatible with the principles of sustainable development' whilst the 1995 Review asserted that 'the emphasis now … must not be on building more roads, but on making better use of the ones we already have' (DTp 1995d Foreword).

7.3 The new realism

In 1988 – before publication of the revised NRTF and *Roads for Prosperity* – the trustees of the Rees Jeffreys Road Fund (which sponsors transport research) came to the view that it was time to undertake a fundamental reappraisal of the direction of transport policy:

> [We] were mindful that no overall view of the place of Transport in Society had taken place since 1963 when Colin Buchanan produced his treatise entitled 'Traffic in Towns'. This clearly recognized the future problems that the unrestricted growth of personal travel would cause. Today, some three decades later, despite action that has been taken massively to increase the supply of road space and other transport capacity, and great advances in the field of traffic management, society faces many major problems in meeting its seemingly insatiable demand for passenger travel and the movement of goods …. A new and wide-ranging report on the subject was clearly timely.
>
> (M Milne Foreword to Goodwin et al. 1991)

The Trustees commissioned a series of reports from a wide range of experts co-ordinated by the Transport Studies Unit at Oxford University. The Unit's own report titled 'Transport: the New Realism' (Goodwin et al. 1991) contained a number of principles on which it claimed there was very wide academic and professional consensus (Box 7.1).

In the face of the Government's plans for an expanded inter-urban roads programme the report's core message was that

> there is no possibility of increasing road supply at a level which matches the growth rates of demand …. If supply cannot be matched to demand, demand has to be matched to supply.

In practice this was a principle which had been followed for many years in connection with urban traffic and transport policy. But its application to the inter-urban context – where at first sight there would seem to be no physical constraint on limitless road-building – challenged the approach which had been followed with the national programme for the previous 35 years.

The report outlined the components of demand management strategies which would include land use planning, 'very substantial' improvements in the quality and scale of public transport, traffic calming and advanced traffic management systems plus consideration of road pricing with its revenues being used as a means of fulfilling the overall programme. As with the presentation of the Buchanan Report almost thirty years previously the likely public resistance to such measures was acknowledged:

Box 7.1 Principles of the New Realism

- There is an intolerable imbalance between expected trends in mobility and the capacity of the transport system.
- This is causing problems to industry, to the environment and also to the ability of people to lead comfortable and fulfilling lives.
- The main problem is the growth in reliance on car use, which no longer succeeds in realising its own objectives.
- It is not possible to provide sufficient capacity to meet unrestrained demands for movement.
- It is necessary to devise systems of managing demand which are economically efficient, provide attractive possibilities for travel for both car owners and non-car owners and give priority to 'essential' traffic.
- Policies to accomplish this are technically feasible, providing they are properly harmonised …. Expansion of road infrastructure will not be the core of transport policy.
- Institutional arrangements must enable a co-ordinated and consistent treatment of all the different parts of the transport system and a 'level playing field' in planning and implementation.

Source: Goodwin et al. 1991 p.3

One of the great difficulties that has been experienced in the past….has been the political resistance from individuals or interest groups who feel their freedom to pursue their private and company interests is under threat from planners or bureaucrats motivated by dogma rather than legitimate social objectives. Perhaps there has been an element of truth in this on occasion. But now the situation is different; it is traffic growth, and inappropriate responses to it, which constitutes the threat to economic efficiency and a decent quality of living. The objective of the 'New Realism' is to make life better, not worse.

(ibid. p. 6)

The impact of the New Realism report cannot be attributed to its individual recommendations which were neither especially novel nor sophisticated, or to the battery of research papers which accompanied them. Rather the appeal of the report lay in presenting a practicable package as an alternative 'brand' to rather tired conventional wisdom at a particularly fortuitous time. The package was cleverly pitched between the positions of key stakeholders and skilfully articulated by the head of TSU, Phil Goodwin. Its message was already well accepted within the academic community and amongst leading practitioners, increasingly acknowledged by the professional rank and file, but just ahead of the Government and many interest groups working within the industry. The New Realism was partly recognition of what had already come to exist (though not perhaps so succinctly conceptualised) but partly also of what had yet to be grasped.

7.4 'Sustainable development'

As in the 1970s, the need to make spending cuts in the inter-urban roads programme happened to coincide with an upsurge in concern for the environment, and Ministers were not averse to using arguments from the latter to 'massage' the former. This time however the environmental concern had acquired greater standing through the concept of 'sustainable development'.

The concept can be traced back to the global environmental concerns registered at the 1972 United Nations Environment Conference in Stockholm and to subsequent work examining anticipatory and preventative policies. This work acquired added impetus in the 1980s following evidence of the effects of acid rain and the depletion of the ozone layer. The term 'sustainable development' itself came into popular use after the 1987 Brundtland Report of the World Commission for Environment and Development in which it was defined as 'development that meets the needs of the present without compromising the ability of future generations to meet their own needs'.

Environmental issues acquired unusually high visibility in domestic British politics in 1989 when the Green Party achieved an unprecedentedly high share of the vote (15%) in the European elections. Mrs Thatcher attached great importance to the subject and to developing an appropriate response to the issue of global warming in particular (Maddison and Pearce 1995). In 1990 she personally led the launch of a White Paper which was the first-ever review of environmental policies across all departments of government (DOE et al. 1990). Whilst there was still disagreement internationally on the need for action the Paper asserted that global warming represented one of the biggest environmental challenges facing the world and committed the British government to reversing the trend of growing carbon emissions. 'In the long term' the measures to achieve this would 'inevitably have to include increases in the relative prices of energy and fuel'.

To many people there was a glaring contradiction between these general expressions of support for reversing carbon emissions and the scale of traffic growth on which the Roads for Prosperity programme was founded. The link was fudged by the Secretary of State for Transport, Cecil Parkinson, who declared that 'it is not the Government's aim to cater for all forecast demand in all circumstances', using city centres and commuting to congested urban areas as rather lame examples (since few such proposals were being contemplated anyway). By contrast he extolled the environmental merits of investment in the strategic road network as a means of improving traffic flow and diverting traffic off less suitable routes.

At the 1992 United Nations 'Earth Summit' Conference in Rio de Janeiro the British Government signed the Convention on Climate Change which required greenhouse gas emissions to be returned to their 1990 levels. The implications for transport policy were potentially severe. The Royal Commission on Environmental Pollution (RCEP) published a report in 1994 which proposed that CO_2 emissions from surface transport *itself* should be limited to the 1990 level by the year 2000 and to no more than 80% of the 1990 level by 2020 (RCEP 1994).

As well as addressing individual environmental impacts the RCEP report took a novel line in promoting the idea of an overall reduction in car travel as contributing to an improved environment in a more general sense. The relevant objective was

> to improve the *quality of life*, particularly in towns and cities, by reducing the dominance of cars and lorries and providing alternative means of access.

In pursuit of this, and complementing the proposed reductions in CO_2, the Commission set out a number of challenging targets for the shares of the different travel modes. To prompt the necessary mode shift it proposed that fuel duty should be raised sufficient to double the pump price of petrol in real terms by 2005. It also proposed that the trunk road programme should be reduced to the construction of bypasses where local need existed, with the financial savings transferred to public transport investment and local transport packages:

> Our recommendations complement and reinforce each other and must be viewed as a whole …. In order to have a substantial effect on the situation after 2000 action must start now and must be vigorously pursued. We have also had constantly in mind the position after 2020. The need is to identify and adopt a strategy which is likely to be sustainable for as far ahead as we can forsee …
>
> (ibid. Chapter 14 para 107)

The vision shown by the Commission contrasted markedly with the absence of any equivalent statement on transport by the Government. Meanwhile the Government was able to plan on meeting its Rio commitment to (short-term) CO_2 reduction without resort to 'draconian' action on car use by virtue of the improvements it anticipated in the other main sources of emission, particularly electricity generation (DOE et al. 1994). The difficulties posed by the concept of sustainable development are nevertheless evident in some rather tortuous prose in the transport section of the strategy:

It is not the Government's job to tell people where and how to travel. But if people continue to exercise their choices as they are at present and there are no other significant changes, the resulting traffic growth would have unacceptable consequences for both the environment and the economy of certain parts of the country and could be very difficult to reconcile with overall sustainable development goals. The Government will need to provide a framework in which people can exercise their transport choice in ways which are compatible with environmental goals.

(ibid. para 26.17)

By coincidence the environmental case for raising motoring costs was being made just at the time the Government badly needed to increase tax revenues to bridge a widening budget deficit. In the 1993 Budget the Chancellor of the Exchequer Kenneth Clarke took the opportunity to increase the duty on petrol by 10% and to make a further commitment to increase it each year thereafter until 2000 by at least 3% in real terms (the so-called 'fuel duty escalator'). How far environmental objectives actually prompted this initiative is a very moot point. Significantly, progress with other fiscal instruments recommended by the Royal Commission, but which did not carry equivalent attractions of revenue gain for the Treasury (e.g. changes in the structure of annual vehicle licence fees and in company car taxation) was noticeably more sluggish.

The concept of sustainable development rapidly acquired hegemonic status. In professional circles almost every policy or proposal had to be explained or justified by reference to 'sustainability' – a mixed blessing since the term quickly became devalued. Nevertheless by the mid-1990s it seemed as though convergence was taking place around a new and quite distinctive set of transport and planning policies framed within the context of sustainable development – policies which, given time, would translate into a very different era of planning practice.

7.5 PPG13 – 'Reducing the need to travel'

Land use policy in relation to transport was another important area in which the Government had begun to introduce radical changes of the kind urged by the Royal Commission. In this case however there was reason to believe there was more genuine support for sustainable development. The Department of the Environment (responsible for land use planning) had previously distanced itself from the Department of Transport when the latter had published its *Roads for Prosperity* and John Gummer (Secretary of State at the DOE at the time of the Sustainable Development Strategy) had an unusual personal commitment to the subject.

Following the 1990 *Common Inheritance* White Paper the Government announced that it would be reviewing all the national planning policy guidance notes (PPGs) to ensure that land use planning contributed to the goal of sustainable development. Preparatory to the review of PPG13 on Transport, the Government commissioned research to identify the ways in which land use planning could contribute to a reduction in transport emissions (ECOTEC 1993). On the basis of this work a revised PPG13 was published in 1994 (DOE and DTp 1994).

Unusually – and a sign perhaps of some 'thawing' in relations between the two departments – the research and the PPG were published under the auspices of both the DOE and the DTp. In truth however comparatively little in the way of policy adjustment was being asked of the DTp – PPG13 was pre-eminently local and urban in orientation and the complementary transport measures it included reflected developments in local transport planning taking place at the same time (7.9 below). The DTp's main fiefdom concerned with national roads and traffic was not being challenged.

The stated objectives of PPG13 were

• to reduce growth in the length and number of motorised journeys;
• to encourage alternative means of travel which have less environmental impact; and hence
• to reduce reliance on the private car.

In this way local authorities will help meet the commitments of the Government's Sustainable Development Strategy to reduce the need to travel; influence the rate of traffic growth; and reduce the environmental impacts of transport overall. These objectives represented a radical change from the original (1988) version of the PPG which dwelt entirely on more mundane highway engineering matters, reflected in its original title: *Highways Considerations in Development Control*. The PPG rapidly acquired totemic status amongst transport professionals such that the phrase 'PPG13' – meaning the 1994 version – came to be used as convenient short-hand for a range of local planning and transport policies concerned with demand management linked to the goals of sustainable development.

The main thrust of 'PPG13' was to promote development within urban areas and to locate major generators of travel in existing centres which are highly accessible by means other than the private car. PPG13 was complemented by revisions to PPG3 on housing which favoured development on previously used (so-called 'brown-field') land within existing built-up areas (DETR 2000b), and to PPG6 on retailing which supported development in or adjacent to existing town centres (DOE 1993).

Together these PPGs signalled a policy initiative which set out to reverse the long-established drift of population and activity from major towns and cities to smaller towns and rural areas. It also represented a complete reversal of the market-led policies adopted by the same Conservative Government a decade earlier which had allowed a rash of peripheral and other non-central retail and office developments to appear in virtually every town (Headicar 1996).

From a sustainable development perspective the Achilles' heel of PPG13 was that it neither contained, nor was accompanied by, any commitment to reducing *actual* car use. The phraseology was very carefully designed to refer only to reducing the *need* to travel and providing the *opportunity* for travel by means other than the car. Politically it was important that *choice* was seen to remain firmly with the individual traveller. The Government's stance on this issue is encapsulated in the reaction given by the Environment Secretary John Gummer to the RCEP report:

> I am not persuaded that the kind of draconian increases recommended [in fuel duty] would have the effects they suggest; people's attachment to their cars is not mere whim but reflects real comfort and convenience. We must design our cities of the future so that choosing not to have a car is made increasingly possible.

From the viewpoint of the development industry, PPG13 represented a radical, probably unrealistic and certainly unwelcome change since it ran against the obvious logic of market forces in a mass car-owning society. The planning profession was generally more sympathetic but there were doubts about whether the policies could be applied sufficiently intensively and over a long enough period to have a significant impact (Ove Arup and Partners 1997). The fear was that development industry would in effect boycott the PPG and seek to force the Government into adopting policies more in line with market forces. There were also doubts about whether the new development policies could be delivered *and* achieve the desired transport outcomes in the absence of national transport policies aimed at reducing overall traffic volumes. Certainly this particular nettle had yet to be grasped.

7.6 Environmental assessment

The overall concept of sustainable development was only the most 'high-level' expression of the increasing attention being paid to the environmental impacts of transport. During the 1970s, concern over the impact of major road schemes had led to the adoption of methods for undertaking and presenting environmental appraisals (DTp 1983a), although these focused on the more immediate (i.e. localised) impacts.

In 1985 the EC issued a Directive (85/337) on the environmental assessment of major projects in general. This included guidance on the preparation of a more comprehensive Environmental Impact Assessment (EIA) and a requirement that its results should be presented publicly in the form of an Environmental Impact Statement (EIS). In the UK regulations were issued in 1988 making it compulsory for certain types of project, including major transport infrastructure proposals, to have an EIA accompanying their planning application.

Considerable controversy followed over the way in which the requirements of the Directive should be incorporated into the planning procedures for major road schemes then in progress. The issue came to a head in 1992 in connection with the proposed final section of the M3 London–Southampton motorway near Winchester. This was an extremely contentious scheme as it involved excavating a deep cutting through Twyford Down – an area of valuable landscape replete with ancient burial sites scheduled as historic monuments. The proposal had a long and difficult history and the Government was anxious to avoid the further delay and uncertainty which would result from reopening investigations into its environmental impact.

Appeals by objectors resulted in the unprecedented step of the EC Environment Commissioner Carlo Ripa di Meana publicly requesting a halt to construction of the scheme. The issue took on wider political significance as the Prime Minister, John Major, was about to assume Presidency of the European Council of Ministers, and relations between the British Government and the EC were extremely sensitive at the time (Haigh and Lanigan 1995). The EC was anxious to gain Britain's acceptance of the Maastricht Treaty and Ripa di Meana's intervention was precisely the sort of 'meddling' in national affairs which the Conservative Government was able to exploit in support of its Eurosceptic position. In the event Ripa di Meana left the Commission and the planning procedure already followed for the Twyford Down scheme was accepted as amounting to an impact assessment.

The Department of Transport's resistance to the possibility that existing road proposals might be open to re-examination was affirmed in its response to a report from SACTRA (1992). The report had emphasised the need for a more strategic approach so that the cumulative effect of successive, linked schemes could be examined (so-called 'corridor assessment'). The Government agreed to issuing revised guidance in connection with future schemes but made clear that this would not affect its current programme (which, at £20bn, would take 15 years or so to complete!).

The significance to be attached to the wider environmental effects of individual road schemes was also causing friction between the Government departments of Environment and Transport. In 1994 the Environment Secretary John Gummer made a notable decision to accept a planning inspector's rejection of a road proposal at Wing in Buckinghamshire. This seemingly innocuous scheme for a village bypass was in fact destined to receive 100% funding from DTp because it formed part of a long-distance Euro-route between Harwich and Swindon! The proposal had only been considered in its local context and no assessment of the long-distance route had ever been undertaken. This was a glaring example of how a major new route might be created by stealth (through linking successive 'bypasses') and the best possible evidence of why corridor assessments were needed.

In 1994, in the context of rapidly changing public opinion, the Department of Transport adopted a noticeably more emollient approach to a subsequent report from SACTRA (1994). This was a momentous report as its recommendations contradicted the Department's long-standing practice that road schemes should be assessed on the basis that they do not add to total traffic – a view which many ordinary members of the public regarded as flying in the face of common sense. In fact recognition of 'induced traffic' did not mean that the benefit of a scheme was necessarily less – it could have a positive or a negative effect depending on local circumstances.

In response the Transport Secretary Brian MacWhinney promised to review all 270 schemes in the national roads programme, including postponement of the controversial Newbury Bypass, whilst other options were explored. In the event allowance for the effects of induced traffic was not assessed to reduce the value of any scheme below the level where it was worth proceeding and MacWhinney himself signed approval for the Newbury Bypass on the day he left office as Secretary of State for Transport!

7.7 The 'Great Debate'

Individually the revision of PPG13 and the RCEP and SACTRA reports were remarkable documents. Together their publication had a synergetic effect at a time when the Department of Transport's 'flagship' programme of trunk road improvements was being scaled down and public opinion appeared to be shifting quite rapidly. There seemed to be a need for a clear, overarching statement in response of Government policy on transport. But whether from political timidity or from scepticism about how deep support for such policies would run, the Secretary of State for Transport Brian MacWhinney decided instead to mount what he called a 'Great Debate'. He promoted this by giving a series of speeches which were published as a Consultation Document (DTp 1995c).

The document posed a series of questions and invited responses on three main themes, viz:

- the balance between economic growth, the environment and personal choice
- the measures to be taken if the balance needed to be shifted
- acceptance of the wider consequences if such measures are taken.

Unusually the Government also commissioned attitudinal research on these themes (3.9).

The instigation of [the Great Debate] appears to have been a genuine attempt to find a way forward with a transport problem increasingly conceived as being one of changing people's travel behaviour in the short, medium and long term. It was also a difficult problem for the Conservatives to resolve as *intervening to manage travel demand ran counter to philosophies of personal choice and personal freedom.*

(Vigar 2002 pp. 76–77)

The Government's credibility in leading the debate was helped by the fact that it had recently hived off its executive responsibilities for trunk roads to a new Highways Agency. This removed the 'lop-sidedness' (in favour of roads) which had long characterised the staffing of the Department of Transport.

Whilst the Great Debate was under way three innovations were made, all very much in line with the RCEP report: the preparation of a National Air Quality Strategy (under the 1995 Environment Act), a National Cycling Strategy, and the publication of sustainable development indicators.

The National Cycling Strategy was prepared by a steering group of representatives from the public, private and voluntary sectors, chaired by a Government Minister (DTp 1996a). It adopted very ambitious targets similar to those proposed by the Royal Commission – for a doubling of cycling journeys by 2005 and a further doubling by 2012. Unlike the air quality strategy however these targets had no basis in legislation and neither central nor local government was under any obligation to pursue their implementation. In practical terms the more prominent action in relation to cycling was a grant of £42m by the Millennium Commission towards the cost of a 4,000-km national network of cycle paths co-ordinated and promoted by the charity Sustrans.

The long-awaited statement of Conservative Government policy on transport was published as 'The Way Forward' in 1996 (DTp 1996b). It set out the Government's views 'on a sensible direction for policies into the next century'. After all that had gone before, this aspiration was somewhat underwhelming. Even amongst groups which might have been expected to be supportive of Conservative policy, the paper generated disappointment.

The absence of specific proposals could be attributed to the fact that a General Election was only a year or so away which the Conservative Government was not expected to (and did not) survive. However the paper did formally embrace the shift away from road investment towards management and restraint measures and contained several initiatives which were carried forward into the programme of the subsequent New Labour Government.

'The Way Forward' was published as the Government's formal response to the RCEP report but on several key issues the hopes of the Royal Commission were dashed. The Commission's recommendations for national traffic targets and for shares amongst the different modes were rejected. The Government made much of the value of economic instruments, but the fact that the effectiveness of its main weapon – the fuel duty escalator – had been badly blunted by the falling cost of fuel itself was ignored (RCEP 1997).

One of the reasons for the Government's rejection of national traffic targets was the extent of variation in local conditions. Its view therefore was that targets for reducing road traffic and encouraging alternative modes were best pursued at local authority level. The pressure group Friends of the Earth advanced their belief in the value of targets by promoting a Private Members Bill, passed as the Road Traffic Reduction Act 1997, aimed at local authorities. A similar Bill relating to national traffic levels was passed in 1998. However in both cases the necessary Government support was only obtained by including amendments which effectively required only the *case* for road traffic reduction to be investigated, i.e. without any obligation on the scale of reduction, if any.

The Royal Commission was frustrated at the lack of progress by the Government in responding to what it saw as a broad consensus about the direction of change needed in transport policy. Anticipating a forthcoming change in government the Commission took the unusual step of publishing a report on developments in transport policy since 1994 and of reviewing its original proposals accordingly:

> Our concern is that recent action has been too little and too slow to provide the prospect of a substantial shift in transport trends. This has left a vacuum in which there is a danger that, if credible alternatives are not being pursued, the pendulum could swing back to demands for a large road-building programme. That is what happened in the late 1980s after a period of reduced road building. There is a need for considerably increased investment in public transport. That is not at present in prospect, from either public or private sources, on the scale required.
>
> (RCEP 1997 para 1.58)

7.8 The revival of planning

A distinguishing feature of the 1990s was a revival in the importance attached to public planning. This is evident in two respects. The first was a strengthening of the mechanisms for development planning (as distinct from the more opportunistic approaches encouraged during the 1980s). The second was a renewed legitimacy given to the role of public authorities working in partnership with the private sector (as distinct from unfettered operation of the commercial market). In both senses many of the actions of New Labour after 1997 can be seen as further steps along this new trajectory.

In relation to development planning, steps were taken to reintroduce strategic direction. 'Guidance notes' issued reluctantly by the Secretary for State for the Environment to local planning authorities in the metropolitan areas (to fill the void created by the abolition of the GLC and MCCs) were extended to regions as a whole and developed on the basis of local 'advice'. A local authority association in the South-East of England known as SERPLAN was particularly active in maintaining what amounted to exercises in regional planning at a time when the Government had effectively declared that such an activity did not and need not exist. The regional planning guidance notes (RPG) – which dealt with issues specific to a particular region – were complemented by the new series of national planning policy guidance notes referred to earlier.

At a local level the structure plans prepared by county councils enjoyed an unexpected reprieve after 1989. The 1991 Planning and Compensation Act did not abolish them, but they were expected to wither away as a consequence of a local government review which was intended to replace the two-tier system of county and district authorities with a unitary one.

The most important feature of the 1991 Act was the inclusion of a clause which restored primacy to the development plan in determining planning applications. This was significant because it strengthened the role of statutory development planning undertaken by local authorities and lessened the probability of the Secretary of State intervening to over-ride local intentions. The corollary was that district councils were required to prepare local plans for the whole of their administrative areas so as to provide guidance on policies and proposals at the 'site specific' level.

As far as urban regeneration was concerned, the Government of John Major adopted a more conciliatory approach to the role of local authorities. In part this was possible because Labour-controlled authorities in the big cities had lost their so-called 'loony left' leaderships of the early 1980s and had abandoned attempts to counter the effects of Thatcherite policies with their own 'municipal socialism'. In 1991 a 'City Challenge' initiative was launched in which local authorities were invited to bid for regeneration funds provided they demonstrated the involvement of the private and voluntary sectors and the local community.

This introduced an important new dimension into the funding of local authorities whereby allocation was not necessarily on the basis of 'need'. Rather, individual authorities were put into a position of overt competition with their peers to mount the most convincing proposal. This 'challenge' procedure became more widely adopted by Government later in the decade, not simply as a means of allocating particular pots of money but as a means of enticing authorities to engage in new types of initiative and methods of delivery.

More generally the Government's restrictions on local authority funding and desire for planning authorities to work in partnership with private developers led to increasing use of so-called 'planning gain' as a means of achieving the provision of facilities which traditionally would have been funded publicly. These included items of transport infrastructure and services beyond the development site itself which the developer would contract to provide or pay for as part of 'section 106' agreements negotiated as part of the granting of planning permission (14.8).

7.9 Local transport planning

During the 1980s local transport planning had been in the doldrums. The annual TPPs submitted to Central Government were dominated by major highway schemes even though the chances of them securing funding approval were slim. The relationship to 'planning' became tenuous and the TPP documents came to be regarded pre-eminently as bidding exercises. Increasingly the schemes being proposed lacked any overall context of the kind that had been provided by the earlier land use/transport studies. The techniques employed in these studies were still being used to fulfil the Department of Transport's requirements to demonstrate the economic value of individual schemes. But these techniques had lost credibility with the public at large – or at least with pressure groups who knew how to expose their limitations. In any case the costs of mounting updated versions of the studies were generally regarded as prohibitive.

As a response to this situation a new style of 'integrated transport study' was devised (May 1991) which owed much to strategic planning methods employed in the 1970s. This attempted to overcome the perceived narrowness of conventional transport modelling exercises by establishing a vision of the overall goals being sought in an area, the transport objectives consistent with it and a realistic assessment of the resources likely to be available. Strategies incorporating both land use and transport were generated and tested for their contribution to resolving identified problems. The broad scope and short timescale of these studies meant that they did not include detailed data collection and model building, relying instead on 'sketch planning' models and professional judgement.

Integrated transport studies were carried out for about 20 cities during the period 1987–91, often to accompany the 'bubble' of light rail proposals which surfaced at the time (6.6). One such study in Birmingham was also used to pilot the development of what became known as the 'package approach'. This was a set of low-cost management measures in an area designed as part of a coherent strategy (as distinct from the disjointed implementation of individual measures as was more common practice).

At the time that the package approach was being piloted the Bus and Coach Council (forerunner of the present Confederation of Passenger Transport) published a report which highlighted the types of investment which local highway authorities could make which would assist bus operation (Bus and Coach Council 1991). The Government initially responded by providing grants for bus demonstration projects and the initiative was later incorporated in the Package submissions within TPPs.

The Department of Transport formally adopted the package approach by inviting local highway authorities to prepare proposals covering whole urban areas in their 1994/95 TPPs. The Government also indicated that it expected this form of submission to become the norm in future. The new approach reflected the Government's view of local transport as requiring 'overall transport infrastructure provision – not simply roads – to encourage a shift from private to public transport' and 'to establish demand strategies'.

Any consideration of urban demand management raised the issue of restraint methods. Reliance thus far on parking policies had been undermined by difficulties in securing adequate enforcement of on-street controls by the Police. Under the 1991 Road Traffic Act powers were given for the designation of Special Parking Zones (SPZ) in which responsibility for enforcement was transferred to local highway authorities. These authorities had a much more direct interest in the effective implementation of parking policies and, working with specialist firms, were able to sub-contract enforcement as part of a self-financing business.

The package approach could be regarded as the reincarnation of management plans which the Ministry of Transport had invited urban authorities to prepare in 1968! (MOT 1968.) The difference 25 years on was recognition of the permanent nature of such an approach – not merely as a temporary expedient pending hoped-for road-building. The associated change in professional culture was an important precursor for the introduction of Local Transport Plans a few years later.

8   A new deal for transport?

New Labour 1997–2004

8.1 Introduction

A *New Deal for Transport* was the title of the White Paper published in 1998 by the incoming Labour Government just over a year after taking office. It was the first of its kind for over twenty years and was intended to provide the policy framework for a series of more detailed proposals to be brought forward subsequently. Section 8.2 explains the context in which it was published and 8.3 summarises its content.

In practice the White Paper was not quite such a new deal as some had hoped for and even so its aspirations quickly began to unravel. *Transport 2010 – The Ten Year Plan* published in 2000 was a much enhanced investment programme intended to demonstrate the Government's commitment to improved transport (8.5). But two extraordinary events later the same year – the road hauliers' campaign against fuel duty increases and the Hatfield rail crash and its aftermath – had the effect of undermining two of the central components of the Government's strategy (8.6). Local authorities' unwillingness to respond to new powers for urban road user charging was a further damaging blow (8.7).

The political damage from the collapse of the Government's intended strategy was such that it decided to publish a second White Paper *The Future of Transport* in 2004 to 'clear the decks' before the 2005 General Election (8.9). The document itself was little more than window-dressing but it marked the transition to an era when transport policy was painstakingly reconstructed. The initiatives taken after 2004 are described in the final part of the book since they form core elements of contemporary policy.

Interspersed between the sections on transport policy are separate sections on changes in governance and development planning during the period (8.4 and 8.8).

8.2 'A consensus for radical change'

It is tempting to regard any change of Government as signifying an important break in the evolution of policy, especially after a period as long as 18 years. In this case not only the change in political control, but the manner of the change – an electoral landslide, a young Prime Minister (Tony Blair), and a fresh administration untarnished by the 'sleaze' and internal wranglings of the Major years – created an air of national euphoria and high expectation.

The appointment of someone as senior as the Deputy Prime Minister John Prescott to head a new combined Department of the Environment, Transport and the Regions (DETR) added to the sense of promise in these particular areas. In practice much of what came to be proposed was traceable to developments in the preceding years and could be regarded as the unfinished business of the previous administration (Goodwin 2003).

In his foreword to the 1998 White Paper Prescott laid claim to this 'consensus for radical change':

> The previous Government's Green Paper [*The Way Forward*] paved the way with the recognition that we needed to improve public transport and reduce dependence on the car. Businesses, unions, environmental organisations and individuals throughout Britain share that analysis. This White Paper builds on that foundation.
>
> (DETR 1998a Foreword)

Politically it was interesting that the new Government should want to justify its proposals on the basis of a consensus, and not on the originality or distinctiveness of its own prospectus. This can be read in two ways – not necessarily mutually exclusive.

The first is that the Government wanted to present itself as occupying the political middle ground and not about to engage in the adversarial politics which had characterised much of the previous 18 years. The Labour Party had been restructured and rebranded as 'New Labour' in the interim in order to overcome the prospect of permanent opposition. Along the way the socialist commitment to nationalisation had been abandoned and the influence of the industrial trade unions weakened through the introduction of 'one member, one vote' as the basis of the Party's constitution. Philosophically New Labour drew upon the 'Third Way' of Anthony Giddens who argued that it was possible to pursue market-oriented economic policies as well as progressive social policies – the political fault-line which had previously divided Left from Right (Giddens 1998).

A second explanation is that, despite its large Parliamentary majority, the new Government lacked confidence that it would do better than its Labour predecessors and survive for more than five years. Hence it wanted to claim wide support for its proposals and certainly avoid creating enemies so as to maximise its chances of winning a second term. Its nervousness was evident in the White Paper's sub-title *Better for Everyone* – an attempt to pre-empt criticisms from the popular press that it was 'anti-motorist'.

Despite the claimed consensus, progress was slow in bringing about practical change. Part of the subsequent sense of disappointment – failure even – was in proportion to the scale of the original expectations which Prescott in particular had talked up. For example within a month of his appointment he was quoted as saying

> I will have failed if in five years' time there are not many more people using public transport and far fewer journeys by car. It is a tall order but I urge you to hold me to it.
>
> (*The Guardian* 6 June 1997)

Whilst typically strong on aspiration and intended commitment, such a statement was unwise (since it was not grounded in any properly analysed course of action) and became a damaging hostage to fortune.

The manner in which the White Paper was produced contained features which came to typify the style of the new Government and which contributed to subsequent disillusionment. A panel of independent experts led by Professor Phil Goodwin (leader of the New Realism project) advised on the content of the new programme. However the final version was doctored by the Policy Unit established in the Prime Minister's own office, forever mindful of how it would be received by the popular press. Such changes were commonplace in the ruthless central political control imposed by the new administration:

> Departmental officials observed that the changes No 10 so systematically made or incited were not concerned with truth and objectivity, but with political saleability.
>
> (Foster 2005 p. 186)

The White Paper was long on aspiration but short on practical detail (Mackie 1998). The rather glossy 'coffee table' format in which it was published and its gushing ad-man's prose heightened the sense that this was more an exercise in 'spin' than a thorough analysis of the situation being confronted. Given the magnitude of the aspiration – to reverse decades of increasing car dependence – the Government was risking riding for a fall. Unfortunately, so it proved.

8.3 The content of the 1998 White Paper

For its starting point the White Paper reiterated the dilemma encapsulated in the Traffic in Towns report 35 years previously – that the growth in transport in general, and car use in particular, has transformed our lives but at enormous cost – in congestion, pollution, road casualties and CO_2 emissions. It acknowledged the 'enormous challenge' presented in delivering a transport system which supported sustainable development and which contributed to people's quality of life rather than detracted from it. In the Government's view the way to achieving this was through an 'integrated transport policy'. By this it meant:

- integration within and between **different types of transport** – so that each contributes its full potential and people can move easily between them
- integration with the **environment** – so that transport choices support a better environment
- integration with **land use planning** – so that transport and planning work together to support more sustainable choices and reduce the need to travel
- integration with **policies for education, health and wealth creation** so that transport helps to make a fairer, more inclusive society.

(DETR 1998a para 1.22)

Concern for the social dimension of public policy was a notable feature of the new administration and was reflected in the creation of cross-departmental Social Exclusion Unit.

The Government also asserted the need for a 'new approach' in achieving change by bringing together public and private sectors in partnership – with incentives to companies to provide new services and raise standards, whilst ensuring cost-effective use of public expenditure and ensuring that services are properly regulated in the public interest. This more pragmatic and 'managerial' view contrasted with the continuing support of many Labour Party members for public ownership and control (for example to reverse bus deregulation and rail privatisation) which the Labour leadership had also argued for when in opposition.

The broader context for transport decision-making was applied straightaway in two important fields. The first was in the Government's review of its trunk roads programme (DETR 1998b) which was conducted using a new set of appraisal criteria (11.4). All proposals inherited from the Conservatives which were sufficiently advanced to be considered for implementation during the subsequent seven years were examined. Of the projects selected five had benefit/cost ratios of less than 2:1 whereas others with much higher economic returns were omitted – apparent evidence of a shift from previous practice in which economic considerations had predominated.

The Government's programme contained just 37 schemes from the 'wish-list' of 156 which it had inherited (LTT 244). However whilst technically the programme was being 'scaled back' it was misleading to imply that the remaining schemes might not at some stage be proceeded with. Most were either to be referred to Regional Planning Bodies for further consideration or were on parts of the network which the Government intended to 'detrunk' and thus transfer responsibility to local highway authorities.

Many schemes were subsumed within a new programme of 'corridor studies' announced by the Government, mostly multi-modal in nature. Whilst the declared aim of these studies was genuine enough (i.e. to secure a broader assessment of schemes and possible alternatives to the original road proposal) it was also politically convenient that they had the effect of putting off the need for a decision for several years.

The second field to which the broader remit was applied was the programmes of local highway authorities. In place of annual TPP submissions authorities were asked to prepare Local Transport Plans (LTPs) for a five-year period, supplemented by Annual Progress Reports (APRs). These plans were presented as 'the key to the delivery of integrated transport locally' to be backed by additional capital funding. They were to be drawn up in consultation with local transport operators and other stakeholders, cover all forms of transport, and include packages of measures designed to meet local transport needs within the five overarching national objectives. Topics to be covered included co-ordination with air quality action plans, the voluntary adoption of green transport plans by major employers, disability issues, public transport interchange, social inclusion, the needs of the countryside and the encouragement of walking and cycling – all of which would not have received explicit attention previously.

Alongside action on the national roads programme the Government took steps to promote the development of alternative modes. The White Paper contained details of its manifesto commitment to establish a Strategic Rail Authority which it claimed would provide 'a clear, coherent and strategic programme for the development of our railways'. The SRA was in effect New Labour's attempt to claim some influence over the future of the railway without engaging in the costly and controversial business of renationalisation.

The SRA was also to assume responsibility for the franchising of passenger services. However since the first round of franchises had only recently been let it was inevitable that in its initial years the SRA would be unable to exercise the intended leverage to secure wider passenger and public benefits. Potentially more significant was the Government's intention to supply additional funds in support of investment in the rail network. The Government also proposed to add to the duties of the Rail Regulator by requiring him to have regard to statutory guidance from the Secretary of State on his broad policy objectives for the railway.

At a national level bus operations were supported by the introduction of a Rural Bus Fund and by a £40m increase in Fuel Duty Rebate to offset the effects of the general increase in fuel duty. In addition a nationally supported minimum half-fare standard for local authority concessionary fares schemes, although not designed to make operators better off, would have the effect of increasing patronage and helping sustain services. A national public transport information system using telephone or internet (subsequently launched as 'Transport Direct') was also commissioned.

At a local level the Government opted to support the development of 'Quality Partnerships' (collaborative schemes of investment between local authorities and bus operators) as the best means of securing improvements in bus services. Legislation would also give local authorities the power to enter into Quality Contracts with operators for the exclusive right to run individual services according to their specification – in effect a version of the franchising system already operating in London. However these would be subject to ministerial approval and it was made clear that they would only be contemplated as a last resort. In practice the QC provisions were merely an empty political gesture to satisfy the many Labour-led local authorities who would have preferred to see regulation reinstated instead.

In terms of promoting more sustainable travel, action was proposed at both national and local levels. The objectives and targets of the National Cycling Strategy inherited from the Conservatives were endorsed, as was the development of the National Cycle Network. Significantly however the intention to produce a national walking strategy was subsequently dropped for fear of engendering ridicule in the popular press.

Nationally the Government had also established a Cleaner Vehicles Task Force and support under the Foresight programme for research and development in more fuel-efficient and less polluting vehicles. It also wanted to extend the use of economic instruments to encourage their take up by manufacturers and consumers. This was reflected in a further 1% annual increase above inflation in fuel duty (to 6%), the introduction of graduated Vehicle Excise Duty for cars, and a review of VED rates for lorries to ensure these reflected the physical and environmental damage they caused.

Notwithstanding the range of initiatives included in LTPs to promote sustainable travel it was acknowledged that they would not be sufficient to tackle the levels of congestion and pollution afflicting many towns and cities. This led to the most innovative feature of the White Paper, namely the proposal to give powers to local authorities to introduce road user charges or workplace parking levies to reduce traffic levels and to retain the revenue for local transport purposes as part of a package of measures contained in an LTP. However in response to business lobbying the Government backed down on original intentions to include retail and leisure attractions within the scope of the parking levies (Walton 2003).

In total the content of the White Paper represented an enormously challenging agenda and the Government acknowledged that there was a lot more work to do. To assist in this it established the Commission for Integrated Transport (CfIT) chaired by Professor David Begg – someone who had had valuable experience at the sharp end of urban transport management as Leader of Edinburgh City Council. The Commission was charged with monitoring the implementation of the *New Deal* and with providing an independent forum through which contentious issues could be examined.

8.4 Changes to local and regional government

A period of frenetic activity followed publication of the *New Deal*, characterised by a blizzard of daughter documents, consultation papers, guidance notes and so forth. In particular the DETR moved quickly to establish the new system of Local Transport Plans in 1999, albeit in 'provisional' one-year form. But as far as legislation was concerned the Government's priorities lay elsewhere. One was constitutional reform embracing devolution from central government, the strengthening of regional decision-making and the 'modernisation' of local government. Changes in each of these affected the context for decision-making in transport and spatial planning thereafter.

The proposals for devolution were the product of manifesto commitments in 1997. Scotland was offered its own Parliament with separately elected Members, legislative and administrative powers in defined fields and a limited tax-raising capability. More significant for transport in day-to-day terms was the transfer of administrative responsibilities from the Scottish Office (previously a department of Central Government) to an Executive answerable to a Minister within the Scottish cabinet. Wales was offered an elected Assembly, with a similar transfer of administrative responsibilities (from the Welsh Office), but without legislative and tax-raising powers (Cole 2003). These proposals were adopted following referenda in the two countries, albeit with only a tiny majority backing devolution in Wales.

The devolution proposals for London were different in that they consisted essentially of the restoration of *local authority* powers lost when the GLC was abolished in 1986. However rather than replicate the traditional council format the Government opted for a new model based on a directly elected Mayor with executive powers – a model again ratified through a local referendum.

In England outside London new bodies (later known as regional assemblies) were created in each of the administrative regions. Their members consisted of elected representatives from each of the region's local authorities plus a minority of representatives from social, economic and environmental interest groups appointed by the Secretary of State. These bodies replaced the previous ad hoc regional planning conferences and were given a strengthened role in the preparation of regional planning guidance. In the field of economic development 'devolution' was achieved, not by transfer of Government office functions to the regional assemblies, but to new Regional Development Agencies (RDAs) run by a Board of appointed members.

The activities of the English Regional Assemblies were constrained by the fact that (unlike the Welsh Assembly) their members were not directly elected and that they had no executive powers. Prescott in particular was keen to remedy this and to bring about more genuine devolution to the English regions. After the 2001 election, working from the Cabinet Office, he published a consultation paper setting out the Government's proposals (Cabinet Office 2001). However the principle of regionalisation within England did not enjoy wide support even amongst Labour Ministers, and there were always going to be practical difficulties in parts of the country where cultural and geographical identities were weak.

In the event the first referendum for a directly elected regional assembly (in North-East England) suffered an overwhelming defeat. This represented a humiliating outcome for Prescott personally and by common consent a sinking of the prospect of English regional government for a generation. One of the reasons was Prescott's failure to negotiate with other Ministers for sufficient powers to be delegated to the putative Assembly, thereby leading to accusations that it would be merely an expensive talking shop. The Department of Transport was notably recalcitrant, refusing for example to devolve investment decisions on major road schemes within the region.

At the local level the Government promised a major shake-up in the functioning of councils geared to 'democratic renewal', improved service delivery and community leadership. Proposals were put forward in a White Paper (DETR 1998d) and legislated for in the Local Government Act 2000 (Stoker and Wilson 2004). Councils were required to abandon the traditional multi-member committee system and to adopt one of three alternatives. Most decided not to adopt the model of a directly elected mayor (as in London), preferring instead a 'cabinet' of elected members from the majority party, with each being given 'portfolio' responsibility for a particular group of services.

The provision of council services, including those relating to transport and development planning, was made subject to a 'best value' regime involving rigorous evaluation and monitoring of performance outcomes following procedures established by central government. The National Audit Office conducted regular Comprehensive Performance Assessments (CPAs) which were used to promote 'earned autonomy' with excellent performers being given greater freedom from central government controls whilst 'failing' authorities were threatened with increased intervention and ultimately takeover.

In relation to community leadership local authorities were charged with producing a 'community strategy' identifying core outcomes and programmes of action for achieving them. In theory this would provide overall direction for the preparation of individual service plans, including LTPs. Authorities were encouraged to establish Local Strategic Partnerships (LSPs) to develop a 'joined-up' approach to policy implementation and delivery across public, private and voluntary sectors. At the same time authorities were granted the general power to promote economic, social and environmental well-being, intended to overcome legal obstacles which might be placed in the way of using any of their more specific powers.

In practice the above changes at both regional and local levels in England served to blur the formal responsibilities of elected councils and to render even more complex the totality of 'governance' operating in particular localities (see Chapter 10).

8.5 The Ten-Year Transport Plan

The *New Deal* proposals requiring legislation did not reach the statute book until two years later (in the Transport Act 2000). The delay did not make much difference in practice as preparatory work continued nonetheless, but gave the impression of a loss of momentum. At a time when the national economy (and hence both traffic levels and Government revenues) were growing strongly, nothing 'new' appeared to be happening which would make much difference to the worsening conditions which people were experiencing on the ground.

Criticisms of the Government's ineffectualness were compounded by personal attacks on John Prescott. Prescott stood out from his Cabinet colleagues because of his working class origins and combative character and presented a ready target for his political opponents in the media. Typical of the ridicule he was subjected to was being photographed at the Labour Party conference in Brighton taking a chauffeured car rather than walking 200 yards from his hotel – a travel choice he explained on the basis of protecting his wife's hairdo from the sea breezes!

In an attempt to restore credibility in 1999 Tony Blair appointed to the post of Transport Minister (nominally under Prescott, but reporting directly to the Prime

Minister) Lord 'Gus' Macdonald – a high-profile Scottish businessman who had a reputation for competence and a 'no-nonsense' approach (LTT 306). Macdonald was charged with overseeing the preparation of a ten-year plan for transport in the context of the Government's Comprehensive Spending Review then under way.

First sight of the technical work underpinning the plan appeared in a document which the Government was required to publish in response to the Road Traffic Reduction (National Targets) Act 1998. The report (DETR 2000d) applied to England only, responsibility in Scotland and Wales having passed to the new devolved administrations. The Government's thinking was conditioned by projections which showed that, if the White Paper measures were applied very intensively, national traffic growth would almost have ceased by 2010, whilst traffic levels in the major cities would have fallen below 1996 levels. However it did not accept the case for a national target, although national traffic levels would continue to be reported as a 'useful broad indicator' as part of the monitoring of sustainable development.

> Our policies focus on improving outcomes that affect people's quality of life in the real world. We already have targets for many of these: climate change, air quality, health and road safety. The issue is therefore whether a national road traffic reduction target would be a useful addition to the current range of targets. Our conclusion is that it would not and that we should concentrate on developing better indicators, and then considering targets for those outcomes for which we do not currently have targets.
>
> (ibid. para 18)

The Ten Year Plan itself was published in July 2000 (DETR 2000f). The notion of a national transport plan embodying particular levels of public expenditure over a period as long as ten years was unprecedented, although strictly there was no formal commitment beyond the three years covered by the Spending Review. In contrast with the financial stringency of New Labour's first term it proposed expenditure of £180bn over the ten-year period – a claimed increase of 75% in real terms. In fact some £56bn of the total was expected to consist of private investment. Within the overall total there were major shifts in spending allocations to rail and local transport which had continuing policy significance (12.5).

In his foreword to the Plan Prescott described it as a 'ten-year route map to take us towards the goals we set for ourselves in the Manifesto and the Integrated Transport White Paper'. This was a fudge since in reality the strategy was completely different. There was no reference to the 'consensus for radical change', nor any emphasis on changing travel behaviour. The claim made just two years previously that there was no longer any need for a large-scale road building programme was conveniently overlooked. Instead the White Paper resorted to the traditional idea that transport conditions are a function of the quality of the infrastructure and that contemporary problems were a product of decades of under-investment. In the interests of the country's economic prosperity it was deemed 'vital' to tackle this legacy and to transform the nation's transport networks. The expected outputs from the Plan are shown in Box 8.1.

Amidst the triumphalist atmosphere surrounding the launch of the Plan it would have been jarring to suggest that all the planned investment would still not cope with the anticipated increase in car use. But tucked away in the back of *Transport 2010* was a chapter which acknowledged the 'difficult challenge' which growing car use would continue to pose. However this was massaged away by discussing it under the heading

---

Box 8.1 Principal outputs expected to be delivered by the Ten Year Plan (to 2010)

- 360 miles of motorway widening
- all 40 schemes in the Highways Agency's Targeted Programme of Improvements, 30 trunk road bypasses and 80 major schemes tackling bottlenecks at other junctions
- 200 major local road improvements including 70 bypasses
- a £30bn programme to eliminate the backlog in local road and bridge maintenance
- completion of the Channel Tunnel Rail Link and the West Coast Main Line renewal, plus upgrades of the East Coast and Great Western main lines
- completion of the Thameslink 2000 and East London line extension projects plus a new east–west rail link in London such as CrossRail
- elimination of the backlog of maintenance and renewal work on the London Underground through a Public-Private Partnership
- 25 new light rail schemes and 100 park-and-ride schemes
- introduction of road user charging in eight of the largest English towns and cities outside London and a further twelve workplace parking schemes.

---

of 'future choices'. Lord Macdonald was also happy to leave the prospect of national road user charging in the long grass – 'a discussion for the second half of the decade'.

The Plan came in for serious criticism on the basis of what were still ostensibly the principles of the Government's strategy. A report by the House of Commons Select Committee was particularly scathing (House of Commons 2002). Whilst acknowledging that the Plan represented a welcome move away from the uncertainty of short-term funding regimes it queried the adequacy of a ten-year period for establishing a 'long-term vision':

> It is essential that the projects put in place form part of a long-term sustainable solution and not just a medium-term fix that moves us further towards car dependence.
>
> (ibid. para 11)

The Committee called for the examination of a range of policy options after 2010 based on rigorous advice from experts in the field. It criticised the Plan's concentration on the issue of congestion and the fact that the Government was willing to see a widening of the gap between the costs of public and private transport:

> It cannot have been the Department's objective to produce a plan that benefits the better off and those who travel the most. However the Plan acknowledges that it does just that. It is in complete contradiction to the Department's desires to reduce the need to travel and the Government's aims to promote equity and social inclusion.
>
> (ibid. para 37)

In conception the Ten Year Plan was seriously flawed and a disingenuous attempt to wrap a rather primitive, albeit grandiose, prospectus within the cloak of the *New Deal*. Unfortunately, as it transpired, the reality was even worse.

8.6 Blown off course: the road hauliers' blockade and the Hatfield rail crash

Even with a fair wind it was unlikely that the Ten Year Plan would have delivered all that was claimed for it. But within only a couple of months of publication the Government suffered two momentous but entirely unexpected events, the like of which it might normally have had to face only during a decade.

The first was a series of demonstrations mounted by truck drivers and farmers in September 2000 over the issue of fuel duty. The 'killer punch' in the campaign was the blockades mounted at the entrances to major fuel depots which prevented the movement of tankers serving the nation's petrol stations. With scarifying speed a state of emergency arose in a matter of days as the motoring public engaged in panic buying and stations literally ran dry.

At the centre of the dispute was the rapid rise in the pump price of petrol and diesel – a combination of increases in the price of crude oil worldwide and the effects of the UK fuel duty escalator. For long-distance truck drivers their particular grievance was the competitive disadvantage which the UK taxation regime was perceived to impose relative to the one borne by firms operating out of mainland Europe (McKinnon 2003).

For motorists generally the impact of the fuel duty escalator had been masked in previous years by falls in the real price of oil. Arguably the Government had sheltered behind this convenient façade and had not sought to convince the public of the need to reduce car use. The 1998 White Paper for example talked in terms of 'choice' and of getting more people to use non-car modes – of minor significance by comparison. Only a single paragraph was devoted to fuel duty and the term 'escalator' was omitted altogether. Hence when motoring costs started to rise sharply the Government had no established argument to fall back on. Significantly Gordon Brown defended the need to maintain fuel tax levels not in the interests of transport demand management, nor even in funding transport improvements, but in terms of providing for health and education services!

The issues which came to public attention during the hauliers' campaign had in fact already been registered a year earlier in submissions to the Chancellor by the CBI and the Freight Transport Association (LTT 276). Gordon Brown had responded by proposing to abolish the fuel duty escalator, saying that decisions in future would be taken on a year-by-year basis with any real increases in duty being channelled to additional transport investment via a ring-fenced fund.

In March 2000, because of rapidly rising oil prices, he opted to raise fuel duty to offset inflation only. Following the demonstrations however he announced further tax concessions which represented a loss of revenue to the Exchequer of over £1.5bn a year (LTT 302). Additional concessions worth about £400m a year were made to appease lorry drivers and farmers. All lorries operating on British roads were also to be subject to a 'vignette' charging scheme to ensure that foreign vehicles contributed to the cost of the road system.

On the railways meanwhile the initial years under privatisation happened to coincide with sustained growth in the national economy. As in the equivalent period of the 1980s, use of the railways rose sharply. However the regime of access charges payable to the infrastructure owner (Railtrack) had not been designed with growth in mind. Hence train operators could run additional trains without incurring significant costs but Railtrack received little revenue for the extra wear and tear (Nash 2003). Railtrack also had little commercial incentive to invest in the capacity of the network which was coming under more and more pressure.

The real Achilles' heel of privatised operations however was in the provisions made for safety. Although the overall safety of the railways continued to improve, two dramatic crashes involving heavily loaded passenger trains – at Southall and Ladbroke Grove (near London Paddington) in 1997 and 1999 – brought to light examples of practices on the railway where this was being compromised (Wolmar 2001). The grisly juxtaposition of railway fatalities with Railtrack's 'fat cat' image of bloated profiteers made railway operations the unusual subject of attention by film-maker Ken Loach and playwright David Hare.

A third high-profile rail crash – at Hatfield in September 2000 – brought to light a catalogue of errors and evidence of a neglectful maintenance regime. The crash took the form of a derailment at high speed caused by a broken rail, although amazingly only four people were killed. Railtrack responded by imposing severe speed limits on hundreds of locations where a similar weakening of rails was feared until a detailed inspection and some immediate remedial work could be done. During this period it was impossible for trains to maintain their schedules, one disruption compounded another and extensive delays ensued. Subsequently Railtrack embarked on an accelerated programme of track renewals which had a continuing disruptive effect on train operations and further damaged patronage.

Railtrack's financial resources were stretched to the limit coping with the immediate consequences of the Hatfield crash (£733m, mostly in compensation payments) and with colossal cost over-runs in its renewal of the West Coast Main Line (WCML) from London to Glasgow. However experience with the WCML was only the most extreme example of more general cost escalation gripping the industry as contractors sought to protect themselves from risk. Excluding costs arising from Hatfield, Railtrack's pre-tax profits for 2000/01 were halved. And yet whilst declaring overall losses of £534m the company announced it would keep dividends to shareholders at the same levels per share as the previous year 'to maintain access to the capital markets'.

> Taxpayers were paying dearly for that continued access – which was notional anyway, given the wrecked state of Railtrack's finances – and virtually any other way of funding the rail industry would have been cheaper.
>
> (Wolmar 2001 p. 229)

With the 2001 general election campaign under way, a £1.5bn advance was paid to Railtrack to keep it afloat, but with strings attached. Six months later Railtrack returned requesting a further £2bn bail-out whereupon the new Secretary of State Stephen Byers decided that enough was enough, refused the application and forced the company into liquidation.

In Railtrack's place a 'not for profit' organisation called Network Rail was established. Network Rail inherited a revised regime of access charges which increased its income by 35% (though requiring a corresponding increase in subsidies for passenger services) and altered the balance to give greater weight to variable costs. A further £100m pa was received to enable freight access charges to be halved – to offset the competitive disadvantage otherwise arising from the VED reduction given to road hauliers and an increase in maximum lorry weights to 44 tonnes.

The circumstances surrounding Byer's dealings with Railtrack were highly controversial and its shareholders subsequently mounted a legal challenge claiming that he had deliberately engineered the company's downfall. To minimise continuing embarrassment to the Government he was replaced as Transport Secretary by Alistair Darling in May 2002.

8.7 *Breaking the Logjam* – urban road user charging

The proposal to allow local authorities to introduce road user charging – and to retain the net revenues – was regarded by John Prescott as his major achievement in the haggling which went on within Government over the measures to be included in the *New Deal*. As the title of the 'daughter document' on the subject implied – *Breaking the Logjam* (DETR 1998c) – the new instrument was seen as central in overcoming the deadlock of urban traffic congestion.

The idea that some form of direct charging of road users should be used to influence urban traffic demand had been debated since the 1960s. However, despite its impeccable credentials as an example of market economics Mrs Thatcher's nose for popular opinion led her to prohibit any official investigation of the subject. Only after her departure did the Department of Transport return to the idea as part of its growing interest in fiscal instruments generally. By a nice irony one of the conclusions of a major research exercise was that, if this new, difficult and potentially fallible measure was to be proceeded with, the one place which should *not* be used to test it was London (MVA Consultancy 1995)!

Following consultation on the 'Logjam' document powers were given to local authorities in the Transport Act 2000 (and separately to the new Mayor of London in 1999). They allowed for two types of charging:

1   direct charges on drivers using roads in their area (which could be implemented in a variety of ways – by cordon pricing, supplementary licensing, electronic metering etc.)
2   workplace parking levies – charges on employers based on the number of private parking spaces they provided for their employees.

The Ten Year Plan and projections of its impact were based on the expectation of road user charging being introduced in eight of the largest towns and cities outside London and a further twelve workplace parking schemes. In terms of practical outcomes as well as credibility of the Government's overall strategy it was therefore little short of calamitous that this initiative proved an (almost) complete failure.

The Government worked with interested authorities behind the scenes in a 'charging partnership' but was careful publicly to emphasise that decisions were a local matter. This appeared as a less than whole-hearted commitment to the principle of charging and gave the impression that the Government was hedging its bets against unpopular or unsuccessful outcomes.

Another impediment to implementation was the absence of 'up-front' funding (LTT 282). Everyone including the Government recognised that tangible improvements would be needed in public transport *before* it would be politically feasible to impose charging on motorists. However the Government was not prepared to sanction additional funding for this purpose and, because of deregulation, councils were unable to determine bus fares or services anyway.

The significance of the public transport aspect is highlighted by what happened in London – 'the one that got away'. Not only is the base level of public transport service and use much higher in Central London but following the transfer of powers to the

London Mayor, local control over bus and tube services existed in a way which had no counterpart elsewhere.

However the Central London scheme would never have happened – or certainly not within such a short time-scale – but for the election of Ken Livingstone as London's first Mayor. Livingstone – the notoriously maverick, populist leader of the GLC in the 1980s – had been manoeuvred from standing as the Labour Party candidate, whereupon he resigned but stood and won as an Independent. Unlike the Conservative and Labour candidates, a 'congestion charging scheme' was a central plank of his manifesto.

The Central London scheme was designed, consulted on and implemented in less than three years from Livingstone's election in May 2000. This period also included extensive publicity, improvements in bus services and changes to the fare system as preparatory measures (LTT 326). The scheme was introduced amidst intense media scrutiny in February 2003. Fortunately the launch went without any major technical hitch and traffic flows on the first day (carefully chosen to coincide with schools' half-term) were reported to be down by 25%.

A few weeks after the launch the Prime Minister, Tony Blair was gracious enough to say:

> I think that it was an experiment that a lot of people were dubious about frankly, including me, and I think he [Livingstone] deserves credit for having carried that through … We have got to work out what its implications are more widely now.
>
> (reported in LTT 365)

Whilst preparation for the London scheme was under way, interest in almost all the other urban schemes faded. Only one other, small-scale scheme was implemented in the special circumstances of the historic core of Durham city. Proposals for a central Bristol scheme were shelved following a change in political control whilst a city-wide scheme for Edinburgh had to be abandoned after a botched public referendum exercise.

The *New Deal* idea of local schemes being generated in what amounted to a national vacuum had come to nothing. This represented another nail in the coffin of the Ten Year Plan as traffic forecasts and expected charging revenues had to be revised in consequence – in both cases in the wrong direction (LTT 356).

8.8 'Sustainable Communities Plan'

The *New Deal* White Paper acknowledged that land use planning was a key component of an integrated transport policy through reducing the need for travel and facilitating sustainable travel choices. The concept of 'urban renaissance' had great political appeal in that it appeared simultaneously to address several concerns – the regeneration of inner cities and the protection of the countryside from 'greenfield' development as well as promoting sustainable travel. However it challenged social and professional norms which associated more intensive urban development with a worsening of living conditions. The architect Lord Richard Rogers was commissioned to lead an Urban Task Force to investigate these issues (DETR 1999c).

The work of the Urban Task Force was reflected in a revised PPG3 (DETR 2000b) which made a notable shift from land availability to 'urban capacity' as the basis for identifying the additional land needed for housing development. (Urban capacity places greater emphasis on the potential for additional housing through more intensive use and re-use of sites and properties, including conversions from non-residential uses.) The Government set a national target of 60% of future housing requirements to be met from development of previously used (so-called 'brownfield') land. To help achieve this the minimum density for new housing developments was raised to 30 dwellings per hectare and planning authorities were required to follow a 'sequential test' in the phasing of major developments, demonstrating that all brownfield opportunities had been exploited before the go-ahead was given on new greenfield sites.

There is a general synergy between this emphasis on the use of brownfield land and the transport interest in promoting development within urban areas so as to lessen car use. However not all brownfield sites are within urban areas (e.g. former military airfields) and of those which are, some of the largest are often relatively inaccessible (e.g. major industrial installations). Hence it was important that a revision of PPG13 *Transport* published in 2001 (DETR 2001) emphasised the need for development sites to offer good accessibility by non-car modes.

Greater emphasis on land use/transport integration was also pursued in the Government's review of arrangements for regional planning guidance (RPG). A new version of PPG11 (DETR 2000c) required inclusion of a separately identifiable Regional Transport Strategy (RTS) which, amongst other things, allowed for consideration of trunk road proposals as part of the overall planning of a region.

The most controversial element in RPGs was typically the projection of future housing requirements and the amount and distribution of proposed 'greenfield' development. The Panel Report on RPG9 (for South-East England outside London) created shock waves by recommending much higher housing provision than the shire counties had proposed. With the 2001 general election in the offing the Government took refuge in a compromise position. However public concern over housing affordability continued to grow along with fears that difficulties in recruiting and retaining 'key workers' in the public services would threaten economic prospects for the capital. The issue rapidly assumed national significance and the Government responded with a bold, but controversial strategy.

As it happened the timing of the Government's initiative came soon after the cabinet reshuffle removing Stephen Byers. The DTLR empire was split and John Prescott was given charge of a resurrected planning, housing and local government department which he insisted should be referred to as the Office of the Deputy Prime Minister (ODPM).

The launch of the 'Sustainable Communities Plan' (ODPM 2003d) provided Prescott with another opportunity (after transport and regional government) to apply his crusading zeal. This was a wide-ranging review of the Department's housing-related activities but its main thrust was to increase the supply of housing, especially in the South-East. This was focused on four 'growth areas' (Milton Keynes/South Midlands, London–Cambridge, Thames Gateway and Ashford) which had previously been identified in RPG9. The Government was now proposing that they should make provision for an additional 200,000 houses up to a total of 900,000 by 2031. Implementation of this very ambitious programme was to be progressed through a variety of 'delivery vehicles' including urban development corporations and regeneration companies (ODPM 2003a).

The environmental credentials of the Plan were suspect, not least because their travel implications were uncertain. Local authorities and regional assemblies flagged their opposition to the proposed population increases in the absence of Government commitment to funding the public service infrastructure needed to turn the aspiration for 'communities' into reality. The Department of Transport appeared not to have been involved in the preparation of the Plan and made clear that it did not anticipate the hard-won resources of the Ten Year Transport Plan being diverted into catering for the needs of growth areas!

The growth areas initiative reflected an increasingly important Treasury view that high house prices could be remedied by additional housing supply (Barker 2004). The planning system was considered one of the major constraints. It had already come in for criticism on account of inordinate delays in plan preparation and because excessive detail and negative, bureaucratic attitudes were said to stifle business enterprise.

All these complaints and more were registered in a Green Paper published at the end of 2001 (DTLR 2001). This proposed wholesale upheaval of the development plan system whose basic form had operated since 1968. Notwithstanding a mix of misgiving and outright opposition the proposals went ahead largely unchanged under the Planning and Compulsory Purchase Act 2004. At a strategic level the main change was the abolition of structure plans and the elevation of RPG to statutory status as a 'regional spatial strategy' (Chapter 18).

8.9 Clearing the decks – the 2004 White Paper

Despite the raft of initiatives from the *New Deal* and the increased investment in the Ten Year Plan it was soon apparent that failure of several key elements meant that most of the hoped-for outcomes would not materialise. The lack of local enthusiasm for urban charging schemes and the impracticability of the procedures set up around statutory Quality Bus Partnerships and Contracts meant that the provisions included in the 2000 Transport Act for these measures took on the status of white elephants.

The Government's change in policy on fuel duty contributed to a situation where after 2000 the rate of traffic growth *increased* compared with the slowing which had occurred previously. Even without this the Department of Transport had had to own up to a technical error which meant that the Ten Year Plan's much-vaunted impact on traffic congestion was a misrepresentation. Instead of achieving an overall reduction by 2010, it was likely to increase by between 11% and 20% (DfT 2002a).

On the railways by 2004/05 the train operators had only recovered half of the losses in punctuality and reliability incurred during the year after Hatfield. The previous growth in rail use was seriously dented and the Government had to abandon the targets it had set in the Ten Year Plan. The bulk of the additional rail investment envisaged had had to be diverted to maintaining and renewing the existing railway, rather than bringing about hoped-for enhancements. Cost escalation also had ramifications for the 25 light rail projects envisaged in the Plan. Schemes which had reached an advanced state of preparation in Leeds and Portsmouth were abandoned whilst extensions to the systems in Manchester and Birmingham were stalled.

The limbo into which railway developments were cast post-Hatfield had the effect of removing them from regional and local transport planning exercises since it was not possible to enter into any forward commitment. In particular the 'multi-modal' credentials of the motorway corridor studies were demolished at a stroke since no matter what they might recommend in the way of rail enhancements there was very little probability of schemes being implemented.

This series of calamities distorted the composition and trajectory of the Government's strategy *actually being implemented*. CfIT noted this imbalance and registered concern that the announcement of a large programme of road schemes arising from the first batch of multi-modal studies had made little reference to supporting public transport schemes or demand restraint measures:

> There is growing doubt about the Government's commitment to all aspects of an integrated transport agenda .... If transport is to play its part in delivering the quality of life that the country needs and deserves for the 21st century then integrated transport, incorporating behavioural change and demand restraint, as well as infrastructure provision, is the essential way forward.
>
> (CfIT 2003)

CfIT, and David Begg personally, were prominent in arguing the case for investigating a nationwide system of road user charging (CfIT 2002). The new Transport Secretary Alistair Darling appears to have been won over by the idea and took the opportunity when announcing his response to a second batch of multi-modal studies to publish a Green Paper *Managing Our Roads* (DfT 2003a). Whilst the DfT's press release headlined a '£7bn blitz of improvements to keep traffic flowing on some of Britain's most congested roads', Darling also announced the commissioning of a Road Charging Feasibility Study.

In deciding on some of the MMS road proposals Darling had shown himself willing to give priority to local environmental issues in certain cases. However there was no evidence that he was prepared to give ground to more global environmental considerations. This impression was confirmed a few months later when he published a White Paper on *The Future of Air Transport* (DfT 2003b). This was a much-delayed fulfilment of a commitment given in the *New Deal* White Paper to apply to the subject of airports the policies 'of sustainable development, integration with surface transport and contribution to regional growth' (DETR 1998a para 3.109).

In the event the airports White Paper did no such thing. Whilst acknowledging that 'we must do more to reduce the environmental effects of aviation' (including promoting an international trade in carbon emissions) the basis of the policies for airport development was essentially 'predict and provide'. Overall projections were for between a doubling and trebling of passenger demand by 2030 with aviation potentially contributing a quarter of the UK's contribution to global warming by that date. Much of the White Paper was concerned with the implications of this growth for development policies at individual airports, but in 'policy silo' fashion. Given the enormous importance of airports in influencing the distribution of economic and spatial development the absence of explicit discussion of these matters, let alone attempt at integrated planning, was stunning.

The Government had always intended to review the Ten Year Plan in 2004 to coincide with the Chancellor's Comprehensive Spending Review. Unexpectedly it chose to do this in the form of a White Paper *The Future of Transport* (DfT 2004f). (For the first time this largely applied to England only.) In terms of analysis and policy the text of the White Paper offered almost nothing new and, except for the restructuring of rail responsibilities (the subject of a separate White Paper – see 23.5), did not preface any legislative proposals.

The White Paper was subtitled *A Network for 2030*. On the face of it this looked like a response to calls by the Select Committee and others for a longer term planning horizon. In fact the Paper contained minimal and superficial consideration of issues over this longer period. The following is typical:

We expect to see further growth in car ownership and use over the next 30 years. The car provides many benefits, but the challenge is to ensure that people have other options, including good quality public transport and the opportunity to walk or cycle.

(DfT 2004f para 1.9)

The theme used to introduce the White Paper was the unoriginal one of the challenge presented by the demand for travel in the context of historic under-investment in infrastructure. On this basis almost any investment programme was justification in itself. The only advance on the Ten Year Plan (apart from a necessary revision of projections and targets) was confirmation of the Government's intention 'to explore new ways of paying for road use which incentivise smarter individual choices about when and how we travel'. Drawing on the results of the Road Pricing Feasibility Study it intended to push ahead with persuading major stakeholders and the general public so as to secure the political consensus needed to translate such a radical proposal into practice:

There is a need for a mature discussion as to which approach we take. The Government view is that the costs of inaction or unrestricted road-building are too high for society. The time has come seriously to consider the role that could be played by some form of road pricing policy.

(DfT 2004f para 3.23)

Overall, with the 2005 general election in prospect, the White Paper sought to put the best possible complexion on events of the previous six years. The Government's 'achievements' were expressed almost entirely in terms of physical outputs and administrative or institutional changes (i.e. not in outcomes). In a manner reminiscent of the former Soviet Union the previous (1998) White Paper was air-brushed out of existence – not only any mention of the document itself, but also several of its distinctive features: notably integration, social inclusion, traffic reduction and even sustainable development. An enhanced spending trajectory had been secured as part of the 2004 Comprehensive Spending Review but, aside from short-term targets, there was no clear sense of what longer term strategy it was contributing to.

Part III

Ends and means

The first two parts of this book have provided much of the context needed to understand the contemporary situation surrounding transport policy and planning. Part 1 described the trends in travel and transport themselves and their impacts. Part 2 charted the involvement of the State over time, altering the physical development of transport networks and the way they are planned, managed and funded.

Had past governments acted differently the starting point for contemporary policy-making – the present mix of transport networks, travel behaviour and attitudes, institutional arrangements and so on – would be different from the one we have today. An interesting illustration of this is the *different* transport conditions which prevail in the neighbouring countries of continental Europe which are broadly *similar* in their social and political traditions and in their economic development. (These differences are not explored here, but see CfIT 2006.)

The physical legacy of past policies is largely incremental so that what exists today is essentially the sum of the developments described in Part 2. Each generation tends to adapt and improve the inherited infrastructure to meet contemporary needs and adds new elements of its own. Only rarely are former transport developments obliterated by new ones.

The situation with what might be termed the institutional infrastructure – the agencies responsible for planning and managing the transport networks, their duties, powers, funding etc. – is rather different. Here too there will be elements which have grown incrementally over time. In this case however, as new elements are introduced, the opportunity is normally taken to amend or withdraw previous legislation, government advice etc. so that the framework within which executive bodies have to work is reasonably coherent and internally consistent. Sometimes, as we saw in Part 2, it is possible for major elements of the institutional infrastructure to be replaced completely. This has occurred most notably in the ownership and regulation of transport industries and in the structure of local government.

The main purpose of Parts 3 and 4 is to describe the cumulative effect of these past initiatives as represented by the institutional arrangements in operation today. Part 3 deals with aspects of policy choice surrounding 'ends' and 'means', i.e. the objectives to which transport policy should be directed and the instruments available to pursue them. These define the broad repertoire of possibilities which are open to decision-takers. Part 4 then deals with planning procedures, i.e. with the requirements or 'guidance' which national governments set for the detailed planning activity undertaken in particular areas or on particular topics in order to determine which combination of ends and means (from the pool of possibilities) is most appropriate to local circumstances. Together Parts 3 and 4 constitute the 'rules of the game' within which planning practitioners operate on a day-to-day basis.

The individual chapters of Part 3 are as follows:

- *the role of the State* (Chapter 9) – considers the fundamental questions which underpin any aspect of public policy: what is the nature of the State and what are the criteria which do or might influence its role as interpreted by a particular Government – in our case with respect to transport?
- *institutional arrangements* (Chapter 10) – the division of functions as between public and private sectors in the provision of transport infrastructure and services and the allocation of responsibilities amongst the public sector
- *objectives and targets* (Chapter 11) – the purposes or 'ends' set for public bodies working in the transport field and the use of indicators to measure their performance in fulfilling them
- *infrastructure investment and its funding* (Chapter 12) – the 'means' available for pursuing these ends in terms of improvements to transport infrastructure and the opportunities and constraints surrounding their funding
- *regulatory measures* (Chapters 13 and 14) – i.e. the means available in the form of legally enforceable rules on vehicles, traffic and development (Chapter 13) or on transport industries (Chapter 14)
- *fiscal measures* (Chapter 15) – the means available via forms of taxation or charging on the one hand or via grants or subsidies on the other to influence the amount or type of travel or transport service provided
- *behavioural measures* (Chapter 16) – referred to by the Government as 'smarter choices' – are a relatively new category of instrument which seeks to secure change in travel behaviour amongst individuals and organisations independently of improvements to the transport system and without application of traditional regulatory or fiscal measures.

9 The State and its role

9.1 Introduction

When we speak of 'public policy' we are referring to the principles adopted in steering the activities of institutions which collectively form, or act on behalf of, the State. In our case we are concerned about activities relating to transport, and in subsequent chapters we will be looking at objectives and instruments which are specifically relevant to them.

However before getting into that level of detail we need to think first about the criteria which should govern State action more generally. What exactly is 'the State' and what determines whether it should initiate action in a particular field? If so, how should the amount and type of action be judged? What distinguishes action by the State from actions undertaken by any other organisation?

These questions are especially relevant to transport because – unlike, say, military intervention or international diplomacy – it is not itself the product of the State. Transport and transport services can be engaged in by private individuals and businesses and it is perfectly possible to conceive of a situation in which their activities were solely a matter determined by social and market forces. (This was very largely the case in Britain until the mid-19th century.) As we saw in Chapter 6 it is also possible for public policy to be pursued with the explicit aim of *lessening* State involvement (compared with that undertaken hitherto) in the belief that these forces, left to themselves, will produce a more beneficial outcome.

We therefore consider first in this chapter the nature and role of the State (9.2 and 9.3). We then go on to explore the various sources of 'market failure' on which State action is predicated (9.4). The economic case underpinning such action is to maximise aggregate welfare but in practice this is moderated by a range of social equity considerations (9.5). Equally concern for the well-being of particular social groups may prompt State action in itself but at the expense of forgoing greater benefits which could be enjoyed by the population as a whole.

The arguments presented here do not resolve what course of action should be followed in a particular case but they do illuminate the criteria by which options deserve to be assessed. Ultimately decisions will depend on the relative importance attached to economic and social considerations, to individual versus collective interests and to the efficacy of public versus private action. Many of the policy differences between political parties on particular transport and other issues derive from ideological differences on these fundamental matters.

9.2 The nature of 'the State'

The State has been defined as 'the sum of *all* the institutions which possess legitimate authority to exercise public power' (Dearlove and Saunders 2000 p. 246). The most politically visible of these institutions is (Central) Government – the collection of Ministers appointed by the Prime Minister (officially by the Crown) from the majority party in the House of Commons. Each Minister directs and is accountable to Parliament for specific aspects of administration undertaken in the various Departments of State. The most senior Ministers – mainly those who head the individual Government departments – collectively form the Cabinet. It is in the Cabinet, or more commonly in the large number of Cabinet sub-committees set up to deal with individual subjects, that overall Government policy is formally decided on.

The day-to-day business of executing Government responsibilities, advising Ministers and carrying out their decisions, is conducted by the Civil Service. This is staffed by career administrators and specialist professionals who are unelected and, in a formal sense, politically neutral. The continuity of the Civil Service from one Government to another (even when it changes political colour) is a very important influence on the evolution of policy – a force for stability or an impediment to change depending on one's point of view.

As was very acutely shown in the TV series 'Yes Minister' the greater knowledge and experience of senior civil servants in a particular field can mean that in practice it is they and not the Ministers who direct the workings of government departments and lead decision-making, subject of course to the niceties of constitutional etiquette. To counter this a system of 'political advisers' – overtly party political appointment of experts – has grown up in order to strengthen Ministers' hands. Increasingly too the Prime Minister's own Policy Unit exerts a controlling influence on the policies and priorities pursued in individual departments.

Much State activity which is not concerned with national policy-making is devolved in some way – to executive agencies (such as the Highways Agency), to non-governmental public bodies (such as the Rail Regulator), or to regional assemblies and local government. (These are discussed further as part of the 'institutional framework' in the following chapter.)

The work of all these bodies carries the authority of the 'Crown in Parliament' and is backed by the State enforcement agencies – the police, the judiciary and the armed forces. This gives them the unique status of having the backing of legitimate coercive force which, if resisted, can be punished by fines or imprisonment. However this force only comes into play occasionally and in rather extreme circumstances. The power which derives from its *potential* use is greater, particularly – in the case of personal behaviour – in the way it reinforces social norms.

The ordinary person is likely to have only a vague idea of what 'the State' consists of and what it actually does. This uncertainty is probably best encapsulated in the all-purpose 'they' which is commonly used to refer to *any* body which exerts a controlling influence over some aspect of their lives. People are likely to remark that 'they' have put up bus fares again, or that 'they' are planning to build a bypass without pausing to reflect on which particular body is responsible – even whether it is a public or a private one.

In fact the public/private distinction is of fundamental importance because it is associated with quite different regimes of accountability which impact on the position of the individual. In relation to private companies this position is normally as a customer who is free to choose whether to use the services on offer but whose influence (with others) is confined to their purchasing power. By contrast, the relationship to public bodies is as a citizen who is *obliged* to accept any requirements which may be imposed, but who also has the right (again with others) to elect representatives who have authority to take action on their behalf. Thus if I want to run a car, I can *choose* which particular make of car I buy, but if I want to use it on public roads I am *required* to pass a driving test and to pay for a vehicle licence.

Private organisations have to work successfully with their suppliers, customers, employees, business partners and so on but ultimately their policies will be determined by their directors and shareholders. In the case of a commercial company (bus and train companies for example) these policies will be geared to securing a satisfactory return for its investors, without which the financial backing necessary to the company's future will not be forthcoming.

In order to advance a company's interests relative to its competitors its dealings are normally confidential and its policies are not open to public debate. Indeed members of the public may not be aware that an issue is under consideration until a decision is announced, or until the results of that decision become obvious. If people want to make representations to a company it is under no obligation to receive or respond to them, although in the interests of good public relations it may choose to do so.

Public bodies by contrast are run by members who are either themselves elected by the population at large or appointed by others who are. The workings of these bodies are open to public scrutiny and the responsible members are obliged to respond to concerns or criticisms that are raised. Service delivery and impartial treatment of all members of the population are over-riding criteria of operations rather than profit generation (although control of costs may be equally important). The ethic of public service is an important factor in public sector employment and in the vast majority of cases the payment of staff is not linked to performance of the organisation as a whole (however this might be measured).

At election time people have the opportunity to vote for their particular MP (Member of Parliament) or local ward councillor but often use this as the occasion to register a more general opinion on how well the country or their local council is being run. There is a very rough justice in all this. Local councillors may be ejected because of some national issue for which they have no responsibility. National governments may suffer because of the decisions of key private companies, or movements in the global economy, over which they have no control.

Nevertheless because the fate of governments is ultimately dependent on public opinion they have a close interest in interpreting and acting upon the 'messages' articulated by the electorate. As far as domestic policy areas such as transport are concerned, governments *do* have the option of taking action to improve conditions, *whether they currently have direct responsibility or not*. Thus even in situations where responsibility lies primarily with the private sector (like the current provision of bus services for example) there are normally powers already available which public bodies can use to influence the behaviour of the firms concerned. If the requisite powers are unavailable or insufficient then – provided the need is considered serious enough – legislation can be introduced into Parliament to remedy the situation.

References to elections and to Parliament are the 'windows' on to the workings of the State which ordinary people are most likely to be aware of. But in truth this gives a distorted impression. Although the democratic process for electing representatives, using them to scrutinise the workings of public bodies and (in the case of MPs) to approve or amend legislation is of fundamental importance, it is in a sense operating at the very limits – the margins if you like – of the actions taken by the State. Most State activity – and much of the policy-making described in this book – takes place in the spaces in between.

9.3 The role of the State

In a democratic society the fundamental justification for State activity lies in the protection of its citizens and the upholding of the rule of law. More extensive involvement in economic and social matters derives from arguments that the conditions which would otherwise result from the workings of civil society – the interaction of households, businesses and other organisations which come about spontaneously – are insufficient or unsatisfactory in some way.

State involvement in transport in the UK has been on a scale sufficient to warrant a separate Government department for almost a century. Given this tradition it requires a considerable degree of intellectual detachment to pose the question 'why is the State involved in transport at all?' But, as we shall see, the answer to this question effectively determines the areas of activity the Government and its agencies are engaged in and sets the parameters for discussion about policy in each of these areas.

The fact that we pose the basic question (and do not take State involvement for granted) derives from our liberal political tradition. This upholds the freedom of the individual citizen to the extent that actions by agencies of the State are only legitimate to the extent that they use powers granted by Parliament.

To speak of 'State action' backed by 'coercive force' invokes images of third-world dictators and civil riots – seemingly far removed from something as comparatively mundane as transport. But in fact the ability of people to move around as and when they please is valued as one of the defining characteristics of a free society. Precisely because it is so intrinsic to our way of life it is not in the forefront of our minds on a day-to-day basis. However, any suggestion of *changing* the status quo will quickly bring this issue to the surface.

The sense of basic freedoms being threatened explains why seemingly minor transport proposals – for example to introduce parking restrictions in a particular street or a traffic management scheme which restricts movements in an area – can meet with vociferous opposition apparently out of all proportion to the actual inconvenience which people will incur. In broader discussions about transport the rhetoric of 'freedom' is also frequently used, particularly by those on the right of the political spectrum – for example:

> We need to expand the capacity of the road system – and for that matter the public transport system too – in order to cater for people's freedoms.
> (Bernard Jenkin, Conservative Party Transport spokesman, BBC Radio 4 Today programme, 29 May 2001)

Debates about the scale and nature of State involvement in transport invoke the same principles as in other policy areas. The dominant principle, consistent with our liberal political tradition referred to above, is that individuals are the best judges of their own welfare. This underpins our general use of markets to determine the allocation of investment and the consumption of goods and services. (One dimension of State activity is in fact to ensure that markets in particular fields operate freely and fairly.) Any suggestion that governments might seek to intervene so as to influence individuals' behaviour beyond what can be shown to be in the *public* interest will be quickly ridiculed as the actions of a 'nanny State' and generate political opprobrium.

However much a Government might favour a course of action (e.g. using funds raised through taxes to improve transport infrastructure or services) it will need to have regard to arguments about whether it adds to the sum of individuals' welfare. These arguments will not of course be rehearsed at length in the pages of popular newspapers or on TV, but will be important in securing the support of key stakeholders and opinion formers in the media and elsewhere. Because transport is essentially a marketable commodity (i.e. its provision can be freely negotiated between suppliers and consumers) the case for State action arises only in those situations where for one reason or another the operation of the free market would not maximise welfare.

In the following section we therefore consider the various kinds of 'market failure' which may arise in practice. It does not follow that in all such cases the State *will* intervene because public action itself has attendant drawbacks. For example there are costs incurred in setting up and running the necessary institutions. There may also be difficulties in ensuring that they are operated efficiently and responsively in meeting people's requirements. The 'cure' might be considered to have worse, or certainly different, consequences than the original disease.

The yardstick of market conditions applies not only to judgements about whether to intervene but also to the *manner* of intervention. As we shall see, many transport proposals involving public funding are assessed in a way which seeks to identify which would perform best if it were subject to market-like conditions on the basis of consumers' willingness to pay.

Although this reference to market principles has become the dominant paradigm in contemporary public policy-making it is not one which is universally accepted. The economic conception of welfare is based on the idea that individuals are essentially self-seeking and in competition with one another. Such a view conflicts with some people's notions of 'community' or 'mutuality' which they believe should have a greater influence in the workings of our society. Much campaigning by social or environmental pressure groups for example cannot be explained in terms of the benefits which the individuals involved can ever expect to gain for themselves. The 'co-operative' spirit also finds expression in community transport organisations and social enterprises more generally.

Concepts of need and mutual responsibility nevertheless still have a critical influence on public policy. This derives from a quite separate set of arguments which will be considered after the next section.

9.4 Sources of market failure

The notion that markets work by means of an 'invisible hand' to secure economically efficient outcomes is dependent on a body of theory which requires a large number of conditions to be satisfied. (An economically efficient situation is one in which it is not possible to increase the welfare of any one person without simultaneously decreasing another's.)

Unfortunately the real world differs greatly from these ideal conditions and it is in this area that a large amount of academic argument takes place. Since these arguments are not conclusive – and the difficulties of applying them to practical situations cannot be fully surmounted – there remain many areas requiring political or professional judgement. Economists would maintain that the intellectual discipline is nevertheless instructive and that decision-makers should pursue these lines of argument as far as they reasonably can, so as to minimise the area in which judgements (of values or about uncertainties) have to be resorted to.

The various types of 'market failure' can be grouped as follows:

1   external effects
2   imperfect information
3   public goods
4   natural monopolies
5   very large investments.

These, and their consequences for the main types of State involvement in transport, are discussed below. (For further reading see Quinet and Vickerman 2004 or Button 1993.)

1) External effects

For markets to produce outcomes which maximise welfare a key condition is that the transactions between producers and consumers should take account of all the costs and benefits arising, not only to themselves but to anyone else who may be affected.

Transport which is supplied in a market form has a price which essentially reflects the *internal* costs and benefits of those involved in the transaction (i.e. producers and consumers). Thus if I make a bus journey I pay a fare which covers the immediate operating costs of the company concerned (staff costs, fuel, vehicle maintenance etc.) plus a share of its fixed costs (vehicles, garage facilities etc.). The revenue received by the company from passengers as a whole, after paying for all its costs, must give a return on the money tied up in the business which is sufficient to attract and retain the funding supplied by its owners (shareholders) or other investors. The fares charged must be less than the value which passengers place on the activity made possible by making the journey (e.g. a shopping trip) or on the travel time savings or other benefits they receive by making the journey by this means rather than any other. (If this weren't the case then they either would not travel at all or else travel by an alternative, cheaper mode, such as walking.) Assuming the transport provision is being made in a freely competitive environment (another key condition) pressure will be exerted on suppliers to keep their prices at the lowest possible level consistent with generating an adequate return. In this way the number of passengers is maximised and therefore the aggregate benefit maximised also. (Economists would put a number of provisos on each of the statements for them to hold true in particular circumstances but this is the gist of the argument.)

However bus travel, or any other form of transport, alters the conditions experienced both by other travellers ('users' of the transport system) and by other groups in society ('non-users'). Thus if I and a proportion of other travellers have opted to make our journeys by bus rather than, say, by car then we will probably be generating benefits to motorists through less traffic congestion and to residents and others in the form of better safety and environmental conditions. Conversely motorists in making their journeys will worsen the conditions experienced by bus users, pedestrians, residents and so on.

If roadspace were charged for directly (which it is not) then it would be possible to adjust the prices paid by the various classes of user to reflect their interacting costs and benefits. However this would still leave the impacts on *non-users* – positive or negative – unaccounted for. Ideally (in the case of adverse environmental effects) their estimated monetary value would be incorporated in user charging also – the so-called 'polluter pays' principle (Pearce et al. 1989 p. 156). If the mechanisms to levy such charges do not exist then there may be a case for the State to intervene using other kinds of (regulatory) measure which impact on travel to produce outcomes different from those which would result solely from the interplay of producers and consumers of particular transport modes. The aim would be to deliver outcomes which reflect more nearly the situation which would arise if the various external effects (so-called 'externalities') *were* included in market transactions – i.e. as if people had to compensate all those whom they disbenefited and were rewarded by all those they benefited.

Impacts on other travellers or on environmental conditions are not the full extent of possible externalities. Two other categories are particularly important. The first is the impact of transport on the economy as a whole (whether at local, regional or national levels). The second is the effect of transport on the pattern of development. Since the State is not indifferent to the social, economic and environmental outcomes in either of these it follows that the public interests involved need to be reflected in regulatory regimes governing both transport operations and investment.

Interactions between the different categories of transport users and between transport and local environments now form part of standard procedures for the assessment of individual transport proposals (Chapter 21). Recognition of broader interactions between transport, the economy and spatial development accounts for the increasing emphasis being placed on the strategic planning of all three (Chapter 18).

2) Imperfect information

Even if mechanisms existed which made it possible for transport suppliers and consumers to pay and receive sums equivalent to the external costs and benefits they generated there would be great difficulties in them knowing what the full extent of these were. (Knowledge of all such factors is another of the key conditions for markets to produce economically efficient outcomes.) The direct provision of adequate, socially responsible information, or the regulation of operators so that they supply it, is therefore another case for State intervention.

Two examples can be given. The first is real-time information about traffic conditions on the highway network. The second is information about the availability of public transport services in an area. In both cases there is a distinction between the private and public interests involved. A commercial supplier of route information may have no scruples about its traffic and environmental effects and how these marry with the management strategies of public highway authorities. In a similar vein an individual public transport operator may be more concerned with attracting users on to his particular services than with providing co-ordinated information that fulfils public objectives of maximising use of publicly available networks as a whole. In both cases therefore there may be a public interest in over-riding the particular private interests.

The issue of imperfect information also arises in connection with safety regulation as far as *users* of particular transport modes are concerned. (Impacts on the safety of non-users is a straightforward externality of the kind discussed earlier.) In an ideal world prospective users of transport services would have full knowledge of the safety features they possessed and what the practical consequences of these were for the risk being taken on any one journey. In a free market levels of safety would then be one of the various attributes (along with speed, cost, reliability, comfort etc.) with which operators would compete for business. In practice, because of the sensitivity of the subject and the technical complexities involved, State intervention is commonplace to impose safety regulations so as to safeguard travellers (i.e. to relieve them of the responsibility of finding the necessary information themselves, and also to protect them from unscrupulous operators).

3) Public goods

Public goods are commodities which cannot be supplied in a way which enables their benefits to be enjoyed only by the people who choose to pay for them. Examples are clean air or public policing. The possibility of 'free-riders' means that, without State intervention compelling people to contribute to their cost, the provision of these things – either at all or to the level which most individuals actually want – would not be forthcoming.

Much activity by the State countering the adverse environmental effects of traffic and transport has a 'public goods' justification, paid for out of general taxation. This is because of the indivisibility of the various environmental attributes (clean air, quiet, landscaping etc.) and the fact that it is not possible to exclude from these benefits individual property owners who, if they had the opportunity, might seek not to pay for them.

Local roads, streets and footpaths are also public goods. As we have seen (in Chapter 4) securing their maintenance was one of the first examples of State intervention in transport matters. It is not practicable to adopt a 'pay as you go' (toll-road) approach to such minor rights of way. In fact these are one of many such local facilities for which an overall charge is levied on businesses and householders in an area (in the form of the business rate or council tax). This leaves open the problem which has existed for centuries that the costs involved may differ greatly from one area to another and that some places are frequented more by 'outsiders' who do not contribute to local taxes. This is resolved by equalisation formulae built into the system of financial support from Central Government to local authorities, funded out of general taxation.

Motorways and other high-standard roads which have been built to supplement the local road network and have few points of connection with it do not fall into the category of public goods even though at present in the UK they happen to be publicly owned and funded out of general taxation. This is because it would be perfectly possible to charge users directly for the benefits they receive (e.g. via tolls, as is the practice in several other countries). In theory this revenue stream would also allow for the development of such roads and their standards of operation to be determined by commercial companies (Newbery 1994).

There are however potential difficulties arising from the interaction between traffic levels and conditions on and off tolled sections of the highway network (i.e. a category of the external effects mentioned earlier) which, if they were developed privately, would imply the need for some over-arching regulation. (Broader effects on the economy, environment and spatial development mean that, as at present, new highway proposals would need to be subject to development permission.) The complexities of this issue are such that the current Government has preferred to retain control over the specification of major new roads (mostly untolled) but in certain cases to invite private sector consortia to bid for the opportunity to finance, build, operate and maintain them over a defined concession period.

4) Natural monopolies

Transport operation tends towards monopoly provision because of economies of scale and the benefits of an integrated network. This was evident in the amalgamation of railway companies in the 19th century. More recently there have been acquisitions and amalgamations of companies formed out of the transport privatisations of the 1980s and 90s, particularly in the bus industry. In such situations intervention by the State is necessary either to prevent monopolies from forming (and hence maintain a competitive operating environment) or alternatively to permit the formation of monopolies but to regulate their operations so as to prevent exploitation of users.

Locally monopoly provision can arise because of the size and 'lumpiness' of investments. For example there is only likely to be economic justification for *one* main road or railway between many towns, or one toll bridge across an estuary. If there is to be such provision it will be important for public agencies to regulate the charges and travel conditions which are applied.

In the case of service provision an operator may only be prepared to tie himself to restrictive conditions if he is protected from possible competition by another company. This was the situation which arose when the franchising of passenger rail services began in the mid-1990s. Commercial train operating companies acted together to prevent the Conservative Government introducing the 'open access' free-for-all it would have preferred.

Local monopolies arise in bus operations partly because of economies of scale, for example the ability to serve a town from a single depot, or to inter-work vehicles between services so as to maximise their utilisation. They also arise because large operators can use their dominant position to offer travelcards, return tickets and the like (on their services only) in a way which disadvantages smaller operators with whom they may be in competition on individual routes. In this situation not only does competition on the individual routes suffer but also the public interest in securing genuine area-wide travelcards and other network benefits may be inhibited. It was these circumstances which led to the Government taking new powers in the Transport Act 2000 (see 13.5).

5) Very large investments

The scale of some transport projects (e.g. a new airport or high-speed rail line) presents difficulties for provision through the commercial market because of the 'lumpiness' of the investment required. Investors faced with a range of project opportunities, each of which had the same prospective rate of return, would normally prefer to spread their risk over a number of smaller projects rather than concentrate it all in one. In effect therefore large-scale investments are discriminated against. It is for this reason that very large projects – even potentially commercially viable ones – have traditionally been undertaken as public sector investments, although the extent of non-user benefits may also be a factor.

It is against this background that the insistence of Mrs Thatcher's Government for the colossal Channel Tunnel project to be funded by a *private* sector consortium was of such symbolic political importance. (The scale of risk was countered by spreading funding over some 200 banks in addition to equity shareholders.)

The strategic significance of such large-scale investments also raises questions over whether a Government can permit the possibility of their commercial failure.

If it cannot (i.e. if the State would ultimately intervene to 'save' a company so that the relevant facility continued to operate) then it is effectively discriminating in *favour* of them (since the commercial risk would be less than in smaller but otherwise comparable investments). This issue has assumed very much greater significance in recent years because of government policy favouring public-private partnerships as the basis of financing many transport projects which previously would have been wholly publicly funded (12.4).

9.5 The treatment of equity

In a market situation the ability of individuals to obtain goods and services of benefit to them depends on the resources at their disposal. Accepting market processes (even if they work perfectly) or the results of policy analyses based on welfare economics therefore begs questions about whether the initial distribution of wealth and other resources amongst the population (knowledge, physical mobility, economic opportunities etc.) is considered to be fair. Similarly there are questions about how far an overall increase in welfare is acceptable if this leads to adverse outcomes for particular sections of the population, or if it widens the gap between those who are well off and those who are not. These issues of distributional equity are not ones which any amount of economic analysis can answer – they are essentially matters of personal or political value judgement.

For the State to intervene to alter the *distribution* of benefits depends on either or both of two arguments. The first is the ethical argument that limits ought to be placed on the ability of the certain groups within the population to benefit from a course of action if this implies worsening the conditions of others in either an absolute or relative sense. The second is the political argument that inequalities need to be limited in order to retain social cohesion and reduce the likelihood of civil disorder. Irrespective of any ethical considerations commercial firms may in fact be willing to engage in welfare policies themselves (or to support redistributive action by the State with similar objectives) on the basis that it provides the stable conditions necessary to continued capital accumulation.

Ethical and political arguments have been brought together in the concept of the 'social contract' (Rawls 1999). This holds that the rules governing distribution should be those which, in a hypothetical 'original position' all members of society would agree to, not knowing what status they would occupy in practice.

Intervention on distributional grounds is of two main kinds. The first is to reduce differences of *income* between sections of the population; the second is to constrain the differences in *outcome* which then arise from the interplay of these (adjusted) incomes.

As far as personal incomes are concerned many elements of the country's tax and benefits system are 'progressive' in that they are designed to lessen the more extreme disparities. As a result people who would otherwise be the poorest have more money to spend on transport (or anything else) than they would without such State intervention – and vice versa amongst more affluent groups.

It also follows that where general taxation is used to fund transport investments and services then its (partly) progressive nature can mean that a positive redistribution of welfare results from transport expenditures by the State as well. However a very important proviso is the amount of use – hence benefit – which different groups derive from these expenditures. For example public payments in support of the country's rail system (funded from national taxation) may appear to be progressive when viewed from the revenue side of the equation. However, as we saw in section 2.9 rail *use* is very much greater by higher income groups so that overall, from a distributional perspective, this form of intervention may be considered highly *regressive*.

An example of transport expenditure designed to counteract the *consequences* (i.e. outcomes) of income differences is the system of concessionary fares operated on local public transport. This stops short of actually giving eligible groups money to spend on transport (although the system of tokens used in some places gets very close to this). Instead it enables them to 'purchase' more of the commodity in question (bus services) than they would otherwise. Opponents of concessionary fares would argue that this is a classic case of the State managing redistributive action wrongly by effectively prescribing what people should spend their money on. If the recipients of concessions are deserving of benefits on the grounds of insufficient income then, so the argument goes, they should be given in a cash form so that the individuals can decide for themselves whether they would benefit most from spending it on public transport rather than anything else.

Standards

Consider, for example, a bypass proposal which improved the safety and environment of many people living in a town but which resulted in the dramatic worsening of conditions for a few people living near the new route. Such a proposal would be economically justified provided that *in theory* the gainers would be willing to pay for the cost of the road (including the amount needed to compensate the losers).

Clearly in this and similar examples, unless some further equity principle is applied, the interests of minorities could be compromised to an unacceptable degree. One way of addressing this is for the State to establish standards so that, irrespective of the aggregate benefit of proposals, these are not obtained by pushing conditions below acceptable thresholds for particular groups of people or at particular places. (The maximum noise levels set under the 1973 Land Compensation Act for households to incur as a result of a highway scheme is an example.) Under such a regime the remedial action actually to achieve these minimum standards and its associated cost has to form part of any scheme. It should be emphasised that these standards are applied on the basis of ethical or political judgements, not economic ones.

Although standards are superficially attractive they are a hazardous concept for policy-makers. This is because the cost of achieving a particular standard is likely to vary widely according to circumstances whilst the number of people benefiting will vary too. It is unrealistic to divorce the desirability of ensuring that individuals enjoy certain minimum standards from the conflicting aim of using available resources to greatest overall benefit. In practice State action often seeks to improve conditions in worst-affected places (beyond what would be justified in economic efficiency terms) but without necessarily accepting a commitment to a particular standard. The support of rural public transport services is a case in point.

Rights

The notion of standards leads on to the more fundamental question of *rights*. Sometimes politicians or others appeal to the notion of rights in order to argue the case for the automatic provision of certain standards, almost irrespective of the costs and benefits involved. (Thus people may speak of the 'right' to enjoy clean air, a safe environment, a decent public transport service or even just to park a car in the street outside their home!) Although this may help to win support for a particular viewpoint it confuses discussion considerably.

There are in fact several different conceptions of rights. We may distinguish three – political rights, human rights and welfare rights. Political rights are basic freedoms which the State protects, but which it may also decide to amend. In the transport field a system of 'rights of way' has been established by law in the UK which confirms freedom of movement over certain designated routes – not merely public highways but also private paths and tracks over which the public has traditionally had access. However these rights can be amended or terminated in particular places, e.g. to allow for the construction of a new road or development. A general right of way can also be amended by traffic regulation which effectively withdraws the right of movement for specified classes of user or limits it at certain places and times. The Special Roads Act of 1949 created a new class of highway – the motorway – from which certain users such as pedestrians, cyclists and horseriders are excluded altogether.

Political rights by definition embody some conception of human rights – i.e. the freedoms which each individual is thought to be entitled to as a matter of natural justice. In recent decades a notable development in the UK has been explicit recognition through legislation of freedom from discrimination on the grounds of race and gender. Particularly important in the transport field has been action to counter discrimination against disabled people (13.2). More generally human rights campaigners have sought for codes to be established and upheld on an international basis. The key feature of such codes is that they may be used to challenge the legitimacy of actions (whether by governments or others) irrespective of whether they are permissible under the legislation prevailing in particular countries. The European Convention on Human Rights, adopted in 1950, was incorporated directly into UK law under the Human Rights Act in 1998. However the full implications of this (in terms of UK policy and practice) will depend on the outcome of test cases being brought and adjudicated upon and will therefore take several years to determine.

It is in the provision of welfare services that the notion of 'rights' comes to assume importance in a more everyday sense. For example the fact that the Transport Act 2000 *required* the operation of a concessionary fares system in all areas (whereas previously local authorities only had the *powers* to do so) means that eligible groups are now automatically entitled to its benefits. Similarly children living beyond prescribed distances from their schools have the 'right' to free transport. However such welfare rights or 'entitlements' need to be distinguished from the more fundamental human rights. It is open to any UK Government, as a matter of policy, to vary the level of entitlement to welfare provision (including removing it altogether) subject of course to it not contravening its own legislation on discrimination or to the provisions of the European Convention.

Inter-generational equity and the use of finite resources

The notion of rights also arises in connection with inter-generational equity, although no formal legislation or judicial procedures exist in this field. Normally present-day transactions do not reflect more than the costs and benefits incurred by users and suppliers over the lifetime of a project. However decisions which involve the consumption of finite resources beg questions about the value to be placed on these by future generations. Some people assert that we do not have the 'right' to compromise the ability of future generations to meet their needs by exploiting resources for our own use instead. Achieving an appropriate balance between the two is the basis of what is now known as 'sustainable development' – a principle to which the UK Government is committed (Defra et al. 2005).

Unfortunately, as with human rights, it is only possible to define this principle in very broad terms and it is in its application to particular policy areas and decisions that a great deal of argument takes place. Plainly we have no way of knowing whether in fact future generations will wish to inherit our present resource stock and the extent to which their welfare would be diminished if they did not. (Behaviour and preferences will obviously change and there is always the possibility of new discoveries, technical advances etc. as alternatives to present patterns of production and consumption.) There is also scientific uncertainty about critical factors such as population levels and about climate change and its effects.

In this situation some argue for the adoption of the 'precautionary principle' (O'Riordan and Cameron 1995), i.e. for a policy of 'safety first'. The interests of resource conservation may be served for example by the State imposing a tax on fuel or on carbon emissions. These may be levied with the aim of acting both as a brake on present consumption and as an incentive to suppliers and consumers to explore renewable or low-carbon alternatives.

Other resources within the natural and built environments, although not 'consumed' in quite the same way, may be damaged or depleted as a result of transport and travel. The quantity of attractive landscape or of countryside unspoilt by urban development or transport infrastructure is finite and effectively non-renewable. The qualities of particular areas may also have 'unique' value in that they have characteristics not replicated elsewhere, including their accessibility to potential visitors. There is only one Peak District National Park for example. The same considerations apply to sites of special scientific interest (SSSIs), listed buildings of historical or architectural interest, conservation areas etc.

The value to society of such places is plainly more than the price at which the land or property is currently traded on the open market, though exactly what that value might be is a moot point. (Depending on the estimated amount remedial works might be undertaken to overcome the adverse impacts of a development, or possibly a more expensive option selected at an alternative location.) Currently debate rages over the future of the A303 trunk road which runs close to Stonehenge, designated a World Heritage Site. 'Doing nothing' involves continued despoilation of visitors' enjoyment of this site and serious delays to users of the road. On the other hand undertaking a road improvement involving anything less than a bored tunnel costing in the region of £500m would involve permanent physical destruction of archaeological features in the area and the landscape setting of the monument itself.

The practical consequences of the precautionary principle are to impose additional costs (or to forgo benefits) for certain today in order to safeguard conditions which may or may not be valued equally highly tomorrow. Clearly this is a difficult position to sustain politically since it is the *present* generation of voters whom politicians have to satisfy and a proportion of them are likely to opt for enjoying their jam today instead. The fact that effective action for sustainable development (notably in relation to global warming) is dependent on international co-operation adds further uncertainty into national debates and compounds the difficulties faced by those who advocate it.

9.6 Conclusion on State action

In this chapter we have considered the various arguments which are used to justify the State having powers of legally enforceable action to intervene in the workings of civil society. In practice there is not always a one-for-one relationship – certain policies can be directed at more than one source of market failure or one aspect of equity. Conversely several different types of adverse impact can occur concurrently, but overcoming them does not necessarily point to a single course of action. Conflicts can occur. In the field of public transport for example there may be pressure on governments to safeguard passengers' interests by maintaining competition between operators whilst at the same time wanting to protect them from a lack of overall co-ordination. Policy-makers have to juggle with these disparate and sometimes conflicting concerns as well as with the different sectional interests represented in the political process.

10 Institutional arrangements

10.1 Introduction

We noted in the previous chapter that some institutions concerned with the maintenance of civil order and the making and enforcement of laws are prerequisites for the functioning of the State. Insofar as it then seeks to intervene in particular fields – transport being one – additional institutions will be needed to provide advice to Government and to implement its policies. The administrative Civil Service is the immediate resource created for this purpose, including staff of the Scottish Executive and the Welsh Assembly in relation to functions transferred to the devolved administrations. The further, more detailed arrangements currently in operation are the subject of this chapter.

The responsibilities of Government are so diverse and the associated workload so great that its activities have to be broken down in various ways. The manner of this sub-division will have implications for general concerns of efficiency, effectiveness and accountability and will also set the context for the way particular policy issues are treated. Setting up a single-purpose body for example may provide clear direction and accountability as far as that particular activity is concerned but at the same time make co-ordination with related activities more difficult. In practice a compromise has to be found.

We have already highlighted the differences of purpose and accountability between public and private bodies. Hence a policy decision of fundamental importance is whether a particular activity should fall within the responsibility of *any* public institution, and if so the role it should perform. A key distinction in relation to transport industries is whether the State should seek to own and operate their infrastructure and services or whether it should seek to regulate or incentivise their operation by private firms.

Although each public body is in some abstract sense working for the public good it will in practice be interpreting this in terms of its statutory responsibilities and of the policy remit set by the Government currently in office. Whether and how an issue falls within its patch will strongly influence how it responds. The issue of fuel taxation for example will be viewed very differently by public bodies with responsibility for transport, environment, industry or public finance. Similarly the view which a local authority takes towards a transport proposal is likely to depend very much on whether this is seen as contributing to or resolving problems within *its* area. Hence the way that public responsibilities are organised – functionally and geographically – is itself a key area of policy choice.

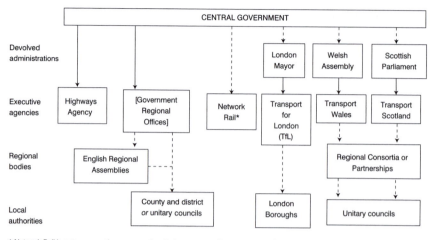

* Network Rail is not an executive agency of central government but operates on the basis of its financial support on terms set out in a High Level Output Statement [see 23.5] Solid lines represent direct policy control.

Figure 10.1 The pattern of devolved administration

In the following sections we look first at the divisions within central government itself (10.2) and at the arrangements made for devolved government and regional administration (10.3). We then look at the division of ownership amongst the transport industries as between the public and private sectors (10.4). (The sections are presented in this order because the public/private split is a *product* of national policy and may be amended at any time.) In sections 10.5 and 10.6 we examine the two main ways in which the bulk of more detailed policy-making and service delivery is managed within the public sector. This is either:

a   to executive agencies or non-governmental bodies which have responsibility for a particular function across the country, or
b   to elected local councils which have responsibility for a range of functions within particular geographical areas.

Figure 10.1 illustrates the pattern of devolved administration.

As an overall guide for this chapter Table 10.1 (p. 160) summarises the division of responsibilities between national, regional and local bodies and the powers each has to influence the main sectors of transport and land use planning.

10.2 The structuring of Central Government

The main areas of Government activity can be thought of as building blocks which are brought together to form Departments of State each headed by a Cabinet Minister who normally has the title of Secretary of State (SoS). The way in which the blocks are combined is altered from time to time – sometimes to reflect changes in workload, sometimes to give expression to new policy priorities.

Smaller, sometimes more transient areas of work associated with particular initiatives have units which are 'tacked on' to the main building blocks and tend to be moved or reformed more frequently. This applies particularly to issues which have significance across a range of Government activities. For example, in the first term of the New Labour Government a Social Exclusion Unit was formed within the Cabinet Office whilst an Urban Policy Unit was located within the then DETR (Department of Transport, Environment and the Regions).

Changes in the structure of Central Government are normally made after a general election and at other times when ministerial responsibilities are being reshuffled. This provides another clue as to the reasoning behind the particular arrangement adopted at any one time, namely to define and distribute the offices of State amongst the most senior members of the governing party in a way which will both utilise their talents and satisfy their egos!

The treatment of transport over the past decade provides evidence of these factors. The bringing together of the Departments of the Environment and Transport to form DETR after New Labour's 1997 election victory fulfilled a number of objectives. It appeared to signal a policy objective of ending the rather narrow, road-building pre-occupations of the formerly separate Department of Transport. At the same time it created a department of appropriate status and character for John Prescott who was Deputy Prime Minister and an important 'Old Labour' figurehead in the new Government.

After the 2001 election Prescott retained his position as Deputy Prime Minister but was shunted off somewhat ignominiously to the Cabinet Office which is mainly concerned with progressing overall Government policy. Prescott was also given responsibility for developing the regional devolution agenda in which he had a personal interest. At the same time the Prime Minister responded to the crisis in agriculture and the rural economy brought about by the outbreak of foot and mouth disease by creating a new Department for the Environment, Food and Rural Affairs (Defra), combining the former environment wing of DETR with the former Ministry of Agriculture, Fisheries and Food (Table 10.2). This transfer of environmental responsibilities meant that for a second time (the first being during the 1970s) the amalgamation of transport with the environment had proved short-lived. As with all such changes it is difficult for outsiders to gauge what policy intent, if any, should be read into it. In this case it might simply have been the consequence of a higher priority being attached to the creation of the new 'rural' ministry. Nonetheless it added to the concerns of environmental groups about the importance that would be placed on environmental issues in the implementation of the national road-building programme included in the Ten Year Plan.

For a brief period the restyled DTLR (Department of Transport, Local Government and the Regions) headed by a new Secretary of State, Stephen Byers, retained all the former department's functions in the fields of planning and transport. However the political controversy surrounding his dealings with Railtrack in the aftermath of the Hatfield crash (8.6) forced his resignation, whereupon DTLR was split into two. (The joining of the planning and transport ministries had therefore lasted just five years.) Alistair Darling, a former Chief Secretary at the Treasury, was given responsibility for a separate Department for Transport (DfT) whilst the non-transport functions were returned to John Prescott in a department titled Office of the Deputy Prime Minister (ODPM).

Darling held the transport portfolio for four years – an unusually long time – until a ministerial reshuffle in May 2006 replaced him and Prescott respectively with new younger Cabinet members Douglas Alexander and Ruth Kelly, ODPM being then renamed the Department of Communities and Local Government (DCLG). They in turn were moved a year later as part of the 'handover' of the Premiership from

Table 10.1 Overview of public bodies and powers in relation to transport and land use

	Road network	Road vehicles	Road passenger services	Rail network and services	Land use/development
EU	Strategic investment in Euro network	Harmonisation of operating and environmental regulations		Strategic investment in Euro network	Environmental assessment regulations
UK Central Government					
DfT (Department for Transport)	Motorways and trunk roads in England HA (Highways Agency)	Licensing of vehicles and drivers DVLA (Driver and Vehicle Licensing Agency)	Licensing of operators, but not services (Traffic Commissioners)	a) strategy for Network Rail & ORR (Office of Rail Regulation) b) franchising of English passenger services	HA (Highways Agency) direction to LPAs (local planning authorities) on dev't applications
DCLG (Department for Communities & Local Goverment)			Revenue support to English LAs (local authorities)		Policy Guidance to English LPAs; decisions on appeals and call-ins
Treasury	Vetting of Department spending and targets	Fuel duty; VED (Vehicle Excise Duty); VAT (Value Added Tax)		Vetting of Department spending and targets	
Scottish Executive/Welsh Assembly	a) Motorways & trunk roads b) Approval/funding of LA major schemes		Revenue support to Scottish/Welsh LAs	Franchising of Scottish/ Welsh passenger services	Policy Guidance to LPAs' decision on appeals and call-ins
English Regions					
Government Regional Offices	Approval/funding of LA major schemes & RTS				Approval of RSS (Regional Spatial Strategy)
Regional Assembly/ London Mayor	Drafting of RTS (Regional/ London Transport Strategy)				Drafting of RSS/ SDS (Spatial Development Strategy)

English Local Authorities

London

Authority				
Mayor	Strategic roads TfL (Transport for London); Congestion charge (TfL)	Public transport promotion;Franchising of bus services (TfL)	Underground services (TfL); Franchising of delegated 'overground' rail services	Major development control
Borough Councils	Local Transport Implementation Plan; local roads, parking, traffic management			Local Development Framework; Development control

Metropolitan areas

Authority				
PTA (Passenger Transport Authority)	Preparation of Local Transport Plan (jointly with metropolitan councils)	PT promotion; Contracting of socially necessary bus services by PTEs (Passenger Transport Executives)	Input to national franchising of local rail services	
Metropolitan councils	Roads, traffic management, parking			Local Development Framework; Development control

Non-metropolitan areas*

Authority				
County councils	Local Transport Plan; roads, on-street parking, traffic management	Contracting of socially necessary bus services		Local Development Framework; Development control
District councils	Off-street parking			Local Development Framework; Development control

*Also known as 'shires'. Non-metropolitan unitary councils and all (unitary) councils in Scotland and Wales perform both sets of functions.

Table 10.2 The structuring of Central Government in relation to transport, planning and the environment 1997–2008 (Secretaries of State shown in brackets)

	Transport	Planning	Environment
1997	DETR – Dept Environment, Transport and the Regions (John Prescott)		
2001	DTLR – Dept Transport, Local Government and the Regions (Stephen Byers)		Defra – Dept Environment, Food and Rural Affairs (Margaret Beckett)
2002	DfT – Dept for Transport (Alistair Darling)	ODPM – Office of the Deputy Prime Minister (John Prescott)	
2005			(David Miliband)
2006	(Douglas Alexander)	DCLG – Dept of Communities and Local Government (Ruth Kelly)	
2007	(Ruth Kelly)	(Hazel Blears)	(Hilary Benn)
2008	(Geoff Hoon)		[Climate change responsibility transferred to separate new DECC (Ed Miliband)]

Tony Blair to Gordon Brown. Kelly was transferred to Transport whilst her post of Communities Secretary was taken by Hazel Blears. Ruth Kelly's tenure at Transport also lasted barely a year, resigning in the summer of 2008. She was replaced in an October reshuffle by the long-serving middle-ranking Minister Geoff Hoon.

DfT, DCLG and Defra are not the only government departments with a significant interest in transport. Transport is a major area of Central Government expenditure, and transport taxation is also an important source of revenue. Policy responsibility for these areas resides with the Treasury and both the Chancellor of the Exchequer and the Chief Secretary (responsible for public spending) are members of the Cabinet. Gordon Brown held the post of Chancellor throughout the ten years of Tony Blair's Premiership and Alistair Darling succeeded him in 2007.

Like other departments DfT is in a supplicant position to the Treasury as far as its share of overall government spending is concerned. Its 'success' will depend on satisfying the *Treasury* view of what constitutes value for money. The Treasury also has a reputation for high-handedness and lack of consultation with other departments when advancing its own proposals. Famously it is known not to have consulted either the Departments of Transport or the Environment before the fuel duty escalator was introduced in 1993 (despite the environmental benefits claimed for it).

> Treasury officials may well discuss specific issues with officials from other departments from time to time … but it suits the Treasury well enough to spread the cloak of budget secrecy over all the key decisions on both spending and taxation, which obliges the Chancellor to take many important decisions within a very small circle of Treasury officials. Such an absence of properly informed debate, even behind closed doors, would be a matter of concern in any circumstances. It is particularly serious when prices (heavily influenced by taxation) are a key component of any transport strategy.
>
> (Glaister et al. 1998 p. 62)

The Department for Business, Enterprise and Regulatory Reform (formerly Trade and Industry) also has a number of specific responsibilities related to transport. These include safeguarding the interests of the vehicle manufacturing and related industries and promoting technological applications to transport through its 'Foresight' programme. It also sponsors the Competition Commission and the Office of Fair Trading – non-departmental bodies which have a significant role in the regulation of transport operations (13.3). In October 2008, reflecting the increasing volume of work associated with the Climate Change Programme (24.3), the Energy Group within BERR was transferred together with most of the Climate Change Group within Defra to form a new Department of Energy and Climate Change (DECC) with Ed Miliband as its first Secretary of State.

The Home Office has responsibility for law enforcement. It is therefore concerned about the practicability of any proposed changes in transport legislation, particularly as far as road traffic is concerned, in terms of public acceptability (hence relations with the police) and in the potential claims on resources for policing. However the observance of traffic and parking regulations – though often important to local communities – is peripheral to the department's main concerns. This has led to some transfers of responsibility from police authorities to local councils (14.6).

Thus far we have considered the structure of Central Government at a broad, ministerial level. More detailed changes take place at administrative level (i.e. within the Civil Service) both at the time of ministerial reshuffles and independently of them.

> The policy directorates are subject to continual reorganisation, partly in response to changing political priorities … These changes also reflect a continual search for the ideal structure … The benefits claimed for such reorganisations are debatable. Fortunately their main impact is on senior managers who are accustomed to adjusting quickly to changing circumstances and priorities. Much of the department's more routine work continues more or less undisturbed, but the constant upheaval in response to the latest pressure could well contribute to the culture of the short-term political fix, which some commentators find to be characteristic of British policy-making, and not only in regard to transport.
>
> (Glaister et al. 1998 p. 53)

Currently the Department's structure is centred on a Board responsible for 'Strategy, Planning and Performance Capability' whose membership consists of the Permanent Secretary (the head official of the Department), five Directors General (DGs), the Chief Executive of the Highways Agency and two non-executive members. The presence of the HA's Chief Executive and a DG overseeing the work of four executive agencies concerned with aspects of vehicle and driver regulation is intended to ensure that they contribute to the shaping as well as delivery of policy. One of the directorates is almost wholly concerned with the rail industry. This reflects the transfer 'in-house' of functions previously carried out by the Strategic Rail Authority and is a notable exception from the general trend of devolving such functions to executive agencies.

Each of the DfT's directorates has a number of divisions. Two (out of about 30!) which are especially important to people working in local transport planning lie within the City and Regional Networks Directorate. One (concerned with delivery) is organised by groups of English regions; the other (concerned with policy) includes groups dealing with the Local Transport Bill and Concessionary Travel which at the time of writing (2007) reflected important government initiatives then in progress. The detailed structure of the Department can be viewed at www.dft.gov.uk/about/

10.3 Devolved government and regional administration

Central Government functions relating to particular parts of the country, and especially its dealings with local authorities, have always been managed through some system of regional offices. For many years these were outposts of individual departments and had an organisation and culture not unlike overseas colonies. (Civil servants working in them who began to show sympathy with the views of their local populations rather than with their masters in Whitehall would be criticised for 'going native'.) Until devolution Scotland and Wales were treated somewhat differently with the range of domestic responsibilities managed collectively by the Scottish and Welsh Offices each answerable to their own Secretary of State who had Cabinet status.

The physical division of England into what are referred to as 'standard' regions is a compromise between geographical and administrative considerations (see Figure 10.2 in section 10.6 below). Functionally and culturally, regions such as the South-West for example might be better described as a set of sub-regions each of which has as much affinity with others in neighbouring regions as its own. The most obvious geographical anomaly is the subdivision of South-East England into three separate regions: London, the South-East (largely south of the River Thames) and the East of England – the latter including East Anglia which was formerly administered as a separate region. The explanation for this is Civil Service concern to devise regions which have comparable status and involve broadly similar scales of administrative responsibility. The current pattern does however have the unfortunate effect of separating London from much of its functional hinterland and means that the overall planning of the nation's most important economic region has to be dealt with by ad hoc arrangements. It also produces the rather confusing outcome of Greater London itself being both an administrative 'region' of Central Government and also a single unit of 'local' government (10.6).

In 1994 an important change was introduced in England in an attempt to break the 'silo' pattern of individual government departments each pursuing their own agendas in the same region. A series of 'integrated' government offices was established in each region (GORs) which brought together staff from the then transport, environment, trade and education departments. (They have since been extended to all domestic departments other than the Treasury.) Although they receive funding from the individual central departments the allocation of this within the region is planned and managed in a cross-sectoral manner.

In dealings with local authorities the work of GORs includes giving comments on development plans and local transport plans (LTPs), discussing grants, loans or borrowing approval required of central government (including the design and progressing of individual major schemes), and the processing of various types of order (e.g. highway, traffic management or compulsory purchase) which require ministerial consent. As well as issuing decisions or observations 'downwards' to local authorities the regional offices act as the source of local information and advice 'upwards' to the headquarters of the individual government departments. Thus regional offices will assemble and forward material to DfT HQ in London relating to LTP bids in their area for example, or transport or development proposals which may be the subject of a public inquiry.

As explained previously the promise of devolving many erstwhile functions of Central Government was an important feature of the New Labour manifesto. The terminology employed in this can be confusing. From a UK perspective all such devolution can be considered 'regional' but the Scottish Parliament and Welsh Assembly are 'national' institutions in the countries concerned. (Further disparities arise as a result – what are referred to as 'regional' planning arrangements in Scotland and Wales would be termed 'sub-regional' in England – see 17.4.)

With the creation of the elected Scottish Parliament and Welsh Assembly the functions of their former Secretaries of State were transferred to the new bodies. Each has a 'First Minister' and a Cabinet of departmental heads drawn from the ruling party or coalition. Having been elected by proportional representation the first Scottish administration was formed by a coalition of Labour and Liberal Democrats, but with the Scottish Nationalists assuming control in 2007. Labour remains the controlling party in Wales.

Traditionally legislation passed by the UK Government often included separate clauses relating to Scotland or Wales and this facility remains in matters which it has reserved for its jurisdiction. In domestic transport matters however the Scottish Parliament has powers to introduce its own primary legislation – the first example being the Transport (Scotland) Act 2001, a version of the Transport Act 2000.

Initially at least, the Scottish Government appeared willing to go along with the legislative framework and general policy direction being set in Westminster, not least because New Labour was the dominant party in both places. Certainly devolution can be considered a mixed blessing politically in such a situation since any significant departure by the devolved administration will be seized on by Government's opponents as evidence of a policy 'split' (Smyth 2003). Arguably the lead taken subsequently by the Scottish Parliament on a 'national' concessionary fares scheme pushed the Westminster Government more quickly in this direction than it might otherwise have done (15.7) whilst, in a broader context, the Scottish decision not to charge university tuition fees has been a source of continuing embarrassment south of the border.

Both the Scottish Parliament and the Welsh Assembly have powers of secondary legislation, that is the detailing of measures allowed for within the terms of the primary Act, the framing of regulations, the issuing of policy guidance and so on. Differences of substance are emerging in these more detailed administrative areas and in the policies being applied to expenditure programmes. Overall funding continues to take the form of a block grant from the UK Government (which retains national tax revenues) although the Scottish Parliament has the discretion to increase this by levying up to 3p on top of the basic rate of income tax.

In England, aside from devolution in London, regional representation was strengthened by the creation in 1999 of regional assemblies and regional development agencies (RDAs). These are established for the same areas as the provincial Government Office regions although some of the RDAs have used distinctive branding names (e.g. Advantage West Midlands, Yorkshire Forward and One North East). However unlike in London (where policy control of its RDA was formally assigned to the elected Mayor) the position of the provincial RDAs is more ambiguous. Formally they owe their allegiance and sponsorship to Central Government although their economic strategies have to be approved by the relevant Regional Assembly. In itself this is problematic since Assemblies are unlikely to mount a significant challenge to strategies geared to securing funds for their region from Central Government. Differences in style as well as substance however tend to characterise the activities of the two bodies. RDAs have a narrower, shorter term, more business-oriented focus than the Assemblies and are unencumbered by the latter's wider remit, statutory planning responsibilities and democratic accountability (albeit indirect) within the region. Significantly, following the Government's failure to extend formal devolution into the English regions, it has concluded that the functions of the Regional Assemblies should be transferred to their respective RDAs rather than the other way round (DTI et al. 2007).

10.4 Public and private ownerships

As a consequence of the privatisation programme pursued by Conservative governments in the 1980s and 90s the extent of public ownership, and hence direct control, of transport industries has returned to the levels of a century ago. With the exception of the public highway network, most of the nation's transport assets are now privately owned, including almost all the companies previously nationalised (London Underground being the conspicuous exception).

The situation with public transport industries which were previously municipally owned (i.e. by local authorities) is less straightforward. Central Government stopped short of introducing legislation *requiring* the sale of these companies but most have in fact been sold. The bulk of the bus industry in Britain is now owned by one of five private companies – Arriva, First, Go-Ahead, National Express and Stagecoach. Their operations are however divided around the country and include services operated under franchise in London. The precise distribution reflects their pattern of acquisition of formerly separate local companies by which they have grown to their present size. All of them have also expanded into operating franchised rail services (15.5). In some areas (e.g. First Group in much of South-West England) this has effectively given them a monopoly of public transport which they can utilise to promote a form of 'company' integration.

The ownership of the country's few urban metro and light rail systems generally lies with Passenger Transport Authorities although in most cases responsibility for infrastructure maintenance and service operation has been transferred to a private operator for a prescribed period (Table 10.3). In some cases (e.g. Manchester Metrolink) the system was designed and built as well as operated and maintained by a private consortium for 25–30 years, funded by either an initial payment or an annual leasing charge. At the end of the period the asset is transferred to the public authority.

The decline in public ownership over the last quarter of the 20th century was partly a function of financial expediency during difficult economic periods – to rid governments of the burden of borrowing for investment and to generate one-off capital receipts (what the former Conservative Prime Minister Harold Macmillan referred to as 'selling the family silver'). It was also a function of ideological commitment to privatisation by the Thatcher Government after 1979, pursued only slightly less stridently by New Labour after 1997. As a result public ownership as an issue of principle has largely disappeared from the political landscape.

The pursuit of privatisation as a matter of principle does not however exclude the possibility of public ownership being adopted on pragmatic grounds, i.e. as the most efficient – or least inefficient – option available for managing the nation's resources. (In 2008 for example the Government was forced into nationalising the Northern Rock Building Society as the only way of saving the business and preventing further damage to financial markets.) At the time of Railtrack's collapse many commentators called for its renationalisation, or at least for the Government to take a controlling stake in

Table 10.3 Owners and operators of light rail and metro systems in the UK

System	Network length (miles)	Owner	Operator
Glasgow Underground		Strathclyde PTA	Strathclyde PTA
Tyne and Wear Metro	49	Tyne and Wear PTA	Tyne and Wear PTA
Blackpool Tramway	11	Blackpool Council	Blackpool Council
Manchester Metrolink	24	[Greater Manchester PTA]	Serco Metrolink
Sheffield Supertram	18	[South Yorkshire PTA]	Stagecoach Supertram
Midland Metro (Birmingham–Wolverhampton)	12	[West Midlands PTA]	Travel West Midlands [part of National Express group]
London Underground		[Transport for London]	Infrastructure: maintained by private consortia for three groups of lines
Docklands Light Railway	17		Serco Docklands
Croydon Tramlink		[As London Underground]	Tramtrack Croydon (Consortium of CentreWest Buses and others)
Nottingham Express Transit	11	[Nottingham City Council]	Nottingham Express Transit (Arrow Consortium)

its ownership. Instead the Government carefully constructed a 'private' company – Network Rail – which is formally independent, although in practice now subject to the overall rail strategy set by the Government (23.5). Network Rail is unusual in that it is controlled by a large board representing various railway interests and is a 'non-dividend' company, i.e. its profits are reinvested in the business and not distributed to shareholders.

Disenchantment with public *management* is also evident in the way the Government has pursued greater private sector involvement in the running and financing of operations which formally remain within public ownership. The Treasury was the dominant force behind the Government pressing ahead with the public-private partnership arrangement for renewing the infrastructure of the London Underground, despite the opposition of all 55 London Labour MPs as well as the London Mayor (nominally the Government's supporters!). Unusually in this case however the operation of services remains within the direct control of the public sector (Transport for London – the executive arm of the Mayor and the Greater London Authority).

Network Rail and the London Underground (technically privately and publicly owned respectively) epitomise the way in which ownership itself has come to assume much less significance as an indicator of public influence in the passenger transport industries. Irrespective of ownership there are degrees of public and private sector involvement in investment and service provision in both. The question of public influence or control therefore increasingly centres on the particular arrangements which are made with respect to funding and regulation instead (Chapters 12, 13 and 15). Unfortunately these are very complex subjects whose practical implications cannot readily be understood by the general public and which ultimately hinge on the legal interpretation of the mass of statutory and contractual documentation.

Whilst the ownership of the passenger transport industries during the 20th century followed a pattern of transfer first into and then out of the public sector, ownership of the highway network remained essentially public throughout. For only a short period after 1989 was the possibility of outright private development and ownership of major new roads seriously contemplated – a phase which led to the construction of the M6 toll road north of Birmingham. Since that time private sector involvement has been confined to designing, building, operating and maintaining roads under public contract, some of which have also been delivered under the Private Finance Initiative (12.4).

10.5 Executive agencies and other public bodies

The function of implementing policies and delivering services which are the responsibility of Central Government is not confined to the Civil Service. In the days of nationalised transport industries British Rail, the National Bus Company and London Transport for example were operated as separate entities with boards of directors appointed by, and receiving their overall policy remit from, the Secretary of State. Currently the devolution of functions is to 'executive agencies' and 'non-departmental public bodies' (NDPBs). These are 'sponsored' (funded) by particular Government departments and the relevant Secretary of State is ultimately responsible for their activities.

The creation of executive agencies can be traced back to an early initiative of Mrs Thatcher to investigate ways of improving efficiency within the civil service. As a concept they are intended to have the twin benefit of helping overloaded Ministers and senior civil servants concentrate on policy issues whilst enabling the executive functions to be 'hived off' to separate agencies each of which could focus in a more business-like way on managing a particular service. The agencies therefore have autonomy in how they organise themselves within the policy remit they are given. Arguably however this reduces ministerial accountability (a key feature of public services) and there is inevitably a grey area between where policy decisions end and management discretion begins.

In the field of domestic transport five main executive agencies have been created in this way (Box 10.1) of which (from our perspective) the Highways Agency responsible for the planning and management of motorways and trunk roads in England is of most importance. In Scotland and Wales the equivalent function is undertaken by the executive agencies Transport Scotland and Transport Wales. The work of the agencies involved in regulating vehicles, drivers and operators across Britain is discussed in section 13.2.

The work of 'Non-Departmental Public Bodies' (NDPBs) is not directly related to the delivery of departmental services. They are divided into executive and advisory categories. As their name implies, advisory bodies are established to enable the Government to receive independent advice. Although their membership is approved by Ministers, selection will have regard to the need to include the main strands of interest, opinion or expertise in the field in order that their work should carry public credibility. An important feature of these bodies is publication of the results of their deliberations – something which the Civil Service is normally constrained *not* to do.

A particularly interesting example of an advisory body is the Commission for Integrated Transport (CfIT) which is made up of members prominent within the

Box 10.1 Executive agencies and non-departmental public bodies sponsored by the Department for Transport (select list)

Executive agencies
- Driving Standards Agency (DSA)
- Driver and Vehicle Licensing Agency (DVLA)
- Highways Agency (HA)
- Vehicle Certification Agency (VCA)
- Vehicle and Operator Services Agency (VOSA,)

Non-departmental public bodies (* = advisory)
- British Transport Police Authority
- Passenger Focus (National representative forum for rail passengers)
- *Commission for Integrated Transport (CfIT)
- *Disabled Persons Transport Advisory Committee (DPTAC)
- *Standing Committee for Trunk Road Assessment (SACTRA)
- Traffic Commissioners and Deputies (a tribunal NDPB operating under quasi-judicial rules),

transport industries, local government, pressure groups and academia. It meets periodically and is serviced by staff from within DfT. Through sub-groups it carries out studies into policy issues which are of contemporary significance, sometimes sponsoring research in the process. (Its publications can be accessed at www.cfit.gov. uk) Under the auspices of CfIT a Motorists' Forum has also been established.

From the Government's perspective the value of the Commission is not just the advice it receives (which it could obtain privately) but the public relations credit it hopes to derive from gaining independent 'support' for its policies or from being seen to respond positively to informed comment. The public relations value of CfIT can be contrasted with the work of the House of Commons Select Committee on Transport whose reports based on the assembly of evidence submitted from a wide range of interests have a similar role, though are somewhat less technical in nature (see http://www.parliament.gov.uk/parliamentary_committees/transport_committee.cfm). A key difference however is that the Select Committee is a creation of Parliament, not Government and comprises 'backbench' MPs only. It is therefore more genuinely independent and, as far as policy recommendations are concerned, can afford to be more critical.

10.6 Local government

Much State activity is concerned with the delivery of local services. For these there is a long tradition of delegating responsibility to local bodies. Transport is a good example. As we saw in Part 2, local highway boards or authorities have existed for centuries; involvement in public passenger transport and responsibility for overall local transport planning is more recent.

Local State activity is carried on through a combination of multi-purpose elected authorities and other public bodies which typically have responsibility for a single main function only (e.g. police and health authorities). These other bodies have members appointed by central government, sometimes including representatives from local councils in the areas concerned. However most local functions in the transport and planning fields which remain in the public sector are discharged by local authorities.

Local authorities are much better placed than central government to appreciate the particular needs of their areas and to be responsive to local public opinion. Even if it wanted to, central government would rapidly become bogged down in excessive detail if it tried to control everything that happened locally. On the other hand the sum of local decisions goes a long way towards determining what conditions are like across the country as a whole, which is something central government clearly has an interest in and will be held to account for. In relations between local and central government there is thus a perennial debate about arrangements which will achieve the best balance between efficiency and accountability in local decision-making on the one hand and effectiveness in delivering national policy objectives on the other.

Local authorities work within a set of duties and powers approved by Parliament and to policy guidance issued by the national government currently in office. Local authorities are also dependent on national government for the bulk of their funding. Their formal duties and powers effectively set limits on what local authorities can or must do; national decisions on policy and funding seek to influence how authorities exercise discretion within these limits. Local authorities have their own political ruling groups (which may have a different party complexion from central government). They also have their own electorates which are likely to differ in socio-economic composition and voting preferences from the country as a whole. There is thus inter-dependence between the central and the local state but also fertile ground for disagreement.

The present pattern of local government in Great Britain is not one which any person of sound mind would design from scratch. In addition to differences between the systems of government there are local anomalies which arise from the boundaries used to define the administrative areas of individual authorities.

Although the pattern has evolved over centuries, the source of present arrangements can be understood from the comprehensive reorganisation undertaken in 1974 (1965 in London). A 'two-tier' system was adopted throughout (i.e. with a number of smaller authorities 'nested' within the area of a single larger one). (Strictly there are *three* tiers of local government since in rural areas there remain parish or town councils as well. These can raise and spend very small sums on local facilities such as footpaths or bus shelters but their main role is as a sounding board for consultation by the larger councils.)

In England the country was – and remains – divided into three types of area (Figure 10.2, p. 172)), viz:

- London
- metropolitan areas (provincial conurbations)
- non-metropolitan areas (also sometimes referred to as 'the shires').

In London the two-tier division was between the GLC and London Boroughs (the latter including the City of London which covers the historic 'square mile'). (Lower-tier district councils within counties, and boroughs within London are not shown.) Elsewhere, including Wales, the division was between county and district councils (although some of the latter retain names as 'boroughs', reflecting their historical status). In Scotland the upper tier was known as regional councils.

As a general principle the upper-tier authority was assigned responsibility for strategic planning, passenger transport and major highways (including control of on-street parking) whereas the lower tier had responsibility for development control (hence provision for parking in new developments), local roads and public off-street parking.

The rationale claimed for the two-tier arrangement was to couple provision for local representation and accountability on the one hand (at the lower level) with the need for units which are sufficiently large geographically and in resource terms to plan strategically and deliver specialised services on the other (at the upper level). However, as subsequent experience demonstrated, a two-tier system can be a source of friction, especially where different political parties reign. It can also be considered unnecessarily costly. This is more pertinent today than when the two-tier system was established because of the reduced role of local authorities arising from the privatisation and contracting out of services, 'self-governing' schools etc. pursued in the interim. In recent decades there has therefore been a general move towards a leaner arrangement of single-tier 'unitary' councils which have responsibility for all remaining local government functions.

Unitary local government was first established in London and the provincial conurbations in 1986 as a product of the abolition of the GLC and metropolitan counties. Many of their former functions were simply devolved to the London borough or metropolitan (district) councils respectively although separate arrangements were made for certain conurbation-wide functions. Of particular importance in the transport field was the retention of single Passenger Transport Authorities (PTAs) in the provincial conurbations, returning to their original form as joint boards of the constituent local councils. PTA functions are carried out by a Passenger Transport Executive (PTE), commonly known by the brand names they use for promotional purposes (e.g. Centro in the West Midlands).

Technically London never lost two-tier government (only two-tier elected representation) since many of the GLC's functions were taken over by Central Government. This applied to passenger transport (carried out through London Transport) and to major roads and strategic land use planning. These functions were returned to local control in 1999 but in a novel form. Statutory responsibilities are vested in a directly elected Mayor with a relatively small Greater London Authority (GLA) made up of elected members for local constituencies plus a 'top-up' based on proportional representation. The GLA only has powers to 'scrutinise' the activities of the Mayor and to vote on his proposed budget. The Mayor's executive functions in relation to transport are undertaken by Transport for London (TfL) under his policy control.

In the non-metropolitan areas a move to replace the two-tier system with unitary councils was initiated by the Conservative Government in the early 1990s. In England the Local Government Commission was charged with hearing representations from people in particular areas as to their preferred model – with hindsight a dangerous hostage to fortune. In practice what began as a move to simplify local government arrangements became bogged down in controversy. The outcome was for different 'solutions' in different areas – partly reflecting local history, geography and politics but also the vagaries of the review process itself.

The resulting situation in non-metropolitan areas can be categorised in one of three ways:

1   Areas where the two-tier county/district arrangement introduced in 1974 has been retained unaltered (e.g. Oxfordshire, Surrey, Lincolnshire).
2   Areas where the former counties have been abolished and replaced entirely by a number of unitary councils based on their constituent districts (the 'new'

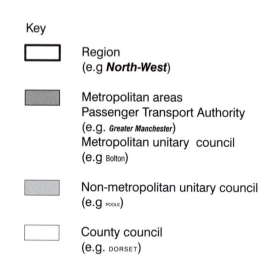

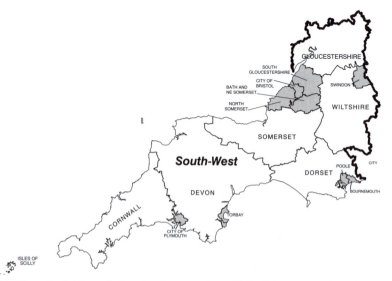

Figure 10.2 The main divisions of sub-national government in England (non-metropolitan district councils and London Bourough Councils not shown)

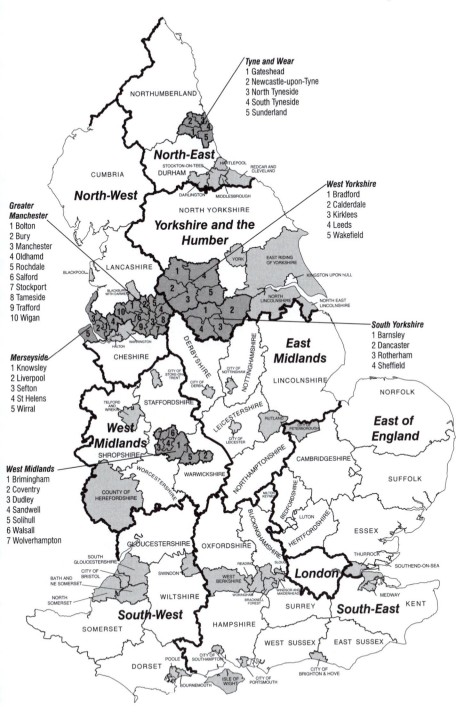

Tyne and Wear
1 Gateshead
2 Newcastle-upon-Tyne
3 North Tyneside
4 South Tyneside
5 Sunderland

West Yorkshire
1 Bradford
2 Calderdale
3 Kirklees
4 Leeds
5 Wakefield

Greater Manchester
1 Bolton
2 Bury
3 Manchester
4 Oldhamd
5 Rochdale
6 Salford
7 Stockport
8 Tameside
9 Trafford
10 Wigan

South Yorkshire
1 Barnsley
2 Dancaster
3 Rotherham
4 Sheffield

Merseyside
1 Knowsley
2 Liverpool
3 Sefton
4 St Helens
5 Wirral

West Midlands
1 Brimingham
2 Coventry
3 Dudley
4 Sandwell
5 Solihull
6 Walsall
7 Wolverhampton

counties of Avon, Humberside and Cleveland created in 1974 plus – peculiarly – Berkshire). There are now 18 unitary councils in these four areas.

3   An intermediate arrangement where the former counties remain but with their boundaries revised to exclude one or more districts which have been given unitary status. Mostly these are the larger freestanding cities (e.g. Southampton and Portsmouth which have been extracted from Hampshire, and Nottingham which has been extracted from Nottinghamshire to leave the county with a hole in its middle!). However one or two other unitaries have also been created (e.g. Rutland, Herefordshire and the Isle of Wight) which owe their existence solely to some geographical or historical quirk and local political pressure. There are currently 28 freestanding unitary councils of this kind.

There remain 34 shire counties (some, like Hampshire and Nottinghamshire, pale versions of their former selves because of the abstraction of their main urban areas) containing 238 districts. A listing of the current arrangement in each former county area is given in Table 10.4.

In Scotland and Wales reviews conducted at the same time were focused on the form that a unitary system should take rather than on *whether* (or the extent to which) unitary councils should be introduced. As a result both the process of reorganisation and its outcome were much more straightforward. Geographically and politically they are much more sharply divided between predominantly urbanised and extensively rural areas, unlike the relatively close juxtaposition of freestanding towns and semi-rural hinterlands in lowland England which gives rise to political friction. As a consequence the unitary councils in Scotland (32) and Wales (22) vary enormously in their physical size, reflecting their extremes in population density. (For further discussion and a comprehensive list of local authorities throughout Great Britain see Cullingworth and Nadin 2006.)

As well as the system of local government prevailing in any area the boundaries designated for individual councils have major implications for planning. This is because the focus of land use/transport planning is on the interaction of activities across space (in a way that, for example, the provision of education or social services is not). Difficulties tend to arise when 'functional areas' (i.e. areas which have cohesion as far as travel to work and other day-to-day activities are concerned) are divided between separate authorities.

Many of the shire county boundaries are mediaeval in origin and unsurprisingly are very variable in how well they happen to relate to present-day functioning. Some, like Oxfordshire or Lincolnshire have territories based on a traditional, dominant county town (Oxford or Lincoln) plus its rural hinterland which is still a dominant feature. Others, like Surrey or Somerset, have no such coherence. Particularly significant for planning is the fact that traditional county boundaries often do not fit well with major modern developments – the division of the Crawley New Town/Gatwick Airport complex between Surrey and West Sussex is a good example. The recently designated Milton Keynes/South Midlands growth area is an even more extreme case as it embraces not only several separate local authorities but also falls within three of the Government's administrative regions!

Attempts to change the status of councils or to revise boundaries to match present-day settlement patterns and functioning are always extremely controversial. 'Logical' outcomes like the one secured at York (where the creation of a unitary council was accompanied by the extension of the city boundaries to include its immediate commuting area) are the exception rather than the rule. For the most part the 1997 reorganisation was *not* accompanied by boundary changes to the former district council areas with the result that unitary councils such as Reading or Portsmouth only control a small proportion of the functional area which utilises these places as their main employment and service centre.

Table 10.4   Local government in England outside London (by geographical county)

Region	Metropolitan areas	Non-metropolitan areas		
	Single PTA + unitary metropolitan councils	Wholly two-tier (county + districts)	Wholly unitary councils	Mixed; two-tier and unitary council(s)
North-East	Tyne and Wear	Northumberland*	Cleveland (Tees-side)	County Durham*
Yorkshire and the Humber	South Yorkshire West Yorkshire		Humberside (Hull/Grimsby)	North Yorkshire
North-West	Greater Manchester Merseyside	Cumbria		Cheshire* Lancashire
West Midlands	West Midlands	Warwickshire	Herefordshire (single unitary)	Shropshire* Staffordshire Worcestershire
East Midlands		Lincolnshire Northamptonshire		Derbyshire Leicestershire Nottinghamshire
East of England		Cambridgeshire Hertfordshire Norfolk** Suffolk**		Bedfordshire** Essex
South-East		Oxfordshire Surrey East Sussex	Berkshire	Buckinghamshire Hampshire Kent West Sussex
South-West		Gloucestershire Somerset Cornwall*	Avon (Bristol/ Bath)	Devon** Dorset Wiltshire*

* As part of the Government's policy of pursuing the further rationalisation of local government it has announced its intention to accept authorities' proposals for replacing existing two-tier arrangements with single unitary councils in these areas (two unitaries in Cheshire) – these to be established in 2009

**Options for reform continue to be investigated in these areas (2008)

11 Policy aims

Issues, objectives and targets

11.1 Introduction

In the previous chapter we looked at the institutional framework within which public policy-making takes place. This has evolved in response to changing views about the role of the State in relation to transport, and its present form reflects contemporary views on the main purposes to which State activity should be directed.

In this chapter we look more explicitly at the issues with which transport policy and planning are concerned and how, within this broad range of concerns, objectives and targets may be set to highlight priorities and steer this activity in the desired direction. For the moment discussion is confined to the national level. The way in which national aims are translated into the planning of transport at regional and local levels is considered in Part 4.

We begin by presenting a comprehensive list of issues which may influence decision-making, both in the sense of prompting action and in providing a framework for assessing its potential impacts (11.2). We then consider the role of objectives in focusing attention on priority issues and the particular objectives which have been adopted by Central Government (11.3 and 11.4). Within this selected trajectory targets may be set to focus action still further and to provide a basis for monitoring achievement of desired outcomes. Again we consider the general role of targets first and some of their implications before reporting on the particular targets which have been set for the Department of Transport (11.5 and 11.6).

11.2 Issues

In the context of this book issues are broad subjects of concern to decision-takers or groups within the public at large whose condition is open to influence through interventions in the form or operation of transport systems. Whether an issue will actually be raised as a matter of concern at a particular place and time will depend partly on prevailing physical conditions but also on levels of awareness of the issue generally amongst groups within the population and the importance they place upon it. One of the main aims of pressure groups is to seek to raise and maintain public awareness of individual issues (such as road safety or protection of the countryside) so as to keep them on the 'political agenda' – this then providing a platform on which campaigns can be mounted for or against particular policies and proposals. (For a discussion of 'agenda-setting' and its significance see Hill 2005.)

There are many more, and more diverse issues than might first be imagined. There is no definitive list. Indeed the range of issues commanding public attention (such as might be gleaned from a search of publications) is changing all the time. For example concerns about increasing obesity within the population generally have brought the issue of physical fitness on to the transport agenda in a way which did not exist a few years ago. To provide a framework for discussion, an illustrative list is offered in Box 11.1.

Readers will have their own experience of transport-related issues and will therefore be more familiar with some than others. However people are mostly conscious of symptoms and tend to talk about problems as they perceive them without recognising that the same condition can reflect quite different issues. For example is traffic congestion a problem because it increases journey times, adds to pollution or provokes unreliable bus services – or possibly all three? Depending on which, or their relative importance, the appropriate policy response will differ. So even familiar items deserve to be considered with care and it is for these reasons that the following explanation is offered structured under the four headings of political, economic, environmental and social/personal issues.

Political issues

There are two kinds of issue under this heading – those concerned with the interests of the State and those with the interests of the political party currently forming the Government.

In the first group is the interest of the State in its transport system as a means of moving armed forces for both internal security and external defence. In England we are conscious that this was *the* objective of the network built by the Romans, whose routes form the origin of many of today's main roads. In modern times information on how transport decisions are influenced by military or civil defence considerations is obviously not in the public domain. In the 1970s and 80s however there was speculation that the national motorway programme was influenced by its potential role in deploying mobile missile launchers.

A similar issue is the cohesion of the State in a political sense, i.e. as a unit of government. Transport investment is often seen as a means of 'tying in' otherwise peripheral or inaccessible parts of a country in order to lessen the threat of secession, particularly where there are separate nationalist parties. In Britain additional public spending (on a per capita basis) goes to Scotland and Wales, part of which can be attributed to concern to uphold the political union. The European Union also funds a programme of major trans-national transport projects which have political as well as economic integration as their aim.

The State is also concerned with civil order and law enforcement, whose implications range from the handling of national emergencies at one extreme (such as the one brought on by the blockade of oil depots in September 2000) to everyday relations between the police and the public in enforcing traffic regulations at the other.

The second group of issues relates to the political interests of the party currently forming the Government. These may involve giving special attention to topics of particular concern to the Government's supporters, or to policies which advance its particular ideology. The Conservative's privatisation programme in the 1980s and 90s was motivated by the ideological view that private ownership was to be preferred and that – like the sale of council houses – an increase in the number of 'shareholders' would also add to the number of the Party's natural supporters.

Such seismic changes only occur occasionally. More common is the selectivity applied in government decision-making in the attempt to influence electoral prospects

---

Box 11.1 An illustrative list of transport-related issues

Political

i) Interests of the State
- Facilities for moving armed forces
- Cohesion amongst 'provinces' within State boundary; political unity
- Civil order and law enforcement; demands on and relations with the police.

ii) Interests of the Government in power
- The pattern of ownership or control of resources
- The social or spatial distribution of transport-related benefits and disbenefits
- Maintenance/promotion of ideological values championed by the political party in Government
- Electoral advantage; political implications of the presentation or perception of transport topics
- Implementation of the Government's priorities; prospects of delay or disruption.

Economic
- Efficiency of travel: journey time, operating costs, information, reliability, comfort
- Losses through accidents: vehicle damage, work time, costs of medical and emergency services
- Maintenance of transport infrastructure and vehicles
- Employment or business opportunities (accessibility of workforce, customers etc.)
- Impact on public finances (revenues and expenditures)
- Direct employment in transport industries (inc. infrastructure companies)
- Spatial distribution of economic activity (esp. utilisation of existing capital and labour)
- Support for regeneration and economic development projects; access to specific sites
- Relationship of transport provision/opportunities to planned development pattern
- Use of finite resources (land, non-renewable energy, aggregates).

Environmental
- Greenhouse gas emissions; pollutants contributing to acid rain
- Local air quality, noise and vibration levels; perceived danger from traffic
- Visual intrusion of vehicles and transport infrastructure; light pollution
- Protection/enhancement of areas of historic, architectural, landscape or ecological importance
- Visual quality of streets and travelling environment.

Social/personal
- Personal mobility/freedom (inc. access for disabled/mobility impaired; personal security in travel)
- Personal accessibility (opportunity to fulfil basic activity/travel needs)*
- Personal health/fitness
- Anxiety and suffering arising from accidents
- Working conditions within transport industries; protection of travellers from unsafe practices
- Community identify and development; protection from severance
- Public awareness of transport issues; involvement in decision-making.

*Limitations on mobility and accessibility, where they are concentrated amongst particular social groups, are currently referred to as a dimension of 'social exclusion'.

in particular constituencies. The largest and most shameless example of this kind was the go-ahead given in 1967 to the Humber Suspension Bridge by the Labour Government in the run-up to the by-election in nearby Grimsby (and which left a legacy of financial losses for decades afterwards). More routinely, issues of political preference arise in the selection and programming of improvement schemes funded by both central and local government, although such considerations are never explicitly acknowledged in any formal policy statement.

Aside from sectional preferences, both the timing and content of Government announcements will be influenced by concern to gain advantage over its political opponents and to present the Government's own actions in the best possible light. Proposals which might provoke delays or campaigns of opposition may be deferred or quietly abandoned. Conversely others may be rushed forward in order to head off criticism or to grab media attention. The sudden appearance of the rural transport element in the March 1998 budget, only a couple of weeks after the mass 'rural lobby' demonstration in London, is an example of this.

Economic issues

The first, and normally the most important, group of issues under this head is the contribution to economic performance made by the efficiency of the transport system. This is either in the form of the conditions experienced by existing or prospective travellers or of the opportunities to make new or different trips which have additional value.

For transport industries maintaining and increasing the efficiency of travel – i.e. with facilitating mobility – is their pre-eminent purpose. Their investment is rewarded by increased revenues from customers who are prepared to pay for savings in time (mainly) or from other gains which can be derived from access to wider markets, consolidated business operations etc. Increased efficiency however is not solely a matter of increased speed (in-vehicle journey time). Reliability of operation, the predictability of journey times and arrangements for interchange or transhipment are also important features.

These issues are incorporated in the appraisal of public investments in transport as are the savings to be derived from reducing the number or severity of accidents (i.e. loss of working time, damage to vehicles, costs of medical treatment etc.).

The case for improving mobility amongst the population at large is less straightforward. The central conundrum is that transport is predominantly a derived demand and therefore improving mobility by itself is no guarantee of overall benefit. In some cases, paradoxically, reducing travel time may be perceived as a disadvantage (Jain and Lyons 2008). More generally, changes in the spatial distribution of population and facilities over time can defeat part or all of the benefits of transport improvements – with people simply travelling further and spending more to do much the same things. Conversely, through telecommunication and information technology, it is increasingly possible for activities and exchanges to be achieved without recourse to physical movement. In these circumstances it is not clear that to travel further or faster necessarily represents a net economic gain, or conversely that to travel less or slower represents a net loss. Ideally a much wider frame of reference is required (Metz 2008).

In the past, improving transport networks at a sub-regional or regional level was a major plank of regional development programmes. Public and private agencies continue to lobby for transport investment in their areas as an impetus to economic regeneration. This is a good example of where differentiating between the issues involved is important to sound decision-making. As highlighted in the Eddington Report (24.5) such proposals need to be examined to determine whether they generate a net gain in national productivity (and if so whether this is being achieved cost-effectively) or whether they are primarily a matter of redistributing it (i.e. of bringing benefits to disadvantaged areas). Both are legitimate concerns but one is economic in nature whilst the other is social and it should be a matter of public debate and political choice as to the relative importance attached to them. The value accorded to a particular investment would vary accordingly.

Environmental issues

Environmental damage of various kinds is an inevitable consequence of motorised transport. A key element in public decision-making is therefore the issue of environmental protection and enhancement applicable to both the impact of existing traffic movements and transport infrastructure and to the adverse effects of additional travel and any new or expanded facility built to accommodate it. In some circumstances the two may apply concurrently. In the case of a bypass proposal for example, the environmental gains from removing through traffic from a settlement have to be weighed against the environmental losses which would be caused by the new road and the redirected traffic along it.

Environmental issues can be viewed at two levels – local and non-local. At the extreme, non-local issues are literally global in nature, as is the case with the emission of carbon dioxide and other greenhouse gases from transport sources. Pollutants which contribute to acid rain have a more geographically specific, but still potentially international significance. Emissions contributing to the formation of smog have a narrower significance, but still more than purely local. Because there is no direct spatial association between source and effect, actions addressing these issues have to be agreed and enforced at national and international levels. Although they are presented here as 'environmental' the concern underlying them may be partly economic in nature, e.g. to lessen losses in capital or productive output, or to avoid resources having to be expended later on remedial measures.

Local environmental issues by contrast vary in their significance according to where the effects are generated and the impacts occur. The importance of drainage, vegetation, micro-climate etc. – features which will be altered by new transport infrastructure – will depend on the ecology of the immediate area. Likewise the importance of local levels of noise, air pollution and perceived danger caused by transport movements will depend on the character of the places affected and the sensitivity of the activities being carried on within them.

With new works there is the opportunity to minimise environmental impacts through a combination of good design and remedial measures. The alignment of new routes is constrained by concerns to protect 'listed' buildings of architectural or historic interest, conservation areas, national parks or other areas of high landscape value and sites of special scientific interest. Listed buildings and the like are the subject of national designation. Central government may also impose noise and air quality standards as a matter of national policy. Beyond these, however, the consideration to be given to local environmental impacts is essentially a matter for local decision since, whatever approach is taken, the results are not normally 'exported' to neighbouring areas.

Social and personal issues

As with environmental issues these are not necessarily devoid of economic significance, but that is not their main source of concern. Rather they derive from concerns about individual welfare, rights and the distribution of opportunities and other transport-related conditions between different groups in society. For example improving the mobility of disabled people may have economic benefits, but this is unlikely to be the main reason it is proposed.

The distributional concern at the root of social objectives is different from the preferences between groups on purely political grounds noted earlier. Although governments will vary in the importance they attach to social issues, once policies have been determined they are normally applied without political preference. For example once national eligibility criteria have been set for people to receive free school transport or concessionary travel, all members of the population who meet these criteria are entitled to the associated benefits.

As we noted in Chapter 9 mobility in the sense of *freedom from restriction* on personal movement is perceived as a fundamental right. Many decisions, particularly at the local level, are concerned with balancing the 'freedom' available to different modal groups where, because of the limitations of space and infrastructure, unimpeded movement by all is impracticable. For example motorists may be restricted in their ability to use certain shopping streets in order to give greater freedom to pedestrians, or in 'home zones' in order to give children and others the freedom to move around safely.

Less noted tend to be restrictions which are not formally 'imposed' but which arise because of the way streets and other transport facilities are designed and managed. Otherwise mobile people can effectively be prevented from travel, for example by the presence of steps, inadequate signing, or by fear of attack – especially after dark.

Mobility in the sense of *freedom to travel* amongst people who for one reason or another do not already have this capability is a more contested policy area. Mobility is something most people are able to 'purchase' and to exercise choice relative to other claims on their time and income. However exactly what they are able to purchase, and what kind of 'lifestyle' they are able to follow as a result, will depend on particular circumstances. These include characteristics of the individual (e.g. physical mobility, income, work or family responsibilities) and of their location (availability of jobs and services, quality of transport networks etc.). Concern arises where the combination of circumstances is such that people are effectively prevented from living what most people would regard as a 'normal' life and may thus be classed as 'socially excluded'.

There are relatively few activities where the ability to travel has been given the status of a right. Travel to school is the most important and is the corollary of school attendance being compulsory. Other transport may be provided as ancillary to publicly-funded welfare services, e.g. to hospitals (for patients) or to day-care centres. However there is no 'entitlement' to transport for other purposes, irrespective of how severe are personal circumstances. Public authorities are able to pay financial support for transport services which fulfil 'social needs', but the definition of these and the extent to which they are provided for is a matter of local discretion and voluntary resources. Hence the *opportunities* available to similar sorts of people living in similar sorts of places varies widely in different parts of the country.

Transport has significance for personal welfare other than through mobility and accessibility. Car dependence can be a factor contributing to obesity and heart disease; conversely walking and cycling may be encouraged as ways of combating these problems and contributing to well-being. Personal suffering and anxiety arises from road accidents and from fear of traffic danger, both on the part of the individual directly affected and of other members of their family. At a neighbourhood level there can be concerns about the effect of transport routes or the presence of traffic flows in inhibiting local pedestrian movement and introducing 'severance' into a community.

The provision of services at the neighbourhood level in a form which involves local people – perhaps through voluntary action – can be an issue for public policy. Especially in disadvantaged areas such services can be designed to strengthen communities and foster individual confidence – possibly to promote independence and reduce reliance on State provision more generally. The provision of some form of community transport service, as well as catering for specific travel needs referred to above, can contribute to these wider aims.

11.3 The role of objectives

The very existence of policy-making and planning reflects the importance we attach to choice and a belief in our ability to exercise it. On the face of it there should be little difficulty in saying broadly what we would like to see in future, particularly in terms of improvements relative to the existing situation. We probably won't be sure exactly what needs to be done in order to bring about the desired conditions – that is the purpose of successive levels of planning to explore and test possible options.

In practice however the business of setting objectives is problematic. The principal reason for this is the divergence between the politician's interest in generality and flexibility and the professional manager's interest in specificity and consistency.

For politicians, 'statements of intent' are in effect their marketing material. In order to win support they need to offer a prospectus which is attractive to their electorate. This means putting forward aspirations which appeal to a wide body of the population and which preferably avoid alienating others. In responding to the concerns of particular groups it may be tempting to offer more than can be delivered (because of insufficient resources or because addressing one issue will in practice conflict with another). In this context a formal set of objectives and priorities, published for all the world to see and pore over, could easily be regarded as unhelpful to political leaders – boxing them in and providing ready ammunition to their opponents for years after to hold them to account.

And yet, in their role as heads of government departments or portfolio holders in local authorities, senior politicians will recognise that some such statement is required in order that administrators or managers responsible for professional teams are given clear direction to guide their work. (In the case of executive agencies, providing them with such directives is a formal requirement.) Because managers are dealing with a complex mix of activities – some routine, some one-off – and with plans and projects which take several years to bring to fruition, consistency is critical.

Objectives therefore provide a first step in fleshing out broad aims into a more detailed, operational form. In doing so they give distinctiveness to a political agenda. They provide a stable framework within which a continuing dialogue can take place between political leaders and senior managers – and with external stakeholders – in developing programmes of action and in responding to problems or opportunities which arise along the way.

Given the important role objectives can play it is perhaps surprising, historically, how rarely they have been used. However the fact that governments may choose not to publish them in a formal list does not mean that they do not have any! The post-1979 Conservative Government for example was one of the most purposive on record, yet it managed to operate for most of its eighteen years without any overall statement of transport objectives and policies.

Even when objectives *are* published it would be wrong to imagine that they are (all) the considerations which are actually being brought to bear on decision-making. Sometimes governments will want to focus on particular issues or priorities which set them apart from their political opponents or predecessors – in other words to highlight distinctive *differences* – even though in reality there is a lot of 'common ground'. Selectivity may also be used to put a favourable 'spin' on the objectives claimed for particular proposals. (It is much easier to change the rhetoric surrounding plans and programmes than it is to change their substance.) So even where objectives are presented for public consumption one needs to do more than simply take them at face value.

Statements about objectives are important not solely in terms of the issues they address but also, implicitly, of those which they omit. In the interests of comprehensibility and 'saleability' to the general public it is almost inevitable that attention will be focused on a few issues only. The fact that others are not represented may simply mean that they are not being actively pursued or given priority. However there is also the danger that when conflicts arise or resources are tight such issues may be compromised or overlooked in the pursuit of objectives which *are* being highlighted. That is why, when reviewing the objectives adopted by any particular administration it is important to keep the full range of issues in mind.

11.4 Objectives set nationally

The 1998 White Paper was remarkable for the extent to which transport was viewed as a means to an end and hence as a potential contributor to Government objectives in *other* policy sectors.

> We need a transport system which supports our policies for more jobs and a strong economy, which helps increase prosperity and tackles social inclusion. We also need a transport system which doesn't damage our health and provides a better quality of life now – for everyone – without passing on to future generations a poorer world.
>
> (DETR 1998a para 2.1)

A 'framework for change' was set out under a series of headings which reflected these broader aspirations (see Box 11.2). Interestingly only one of these was expressed in terms of transport itself. The presence of economic and environmental components reflected traditional concerns of transport policy although within these categories there were some notable innovations – to have regard to the economic vitality of particular areas for example and to reduce traffic growth and respond to the challenge of climate change. However the status accorded to health and social inclusion issues as distinct categories was novel. So too was the approach taken to issues associated with transport operation – as part of an integrated system developed in the public interest.

Politically however this enlightened approach to transport issues was vulnerable and the fact that little priority appeared to be given to serving the more immediate

---

Box 11.2 'The New Deal for Transport'

'A long-term strategy to deliver sustainable transport':

- better health
- more jobs and a strong economy
- a better environment
- a fairer, more inclusive society
- a modern, integrated transport system.

Source : DETR 1998 Ch 2

---

interests of motorists was to prove its Achilles' heel. The attempt was made to alter this impression in John Prescott's Introduction:

> As a car driver I recognise that motorists will not readily switch to public transport unless it is significantly better and more reliable. The *main aim* of this White Paper is to increase personal choice by improving the alternatives and to secure mobility that is sustainable in the long term.
>
> (DETR 1998a p. 3, emphasis added)

As with the Conservatives previously, the language of 'choice' was being used in a carefully selective manner – in effect a politically acceptable way of presenting the more unpalatable concept of demand management. Motorists were being offered better options for *not* using their cars whereas many would have chosen to have better options for using them!

Whilst this policy rhetoric was being set out in the White Paper the practical development of the Government's transport programme was being pursued through application of a 'New Approach to Transport Appraisal' (NATA). This attempted to summarise all the impacts of a scheme under a series of headings which, it was claimed, reflected the Government's overarching objectives, viz:

- environment
- safety
- economy
- accessibility
- integration.

The full list is shown in Table 11.1. In character it is similar to the list of issues presented earlier. However the use of the terms objective and sub-objective can be considered misnomers in that they fail to fulfil the function of objective-setting in steering action as explained in the previous section. Rather the framework is intended to act as a 'neutral' technical device – a comprehensive impact statement – to which Ministers can apply their own relative priorities in arriving at decisions. However this begs the important question of what objectives have *actually* been used, consciously or otherwise, in generating the proposals brought forward for Ministers' attention!

Because the NATA framework is used as part of a process of selecting (and hence also of rejecting) transport proposals the interpretation of issues and objectives which it

Table 11.1 Objectives and sub-objectives in the NATA framework (source: TAG unit 3.2)

Objective	Sub-objectives
ENVIRONMENT To protect the built and natural environment	To reduce noise To improve local air quality To reduce greenhouse gases To protect and enhance the landscape To protect the heritage of historic resources To support bio-diversity To protect the water environment To encourage physical fitness To improve journey ambience
SAFETY To improve safety	To reduce accidents To improve security
ECONOMY To support sustainable economic activity and get good value for money	To get good value for money in relation to impacts on public accounts To improve transport economic efficiency for business users and transport providers To improve transport economic efficiency for consumers (users) To improve reliability To provide beneficial wider economic impacts[1]
ACCESSIBILITY To improve access to facilities for those without a car and to reduce severance	To improve access to the transport system To increase option values[2] To reduce severance[3]
INTEGRATION To ensure that all decisions are taken in the context of the Government's integrated transport policy	To improve transport interchange To integrate transport policy with land use policy To integrate transport policy with other Government policies

Notes

1 Wider economic impacts are effects on employment and productivity additional to those arising directly from changes in travel times and costs represented by transport efficiency.
2 Option value is the importance which non-users place on the presence of transport opportunities – for example by businesses on the presence of a public transport facility to bring workers or customers, or by car owning residents as a fall-back when their car is not available.
3 Severance is the impairment of local accessibility (normally as experienced by pedestrians or cyclists) arising from the physical barrier of a transport route (e.g. motorway or railway) or from the deterrent effect of traffic volumes or speed.

embodies has a strong conditioning effect on 'Government policy in practice'. Probably the most notable feature of NATA is that two of the five main aspirations of the 1998 White Paper ('better health' and 'a fairer, more inclusive society') do not figure as main objectives. Health issues do appear – rather incongruously – as sub-objectives under the Environment objective (local air quality and personal fitness). Narrowly defined attributes which have relevance to social inclusion are included under the sub-objectives of security, severance and access to the transport system but the more significant attribute of personal accessibility is omitted (i.e. the opportunity for people to access the facilities they need). The reason for this is that, for the population as a whole, changes in accessibility are taken to be reflected in people's *actual travel behaviour* and hence subsumed within the economic efficiency calculations. However

---

Box 11.3 Roads: 'Where we want to be'

Looking ahead thirty years we need to be in a position where
- We continue to improve safety
- We identify, fund and deliver promptly improvements in road capacity where justified – balancing the needs of motorist and other road users with wider concerns about impact on the environment, including impact on the landscape
- We get ever greater performance out of the road network through improved management
- We facilitate smarter individual choices about the trips we need to make, giving people alternatives to using their car, particularly for short journeys, and
- Promote these choices by ensuring that new ways of paying for road use are developed so that they become practical options.

Source: DfT 2004f Future of Transport para 3.5

---

policy-makers' particular concern with the opportunities available to otherwise socially excluded groups is not reflected in the framework.

Although NATA has continued to have a central role in investment appraisal and is currently being updated (24.8), the intervening 2004 White Paper seems to have been written in a parallel universe. It marked a complete change in style and substance from its 1998 predecessor. There was no discussion about the rationale for transport policy and the contribution it can make to other policy sectors. Equally there was no explicit consideration of overall objectives. Rather the text is written more narrowly around individual travel modes. For each of these there is a short section headed 'where we want to be' which mixes both ends and means. The section in the Roads chapter is reproduced in Box 11.3 as an example.

At one level such statements can be regarded as unexceptional. (Only the pursuit of road user charging was controversial and hence cosmetically presented as 'new ways of paying for road use'.) On the other hand as evidence of the strategic steer on national transport policy over a period as long as thirty years they are seriously lacking. (This void will be returned to in the discussion of contemporary policy in Part 5.)

Some evidence of the 'real' change taking place in the evolution of policy (as opposed to the rhetoric of policy statements) can be seen in the *targets* which were published to accompany the 2004 White Paper. Before considering these however we need to reflect on the role of targets in general.

11.5 The role of targets

Objectives are typically expressed in terms of *directions of change* – for example to lessen pollution or to increase reliability. They do not normally prescribe a particular outcome or degree of improvement by a particular date. Traditionally these future conditions have been left undefined in policy documents. This is partly because of uncertainty about the level of resources and other factors which will have a bearing on the rate of implementation. It is also because more detailed work usually remains to be done to explore the practical options available for making such improvements.

From a politician's point of view expressing aspirations only in the generalised form of objectives retains flexibility but does not convey much idea to the public of the progress to be made or the actual improvements they are likely to see. One device aimed at winning greater support is to couple objectives with proposed levels of spending – the implication being that, say, to spend more than in the past, or more than one's political opponents is a measure of how much better conditions are likely to be. However reference to increased spending is normally politically hazardous, and in any case confuses inputs with outputs and outcomes. A counter-argument might be that public money was being wasted and that it is possible to secure the same outcomes with less expenditure by improving cost-effectiveness instead.

Targets can be used to strengthen both kinds of argument. Instead of quoting levels of spending (i.e. inputs), targets can be specified to indicate what this is expected to deliver, measured either in terms of *outputs* (what the money is to be spent on) or *outcomes* (what changes in conditions are planned to result). If coupled with a spending budget these can also be used to demonstrate the level of effectiveness achieved. (Output-related measures quantify efficiency; outcome-related measures quantify effectiveness.)

Targets can also act as benchmarks for monitoring or comparing management performance. They can therefore help focus the activities of an executive agency on political priorities and encourage innovation in devising ways of solving problems and delivering the desired outcomes. By linking performance assessment to grant funding or contract payments the 'incentive' element of using targets is enhanced (Marsden and Bonsall 2006).

Since 1985 the Government has set targets for reductions in road accidents, and the effectiveness of road safety programmes, nationally and locally, are judged in terms of actual accident reductions. In principle this is a field for which the application of targets is well suited since outcomes are clearly measurable and not affected by extraneous factors likely to change greatly over time. However the use of targets is far from straightforward and this example of road safety can be used to illustrate some of the difficulties they pose. These apply equally in other fields to which the use of targets has been extended or proposed.

The first difficulty is the selection of which aspect of an issue is to be the subject of a target. Road safety for example embraces a range of different types of accidents, from those which do not involve injury through to those which result in fatalities. Accidents can be also categorised according to the type of road user involved (pedestrian, cyclist, motorist etc.), the type of person injured (child, elderly person etc.) or the type of road on which the accident occurs (urban, rural, motorway, all-purpose road etc.). Statistics are maintained for each of these categories. The trend in accidents in each of these categories will differ and in some cases may be moving in opposite directions. For the purpose of setting targets, simply taking all injury accidents for example, by mixing up these different trends, may therefore obscure more than it reveals.

For management purposes many different aspects will be monitored, but politically (i.e. for consumption by the general public) more than just one or two would be confusing. Which one(s) should therefore be selected? There is clearly the temptation for politicians – and managers – to focus on the ones which offer the greatest potential for improvement, but which in practice are relatively easy to achieve. Aspects which are more important, or which are a more exacting test of management performance, may be ones which offer relatively limited scope for improvement and therefore run the risk of being sidelined.

There is then difficulty in the precise way a target should be specified. In the case of road safety for example should one be concerned about the number of accidents or the accident rate (say, per vehicle mile) since, all other things being equal, more traffic will imply more accidents? Should conditions be recorded at their face value or take account of the secular trend (i.e. the combined effect of external factors) which will be causing changes anyway? Again there is the temptation to choose the specification likely to give the *appearance* of producing the greatest improvement in conditions.

With many issues difficulties arise in identifying indicators which accurately represent their condition and for which it is practicable to generate the necessary information. (Indicators are quantified measurements or some systematically organised form of description and classification.) Road accidents are relatively straightforward and comprehensive records are maintained by police authorities. At the other extreme issues like personal security are very difficult to measure – there is no recognised methodology and no generally available source of data. Adopting targets, or developing monitoring procedures more generally, therefore runs the risk of focusing attention on issues which *are* susceptible to quantification and/or on ones for which information is readily available.

Whatever aspect of an issue is chosen and however the target is specified there is the conundrum that it will tend to skew expenditure and professional activity in that field. If one of the purposes of targets is to *focus* effort on achieving particular outcomes ,inevitably aspects which are not the subject of targets will tend to suffer. This can have unintended and sometimes rather perverse consequences. For example public concern about road safety is not simply confined to actual accident reduction, but to lowering the risk of accidents, and – even more important – lowering the *perceived* risk. People campaigning for a particular road safety improvement will not welcome being told that the accident record at the place concerned is not bad enough to justify the expenditure involved. They are likely to interpret that as meaning they will have to wait for somebody to be killed before anything is done!

Targets are likely to be most effective where they are closely linked to the problem needing to be solved. Targets for reducing CO_2 or road casualties fall into this category, but targets for, say, increasing public transport use do not. Such targets may 'miss the point' if, for example, they succeed in increasing travel by public transport but do not in fact reduce travel by car – and hence do not contribute to the end in view, i.e. to reducing traffic congestion or CO_2 emissions. The Government adopted a similar line of argument in rejecting the case for a national target for road traffic reduction (DETR 2000d).

Without sufficient analysis there is also the risk that the economic costs involved in achieving a particular target may be more than the benefits derived. The balance of costs and benefits can depend on local circumstances. Hence if targets are to be set, they need to take account of these local variations. This reasoning underpinned CfIT's approach to national traffic reduction in which they maintained that it should be built up from local and regional assessments rather than applied 'top-down' (CfIT 1999). Finally the Government has commented that with issues which are not solely transport-related it is more efficient to set targets across all policy sectors and not specifically for transport. This leaves open its ability to choose between options which in aggregate offer the most cost-effective course of action. This was – and continues to be – the reason given for the Government's carbon emission targets being specified across the range of relevant policy sectors and not for transport alone. In practice these arguments have to be set against the political and management difficulties of trying to function successfully in a particular field such as transport without targets.

The growing use of targets within a 'performance management' culture has been one of the distinctive features of governance over the last ten years. It has been strongly linked with the trend towards contracting out the provision of public services and even viewing local government and other public agencies as essentially 'purchasers' of services. Targets then become instruments of control and – particularly in central/local government relations – undermine the opportunity for local administrations to exercise meaningful discretion.

11.6 Targets set nationally

The 1998 White Paper proposed that, in addition to the new appraisal framework, further work would be done to develop indicators and targets. The Ten Year Plan published two years later marked the first time that a series of targets were announced concurrently across a range of issues. They were complemented by the introduction of target-setting procedures in Local Transport Plans on issues which were more appropriately monitored at the local level (see Chapter 20).

The increased attention given to targets was part of a general move by the New Labour Government to focus attention on 'delivery'. This was manifested in an initiative mounted by the Treasury to link the funding of government departments and local authorities with performance measures, developed through a system of national and local Public Service Agreements (PSAs).

The targets included in the Ten Year Plan were revised at the time of the 2004 White Paper and their presentation altered so as to link them with objectives which were more selective and focused than the 'all-purpose' set of objectives listed in the NATA framework (Table 11.2).

- The target for road traffic congestion was revised after it became apparent that the original intention (to reduce it below 2000 levels by 2010) was impracticable. The formulations presented in the 2004 Paper are skilful in that they give the impression that conditions are being improved whereas strictly this is not the case.
- The target for increased rail patronage was dropped (because it became unachievable as a consequence of the Hatfield crash and its aftermath); emphasis was placed on improving reliability instead.
- Targets for bus and light rail use were combined and a rider added about growth in every English region (responding to criticism that the Ten Year Plan target for bus use was likely to be achieved through the exceptional growth in London alone).
- The target for London Underground was removed from the Department's PSA – responsibility having been transferred to the London Mayor.
- Ancillary targets (not forming part of the DfT's PSA) were omitted.

The DfT acknowledged that 'PSA targets are used sparingly and do not cover the full range of the Department's responsibilities' (2005/06 Annual Report Appendix D). This nevertheless raises the question of whether, as seems likely, issues which *are* included in the PSA receive disproportionate attention. Ideally performance relative to these short-term targets would be complemented by a more stable set of indicators covering a wider range of issues, so that a more comprehensive and longer-term assessment of 'progress' could be maintained. This principle is acknowledged in the monitoring of the Government's Sustainable Development Strategy (Defra et al. 2005) although it includes only a small number of transport-related indicators.

The list in Table 11.2 follows the traditional pattern in which objectives are presented in terms of a trade-off (or 'balance') between the economic interests in

Table 11.2 Objectives and PSA targets published in 2004 (source: 'The Future of Transport' Annex B as updated in *DfT Annual Report 2005/06*)

Issue/topic	DfT Public Service Agreements CM 6234
Road congestion Rail	Objective I: Support the economy through the provision of efficient and reliable inter-regional transport systems by making better use of the existing road network; reforming rail services and industry structures to deliver significant performance improvements for users; and investing in additional capacity to meet growing demand.
	PSA1 By 2007/08 make journeys more reliable on the Strategic Road network.
	PSA2 Improve punctuality and reliability of rail services to at least 85% by 2006, with further improvements by 2008.
Bus Light rail London Underground	Objective II: Deliver improvements to the accessibility, punctuality and reliability of local and regional transport systems through the approaches set out in Objective I and through increased use of public transport and other appropriate local solutions.
	PSA3 By 2010, increase the use of bus and light rail by more than 12% in England compared with 2000 levels, with growth in every region.
	PSA4 By 2010–11 the ten largest urban areas in England will meet the congestion targets set in their LTPs relating to the movement on main roads into city centres.
Road accidents Air quality Greenhouse gases	Objective III: Balance the need to travel with the need to improve quality of life by improving safety and respecting the environment.
	PSA5 Reduce the number of people killed or seriously injured in GB in road accidents by 40% and the number of children by 50% by 2010 compared with the average for 1994–98, tackling the significantly higher incidence in disadvantaged communities.
	PSA6 Improve air quality by meeting the Air Quality Strategy targets for carbon monoxide, lead, nitrogen dioxide, particles, sulphur dioxide, benzene and 1,3 butadiene. [Joint with Defra]
	PSA7 Reduce greenhouse gas emissions to 12.5% below 1990 levels in line with our Kyoto commitment and move towards a 20% reduction in CO_2 emissions below 1990 levels by 2010, through measures including energy efficiency and renewables. [Joint with Defra and DTI]
	Objective IV: Improve cost-effectiveness through sound financial management, robust cost control, and clear appraisal of transport investment choices across different modes and locations.

improving the efficiency of travel and catering for increased demands on the one hand and protecting or improving safety and environmental conditions on the other. What is striking about the list however is the way that the economic objective should be framed in such a way as to concentrate so heavily on congestion and reliability. This reflects a shift to more visible instances of poor performance in particular situations rather than less easily assimilated notions of economic performance or accessibility across transport systems as a whole (Box 11.4).

Box 11.4 PSA targets relating to road traffic congestion

PSA1 [Applicable to the strategic highway network managed by the Highways Agency]
For the purposes of this target the indicator is based on the whole of the motorway and trunk road network, broken down into 100 or so 'routes', each averaging some forty miles in length. The traffic speed on each of these routes is measured on a series of links in both directions for 15-minute periods between 06.00 and 20.00. The indicator is the average delay experienced in the worst 10% of situations (defined by route, direction and time period). Delay is expressed as minutes per vehicle per 10 miles as compared with the 'reference speed', i.e. the speed at which motorists could expect to travel in free-flow conditions. The target will be considered met if the average delay in 2007/08 is less than that in the baseline period (2004/05). Because the delay is expressed per vehicle an improvement will have to more than offset the effects of likely increases in traffic volume.

PSA4 [Applicable to the networks managed by local authorities in the ten largest urban areas in England, viz London and the six metropolitan areas (see Fig 10.2) plus Nottingham, Leicester and Bristol]
For the purposes of this target the indicator is based on only a small proportion of main roads within each area – in this case the routes are typically 2–5 miles in length.

Unlike the indicator for the strategic network, conditions are only measured during the 'morning peak period' and may be in one (peak) direction only. Measurements are of the average journey time per person (minutes per mile) and therefore require separate observations of the number and speed of buses and other vehicles and of their average occupancy.

The targets for each area have been developed as part of the LTP2 process and explicitly incorporate the expected increase in local travel to 2010/11. The target increase in average journey time during this period (on a nominal 2005 base) ranges from 0% in Greater Manchester to 14% in Bristol. The national target is an average of these area figures weighted according to their total traffic flow on all major roads. The national target will be deemed to have been met if by 2010/11 an average increase in travel of 4.4% has been accommodated in these areas with an increase of not more than 3.6% in person journey times per mile.

12 Policy instruments (1)

Infrastructure investment

12.1 Introduction

We now proceed to consider the instruments (or 'means') available to Government to influence conditions in pursuit of the objectives and targets (or 'ends') that were discussed in the previous chapter. These instruments are of two main kinds:

1   action to alter the physical nature of transport networks
2   action to alter the behaviour of travellers or transport operators in their use of these networks.

Both types of instrument are used to:

a   improve the operational performance of networks (improving the speed, safety, reliability etc. of journeys made on them), and/or
b   lessen their adverse environmental or social impacts.

The two types of measure may be utilised in complementary fashion. For example the building of a bypass is likely to produce greater benefits if it is accompanied by management measures (e.g. direction signing or weight restrictions) to maximise its use by through traffic and in the bypassed settlement (by traffic calming and promotion of walking and cycling) to ensure that the opportunities created for environmental improvement are secured. Alternatively it is possible that management measures alone could be introduced to improve traffic and environmental conditions in the existing settlement *instead of* building a bypass. Indeed it is possible to conceive of a range of options involving different mixes and scales of 'hard' and 'soft' measures which could be tested for their cost-effectiveness in addressing issues within an area. Unfortunately such an approach is inhibited by current funding mechanisms which make a very sharp distinction between 'major' and 'minor' investments and between capital and revenue expenditure.

Having drawn attention to the way in which the different types of instrument may be linked we are now going to consider each of them in more detail. In this chapter we focus on investment in transport networks whilst in the following four chapters we explore the various types of instrument available for controlling or otherwise influencing travel behaviour.

In this chapter we begin by considering the nature of 'investment' and the rationale for public investment in transport projects (12.2 and 12.3). We then consider the sources of funding for these projects and the scope for private sector involvement in their delivery, operation and finance (12.4). We go on to review recent government policy on transport investment to identify important changes in its amount and pattern of allocation (12.5). Cost-benefit analysis is a technical tool used to guide the allocation of spending both within and between categories of investment and we outline its main features in section 12.6. Detailed guidance by the Department of Transport on the use of this tool is however deferred to Part 4 as part of the consideration of planning procedures, whilst discussion of the Government's current investment plans is contained in Part 5.

12.2 The nature of investment

'Investment' refers to expenditure in assets from which benefits are enjoyed over a period of time. In a transport context it encompasses both physical infrastructure (track, interchanges and signalling or other control systems) and vehicles. Infrastructure is fixed at a particular location whilst vehicles for the most part are not. (Some vehicles are designed for use on a particular route or network, such as the London Underground, and are effectively fixed as well.)

The distinction is important in influencing how assets may be provided. Those which are transferable can have their nature and volume determined by an ongoing competitive market (as is the case with most road and rail vehicles). By contrast investment in transport infrastructure is usually the product of a 'one-off' decision and, in its particular locational context, possesses something approaching monopoly status. Coupled with this is the fact that, like other utilities such as water, energy or sewerage, the value of any individual facility is usually a product of the network of which it is part. This and the associated economies of scale reinforces their 'natural monopoly' characteristics and explains why systems are typically owned by a single agency, either within the public sector or subject to a special regime of public regulation.

Initial investment in the land, track, buildings etc. needed to create a transport facility has to be accompanied by on-going spending on maintenance and operation to render it functional. These two types of expenditure are known as 'capital' and 'revenue' respectively and, as we will explain later, are funded in different ways. Once a facility is in existence however further investment may be carried out:

1 in structural maintenance or infrastructure renewal (where the life of a facility is being extended but its performance is essentially unaltered) and
2 in enhancements (where its capacity, safety, speed etc. or ancillary impacts are being improved).

In a developed country like the UK with well-established rail and road networks, most infrastructure investment falls into these two categories rather than into wholly new facilities. In this chapter we will be focusing on enhancements since this is the main area of policy choice. Structural maintenance and renewal are nevertheless extremely important since they enable continued use to be made of the very large asset represented by the inherited physical stock. Although 'unglamorous' as a form of spending, they normally deserve to be treated as commitments or 'first calls' on any investment budget even though – during times of financial stringency especially – there is the temptation for decision makers to cut back on them so as to maintain a programme of more visible 'improvements'.

In some cases there are links between renewal and enhancement as variants of an investment strategy. In Tyneside and Greater Manchester for example the 'like for like' replacement of life-expired former electrified suburban rail lines was not considered an economic proposition and the opportunity was taken to introduce new light rail systems instead. On the national rail network the degree of disruption caused by track and signalling renewal schemes means that these are normally combined with planned enhancements wherever practicable. Disruption to traffic during highway (re-)construction can also be an important factor in weighing up the relative merits of improvements on or off the present road alignment.

As the general standard of transport networks is improved over a long period of time, so the scale of investment involved in making a significant improvement increases (whether this is by the remodelling of an existing facility or the building of a new one). This has several important implications:

- **Enhanced facilities will be fewer in number.** (There are fewer motorways than all-purpose main roads, fewer high speed rail lines than ordinary main lines.) The gap in opportunities between places which do or don't benefit from enhanced facilities widens and economic activity increasingly focuses on the corridors and urban centres which have received major transport investment. (Access to major airports is a further dimension of this spatial phenomenon.)
- **The costs involved in achieving a 'step-change' improvement are very large,** as are the potential risks and wider consequences (good and bad). Inevitably any group of decision-makers will be very wary about committing themselves to such a change when the lead-in and pay-back times are long and there are typically few 'get out' opportunities along the way. (The plight of Eurotunnel shareholders following the introduction of cheap short-haul flights and the resulting collapse in forecast use of the Channel Tunnel provides a very salutary lesson.) On the other hand prolonged procrastination can produce widespread uncertainty and blight in related transport and development decisions.
- **Greater attention deserves to be focused on optimising existing networks,** both through managing their use and through carefully targeted, relatively small-scale enhancements. As well as entailing fewer risks (including the potential for significant political opposition) this is likely to represent the most cost-effective use of available resources. This message underpinned both the Route Utilisation Studies initiated by the SRA and the new 'charter' set for the Highways Agency in *Managing Our Roads* (DfT 2003a). The same message was reaffirmed in the context of longer term planning in the Eddington Report (24.5).

12.3 The rationale for public investment

The rationale for public investment in transport can be linked to the more general arguments about the role of the State discussed in Chapter 9. There are two main strands. The first relates to the general road network as a result of its special characteristic as a 'public good'. The second relates to all transport modes and concerns the capturing of benefits which are either not reflected in market transactions or whose market price does not reflect their full social value.

The general highway network

Public highway authorities own and manage the general highway network because, in the absence of a national system of electronic charging, it is not practicable for the costs of investment to be recouped directly from its users. (To prevent 'free-riders' it would be necessary to install toll-booths at the end of virtually every street!) Nevertheless, as far as investment in new or improved roads is concerned, public investment is still directed *as if* individual motorists paid tolls for each journey they made, using the evidence from cost-benefit analyses (12.7).

Given the existence of an ordinary highway network which provides for general mobility it is however feasible to consider the provision of new or improved facilities on a separate basis (i.e. where they offer *additional* opportunities) and for the associated investment to be recouped by tolls from motorists on the routes concerned. (In effect this follows the practice established in the 18th century with the building of turnpike roads.) This is economically feasible in the case of inter-urban motorways (as in France and Italy for example) and has been adopted in England with the Midland Expressway (the M6 relief road north of Birmingham opened in 2003). The idea has also been explored of tolling additional lanes as part of widening schemes for motorways such as the M25.

In the British context the combination of the density of the existing main road network and the relatively short distance of many motorised trips means that there are relatively few opportunities for new roads or lanes which it would be practicable and commercially viable to operate on a tolled basis. (The extension of the M6 relief road northwards towards Manchester was one such possibility recently studied.) Commercially the best prospects arise in situations where traffic demand is sufficiently high that conditions on the existing (nominally 'relieved' road) remain congested – as in Birmingham – so that there is a strong incentive for its users to switch to the alternative, tolled route. However given motorists' antipathy towards congestion and the high levels of motoring taxation they incur already this is not a very attractive feature to emphasise as a matter of public policy!

This dilemma can be overcome in the special circumstances of river or estuary crossings where a toll has been applied from the outset on the original bridge or tunnel. In the case of the 'second' Severn Bridge and Thames crossing at Dartford an additional facility has been provided as a private venture but with the consortium also assuming the debt (and taking the tolls) of the original bridge/tunnel. The pair of crossings are then operated 'as one' (in fact one in each direction) so that the imbalance in conditions between one tolled and one untolled facility does not arise.

Capturing additional benefits

With toll roads and any other transport facility for which users are charged, the bulk of user benefits are expected to be recouped through charges or fares leaving the case for public investment to depend primarily on *non-user* benefits. With the general road network however non-user benefits are additional to the benefits received by motorists noted above which normally provide the main justification for investment.

The context in which the possibility of public investment arises differs as between private and publicly owned facilities. Private companies have their own sources of capital whereas public agencies are mostly dependent on central government. A company will have to satisfy its investors on the financial return it expects to obtain, but how it does this is a matter for private negotiation. As a general principle the gains and losses (financial and other) which might arise for other businesses and the wider public are not a factor in the investment decision. Subject to the availability of funds a project which is consistent with the company's strategy and offers a satisfactory rate of return can be expected to proceed and not otherwise.

Public agencies on the other hand have to submit their major proposals to a standardised and publicly visible appraisal process (Chapter 21). This consists of a financial and economic assessment of the project's costs and benefits *plus* an analysis of all other types of impact, positive and negative. A decision is made on the basis of all these factors. This can mean that a road scheme designed on the basis of the benefits it brings to motorists (and which in theory they would be prepared to pay for) may not be approved because of the disbenefit it brings to others. Conversely a scheme which would not be justified on the basis of its user benefits may nevertheless win approval if it delivers other gains.

Private companies – a train or bus operator for example – may seek some element of public funding for an investment which is not viable commercially but which brings wider public benefits (e.g. by attracting car users and hence improving traffic conditions). Alternatively companies may promote a scheme in partnership with one or more public agencies and jointly seek government funding. Either way the project will be subject to the public appraisal process and the wider impacts of the proposal *will* influence whether it is approved.

Regional policy

As a general principle the rationale for public investment in transport is the same irrespective of where it happens to be located. (Spatial and other distributional impacts are considered in the appraisal process, but as ancillary factors.) In theory, investment is allocated where it brings greatest benefit. In practice however the balance of expenditure between regions is influenced both by a degree of political expediency (so that each region receives its 'fair share') and by overarching Government and EU policy concerning regional economic development.

In the 1960s and 70s transport investment was deliberately targeted at areas such as Tyneside and Merseyside in the belief that this would promote their economic development. Subsequent research has demonstrated that the benefits of this were exaggerated – transport was only influential where a broader range of conditions necessary for regeneration were satisfied (Banister and Berechman 2000). In terms of the workings of the economy as a whole the effect of transport improvements is in any case a two-way affair. Investment which improves the relative accessibility of a city or region opens up a wider market for its goods and services, but at the same time makes it more vulnerable to competition from businesses in other areas who may be operating at a higher level of efficiency. Branch offices, factories and distribution outlets may be closed in remoter areas and served from main centres of population instead.

Similar arguments apply at the European level even though it has long been a feature of EU policy that a significant element of its budget should be directed to transport and other forms of investment in the relatively poor peripheral regions of the continent. Some of this is disbursed under a 'cohesion' or 'convergence' heading. However these mainly political and distributional considerations can be seen to conflict with other policy aspirations concerning the economic performance of the EU as a whole which would be better served by directing investment to the most populated and economically successful regions.

This concern with the performance of the main centres of activity (in the context of increasingly globalised competition) has prompted a different kind of economic argument being advanced by the CBI and others. This holds that continued growth in more *buoyant* areas is threatened by increasing congestion on transport networks (particularly in London and the South-East) and that this has a potentially damaging effect on the national economy as a whole. Additional funding for transport infrastructure in the housing 'growth areas' to cater for an increasing number of households and to prevent an 'affordability' crisis for workers is a further dimension of this argument.

There is clearly a tension in the spatial implications of an investment policy focusing on 'congestion-busting' and infrastructure in growth areas and one which, on equity or economic development grounds, gives equal (or possibly more than equal) treatment to remoter and/or less economically buoyant areas. Significantly the Government objective of 'reducing the persistent gap in economic growth rates between the English regions' is shared between HM Treasury, DTI and DCLG but not the DfT, and the subject of transport investment allocation as between the regions did not feature in the 2004 Transport White Paper.

12.4 The financing of public investment

It is in the nature of investments that they involve a high initial capital cost with benefits (including any benefits recouped through user charges) derived over many years thereafter. The presence of an asset of continuing value enables the cost of investments to be spread over a period by borrowing. Public investment has the advantage that loans to the Government are obtained at the lowest level of interest within the prevailing financial market, because of their almost complete absence of risk (regardless of the success or failure of individual schemes). In principle therefore the overall cost of financing an investment (capital plus interest) should be less when undertaken by the public rather than the private sector.

However the capability of the Government to service the debts generated by investment programmes is not infinite. Higher borrowing pushes up interest rates and 'crowds out' resources available for private investment. Gordon Brown, when Chancellor of the Exchequer, introduced a series of self-imposed 'rules' designed to demonstrate prudence in the management of the nation's finances. His so-called 'golden rule' was that, over the period of an economic cycle, borrowing should be limited to capital expenditure only. (Borrowing for revenue expenditure – rather like a family borrowing to pay for its housekeeping – is therefore confined to dealing with short-term fluctuations only.) A second 'sustainable investment rule' was that the total amount of Government borrowing at any one time – the 'Public Service Borrowing Requirement' or PSBR – should be kept below 40% of the nation's Gross Domestic Product (GDP).

A combination of good fortune and skilful management meant that the decade 1997–2007 was one of unprecedented economic stability in the UK. This has enormous importance for the planning and management of public investment since it is undertaken within a well-established overall profile and not subject to short-term fluctuations in the face of economic crises. During this time the apparently irreconcilable objectives of containing public borrowing whilst investing in improvements in transport and other public services have been met by exploring opportunities for privatisation and private financing. In the case of rail rolling stock for example privatisation has enabled an extensive replacement programme to be achieved (by private investment and leasing to the train operating companies) on a scale which would not have been open to British Rail. Network Rail – the successor to Railtrack – was carefully designed so that technically it remains a private company, and hence – critically – its very large debts are kept off the public accounts. However the company is only able to sustain these on the basis of the funding commitments given by the Government since 2002 to keep it afloat. As this demonstrates, privatisation does not preclude the Government from contributing to investment in rail or other private industries (although this was not part of the original Conservative prospectus).

With London Underground the New Labour Government did not pursue full privatisation but negotiated a public-private partnership (PPP), i.e. a private finance deal. This transferred responsibility for financing and managing a programme of maintenance and renewal of trains and infrastructure over a finite period to private consortia in return for a series of performance-related payments. (The renewed physical asset is returned to public ownership at the end of this period.)

PPPs generally have the advantage that they enable additional investment to be secured without increasing public borrowing and do not involve 'selling off' public assets – indeed adding to their stock over the long term. They also have potential advantages as a form of procurement in that the design and delivery of the investment is overseen by specialist companies. Many of the risks which would otherwise fall to the commissioning public body are thereby transferred to the contracting consortium. However because at least some of these risks are within the contractor's control there is a commercial incentive to manage them as efficiently as possible. Likewise the consortium has the incentive to achieve reliability in the design, construction and operation of the facility, thereby reducing its liability for maintenance expenditure and maximising income through performance-related payments.

PPPs nevertheless remain controversial on several counts. From the public perspective a great deal of their potential 'success' depends on negotiating appropriate details of the contract, which is an extremely complex and time-consuming business. If difficulties arise during the period of the contract then the public client may still find itself having to shoulder the ultimate burden of responsibility (since the facility cannot be allowed simply to cease functioning). This aspect was highlighted in 2007 when Metronet (the larger of the two consortia running the PPP for the London Underground) went into liquidation with debts of around £2bn.

There are also doubts as to whether the overall cost to the public sector is higher – in effect whether the benefits of specialised management, incentives and risk transfer of privately delivered schemes offset the higher costs of private borrowing, the contractor's profit element and the costs involved in setting up the contract in the first place (National Audit Office 1999). In the case of London Underground, Ken Livingstone maintained that the alternative of issuing bonds to raise the necessary money would have been cheaper and retained overall public control. It would however have added to the PSBR.

Aside from arguments about PPPs as a form of financing there is a further dimension of concern. One of the attractions of private finance to both Conservative and Labour governments as they struggled with cuts in investment programmes during the mid-1990s was that it enabled *additional* publicly funded schemes to be introduced. The cost of these is not reflected in capital accounts but in annual revenue expenditure (i.e. as a result of the payments which are made for use of the new facilities). However taking on additional projects via private finance results in an ever-greater proportion of current expenditure being taken up meeting previous commitments. (Over the period of the Ten Year Plan the proportion of revenue spending consumed by these commitments is expected to increase from 8% to 25%.) Given the need to contain overall revenue spending to what can be financed by income on a year-to-year basis it follows that PFI projects are likely to be best suited to situations where they are able to generate their own income streams and/or where they enable major savings to be made in operating or maintenance costs that would otherwise fall to public revenue accounts.

As far as local authorities are concerned, debates about private financing are of limited significance since the approval of major schemes by central government carries with it agreement to additional revenue grant payments regardless of whether these are used to service traditional loans or to pay for private finance contracts. (Concern may of course arise over the complexities of negotiating the contract or if it is believed that being required to follow the PFI route results in an overall increase in cost which places the viability of the scheme in jeopardy.)

Local authorities are not always dependent on government funding for major schemes. They may also use their own capital receipts (for example from the sale of property or former municipally owned bus companies) and developer contributions secured through the planning process. The availability of these sources is however highly variable from one authority to another according to the level of development activity within its area. Projects within certain defined areas may also be eligible for an element of EU funding as part of its regional and economic policies referred to earlier, and similarly contributions from Regional Development Agencies. There are also special 'funding pots' established by central government from time to time targeted at specific objectives which have their own eligibility criteria – for example the Communities Infrastructure Fund (CIF) in the growth areas (23.8). From 2010 local authorities will also be able to levy a supplement on business rates in their area to help pay for new transport and other projects which foster economic development (LTT 479).

The ability to draw on all these funding sources – as well as possible contributions from transport operators and other partners – is nevertheless very much a mixed blessing since it makes the putting together of an overall funding package an extremely complex and uncertain business. Agreement will be needed from a variety of sources, but each party will have its own criteria and priorities, and the decisions it takes – if unfavourable – can have a veto effect on the project as a whole. Financial contributions have to tie in with their own, separate investment programming. Even if initial agreement is obtained, all parties have to be 'kept on board' during the protracted period when details are being worked up, consultation is undertaken, Government approval is sought, planning permission obtained and so on. Actual delivery of a project in these circumstances can rightly be regarded as little short of a miracle!

Most of the transport investment made by local authorities is on the structural maintenance of highways and on relatively minor improvement schemes (those costing less than £5m). Central government funding for these purposes is not dependent on the approval of individual projects. Instead funds are allocated largely on a formula basis (according to the characteristics of an authority's area) in the context of five-yearly programmes prepared and monitored as part of a Local Transport Plan (20.4).

12.5 Recent government policy towards transport investment

Patterns of public expenditure are a mixture of design and accident (i.e. enforced response to unanticipated events). For long periods in the second half of the 20th century levels of public spending fluctuated unpredictably in response to a series of 'boom and bust' cycles in the national economy.

Investment programmes are especially vulnerable to such fluctuations. When the economy slows, government income falls whilst demands for expenditure rise. If the decline takes the form of a recession or 'slump' there is pressure on public accounts and borrowing. Commitments can be reduced most easily by cutting capital rather than revenue budgets – the latter typically have a high proportion of staff costs involved in delivering basic services. To focus on these would aggravate unemployment and provoke inconvenience and hardship amongst service users which would be very visible and politically damaging.

By contrast, deferring structural maintenance and renewals is relatively painless (providing the deficit is made good when the economy recovers) and deferring new projects especially so. (Potential beneficiaries may be disappointed but their immediate conditions are not actually worsened.) However the fact that capital spending on any major project extends over several years means that, to achieve significant savings at any particular point in time, a quite dramatic cut has to be made in the number of new starts. This was the situation with major road schemes in the mid/late 1990s, giving an exaggerated impression of a change in transport policy rather than a response to expenditure constraints.

Because of these cyclical fluctuations, identifying genuine changes in transport policy over the medium term from bald figures of public expenditure is not an easy matter. The situation is complicated by the fact that government expenditure is published in money terms for the year in question (so-called 'out-turn prices'). As a first step therefore all figures need to be converted to a common price base in order that the real changes in spending can be determined. In the case of future spending this involves making assumptions about future levels of inflation.

The Ten Year Plan provided information on actual expenditure for the previous decade (i.e. 1991–2000) and planned spending for the decade to come (i.e. to 2010). Total spending was divided into public investment, public resource (i.e. revenue) and private investment. The resource figure omits capital charges (including support payments for privately financed investments) so as to avoid double counting.

In Figure 12.1 these expenditure figures have been converted to constant prices and presented as a series of indices with 1991–92 = 100. For comparison the actual growth in the national economy (GDP) to 2005–06 has been shown in a similar manner. Private investment is not shown separately but is the difference between the 'ALL public' and 'Private investment and ALL public' components.

Points to note are:

- Planned public spending in the latter part of the 20-year period is almost exactly the same as actual spending in the early years. (It does not rise in line with GDP which has increased at a fairly stable rate during most of the period to date.)
- Private investment began to make a significant contribution from 1995/96, increasing rapidly to 2001–02 , but held at much the same level thereafter.
- Public expenditure fell markedly during the four years from 1994 to 1995 but this was directed almost entirely at cuts in investment.

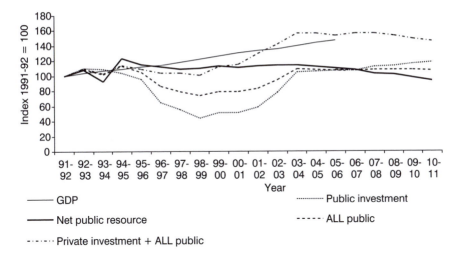

Figure 12.1 Indexed comparison of GDP and transport expenditure: actual GDP 1991–2005; actual expenditure 1991–2001; planned 2001–2011

- Major increases in public spending were planned for the first three years of the Ten Year Plan period (2001/02–2003/04). However this consisted almost entirely of investment spending, (remedying the cuts made in the mid-1990s) with no further increases thereafter.
- By adding private investment and public expenditure together, overall spending on transport by 2005/06 is roughly in line with the growth in GDP.
- Annual payments for the privately financed investments elements have the effect of depressing the amount available for public resource spending generally in the latter part of the period.

Analysing expenditure in this way puts into a rather different perspective the claims of increased investment made for the Ten Year Plan at the time it was launched. For public spending it did no more than restore the position pre-1994 (although this in itself was very important). Overall spending was brought in line with growth in GDP but this was achieved entirely by the introduction of private investment (largely through privatisation of the rail network). Utilising this source does however mean that, in principle, public spending can be increased disproportionately in other policy sectors where the same opportunity for private investment does not exist.

Each of the three expenditure types was subdivided into the main blocks by which funding is allocated: strategic roads, rail, local transport (excluding London) and London. Figure 12.2 shows the total investment (public and private) for these blocks.

As can be seen all the blocks benefit from a significant increase from a low point at the end of the 1990s, but the rate of growth is markedly different.

- Strategic roads are only expected to regain about half the spending lost during the 1990s (i.e. to 75% of their former level).
- London is expected to receive about 12% additional investment over the ten-year period compared with the previous decade.

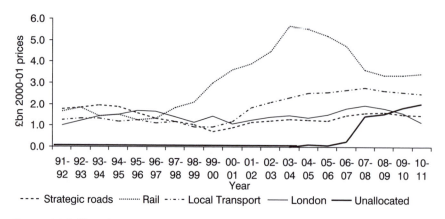

Figure 12.2 Public and private investment 1991–2001 and planned 2001–2011 (source DfT Transport 2010)

- Local Transport benefited disproportionately, increasing steeply to about 150% of former levels by 2004/05.
- Rail benefited from an even greater increase in investment (including in rolling stock) – up 200% in the five years to 2003/04. (The extent of decline shown for Rail after this time is misleading since it was likely to receive the bulk of the expenditure unallocated thus far.)

In practice the aftermath of the Hatfield rail crash and Railtrack's liquidation meant that plans for the rail component of the investment programme had to be completely revised. The combined effect of much-inflated costs and a greater need to invest in infrastructure maintenance and renewal meant that previously anticipated enhancements were squeezed out. Even so by 2004/05 it had become necessary to increase the public investment component (i.e. additional to that made by Railtrack's successor, Network Rail) by some £600m a year more than planned.

In the 2004 Comprehensive Spending Review the original plan for public spending on transport was maintained (i.e. at a roughly constant level in real terms beyond 2004/05) and extended to 2014/15. However an additional £1.7bn was allocated for the three years 2005/06–2007/08 to cope with 'immediate pressures' (i.e. in the rail industry) – an example of an enforced change in spending plans. To these were added an extra £500m a year cumulatively beginning in 2006/07. This represents a genuine policy shift since overall expenditure is now expected to increase broadly in line with growth in the economy (i.e. around 2.5% a year in real terms) and not simply to offset inflation.

Significantly however this growth increment was not added to existing funding blocks but kept separate in the form of a 'Transport Innovation Fund' (TIF) administered centrally by DfT. This is designed to promote road user charging schemes and investments which contribute to national productivity. Further details of TIF and its application are given in section 23.4.

In the next section we go on to describe techniques of cost-benefit analysis which are used to assist in investment allocation decisions.

12.6 Investment appraisal and cost-benefit analysis

In the previous chapter we noted that one way of steering decision-making is for the Government to establish overarching objectives and priorities and then to translate these into particular objectives and targets for individual Departments.

If pursued in isolation a drawback with this approach is that it does not take account of the relative effectiveness of different avenues of spending, whether this is measured in terms of the use of public money or in terms of resources employed within the economy as a whole. Because both are in short supply any proposed investment has an 'opportunity cost' which is the value of the benefits which are being forgone by not investing in the next best alternative. From an economic point of view it does not make sense to pursue a particular investment programme if greater benefit could be derived from the same resources directed differently. Rather the ideal is to achieve an 'efficient' allocation, i.e. one in which no possible alternative would offer any additional benefit.

To assist with this dimension of decision-making, techniques of cost-benefit analysis (CBA) are employed. The principles of CBA can be applied to any type of intervention but are discussed here in the context of major investment proposals. CBA can be used to provide evidence of the cost-effectiveness of spending both between and within policy sectors. It can also be used to assess the merits of individual schemes and to aid the process of prioritising proposals seeking funding from a particular budget (22.6).

CBA has a long tradition in transport planning. The development of techniques in this field was an important factor in gaining Treasury backing for large-scale transport investment in the 1960s and has remained central to the credibility of the Department of Transport's programme ever since.

The Treasury's definition of CBA is

> Analysis which quantifies as many of the costs and benefits of a proposal as feasible, including items for which the market does not provide a satisfactory measure of economic value.
>
> (quoted in DfT Transport Analysis Guidance (TAG) unit 3.5.4)

The ability to quantify impacts in terms of their monetary value is a pre-requisite for inclusion in CBA. The fact that monetisation can be applied to savings in journey time and costs which are often the main consequence of transport interventions explains the core role of CBA in appraisal. However such interventions can also have significant impacts on items which are not monetised. Equally some interventions may be targeted at these other items (though their net economic impact on journey times etc. will also need to be identified). In such situations the Department acknowledges that

> [CBA] does not provide a good measure of value for money and should not be used as the sole basis of decisions .... Impacts not included in monetised cost-benefit analysis must be taken into account in assessing overall value for money.
>
> (ibid. paras 2.1.3 and 2.1.5)

Concern that the ability to monetise certain types of impact and not others might prejudice the overall assessment of schemes was the key reason for changing to the comprehensive presentation of impacts in NATA. However the distinction between 'value for money' (in the limited sense of the results of CBA) and *overall* value for money (relevant to decision-taking) remains a very important one and a subject we will return to later when considering procedures for scheme approval (21.5).

Social cost-benefit analysis, as undertaken by public agencies, is distinctive in that all identifiable impacts are included – whoever happens to be the recipient. Nevertheless the Government has a particular interest in how its own resources are affected (as represented by public income and expenditure). Investment appraisals therefore include an assessment of impacts on public accounts. As we saw previously in the NATA framework (Table 11.1) one of the sub-objectives included under the Economy heading was to achieve 'value for money' in terms of these impacts, i.e. to obtain maximum benefit from the net cost to the public purse.

Conceptually CBA is limited in that 'welfare' is defined in the specific sense of economic efficiency only, i.e. with well-being in total. Benefits and costs are aggregated whoever happens to gain or lose and wherever the impacts happen to occur. Logically this can be justified on the basis of the 'compensation principle', i.e. that if overall gains outweigh overall losses it would be possible in theory for the gainers to compensate the losers (or for the Government to introduce some pattern of fiscal regulation, i.e. taxes and subsidies, which would have the same effect). However this is a rarified argument which is difficult to sustain in the real world if – as is commonly the case – little in the way of direct compensation actually occurs.

In practice decision-takers will be very concerned about the distribution of impacts. This is partly out of a general respect for the principle of equity and partly because of political sensitivity to the likely response from locally elected representatives and other stakeholders who have particular constituencies of interest. It is this distributional dimension (i.e. who benefits from the use of scarce resources) and the choice exercised over it which often dominates public debates.

Appraisal in general and CBA in particular can therefore be considered a technical, ostensibly 'neutral', method of presenting to politicians and others the implications of possible courses of action. This then enables value-judgements about distributional priorities to be superimposed before arriving at a final decision. The appraisal process followed by DfT includes supplementary analyses of distributional and other effects to help in this (21.7).

Providing its limitations are explicitly recognised, CBA can be of great practical assistance in decision-making. This is because *within the range of items included in the analysis,*

a   Different kinds of impact are measured using a common unit (i.e. money) enabling their effects to be aggregated. As a result the decision-taker is relieved of the task of trying to gauge the net outcome of a variety of gains and losses (e.g. the loss of property needed to secure the traffic benefits of a road widening scheme)', or at least to limit this to impacts which cannot be measured in monetary terms.
b   Because money is a unit which we utilise to represent value the relationship of aggregated benefits to aggregated costs can demonstrate whether an investment is economically worthwhile (i.e. whether it results in a net gain) and if so the extent to which it is better or worse than other spending options available.

Individual projects vary in the time taken to achieve their implementation and in the period during which they will generate costs and benefits (their 'economic lifetime'). To enable projects or programmes to be compared on a like basis, two adjustments are made to all monetary measurements included within a CBA:

- All figures are shown net of inflation and expressed in £s for a common base year.
- All future costs and benefits are discounted at a standard annual rate. (The 'discount rate' reflects the extent to which we prefer benefits to be enjoyed – or costs avoided – in one year rather than the next.)

The discount rate which the Government chooses to use in its investment appraisal is a policy decision which is significant in a number of ways:

1 In a technical sense – the lower the discount rate the longer into the future impacts have to be estimated since they will have a significant bearing on the assessment of overall economic performance.
2 In a practical sense – the choice of discount rate will alter the relative performance of schemes (even schemes which are superficially similar) according to the profile of costs and benefits over time.
3 In an ethical sense – any discount rate greater than zero potentially leads to the selection of schemes which give benefits to the current generation at the expense of losses to future ones. This raises issues of inter-generational equity which are central to the concept of sustainable development. (Hanley and Spash 1993 chapter 8)

In 2003 the Treasury introduced a major change by revising down the discount rate from 6% to around 3%, thus giving considerably more weight to costs and benefits experienced over the medium and longer term.

The overall worth of an investment (within the terms of CBA) can be summarised in one or more of the following ways:

- the net present value (NPV), i.e. the sum of discounted benefits minus the sum of discounted costs
- an overall benefit-cost ratio (BCR), i.e. the sum of the discounted benefits divided by the sum of the discounted costs, or
- a public sector benefit-cost ratio, i.e. the sum of the discounted net benefits to users, business and private sector providers divided by the sum of discounted net costs to the public sector.

The same NPV can derive from a small difference between the benefits and costs of a very large project, or a large difference between the benefits and costs of a smaller one. The latter will have a higher BCR and, £ for £, represents a more productive use of scarce resources. This can be extended a stage further with the public sector BCR to identify the rate of return derived from the public investment component alone.

In practice the scope of any appraisal is limited by the ability to identify and measure the full range of impacts in a systematic manner. CBA is further limited by the ability to assign monetary values to these impacts. To date the application of CBA in transport planning has been limited to a small sub-set of the issues included in the NATA framework (see Box 12.1) although in practice these are frequently taken to comprise the most important impacts relevant to a decision. Nevertheless DfT sees it as desirable to extend the range of issues for which monetary values are incorporated in the CBA and has commissioned research on noise, greenhouse gases, journey time reliability and option values. The results of this work are progressively being included in the Department's guidance on scheme appraisal (Chapter 21).

Box 12.1 Monetised items included in DfT's cost-benefit analysis

Impacts included in value for money assessment			
Qualitative/quantitative assessment		Monetised values (NATA BCR)	
Areas for development	Some valuation evidence		
Townscape Water environment Accessibility Social inclusion Integration Biodiversity Heritage	Wider economic benefits Landscape Reliability Air quality Journey ambience Regeneration	Risk of death or injury Noise Carbon Physical fitness	Time savings Operating costs Private sector impacts Cost to the Exchequer

Source: Figure 4.4 of DfT 2007s Towards a Sustainable Transport System

13 Policy instruments (2)

The regulation of vehicles, operators and services

13.1 Introduction

In the previous chapter we saw how governments are able to invest in the nation's transport systems, either directly or in partnership with private companies, to maintain and improve their functioning. Major enhancement schemes attract a great deal of attention because of the scale of the works involved and the visible 'step-change' in conditions they offer. However the cost of such schemes means that they are relatively few and far between. The corollary is that the conditions experienced on a day-to-day basis by the majority of people are the product of *past* investment and the way it is *currently* managed. Concern to achieve more effective utilisation of inherited networks plus recognition of environmental constraints means that growth in travel demand has to be responded to increasingly by more extensive and sophisticated management regimes.

The repertoire of powers available are of four main kinds:

1 regulations governing vehicles, operators and services
2 regulations for the control of traffic and development
3 a variety of fiscal measures – charges, taxes and subsidies – some of which are linked to the regulatory powers
4 powers to promote change in travel behaviour, primarily through marketing and the adoption of travel plans.

These topics are the subject of this and the following three chapters.

In this chapter we deal with the regulation of vehicles, operators and services. 'Regulation' refers to legally enforceable conditions required of people engaging in transport, including households and businesses which run motor vehicles for their own use as well as firms providing transport services. As we saw in Part 2 this form of State intervention has a very long history. It is concerned with protecting the public from unwanted safety and environmental impacts as well as controlling the volume, pattern or price of transport services where market processes are seen to be deficient in some way and/or where distributional outcomes need to be safeguarded.

We begin by considering the licensing of motor vehicles, drivers and road transport operators (13.2) and the overall regulation of transport industries in terms of general competition legislation (13.3). We then detail the provisions applicable to individual passenger modes – rail (13.4), bus and coach (13.5), and taxis and other forms of demand-responsive transport (13.6) – and finally the specific provisions surrounding community transport (13.7).

13.2 The licensing of motor vehicles, drivers and operators

The licensing of motor vehicles

The licensing of motor vehicles was originally introduced as a means of generating revenue for the Road Improvement Fund. Since the 1960s the issuing of an annual licence has been conditional on the production of a certificate from an approved test centre as to a vehicle's roadworthiness (currently applicable to vehicles more than three years old). The checks applied have been extended to include seat-belts, noise and exhaust emissions. Likewise a current insurance certificate is required. The issuing and renewal of licences is administered by the Driver Vehicle and Licensing Agency.

Vehicles are required to carry plates displaying their unique registration number and a tax disc in the windscreen as evidence of a current licence. This enables the owner (or strictly the 'keeper') of a vehicle to be traced and is fundamental to the enforcement of parking and speed restrictions and other traffic offences. Number-plate recognition is also used as the means of checking payment of the Central London congestion charge.

The overall cost of licensing a vehicle, including the repairs and maintenance expenditure needed to obtain a test certificate, can run into many hundreds of pounds. The very rigour of the licensing regime may be counter-productive if increasing numbers of people opt to drive illegally by not renewing a licence. The owner of an unlicensed vehicle may also drive with a sense of impunity and be more likely to contribute to other traffic offences. Since 2004 new licensing rules have been introduced in an attempt to reduce evasion and improve the accuracy of licensing records.

New vehicles have to meet minimum standards of performance affecting safety and emissions. Testing is undertaken by the Vehicle Certification Agency which publishes definitive data available for purchasers and for the Inland Revenue to apply in the application of Vehicle Excise Duty (15.2). A continuous programme of improvement is pursued. Many features have commercial potential and the Government is keen to promote consumer information on them so as to foster competition amongst vehicle manufacturers. This it notes 'should act as a faster lever for change than regulation' (DfT 2007k para 220).

In relation to emissions EU regulations applied over the last 20 years requiring the fitting of catalytic converters and particulate traps have been instrumental in achieving dramatic reductions in nitrogen oxide and particulate matter (PM10) from the vehicle fleet (3.6). However in relation to fuel consumption and hence CO_2 emissions a voluntary approach has been pursued instead. Agreements with motor manufacturers are intended to deliver a 25% improvement in the fuel efficiency of cars between 1995 and 2008–09.

In 2002 the UK Government adopted a strategy aimed at promoting the development and take up of low-carbon vehicles and fuels through the Low Carbon Vehicle Partnership (DfT 2002b). It includes the target of 10% of new cars sold in 2012 being 'low carbon', i.e. producing 100 grams or less of CO_2 per km compared with the current new car average of 178 gm. More recently a technology-based strategy for reducing CO_2 emissions in the transport sector generally was published (DfT 2007f).

A further aspect of vehicle design which assumes policy significance from time to time is the maximum size and weight of lorries. In 1998 dispensation was given to trucks of 44 tonnes with six axles travelling to and from inter-modal depots – a restriction which was lifted two years later on the recommendation of CfIT. The environmental as well as the economic case for the higher limit rested upon the reduced number of lorry movements that it permitted. Research conducted at the end of 2003 concluded that the benefits had in fact been 'greater than expected' (LTT 409). This provided ammunition for road hauliers lobbying for trials of the 'road train' concept (involving the addition of a second trailer) which could potentially involve vehicles weighing up to 84 tonnes (LTT 424). This has reawakened the fears of environmental groups who are concerned that initial stipulations on the routes to which such vehicles might be confined would not be maintained. The rail freight industry is also vehemently opposed, not merely because of the potential transfer of business (and loss of income supporting the rail network generally) but because any uncertainty over future permitted limits on road freight vehicles would have extremely damaging consequences on the prospects for securing private investment in rail freight facilities.

In relation to public service vehicles the Secretary of State is empowered under the 1995 Disability Discrimination Act to issue Regulations to ensure that they are accessible to disabled people. Regulations issued in 2000 prescribe the features to be incorporated, including wheelchair access and dedicated space, the size and height of steps and colour-differentiated features (DfT 2005h). These apply to all new vehicles but buses and coaches built previously will be permitted to continue in operation until 2017 and 2020 respectively. In practice the introduction of 'low-floor' buses has represented a quantum improvement for the convenience of passengers generally, particularly those with young children, push-chairs, shopping trolleys etc.

The licensing of drivers

The requirement to pass a driving test as a pre-condition of being able to drive a motor car unaccompanied by a licensed driver has existed since the 1930s. Since 1996 a separate theory test has been introduced which has to be passed before application is made for the practical test. Test centres are currently managed by the Driving Standards Agency which also trains and certifies driving instructors. Separate licensing regimes (typically with a minimum age of 21 instead of 17) apply to drivers of Heavy Goods Vehicles and Passenger Service Vehicles.

As well as ensuring a basic initial competence the licensing system is used as a means of sanctioning drivers convicted of traffic offences. A points system is applied, varying according to the severity of the offence, which can cumulatively lead to disqualification. In some cases a medical examination and/or retesting is required before relicensing is permitted.

Separate regulations apply to the licensing of motorcyclists. Motorcycling as a mode presents a conundrum for policy-makers. In many respects it has much in its favour. It is economical in fuel consumption and roadspace and provides a cheap form of motorised mobility for people who may not have any other options, especially in getting to work. Set against this are its appalling accident statistics – the overall fatality rate for motorcyclists is 25 times higher than for car users and 5 times higher even than for pedal cyclists. As with pedal cycling the attitude of successive governments over decades has been ambivalent at best, but more commonly neglect as if to avoid giving it the status of official recognition and implicitly hoping the 'problem' will go away.

Against this background the New Labour Government achieved the distinction of confronting the subject head on. It set up an Advisory Group on Motorcycling and published a comprehensive strategy in 2005 (DfT 2005j):

The principal aim of our strategy is to 'mainstream' motorcycling so that all the organisations involved in the development and implementation of transport policy recognise motorcycling as a legitimate and increasingly popular mode of transport.

(ibid. Foreword)

The licensing of operators

Politically the safety issues surrounding heavy goods vehicles (HGVs) and passenger carrying vehicles (PCVs) are especially sensitive. In these cases a licence is required by the operating company or organisation as well as for its individual vehicles and drivers. (Special provisions apply to taxis and community transport, discussed later.)

Applications for operator licences are considered by Traffic Commissioners who are appointed by the Government and organised on a regional basis. Initially an applicant has to demonstrate their suitability in terms of financial standing, professional competence, absence of criminal record, appropriate vehicle storage and maintenance facilities etc. Licences specify the maximum number of vehicles which can be run by an operator, and vehicle licences are controlled accordingly. Vehicles and maintenance facilities are inspected on a regular basis by the Vehicle and Operator Services Agency (a sister agency of DVLA) which acts as a source of intelligence and advice to the Traffic Commissioners. The Agency also conducts random roadside tests including checks on tachographs used to monitor drivers' hours.

Commissioners may investigate complaints against licensed operators brought by VOSA, the police or other organisations, e.g. concerning breaches of restrictions on vehicle weights, speeds or driver hours. In the case of bus services, non-compliance with the terms of service registration (13.6) is also grounds for investigation. An inquiry may be held to adjudicate on the situation and, if a complaint is upheld, result in fines, an alteration to the conditions of a licence or, in the extreme, its removal altogether.

13.3 Competition in the transport industries

The shift to a predominantly 'deregulated' regime for transport industries (as far as quantity and price are concerned) is based on the presumption that the incentives and strictures of a free market will deliver services more in line with consumer preferences.

In practice however, even where privatisation and deregulation have been introduced, the structure of the industry and/or the behaviour of individual companies may have the effect of inhibiting competition. This is not a situation unique to transport, and a body of general competition legislation has been developed to safeguard and promote it. However public passenger transport has certain special features which renders open competition problematic. This has led to elements of regulation and other forms of intervention being retained which do not sit easily in a more general business environment predicated on competition.

In practice there is no such thing as perfect or optimum regulation. The relevant question is always whether an imperfect system of regulation will achieve a better outcome than an imperfect, less regulated market over a long period of time.

(Glaister et al. 1998 p. 228)

The promotion and protection of consumer interests generally is carried out by the Office of Fair Trading (OFT) which can take enforcement action under the 1998 Competition Act. Its work is complemented by the Competition Commission which undertakes inquiries into the workings of particular markets. The OFT has no direct concern with substantive outcomes in transport or anything else (provided these are a product of genuine competition). If these outcomes conflict with some other aspect of the 'public interest' then it is for the Government, or industry-specific regulators to take appropriate action.

The OFT cannot ensure that competition *does* take place in a particular market but rather that the conditions exist where it can. This has three important ramifications:

• for the structure of the industry concerned
• for the behaviour of operators within the industry
• for the behaviour of regulators and other public bodies in their relationship with the industry.

The structure of passenger transport industries

In principle competition requires there to be a number of suppliers in a market without any one acquiring a dominant position such that it can exert a controlling influence. Alternatively where in practice there is only a limited number – possibly a single supplier – then competition should still be possible, i.e. there should be no insuperable barriers to entry into the market by new suppliers. In Great Britain at the present time the majority of road passenger services are run by five major companies. In theory competition prevails between them and any further merger would almost certainly prompt an investigation by the Competition Commission.

In many parts of the country however one or other of these companies enjoys a 'territorial monopoly' by virtue of its ownership of the garaging facilities and associated vehicle fleets based in the larger towns. (There may be additional independent companies in each case but these typically operate on a small scale on minor routes or in more rural areas.) In practice it would be very difficult for another company to break into such territories and mount a significant competitive challenge.

This situation is a very long way from the textbook version of competition envisaged in the 1984 *Buses* White Paper (DTp 1984). Ironically however from a passenger perspective the stability which now characterises local bus services is much preferable to the 'bus wars' which afflicted some towns in the early years following deregulation. A pragmatic compromise prevails, sustained by the major companies not exploiting situations where they enjoy dominant positions (e.g. by adopting differential fare levels). Such practices exist on a modest scale but are kept in check by commercial self-interest for the longer term as well as the threat of potential OFT investigation.

In the rail passenger industry (and buses in London) the introduction of franchising arrangements rather than full deregulation means that competition is 'for' the market rather than 'in' it. Instead of companies competing on a day-to-day basis through the provision of services, they compete only intermittently for the award of a franchise to run services. Once an award is made the successful company typically enjoys a territorial monopoly on the routes concerned but consumer protection is achieved through the terms of the franchise.

Although bus and train companies compete amongst themselves they are of course operating in a much bigger passenger travel market dominated by the use of the private car. This is a further constraint on possible exploitation of local monopolies. The significance of a wider market is illustrated by long-distance coach services which operate under no regulatory regime as far as quantity or price are concerned and yet are provided almost exclusively by single companies (National Express in England and CityLink in Scotland), although in this case the competition is primarily with rail.

The behaviour of operators

Operators within a particular industry are subject to two important constraints as far as anti-competitive behaviour is concerned. The first outlaws collusion unless formal agreements are registered with OFT. The second outlaws predatory practices.

'Collusion' between suppliers is rightly proscribed where this limits competition to the detriment of consumers. As a general principle the OFT expounds the virtues of choice. However whereas this has obvious relevance in terms of goods on sale in the High Street it is very questionable in the context of public transport. Most passengers do not wait at bus stops contemplating the merits of the rival company services on offer. Rather they are concerned with the overall standard of service available for their journey, including opportunities for interchange and inter-available ticketing. Yet any arrangement between operators to co-ordinate services in such ways is in principle deemed anti-competitive. As we will see below, some attempts have been made to overcome these anomalies in the form of legal 'exemptions', but the fundamental stumbling block remains.

'Predatory practice' is another term which has peculiar interpretation in relation to the bus industry. One company may choose to time its services on a route just in front of another's (with the intention of creaming off its patronage), or to duplicate a bus route where patronage has been built up over years through careful investment by the established operator. Such actions are not deemed predatory even though they may weaken the position of the incumbent without adding anything to the quality of service overall. Fortunately, with the greater stability in the industry, such practices are rarer than previously, although legally they are still possible.

In theory the charge of predatory practice could be brought against an operator who tries to force a competitor out of business (or off his patch) by utilising methods which cannot be sustained commercially. A notorious example of this occurred in Darlington where Stagecoach literally set out to take over the town and bankrupted the local company in a matter of weeks. In practice the speed with which this occurred completely outstripped the ability of OFT to intervene to prevent it.

The behaviour of regulators and other public bodies

The principle of fair competition also applies to the behaviour of regulators and of other public bodies in their dealings with companies. The role of regulators is as umpires of a game, and to enjoy the confidence of its players independence is essential. This implies that no preference can be given to the interests of any party, especially Government, beyond that which is established in law. Their decisions may therefore be politically inconvenient or embarrassing. One example was the Rail Regulator's decision in favour of an 'open access' operator utilising an available track slot on the East Coast Main Line (providing a direct service to London from places which otherwise did not have it) rather than giving an extra slot to the then franchise-holder GNER. The decision removed an opportunity for GNER to generate additional revenue and meant a significant shortfall in the planned premium payment received by the Treasury.

In awarding rail passenger franchises (DfT), London bus service licenses (TfL) or tendered bus service contracts (PTEs and local authorities), these public bodies have to provide for fair competition between bidders. This means that the service levels being sought (and any associated features such as vehicle standards) have to be clearly specified in a way that does not discriminate against any particular bidder and are not a matter for private negotiation.

13.4 Rail regulation

The regulatory arrangements under which the national railway network operates remain basically the same as when it was privatised, although the policy context in which they function has altered radically.

The Office of the Rail Regulator (ORR) is a non-departmental public body with Board members appointed by the Secretary of State DfT. It was established to regulate companies within the privatised railways industry and in particular the owner of the national network infrastructure (now Network Rail) which has a monopoly position. Except for this all other parts of the industry were broken up and expected to operate in competition.

Under the Railways Act 1993 ORR's main functions are:

- to licence network providers (primarily Network Rail), train and station operators and to monitor compliance with the terms of these licences
- to determine the access charges payable for use of network facilities
- to issue directions on proposals for access to network facilities
- to promote the efficient functioning of the railway (e.g. through the development of model clauses for inclusion in contracts within the industry).

To these original responsibilities have been added:

- to promote and monitor compliance with health and safety standards (formerly undertaken by the Railways Inspectorate within the Health and Safety Executive)
- to evaluate applications for closure of lines, stations or passenger services.

Although ORR is required to 'contribute to the achievement of sustainable development' and to 'have regard to the effects on the environment of railway activities' it is important to recognise that rail regulation itself was not conceived as part of what would now be termed a 'sustainable transport strategy' (Shaw and Farrington 2003). Action to this end only came about later under New Labour with the establishment of the Strategic Rail Authority (SRA).

To ensure provision for 'minimum passenger requirements', franchises are let through government-funded contracts. In England these are now let by DfT. The franchise for services in Scotland is determined by the Scottish Executive and in Wales by the Welsh Assembly jointly with DfT. Responsibility for franchising the 'Merseyrail Electrics' and the North London line group of local services has been devolved to Merseytravel (Merseyside PTE) and TfL respectively. Franchised operators are able to offer commercial services above the minimum specified but have to abide by requirements in respect of regulated fares (15.5), through ticketing and inter-operator ticketing availability on shared routes.

Within the overarching framework of regulation the consequences of the fragmentation introduced to bring about competition within the rail industry remain profound. Unlike the situation in the bus industry (where an operator is essentially a free agent able to deploy vehicles and run services as he thinks best) no train service can run without the agreement of at least three parties (the operator, Network Rail and the Rail Regulator). If there are implications for franchised services then the assent of relevant funding bodies will also be required. A change in service pattern involving the deployment of new or reassigned stock or alterations to track or signalling is likely to require the additional involvement of train leasing companies and other train operators. Every change has to be formalised in contracts between all the parties, and since every organisation has a sectional interest to protect, progress can be extremely slow and difficult.

Arrangements for the issuing of franchises have undergone a roller-coaster ride during their relatively short period of existence. Most of the franchises issued at the time of privatisation were for about seven years. However in the aftermath of the Hatfield crash a holding operation had to be mounted with the initial franchises extended by a year or two operating on a 'cost-plus' basis set by the SRA.

Even before Hatfield, concern had been growing about capacity and reliability on the network. The limited prospects for infrastructure enhancement meant that it was essential to put existing capacity to best use. Far from the original vision of a free-for-all of operators competing for track paths, the way forward was seen to lie instead in detailed planning and service delivery under a unified operating regime wherever practicable. A series of 'route utilisation studies' were undertaken by the SRA and their results used as the basis of the service specifications set for the second round of franchises.

The revised pattern to emerge from the protracted second round of franchises is shown in Table 13.1. Further details on the financial aspects of rail franchising are given in section 15.5, whilst changes arising from the 2005 Railways Act are reported in section 23.5.

13.5 Regulation of bus and coach services

The deregulation of bus and coach services

Long-distance coaches were exempted from the requirement to obtain road service licences under the 1980 Transport Act and regulation of fares on bus services was removed at the same time. Other than these and some very minor experiments in liberalisation within 'trial areas' there was no experience on which to base the wholesale deregulation of bus services. This was introduced under the 1985 Transport Act with 'D-day' itself occurring in October 1986. Both the principle of deregulation and the sweeping manner in which it was introduced were highly controversial. Although the moribund state of much of the publicly owned bus industry and its attendant operating inefficiencies invited reform, the scale and nature of the changes threatened to throw the baby out with the bath water.

The Act applied to all 'local bus services' outside London, defined as services carrying passengers at separate fares between stops less than 15 miles apart. Operators were merely required to 'register' with the Area Traffic Commissioner the route and

Table 13.1   Rail passenger franchises

Franchise	London terminus	From	
Long distance			
East Coast Main Line (ECML)	Kings Cross	West Yorkshire, NE England, Scotland	
Greater Western	Paddington	S Wales, SW England, Thames Valley	Includes all local services
Cross Country	[Via Birmingham]	Plymouth/ Bournemouth– Manchester/ Edinburgh	
West Coast Main Line (WCML)	Euston	West Midlands, NW England, Glasgow	
Regional to/from London			
Capital Connect	Faringdon (through)	Bedford/Cambridge– Gatwick/Brighton	
One	Liverpool Street	Essex, East Anglia	
C2C	Fenchurch Street	Southend	
South Eastern	Charing X/Victoria	Kent*	
Southern	Victoria/London Br	Sussex	
South West	Waterloo	Surrey/Hampshire	
Chiltern	Marylebone	Bucks/Warwickshire	
London Midland	Euston	West Midlands	Inc. outer suburban services to/from Euston on WCML
East Midlands	St Pancras	East Midlands	Inc. main line services between London and Sheffield/Nottingham
Other regional			
Trans-Pennine		NE England and Yorkshire to NW England	Express services
Northern		Local services within above	
Scotrail		Services within Scotland	
Wales & Border		Services within and bordering Wales	

Note: Additional smaller franchises include Merseyrail (within Liverpool conurbation), North London and Isle of Wight

* High-speed services from East Kent into London St Pancras via CTRL to be franchised separately

timing of services they intended to run commercially (i.e. without subsidy). After D-day only 42 days notice had to be given of any change to registered services (including additions and withdrawals). Fares were a matter of commercial discretion and public authorities lost the ability to subsidise them.

Registration was and remains automatic – there are no public-interest criteria applied as far as service patterns are concerned and there are no powers available to modify directly whatever operators propose. The only exception is that the Commissioners can attach Traffic Regulation Conditions concerning route or stopping arrangements if objections are raised by the police or highway authorities on the grounds of safety or traffic congestion. In theory operators could be sanctioned if they proved not to be running services reliably and punctually in accordance with registrations but neither the Traffic Commissioners nor local authorities have had the resources to monitor conditions comprehensively.

The *Buses* White Paper was unequivocal about the benefits which would flow from the competition created by the combination of deregulation and privatisation:

> The legislation will make major changes to arrangements for the bus industry so that it is set free to give a better service to the passenger at less cost to the ratepayer and taxpayer.
>
> (DTp 1984 para 1.13)

In practice the outcome was much more mixed. Certainly the profit motive and exposure to competition had the effect of driving down unit costs (Glaister et al. 2006 chapter 7). These economies together with more efficiently designed routes and schedules enabled about 85% of previous services to be registered commercially. Comparatively few 'gaps' (other than in rural areas) were therefore left for local authorities to fill by competitive tendering for 'socially necessary services'.

However despite additional bus mileage being operated, in total the hoped-for gains in patronage did not materialise – in fact the reverse. The haemorrhaging of passengers was particularly serious in the metropolitan areas where the removal of subsidy resulted in an initial hike in real fares of more than 20%. In addition wasteful competition on profitable routes, loss of co-ordinated ticketing and information and confusion arising from frequent service changes were further negative influences.

London escaped the 1985 Act largely because of an accident of timing, since the Government had recently taken control of London Transport from the GLC and was already embarked on a different plan. A combination of route franchising and the break-up and sale of London Transport Buses was pursued instead. Unintentionally a live experiment in contrasting regulatory regimes was thereby set in motion (Preston 2003).

Not only was the London model very different in kind (based on a planned network with control of services, fares and ticketing) it was also introduced incrementally over a 10-year period. Until the late 1990s London experienced similar increases in bus mileage and real fares as the metropolitan areas but in a co-ordinated manner. The outcomes for patronage were strikingly different (Figure 13.1). Although there are special factors at work in London (e.g. its much higher proportion of tourists) the scale of the difference has provided ready ammunition for those arguing in favour of introducing a similar regulatory model elsewhere.

Partnerships

Prior to the 1997 election the Labour Party was proposing re-regulation of some kind, but once in government rejected this in favour of the more business-friendly model of voluntary partnerships which had already been established in some places (DETR 1999b).

'Quality Partnerships' (QPs) are agreements between one or more operators and a local transport authority designed to bring about complementary investment

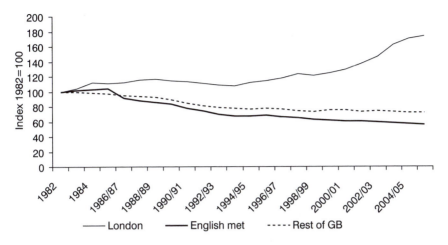

Figure 13.1 Bus passenger journeys in London and other areas 1982–2005

– typically in new vehicles by operators and in passenger facilities and bus priority traffic management measures by authorities. Joint investment in real-time information systems is also becoming more common, with operators and authorities providing on- and off-bus equipment respectively. To encourage a pro-active approach by local authorities towards improving bus services the new system of Local Transport Plans required statutory inclusion of a Bus Strategy under the Transport Act 2000. The Act also included a number of clauses which attempted to remedy some incidental, but not insignificant, adverse features of the 1985 Act regime (Box 13.1).

As a sop to the PTAs, the 2000 Act included powers for local authorities to propose Quality Contracts (QCs) within a defined area where, unless a service was specifically excluded, the normal registration arrangements would be replaced by comprehensive service contracts specified by the local transport authority (i.e. similar to the London model). However QCs were only to be contemplated as a last resort – where all other means of achieving desired outcomes (e.g. via Quality Partnerships) had been shown to be impracticable. This killer clause was accompanied by a very convoluted application procedure ultimately requiring the approval of the Secretary of State – a combination which resulted in no QCs actually being proposed.

The Act also contained clauses which enabled individual QPs to be made statutory. This was intended to guard against the risk of 'free riders' but in practice this provision has scarcely been used.

A more significant inhibitor to QPs was the fact that neither service levels nor fares could be included in the agreements. This made many authorities reluctant to invest in them, since there was no means of guaranteeing what the service outcome would be. Some authorities also object in principle to the idea of taxpayers' money being used as they see it to enable commercial operators to cream off extra profits (given that they could be expected to invest in new vehicles anyway). The converse also applies, i.e. that operators are only likely to commit investment in places which offer the prospect of a good financial return. An added complication in the conurbations is that the PTAs seeking to promote bus use are not highway authorities and therefore cannot guarantee the participation of metropolitan councils necessary to deliver traffic management measures.

Box 13.1 Changes relevant to provision of bus services within the Transport Act 2000

Local transport authorities are required to:

- prepare a Bus Strategy as part of the Local Transport Plan containing policies as to how best to carry out their functions to secure the provision of appropriate bus services in their area
- determine what local bus information should be made available and how, and to seek to arrange with operators for its provision.

Local transport authorities are empowered to:

- establish joint ticketing schemes (i.e. providing for inter-operator availability of tickets and travelcards) and to require operators to participate in them
- recover from operators the costs of providing information if satisfactory provision is not made by the operators themselves
- subsidise public transport services having regard to the interests of public and operators, rather than being constrained by the previous requirement to act 'so as not to inhibit competition'.

Local transport authorities were also empowered to set up statutory Quality Partnership and Quality Contract schemes [see text] although in practice these provisions were almost completely unused.

In exercising the above powers authorities are exempted from the Competition Act provided that their actions fulfil the criteria of a specified 'competition test' which include that the effect on competition is proportionate to the achievement of their intended purpose. [The OFT can give directions and provides guidance on compliance with this test – see 'Guidance on the Competition Test' OFT 2003.]

All in all, therefore, QPs are far from plain sailing. They tend to materialise in places where prospects are favourable anyway and not otherwise. This accounts for the patronage growth achieved in places such as Oxford, Brighton and York which are regularly quoted as examples of what can be achieved under the existing regime. But of course these towns are not typical and there are unfortunately many more places which start from the position of extremely low bus use and are caught up in a seemingly unending spiral of decline.

Socially necessary services

When deregulation was introduced, the task facing local transport authorities in contracting socially necessary services was very difficult. Commercial registrations are made by individual operators on a route-by-route basis with possible variations by section of route, hour of day and day of week. Putting them altogether to discover what service gaps might be left in an area of the size of the metropolitan areas or the more urbanised counties was an immense undertaking. Tenders for individual services then had to be designed and contracts awarded and, if possible, timetables prepared which showed the combination of commercial and tendered journeys along a route (sometimes run by different operators).

The scale of this problem reduced once the turbulence of the initial post-deregulation period died down. In essence however the problem is still present and can be triggered for example by an operator's sudden decision to de-register particular services or journeys. Not only do travel opportunities have to be maintained in a physical sense but the public needs to be informed of forthcoming changes so that they retain the confidence to continue using the service.

To alleviate these difficulties the Bus Partnership Forum published a Code of Conduct on Service Stability in 2003 which encourages the practice of limiting the number of dates in a year on which service changes can take place. It also sets out model timetables for the exchange of information about changes in registrations and tendered services between individual operators and a local transport authority on an 'in confidence basis' well before the formal notice period (now extended to eight weeks).

There is no statutory definition or official guidance as to what constitutes a 'socially necessary service' and hence no minimum standard which any type of settlement or neighbourhood can expect to receive. Authorities typically establish their own criteria although these will only be expressed in fairly general terms or with added provisos in order to retain a degree of political and financial flexibility.

In practical terms securing additional socially necessary services through separate contracts works best in situations where there are either few gaps to be filled within a particular time period or conversely where there are few, if any, commercial registrations – i.e. typically at either end of the urban–rural spectrum. In the former case authorities can utilise what are known as 'de minimis' provisions which allow them to negotiate contracted services with individual operators (including alterations to commercially registered services) without going through formal competitive tendering procedures.

Where a separate contracted service needs to be provided, the task of designing these has also been eased by replacement of the previous constraint imposed under the 1985 Act 'not to inhibit competition' by a broader public-interest criterion which avoids tortuous routes having to be specified so as not to duplicate commercial services at any point.

In rural areas the task of specifying contracted services is comparatively straightforward where the local authority is starting with something approaching a 'clean slate'. (There are financial and other constraints in such places, but these are separate issues.) Complications can arise nevertheless – for example if a commercial service is registered along a main inter-urban route which the local authority would like to see operated in a particular way to enable contracted services to connect with it to and from surrounding villages and small towns. The Interconnect scheme introduced by Lincolnshire County Council in the Lincoln–Skegness corridor is an excellent example of the scope which exists for such an integrated operation. However this was dependent on the voluntary participation of the commercial operator on the main inter-urban route and the not-insignificant incentive of a special grant from DfT worth £2.8m!

Another example of difficulty designing contracted services arises in areas which can only support a limited bus service overall but where a few 'haphazard' journeys are registered commercially at odd days and times (typically by small operators whose main business lies in running school contract journeys). In this situation it may be difficult for the local transport authority to identify a pattern of journeys which can be operated cost-effectively as subsidised contracts and which, in combination with the commercial journeys, offers a coherent set of travel opportunities overall. To overcome these problems ATCO (the Association of Transport Coordinating Officers) proposed that the draft Local Transport Bill published in 2007 should enable authorities to designate 'Tendered Network Zones' where the majority of services were already operated under contract in which the local authority would take responsibility for planning the network as a whole (LTT 471).

13.6 Taxis and other demand-responsive transport

The local bus services considered in the previous section are defined by their characteristics of a fixed route and journeys operating to a set frequency or timetable. Their provision is confined to corridors and times of day and week when there is a sufficient concentration of passenger demand to enable operation on a commercial basis or under public contract (subject to value-for-money criteria). Complementing this are various forms of demand-responsive transport (DRT) which cater for more individual requirements. Typically these provide a superior (quicker, more convenient, door-to-door) but more expensive service. They also provide a 'fall-back' facility at times or places when little if any other public transport is available (mainly during evenings and nights and generally in more rural areas).

Taxis and private hire vehicles (commonly known as minicabs) operating commercially are the most widespread form of DRT. The principal difference between them is that taxis may be hailed in the street or hired from designated ranks whereas PHVs have to be pre-booked. Perhaps surprisingly taxis and PHVs are used disproportionately by members of lower-income households; they are also used more frequently by disabled people.

The use of taxis and PHVs is not necessarily confined to a single individual or group of people making the same end-to-end journey. Sharing is common (significantly reducing the fare differential relative to buses) but the distinctive feature of taxis and hire cars is that such sharing has to be co-ordinated by the hirer. In this they are different from 'jitney' services operated in some other countries where a driver sets out with one person or group travelling in a certain direction and then plies for additional passengers as he goes along, adjusting his route accordingly.

Taxis are referred to legally as 'hackney carriages' (reflecting their existence long before motor vehicles). Outside London they are licensed by district or unitary councils who have traditionally exercised control over quality, quantity and maximum fares. Only quality licensing is applied to PHVs. Within London the vehicles, drivers and fare tariff of 'black cab' taxis are licensed by the Public Carriage Office under the GLA, but no control has ever been exercised over the number of taxis operating.

Taxis, private hire cars and other forms of DRT may be utilised to meet social needs. In these cases the eligibility of users is determined by the public authority or charitable organisation which arranges the time and route of the journeys and provides all or part of the necessary funding. Examples are journeys arranged by or on behalf of education, social service or health authorities to enable pupils, clients or patients to access their facilities, and 'dial-a-ride' services operated to meet the special needs of elderly or disabled people.

In more rural areas there is an especially wide gulf between the limited availability of bus services on the one hand and the high cost of commercial taxi services on the other. This has led to a plethora of experiments beginning in the 1970s seeking to bridge the gap (Nutley 1990). As a result a number of regulatory changes were introduced in the 1985 Transport Act to facilitate various forms of 'unconventional' service. The current legal position is explained in DfT (2002c) and examples of the various types of service are given in Sloman (2003) and Countryside Agency (2000).

Since 2004 the registration requirements for conventional 'fixed route' bus services have been relaxed, subject to discretion exercised by the Traffic Commissioners. Buses operating on flexible routes between two or more named points at specified times in theory enable a better (or any) public transport service to be offered to a group of villages than would be possible using one or more fixed-route services operating infrequently. (See for example the websites for Wigglybus and Cango services supported by Wiltshire and Hampshire County Councils respectively.) However because of route deviations and variability in timing, more cost-effective vehicle utilisation (passenger journeys per vehicle hour) is not necessarily forthcoming and additional costs are incurred in handling bookings and organising routeings for each bus journey. Most such services are at the margins of viability in terms of public funding and have only come into being through special (and limited term) funding initiatives such as Rural Bus Challenge. The maintenance of these services over the longer term and the potential for 'roll-out' into more general use elsewhere is therefore questionable.

13.7 Community transport

The high cost per passenger journey of running conventional bus, DRT or taxi services in situations of low demand has prompted increasing interest in the development of 'community transport'. This is an umbrella term covering a wide range of services which, as transport modes, includes those described in the previous section. However their distinctive features are that they are run on a 'not-for-profit' basis, utilise volunteers for all or part of their operation and are managed by a local organisation independent of (though possibly receiving financial support from) the local authority.

Formalised community transport has generally derived from – and still consists in large part of – schemes with very humble beginnings linked to the activities of local social and welfare clubs and village associations. At a town or district-wide level however a larger purpose-specific community transport operation may be run, for example by the local CVS (Council for Voluntary Service). The Community Transport Association (cta.org.uk) is a national body which provides information and support to local groups in this specialist area and acts on their behalf in dealings with central government.

The involvement of the State in community transport derives from two main sources. The first, as with passenger transport generally, is a 'passive' interest in public safety and – where payment is involved – retaining a fair competitive environment for the provision of commercial transport services. The second is a pro-active interest in developing community transport to cater for local needs which cannot be met cost-effectively by commercial bus or taxi companies, even operating with public subsidy.

Three forms of community transport are widespread:

- **Community car schemes** – operated by a pool of volunteer drivers using their own private cars catering for pre-arranged journeys by individuals who are unable to use (or do not have the option of) public transport – typically for 'socially necessary' journeys such as to hospitals and other health facilities. Drivers are reimbursed for their expenses, normally on a mileage basis, and passengers may be required to make a contribution. Subject to these conditions no special licensing is required.

- **Group bus services** – non-profit-making organisations can provide a service using minibuses (normally 9–16 passengers) and volunteer drivers for particular social and community groups (typically for outings and dial-a-ride services). A 'section 19' minibus permit is required from the local Traffic Commissioner or other nominated body which attaches conditions as to the vehicle and driver. However no operator's licence or route registration is required. These services are not available to the 'general public' but this does not preclude them being made available to specified categories (e.g. residents of isolated communities who have no other transport option). In the 2007 Local Transport Bill it is proposed that section 19 permits are extended to allow vehicles with less than 9 passenger seats to be used with separate fares charged.
- **Community bus services** – social and community organisations using minibuses and volunteer drivers can run local bus services for the general public which complement existing services or provide one where no other exists. A 'section 22' permit is needed from the local Traffic Commissioner and registration of the route and journeys is required, but no operator's licence. In response to lobbying by the CTA over many years the 2007 Local Transport Bill includes amendments allowing these services to be driven by paid staff and to be operated by vehicles with more than 16 seats.

The skills and knowledge required to operate successful community transport (including the ability to identify and sustain appropriate funding) mean that it is evolving as a professional activity in its own right. Interesting recent developments include the growth of 'social enterprise' organisations operating in a more business-like, entrepreneurial manner (LTT 437).

Another is the development of 'brokerage' services, i.e. concerned not with the operation of transport itself but rather the procurement and co-ordination of services run by others.

Overall there has been an enormous growth in community transport over the last 30 years. However the situation in rural areas (where community transport fulfils a more prominent role in catering for general transport needs) remains problematic. This is partly because of the inherent unpredictability and instability surrounding organisations dependent on voluntary workers and uncertain sources of funding. There is also the conundrum that the places where such organisations exist and the services they provide are not necessarily the ones where they are most needed – there are likely to be 'gaps' by place, time and purpose which no one has the resources (or even the locus of interest) to fill.

This situation arises because – taken as a whole – the regulatory framework for road passenger services has developed in terms of separate modes (bus, DRT, taxi) and separate operating regimes (commercial, contracted, and non-profit-making). This framework creates a series of envelopes within which each is permitted or required to function but what actually materialises in terms of the overall pattern of services in any area is entirely unpredictable. It is not merely the 'rural transport problem' which is intractable but the difficulty of contriving an appropriate institutional framework to address it (Headicar 2004).

14 Policy instruments (3)

The regulation of traffic and development

14.1 Introduction

In this chapter we deal with the *physical* regulatory instruments which are available for influencing traffic conditions on individual parts of the highway network. In some cases control over the traffic using a particular road may be applied solely to reflect its own characteristics (e.g. a limit on vehicle weight or dimensions because of a sub-standard bridge). In others the controls applied to individual roads are conceived as part of a strategy for managing traffic over a wider area.

More ambitiously physical measures may be used in conjunction with fiscal instruments (notably the pricing of parking) and the provision of alternatives to car use as a means of limiting the total amount of traffic within an area, i.e. as part of local strategies of demand management (May et al. 2006; Marsden 2006). These apply in many larger town centres but can also be used on a permanent or temporary basis to deal with excessive traffic in the vicinity of other major attractors – e.g. hospitals and universities, tourist hotspots, sporting venues and so on.

Although individual highway authorities exercise discretion over exactly where, when and how to introduce traffic regulation measures in their area, they do so within the context of national legislation and DfT guidance as to both the objectives to be pursued and the precise nature of the instruments to be employed. In particular, signage is standardised. More generally a degree of consistency is sought so that, broadly speaking, motorists can expect to experience similar measures in similar situations, regardless of where in the country they happen to be.

Safeguarding traffic and associated safety and environmental conditions in an area is not solely a matter of regulating the vehicles passing through it. Another important dimension is the traffic generated by the land uses and development within the area itself – both the overall volume and timing of demand and the particular amount and type of traffic drawn or discharged on to individual streets. Problems arising from established developments can only be addressed, if at all, through voluntary negotiation and travel plans (Chapter 16) but with new proposals highway authorities have the opportunity to influence outcomes through the development planning and control processes.

In this chapter we consider first the changing role of traffic management (14.2) and the basic framework of responsibilities and powers under which it is executed (14.3), including the more recent concept of network management (14.4). We then go on to examine in more detail the arrangements surrounding the control of on-street parking (14.5), speed limits and their enforcement (14.6) traffic calming and street management (14.7) and air quality management (14.8). Finally we review the opportunities available to influence traffic conditions through the regulation of development, including private off-street parking (14.9).

14.2 The changing role of traffic management

'Traffic management' began as a set of techniques used independently of one another to address problems at particular points on the highway network – establishing priorities at junctions and introducing traffic lights, pedestrian crossings, parking restrictions, one-way streets and so on. As noted in Chapter 5 a major advance took place in the 1960s in its role in accommodating growing volumes of traffic within urban areas more generally, particularly in town centres. Comprehensive schemes were implemented in congested localities comprising a combination of measures designed to 'get the best' out of the existing road system in advance of major road-building. The control of on-street parking was a central feature of such schemes.

Rather than simply address a succession of localised problems, the Traffic in Towns Report (MOT and MHLG 1963) identified a broader vision within which traffic management measures should be designed. This offered the potential to bring about a hierarchical pattern of traffic movement in an area which reflected the suitability of individual streets to accommodate it rather than merely respond to the pattern which occurred spontaneously or which derived from the routes which had been used historically by through traffic. (The current application of a hierarchical approach to the planning and management of urban networks is explained in section 11.7 of IHT 1997.)

The difficulty with seeking to apply this approach in many older urban areas is the fact that there are few if any roads built to modern design standards (with little or no frontage access) on to which the main flows of traffic can be redirected. In rural areas too, calls by villagers for action to deter 'rat-running' by through traffic have to be set against the fact that classified B and minor A roads in the vicinity are often little better in their suitability to accommodate heavy traffic. In both urban and rural areas therefore the issue of traffic management across a network quickly raises controversial questions about the distribution of benefits and disbenefits – of gainers and losers – not only in terms of safety and environment but also of motorists' convenience of access and through movement. It is for these reasons that in places where it is not practicable or acceptable to alleviate problems by the redistribution of traffic the application of traffic calming techniques has increasingly been followed instead (see 14.7).

The extent and sophistication of traffic management schemes was subsequently extended through the linking of traffic signals according to predetermined programmes appropriate to traffic conditions at different times of day (Urban Traffic Control). These in turn have been superseded by Intelligent Systems governing traffic movements across whole networks in real time. Likewise the control of parking has extended from relatively narrow concerns about safety and obstruction at particular locations to comprehensive strategies embracing both on- and off-street facilities across wide areas, and concerned as much with the volume and type of traffic which is generated by the available facilities as with the physical manner in which provision for parking and loading is made. An important dimension of more modern traffic management schemes has been their inclusion of public transport priorities, whether this is in the amount of 'green time' allocated to roads which function as main routes or to the timing of signals at individual junctions in order to respond to approaching buses or trams.

In addition to the control of traffic through enforceable regulations indicated by static road signs, electronic 'variable message' information has been introduced to help motorists respond appropriately to changing conditions. Advisory signs at the roadside or on overhead gantries can give notice about the availability of parking spaces within town centres for example or on major routes to give advance warning of adverse weather or traffic conditions. Comparable information on recommended routeings and traffic incidents is also now offered in-vehicle by commercial suppliers.

Variable message signs which are adjusted in response to prevailing traffic conditions are also being used to introduce mandatory speed limits on congested motorways. (These enable improved safety and throughput to be achieved by standardising vehicle speeds at lower levels than would otherwise nominally apply.) As we shall see, having broadly achieved all that can be done by 'fixed' management techniques, attention is turning increasingly to the potential offered by 'active' traffic management. This involves the monitoring of conditions in real time and the adaptation of management strategies accordingly, particular so as to deal with roadworks, collisions and other out-of-course events which can have a disproportionate impact on traffic conditions across a wide area.

14.3 Traffic management: responsibilities and powers

Irrespective of any management measures introduced on individual roads it is the responsibility of motorists to drive and park appropriately at all times having regard to prevailing circumstances (e.g. weather, volume and speed of traffic). The Highway Code, first published in 1931, is a compendium of good practice (including such rudimentary advice as driving on the left!). Although failure to comply with the Code is not an offence in itself, it may be quoted by police authorities in bringing charges, for example of dangerous driving or of causing an obstruction.

Although it is for traffic authorities (broadly local highway authorities and the Highways Agency) to propose and implement traffic regulations on the roads for which they are responsible, it is the police who act as the enforcement agency. (There are some exceptions to this in relation to on-street parking which we explain later.) The role of police authorities (which are separate from local authorities and which report directly to the Home Office) is critical in two major respects. First, during consultation by traffic authorities the views of the police (e.g. concerning the practicability of enforcement) will typically have over-riding importance in determining whether an initiative goes ahead and, if so, in what form. Second, after implementation, its *actual* enforcement will depend on the attitude and priorities of the local police force (which may well differ from residents and councillors). Because of the vast number of individual regulations now in being it is essential that measures are likely to be respected by motorists so that they are, or can be made to be, effectively self-enforcing.

Formally, traffic authorities operate under the Road Traffic Regulation Act 1984 which places a duty on them to secure the expeditious, convenient and safe movement of vehicular and other traffic and the provision of suitable and adequate parking facilities both on and off the highway. Direction signs and certain rudimentary regulations such as 'stop', 'give way' and yellow box junction marking can be introduced in accordance with technical guidelines but more exceptional interventions can only be made through the use of Traffic Regulation Orders (TROs) which impose controls on the speed, movement or parking of vehicles. The making of orders has to follow set procedures which involve consultation, advertisement and the consideration of objections. A public inquiry may, and in certain cases (such as following an objection by a local bus operator) must, be held before a decision is made on whether to implement the order, possibly with modifications. If a TRO has the effect of preventing vehicular access to premises for more than 8 hours in any 24 hours and is the subject of an unwithdrawn objection then the approval of the Secretary of State is required.

In situations where the outcome of a proposed scheme is uncertain an authority may introduce an Experimental Order for a period of up to 18 months. This requires consultation to be followed but not the formal advertisement and objection procedures. If however the authority subsequently proposes to make the scheme permanent then these procedures must be followed.

The purposes for which a TRO may be made are very wide-ranging and reflect the interests of different classes of road user, the occupiers of frontage properties, the protection of infrastructure, the character of the area and of air quality (Box 14.1). Of itself the legislation does not determine whether or how streets in a particular area should be managed. The way in which traffic management measures have been applied to a given area has often changed over time, particularly in town and village centres, reflecting different views on relative priorities. In fact many earlier schemes have been modified quite radically as part of recent moves to improve the urban environment and 'reclaim the streets' (see 14.7).

Traffic regulation orders are commonly used to control the presence of all or certain types of traffic within or along individual streets, the turning movements at junctions and the direction of flow along one-way streets, often as part of more comprehensive schemes. (The control of parking and traffic speeds which may be further components are discussed in subsequent sections.)

Orders may be made to prohibit all traffic from using a street (or all motorised traffic – thus allowing cyclists and horse-drawn traffic continued access) either permanently or during specified periods. Permanent pedestrianisation may also be achieved by separate powers under the 1990 Town and Country Planning Act. The prohibition can be confined to certain classes of vehicle specified by weight, width or length or by type. Conversely explicit exemptions may be made for certain types of vehicle, notably

---

Box 14.1 Purposes for which a Traffic Regulation Order may be introduced

- To avoid danger to persons or other traffic using the road or any other road or to prevent the likelihood of such danger arising
- To prevent damage to the road or to any building on or near the road
- To facilitate the passage on the road or any other road of any class of traffic (including pedestrians)
- To prevent the use of the road by vehicular traffic of a kind, or in a manner, which is unsuitable in relation to the character of the road or adjoining property
- To preserve the character of a road where it is specially suitable for use on horseback or on foot
- To preserve or improve the amenities of the area through which the road runs
- In the interests of conserving air quality [added by the 1995 Environment Act].

Source: Road Traffic Regulation Act 1984

buses or for vehicles requiring access to frontage properties. Otherwise a standard set of exemptions is normally applied for emergency and utility vehicles.

Restrictions on turning movements at junctions may need to be imposed in order to complement traffic restrictions operating in the streets to which they give entry. They may also be introduced to alleviate safety or congestion problems at the junction itself. In two-way streets the presence of significant flows of right-turning traffic is particularly problematic. The potential conflict this represents with oncoming traffic is hazardous. This can be alleviated at signal-controlled junctions by the provision of a separate right-turning phase, although usually at the expense of overall traffic capacity. Unless the width of the carriageway allows for a separate lane the presence of queuing right-turning vehicles also reduces the throughput of vehicles travelling straight ahead. This situation may be overcome by banning the right-turn and displacing the turning movement via alternative routes before or after the principal junction instead. Exemptions to the ban are likely to be needed for buses in order to avoid extending route-lengths and bypassing important stopping points.

Conflicts associated with right-turning vehicles are one of the principal reasons for introducing one-way systems in congested urban locations where the nature and configuration of streets is suitable. Instead of a series of prohibited turns, traffic is directed instead to follow a mandatory pattern of movement (using blue arrow signs). One-way systems can achieve better traffic utilisation of available carriageway space but have the disadvantage, partly through higher speeds, of making pedestrian crossing more difficult. Unless special arrangements are made for buses (e.g. by use of contra-flow lanes) these systems are also likely to reduce accessibility to key destinations.

Within streets the marking of the carriageway into separate lanes, although only advisory, is a core feature of contemporary practice. It is especially important at the approaches to intersections in order to segregate the different turning movements and, in conjunction with the phasing of traffic lights, to maximise the traffic throughput and/or to allow opportunities for protected pedestrian crossing or public transport priority movements on other arms of the junction.

Mandatory regulation may restrict certain lanes to particular classes of user, most commonly with-flow bus lanes at the kerbside. Typically these are introduced as a way of enabling buses to bypass other traffic which is queuing back from a congested junction or other restriction on the highway. Bus lanes are normally terminated short of a signalised junction so that the full approach width is available as a reservoir for all traffic to use in the next green phase in the cycle. Signals acting as 'bus gates' can also be used to give buses preferential access into constricted sections of road where continuation of a bus lane is not possible.

In principle it is possible to expand the utilisation of bus lanes by making them available to other classes of vehicle without significantly undermining their prime objective. The most likely additional category (allowed for in some places) is taxis. However because the private hire vehicle variety is virtually indistinguishable from ordinary cars this can create the impression that infringement is taking place, inviting other motorists to follow and thereby causing enforcement problems.

A similar objection might apply to the inclusion of cars with more than one occupant – creating 'high occupancy vehicle' (HOV) lanes. Nevertheless in the interests of improving the economic performance of bus lanes this is an option which highways authorities have been recommended to consider (DfT 2006d). Remarkably (in view of their apparent merits and extensive use in other countries) there have only been three examples of HOV lanes in Britain, the most recent being in conjunction with a 'Park and Share' site on the M606 on the outskirts of Bradford (LTT 403).

14.4 Network management

A combination of growing technological capability, worsening congestion and a changing policy context have expanded the role of management applied to inter-urban as well as urban networks. The arguments were articulated in *Managing our Roads* (DfT 2003a). As both current and prospective conditions deteriorate, especially on the purpose-built motorway and trunk road network, so it becomes more critical to examine ways in which its physical capacity can be maximised. Likewise, because any out-of-course event such as roadworks, collision or vehicle breakdown can rapidly provoke 'gridlock' conditions, it becomes essential to monitor conditions on a minute-by-minute basis and to plan and initiate response measures to minimise the resulting inconvenience and costs incurred.

In relation to the strategic road network the Highways Agency has been charged with developing its role as the 'network operator'. Following a collaborative review with the Association of Chief Police Officers, a series of Regional Control Centres has been established staffed by both police and Agency personnel. These monitor and manage traffic on the network and deploy response teams on the ground. An agreement also provides for the transfer of some traffic management tasks from the police. In support of this the Traffic Management Act 2004 provides for the Agency to establish a uniformed force of 'traffic officers' with powers to stop and direct traffic (currently exercised by the police) in order to assist traffic movement, avoid danger or prevent damage.

The 2004 Act also places a duty on every local traffic authority in England and Wales to manage its road network to secure 'the expeditious movement of traffic' insofar as this is practicable, and having regard to its other obligations and objectives. New powers to regulate streetworks through a permit system are introduced in support of this although, perhaps unsurprisingly, this has been criticised by a representative of the utilities' industries as 'a sledgehammer to crack a nut' (LTT 420).

In fulfilling its duty an authority must, amongst other things, appoint a 'Traffic Manager'. The Secretary of State and the National Assembly for Wales are empowered to issue guidance on the exercise of this duty and to require an authority to provide information in connection with its performance. The Act also goes as far as providing for an Intervention Order enabling the imposition of a 'Traffic Director' in the event of an authority failing to perform its duty satisfactorily.

The strategy to be adopted by an authority was to be spelt out within its second Local Transport Plan (20.5). However a review of these plans revealed a mixed picture:

> there is a variance between those authorities who simply acknowledge the duty and those who have committed themselves and formed strategies to address the duty requirements.
>
> (Halcrow Group 2007)

The respective duties of the Highways Agency and local authorities raises difficult questions about the relationship between the management of 'strategic' and 'local' networks given that in practice motorists use both and can move between either at will. For example the Agency is able to inform motorists that congestion lies ahead on a motorway but does not indicate alternative routes if these would involve using 'local' roads (and hence potentially worsen conditions on them). Similarly the Agency is investigating ramp metering (i.e. introducing signalised controls at motorway access points to ensure that its overall volume of traffic is kept within capacity) but this potentially could create havoc in the management of local networks. A consultation exercise has been initiated between the Highways Agency and local authorities in relation to the north-western part of the M25 (where widening to four lanes commenced in 2008) in an attempt to 'lock in' the benefits of the investment and to link Agency and local authority control systems 'to produce a better net outcome than would otherwise be the case' (LTT 448).

14.5 Control of on-street parking

Traditionally highways have served two main functions – to provide for the passage of traffic and to offer the means of access for servicing adjacent properties. Much development built before the era of statutory planning control lacks provision within the curtilage of the site to accommodate the storage of vehicles and for loading and unloading goods. On-street parking and loading from the kerbside is utilised instead. Kerbside facilities may also be used for parking by visitors, for picking up and setting down passengers and for associated waiting. In residential areas with conventional streets the carriageway typically continues to be used for delivery vehicles and for a proportion of both residents' and visitors' parking.

In streets with an important traffic function or with frontage uses which generate significant numbers of access vehicles kerbside parking may be controlled for one or more of the following main reasons:

• to prevent obstruction (of traffic or access) and to ensure safe operating conditions
• to encourage the use of off-street facilities
• to ration the available on-street space between competing users.

In controlled areas parking is prohibited at and approaching junctions to ensure adequate sightlines, to maximise throughput at signalised intersections and to protect turning opportunities for larger vehicles. All stopping is banned in the vicinity of pedestrian crossings and may be banned at bus stops.

How far remaining kerb-side space is utilised and whether and how it is rationed will depend on the availability of alternative off-street space (public and private) within an area and on local authorities' overall parking strategies. Particularly in commercial centres the total parking provision may deliberately be kept below the potential demand, particularly for long-stay commuter spaces, as a means of limiting the volume of traffic with a central destination and thereby aiding congestion or environmental objectives.

Control of on-street parking is exercised through orders made under the 1984 Road Traffic Regulation Act and subsequent amendments. Waiting may be prohibited along defined sections of road for all or part of specified days of the week and any permitted waiting may be subject to a time limit and/or charge. Additionally restrictions may be placed on kerbside loading and unloading although normally these are for shorter peak periods only in order to minimise inconvenience to local businesses. (These periods may coincide with the operation of a peak-time kerbside bus lane.) The presence of waiting and loading restrictions is indicated by yellow line markings along the edge of the road and at intervals on the kerb respectively. Details are contained on signs affixed to adjacent buildings, lamp-posts or poles.

Areas such as town centres which have a consistent regime of on-street parking restrictions applied throughout may be designated as a Controlled Parking Zone (CPZ). Entry points to the zone are marked with a special sign which indicates the periods in which restrictions apply. This enables a large number of time-plate signs within individual streets to be dispensed with.

More stringent restrictions apply on designated priority (red) routes in London and Birmingham which have a strategic function as traffic and/or bus routes. These prohibit stopping of any kind (other than by buses) either throughout the route or except in designated bays where parking and loading restrictions apply. No-stopping conditions also apply on signed 'clearways' imposed for capacity and/or safety reasons on selected major roads in both urban and rural areas.

Special arrangements are made for the needs of disabled people through operation of a Blue Badge scheme in England and Wales, administered through local authorities. Badges are issued to eligible individuals (not vehicles) and hence may be used by people travelling as drivers or passengers. Authorities making parking orders are required to include exemptions for badge-holders enabling them to park without time limit or charge in bays which have these restrictions and on yellow lines at times when loading and unloading is permitted.

In town centres and around other major attractors where demand for on-street parking exceeds supply, the available space is typically rationed according to the following priorities, working outwards from the area of maximum demand:

- bus stops, other loading and unloading, disabled persons' parking and areas for motorcycles and for bicycle stands
- short-stay parking (with limits of 1–4 hours) supplemented by charging
- short-stay parking, time-limited only
- unlimited time period, though possibly with a restriction before, say, 0930 to prevent use by all-day commuter parking.

Payment is generally by the cash purchase of time-marked tickets in machines at intervals along streets which are then displayed in the parked vehicle ('pay and display'). In Central London kerbside meters alongside individually marked bays have been retained as these provide more readily for the enforcement of very short time-limited periods.

The introduction of controlled zones in town centres results in the displacement of many parked vehicles, especially commuter parking, into adjacent areas. To protect the amenity of these areas, to safeguard the on-street parking requirements of their residents and to encourage the use of park-and-ride and other modes by people travelling to the town centre, successive zones have normally been introduced working outwards from it. These typically incorporate permit schemes for residents which enable them to park in designated bays (sometimes shared with time-limited visitor parking). The number of permits issued may be rationed per dwelling and/or by charge. The issuing of a permit does not entitle the holder to a particular, or indeed any, space. In densely populated inner areas with little if any off-street parking the competition for the available space can have a restraining effect on both car ownership and use – people will be reluctant to use their cars for short trips if they 'lose' their parking space as a result! These are areas where there is clear potential for the development of car clubs which utilise specially reserved parking bays.

In the dynamic and often pressurised circumstances surrounding on-street parking effective enforcement is critical. The progressive extension of controlled areas has been made possible only by the authorisation of enforcement personnel additional to Police officers. This has been achieved by the introduction of decriminalised parking areas under the 1991 Road Traffic Act. In these areas most violations of parking regulations (except those invoking danger or obstruction) cease to be a criminal offence and the power of enforcement is transferred instead to the local traffic authority. Parking attendants working for, or on behalf of, the authority can place parking tickets ('penalty charge notices') on offending vehicles or in appropriate cases authorise them to be wheel-clamped or towed away. Authorities retain the revenues they receive and use them to fund enforcement activities.

14.6 Speed limits

As noted in Chapter 4 the early decades of motoring were marked by fierce debates over the principle of mandatory speed limits. The outcome settled upon – of a 30 mph limit in all built-up areas – has proved remarkably long-lasting. Originally these 'restricted roads' were differentiated from the remainder (i.e. rural roads) where speed was unrestricted, regardless of their character. On leaving built-up areas the round white sign with the black diagonal line is still commonly referred to as the 'de-restriction' sign. In fact, since the 1960s, roads outside built-up areas are subject to a national limit of 60 mph on single carriageways and 70 mph on dual carriageways and motorways. (Lower limits apply to HGVs, coaches and some other classes of vehicle.)

A review conducted for the Government's Road Safety Strategy concluded that

> the 70 mph and 30 mph limits are well established and well understood and there is no case for a blanket change on safety or environmental grounds.
>
> (DETR 2000e para 6.15)

However the national limit on motorways continues to be challenged by some motorist groups quoting amongst other things the improved performance of vehicles and the fact that it is routinely exceeded in practice. (The *average* speed of cars on motorways is only 1 mph less than the legal maximum!) More recent research conducted for the Highways Agency suggests that overall time, fuel and accident costs would be minimised at a speed of 78 mph (TRL 2006). Given that emissions increase above 70 mph and that safety benefits are reduced, the Agency nevertheless argues that target speeds at the current national level remain appropriate (LTT 460).

No signs mark the national limits but signs are required wherever motorists enter or leave sections of road with lower limits. Within the national framework traffic authorities have the discretion to set different ('local') limits where they consider appropriate, taking account of guidance issued by the Department:

> Speed limits are however only one element of speed management. Local speed limits should not be set in isolation. They should be part of a package with other measures to manage speeds which includes engineering and landscaping standards that respect the needs of all road users and raise the driver's awareness of their environment ....

> Indeed, if a speed limit is set in isolation, or is unrealistically low, it is likely
> to be ineffective and lead to disrespect for the limit …. This may also result in
> substantial numbers of drivers continuing to travel at unacceptable speeds, thus
> increasing the risk of collisions and injuries.
>
> (DfT 2006h paras 21 and 22)

In determining appropriate speed limits the aim should therefore be to provide a consistent message between the geometry of a road and its environment and for changes in the limit along a route to reflect changes in these characteristics. Where the basic physical characteristics of the highway suggest a higher speed than is appropriate given its accident record, additional engineering and/or landscaping measures as well as the imposition of a (lower) speed limit will be necessary. The costs of these as well as the effects on traffic capacity and journey times will need to be weighed against the prospective benefits. Only where the requisite engineering measures are impracticable or unsuitable should reliance on camera enforcement be resorted to (see below).

At present within rural areas the vast majority of the network is subject to the national 60 mph limit for single-carriageway roads. However in many cases drivers do not reach this speed because the characteristics of the road make it impractical or unsuitable. Nevertheless almost a half of all serious casualties take place on these roads and excessive traffic speed is a common complaint amongst rural communities. Authorities are therefore encouraged to adopt a two-tier approach to local speed limits based on whether roads have a predominant traffic flow or a local access or recreational function (Table 14.1; also IHT 1999) and are currently required to review the speed limits on all A and B roads in these terms by 2011 (DfT 2007k).

A hierarchical approach is also recommended for use in urban areas to ensure that the speed and other characteristics of traffic on individual roads is appropriate to local circumstances (IHT 2003). The standard limit of 30 mph in built-up areas is the default limit but authorities may impose higher or lower limits in particular places. A higher limit of 40 mph may be appropriate on higher quality main roads in suburban areas or on the outskirts of towns where there is little development and few vulnerable road users. Exceptionally a 50 mph limit may be appropriate for purpose-built dual carriageways such as ring roads or major radials which have little or no frontage development and an absence of non-motorised users.

In places where there is a significant presence of non-motorised users (e.g. shopping streets, residential areas or in the vicinity of schools) consideration should be given to a lower, 20 mph limit. (At an impact of 20 mph a pedestrian has a 95% chance of surviving whereas at 30 mph it is approximately 65% and at 40 mph only 15%.) Limits of 20 mph may either be applied to individual sections of road (except main traffic routes) or to local areas so as to form a 20 mph 'zone' (DETR 1999a). These lower limits are unlikely to be complied with where existing speeds are substantially higher and in these situations it is necessary to complement the lower limit with traffic calming measures so that the arrangement becomes self-enforcing.

Under current arrangements speed cameras cannot be used to aid the enforcement of 20 mph limits. This coupled with the expense and unwanted side-effects of the traffic calming measures needed to create 20 mph zones has led to a revival of debate over whether 20 mph rather than 30 mph should be adopted as the default limit in most residential streets (LTT 480).

Table 14.1 Recommended speed limits for single-carriageway roads in rural areas* (source: Adapted from DfT Circular 01/2006 Appendix D)

Speed limit (mph)	Roads with predominant traffic flow function	Roads with important access or recreation function
60	Most high-quality strategic A and B roads Accident threshold below 35 injury accidents per 100m vehicle km**	Only for best C and unclassified roads with a mixed (partial traffic flow) function In the longer term should be assessed against upper-tier criteria
50	Lower-quality A and B roads with relatively high number of bends, junctions or accesses Accident threshold above 35 injury accidents per 100m vehicle km at higher speeds** Also for consideration where mean speeds are below 50 mph	Lower-quality C and unclassified roads with a mixed function where there are a relatively high number of bends, junctions or accesses Accident threshold below 60 injury accidents per 100m vehicle km**
40	Roads with high number of bends, junctions or accesses, substantial development Where there are strong environmental or landscape factors or presence of vulnerable road users	Roads with predominantly local, access or recreational function, or if part of a recommended route for vulnerable road users Accident threshold above 60 injury accidents per 100m vehicle km**
30	The norm in villages	

* Limits to which traffic authorities are encouraged to move over a period of time, subject to their meeting local needs and considerations.

** When the assessment framework (Appendix E) is being used

Since 1991 police authorities have been able to use photographic evidence uncorroborated by a police officer to bring charges against motorists exceeding the speed limit. The subsequent introduction of speed cameras has provoked prolonged, often hysterical coverage in the national press. Evaluation of the first three years of a national safety camera programme begun in 2000 indicated that the number of vehicles exceeding the speed limit at over 200 fixed camera sites had dropped by 71% (DfT 2004g). At all 2,300 sites monitored there was a 33% reduction in personal injury collisions representing 870 fewer KSI (killed or seriously injured) per year. However although the general impact of cameras in reducing speeds and collisions in their vicinity has been demonstrated, the selectivity employed in choice of sites and other factors makes assessment of their overall effectiveness difficult to determine (LTT 405 and 434).

14.7 Traffic calming and street management

'Traffic calming' is a term used to refer to a collection of mainly engineering techniques which alter the character or appearance of the highway and have the effect of reducing the speed of motor vehicles. These techniques are typically employed to improve safety amongst vulnerable road users, sometimes in combination with local reductions in the speed limit as mentioned in the previous section. They may also be used as part of schemes to discourage through movement by all or certain classes of traffic on minor roads (i.e. to deter 'rat-running') and thereby add to the quality of the local environment.

In spirit, traffic calming is analogous with 'environmental traffic management' which began to be introduced in Britain in the 1960s. However environmental management was limited by what could be achieved through the use of traffic regulations – banning entry to streets for example and utilising opposing one-way streets as a way of slowing traffic and discouraging through movement. These measures can still be utilised (although taken to an extreme they can make access very inconvenient for local traffic) but supplemented by alterations to the highway itself which is the distinctive feature of traffic calming. Alternatively, calming techniques can be used instead (e.g. as a way of reducing speeds without inhibiting access) and are particularly useful in situations where it is not possible to re-route or otherwise reduce the offending traffic flows.

Powers were introduced at the beginning of the 1990s to enable highway authorities to install road humps but these were soon extended to permit a wide variety of physical measures. These include speed cushions and speed tables which generally have a less adverse effect than humps on buses and other larger vehicles. They also include road narrowing (sometimes combined with traffic regulation to indicate a priority direction of flow) or possibly road marking or other surface treatment which has the same psychological effect. At the entry to villages or other built-up areas 'gateway' features can be built which have the effect of registering with drivers that a change is taking place in conditions even if the physical character of the road itself does not alter. In urban areas traffic calming features can often be combined with pedestrian refuges or build-outs at crossing points and with sections of permitted on-street parking, bus and loading bays etc. as part of an overall design for the use of the carriageway. A short description of the various techniques and associated guidance is given in Appendix B of DfT Circular 1/2006.

Given the large number of streets which merit calming treatment the measures authorities adopt are often the minimum necessary to comply with the regulations and to achieve the desired alteration in traffic conditions. However there is increasing recognition that 'damage limitation' from the unwanted effects of traffic is an unduly narrow objective that fails to acknowledge the opportunities available for designing and managing streets as spaces which can make a positive contribution to the quality of life.

For many years attention was focused on shopping streets in town centres using a combination of traffic and environmental measures to create partially or wholly pedestrianised areas. At the other end of the spectrum – in both urban and rural locations where traffic volumes are very low – initiatives have been taken to assert the interests of non-motorised users through a combination of traffic management measures and roadspace treatment. The former Countryside Agency promoted the concept of Quiet Lanes where the roads concerned were a recreational asset for use by walkers, cyclists and horseriders. In urban residential areas the concept of Home Zones extends traffic calming to include measures designed to improve the street environment more generally and to allow for a range of activities other than simply the movement or storage of vehicles. Currently Quiet Lanes and Home Zones can be designated under the Transport Act 2000 which then allows complementary use and speed orders to be introduced.

More ambitiously the objective of 'improving the urban realm' and techniques of street management are being extended to places where significant traffic volumes continue to exist. In this context the traditional priority attached to the interests of moving traffic no longer applies and the division of the highway into 'carriageway' and 'footway' is itself reviewed. The full area of the highway (i.e. the public area between frontage properties) is considered for 'roadspace reallocation' according to the relative importance attached to the needs of its users, i.e. through traffic, buses, cyclists, pedestrians, disabled motorists, parking and loading etc. Different combinations of 'shared space' are also considered. Comprehensive redesign is typically accompanied by a review of street lighting and other elements of 'street furniture' – usually an unco-ordinated and unsightly clutter of signs and installations of utility companies and others which has accumulated over time and which often seriously impedes visibility and pedestrian movement.

Design considerations recommended for both new and remodelled streets (though predominantly the 'easier' residential variety) are set out in DfT (2007g). More comprehensive, though unofficial, guidance on the design of mixed-use urban streets is given in Jones et al. (2007).

14.8 Air quality management

As noted earlier, air quality was added to the list of purposes for which traffic regulation orders can be made as a consequence of the 1995 Environment Act. The obligations which derive from the Act are distinctive in two ways:

1   they are linked directly to a set of obligatory standards (unlike, say, noise where, except in the case of new highway works, action by local highway authorities is entirely discretionary)
2   these standards are derived from an EU directive (even though the impacts are local in nature unlike, say, greenhouse gas emissions which are of international significance).

Because of these obligations a set of procedures has been developed which is unique in the field of traffic management. This is not because the instruments employed are very different from those used to fulfil other objectives (although there are one or two distinctive features) but because their application is undertaken in a much more comprehensive and systematic manner.

Under Part IV of the Act. metropolitan and other unitary authorities as well as district councils in two-tier areas in England are required to carry out regular reviews and assessments of air quality in their areas. These are conducted in the context of the prevailing national Air Quality Strategy (and in London according to the Air Quality Strategy which the Mayor is required to prepare) and in terms of standards prescribed in regulations made under the Act. (The standards set are for the seven pollutants shown previously in Figure 3.8). The standards for the individual pollutants differ in the time period over which concentrations are measured, e.g .as between hourly, daily and annual means (Defra 2008a Table 1). In practice concentrations vary according to local climatic conditions as well as variations in emissions from the relevant sources, notably motorised traffic. For nitrogen oxide, particles (PM10) and sulphur dioxide there are standards for more than one time period, with maximum levels set at higher levels for the shorter time periods. In the most recent national strategy. standards have been revised to focus on an 'exposure reduction' approach which is considered to be a more cost-effective way of delivering improved public health (LTT 441).

Since 2003 authorities have been required to carry out their duties in accordance with published guidance. Separate policy and technical guidance was published in that year (Defra 2003a/b) and an updated version has recently been published for consultation (Defra 2008a). The Review and Assessment process is conducted in three-yearly cycles, the immediate one being 2009-11. In the first year all authorities are required to undertake an Updating and Screening Assessment whose purpose is to identify locations where there is a risk of an air quality objective being exceeded. (These 'locations' are places outside buildings or other structures where members of the public are regularly present.). During the second year, a Detailed Assessment is undertaken at the vulnerable locations to establish whether a new Air Quality Management Area (AQMA) is needed or an existing Area amended.

AQMAs have to be designated by an official order following consultation involving, amongst others, the county council as highways authority in two-tier areas. Authorities then have to follow this with a remedial Action Plan (again subject to consultation) and subsequent Progress Reports. (The prescribed content of such Plans is shown in Box 14.2.) These documents have to be submitted to Defra or the Mayor of London who may challenge their findings and, in the extreme, initiate remedial action themselves.

Road traffic accounts for over half the total emissions of nitrogen oxides and particles (PM10) and around 95% of the AQMAs designated thus far are primarily transport related. The Government therefore strongly recommends that, where transport is the primary factor, Air Quality Action Plans should be integrated with the Local Transport Plan (LTP) for their area (LIP within London). Indeed for a brief period the Government proposed to remove the need for authorities to prepare separate air quality reports (Defra 2005) with them being incorporated in the relevant LTP and associated Annual Progress Reports instead. (Air quality was one of the 'shared objectives' adopted for LTP2s – see 20.6.) However these reporting arrangements have since been abandoned and air quality is now recognised as a suitable subject on which neighbouring authorities may work together within the framework of new Local Area Agreements (19.8). In this

---

Box 14.2 The Content of Air Quality Action Plans

- Quantification of the source contributions to the predicted exceedences of the Objectives
- Evidence that all available options have been considered on the grounds of cost-effectiveness and feasibility
- How the local authority will use its powers and work in conjunction with other organisations in pursuit of the objectives*
- Clear timescales for proposed implementation of measures in the Plan
- Where possible, quantification of the expected impacts of the proposed measures and an indication of whether the measures will be sufficient to meet the objectives
- How the local authority intends to monitor and evaluate the effectiveness of the Plan.

Source: Defra 2008a para 4.2

*If the Action Plan includes conditions which will influence a Development Plan (e.g. require or preclude certain projects at certain locations) then a Strategic Environmental Assessment is required (21.8)

context authorities are encouraged to prepare local air quality strategies in a multi-disciplinary manner which

- outline the management structure for delivering air quality improvements
- identify the groups which will be engaged in consultation, e.g. organisations represented in the Local Strategic Partnership (19.7)
- agree on the integration of functions such as transport planning, land use planning and air quality action planning (Defra 2008a para 2.5)

The guidance reviews the various transport-related measures which local authorities can implement to improve air quality. These include many types of traffic management considered previously in this chapter, viz the regulation of traffic or particular types of vehicle, traffic control systems, speed limits, traffic calming, the restriction of access into certain areas and complementary measures such as parking controls. Additional measures include powers for local authorities (on application to the Secretary of State) to conduct roadside vehicle emissions testing and DFT sponsored programmes to promote the availability and use of clean fuels, particularly amongst organisations' vehicle fleets. Conditions on vehicle usage may also form part of s106 agreements negotiated as part of granting planning permission for development (ODPM 2004c).

The various measures may be used selectively in combination to bring about a Low Emission Zone (LEZ) which is 'a geographically defined area where the most polluting of vehicles are restricted, deterred or discouraged from access and use'. LEZs tend to be focused on town or city centres where land use is dense, traffic is heavy and population exposure is high. The most common vehicles to target are diesel powered Heavy Duty Vehicles due to their cost-effectiveness relative to schemes that would restrict other vehicle types. The most significant scheme to date in the UK is the London LEZ which from July 2008 required that all heavy duty vehicles achieve at least Euro III standards for PM10.

> Given constraints on revenue budgets a scheme which has low operating costs will tend to be more attractive from a whole-life cost viewpoint. However this needs to be carefully balanced against the resulting level of compliance by users with the scheme emission standards, or the purpose and value of the scheme is undermined.
> (Defra 2008b)

14.9 Control of development (including private off-street parking)

The amount and type of traffic in an area, away from the main through traffic routes, is predominantly a function of its land use characteristics. Hence the number of trips arising from a proposed development (whether as a generator or attractor) and their impact on local traffic and environmental conditions is one of the principal factors considered by local authorities in determining applications for planning permission.

In areas of two-tier local government the district council (which determines these applications) is required to notify and take into account the observations made by the county council as local highway authority. In situations where development affects conditions on a trunk road the planning authority is required to notify the Highways Agency, although in this case the Agency is able to issue directions which the authority has to abide by. A planning authority may approve or refuse an application or – more usually – approve it subject to specified conditions being met. (Legal enforcement action may be taken against development which does not conform with a planning permission.) A developer who is aggrieved by an authority's decision and who believes he has grounds for challenging it may appeal to the Secretary of State (DCLG), but at the risk of having costs awarded against him in the event of the appeal being dismissed.

This is a bald statement of the legal position but in practice, in connection with a development of any significance, there will usually be a period of discussion and negotiation prior to the submission of an application between the applicant, the planning authority and other interested parties such as the highway authority. This is to ensure that all relevant information necessary to determining the application is available and that, as far as possible, objections raised have been overcome. This can be achieved by modifications to its original content or design and/or by a legal agreement on the part of the developer to undertake or pay for certain complementary 'off-site' measures (technically termed 'planning obligations' but more commonly referred to as 'section 106 agreements'). Alterations to the layout or management of the highway network or other elements of the transport system in the vicinity of a development are a common component of these obligations. A separate legal mechanism – section 278 of the 1980 Highways Act introduced previously – continues to be available for the private funding of works on the strategic road network (DfT 2006b).

What constitutes 'development' in this context is defined in the 1990 Town and Country Planning Act. In essence it consists of physical development and/or of material changes of use to land or buildings. Hence the conversion of a house into flats or a warehouse into offices constitutes development even if there is no external change in the building itself.

Many small-scale or otherwise uncontroversial changes which would otherwise require planning permission are excluded by means of a General Permitted Development Order. Likewise a Use Classes Order allocates various types of land use into classes such that changes within a particular class do not require planning permission – between different varieties of shop for example (but not between shops, banks, restaurants and takeaways). For a fuller guide on these and the development control system more generally see Chapter 5 of Cullingworth and Nadin (2006).

By law, decisions on individual planning applications have to be made in accordance with the prevailing development plan, unless material considerations indicate otherwise. Hence strategic issues on whether significant new or additional development is appropriate in any area, and if so of what type and density, will normally have been debated and resolved through the development plan process (see Chapter 19). In particular, in line with PPG13 (DETR 2001) the spatial patterning of development should have been framed with the objective of 'reducing the need to travel' and facilitating the use of modes other than the car.

To assist authorities and other interested parties in understanding the basis on which an individual application (other than a change of use) has been prepared, applicants may be required to submit a 'design and access statement'. The access component of this refers to access to the development (i.e. not within buildings). It should explain how relevant development plan policies have been addressed and how the proposal ensures that all users will have convenient and equal access to buildings and spaces and to the public transport network (DCLG 2006a).

Nevertheless with the exception of designated areas where explicit constraints apply (e.g. conservation areas, Green Belts, National Parks) the policy statements in development plans deliberately allow for a degree of flexibility. This reflects the fact that development proposals involve weighing up a number of different objectives and may require trade-offs to be made in order to arrive at a decision (e.g. between promoting economic activity and safeguarding the environment). This means there is often room for manoeuvre in relation to particular sites (which developers and others will seek to exploit) whilst still being able to claim conformity with the development plan.

Under the 2001 revision of PPG13, development proposals with significant transport implications are required to prepare and submit a 'Transport Assessment' (TA) along with their planning application. This replaces the narrower Traffic Impact Assessments (TIAs) required previously. TAs supply information on the accessibility of the site by different modes and the likely modal split of journeys to and from it. In addition they should identify the scope for improving access by non-car modes, for reducing parking requirements and for mitigating transport impacts. (Guidance on the preparation of Transport Assessments has since been published – see Box 14.3.) Evidence from a TA forms the basis of negotiations with the developer in determining the amount of parking to be provided (in the context of the policies contained in the development plan), the nature and scale of any planning obligations and the preparation of a Travel Plan designed to bring about desired travel outcomes (16.5).

In the case of development affecting trunk roads the Department has made it clear that

> developers can no longer expect that all the traffic they might produce will be allowed without constraint. This would lead to ever-increasing congestion, which poses a threat to economic growth and the environment.
>
> (DfT 2007h para 27)

Developers are therefore required to consult with the Highways Agency about the operational capacity of a trunk road affected by a proposal and how this compares with the forecast traffic demand during a period ten years after the registration of a planning application. (This forecast includes existing demand plus forecast general traffic growth, demand likely to be generated by development commitments in the area and demand from the proposed development net of any reduction obtained through the TA procedure.) Where the operational capacity of the road will be exceeded, capacity improvements may be agreed, normally at the developer's expense, subject to environmental and deliverability considerations. The aim of this is to ensure that traffic conditions on the trunk road throughout the period are no worse than if the development had not taken place.

In areas within and surrounding centres where on-street parking is controlled, a key factor influencing the volume of attracted traffic is the amount of private non-residential (PNR) space available. In 1994 government policy switched from requiring planning authorities to set minimum standards of provision (originally intended to reduce the demand for on-street space) to setting maximum standards (as a demand-management tool). This was complemented later by publication of (undemanding) national maximum standards for different classes of non-residential development and inviting regional planning bodies and local planning authorities to adopt more rigorous standards 'where appropriate':

> Reducing the amount of parking space in new development (and in the expansion and change of use in existing development) is essential as part of a package of planning and transport measures to promote sustainable travel choices...

Box 14.3 Transport Assessments of development proposals

Guidance on Transport Assessments DCLG (2007), adapted from paras 1.18–1.20

A properly prepared TA will help LPAs assess the development's compatibility with the relevant planning policy framework and, in particular, the relevant transport strategy (usually the Local Transport Plan). It will allow the transport implications of proposed developments to be properly considered and, where appropriate, will help identify suitable measures to achieve a more sustainable and environmentally sound outcome. A TA can also address issues likely to be of concern to the local traffic authority and/or the Highways Agency in performing their network management duties.

In preparing a transport assessment the following considerations will therefore be relevant.

Encouraging environmental sustainability

- Reducing the need to travel, especially by car
- Tackling the environmental impact of travel
- The accessibility of the location
- Other measures which may assist in influencing travel behaviour.

Managing the existing network

- Making best possible use of existing transport infrastructure
- Managing access to the highway network.

Mitigating residual impacts

- Through demand management
- Through improvements to the local public transport network, and walking and cycling facilities
- Through minor physical improvements to existing roads
- Through provision of new or expanded roads*
- * ... it is considered good transport planning practice to demonstrate that the other opportunities above have been fully explored before considering the provision of additional road space such as new roads or major junction upgrades.
- Consideration of these matters should take place at an early stage in the process of preparing a development proposal. Work on developing the transport assessment can then help inform, and be informed by, discussions about the location of the site and the scale and mix of uses proposed.

A consistent approach on parking should be set out in the RTS (Regional Transport Strategy) to avoid wasteful competition between different locations based around the supply or cost of parking to the detriment of sustainable development.

(DETR 2001 paras 49 and 50)

A similar attempt to set national standards was applied in relation to parking provision within residential development. PPG3 (Housing) published in 2000 asked *all* authorities to plan on the basis of an *average* of 1.5 spaces per dwelling within their areas. This carried no acknowledgement of the widely different circumstances (from cities to rural districts) to which this would supposedly be applied. In practice many authorities had little appetite to pursue this objective in situations where it represented sub-demand levels. Except in inner urban areas covered by controlled parking zones, restricting parking provision in this way would only provoke problems of overspill parking in surrounding streets (White 2006).

Research was commissioned to provide evidence for a more sophisticated methodology based on a range of criteria (WSP Ltd 2007) but ran into ministerial objections on the principle of 'dictating' standards (LTT 432). The issue was neatly bypassed in 2006 by simply removing any reference to numerical standards in revised guidance. Indeed the bland statement included on parking was conspicuous for omitting transport considerations altogether, despite the ostensible over-arching objective of 'creating sustainable communities':

> Local Planning Authorities should, with stakeholders and communities, develop residential parking policies for their areas, taking account of expected levels of car ownership, the importance of promoting good design and the need to use land efficiently.
>
> (DCLG 2006b para 51)

15 Policy instruments (4)

Fiscal measures

15.1 Introduction

Fiscal measures are interventions by the State to affect the payments made or received for transport goods and services. They include:

- taxes levied as a means of generating income for public expenditure, either generally or hypothecated (i.e. 'earmarked') for a particular purpose
- variations in the detailed application of these taxes (plus or minus) as a means of discouraging or incentivising particular forms of vehicle ownership or travel behaviour
- charges made for the use of publicly owned transport assets or services (e.g. public car parks)
- fines imposed as a means of enforcing other regulatory regimes (e.g. licensing conditions or traffic management measures)
- regulation of charges set by private transport companies
- subsidies paid for the provision of transport services or concessionary fares.

As a means of influencing travel behaviour, fiscal instruments have much to commend them. They are comparatively cheap and swift to implement and can be 'fine tuned' to reflect changing conditions. A decision by the Chancellor of the Exchequer to alter fuel duty for example is reflected in a matter of hours in filling stations across the country. They are also distinctive in that they retain discretion amongst individual travellers or firms as to how they respond in the light of their particular circumstances. For example controlling access into a city centre through some form of charging rather than by physical management measures allows people to decide on a day-to-day basis whether the trip they are making warrants the payment involved. This 'advantage' is countered by concerns that this form of management may be socially discriminatory – i.e. that it is conditioned by individuals' ability to pay. Certainly as a form of intervention it more obviously invokes equity considerations.

The fact that fiscal measures alter the distribution of costs and benefits in explicit monetary terms does however make them especially contentious. Undoubtedly the most intractable policy issue in this field at the present time is the legacy of motoring taxation and the extent to which the resentment (and misunderstanding) which surrounds it affects public debate on possibilities for road pricing and fiscal measures more generally.

In this chapter we provide a description of the fiscal measures which are of policy significance in various transport fields. As with the other instruments we have discussed these have evolved in a fragmented, incremental manner over many decades. Changes which might be seen as desirable in the interests of greater coherence and effectiveness from the viewpoint of transport policy have to be set in a wider context and weighed against issues of legal and administrative practicality and political acceptability.

We begin by explaining the key topic of motoring taxation (15.2) and related issues of parking charges and road pricing (15.3 and 15.4). We then deal with fare regulation and service subsidy on the national rail network (15.5), the subsidy of bus services (15.6), concessionary fares (15.7) and finally (because of its significance and close links with subsidised bus services) with transport for the journey to school (15.8).

15.2 Motoring taxation

Motoring taxation comprises two main elements. The first, represented by VAT (Value Added Tax), is simply the application of a general form of taxation to all transactions involving motor vehicles and to transport goods and services (with an exemption for public transport fares). The second, more controversial, element comprises taxes which are specific to motoring. This is represented by fuel duty and vehicle excise duty (VED – the annual licence fee). Until 1992 there was also a special purchase tax on the list price of new cars.

Duties are levied as a fixed charge (e.g. pence per litre of fuel) whereas taxes are levied as a percentage of the sale price. This explains why fuel and vehicle duties – along with duties on tobacco and alcohol – feature regularly in Budget day statements. It is necessary to raise them periodically in order to maintain their real value (unless the Government makes a policy decision otherwise) whereas the real value of VAT rises automatically with retail prices.

As explained in Chapter 4, fuel duty and VED originated as a means of generating revenue to pay for road improvements to cater for motor vehicles. Although a separate Road Improvement Fund was abandoned at the end of the 1930s there remains a commonly held view that the level of motoring taxes is, or should be, linked to public expenditure which benefits motorists. In the post-war decades fuel duty and VED were retained as part of a group of taxes imposed on 'luxury' consumer items as a means of general revenue raising.

In the early 1990s there was increasing Government interest in the idea that the pattern of taxation might be utilised more creatively in contributing to public policy objectives, and specifically in relation to sustainable development (what we would now refer to as 'green taxes'). Three linked decisions were made:

1   the phasing out of the remaining special purchase tax on new vehicles (an economic response to lobbying by the motor industry then experiencing a slump in sales)
2   more generally, a policy of shifting the balance of motoring taxes from taxes on ownership to taxes on use (i.e. from fixed to variable costs). As a result they would become 'fairer' (in that the overall amount motorists would pay would relate more closely to miles driven) and also act as an incentive to improve fuel economy
3   the introduction in the 1993 Budget of the 'fuel duty escalator' – an annual 5% increase above the rate of inflation in the level of duty. This was a means of gradually restoring the tax revenue lost through the ending of the special purchase

tax, but in a way which contributed to environmental objectives, encouraging more energy efficient vehicle design, vehicle purchase and vehicle use.

As an instrument of environmental policy the effectiveness of fuel duty is limited because of the relatively low elasticity of travel demand to fuel prices. (A 10% increase in price only reduces car mileage by 2%.) In addition any reduction in emissions through higher fuel prices are quickly offset by increases in demand due to other factors (Banister 2005).

In practice the effect of the fuel duty escalator was offset in its first few years by a decline in oil prices so that the overall pump price increased little (see Figure 15.1). It also meant that the principle of the escalator became established without generating great political opposition. Unfortunately the reverse occurred at the end of the 1990s when oil prices leapt by over 50% in a single year. Together with increases in fuel duty and VAT this raised the cash price at the pump by 14% (from 70p to 80p per litre) at which point the taxes on vehicle use in the UK were the second highest in Europe. This prompted the protests reported in Chapter 8 which led not merely to a postponement of planned increases in duty but to a fundamental change in policy. After the 3p per litre cut in fuel duty in 2001 it was increased only once in the subsequent six years (by 1.3p to 47.1p in 2003). In effect the escalator was put into reverse.

In his 2007 Budget statement Gordon Brown announced that fuel duty would be increased by at least the rate of inflation for the next three years, although by 2009/10 this would mean that duty was still 11% less in real terms than in 1999. (In revenue terms the Government enjoys some compensation from the higher VAT receipts through increased oil prices.) As in previous years however one might expect these plans to be reviewed in the event of exceptional changes in world oil prices and/or the state of the economy, and 12 months later his successor Alistair Darling in fact deferred the proposed 2p increase for six months.

In relation to VED an important change was introduced in 2001 whereby the flat-rate annual fee was replaced by a banded scale linked to CO_2 emissions for all cars registered subsequently (and to engine size for those registered previously). Minor differences were also made for diesel engined cars (higher) and alternative fuels (lower). The initial range of fees was however very narrow (£90 to £160) and criticised on the basis that it would have no impact on the behaviour of car purchasers. Some acknowledgement of this was reflected in subsequent changes to differentiate further between the more polluting vehicles. In the 2007 Budget the fee for the most polluting

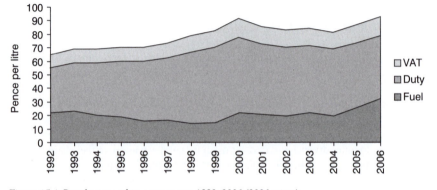

Figure 15.1 Petrol price and its components 1992–2006 (2006 prices)

vehicles (band G) was increased disproportionately – to £300 in 2007/08 and £400 in 2008/09. However this is still a paltry sum compared with £1800 for the top band and a £300 differential between all other bands recommended by the House of Commons Environmental Audit Committee (2006b).

The 2007 announcements about motoring taxes were presented on the basis that they would 'sharpen the signals to motorists to purchase more fuel efficient vehicles'. However this invites the obvious rejoinder that if influencing vehicle purchase is considered the principal aim (since it pre-determines the emission rates of the vehicle stock) then it is to vehicle purchase that banded taxation should be applied (Potter et al. 2003). A step in this direction was made in the 2008 Budget when the most polluting vehicles were required to pay double rates of VED in their first year. In effect this is a purchase tax by other means although the sums involved only represent a tax of about 1–2% on the purchase price of the cars concerned.

In addition to the motoring taxes discussed thus far it is also relevant to note the treatment of motoring costs within company and personal taxation. For many years the general taxpayer subsidised the growth of a 'company car culture' in which employees enjoyed what was in effect a salary perk by having personal use of a company-owned car. This had the unfortunate effect of stimulating the purchase of larger engined cars which then skewed the nation's vehicle stock towards lower fuel efficiency. A system of tax relief discounts was then introduced linked to the volume of business mileage undertaken but this had the perverse effect of encouraging car use in order to qualify for a higher discount. In 2002 the tax levied on company cars was revised to relate to their emission standards (to encourage purchase of more fuel-efficient vehicles) and business mileage discounts were abolished.

15.3 Parking charges

The supply of parking available to the public has two main components – off-street car parks and on-street spaces. The principle of payment for the former is accepted as a service charge and is reflected in the commercial operation of car parks developed in town centres, at transport interchanges and other locations of high demand. (Local authorities are more general providers.) Payment for on-street spaces on the other hand is contentious – it invokes questions of the 'right' to use the public highway and concerns in some quarters that motorists are being exploited for additional 'stealth taxes'.

On-street charging was first applied through the introduction of kerbside meters in Central London in the 1950s as an additional means of rationing the limited space available beyond restrictions on length of stay. Overall control of the amount and pricing of parking space was officially recognised as the most appropriate means of managing traffic demand in town centres in advance of developments in road pricing (MOT 1967a). Outside London however it was many years before this idea began to exert a significant influence on the management of on-street space, partly because of local political resistance but also because traffic conditions were eased by a combination of urban road-building, improved traffic management and industrial decline in inner urban areas. The presence of vacant and derelict sites within walking distance of town centres which could be used informally for car parking was a further factor. In some less economically buoyant areas this situation has not changed greatly to this day.

The role of charging as a component of integrated demand management came to assume more general prominence in the early 1990s particularly through the practical opportunities created by decriminalised parking described in the previous section. For metropolitan authorities and the new urban unitaries created in 1997, councils assuming DPE powers achieved unified control of charging policy and enforcement over both on-street and public off-street spaces. Schemes are expected to be self-financing but any surpluses can be used for other transport-related purposes (DTp 1995b).

Motorists' concerns that such schemes are being used as a source of revenue generation by local authorities have been compounded by the decision of some councils to introduce a charge for residents' permits within controlled parking zones. However the level of charge is typically a very small fraction of the cost of renting a private parking space in the same area. The London Borough of Richmond has gone one step further in introducing graduated charges linked to the CO_2 emissions of the vehicle concerned (i.e. as adopted for VED).

Achieving a coherent, workable and politically acceptable regime of parking charges given the inevitably haphazard legacy of the amount and distribution of parking space within any area represents a considerable challenge. (For a compendium of advice and examples of best practice see IHT 2005.) In areas of two-tier local government especially there is likely to be a conflict of objectives between the county council's interest in parking as an instrument of demand management and the local council's interest in maintaining the attractiveness of its commercial centres.

An added dimension arises with demand management strategies which include a Park and Ride (P&R) component. For these to operate successfully it is essential that the structure and level of parking charges is consistent between the three main choices presented to the motorist, viz:

- on-street parking spaces in the city centre
- car parks in the city centre
- the combination of P&R car park and dedicated bus service.

In most places the bus service operates as a tendered contract to the authority owning the P&R car park and this provides the means of determining the overall amount paid by users (TAS 2007).

A further complication is the extent of *private* non-residential (PNR) space. This is significant in two contexts. Firstly the amount of free parking space included in out-of-town retail and leisure developments presents councils seeking to promote traditional town centres with a conundrum. On the one hand they need to provide efficient access for motorists who might otherwise be attracted to the out-of-town sites; on the other hand using parking charges as part of a strategy to achieve this would have a deterrent effect. Secondly the effectiveness of local authority action to limit the number of public parking spaces and price them so as to deter commuters is undermined if there is a large pool of private spaces attached to offices and other workplaces which are made available free to employees. It was in this context that the powers for authorities to propose Workplace Parking Levy (WPL) schemes were included in the 2000 Act.

In practice the WPL concept has proved almost wholly unappealing. Only one city – Nottingham – has pursued the idea of a WPL, and in a rather special set of circumstances. It has been developed, not as an instrument of demand management in itself, but as a means of funding extensions of the city's tram system as part of an overall strategy for tackling congestion. In effect therefore the levy has been refashioned as a form of the *Versement Transport* public transport tax which is levied on businesses in a number of French cities.

15.4 Road user charging

As a general principle road space in Great Britain is provided free at the point of use. However, as noted in section 15.2, motorists make a very substantial financial contribution to the Exchequer through fuel duty and this can be interpreted as a form of surrogate payment. If so then it has the merit of being easily collected and 'fair' in that payment is broadly proportional to use. As an instrument of road user charging however it has the disadvantage that the broadly constant rate of payment (i.e. pence per mile) is unrelated to the costs of provision and to the external costs which are generated – principally in terms of delay to other road users and of environmental impacts. These are factors which vary greatly by place and time. It is principally in response to growing congestion and the impracticability and/or undesirability of overcoming this by increased road capacity that interest has arisen in more direct charging methods which can take these factors into account.

The theoretical case for direct user charging as a means of securing economically efficient use and provision of road space had been argued since the early years of the 20th century (Bonsall and Milne 2003). The possibility of pricing as means of restraining the projected growth of traffic demand in urban centres was acknowledged in the Traffic in Towns report (5.5) although the political limitations were anticipated:

> The political limitations derive from the fact that, before long, a majority of the electorate will be car-owners....
>
> It is calculated [in the Report] that there will be room for only about 1 in 4 – in London 1 in 10 – of the cars that would come in if there were no restriction. What licensing system could be devised, in a democratic society, that would turn away 75% or 90% of the applicants?
>
> (Sir Geoffrey Crowther: Preface 'Traffic in Towns' MOT and MHLG 1963)

This led to their conclusion about the importance of urban public transport which would enable people to be 'persuaded' not to use their cars (since it was not realistic to imagine that they could be compelled).

Although there are inevitably practical difficulties with any pricing scheme (defining boundaries, determining exemptions, devising charging systems, securing enforcement and so on) it has essentially been the issue of political acceptability which has prevented the economic logic of road user charging from being converted into practical implementation.

As we saw in section 7.3 the prospect of road pricing in the UK, and the logic underpinning it, was an important component of the 'New Realism'. Hence, by the time it came to be included in the 1998 White Paper:

> The concept of charging had been championed in academic and local authority circles for more than a decade but the potential political fall-out from introducing 'new taxes' on motoring together with opposition from the Treasury to the concept of 'hypothecation' meant that it never really became a serious policy proposal. [Hypothecation is the use of revenues for predetermined purposes –

in this case transport improvements – rather than adding to Exchequer income generally.]

(Begg 2003)

New Labour legislated for the concept (8.7) but only on the basis that individual local authorities took the brunt of any political flak. Significantly it was only Ken Livingstone, characteristically operating outside the bounds of normal political behaviour (and with the unique authority available to the London Mayor) who had the temerity both to propose the Central London 'congestion charge' and to push through its implementation within his first four-year term.

Strictly, the Central London scheme is not a 'congestion' charge, nor is it one which reflects the finer points of economic theory. In essence it is remarkably similar to a supplementary licensing scheme proposed in the 1960s – the prime difference being that it is enforced using camera recognition of vehicle number plates rather than as an ordinary paper licence. However the bluntness of a single daytime charge is one of the reasons for the current scheme performing less well in economic terms than might be expected. TfL claims a benefit-cost ratio of 1.4 although this has been disputed (LTT 419). The main problem is the high costs involved in installing and operating the scheme which amount to around two-thirds of the estimated benefits.

> The conventional wisdom is that, in heavily congested conditions, it is economically desirable but socially unacceptable. The irony … is that a scheme which has gained a fair degree of social acceptance is economically unsatisfactory.
> (Prof Peter Mackie, quoted in LTT 419)

An important corollary is that urban schemes outside London are likely to show even poorer economic returns and, if so, are unlikely to pass the DfT's own 'value for money' criterion (LTT 465). They will also not possess the relatively small charging zone compared with the area from which motorists are drawn which makes it practicable for Central London residents to be given a 90% discount – a key factor in gaining public acceptability.

Monitoring of the London scheme indicates that in 2005 congestion was 22% less than in 2002. About 5% of traffic capacity has been re-allocated to improve safety, assist pedestrians and cyclists and make greater provision for buses. In 2005/06 the scheme also generated an income of £122m for transport investment in London (TfL 2006).

Interest is currently focused on a series of pilot studies being conducted in cities and towns which have come about as a result of the Government's interest in a *national* pricing scheme. The Road Pricing Feasibility Study commissioned by Alistair Darling in 2003 investigated the possibility of a scheme in which central government designed and operated a national distance charge (offset by a reduction in other motoring taxes) with the facility for local variation to reflect congestion levels and other external costs (DfT 2004b). Such a scheme was 'becoming' technically feasible, and 'certainly' would be by 2015–20 based on the market-led development of in-vehicle satellite navigation equipment. Contemporary developments with the pilot studies are reported in section 23.3.

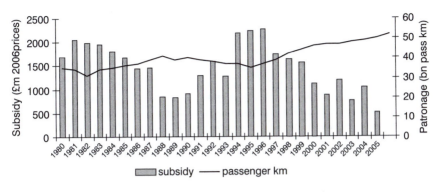

Figure 15.2 Rail subsidy and patronage 1980-2005 (see explanatory comments in text)

15.5 Rail passenger service subsidies and fare regulation

As explained in section 5.8 government subsidies to maintain rail passenger services – and avoid further line closures – were introduced at the end of the 1960s. As a nationalised industry fare structures were standardised across the network and overall fare levels determined as a matter of Government policy. PTAs were also able to support local services and fund higher service levels (and subsidise fares) as part of overall transport policies in the provincial conurbations. This facility was never available in London to the former GLC and elements have only recently been introduced in the refranchising of a group of North London lines (branded as the 'Overground').

Overall the subsidy requirement was linked to fluctuating economic cycles, with peaks during the recessions of the early 1980s and 90s when passenger levels fell (see Figure 15.2). In 1995 subsidy leapt by over 70% because of the change in the basis of accounting for infrastructure costs prior to privatisation. This amounted to a short-term increase in public expenditure which was planned to be offset in the following years by a reducing profile of subsidy payments to the train operating companies (TOCs) awarded the first round of franchises. After 2000 national (GB) liabilities were also reduced because of the transfer of responsibilities to the devolved administrations.

However the payments to operators give a very misleading impression of the public cost of maintaining the nation's rail network after 2000. From this time the Government began to make very large additional payments, directly to Railtrack and then its successor Network Rail, to support a programme to remedy the backlog of track maintenance and renewals. Costs within the industry were also rising rapidly. These included meeting the requirements of the Disability Discrimination Act (for which no special payment was made), the increasingly stringent – arguably excessive – standards set by the Health and Safety Executive and the rocketing costs of insurance and other expenditures associated with the litigation-ridden commercial regime. Overall by 2006 the national rail network was costing the taxpayer in excess of £5bn. Forty percent of the DfT's budget was being spent on a mode which served only 8% of the nation's travel.

The payments to operators remain very heavily skewed towards the former Regional sector of British Rail. This includes most of the country's rural lines which escaped the Beeching axe whose financial performance remains dire. For example the short (barely 10 miles) section of railway which continues to operate on the Isle of Wight has annual costs in excess of £3m but revenues less than £1m – the subsidy therefore being greater than the *total* support for socially necessary bus services in many shire counties.

Such lines are of course often greatly valued (or claimed to be so) by the local communities they serve, and in recognition of this the SRA published a 'Community Rail Development Strategy' since adopted by DfT. This seeks to establish partnerships with local authorities, business and community groups to promote the use and development of individual lines (see the work of ACORP – the Association of Community Rail Partnerships – at www.acorp.uk.com). The strategy states that with local support it should be possible to double fare income originating from these lines over a five-year period and to reduce subsidy per passenger by a half, thereby putting the lines on 'a more sustainable basis' for the future (DfT 2007j).

Since privatisation, operators have had the freedom to determine both the level and structure of fares on their services with the exception of season tickets and off-peak Saver tickets for longer distance journeys, which remain regulated. Price rises on these were limited to 1% below inflation in the period to 2003 and 1% above inflation since. Revenue from these regulated fares represents about 40% of the total.

Operators have responded by introducing enormous variety – some would say chaos – into the system of rail fares and ticketing. Each has exploited the opportunities in its own patch in its own way. These practices, combined with the effect of the regulated fares, have not altered the long-term trend of the average cost of rail travel (Figure 1.6 earlier) – if indeed this remains a meaningful concept. They have however offered choice to the consumer and enabled operators to maximise their revenue, thereby contributing to the profile of falling subsidy payments. The disadvantage is confusion amongst passengers trying to understand the different products and procedures offered by the various companies and annoyance at paying extra (or being caught out by some restriction) if they do not. The price-setting policies of commercial railway companies also bears no relation to any wider public interest. The opposing arguments are clearly contrasted in the Government's response to the Select Committee's report on this subject:

> The Government does not believe that encouraging modal shift to rail is a cause for subsidy in itself. However the Government does have wider objectives including those related to environment or congestion towards which rail is well-placed to make a contribution. These wide objectives are reflected in the fact that currently over 40% of all rail costs are met though subsidy.
>
> … The Government's approach to regulation (compatible with wider policies) is only to regulate where we believe that market elasticities are such that passengers do not have realistic alternative travel choices. Predominantly this is commuter markets (with travel choices being linked to home ownership). Issues of Saver regulation are more complicated.
>
> (House of Commons 2006a)

The Government would almost certainly like to do away with regulated Saver fares but is inhibited by opposition from consumer groups and by public scepticism about the behaviour of operators on ticketing generally. Nevertheless it is sympathetic to the concerns highlighted by the Select Committee and has therefore been working with operators to devise a standardised ticketing framework within which all companies would work (see Box 15.1). Interestingly the proposed framework would allow for subdivision of the 'off-peak' time period, for example to include separate periods

---

Box 15.1 Proposed simplified national rail fare structure

Name	Validity
(Day Anytime)	Any train
(Day) Off-peak	Any train outside peak period
(Day) Super off-peak	Any train at least-busy time of the day
Advance	One specific train (pre-booked up to 1800 the day before)

(with higher fares) for the 'shoulders' either side of the conventional peak periods. Stagecoach recently pioneered this on SouthWest trains by introducing a separate category for trains arriving at London Waterloo between 10am and noon – amounting to a 20% increase in fares for journeys at that time.

15.6 Bus service subsidies

As with rail services, public subsidy of bus services has existed since the 1960s. Currently it takes three main forms:

- national government rebate to operators for fuel duty paid
- local government support for socially necessary services
- grants from national government for particular categories of service.

In addition local authorities pay rebates to operators from the income forgone in running concessionary fare schemes (15.7). Public expenditure on these four items is estimated at £2.2bn in 2007/08 (Table 15.1).

Fuel duty rebate was introduced in 1965 but since 2002 has been retitled 'bus service operators' grant' (BSOG). The original title still reflects what the subsidy consists of; with 82% of the duty being rebated, currently worth 41p per litre.

What the grant is 'for' exactly – other than a generalised means of supporting the bus industry – is a moot point. For several years the Government has recognised that the basis of BSOG is unsatisfactory since it does nothing to incentivise operators to run services in a way which contributes to its policy objectives and actually rewards fuel

Table 15.1   Sources of bus service support in England 2007/08 (source: estimates as published in DfT 2008c *Local Bus Services Support: Options for Reform*)

Bus service operators' grant (fuel duty rebate)	£413m
Services contracted by local authorities	
outside London (tendered socially necessary services)	£330m
within London (services franchised by TfL)	£650m
Grants from Central Government	
rural bus subsidy grant	£56m
Challenge and Kickstart awards (remaining commitments)	£11m
Reimbursement for concessionary fares	£725m
TOTAL	£2,185m*

* An additional £300m is spent by local authorities on capital items supporting bus services.

inefficiency. Alternative formulations have been put forward, for example based on the number of passengers carried (CfIT 2002b).

The Government's intention to reform BSOG was reiterated in 2006 (DfT 2006e 'Putting Passengers First'). A consultation paper has since been published setting out options for reform of the grant in the short term linked to fuel efficiency standards with more radical options, including possible rationalisation of BSOG and concessionary fare payments, for consideration from 2011/12 (DfT 2008c).

The context for local authorities' support of bus services outside London changed radically following deregulation in 1986 when they ceased to pay incumbent operators for the maintenance of whole networks and arranged contracts for individual socially necessary services through a competitive tendering procedure instead. Overall support costs were almost halved between 1984/85 and 1987/88 with especially large reductions in the metropolitan areas because of the ending of subsidised fare regimes.

During the subsequent decade the costs of bus tendering continued to fall on a per-mile basis and in total. Since the late 1990s however the situation has become more difficult both for the bus industry as a whole and for local authority tendering. The main factors are increases in the costs of labour, pension provision and fuel. Previous gains in productivity (bus miles per member of staff) have also been lost, partly because of worsening traffic congestion and greater emphasis by operators in scheduling services to achieve greater reliability. Profit margins in 2005/06 were only 7% on average, having fallen in seven out of the previous eight years (Cheek 2008).

Over the last decade local authorities have been faced with the double whammy of increased demand for tendered services (arising from the de-registration of commercial services) coupled with higher prices for maintaining existing ones. On average the cost of contracts has risen by about 2% a year above inflation.

The rise in contract prices has been greatest in London. However the effects of this are subsumed within the huge increase in payments made by the Mayor as part of his policy for securing rapid growth in bus mileage and patronage within the capital in complete contrast to the previous policy of zero support when London Transport was controlled by Central Government (Figure 15.3).

Rising costs would have had more serious repercussions for rural areas but for a hastily arranged initiative by the Government in response to the mass rural demonstration in 1998. A new rural bus services grant (RBSG) was paid annually to local transport authorities on the basis of their population in settlements of less than 10,000 people (later increased to 25,000). The grant was introduced at the level of around £20m p.a. and for some authorities represented more than a doubling of the amounts they were contributing to rural services previously. Although the grant was originally confined to service enhancements, the rules were relaxed in 2001 in response to the more difficult tendering environment, allowing up to 20% of the grant to be used to support services operating prior to that date. General opinion of the grant has been very favourable and the Government has continued to fund it at increased levels since (DfT 2004a).

A Rural Bus Challenge (RBC) fund also introduced at the end of the 1990s had a more mixed reception. It was distributed on a competitive basis in response to bids from authorities for innovative forms of service. However several features of the grant were criticised – the costs and uncertainty involved in the bidding process, the unnecessary and (as some considered) inequitable requirement for 'innovation' and the three-year limit on funding for each scheme. The last round of RBC awards was made for projects beginning in 2004/05.

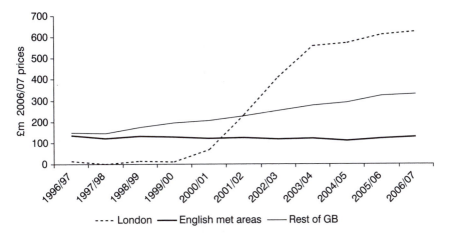

Figure 15.3 Local authority support for local bus services by area 1996/97–2006/07

For a short period between 2002 and 2004 the Government also introduced an Urban Bus Challenge fund to support projects designed to increase opportunities from disadvantaged communities in line with the recommendations of the Social Exclusion Unit (ODPM 2003b). In the event part of this fund was utilised – hijacked might be a better word – to trial a new type of project labelled 'Kickstart' proposed by the bus operator Stagecoach. This had entirely different objectives and was applicable to any type of area. A further round of Kickstart awards (only) was made in 2005. Projects are designed to pump-prime new services capable of achieving patronage and modal shift and to 'have a clear prospect of becoming commercially viable or otherwise fully sustaining with a guarantee of local authority support' (DfT 2005d).

All forms of grant for specific bus services (i.e. other than BSOG and RBSG) have now come to an end. This can be seen as clearing the decks to allow for the introduction of more radical reforms referred to earlier.

15.7 Concessionary fares

Provision for concessionary fares was originally made under the 1968 Transport Act, re-enacted (but with essentially the same effect) under s93 of the 1985 Act. This gives district and unitary authorities outside London (PTEs in the conurbations) the discretionary power to provide concessionary travel on local bus services for elderly and disabled persons. Each authority determines its own scheme (known as s93 schemes) and reimburses operators for the net cost to them of participating in it. Separate arrangements apply in London where a unified scheme is operated by TfL under the 1999 Greater London Authority Act.

The 1985 Act allows authorities to specify:

- the concession to be offered (e.g. half fare, flat fare, pre-paid tokens)
- the eligible categories of passenger
- the times when the concession is to be available
- the area within which the concession applies
- the method by which reimbursement is to be calculated
- arrangements for making payment to operators.

Concessions may only be offered to groups identified within national regulations although authorities may choose to be more selective.

In principle all operators of registered bus services have the right to participate in an s93 scheme within their area although there is provision for exemptions, e.g. for tourist or express services. Likewise authorities have the power to enforce participation on operators. Authorities may choose to offer concessions on modes other than local bus services but in these cases the rights of participation and powers of compulsion do not apply.

The basis of reimbursement should be that operators are 'no better and no worse off' as a result of participation in the scheme. Hence they are paid for the revenue forgone as a result of issuing concessionary fares and for any additional costs which can be demonstrated (e.g. through having to provide additional capacity). This requires estimates to be made of the number of concessionary trips, the full-fare equivalent of these trips (or at least an average fare) and a generation factor (to identify the number of *additional* trips which are made as a result of the concession being available). The methods which may be employed in this are explained in DfT (2005a).

Achieving an accurate estimate of the appropriate amount of reimbursement for each operator participating in an authority's scheme is potentially an extremely complex and costly undertaking. In practice the amount decided on is more a matter of negotiation settled to the satisfaction of the parties involved. Operators have the right of appeal to the Secretary of State for Transport if they consider they are being inadequately reimbursed. The level of reimbursement is frequently a bone of contention, in part because the starting point of operators and local authorities is fundamentally different. Local authorities are under a duty to follow the 'no better, no worse off' principle but operators have no such scruples – they have a commercial incentive to utilise whatever evidence and argument will secure them maximum payment.

In addition to these discretionary powers central government has legislated that certain concessions *must* be made available and, in principle at least, is paying individual authorities for the additional costs incurred. Initially, under the Transport Act 2000 authorities had to provide for half-price bus fares as a minimum during off-peak periods for concessionary travel within the authority's area. (This reflected a commitment given in the 1998 White Paper towards 'a fairer, more inclusive society'.) Subsequently this requirement was extended so that, as from April 2006, such travel would be free. A further extension has been introduced under the Concessionary Bus Travel Act 2007 which requires the free travel concession to be available anywhere in England from April 2008.

These moves follow previous decisions by the Scottish Parliament and Welsh Assembly to provide for free concessionary bus travel in their countries which were early examples of their use of devolved powers. However whereas in Scotland and Wales reimbursement is organised centrally, in England it continues to be administered by individual authorities which causes considerable practical difficulties (LTT 458). The 2007 Act does include clauses which will allow the Secretary of State to take over responsibility for reimbursement at some point in future without further primary legislation. It also enables the SoS to take powers to determine how operators should be reimbursed (i.e. not as a matter of negotiation), and to extend the availability of a national concession to 16–18 year olds in full-time education and to modes other than local bus services.

On the face of it concessions are most important to safeguarding the accessibility of people with low incomes, yet low income or unemployment do not figure in the definition of eligibility. Neither is high income a disqualification for the receipt of concessions amongst elderly and disabled people. That said, there is a strong correlation between old age or disability and low income. It is also true that higher income groups (of whatever age) use buses little. So even though concessionary bus fares do not benefit low-income groups as a whole, most of those who *do* benefit are likely to be on lower incomes.

The introduction of the statutory concession for travel anywhere in England has greatly reduced the 'postcode lottery' which operated previously – both in terms of lessening the differences between individual schemes and removing the disadvantage which some residents experienced through living near the boundary of their authority's area. However significant anomalies remain in that the national concession is of no value to people who live in places without bus services or who, on account of walking difficulty or other disability, are unable to use them. One of the rather perverse outcomes of concessions – particularly since they have been extended to free travel – is that they facilitate 'joy-riding' by people living in areas with good facilities and bus networks whilst not doing anything to alleviate the condition of people with the worst accessibility.

Individuals who are entitled to the statutory concession may elect to forgo their rights to it if they prefer to take advantage of an alternative form of concession offered by their local authority instead (such as travel tokens which can be used for taxis or other modes). However because such alternatives add to the cost and administrative complexity of local schemes their availability is patchy.

Some evidence of the unevenness in the value of concessionary travel by area can be seen in the expenditure by the main categories of authority within England (Figure 15.4). Total expenditure in the shire counties is less than in the metropolitan (PTE) areas or London, even though their population is some 50% greater than both put together. However several other important factors contribute to this – the lower proportion of non-car-owning households in the counties and the more generous schemes provided in the conurbations, in turn a reflection of their difference in political colour.

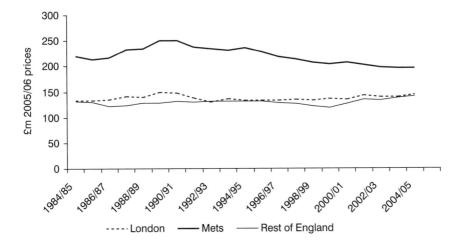

Figure 15.4 Concessionary fare reimbursement by area 1984/85–2005/06

These arguments cast doubts on the wisdom of the Government's introduction of the full-fare concession (costing an extra £350m in 2006/07) and its extension for travel anywhere in England (a further £250m a year from 2008/9) as compared with alternative, better targeted uses of the same money (White 2008). However now that these decisions have been made it is inconceivable that it will ever be practicable politically to reverse them.

15.8 School transport

The provision of free travel to and from school for eligible children might appear as another form of public transport concession but its origins are very different. Unlike other publicly funded concessions it is not treated as an item of transport expenditure but of *education* expenditure.

Present arrangements derive from an Act of 1870 which made school attendance obligatory for children living up to two miles away who were aged 5–7 and up to three miles for older children. Under the 1944 Education Act local authorities were given comprehensive duties and powers as education authorities (LEAs), including the power to provide transport to school free of charge where necessary. This has been interpreted as catering for children of compulsory school age (currently 5–16) living beyond the statutory walking distances in travelling to the nearest available State or voluntary-aided school. Free travel is also provided irrespective of distance for children with special educational needs or mobility handicap.

Most LEAs exercise discretion to arrange transport additionally for children attending a religious denominational school beyond the statutory walking distance even though it is not strictly their nearest school. Discretion is also exercised over whether to arrange transport, free or otherwise, to children staying on at school after 16 or attending further education colleges.

'Free travel' can take a number of forms:

- a season ticket or 'pass' for use between home and school on bus or train services provided for the general public
- free travel on a specially contracted school bus, minibus or taxi
- reimbursement of travel expenses.

In rural areas many ordinary bus services are themselves tendered services – hence a duty is placed on local authorities to cooperate with education and social service authorities in relation to tendering under the 1985 Transport Act in order to achieve best value for money overall.

The principle of parental choice of school which was introduced in the 1980 Education Act conflicted with the presumptions on which the 1944 Act arrangements were based. Choice of school beyond the statutory walking distances could only be said to exist insofar as transport was available and affordable. Arranging transport for all possible 'choice' combinations of origin and destination (as opposed to the traditional approach of serving a single nearest or catchment school) was clearly impracticable and LEAs were encouraged to pay 'equivalent fares' on a discretionary basis instead. However, in rural areas particularly, LEAs proved unresponsive – typically they would not have derived any saving in the cost of contracted transport for children continuing to travel to the nearest school and hence would simply have incurred an additional cost.

The issue of transport as a potential constraint on educational choice amongst poorer families has only recently been revisited by New Labour. Under the Education and Inspections Act 2006, children aged 11+ from these families are now entitled to free travel to a choice of three schools more than two and up to six miles from their home and to their nearest school by reason of parents' religion or belief up to a maximum of 15 miles. In addition children aged 8–11 from these families are to receive free travel to their nearest school beyond two rather than three miles.

However there remains the long-standing conundrum surrounding the use of the 1870 walking distances to determine entitlement to free travel generally. Mindful of the political hazards involved in seeking to tackle this issue head-on, the Government has adopted a now favoured device of inviting individual LEAs to apply to become one of a limited number of 'pathfinder' authorities (DfES 2007). These will have the obligation removed to provide free travel for the generality of children living beyond the statutory distances. Revenue raised from charging for their use of transport services will be used to subsidise measures designed to encourage children living nearer school to travel by means other than in private cars, i.e. as part of the Government's more general programme for sustainable travel to schools (16.5).

Some groups have lobbied for a national network of dedicated school buses to be available free for every child, based on the 'yellow buses' operated in the United States. Such a system would greatly increase the financial costs of school transport and weaken public transport more generally. On the other hand the system has an excellent safety record and experience of yellow bus schemes already operating in the UK shows strong parental support (LTT 420). In terms of conventional transport assessment the resulting reduction in congestion, vehicle operating costs, accidents and emissions, coupled with savings in the travel time of escorting drivers, would imply a substantial economic return overall. One study estimated that a national scheme for primary school children would cost around £184m a year but generate benefits 2.5 times greater (Sutton Trust 2006).

16 Behavioural change measures ('Smarter Choices')

16.1 Introduction

Thus far in Part 3 of the book we have followed the trajectory of transport planning itself in seeing problems and opportunities arising from (mainly) increasing demand being responded to by improvements through investment where it is cost-effective to do so, and by a variety of 'stick and carrot' measures to alter the scale and pattern of demand where it is not.

Possible ways of influencing motorists' behaviour, other than by major investment or by physical or fiscal instruments, is a more recent development. The term 'soft measures' used originally was never defined precisely, nor has its successor 'smarter choices' preferred by the Government. Their common feature is that they aim primarily to alter the way travel opportunities are *perceived* and *responded to* (as distinct from the more traditional approach of seeking to change behaviour by altering the opportunities themselves). They can be used in conjunction with these traditional measures (i.e. to help bring about the behavioural change intended) or more intriguingly, to bring about change in behaviour with little or no change in the transport system.

A further feature of these measures is that, except for those secured through the development planning process, they are not based on any legal sanction or reward. In essence individuals and businesses are free to adopt them or not as they think fit. That is both their strength and their weakness. Nobody can object to them because nobody is being forced to do anything they don't want to do. But equally of course if the scale of 'voluntary' change does not achieve the desired outcomes then this begs the question of whether some system of rewards or sanctions should be invoked.

In this final chapter of Part 3 we therefore consider this most recent set of instruments available to transport planners. As essential background we begin by explaining the nature and significance of car dependency (16.2). We then review the overall stance taken by central government towards 'smarter choices' (16.3). This is followed by an overview of the range of measures available and evidence of their cost-effectiveness (16.4). Experience to date with many of these, it should be emphasised, is the product of *private* initiative. In the remainder of the chapter we focus on measures where significant *public* intervention has taken place, dealing first with travel plans of various kinds (16.5) and marketing (16.6). As part of the latter we report on the Government's recent 'Sustainable Travel Demonstration Towns' initiative – the only attempt yet to study the effect of a range of 'smarter choices' being introduced in the same locality as part of a concerted programme.

16.2 Car dependency

There are a number of different attributes to which the term 'car dependency' can be applied. All have some bearing on the propensity of particular individuals or groups to utilise cars for their travel. Here we are concerned with the way these act as barriers to the use of alternative modes (i.e. conflict with the prospective take-up of 'smarter choices'). We will be distinguishing between car use, car reliance and car habit.

People can be differentiated simply on the basis of their *car use*, i.e. the proportion of their travel they make by car (especially as a car driver). Used in this way the term 'car dependence' conveys nothing about whether it is practicable for the journeys to be made by means other than a car and if so whether the individual concerned would recognise the fact and be willing to do so. Nevertheless the mere extent of car use has important implications for the pattern of travel choices over time (Goodwin et al. 1995). (Evidence of the significance of car availability as a factor in car use was presented earlier in section 2.9.)

By definition the higher the level of car use amongst any community the less use will be made of other modes and the fewer and/or poorer the standard of these will be as a result. The starting point from which any other mode may be promoted as an alternative to the car is therefore objectively lower. Furthermore, given the status conventionally associated with cars, the prevalence of car use will have a strong conditioning effect as a social norm.

Increasing levels of car ownership also affect the behaviour and attitudes of non-drivers because of the greater opportunity for them to travel as car passengers, courtesy of lifts given by friends or family members. This is especially important in the conditioning effect upon children. Those who have not learnt how to use walking, cycling and public transport as part of a range of options to fulfil their travel needs are not in a neutral position to exercise 'choice' when they reach adulthood.

Increasing car ownership also tends to generate *car reliance*. Households without cars or with only one car between two adults will be more concerned to choose places to live, work and shop in ways which enable them to function without being reliant on driving or getting a lift. If they get a (second) car this constraint no longer applies – in fact it may be acquired deliberately in order to free up such choices. A pattern of activities will then evolve which, to a greater or lesser extent, is predicated on each adult able to use a car independently.

The car reliance which is built into people's choices about the spatial patterning of their lives acts as a practical barrier to them changing mode, even if in principle they were willing to consider such a thing. Table 16.1 shows the results of a Scottish study which asked people who currently drove for four main activities whether it would be practical to use other forms of transport (reported in Stradling 2003). Car reliance was demonstrated to range between 28% and 57% for these trip purposes. The scope for attracting drivers out of their cars for short trips (under 5 miles) more generally is reported in Mackett (2001).

The fact that a large proportion of drivers report that they have 'no option' but to use a car accounts for the widespread hostility generated by national or local policies which seek to make car use more difficult or expensive. In these circumstances what may be presented as a stimulus for people to make 'smarter choices' in their travel behaviour is actually implying that they restructure their lives! Unsurprisingly this is not welcome if accompanied by a metaphorical gun to their heads. However there is scope to present restructuring in a much more constructive manner if it can be tied in

Table 16.1   Car reliance: percentage of drivers for whom it would not be practicable to use other modes to undertake selected activities (source: adapted from Stradling 2003)

Activity	Bus	Train	Walk	Cycle	Any non-car
Take children to/from school	84	> 99	41	97	28
Town centre shopping	57	87	77	98	31
Travel to work	72	91	85	90	55
Supermarket shopping	74	> 99	81	97	57

with the times in people's lives when for one reason or another they are contemplating change (16.8).

High car use – whether the product of 'reliance' or not – contributes to the development of a *car habit*. 'Habitual' behaviour does not mean merely that the same (car driver) mode is used regularly and frequently but that its status as a 'choice' ceases to be recognised (Verplanken et al. 1994).

Like the many activities with which it is linked, day-to-day travel is not a matter of rational choice, constantly reappraised. Once an individual has found that car use is convenient (or that in their experience it has always been used for certain types of journey) they are unlikely to alter it, or even to contemplate doing so. In any case car use often is the most advantageous mode at a personal level – especially once the financial hurdle of car ownership has been overcome. Nevertheless it is important not to overstate 'objective' explanations for travel behaviour – in practice every individual will be operating according to a complex personal set of relationships between beliefs, attitudes and intentions (Mann 2005).

Although the travel behaviour of car drivers is dominated by car use it is also the case that almost nobody is wholly car dependent. The Scottish study referred to above found that only 1 in 125 drivers did literally all their travel by car. Walking (for at least 10 minutes) and car passenger were used at least once a month by 88% and 67% of drivers respectively. Less used but still significant were taxi (32%), bus (26%) and train (15%).

These statistics highlight the fact that car dependency is not an absolute condition but a matter of degree. As we saw in Chapter 1 car ownership and use varies geographically and between socio-economic groups, but amongst people in each of these categories car dependence will vary according to the nature of the trips being made (by purpose, length and destination). The pattern of variation will also reflect the attitudes of the individuals concerned to the alternatives on offer, even amongst people travelling to the same place for the same purpose (see Box 16.1).

From this the general point emerges that in considering behavioural change there is little value in talking about transport and travel in aggregate. To be effective one needs to understand the characteristics of the market in which intervention is proposed and target measures accordingly.

Nevertheless the cumulative weight of all the factors discussed – economic, social, cultural, practical and psychological – in biasing the scales *against* the probability of behavioural change is immense. Evidence of travel behaviour over the decade to 2004 seems to confirm this:

It is clear from this research that we are just as car dependent today as we were in the early 1990s. Trying and experiencing new things is part and parcel of our everyday lives but where transport is concerned we tend to stick with what we know.

(Leibling 2007)

Nevertheless whilst there is a large number of motorists psychologically as well as practically committed to using their cars it is also true, as the segmentation research demonstrates, that there are groups who are willing and in some cases keen to use other modes, given the right opportunities. It is to these groups that 'smarter choices' are particularly directed.

Box 16.1 Segmentation of the population into attitudinal types

This research was conducted on the basis of a survey of 666 visitors to National Trust properties in the north west of England. Statistical clustering techniques were used to segment the population into four car-owning and two non-car-owning groups according to four sets of variables:

- attitudes towards car use
- attitudes towards alternatives to the car
- attitudes to the environment
- 'green behaviour'.

The research revealed very wide differences in terms of attitudes and behaviour between the groups in relation to potential use of modes other than the car for this type of trip. (Each group was given a descriptive label – e.g. 'malcontented motorist' – which summarised their distinctive features.) It also showed that although there are socio-economic differences between the car-owning and non-car-owning groups there are very few statistically significant differences within them (education being the only distinguishing variable). This suggests that personal characteristics are not an important determinant of attitude or differences in behaviour between segments of equivalent vehicle availability.

	Car-owning segments				Non-car-owning	
	Malcontented motorists	Complacent car addicts	Die-hard drivers	Aspiring environ'talist	Car-less crusaders	Reluctant riders
% of respondents	30%	26%	19%	18%	4%	3%
Vehicle availability*	0.87	0.83	0.88	0.77	0.29	0.42
Intention / Behaviour**	18% / 2%	12% / 4%	7% / 1%	50% / 19%	100% / 85%	72% / 52%

*Number of vehicles in household divided by the number of adults with driving licences
** Intention = % concurring with statement 'I will try and use an alternative to the car to visit a National Trust property in the next 12 months. Behaviour = % using car to travel to the NT property on the survey day

Source: Anable 2005)

16.3 The stance of central government

On the face of it behavioural change measures should be like manna from heaven to a stricken Department for Transport. Here are a range of instruments which contribute to all the 'right' objectives, which are relatively cheap and easily implemented, have no undesirable side-effects and which generate no significant opposition. One might expect them to be thrust centre stage in both national and local policy agendas. And yet, to date at least, they have not been. The DfT's attitude to them remains ambivalent and their significance within its overall spread of activities highly marginal. What is the explanation for this?

'Soft measures' as they were originally called are an interesting example of the difficulty faced by a bureaucracy in responding to a novel issue which does not conform with the presumptions on which its established activities and organisation are based. Significantly the first formal recognition of this type of measure came not from within central government but from a group of local authorities originally led by Hertfordshire CC who came together as the 'Travelwise' consortium to develop and share travel awareness and other promotional techniques using this as their 'brand name'. (They have recently merged with ACT – the Association of Commuter Transport – to form what is in effect a 'sub-profession' of people and organisations engaged in travel planning and mobility management.)

Compared with long-standing DfT practice, soft measures were novel in at least three respects:

- in their aim: they are wholly concerned with reducing car use and promoting alternative modes
- in the focus of their activity: on promotion and marketing (rather than construction and maintenance of infrastructure, or operation of services)
- in their funding requirement: using revenue rather than capital spending as a form of 'investment' to bring about improvements in the functioning of the transport system.

The conflict over aim is critical. As we have noted elsewhere, the DfT has thus far 'succeeded' in resisting calls for target levels of traffic nationally, or of traffic reduction. Its argument is that the amount of traffic is not itself an issue relevant to the setting of objectives. Hence as far as 'smarter choices' are concerned it is prepared to endorse and indeed encourage their use in appropriate situations (i.e. where they contribute effectively to other, substantive objectives) but not to alter the national policy framework in ways which, in its view, would effectively favour their adoption in inappropriate ones.

Soft measures present a more fundamental, philosophical challenge to the Department concerning the nature of travel demand. Traditionally this was something it observed, modelled and predicted as an 'onlooker'. If projected demand led to unwanted outcomes then interventions would be planned which would result in people travelling differently – more or less, by a different route, mode or whatever. The change was achieved by altering the nature and pricing of the transport system – the criteria by which travellers were expected to respond were unchanged. Physical and economic levers were pulled, not social and psychological ones.

If however conditions can be improved by altering the way people perceive and respond to them, what is the significance to be attached to any initial observation of 'travel demand'? How far should national or local governments intervene to seek to alter demand (by changing people's perceptions of the available choices) before intervening with physical or economic measures to address any excess demand which remains? This may seem a rather esoteric point if, as is commonly believed, there is little realistic scope for change. In practice the situation is more fluid. Research conducted by the UCL Transport Studies Unit highlighted the large amount of 'churn' which takes place each year in the population's car ownership and travel habits which is overlooked because of statistics which report only the net outcome (LTT 401).

This issue surfaced in practice in the context of the Multi-Modal Studies when the question arose as to what adjustments should be made to the output of the National Transport Model to allow for the new breed of instruments supported in principle in the 1998 White Paper (W S Atkins 1999). Many of the consultants undertaking the studies also took the view that greater investment in these measures would generate better value for money than some of the large-scale infrastructure schemes they were being asked to consider.

In an attempt to calm what became quite fiercely contested waters, the Department in 2003 commissioned a further study from a mainly academic consortium which reviewed all the published evidence on the cost-effectiveness of soft measures and additionally conducted a series of more detailed case studies. The results of this are reported in the next section. It was in publishing this work that the switch in official terminology to 'smarter choices' was made (Cairns et al. 2004).

16.4 Overview of 'Smarter Choices'

The 'Smarter Choices' research identified ten types of measure (Box 16.2). To this may be added residential travel plans which have been the subject of separate research. All the measures are commonly introduced independently of one another and by different agencies. In theory all could be subject to public influence as a matter of policy through regulatory or fiscal means, but for the most part have not been thus far.

Perhaps surprisingly only two types of measure – personalised travel planning and travel awareness schemes – necessarily depend on public authorities for their initiation and funding. All the rest can and have been introduced by businesses or other organisations either as a commercial venture (e.g. public transport marketing, car clubs and home shopping) or to improve their own functioning (e.g. teleworking and teleconferencing). Workplace, school and residential travel plans fall into this category too although they may also be prompted by public action, either through promotional activity or through legal requirements. Local transport authorities may help initiate, fund or promote some of the other types of measure (e.g. public transport marketing and car clubs).

Having analysed individual examples of all the types of measure listed it was estimated that the potential overall reduction in traffic obtainable from these measures could range from 4–5% nationally at the low end (assuming 'business as usual') to 10–15% nationally and 15–20% locally under a more supportive policy environment. These two scenarios were labelled 'low' and 'high' intensity respectively (Table 16.2).

Estimates of the traffic reduction effect of individual types of soft measure are shown in Table 16.3. Note that in this table a different basis is used to report measures which address a particular journey purpose from those which apply to travel in general. The latter's much lower figures do not signify that they are necessarily any less effective in reducing overall car mileage. (In fact their cost-effectiveness in these terms appears to be better.) However the difference does illustrate a very important point, namely that the purpose-specific measures can show 'visible' reductions for

---

Box 16.2 Types of soft measure

Workplace travel plans – a package of measures introduced by employers (singly or collectively at a particular location) aimed at encouraging and enabling their employees to reduce their car mileage (These measures may include car sharing, teleworking and teleconferencing below, and car pools for business use)

School travel plans – a package of measures introduced at an individual school to encourage and enable children to travel to school more sustainably. (Particularly likely to include the promotion of walking and cycling)

*Residential travel plans – a package of measures introduced within a housing development aimed at lowering personal car ownership and/or encouraging and enabling residents to travel more sustainably. (May include car club or car sharing schemes below)

Personalised travel planning – offer to individuals of information carefully targeted to their personal and locational circumstances to encourage and enable them to travel more sustainably. (May be included as part of workplace and residential travel plans)

Public transport information and marketing – advertising campaigns, the provision of information in more accessible formats and simplified ticketing schemes

Travel awareness campaigns – a range of media aimed at improving general public awareness of the implications of transport choices, and information about problem solving including changing travel behaviour

Car clubs – an alternative to private car ownership where individuals are encouraged to join a club which gives them access to a number of vehicles parked in their neighbourhood on a 'pay as you go' basis

Car sharing scheme – where individuals are encouraged to share their private vehicles for particular journeys (also known as 'car pooling')

Teleworking – where employers encourage employees to adopt a range of working practices remote from their main workplace, including working at home, for all or part of the time

Teleconferencing – where telecommunication is used to facilitate contacts/meetings that would otherwise have involved business travel

Home shopping – where customers purchase goods which are subsequently delivered directly to them rather than purchasing and transporting them from a store

* Not included in the Smarter Choices report – see 16.5

Source: Based on S Cairns et al. (forthcoming)

---

the organisation concerned and for traffic levels in the vicinity of its site. These can act as strong motivators in promoting and gaining acceptance of such schemes on a voluntary basis. By contrast the traffic benefits of personalised travel planning and travel awareness schemes are dispersed over place and time – hence their dependence on public funding.

Table 16.2 Impact of soft factors on future traffic levels (source: Cairns et al. 2004 Table 7)

Impact on….	Low-intensity scenario	High-intensity scenario
National traffic:		
All time periods	2%	11%
Peak time	4%	17%
Off-peak	2%	10%
Urban traffic:		
All time periods	3%	14%
Peak time	5%	21%
Off-peak	3%	13%
Non-urban traffic:		
All time periods	2%	8%
Peak time	3%	14%
Off-peak	1%	7%

Table 16.3 Impact (car travel reduction) of different types of soft measure (source: Cairns et al. 2004)

Journey purpose	Soft measure	Impact* Non-urban		Urban	
		Low	High	Low	High
Journey to work	Workplace travel plans	2%	4%	2%	4%
	Car sharing	0.6%	11%	0.6%	11%
	Teleworking	3%	12%	3%	12%
Combination of the above allowing for double-counting		5%	24%	8%	26%
Journey to school	School travel plans	4%	20%	4%	20%
Business journeys	Teleconferencing	2.5%	18%	2.5%	18%
Shopping trips	Home shopping for groceries	1%	4%	1%	4%
Personal business trips	Local collection points	1.5%	1.5%	1.5%	1.5%
Multiple purposes	Personalised travel planning	< 1%	< 1%	1%	3%
	PT information and marketing	0.1%	0.3%	0.3%	1.1%
	Travel awareness campaigns	0.1%	1%	0.1%	1%
	Car clubs			0.03%	0.06%**

Notes
* For measures affecting multiple journey purposes the impact is expressed relative to all car travel; for single purposes it is relative to car travel for that purpose. For car clubs, car sharing, home shopping and local collection the impact is expressed as a percentage reduction in car kilometres, otherwise as a percentage of car trips
** Up to 3% longer term

Box 16.3 Policy initiatives important in fulfilling the potential of Smarter Choices

- A clear national strategy in favour of traffic reduction, with recognition that smarter choice measures could make a valuable and concrete contribution to this
- The availability of new revenue funding streams for local authorities [Note smarter choice measures depend on revenue expenditure, including a high staffing component, whereas Local Transport Plans and their attendant funding increases have been focused on infrastructure (capital) spending
- Specific national policies to support particular initiatives, including
  - more tax breaks for workplace travel plans
  - a statutory requirement for schools to have travel plans [introduced in 2006 – see next section]
  - stronger planning guidance requiring implementation of smarter choices in parallel with new development
  - greater regulation of public transport and fewer restrictions on cooperation between operators
- Greater implementation of local policies, including
  - reallocation of road capacity, parking restraint, congestion charging and workplace parking levies to encourage workplace travel plans
  - traffic calming, 20mph limits, safe crossings and parking restrictions outside schools to complement school travel planning
  - fast-tracking traffic orders for dedicated car club spaces and new national parking arrangements for car sharers
  - specific parking rights and investment in local drop-off facilities to encourage home shopping and less polluting logistics systems

Source Cairns et al. 2004

Evidence of the cost of the measures investigated varied widely both within and between categories, from 0.1 pence to 10 pence per vehicle kilometre removed with most cases being towards the lower end of this range. This suggested that their benefit:cost ratio could be of the order of 10:1 (and higher still in congested urban conditions). As a form of policy instrument therefore 'soft measures' appeared to offer very good value for money. However realising this potential is dependent on the policy context in which they are set and, for the present, a 'chicken and egg' situation prevails. The key policy initiatives identified as important to achieving the full potential of smarter choices are listed in Box 16.3.

16.5 Travel plans

In this and the following section we look at aspects of the Smarter Choices repertoire where public intervention is or potentially might be significant. We look first at the various forms of travel plan which here are grouped into three main types:

- workplace travel plans
- school travel plans
- residential travel plans.

Workplace travel plans (WTPs)

The term 'workplace' is used here in a very broad sense and covers almost all types of non-residential use other than schools. The main component is businesses (hence sometimes 'business travel plans') where the focus is on the travel behaviour of staff. However travel plans are also appropriate for other major generators of travel including hospitals, universities, freestanding retail developments, sporting venues and leisure attractions where the additional and often prime concern is the travel of visitors (hence sometimes 'visitor travel plans'). Government and local authority offices are also important, not least because of the example they set to others.

As noted previously, these organisations may introduce measures influencing travel behaviour for their own benefit, whether these are 'one-off' initiatives or a package of measures designed and implemented as part of a formal travel plan. Typically these arise because of parking and congestion problems on the site itself or in the immediate vicinity. They may also reflect concerns to utilise the available space most efficiently in meeting the relative needs of staff and visitors or as between different categories of staff (e.g. shift workers or those who need to use cars as part of their work). Potential cost-savings through teleworking, 'hot-desking', reduction in space needed for employee parking etc. are further incentives.

Public involvement in WTPs arises from two main sources:

1   promotional activity designed to encourage the voluntary adoption of measures amongst relevant organisations
2   negotiation on measures to be introduced within a new development as part of a condition of planning permission (as explained earlier in section 14.9).

In these cases the public objective will typically be to improve the travel choices on offer and to seek to reduce the amount of car travel generated. Emphasis is on the preparation of formalised travel plans, both to ensure that the objectives and options appropriate to the particular situation are examined in a comprehensive and systematic manner and so that a framework of targets is set against which travel behaviour can be monitored subsequently. In the case of travel plans prepared in connection with proposed developments, targets will be linked with the level of car parking or other facilities being provided so that the level of generated traffic is kept within the limits of what are considered acceptable conditions.

The travel plan will contain a mix of measures appropriate to the site and organisation in question but may include:

*   publicity and incentives (e.g. season ticket loans) for use of public transport (sometimes complemented by enhanced services to/from the site)
*   car-sharing scheme
*   promotion of opportunities and facilities for walking and cycling
*   alternative working practices (e.g. flexitime, home-working)
*   car parking management (which may include pricing or prioritising elements or 'cash-out' payments for employees who forgo a parking space)
*   car pools for business use (to obviate the need for employees to drive to work on the off-chance that they might need a car during the course of the day).

Much of the early work by local authorities in this field was concerned with engaging with major employers and encouraging the production of travel plans.

National guidance on Best Practice has also been published (DfT 2007n). By 2007 it was estimated that 11% of employers with 100 or more staff would have travel plans, 22% of hospitals and 51% of further/higher education establishments (Cairns et al. 2004 Table 3.3).

However this apparent progress is subject to two very important qualifications:

1   a large proportion of private firms have yet to engage with travel planning and there is a fear that those already participating represent the 'easy wins'
2   the production of travel plan documents should not be equated with achieving *actual changes in travel behaviour.*

Although individual examples of significant behavioural change can be cited, the norm is typically very modest (a reduction in car commuting by a few percentage points). 'Promoting travel choices' by itself is insufficient. To be effective this needs to be complemented by sticks or carrots (i.e. penalties for car use or rewards for forgoing it) and these are much more difficult to achieve – both in terms of support by the firm's management and acceptance by the workforce (G Emmerson in LTT 441).

In theory it should be possible to enforce the car use reductions anticipated in the travel plans produced as a condition of planning permission. However there are several barriers to this.

> ... the concept of the 'ideal travel plan' as developed for major single-occupier organisations does not easily translate into the planning context, particularly where multi-occupation, speculative development and commercial factors are major issues.
>
> (DfT 2005n)

A recent survey of highway authorities undertaken by Napier University indicates that almost 75% of travel plans currently produced are the product of a requirement for planning permission (LTT 487). However only four authorities had ever taken enforcement action in this field and, when asked how they would enforce such plans, the remaining 82 respondents said they were not sure or did not answer the question! The process is complicated by the fact that travel plan officers working for highway authorities are not responsible for dealing with breaches of planning permission, whilst travel plans feature very low in the list of issues to be monitored by enforcement officers working for planning authorities. Monitoring of travel behaviour is in any case a much more difficult proposition than monitoring the physical nature of developments, and unless funding for monitoring is included in the original section 106 agreement the necessary data will not be available.

Overall the evidence suggests that using the planning system as a 'back door' means of securing WTPs is not only unsatisfactory in coverage (by definition) but ineffective in outcome. Certainly there is no prospect of achieving the sort of national reductions in traffic suggested in the Smarter Choices report without a major overhaul in the instruments available.

School travel plans (STPs)

To date, the journey to school has prompted more public action than with any other type of soft measure. Two factors would seem to account for this:

1   a very distinctive set of issues surrounding children's journeys which gives them unusual prominence as candidates for intervention
2   the institutional character of schools, both as individual organisations closely linked to their local communities and collectively (as far as State schools are concerned) as subject to direct policy control by central government.

Unlike other forms of soft measure the motivation for school travel plans does not derive primarily from concerns about the general volume of car traffic or practical difficulties with staff or visitor parking. Rather the 'school run' generates public attention because it involves a concentration of journeys at particular places and times which can create chaotic conditions in the vicinity of school gates as well as conspicuously adding to congestion and safety hazards on local road networks. The welfare of the children involved is also a very sensitive political issue. Broader concerns about their development (lack of independence), poor preparation for adulthood, and – more recently – lack of physical activity contributing to obesity are further factors which have prompted Government involvement.

Initial work on school travel focused primarily on physical improvements such as traffic calming, 20 mph zones, cycle lanes and safe crossings.

> Over time the approach developed to include greater coordination on consultation with the school and local community, education and information measures, road safety training, changes within the school and initiatives such as 'walking buses' and, more recently, 'cycle trains'. These involve volunteer parents escorting children in groups on foot or by bike on a fixed route.
>
> (Cairns et al. 2004)

In 2001 Government funding was provided to enable travel co-ordinators to be appointed in local authorities to work on school travel and to provide free advice to schools. The scheme was extended in 2003 as part of a comprehensive Action Plan (DfES and DfT 2003a). This included the offer of capital grants of £5,000 and £10,000 to primary and secondary schools respectively who prepared an authorised travel plan and was accompanied by a good practice guide (DfES and DfT 2003b). A target was set of 40% of schools having travel plans by 2006 and all by 2010. Some of these may be plans prepared by schools as part of applications for planning permission.

An initial evaluation of the initiative suggested that, whilst some schools had reported achieving reductions in car use there were as many that had reported increases at primary school level and a higher number reporting increases (at secondary level) (DfT 2005m). By comparison with workplace plans it should be noted that the individual components of STPs are essentially of the 'carrot' variety, there being little opportunity to impose sanctions through the rationing or pricing of parking spaces. Significantly however the results of case studies listed 14 types of benefit which were being obtained, other than modal shift. These include raising environmental awareness, involving pupils in travel planning work through the curriculum, and opportunities for working with the local community.

As from 2007 the context for STP work has been strengthened through a statutory duty on local education authorities to promote the use of sustainable travel and transport. This is to be achieved through

- an assessment of needs within the authority's areas
- an audit of the sustainable travel and transport infrastructure available when travelling to, from or between schools or other institutions
- a strategy to develop this infrastructure so that needs are better catered for (in the context of the authority's community strategy, LTP and accessibility action plan – see Chapters 19 and 20)
- the promotion of sustainable travel.

Further details are given in Part 1 of DfES (2007).

Residential travel plans (RTPs)

Sadly residential travel plans are very much the poor relation of the travel plan family, despite the need and opportunity which exists for implementing them (Addison 2006). Unlike the other forms of travel plan, RTPs are almost exclusively associated with planning and negotiation of large new developments.

In theory managing the travel of people moving to new residential developments should be a focal point of any sustainable transport programme because such moves are typically linked with key points in individuals' 'life-cycles' such as getting married, having children or changing jobs (Jones et al. 1983). These are points at which previous habits often have to be reviewed, including the pattern of journeys made, the mode of travel and the number and use of household cars. Unfortunately instead of planned developments being viewed as the opportunity to bring about more sustainable patterns of travel, the reverse seems to occur with sharp increases in car dependency being reported amongst residents moving to new estates (Headicar and Curtis 1996).

Work undertaken as part of the preparation of good practice guidelines revealed that relatively few authorities are utilising RTPs and those that are face an uphill struggle. One of the reasons for this is the absence of official recognition of their role – they are not referred to in PPG13 (which quotes the need for travel plans only in relation to major *non-residential* development), nor in PPS3. There is also widespread misunderstanding of the character of RTPs. Unlike workplace plans they cannot simply take the form of management measures applied to existing developments (or 'bolted on' to the building of new ones). Rather they involve consideration of range of 'hard' and 'soft' measures throughout the development planning process (DfT 2005f).

As with travel plans generally the critical feature to securing lower levels of car use is likely to be the inclusion of 'sticks' as well as 'carrots'. However in the context of residential plans this implies restraint on car *ownership* and not merely car use for a particular trip purpose – clearly a more contentious proposition.

A way out of this conundrum, particularly in more densely developed urban areas, is through operation of a car club, either integral to the development or as part of a scheme already in the area. This is likely to be an attractive proposition to some residents if, by forgoing use of a parking space, the cost of their housing is reduced. The need for fewer parking spaces also offers benefits to developers through what can be achieved in terms of design and costs on the site as a whole. If the development consists of a block of flats or similar with a range of communal facilities, then almost certainly a management company will be established anyway which can include operating a travel plan, car club etc. as part of its responsibilities. Car clubs offer potentially the greatest benefits to all parties in the context of so-called 'car-free' developments (Morris 2005).

From a public perspective the operation of car clubs (whether as part of a travel plan or more generally) has the benefit that members who were previously car-owning (but who now adopt a 'pay as you go' approach) are likely to reduce their car mileage by around 60–70% (Cairns et al. 2004). The average change in mileage for all car club users is 33%. This lower figure reflects the fact that car club membership also offers the opportunity of car use to people who would otherwise not have had it, i.e. non-car-owners or people seeking occasional use of a second car. Advice on the setting up of car clubs and car sharing schemes and the role of local authorities in supporting them is given in ITP Ltd (2005).

16.6 Marketing and the 'Sustainable Towns' initiative

Marketing is a feature of all forms of soft measure as well as being a discrete activity in itself. It extends from the passive provision of information, through advertising and promotional campaigns (often involving the product branding of particular facilities or services) to the selective presentation and targeting of information at certain groups or individuals with a view to achieving attitudinal and/or behavioural change in their travel behaviour. Marketing can also be utilised in the branding of overall behavioural change programmes of which those undertaken as part of the Government's recent Sustainable Towns initiative are important examples.

Travel information

The availability of information about alternative modes is recognised as one of the major barriers to securing changes in travel behaviour amongst car users. Unlike other barriers such as cost and unreliability it is a shortcoming which can be rectified relatively quickly and cheaply. In line with its 'Integrated Transport' agenda the New Labour Government took two major initiatives in this field:

1   placing a statutory duty on local transport authorities (under the Transport Act 2000) to ensure the availability of bus service timetables
2   to establish (as part of the 2000 Ten Year Plan) a new national web-based journey information service (launched in 2004 as 'Transport Direct') embracing all modes and offered on a 'door to door' basis.

A further important information facility – for rail journeys – had been established previously as part of the privatisation of the network, through a National Rail Inquiry Service.

By 2006 Transport Direct had achieved its initial target of 6 million users a year. However the value of the service, both in meeting the needs of its users, and in serving public objectives of promoting choice and securing behavioural change is open to question. Prior to considering the next phase of its development DfT commissioned a review of research in the field of travel information generally (Lyons et al. 2007). This highlights the importance of understanding the reasons why individuals do (or do not) seek information and what their interpretation and response is to the information they receive. These factors cast a very different light on the 'rational/comprehensive' assumptions which underpin Transport Direct and similar facilities whose development has tended to be dominated by issues of data supply. The future of Transport Direct also has to be placed in the context of the much-expanded information environment in which it now operates, including real-time 'sat-nav' systems geared solely to the requirements of motorists.

Personalised travel plans (PTPs)

Utilising the above sources, targeted information about non-car options can be generated to meet the needs of people travelling to or from the sites where travel plans are in operation. A more sophisticated concept is of 'personalised travel plans', otherwise known as 'individualised travel marketing' (ITM) pioneered in Germany and Australia (Brog 2003).

This technique seeks to establish a dialogue with each person, sometimes on the basis of an initial travel diary, to determine whether

a   the respondent would be interested in exploring alternative travel behaviour and, if so,
b   what the options would be for them (given their particular activity needs) and their implications in terms of travel time, cost, health, emissions etc.

The dialogue is undertaken on the basis of partnership – a 'homoeopathic' approach – focusing on motivation and empowerment. Respondents are invited to consider transport-related issues which may be of concern to them, not merely those of public interest. Consistent with this approach, if a particular respondent expresses no interest in participating then they are not involved further. Amongst the remainder a process of segmentation is adopted with different groups receiving different types of information, travel incentives and further forms of contact according to their circumstances. A major benefit claimed for this approach is that, because it is entirely defined by individuals' own needs and inclinations, an overwhelmingly positive reaction is obtained.

In the UK in 2002 the DfT awarded grants of up to £50,000 to 14 local authorities in England to run pilot PTP projects in a variety of settings. Subsequent evaluation of these pilots reported that those targeted at residential populations were consistently the most effective in reducing car kilometres and increasing the use of sustainable modes. The cost per car km saved in these pilots varied between 3p and 18p, or between 2p and 10p if monitoring and evaluation costs were excluded (Operational Research Unit 2005).

'Sustainable Towns'

Following the 'Smarter Choices' research reported earlier, the DfT held a competition for towns to become showcases for the development of soft measures (Sustainable Travel Demonstration Towns). The three winners, Darlington, Peterborough and Worcester, were jointly allocated a total of £10m for five years beginning 2004. The aim was to establish whether the results identified in the various case studies and pilot exercises conducted previously could be replicated on a larger scale in single towns, and indeed whether additional synergy might be created. The results of an EU project were also brought together to provide guidelines for local authorities generally in mounting 'Smarter Choices' campaigns (DfT 2005e).

Each town developed their own brand names, images, logos and slogans for use in creating a recognisable 'theme' within which individual initiatives could be promoted (LTT 415). ITM programmes were planned as a major component, on a scale not previously seen in the UK. However the towns are relatively small and freestanding with a large proportion of short-distance trips, so that the potential for mode shift is higher than average. Reflections on experience to date in Darlington are given in Higgitt (2007) whilst experience and prospects more generally within the three towns are reviewed by R Thomas in LTT 481.

In May 2007 Transport Minister Gillian Merron appears to have been so impressed with the interim results from the Demonstration Towns that she wrote to all local authorities inviting them to give Smarter Choices 'strong consideration' when setting their budgets. Authorities might reasonably have countered that if DfT was so impressed it could conceivably have found rather more than the microscopically small amount from its own budget! Nevertheless changes are in prospect:

> Subject to value for money tests we will be increasing our investment in initiatives like these [Demonstration Towns] significantly in coming years and will publish detailed plans shortly.
>
> (DfT 2007s para 3.13)

Closely linked with the 'smarter choices' agenda is the scope for promoting walking and cycling (Sloman 2003a). In 2004 the Government published an Action Plan which identified 37 initiatives to be pursued and monitored by the Government with local authorities and other stakeholders (DfT 2004h). In practice the programme represented a 'realistic' replacement for the wholly unfulfilled aspirations of the New Deal in this field.

A programme of six cycling demonstration towns was initiated and this has recently been added to with the announcement of a much enhanced (£140m) programme over the three years to 2010/11. This will include training for an extra 500,000 children across England, links connecting around 500 more schools to the National Cycle Network and up to ten further cycle demonstration towns (LTT 486). Significantly the funding includes a contribution from the Department of Health that will be targeted at areas with high levels of obesity.

Part IV

Strategies, plans and planning procedures

In Part 3 we examined the repertoire of choices available to public decision-makers seeking to influence transport and travel. In this part of the book we explore the formalised mechanisms which have been established to guide and control the making of these choices which we refer to collectively as planning procedures. By 'procedures' we mean the *administrative* processes followed, either as a statutory requirement or as set out in guidance issued by national government. For the most part we are not concerned here with *technical* procedures (aimed at generating information in support of the planning process) except where these are required as part of it.

All planning is geared to the making or informing of decisions but not all decisions can be linked directly to a particular planning process. As we shall see, a number of different processes are followed at different levels of government and in relation to different sectors of public policy. Many overlap in place and time. Different agencies engage with different elements adopting different stances according to their individual responsibilities and constituencies of interest. All in all it is a very complex picture. For people concerned with outcomes in a particular locality it is extremely difficult to identify where, within the variety of planning activities conducted over time, key steps are taken which will ultimately have a defining influence.

And yet simply describing the formalised elements of planning, as presented in this part of the book, runs the danger of giving too neat and tidy an impression of what is actually going on. It needs to be emphasised that the brokering of power and decision-making continues both *within* the interstices of the planning framework (where flexibility is deliberately allowed for) as well as above and beyond it – in effect the field of policy studies. Exactly when, where, how and why decisions are made which account for the outcomes we all eventually experience 'on the ground' is a separate research area, of which, in relation to transport, there are sadly few examples. Readers are encouraged to explore general texts (Parsons 1995; Hill 2007) as well as Banister et al. (2000), Dudley and Richardson (2000) and Vigar (2002) which attempt to develop theory on the basis of case studies of transport planning.

In Part 4 we

- provide an overview of planning arrangements within Great Britain and explain the nature of 'national planning' as currently operated in England, Scotland and Wales (Chapter 17)
- explain the form and content of regional strategies and of local development and transport plans and the administrative requirements surrounding their preparation (Chapters 18–20)

- report the guidance published for the appraisal of transport projects seeking Government funding (Chapter 21)
- describe the formal examination regimes which apply to certain types of plan and project before approval is granted (Chapter 22).

17 National planning

17.1 Introduction

'Planning' and 'plans' are terms used in a variety of settings, including everyday speech, and can have rather different meanings. The reader's own interpretation is likely to be influenced by whether they have had experience of planning as a professional activity and, if so, which part of it. We therefore begin with a discussion of these terms and their role in governance (17.2).

In relation to transport and spatial planning we are particularly concerned with the way that generalised aspirations are translated into physical outcomes 'on the ground' in particular places. This involves a broadly hierarchical sequence of planning processes at national, regional and local levels. We explain the general character of this in section 17.3.

Overall responsibility for these processes in relation to inland surface transport is currently divided between the UK Government (but in this case concerned only with England) and the devolved administrations of Scotland and Wales. We explain what is meant by 'national planning' in this context in section 17.4 and describe the processes associated with it separately for each country in sections 17.5 to 17.7.

These national processes set the 'terms of reference' within which much of the executive activity in transport and spatial planning is carried out by sub-national (i.e. regional and local) bodies. In the final section we provide an overview of these sub-national planning arrangements (17.8) which acts as an introduction to the more detailed chapters which follow.

17.2 The nature of planning

National governments have ultimate responsibility for transport and travel conditions, but as we have seen, many of the instruments for influencing these lie with local authorities and other public agencies. Any government therefore has close interest in the effectiveness of what these other bodies are doing (relative to its own objectives) and – since it is the main paymaster – the efficiency with which they are doing it. But why should this translate into a requirement to prepare *plans*? For professionals already working in a planning environment the reasons may seem obvious but it is not so for the rest of the human race (witness the bafflement encountered in social situations when people ask what you do and you say you are a planner!).

Planning generally may be defined as an intelligence-generating activity aimed at improving the quality of decision-making. In essence it involves estimating the future circumstances in which initiatives might be brought into play, identifying the available choices and offering informed judgements on their relative merits to decision-takers – be they political leaders, board members or whoever.

Planning within government organisations is more problematic because of the context of political accountability in which it takes place. The 'validity' which members of the public ascribe to decisions is likely to depend on the manner in which choices are *seen* to have been identified and evaluated along the way, and the opportunity people have had to contribute. Decisions involving development (including transport developments) are especially contentious because they typically involve very visible changes in local environments and/or freedoms of movement. It is also almost inevitable that they involve shifts in the balance of benefits and disbenefits enjoyed at different places by different social groups – factors which can impact on property values, the profitability of businesses and individuals' quality of life.

Public planning in this field necessarily engages with, and impacts upon, a variety of groups (e.g. developers, transport operators, businesses, residents). The choices under consideration have to be developed in ways which are practically deliverable and which ultimately can command public support. Overall planning in relation to development therefore needs to be conceived as a broader process for facilitating the translation of aspirations into effective actions, taking account of opportunities and constraints and mediating between disparate interests and stakeholders.

There is a body of literature on the nature of planning in this context. Some of this is normative in character (i.e. seeking to identify those features which will enable the planning contribution to be most effective) – see for example Faludi (1989) and Healey (1997) as representatives of very different theoretical positions. Some is more behavioural in nature (i.e. seeking to identify what processes are actually followed in the name of planning) – see Vigar et al. (2000).

Within the 'proceduralist' tradition represented by Faludi the norm is taken to consist of a 'rational' planning process involving the explicit identification of aims followed by a systematic examination of possible choices and their merits relative to these (Box 17.1).

Although this lends itself to 'technical' planning exercises conducted in the back-offices of public authorities or consultancie,s its efficacy rapidly diminishes in the face of the real-world complexities posed in seeking to reconcile a variety of different conceptions and aspirations amongst different stakeholders. The 'communicative' approach advanced by Healey offers an alternative conception, viewing planning policies and their implementation as 'active processes of social construction, that is of human invention':

> Public policy-making, and processes of local environmental planning, may thus be reconceptualised as processes of intersubjective communication in the public sphere, through which mutual learning takes place.
>
> (Healey 1997 p. 55)

As we will see, the official requirements set for formal planning exercises embody elements of both of these approaches, with systematic, evidence-based procedures being coupled with practices aimed at public engagement and consensus-building. Both dimensions of planning activity are extremely demanding and professional planners are typically faced with pursuing them in the context of imposed timetables under a variety of resource constraints. In reality their task is better expressed as designing and

---

Box 17.1 Stages in an idealised planning process

- Reviewing existing and prospective future conditions
- Agreeing aims and objectives
- Identifying opportunities/constraints for achieving these
- Generating possible options (packages of complementary measures)
- Establishing the likely consequences of pursuing each option
- Appraising options relative to objectives and in the light of political, financial and practical issues surrounding their delivery
- Selecting a preferred option.

---

managing processes which marry political aspirations with administrative and legal requirements whilst minimising the adverse effects of technical and communicative sub-optimality.

As planners we need to be careful not to overstate the significance of formalised planning exercises within the wider context of governance (Figure 17.1). The 'mainstream' activity of organisations is the ongoing business of responding to conditions, deliberating on choices, making and then implementing decisions. Planning exercises proceed in parallel, often over a longer time-frame. Those that are required by law or which are an administrative requirement of Government will feed into deliberations, both as specific proposals and as a general policy background against which day-to-day decision-making is conducted. Authorities may of course commission additional planning studies to inform their decision-making (including a general monitoring and intelligence capability) but not everyone will view these as a fruitful use of time and money – some politicians and promoters have a clear idea of what needs doing and just want to get on with doing it!

Without the requirement to produce plans and to act in accordance with them, decision-takers will certainly find themselves under pressure to 'cut corners' and 'muddle through'. They are more likely to focus on a succession of immediate problems and deal with them on a one-off basis within a narrow set of criteria. Possible alternatives and inter-relationships will not be properly explored and no systematic assessment undertaken of effectiveness and wider impacts. In the interests of trying to get something done they may well seek to press ahead with a particular proposal only to find that, when it comes to the nitty gritty of implementation, the necessary public support and cooperation of other stakeholders has not been secured. Issues come to light which suggest that perhaps the proposal is not such a good idea as it seemed at first. Opposition mushrooms and very likely the whole scheme backfires and has to go 'back to the drawing board'.

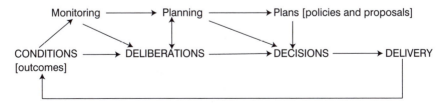

Figure 17.1 Planning and plans in the wider context of governance

Planning is no panacea – it cannot guarantee that a consensus will be reached and that a decision will prove to have been the most appropriate in the light of subsequent events. It may achieve better, more 'joined-up' and more acceptable outcomes and help fulfil wider and longer-term aspirations. But it is also likely to draw attention to difficult issues that most people, especially elected politicians, might prefer not having to face. Examples are the likely scale and nature of change taking place in an area, the conflicting views which people have of how this should be responded to, and the limited capability which public agencies may have to deal with problems and opportunities anyway.

Planning can also consume a great deal of time and resources, particularly where formalised procedures involve long periods devoted to public consultation, examination and approval. The resulting delay can be criticised for having the effect of prolonging unsatisfactory conditions, adding to costs and deferring desirable improvements. Hence the planning procedures which are established have to embody a balance between two sets of considerations and at any one time there will groups lobbying for 'speeding up the process' on the one hand and those arguing for more time to allow for fuller investigations, wider consultation, more rigorous scrutiny of proposals etc. on the other.

17.3 The pattern of plans

In the public sphere planning is undertaken at several levels. For illustrative purposes in relation to transport and development three main levels can be identified (the exact arrangements and terms used in each field will be described later):

- national policy statements
- regional strategies
- local plans.

At each level costed *programmes* may also be prepared summarising the intended initiatives to be undertaken within a specified time period, often subdivided by objective (e.g. road safety or economic regeneration), mode and/or delivery agent.

There is a hierarchical relationship between these plans in that the (more strategic) policies and proposals determined at a higher level create a framework within which bodies at lower levels have to work (Figure 17.2). (Even national governments have to work within the framework of EU and other international agreements they have signed up to.) At regional and local levels policies and proposals are developed in more detail, taking account of the implications of national policies for their areas and at the same time injecting their own policies and priorities.

Note however that, because there is no system of regional government in Great Britain, national policies impact directly on the work of local authorities as well as on regional assemblies (in England outside London) and regional partnerships (in Scotland and Wales). Likewise because these bodies have few, if any, executive powers, responsibility for delivery of their policies and proposals falls either to separately created executive agencies (such as the Highways Agency) or to local authorities. (London is a separate case and its position is explained later.)

Although the pattern depicted above provides a useful conceptual framework it is important to recognise that its form in practice has varied over time. There are also differences in the way it is manifested in the fields of transport and development

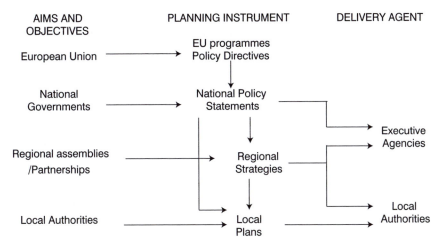

Figure 17.2 The hierarchy of plans 'translating aspiration into action'

planning and in England (outside London) and in the three areas of devolved administration – Scotland, Wales and London.

Some of the changes have taken place as a result of changes in the structuring of government. For example early development of the concept of spatial planning was pioneered by the European Union (concerned with cross-border issues and trans-national cooperation). However the practical implications of this were forestalled by the desire of national governments (especially in the UK) to protect their own jurisdictions and to assert the principle of 'subsidiarity'. (For a discussion of this see Chapter 4 of Cullingworth and Nadin 2006.) The political project of devolution undertaken by the New Labour Government provided impetus for 'national' planning projects in Scotland and Wales and for a much higher profile of planning activity in the English regions. Reforms in the pattern of local government have impacted on the forms of local development and transport planning.

Other changes have occurred as a result of shifts in the importance of public planning as perceived by the Government of the time. For example during the 1980s the statutory development plan system was allowed to fall into a substantial degree of neglect and parts were threatened with extinction. Privatisation of the bus and rail industries was also conceived in a manner which, bar the protection of socially necessary services, effectively amounted to the Government leaving outcomes to be determined by the market. Local transport plans, initially hailed by New Labour as the key instrument for bringing about integrated transport locally, have since operated under a degree of uncertainty as the Government has vacillated about mechanisms for local government funding and performance monitoring generally – quite separate considerations.

Whatever the details at any point in time the overall pattern of transport and development plans has been concerned with translating aspirations – national, regional and ultimately local – into actions 'on the ground'. In the process these physical changes have a strong influence on the character of particular places, including their economic, social and environmental attributes, although this often occurs in a disjointed fashion. In recent years the Government has therefore promoted a reconceptualisation of development planning as 'spatial planning'. This seeks to take a rounded, place-related view of *all* development and related activities (not merely those which are subject to the statutory development planning system), transport being one. This is in order to improve the efficiency and coherence of publicly sponsored programmes in contributing to the qualities of individual places and the opportunities available to their local populations.

> ... the spatial planning approach concentrates on establishing better coordination of territorial impacts *horizontally* across different [policy] sectors, *vertically* among different levels of jurisdiction and *geographically* across administrative boundaries.
> (Cullingworth and Nadin 2006 p. 91)

Despite its concern with spatial outcomes the overall planning process described thus far is nevertheless 'top-down' in character. A very different conception of 'place-shaping' derives from harnessing the energies and aspirations of people who live and work in an area in contributing to its well-being – very much a 'bottom-up' approach.

> At the centre of the place-shaping idea is the notion that local leadership is crucial to the economic, social and physical fabric of a locality. Places that are successful have economies where business investment, labour markets, public infrastructure and services share a set of objectives ... Such places create civic pride, partnerships between public and private sector, a belief in the importance of the public realm and a willingness to tackle complex social and environmental problems.
> An integrated approach to a locality and its problems is only possible in the locality and is most successful when locally owned.
> (Briscoe 2007)

Place-shaping is central to a distinctive agenda focused on 'communities' that has been developed in recent years by ODPM/DCLG, linked to its programme of reform in the workings of local government. Local Strategic Partnerships – voluntary associations comprising a local authority and representatives of other interests in an area – have been formed, charged with preparing 'Community Strategies'. These are designed to articulate local needs and priorities and to co-ordinate the actions of public, private and voluntary agencies in an area in fulfilling them. Local transport and development plans in England are now required to take account of these strategies as well as operating within the more established framework of 'top-down' policies and plans noted above, although the extent to which it will prove practicable to marry these two very different processes is unclear.

17.4 The meaning of 'national planning'

The term 'national planning' is somewhat confusing in the context of the political union that is Great Britain. Much legislation embodying transport policy – for example concerning traffic regulation, vehicle licensing and motoring taxation – was, and continues to be, framed for the whole of Great Britain.

Critically fiscal policy remains with central government, both in terms of revenue (taxation) and expenditure (although Scotland has a degree of discretion over income tax levels which it has not yet exercised). For Scotland and Wales – and also for London – payment comes in the form of a block grant which these devolved administrations have the discretion to allocate between 'domestic' services (including transport) as they see fit. Central government also retains responsibility for overall policy towards Britain's rail network, including the franchising of long-distance 'cross-border' services and for aviation. These are topics which are especially important to the circumstances of Scotland (Smyth 2003) and, in that sense, constrain its discretion.

At the level of the devolved governments the context for 'national planning' is also very different. In terms of population and geographical size the 'nations' of Scotland and Wales are akin to the 'regions' of England. Yet Scotland and Wales have elected governments which have discretion over the policies they adopt and the procedures through which they implement them (MacKinnon et al. 2008). By contrast the English regions outside London have no such status and essentially work within the policy and administrative frameworks set by national (central) government. This is the situation in which 'regional' bodies operate in Scotland and Wales, except that the areas they cover are more like the shire counties in England. Politically these regional bodies are akin to the 'joint boards' of constituent local authorities which form the Passenger Transport Authorities in the English metropolitan areas.

Finally London is an exception even to this very complicated pattern. In geographical size it is comparable with a Scots/Welsh region or an English county but in terms of population and economic significance it is much greater than either the *whole* of Scotland or Wales or any English region. In policy-making it has much of the discretion available to the devolved nations (and similarly has directly elected representation) but constitutionally is no more than a local authority!

Scotland has traditionally operated variants of the planning procedures applied in England and Wales. Since devolution in 1999, more distinctive regimes have been developed in both Scotland and Wales. Hence the current arrangements for the three countries are presented separately in the following sections.

In each case there are sub-sections on transport and on development or spatial planning. However their relationship is different. In England there is no single strategy or 'plan' at national level (and was none even during the time when DETR functioned as a single government department). Hence in England transport and development planning at national level is operated through separate vertical 'silos' with no formal relationship between them. (Policy development may involve a degree of collaborative working, but on an ad hoc basis; in essence the relationship between these two policy sectors is no different from any other.) In Scotland and Wales (and, as we will see later, in London) the situation is quite different with transport planning being treated as integral to, and ultimately a subordinate component of, overall spatial planning.

17.5 National planning in England

National transport planning in England

During the last quarter of the 20th century the concept of a national plan in any sector of public activity was decidedly unfashionable, inviting comparisons with Stalinist exercises of the 1930s or monolithic State enterprises in Britain in the 1950s and 1960s. Interestingly in the transport field national planning has only enjoyed continuous status in relation to motorways and trunk roads, although even here the possibility of fragmentation through privatisation was only narrowly missed in the early 1990s.

Unlike the situation now in Scotland and Wales, central government (in acting as the government for England) is under no statutory obligation to prepare or maintain a national plan for transport. Hence whether it publicly reviews existing and prospective conditions and links these to policy statements or strategies is very much at its own discretion.

The revival of interest in the national planning of transport during the mid/late 1990s can be attributed in part to the 'consensus for radical change' commented on previously (8.2). However the major planning initiatives undertaken in New Labour's early years – the 1998 White Paper and the Ten Year Plan – undoubtedly drew also on the political motivation to be seen to be 'making a difference'. Unfortunately this political dimension placed disproportionate significance on the presentational character of these documents which diminished their quality as planning instruments.

Ironically during the very time when the Government was exhorting others – notably local transport authorities – to demonstrate objective-led planning and stakeholder consultation as the basis of their programmes the Government found itself unable to apply these disciplines to its own work. Although the Ten Year Plan was backed up by extensive technical work no opportunity was afforded to debate this work or its policy implications. When published much of it was relegated to a background report so that the main document could focus on 'selling' the physical deliverables. Attention was thereby diverted from the process to the product.

As explained in section 8.5 the Plan was innovative in establishing 10-year profiles for the main sectors of transport spending (a feature which has been maintained following subsequent Spending Reviews). In each sector the Government's broad intentions and priorities were identified with an indicative outline of the number and type of major investments. With the exception of London (which was one of the expenditure sectors) there was no explicitly spatial dimension to the Plan. For the first time however a selected set of operational objectives and targets were published at national level.

Good intentions were signalled for monitoring the Plan:

> We will monitor closely the performance of the agencies involved in delivering the objectives and outcomes set out here and take regular stock of progress …. We will also ensure that the Plan continues to provide the most cost-effective and efficient means of delivering our strategy and that it takes account of new pressures and developments. We will therefore review the Plan periodically.
>
> (DETR 2000f paras 10.2–3)

In the event a single Progress Report was published in 2002 but as events proved not to materialise 'according to plan', the process of explicit, comprehensive reporting was abandoned thereafter. Hence instead of building an evolving, evidence-based process through successive reviews of the Plan the Government bowed to the political imperatives of presentation and published a 'new' strategy in the form of the 2004 White Paper. Thus began an unfortunate era in which the notion of a national 'plan' (other than purely a set of spending allocations) was dropped. Initiatives were simply 'layered' on top of what had been announced previously without any attempt to maintain a coherent narrative linked to systematic monitoring and updated projections. The Department's attention focused instead on the narrower set of short-term objectives and PSA targets agreed with the Treasury (11.6).

The importance of setting shorter-term programmes within a longer-term strategy now appears to have been accepted and a more considered process is currently being embarked on in preparation for the programmes to be delivered post-2014 (24.8).

National spatial planning in England

All governments in England have resisted the idea of a national spatial plan or framework, although they are regularly called on to prepare one by organisations such as the Royal Town Planning Institute and the Town and Country Planning Association. This does not mean that Government decisions do not have inter-regional or cross-boundary implications that would logically indicate the case for a national plan. Rather not having a plan appears to have the over-riding merit of not drawing attention to the extremely difficult and controversial issues involved and requiring them to be explicitly addressed.

Two of the most important issues are the future of the London metropolis (which in functional terms extends across at least three of the English regions) and the relationship of developments in this dominant area to the rest of the country, and indeed the rest of the UK. The absence of a plan also enables decisions which have inter-regional implications to be made on a one-off basis and kept 'under the radar'. Examples are the selection of housing growth areas in the Sustainable Communities Plan, the development of individual airports and the spatial patterning of investment by the Highways Agency and Network Rail.

National policy is contained instead in a series of generic Planning Policy Statements (which are progressively replacing the former Planning Policy Guidance Notes). Again the Government is under no obligation to publish documents of this kind. However in the field of spatial planning if it does so these have statutory significance in the preparation of regional strategies and local plans and are a material consideration in the determination of planning applications. There are currently about two dozen PPSs or PPGs on various subjects, the transport aspects of development being one (Box 17.2).

Ironically, given their significance for spatial planning at regional and local levels, it is the *absence* of spatial references in this national guidance which is one of its main weaknesses. For example policies such as the location of development in relation to

---

Box 17.2 The role of land use planning in relation to transport

Land use planning has a key role in delivering the Government's integrated transport strategy. By shaping the pattern of development and influencing the location, scale, density, design and mix of land uses, planning can help to reduce the need to travel, reduce the length of journeys and make it safer and easier for people to access jobs, shopping, leisure facilities and services by public transport, walking, and cycling. Consistent application of these planning policies will help to reduce some of the need for car journeys (by reducing the physical separation of key land uses) and enable people to make sustainable transport choices. These policies are therefore part of the Government's overall approach to addressing the needs of motorists, other road and public transport users, and business by reducing congestion and pollution and achieving better access to development and facilities. They will also help to promote sustainable distribution. In this way, planning policies can increase the effectiveness of other transport policies and help maximise the contribution of transport to improving our quality of life.

Source: DTLR 2001 PPG13 Transport para 3

accessibility by public transport have to be expressed in a way which is as applicable in Whitehaven as in Westminster! As a result the statements are inevitably rather generalised. Whilst they have been welcomed for introducing a degree of consistency into the workings of the development planning system they nevertheless leave plenty of room for argument in their precise application to local circumstances.

A further difficulty faced by users of national guidance is the proliferation of material and the problem of distilling all the elements from the various documents which are relevant to a particular situation. In making the transition from PPGs to PPSs the Government has therefore attempted to shorten the documents and to focus more explicitly on items of policy (i.e. those which *have* to be taken account of) as opposed to 'good practice' advice which is now generally published separately. A further focusing of policy, possibly with spatial references, is anticipated in connection with infrastructure of national significance (22.5).

17.6 National planning in Wales

National transport planning in Wales

Following devolution the Welsh Assembly Government (WAG) produced an overall *Plan for Wales* (2001a) and within this a range of strategies for individual topics – transport being one (WAG 2001b). This set out the overall objectives and priorities of the new Government and signalled its intention to review, adapt and develop the inherited legal and procedural arrangements for delivering them. These arrangements included the provisions of the Transport Act 2000 which applied to Wales.

A Welsh Transport Forum was established comprising representatives of about two dozen national transport-related organisations in Wales. As with the Commission for Integrated Transport set up by the UK Government this acts as a consultative body in the development of national policy and, via working sub-groups, acts as a mechanism through which options for the delivery of policy in particular fields can be investigated. An Executive Agency – Transport Wales – was established to deliver national policy, which (under the inherited arrangements) was responsible primarily for the development and management of trunk roads in the country.

In its early years WAG's aspirations were constrained by a combination of limited powers at a national level and fragmented decision-making at the local level, consequent upon the pattern of unitary local government introduced in the late 1990s. A series of voluntary regional consortia of local authorities was formed to promote integration and develop services across their individual boundaries. It was through these consortia that WAG invited bids for grant funding of major projects. These arrangements have been used as the basis of more recent sub-national reform (18.7).

As a result of the Transport (Wales) Act 2006 a duty has been placed on the Welsh Assembly to develop transport policies and to carry out its functions in pursuit of these policies. It is required to consult on and publish a Wales Transport Strategy to be approved by the full Assembly and to be kept under review. (This will replace the non-statutory Framework published in 2001.) A consultation document on this Strategy was published in 2006 (WAG 2006) and the 'outcomes and themes' identified in this have been used to provide a policy context for new Regional Transport Plans. The final version was published in May 2008 (WAG 2008b).

The 2006 Act also provides for subordinate legislation to be passed to enable Welsh Ministers to revise the pattern of transport authorities and procedural arrangements at sub-national level. It also gives the Assembly additional powers for directly funding transport infrastructure and services within Wales, including the passenger rail franchise (currently operated as Arriva Trains Wales).

National spatial planning in Wales

The Welsh Assembly Government began consultation on a national spatial framework in 2001 and the final document – the Wales Spatial Plan – was published in 2004 (WAG 2004). As a policy document it set out to:

- Provide a clear framework for future collaborative action involving the Welsh Assembly Government and its agencies, local authorities, the private and voluntary sectors to achieve the priorities it sets out nationally and regionally
- Influence the location of expenditure by the Assembly Government and its agencies
- Influence the mix and balance of public sector delivery agencies' programmes in different areas
- Set the context for local and community planning
- Provide a clear evidence base for the public, private and voluntary sectors to develop policy and action. (ibid. p. 4)

As well as steering programmes in 'top-down' fashion the Plan outlined strategies for six areas of Wales which interpreted the national vision and provided a framework for more local action. The six areas are North West, North East, Central and South East Wales plus Swansea Bay and Pembrokeshire. These areas are deliberately not defined in precise geographical terms so that individual issues, and the organisations involved, can be addressed on a cross-boundary basis as appropriate. Unlike in Scotland the reorganisation of local government on unitary lines in Wales was not accompanied by the retention of joint structure plans and hence there was a particular need to establish a wider context for the work of individual local planning authorities.

As part of the reform of the development planning system in England and Wales the 2004 Planning and Compulsory Purchase Act required the preparation of a spatial plan for Wales, to be approved by the Assembly. The Wales Spatial Plan referred to above was given statutory status for the purpose of steering the new breed of local development plans to be prepared under the Act (19.6).

Within this new statutory context preliminary outputs from an update of the Spatial Plan were published in 2007 including an Interim Statement for each of the six areas. Consultation on the Spatial Plan update was planned to continue into 2008.

Generic national planning policy guidance in Wales is published in the form of a single overarching statement (WAG 2002) complemented by a series of Technical Advice Notes (TANs). TAN18 (WAG 2007b) contains very similar material to PPG13 in England in providing the policy context for the transport aspects of local development planning. It also includes guidance for the integration of land use and transport planning at the regional level and on the transport assessment of development proposals which in England are published as separate documents.

17.7 National planning in Scotland

National transport planning in Scotland

At around the time of the 'New Deal' a separate Transport White Paper (Scottish Office 1998) and Transport (Scotland) Act 2001 were produced for Scotland although their content closely paralleled their English equivalents. However as in Wales there was no equivalent of England's Ten Year Plan – if only because, in the early years of devolved government, it would not have been practical politically or technically to have undertaken such an exercise. The first overview of transport developments in Scotland which reflected directions set by the new administration was published in 2002 (Scottish Executive 2002).

Political energies were focused more on bringing about institutional change (LTT 377). These were particularly concerned with creating mechanisms through which the policy priority of major public transport investments could be delivered. A 2004 White Paper (Scottish Executive 2004b) contained proposals enacted in the following year (Transport (Scotland) Act 2005). This created a new national transport agency for rail and trunk roads (Transport Scotland) together with powers for statutory Regional Strategic Partnerships (18.8). The 2005 UK Railways Act also transferred policy control of the rail network in Scotland to Scottish Ministers.

The 2004 White Paper signalled the intention to develop a National Transport Strategy and contained the objectives which were to form its guiding principles. A consultation exercise was mounted which invited responses on a large number of policy choices (Scottish Executive 2006a). On the face of it this represented a welcome contrast to the process followed in England, but in practice generated widespread criticism for its lack of focus. For example:

> We feel that it would have been of more value for the Scottish Executive to have led a consultation on a proposed strategy, rather than consult on a document that is basically a long and open-ended discussion paper.
>
> (Comments of TRANSform, the Scottish campaign group for sustainable transport, reported in LTT 450)

The final version of the Executive's strategy contains a series of policy packages directed at three 'strategic outcomes' together with action plans for rail, buses and freight (Scottish Executive 2006b). However unlike the situation in England the strategy does not have the backing of an agreed medium-term expenditure plan and progress will therefore be dependent on the outcomes of the Executive's Spending Reviews. The Executive intends to develop a range of indicators for measuring progress against the strategic outcomes and the strategy is planned to be reviewed every four years.

The strategy provides the policy framework for the range of planning processes in the country (Figure 17.3). These include a national review of major projects (Transport Scotland 2008b) which is the first ever nation-wide, multi-modal evaluation aimed at recommending a programme of interventions for implementation between 2012 and 2022.

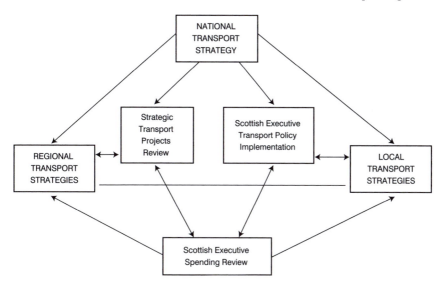

Figure 17.3 The relationship of the National Transport Strategy to other planning instruments in Scotland (source: after Scottish Executive 2006)

National spatial planning in Scotland

As in England and Wales statements of national policy were for many years confined to National Planning Policy Guidelines, and more technical Advice Notes. NPPG17 (Scottish Office 1999) followed PPG13 south of the border in promoting integrated land use/transport planning, and was later complemented by details of maximum parking standards in new development (Scottish Executive 2003). (NPPGs, as they come to be reviewed, are being retitled SPPs – Scottish Planning Policy.)

Following devolution a first National Planning Framework was produced, drawing into a single document evidence on Scotland's development and the factors influencing spatial change across the country (Scottish Executive 2004a). The motivation for producing the Framework was generated both externally and internally (Lloyd and Peel 2007). Externally it sought to promote Scotland's position as a nation within a European context and to demonstrate its readiness as a recipient of EU Structural Funding. Internally it was aimed at addressing regional disparities, including commuting patterns, city-region building and political commitment to sustainable development. The Framework offers a broad vision and non-statutory guide to enhance development planning by local planning authorities and to influence spending priorities in transport and other programmes.

The role of the Framework is being extended and given statutory status as part of the overall reform of the Scottish Planning System, comparable in significance (but different in content) to the 2004 Act in England. Proposals set out in a White Paper (Scottish Executive 2005a) were legislated for in the Planning etc. (Scotland) Act 2006. This requires the Framework to be approved by the Scottish Parliament and reviewed at not more than five-yearly intervals. New arrangements are also being introduced for the determination of applications for development of national strategic importance (so-called 'national developments') which will include transport infrastructure (Scottish Executive 2007a).

A second Framework document, due for publication in 2008 and covering the period to 2030, is undergoing an extensive programme of stakeholder involvement.

17.8 Sub-national planning: an overview

In this final section we give an overview of planning arrangements below national level throughout Britain to provide the context for consideration of the individual elements in the following chapters.

Although the nomenclature is confusing there is in fact a great deal of similarity in the current arrangements for sub-national planning in its four main constituent areas, viz:

- England (outside London)
- London
- Wales
- Scotland.

The key to understanding this is to recognise that the *same* types of planning activity are undertaken at *different* administrative levels. This is illustrated in Figure 17.4. The shaded cells highlight the levels at which the strategic relationship between transport and land use is considered and major transport projects are assessed. In Scotland and Wales this is at national level, in England it is at regional level (London in this context being classed as a region).

The precise form this strategic relationship takes in planning terms is slightly different. In the English regions outside London there is a separately identifiable Regional Transport Strategy, but it is embedded within a single Regional Spatial Strategy (RSS) document. In Wales and Scotland there are separate planning processes for transport and land use but there is a hierarchical relationship between them with the transport strategy delivering the major elements needed to fulfil the Spatial Plan/ National Planning Framework which in turn seek to deliver the strategic aims of the Assembly/Parliament. A similar situation exists in London where the Transport Strategy and the Sustainable Development Strategy (SDS) are separate entities and formally are two of several topics for which strategic policies are prepared. In practice however the Mayor has chosen to give the SDS primacy (and has titled it the 'London Plan' accordingly) such that the Transport Strategy takes on the character of a delivery mechanism.

Beneath this strategic level (i.e. below the shaded cells in Figure 17.4) there are two further levels of planning in most parts of Britain. In England this does not appear to be the case because the higher level is incorporated in the strategic document – sub-regional insets in the case of RSS and sub-regional frameworks (sectors) in the case of London's SDS. In Scotland and Wales the equivalent plans are freestanding.

Except for the four Scottish city regions a single tier of sub-national development planning operates at (unitary) local council level in Scotland and Wales. In these mostly rural areas there is insufficient spatial change to warrant an intermediate level of statutory planning between the national and local development plans.

In Wales there is also a single tier of sub-national transport planning. The former local transport plans of individual local authorities are being replaced by regional transport plans prepared by these authorities acting jointly through four consortia.

Within London a unique situation exists in which the body responsible for its strategic planning (the London Mayor) also has significant executive powers in the

	England Outside London — Transport	England Outside London — Development	England London — Transport	England London — Development	Wales — Transport	Wales — Development	Scotland — Transport	Scotland — Development
National governments	Ten Year Plan Road/Rail White Papers	Sustainable Communities Plan			Wales Transport Strategy	Wales Spatial Plan	National Transport Strategy Strategic Transport Projects Review	National Planning Framework
	Guidance on RTS and LTPs	Planning Policy Statements			Guidance on RTPs	Planning Policy Wales Technical Advice Notes	Guidance on RTS and LTS	Planning Policy Statements
Regional bodies/ London Mayor	Regional Spatial Strategy including Regional Transport Strategy		Transport Strategy	Sustainable Development Strategy ('The London Plan')	Regional Transport Plans	[Area strategies of Wales Spatial Plan]	Regional Transport Strategy	[Strategic Development Plans*]
	Sub-regional insets of RSS		Sub-regional frameworks of London Plan					
County Councils OR	Local Transport Plan							
Unitary councils	Local Transport Plan**	Local Development Frameworks	Local Transport Strategies	Local Development Plans		Local Development Plans	Local Transport Strategies	Local Development plans
District Councils / London Boroughs		Local Development Frameworks		Local Development Frameworks				

* Strategic development plans in Scotland are prepared for city-regions only

** In English metropolitan areas a single Local Transport Plan is prepared jointly by the constituent unitary councils and the Passenger Transport Authority

Figure 17.4 The pattern of plans for England (outside London), London, Wales and Scotland. Shaded cells show main locus for strategic integration of transport and development planning

fields of transport and development planning. The Mayor directly funds investment programmes, including the transport programmes of the London Boroughs. As a result the local transport and development planning undertaken by the London Borough Councils, although broadly similar to that undertaken by unitary councils elsewhere, operates within a tighter policy remit (as set by the Mayor).

In the shire counties of England local transport plans (LTPs) are prepared by county councils and local development frameworks by district councils. Elsewhere (outside London) both types of local plan are prepared by unitary councils. (In the case of the metropolitan areas LTPs are prepared jointly with the Passenger Transport Authority for the conurbation concerned.) However these local plans do not 'nest' neatly (geographically speaking) within the sub-regions defined in the regional strategies. This is because they are prepared for the whole of the administrative area of each authority whereas the sub-regional strategies are prepared for areas defined on a functional basis. As far as transport is concerned an improvement on this arrangement may come about in future as a consequence of the Government's proposals for 'Integrated Transport Areas' within the current Local Transport Bill (23.7).

18 Regional strategies

18.1 Introduction

In this chapter we consider the nature of the regional planning processes operating in different parts of Britain. The status of the different processes with this title was explained at the end of the previous chapter as part of an overview of sub-national arrangements.

We begin by noting the relationship between spatial, transport and other strategies in the English regions outside London (18.2) and then describing the requirements for Regional Spatial Strategies and Regional Transport Strategies as set out in Government guidance (18.3 and 18.4). In section 18.5 we comment on the Government's proposals arising from its Sub-National Review to abolish the English Regional Assemblies and to transfer their responsibilities in this field to Regional Development Agencies.

In the following three sections (18.6 to 18.8) we review the regional planning processes in London, Wales and Scotland highlighting their distinctive features.

18.2 Strategic planning in the English regions

Although the English regions outside London did not benefit from formal constitutional devolution in 1999 there has nevertheless been a sharp rise since in the significance of this regional tier of governance. In particular the perspectives of regional stakeholders have been brought to bear on public decision-making through the activities of the Regional Assemblies and Regional Development Agencies created at that time.

Responsibility for drafting Regional Planning Guidance was transferred from Government Regional Offices to the Regional Assemblies – consisting mainly of elected members from local authorities in the region. Over the last decade the role of these documents has evolved from a comparatively narrow remit concerned with guidance to local planning authorities on land use policy to an overarching strategy aimed at delivering the spatial component of public policies and programmes more generally. Of particular importance from our perspective is the fact that, since 1999, they have been required to include a separately identifiable Regional Transport Strategy (RTS). As a result of this and the subsequent abolition of Structure Plans the current Regional Spatial Strategies (RSS) provide the strategic policy framework for both Local Transport Plans and Local Development Frameworks.

During this period regional planning has also been important as far as the Government is concerned in helping drive key changes in policy within more local areas – towards sustainable development generally and to urban renaissance, the acceleration of housing provision in urban areas, and support for business development in particular (Marshall 2004). That said the Government is not averse to riding roughshod over regional planning exercises where it considers national needs dictate. This applied to the designation of 'growth areas' as part of the Sustainable Communities programme (8.8) and is currently threatened with the Transport Innovation Fund (23.4) and the Infrastructure Planning Commission (22.5). These reflect the absence of a national spatial strategy noted in the previous chapter.

In theory at least, Regional Spatial Strategies (RSS) occupy a pivotal position in planning within the English regions outside London. They are the first level at which national development and transport policies are translated into spatial effect and hence where attention to physical and functional integration begins to assume prominence. As a single document they then provide the spatial policy framework for the preparation of more local plans, especially via sub-regional insets for the more urbanised areas.

Regional strategies are also the level at which the case for or against the major proposals of individual local authorities has to be argued. Because there are no directly elected regional councils, the work of the Regional Assemblies provides a forum in which the individual and collective aspirations of local authorities and other stakeholders within the region can be debated and articulated to central government via its Regional Office. Equally it provides a medium though which central government can seek to engage these bodies collectively within a region in advancing its own policy agenda (although Regional Office staff also maintain a dialogue with individual authorities).

RSS also provides the strategic spatial context for the work of the Regional Development Agencies (RDAs) and other delivery agencies such as the Highways Agency and the Homes and Communities Agency (the successor to English Partnerships and the Housing Corporation concerned with delivering social housing). Figure 18.1 shows the relationship of RSS to these other plans and agencies at the regional level as well as to the planning processes of local authorities. As can be seen, the overall pattern is complex. The fact that it is not always clear where a particular process begins or ends or which parts follow or are conditional upon others is not a fault of the diagram!

However the nominally central position occupied by regional strategies somewhat misrepresents their significance within the totality of planning activity within a region – for two main reasons:

1   The regional assemblies which have prime responsibility for preparing RSS/RTS are relatively weak bodies. They have no independent political mandate and their ability to exert a distinctive policy influence is dependent on the degree to which it is possible to secure a degree of consensus amongst their constituent local authorities. They also have very limited resources and executive powers of their own. They are therefore heavily dependent on other agencies for contributing information and 'intelligence'. These include local highway authorities and other transport providers for operational data and for the generation and working up of proposals – a role which in practice gives these 'lower' bodies considerable leverage. In fact, because regional assemblies are not directly elected, special provision is made for the principal local authorities to formally initiate strategic proposals for their areas – i.e. a 'bottom-up' process.

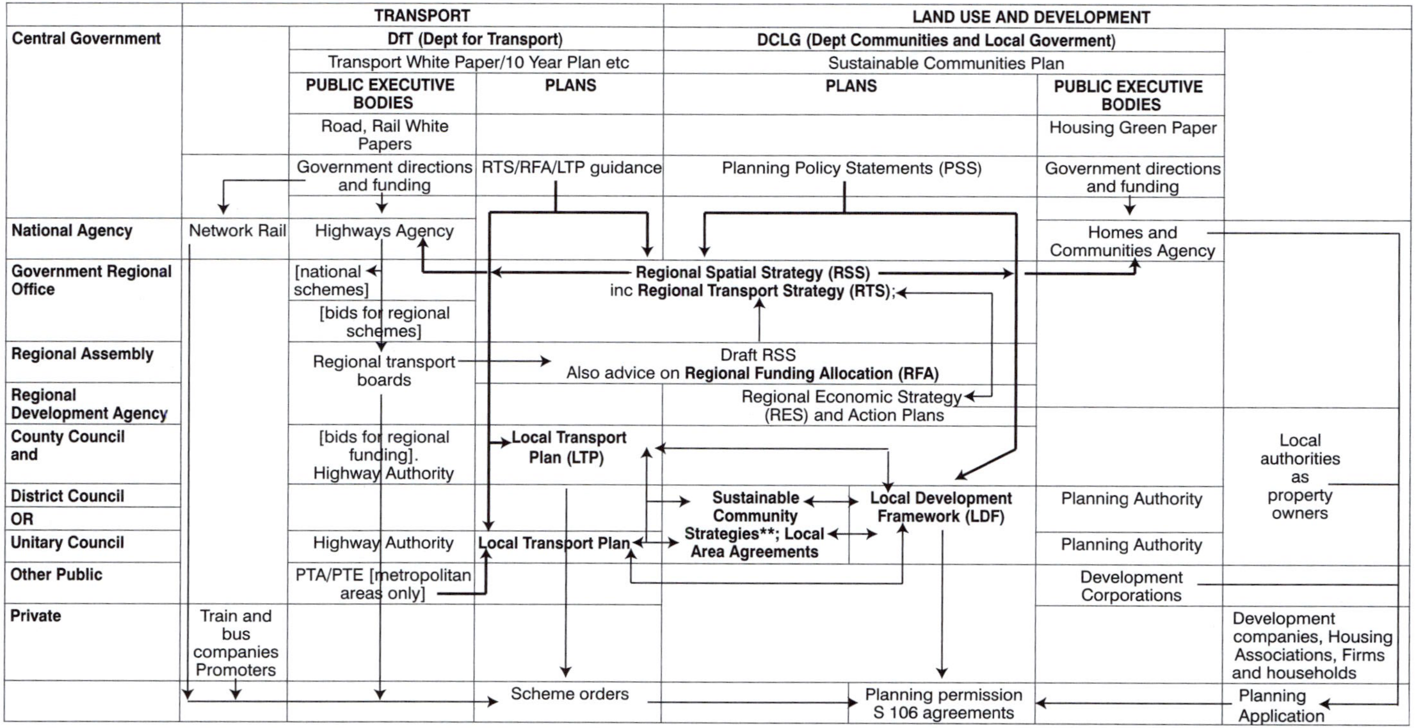

Figure 18.1 — The relationship of Regional Spatial Strategies* to other planning processes [England outside London]

	TRANSPORT — DfT (Dept for Transport) — Transport White Paper/10 Year Plan etc		LAND USE AND DEVELOPMENT — DCLG (Dept Communities and Local Goverment) — Sustainable Communities Plan	
	PUBLIC EXECUTIVE BODIES	PLANS	PLANS	PUBLIC EXECUTIVE BODIES
Central Government	Road, Rail White Papers	Government directions and funding — RTS/RFA/LTP guidance	Planning Policy Statements (PSS)	Housing Green Paper — Government directions and funding
National Agency	Network Rail — Highways Agency			Homes and Communities Agency
Government Regional Office	[national schemes] — [bids for regional schemes]	Regional Spatial Strategy (RSS) inc Regional Transport Strategy (RTS)		
Regional Assembly	Regional transport boards	Draft RSS — Also advice on Regional Funding Allocation (RFA)		
Regional Development Agency			Regional Economic Strategy (RES) and Action Plans	
County Council and	[bids for regional funding]. Highway Authority	Local Transport Plan (LTP)	Sustainable Community Strategies**; Local Area Agreements	
District Council OR			Local Development Framework (LDF)	Planning Authority
Unitary Council	Highway Authority	Local Transport Plan		Planning Authority
Other Public	PTA/PTE [metropolitan areas only]			Development Corporations
Private	Train and bus companies Promoters	Scheme orders	Planning permission S 106 agreements	Development companies, Housing Associations, Firms and households — Planning Application — Local authorities as property owners

* Note that by 2011 the Government proposes that the Regional Spatial and Economic Strategies will have been integrated into single strategy drafted by the RDA – see 18.5
** Sustainable Community Strategies are prepared by Local Strategic Partnerships – a mix of public, private and voluntary agencies led by the relevant local council (see x.x)

Figure 18.1 The relationship of Regional Spatial Strategies* to other planning processes [England outside London]

2   Although the transport and development planning processes are formally joined at the regional level it would be more accurate to describe them as being mutually 'aligned' rather than genuinely integrated. As we will see, there are distinct differences other than just subject matter which characterise the two processes and which reflect their different origins. The attempt to integrate them at regional level is relatively recent and procedures remain in place for both which would enable them to function perfectly well in an administrative sense independently of the other.

18.3 Regional Spatial Strategies

Government guidance on RSS is set out in PPS11 (ODPM 2004a) and will be described here under the headings of

* purpose
* form and content, and
* administrative procedures.

Purpose

The Government's ambition for RSS is expressed in the opening sentence of PPS11:

> The main principles of the new arrangements are to deliver policy better at the regional level and contribute to the culture change necessary to deliver the Government's Sustainable Communities Plan.
>
> (ibid. para 1.1)

The purpose of the RSS is to provide a broad development strategy for a region over a 15–20 year period, taking into account

* the scale and distribution of provision for new housing
* priorities for the environment
* transport, infrastructure, economic development, agriculture, minerals extraction and waste treatment and disposal.

From a transport perspective the strategy has an important role in identifying planning policy levers which can contribute to more sustainable travel patterns. In steering policies within local development plans it will also help deliver more appropriate locations in relation to the existing and planned future transport network.

RSS has to be prepared in the context of a Regional Sustainable Development Framework which is intended to have a 'key role' in resolving any conflicts between individual strategies prepared by regional bodies. These include the Regional Economic Strategy prepared by the Regional Development Agency (the only strategy other than RSS to have a statutory basis) as well as strategies for health, higher education and skills, housing, environment, culture and other policy areas. The Framework also seeks to ensure a 'fully integrated approach to sustainable development' – a rather optimistic aim except at a very generalised level commensurate with its 'vision' status.

RSS also has to be consistent with, and supportive of, these other regional strategies. The Guidance is careful not to give RSS any primacy amongst these other strategies; rather there is intended to be a 'two-way relationship' between them all. No indication is given as to what this phrase actually means. In practice the relative importance attached to the different strategies and the issues they address will have a significant bearing on the character of the RSS. However the fact that they are prepared by a variety of agencies over different timescales with different resources, status and so on means that the interaction takes place on a very uneven playing field. There is no formal mechanism for testing whether they 'join up' or how they might be amended if they do not.

Nevertheless the Government has taken steps to try and improve prospects for integration at regional level. For example the Regional Assembly is encouraged to explore with other agencies whether it is feasible to 'join up' consultation exercises, potentially achieving economies and reducing 'consultation fatigue' as well as promoting integration. The Regional Assembly and other bodies also have to come together to provide co-ordinated 'advice' on the regional funding allocation for transport, housing and economic development (22.6).

The particular issue of integration between land use and transport strategies illustrates the difficulties which have to be overcome more generally. Although, uniquely, the transport strategy is included as an integral part of the RSS *document* ,research on the first round of RTS discovered that there were problems in achieving integration in substance, with it rather being 'bolted on' as a separate chapter instead (MVA 2004). This arose in part from the inertia of separate working inherited from the previous era and partly from practical constraints surrounding production of the RTS – it often being dependent on a small group of local authority professionals who had to continue to fulfil their 'day job' at the same time. It is even more difficult to achieve meaningful engagement from transport organisations who are not themselves members of the Regional Assembly (e.g. Network Rail and bus and train operators), who determine their own policies and programmes and may see no advantage from participating in the RSS process.

Form and content

PPS11 states that the RSS should provide a spatial vision for the region plus a concise spatial strategy for achieving it including an agreed implementation plan. The detailed requirements are listed in Box 18.1.

In its format the RSS is required to make clear whether its policies relate to strategic development control, delivery through local transport or development plans, or delivery through other means. Policy statements have to be distinguished from supporting text and accompanied by a key diagram. Advice on the approach to be taken on substantive topics other than transport is given in Annex A of PPS11. For the transport component – i.e. the Regional Transport Strategy – it is contained in a separate guidance note (considered in the next section).

The implementation plan for the RSS has to identify which organisation(s) are responsible for delivery of each policy and proposal, their current formal status and timescale for delivery including any output targets. This information is said to be necessary in order to be able to test the realism of the strategy. However we may note that this is dependent on sufficient cooperation and input being received from 'external' agencies who in practice are under no obligation to supply it.

For transport issues targets need to be developed within a framework which takes account of the national targets set by Government and the local targets incorporated in LTPs (20.7).

Box 18.1 Requirements of a Regional Spatial Strategy

Based on PPS11 2004 para 1.7

The RSS should:

- articulate a spatial vision of what the region will look like at the end of the period of the strategy
- provide a concise spatial strategy for achieving that vision, defining its main aims and objectives, illustrated by a key diagram, with the policies clearly highlighted
- address regional or sub-regional issues that will often cross county or unitary authority and, on occasion, district boundaries, and take advantage of the range of development options that exist at that level
- be consistent with and supportive of other regional frameworks and strategies, including the RSDF and the regional cultural, economic and housing strategies
- provide spatially specific policies applying national policies to the circumstances of the region
- be locationally but not site specific, while not going into the level of detail more appropriate to a LDD
- be focused on delivery mechanisms which make clear what is to be done by whom and by when
- provide a clear link between policy objectives and priorities, targets and indicators
- should apply the test of adding value to the overall planning process, and
- contribute to the achievement of sustainable development in line with section 39 of the Act.

The draft RSS has to be accompanied by details of proposed monitoring arrangements, including the establishment by the regional planning body of partnership arrangements with local planning authorities, the RDA, the Regional Observatory (itself a partnership provider of data and intelligence) and other regional bodies as appropriate.

The structure of the Annual Monitoring Report is for each region to decide but indicators should be used to address the following implementation issues (see also DCLG 2008d):

- whether policies and related targets have been met or progress is 'on track' (or, if not, why)
- what significant impacts policies are having on the social, environmental and economic characteristics of the area and whether these are as predicted by the Sustainability Appraisal
- whether policies need amending because they are not working as intended or because national policy or regional circumstances have changed
- whether the way the RSS is being implemented needs alteration in order to ensure delivery.

Administrative procedures

As a result of the 2004 Planning and Compulsory Purchase Act the planning documents previously known as Regional Planning Guidance have been re-titled Regional Spatial Strategies and now form part of the statutory development plan for an area. Technically therefore new strategies are classed as 'revisions' of these initial documents. A single strategy is prepared for each of the English administrative regions outside London.

Regional Planning Bodies (RPBs – to date the Regional Assemblies) have the principal responsibility for preparing revisions to an RSS. Formally these are 'draft' revisions since the final version has to be issued by the Secretary of State (DCLG).

The issues to be addressed and a timetable for the revision process have to be agreed between an RPB and the relevant Government Regional Office. The main stages in the revision process are:

- identify revision issues and prepare a project plan
- develop options and policies, assess effects and prepare draft RSS
- publish draft RSS and provide for formal consultation
- examination in public conducted by independent Panel
- publication of Panel report and consultation on proposed changes to draft RSS
- Secretary of State issues final RSS.

A maximum overall timescale of three years is envisaged of which only 15 months is allocated to the preparation of the draft RSS itself.

Although the RPB has the leadership role in the preparation process this has to be carried out on the basis of partnership working with regional stakeholders and community involvement. RPBs are encouraged to establish topic groups of stakeholders reporting to a central steering group – these to include representatives from the Regional Development Agency and other bodies producing strategies at the regional level as well as organisations responsible for key infrastructure and services critical to RSS delivery. The RPB is also statutorily required to prepare, publish and keep under review a statement of public participation. The PPS makes clear that 'consultation' in this context is not viewed as a one-off exercise but rather a continuous process of pro-active involvement.

Primarily because of the abolition of Structure Plans and the consequent loss of direct planning powers by County Councils, the 2004 Act made specific provision for the involvement of these and other principal councils (so-called section 4(4) authorities) in the preparation of draft RSS. RPBs are required to seek the *advice* of these bodies with strategic planning expertise. They may also enter into *arrangements* with them in commissioning items of technical work. (Land use/transport studies cutting across individual local authority boundaries are highlighted as an example.) Where an RPB decides to include policies which are specific to particular parts of a region (e.g. for individual city regions or growth areas) then the relevant 4(4) authorities also have the right to prepare what are known as 'first detailed proposals' for these sub-regional elements.

There are requirements for publication of the draft RSS and associated documents, including to all councils in the area affected by the revisions and to other consultees. A period of between 6 and 12 weeks (depending on the scale of revision) is then allowed for representations to be submitted on the draft. Except where only minor revisions are involved, an Examination in Public (EIP) then follows undertaken by a Panel appointed by the Secretary of State (22.2).

18.4 Regional Transport Strategies

Guidance on the transport component of RSS is contained in Annex B of PPS 11 and in a separate guidance note from DfT (DfT 2006g).

Purpose

The declared purpose of the Regional Transport Strategy (RTS) is to

- set out how national transport policies and programmes will be delivered in the regions
- outline the transport and related land use policies and measures required to support the spatial strategy
- provide a long-term framework for transport in the region
- steer the development of local transport plans and local development policies.

In relation to Local Transport Plans the RTS has a specific role by focusing on policy priorities at the sub-regional level (including addressing intra-regional and cross-boundary issues) and by identifying transport measures of a regional significance to be taken forward as part of the LTP process. The aim of RTS should also be to 'add value' to the national guidance on LTPs and emphasises that local authorities should consider the feasibility, affordability and value for money of measures identified in the RTS *before* including them in their LTPs.

Form and content

RPBs are advised that the requirement for RTS to be 'an integral and clearly identifiable part of RSS' is likely to be best served by making them a separate chapter with cross-references to policy material in other chapters and contextual material, analysis etc. set out in a background document. The list of requirements concerning content is given in Box 18.2.

Objectives should be focused on the wider policy priorities of the spatial strategy and not on narrow transport issues. They should also be regionally-specific and add value to national policy.

The RTS is required to set out policies and proposed solutions for addressing the identified problems and objectives, with in each case a brief explanation of their rationale and analytical basis. The DfT guide is careful to point out that RPBs should consider *first* a range of options for ensuring the effective use of existing transport assets and for influencing patterns of travel through demand management and alternative land use strategies. They should also consider the scope for encouraging investment by the private sector. Where public sector investment is being considered, attention should not simply be focused on major items of new infrastructure but on network management and small-scale infrastructure enhancements. However we should note that except where measures of this can 'bundled' into a package which the DfT is prepared to consider as a major scheme, there can be a perverse incentive for local highway authorities to pursue the 'big bang' approach of bidding for a

---

Box 18.2 Requirements of a Regional Transport Strategy

The RTS should provide:

- regional objectives and priorities for transport investment and management across all modes to support the spatial strategy and delivery of sustainable national transport policies
- a strategic steer on the future development of airports and ports in the region consistent with national policy and the development of inland waterways
- guidance on priorities for managing and improving the trunk road network, and local roads of regional or sub-regional importance
- advice on the promotion of sustainable freight distribution where there is an appropriate regional or sub-regional dimension
- a strategic framework for public transport that identifies measures to improve accessibility to jobs and key services at the regional and sub-regional level, expands travel choice, improves access for those without a car, and guides the location of new development
- advice on parking policies appropriate to different parts of the region, and
- guidance on the strategic context for local demand management measures within the region.

Source: PPS11 Annex B para 4

---

single large project as this potentially increases their chances of receiving additional funding.

RPBs are expected to include in their strategies a 'framework' within which affordable priorities for public sector investment can be determined. The implication is that RTS will refer to more potential investments during the plan period than will be affordable in practice – in effect presenting a 'long list' or 'preparation pool' from which individual schemes will subsequently be selected and brought forward for implementation. This occurs because neither the likely level of funding nor the cost, practicability or value for money of proposals will be known beyond the initial few years. This may be a realistic reflection of the uncertainties involved in planning and managing major investment programmes but it does raise questions about what exactly is 'included' in an RSS/RTS and whether this is sufficient for its impacts to be identified and its soundness and deliverability to be assessed.

For all the emphasis placed on public involvement in the preparation of the strategy it is decisions made subsequently about the progressing and funding of individual schemes which determines what actually materialises. The prioritisation undertaken within the medium-term Regional Funding Allocation (RFA) is a critical subsequent stage (22.6).

For evidence of case studies and commentary on the RSS/RTS process in practice readers are referred to Glasson and Marshall (2007).

Administrative procedures

Administratively the Regional Transport Strategy (RTS) is handled as an integral part of RSS and is therefore subject to the same arrangements. However the RTS is a component which lends itself to revision separately from the remainder of the strategy if the need arises. For example this could be done to incorporate decisions made by DfT about the approval and timing for implementation of major transport investments in the region – decisions which in an administrative sense are made independently of the approval and publication of any region's RSS/RTS.

18.5 Changes consequent on the Sub-National Review

The Sub-National Review (DTI 2007) has its origins in the Government's failure to achieve public backing for its earlier intention to progress the devolution agenda through directly elected regional assemblies (8.4). An alternative pattern of reform was seen to be needed which would improve upon the initial arrangements for governance in the English regions introduced in 1999.

Significantly the Review was focused on economic development as the driver of change. It was led by the former Department of Trade and Industry (re-named the Department for Business, Enterprise and Regulatory Reform in 2007) with some input from DCLG. Publication of the Review itself was followed by a consultation document on its proposals (BERR et al. 2008a). If carried through, the regional institutions and planning procedures described thus far are expected to be reformed by 2011 although transitional changes are expected to begin before then:

> The challenge for central and local government is to organise itself to facilitate better outcomes at the most appropriate level through more focused decision-making in competitive, dynamic localities, sub-regions and regions. The SNR is a vehicle for reforming public institutions to enable them to achieve sustainable economic growth, development and regeneration at every spatial level through better alignment of economic and spatial planning within a sustainable development framework.
>
> (ibid. para 2.3)

The principle of 'promoting sustainable growth' underpins the reforms. This is defined as

> economic growth that can be sustained and is within environmental limits, but also enhances the environment and social welfare and avoids greater extremes in future economic cycles.
>
> (ibid. p. 15)

The SNR also places strong emphasis on devolved decision-making to the most appropriate level. Its proposals are being introduced as part of a wider programme of governance reform including the changes consequent upon the Local Government and Public Health Act, the Planning Bill and the Local Transport Bill (Chapter 23).

The proposed SNR reforms are:

• to streamline the regional tier of governance and to introduce single integrated regional strategies (IRS)
• to strengthen the local authority role in economic development
• to support collaboration by local authorities across economic areas.

(The reforms affecting local authorities are explained in the next chapter.)

As noted previously the arrangements introduced in 1999 created a somewhat ambiguous relationship in the English regions between the Regional Development Agency (RDA) responsible for the Regional Economic Strategy and the Regional Assembly responsible for the Regional Spatial Strategy. (In London the Mayor has responsibility for both.) Structural change to secure better integration was a logical development. However the manner in which the Government proposed to do this was highly controversial. Consistent with its emphasis on economic development the Government proposed to give the RDA responsibility for preparing a single strategy and to abolish the Regional Assembly. The RDA would become the regional planning body (RPB) and the IRS would then incorporate all strategies currently prepared at regional level, not merely RES and RSS/RTS. The IRS would assume the status of the regional component of the 'development plan' and thus form part of the statutory framework for local development planning and development control.

If proceeded with this would mean the role of RPB being transferred to a body which

a   is in the nature of an executive agency traditionally concerned with short/medium-term delivery rather than longer-term planning
b   is business-led in character, charged with pursuing a particular sectoral objective (promoting sustainable economic growth) rather than managing the interplay between a range of objectives
c   is run by a board of Government appointees rather than by an assembly of elected representatives from within the region.

To maintain the link with elected representatives (following the abolition of Regional Assemblies) the leaders of councils in each region were expected to organise themselves into a 'forum' which would 'sign off' (i.e. agree to) the draft IRS before it was submitted to Ministers. Following consultation however the Government has accepted the case for a collaborative approach to producing the draft regional strategy with the RDA and the Local Authority Leaders Board having joint responsibility for its drafting, implementation plan and monitoring of delivery (BERR and DCLG 2008b).

The IRS are intended to be 'succinct documents setting out the regions' vision for how and where sustainable growth should be delivered'. They are also intended to be produced according to a 'streamlined' process taking just 25 months to ministerial approval (Figure 18.2) – i.e. about two-thirds of the time set for the current RSS. The practicality of these two aspirations is scarcely credible – or if they are to be achieved then they imply much more cursory intelligence gathering and stakeholder involvement.

The SNR Consultation Paper does not refer to any 'separately identifiable' RTS component (though transport will be one of the mechanisms for delivering growth) nor to sub-regional strategies forming part of the IRS. If omitted this would remove the more detailed area-specific policies which are critical for effective local development and transport planning. (In the current draft RSS for South East England this sub-regional component occupies almost a third of the 340-page Core Document.) Such omissions would merely defer consideration of cross-boundary issues and provoke additional uncertainty, contention and delay within the overall planning process. It is possible that these voids might be filled by joint local authority working but whether and how the various pieces of the jigsaw for economic development, spatial planning and transport might be made to 'fit' in time and place at the sub-regional level is unclear.

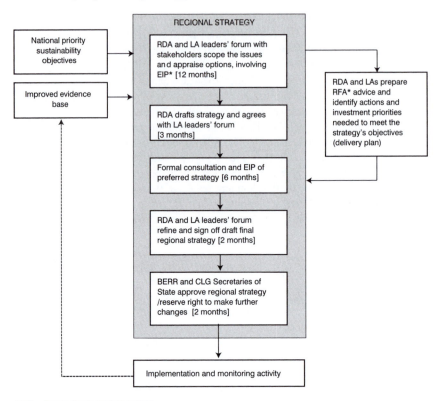

* EIP = Examination in Public [see 22.2]
RFA = Regional Funding Allocation [see 22.6]

Figure 18.2 The 'streamlined process' proposed for Integrated Regional Strategies (source: based on BERR and DCLG 2008 p. 35)

18.6 Strategic planning in London

Strategic planning in London is undertaken by the Mayor with scrutiny from the elected members of the Greater London Authority (GLA). Under the GLA Act of 1999 the Mayor is charged with producing a number of strategies, two being the Spatial Development Strategy (SDS) and the Transport Strategy. The Mayor has chosen to give primacy to the SDS which is referred to as the 'London Plan'. The first version was published in 2004.

Formally the SDS occupies a similar position within the statutory development planning system as the English Regional Spatial Strategies. Plans prepared by local planning authorities (in this case London Boroughs) have to be in general conformity with it and legally its policies constitute a material consideration in their determination of planning applications. The Mayor has to be consulted on defined classes of major applications and – unlike the Regional Assemblies – has the power to direct refusal. The Mayor also leads on several strategic initiatives including the Thames Gateway Growth Area, the Lower Lea Valley regeneration area and planning for the 2012 Olympic Games.

In 2006 the Mayor supplemented the policies in the SDS by publishing five non-statutory Sub-Regional Development Frameworks. These cover Central London and four geographical sectors and are intended to provide a bridge between the general policies in the SDS and the particular circumstances of each sector. Also in 2006 an 'early alteration' to the SDS was published which amended a limited range of policies, notably in respect of the scale of housing provision.

The Mayor is also party to an Inter-Regional Forum which has been established with the South-East and East of England Regional Assemblies to advise on planning issues in the wider London region.

The transport component of the SDS is subject to public examination but the Transport Strategy itself is not. The first strategy was published in 2001 and has been revised on two occasions since – in 2004 (to include the western extension of the Central London congestion charging zone) and in 2006 (to include the Transport and Air Quality Strategy).

The nature and role of London's Transport Strategy is very different from the RTS of the English regions. It is more fully developed and is in the nature of a strategic investment programme. This derives from the unique institutional position of the Mayor. His overall autonomy is similar to that of the devolved governments in Wales and Scotland but his executive powers are more wide-ranging and bring him into much closer contact with delivery at the local level.

1   The Mayor has discretion over the allocation of block funding received from central government, both within transport and between transport and other programme areas. He therefore does not have to offer 'advice' on RFA (Regional Funding Allocation) and is not dependent on Government's response on this or on the approval and prioritisation of individual major schemes.

2   By virtue of his directly elected position the Mayor is able to exercise sole decision-making – the London Strategy and the prioritisation of schemes is not dependent on a consensus being brokered between regional stakeholders and individual local authorities represented in a Regional Assembly.

3   The Mayor has several major executive functions in the field of transport and can therefore implement his policies directly rather than being dependent on other agencies. He controls bus, tram and Underground services and fares in the capital as well as 580 km of strategic roads and all of London's traffic signals. (The main functions over which he does *not* have direct control are National Rail services and sections of trunk road and motorway in Outer London.) From a funding perspective the Mayor also has the advantage of access to the revenue streams from bus and Underground services and from the congestion charging scheme.

4   The Mayor has much greater leverage over the activities of London Boroughs than do the English Regional Assemblies over their constituent local highway authorities. This is because statutorily the Boroughs act as implementation agencies for the Mayor's Strategy and it is from the Mayor rather than the Government that they receive grant funding for minor works programmes. The broad policy framework provided by the Transport Strategy is supplemented by advice on individual programme areas contained in separate guidance (20.9).

18.7 Regional Transport Strategies in Wales

Unlike England, Wales is not divided administratively into a set of regions and there is no sub-national equivalent of the English Regional Spatial Strategies. As noted in the previous chapter Wales has divided the country into six areas for the purpose of progressing its Spatial Plan. Meanwhile the transport planning previously undertaken by individual local authorities is being reorganised through regional consortia. This work is being conducted in the context of the emerging Wales Transport Strategy which serves to support and promote the outcomes sought in the Spatial Plan (17.6).

Following devolution sub-national transport planning in Wales centred on the production of Local Transport Plans by its individual unitary authorities, like their English counterparts. However the Transport (Wales) Act 2006 modified the Transport Act 2000 and the National Assembly passed an order which replaced LTPs with new Regional Transport Plans. These are being prepared by four consortia, operating in their established form as voluntary joint committees:

- TAITH – North Wales
- TRACC – Central Wales
- SWWITCH – South West Wales
- SEWTA – South East Wales.

These areas are shown in Figure 18.3.

In their current form these consortia do not assume the executive functions of their constituent councils as highway authorities. Rather they prepare RTPs on a

Figure 18.3 Regional Transport Consortia in Wales (reproduced by permission of Ordnance Survey on behalf of HMSO © Crown copyright 2009. All rights reserved. Ordnance Survey Licence number 100045659)

cross-boundary basis on behalf of these councils and seek funding from the National Assembly.

Guidance prepared by the Welsh Assembly asks that RTPs set out a *vision* for the medium and longer term to integrate it with the horizons of the national Spatial Plan and Transport Strategy as well as a detailed five-year *programme* beginning in 2008/09 (WAG 2007a). As in England, bids for national funding of new major schemes (over £5m) may be included, supported by evidence from project appraisal.

In the absence of formal arrangements for land use/transport integration at the regional level the Guidance goes to some length to promote collaborative working:

> Each spatial plan group has embarked on a series of projects that seek to establish the strategic agenda for economic, social and environmental development at a sub-regional level in order to meet the area visions. This work will identify the role and function of places and set the basis for policy and investment in a whole range of sectors ....
>
> It is therefore essential that the Consortia work closely with each spatial plan group in developing this strategic agenda in each area. **Consortia should not regard the WSP and RTPs as separate strategies and the transport content of both ought to originate from the same basis of thinking as far as possible.** The spatial priorities need to inform the strategic transport proposals at regional and local levels, but at the same time be informed by what is realistic in transport terms. The Welsh Assembly Government, in funding key regional transport schemes, will look for evidence that this iteration has taken place in practice, assessing schemes for 'fit' with the regional strategic agenda set out in the Spatial Plan.
>
> (ibid. paras 2.19 and 2.20; emphasis in original)

The RTP is envisaged to be a 'dynamic framework' for transport planning and 'not just a reference map'. This will be reflected in four continuing activities:

- monitoring programmes
- annual progress reporting
- possible responsibility for developing Welsh Assembly Government initiatives in their area (e.g. prioritisation of trunk road improvements alongside local authority interventions, similar to the transport element of the English RFA process)
- implementation management.

To fulfil these tasks the Guidance rather pointedly notes that the Consortia will need to develop the capability to take on greater responsibilities involving spending, employment and project management:

> These changes will mean that more clarity and robustness may be needed to govern the cooperative relationships between Local Authorities and their respective Consortia. This will require consideration of whether the respective constitutions are appropriate or in need of strengthening ...
>
> The Assembly Government will support the Consortia so that they continue to develop to become an effective vehicle for implementing the RTPs. It has however made clear that it will consider establishing a Joint Transport Authority

if the current voluntary arrangements are not making sufficient progress in delivering integrated solutions in any part of Wales.

(ibid. paras 3.18 and 3.19)

If proceeded with, such authorities would be similar to the Integrated Transport Authorities being legislated for in the English conurbations (23.7).

18.8 Regional Transport Strategies in Scotland

Scotland is similar to Wales in that it has no formal mechanism for a single integrated strategy at the regional level, but does have regional transport partnerships.

The Transport (Scotland) Act 2005 placed a duty on Scottish Ministers to create regional transport partnerships (RTPs) covering the whole of Scotland. The preceding White Paper had stated that the purpose of these new statutory partnerships was 'to facilitate the planning and delivery of our transport in a more strategic way within local government'. In essence this was rectifying the consequences of abolishing the regional councils a decade earlier when unitary local government had been introduced.

Seven statutory RTPs were created for the areas shown in Figure 18.4, superseding the four areas in which voluntary partnerships had been operating previously. Membership of the RTPs is similar to that of the English Regional Assemblies with about two-thirds consisting of elected members nominated from the constituent local authorities and the remainder appointed to offer additional expertise, with a regional rather than a local perspective and without party political affiliation.

Under the Act RTPs were required to prepare regional transport strategies (RTS) by March 2007. Guidance issued by the Scottish Executive identified the following purposes for these strategies:

- To provide a vision and objectives for transport in the region over a long-term (10–15-year) time horizon
- To provide an analysis of the current situation, covering transport needs and problems in the region
- To set out a programme of activities, projects and interventions by the RTP, its constituent councils and other stakeholders, that is prioritised and costed, and which will contribute to the achievement of regional transport objectives
- To inform the RTP's implementation and investment planning, setting out how the strategy will be achieved and its programme of activities delivered using funding at the RTP's disposal
- To identify any additional measures that would be dependent on further contributions from a range of possible stakeholders and to make the case for any additional contributions from those stakeholders (including the Scottish Executive)
- To provide a key steer for local transport strategies by setting regional transport objectives, outlining how the exercise of functions is to be shared between the regional and local levels
- To support the National Transport Strategy and provide an important input to the Strategic Projects Review.

(Scottish Executive 2006c para 14)

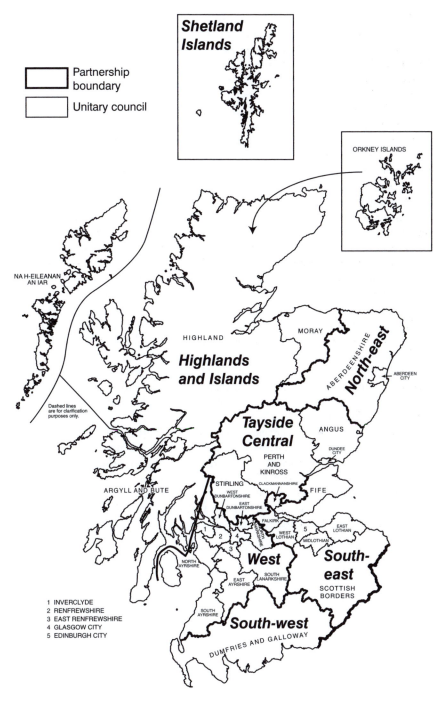

Figure 18.4 Scottish Regional Transport Partnerships (reproduced by permission of Ordnance Survey on behalf of HMSO © Crown copyright 2009. All rights reserved. Ordnance Survey Licence number 100045659)

Regional strategies were encouraged to be 'aspirational but also realistic'. RTPs are independent statutory bodies and it was for them to set their budgets and agree priorities. Where additional funding or other intervention was sought from the Scottish Executive ,the strategies needed to make the case to Ministers.

RTPs already have the power to give grants or loans for any purposes that will contribute to implementation of the RTS. However the 2005 Act also enables them to apply for executive functions, linked to the RTS, which may be transferred to them from an existing authority or operated concurrently. RTPs will also be able to act as agents of some or all of their constituent councils or of Scottish Ministers. Clearly the level of expenditure anticipated in the RTS will reflect the position taken on possible transfer of functions. The Strathclyde Regional Partnership is unusual in this respect since from the outset it has assumed the passenger transport functions of the former Strathclyde PTE (the only one in Scotland).

Regional strategies require the approval of Scottish Ministers which will have regard to both the preparation process and content. It was envisaged that Ministers would approve or return a submitted RTS within three months. In the event a change of political control of the Scottish Parliament in May 2007 (to the Scottish Nationalists) stalled this aim. In the new Government's first budget it was announced that the capital grant for RTPs (worth £35m in 2007/08) would in future be paid to their constituent local councils and would not be ring-fenced. (An exception was made in the case of the Strathclyde Partnership because of its direct operation of the Glasgow Underground and other services formerly provided by the PTE.)

The effect of this was that RTPs would need to make their case to each constituent local authority for them to forward their share of the government grant. In practice this means influencing the Single Outcome Agreement which these authorities have to negotiate with the Scottish Government – the equivalent of the Local Area Agreement in England (19.8).

Meanwhile the regional strategies remain in their unapproved state. It has been reported that Government officials were critical of the submitted documents for lacking a realistic view of available funding (LTT 484). This is unsurprising since the Director of the South-East Partnership acknowledged that even if his RTP succeeded in extracting from constituent councils the same amount as had previously been received directly this would only amount to £29m over the subsequent three years whereas the RTS had identified a capital spend of £131m!

19 Local development frameworks, community strategies and area agreements

19.1 Introduction

National policies and regional strategies provide the framework for local planning in the hierarchical translation of overall aims into particular outcomes described in Chapter 17. However transport proposals do not merely have to be aligned 'vertically' with this strategic policy context, but also 'laterally' with other actions being taken locally.

This need for local integration can be visualised most obviously in physical terms. Transport infrastructure is not only a major component of the physical fabric of settlements; the operation of transport systems is critical to the functioning of activities within them. This applies at the level of access to individual sites and premises as well as in the connectivity (opportunities) it offers for economic and social interaction and the fulfilment of individual needs within neighbourhoods, towns and city regions.

Establishing the appropriate manner in which transport systems should be developed and managed at this local level requires them to be planned within their particular spatial contexts. Transport is therefore a major component of the 'spatial planning' activity pursued by local planning authorities. Much of this chapter is devoted to explaining the nature of this activity and the particular plans and procedures through which it is currently executed.

In Part 2 we charted the way in which arrangements for development (now spatial) planning evolved largely independently of transport planning. Readers who already have some familiarity with local transport planning should note that these processes are not merely different in subject matter but also – largely for historical reasons – different in nature and purpose. As a preface to the detailed discussion which follows we therefore begin by highlighting some of the distinctive features of the development planning system (19.2).

We then consider the role currently set for local development plans in England (19.3) and the nature of Local Development Frameworks (19.4) and Development Plan Documents (19.5). Significant differences in local development planning as operated in Wales and Scotland are noted in section 19.6. Increasingly the Government is viewing these plans (and local transport plans too) as instruments for delivering outcomes identified in Sustainable Community Strategies. We therefore explain the nature of these strategies in section 19.7 and the role of Local Area Agreements in the new performance framework being set for local government in section 19.8.

19.2 Distinctive features of the development planning system

We begin by highlighting four overarching features of the development planning system which are distinctive relative to local transport planning, viz:

- the status of the plan-making process
- the role of authorities as developers
- the control of activity
- the division of development and transport planning responsibilities.

The status of the plan-making process

The functions of local planning authorities, like transport authorities, are dependent on the granting of legal powers. But in the case of planning authorities the *process of plan-making* is itself central to these functions and is prescribed by statute and accompanying regulations. This makes it subject to much greater public scrutiny (and is much more protracted as a result).

One of the main reasons why this difference exists is because the provisions of a development plan have a direct effect on the rights of landowners to develop their property (and hence the value attaching to it). The development planning system therefore has to allow for the hearing and defence of these rights. The provisions of a transport plan generally do not have such an effect, or not to the same degree. Individual transport or traffic management proposals may affect the rights of travellers or property owners (mainly in terms of access to premises), but their legal safeguard is provided for in the procedures authorities have to follow to gain approval for a particular *scheme* – see 22.4. With only one or two exceptions (e.g. school transport or rail closures) no statutory rights have been established for the protection of accessibility in a broader sense.

The role of authorities as developers

Local planning authorities are not themselves managers and investors in infrastructure in the way that transport authorities are. Hence development plans are not primarily mechanisms for formulating their *own* development programmes. Unlike local transport plans they are not prepared primarily as an administrative exercise established by central government to control local authority capital spending.

Instead a key feature of development plan preparation is authorities' role in mediating between *other* parties who have interests in development. These will include landowners and developers competing for the opportunity to undertake development on individual sites as well as sections of the local community who are seeking the promotion or restriction of development in particular places or more or less of particular kinds of development. Development planning is therefore innately more outward-looking in character and is a further reason for the prominence given to community and stakeholder involvement in the plan preparation process.

The control of activity

The statutory definition of 'development' includes not merely building works but also the *use* to which land or buildings are put. Development control effectively limits the amount or type of activity which an occupant can engage in. (For example a house cannot be converted into flats or offices without planning permission.) This potentially has a highly constraining effect and is therefore subject to legal safeguards. By contrast local transport authorities do not exercise any equivalent *general* constraint on the amount or type of travel which households or businesses may undertake. (Occupants do not have to seek permission to own an additional vehicle or to travel more than their predecessors in the way they do if they wish to increase their land use activity.)

Development control applies universally whereas constraints on travel only apply indirectly and in particular situations (e.g. controlled parking zones where – in similar fashion – formal provision is made for the hearing of objections). Interestingly the prospect of road user charging has brought a new dimension to the potentially constraining effects of local transport policies. This is reflected in the contested debate which has surrounded the legal procedures under which it might be introduced (23.3).

Division of local authority responsibilities

In non-metropolitan areas where a two-tier system of local government prevails, development planning is undertaken by the lower-tier district councils whereas transport planning is undertaken by the upper-tier county councils. In these areas therefore the two functions (which ideally would be integrated) are exercised by authorities which have different combinations of responsibilities for different areas with different electorates and different political administrations. The perspectives they bring to development and transport and their inter-relationship will therefore be different – often quite markedly so. Broadly speaking, planning authorities will be less concerned with the operation of the transport system as such in their areas but more with the opportunities and constraints it places on other types of activity and development and with its impact on environmental conditions. By contrast transport authorities will view the development policies for an area primarily in terms of resulting patterns of travel demand and their implications for the functioning of the transport system.

As far as planning in England is concerned the following sections are written in terms of the 'new' development planning system which came into effect from 2007, consequent on the changes arising from the Planning and Compulsory Purchase Act 2004. (In practice many of the policies in previous plans, where they have been explicitly 'saved', will continue to apply for an interim period.) The terminology used in the new system is somewhat confusing and for convenience we will often refer to them here simply as 'plans'. However a particular feature to note is that the term 'development plan' is not a single planning document at all but is reserved for the collection of documents applicable to an area which have development plan *status* and thus have statutory significance in development control decisions.

19.3 The role of local development plans

Historically 'town and country planning' has been concerned with regulating the use and development of land in the interests of improving the functioning and environmental quality of built-up areas and with protecting the countryside. This traditional role is reiterated in current Government policy:

Planning shapes the places where people work and live. The planning system operates in the public interest to ensure the development and use of land results in better places for people to live, the delivery of development where communities need it, as well as the protection and enhancement of the natural and historic environment and the countryside.

(ODPM 2005d para 40)

This aspiration is now framed in terms of 'sustainable development' which is held to be the 'core principle' underpinning planning.

National policy statements, regional strategies and local development plans together provide the framework for the planning and management of sustainable development. Local planning authorities are charged with using their regulatory powers over development in accordance with this framework – the so-called 'plan-led system'. (Details of these powers were given in section 14.9.)

At one level therefore the purpose of the development planning system can be considered as fundamentally unchanged and the reforms under the 2004 Act viewed as just one more example of 'tampering' with the mechanics of the system which successive governments have engaged in over the years. Ironically, given the claims made for improving speed, efficiency and transparency, it is in this aspect that its likely success is most questionable (Wood 2007).

Local communities, businesses, the voluntary sector and individuals have a right to a high quality service that is fast, fair, open, transparent and consistent and respects the costs, effort and commitment that has gone into engagement in plan-making and in preparing and submitting applications. Planning authorities must ensure that plans are kept up to date and that planning applications are dealt with expeditiously, while addressing relevant issues.

(ODPM 2005d para 9)

This aspect is obviously important, not least because failure of the development planning system to function efficiently in an administrative sense provides ready ammunition to those who would wish to diminish its scope. More interesting though are the 'softer' changes surrounding the context in which the new system is expected to function and the culture which is intended to characterise its operation.

Simply focusing on the changed plans and procedures of the new system would overlook the fact that pursuing 'place-shaping' involves many processes and agencies beyond the reach of the development planning system (Morphet 2007). It is this which accounts for the intended transition to a 'spatial planning' approach:

Spatial planning goes beyond traditional land use planning to bring together and integrate policies for the development and use of land with other policies and programmes which influence the nature of places and how they can function. That will include policies which can impact on land use, for example by influencing the demands on or needs for development, but which are not capable of being delivered solely or mainly through the granting or refusal of planning permission and which may be implemented by other means.

(ODPM 2005d para 30)

Box 19.1 The nature of local spatial planning

Source: DCLG 2007 Draft PPS12 para 2.1

Spatial planning is a process of place shaping and delivery. It aims to:

- Produce a vision for the future of places and communities that responds to the local challenges and opportunities, based on evidence and community derived objectives, within the overall framework of national policy and regional strategies
- Translate this vision into a set of priorities, programmes, policies, and land allocations together with the public sector resources to deliver them
- Create a framework for private investment and regeneration that promotes economic, environmental and social well-being for the area
- Coordinate and deliver the public sector components of this vision with other agencies and processes [e.g. LAAs and MAAs]
- Create a positive framework for action on climate change.

This approach cannot be fulfilled simply through passive operation of the regulatory system but requires a more pro-active stance by planning authorities and greater attention to 'delivery'. One of the procedural changes designed to promote this is the requirement for authorities to produce an annual monitoring report indicating the extent to which the policies and targets set out in the new plans are being achieved. In practice planners are being challenged to work more effectively with other agencies in achieving desired outcomes. Arguably however they are being presented with responsibility without commensurate power. Indeed responsibilities are being added to all the time and the Government's latest articulation of aims for local spatial planning incorporates the not-insignificant task of providing a positive framework for action on climate change (Box 19.1)!

Whilst reforming the planning system the Government is also in the process of introducing other mechanisms for delivering outcomes which are not encumbered by the rigours of direct political accountability, public examination and elaborate legal safeguards. In both political and delivery terms this overlapping of responsibilities and proliferation of ad hoc multi-agency arrangements does not ease the planning task! The increasing complexity of governance also does not make for transparency and for public involvement in, and comprehension of, decision-making processes. Yet, as we will see, development planning itself is being tasked with greater attention to community involvement, both in the process of plan preparation and in the link between development plans and community strategies.

19.4 Local Development Frameworks

A key feature of the new development planning system in England is that district, unitary and London Borough councils, instead of being required to prepare a single 'local' or 'unitary' plan for the whole of their area, prepare and progressively add to a portfolio of separate documents, as appropriate to their circumstances. This is intended to provide greater flexibility in both form and timing. The more important elements can be introduced more quickly and professional resources used more effectively by being phased over successive exercises.

The portfolio is known as the *Local Development Framework* (LDF) and includes several different types of plan together with documents concerned with the management of the planning process (Figure 19.1).

The plans are collectively referred to as 'local development documents'. They are subdivided into

- *development plan documents* (which form part of the statutory development plan), and
- *supplementary planning documents* (such as design briefs for individual sites) which are advisory in nature.

(Details of the development plan documents are given in the next section.)
The other documents which are obligatory comprise

- a *local development scheme* (a timetable for the preparation of plans)
- a *statement of community involvement*
- an *annual monitoring report.*

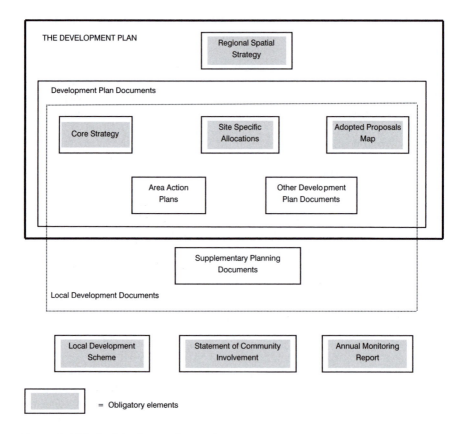

Figure 19.1 The local development framework

Development plan scheme

Each authority is required to publish a statement giving a brief description of the local development documents it intends to produce and the timetable to be followed for each of them. This is submitted to the Government Regional Office who need to be satisfied that the programme is appropriate and deliverable and is consistent with PSA targets in this field. In the past, unlike Local Transport Plans, there has been no pre-ordained timetable for the production of development plans or the period within which they needed to be reviewed. Currently however, in order to fulfil a cross-government Public Service Agreement for additional housing, local planning authorities have been urged to adopt the necessary planning documents by March 2011.

Publication of the Local Development Scheme enables principal stakeholders and members of the public to identify when the planning of particular topics or areas will come under consideration. This has particular importance given the emphasis which is placed in the new system on community involvement.

Statement of Community Involvement

Authorities are required to prepare an overarching Statement of Community Involvement (SCI) which sets out the standards it intends to achieve generally in involving sectors of the community in the preparation and review of planning documents. The SCI has to be published and is open to 'representations' (i.e. objections and requests for changes). Initially the SCI was to be subject to independent examination (as are the plans themselves) but the Government has since stated its intention to rescind this requirement because of the more general duty being imposed on local authorities concerning public consultation (19.7 below).

Annual Monitoring Report

Authorities are also required to produce an Annual Monitoring Report which assesses progress:

a   in implementing the local development scheme
b   in achieving the policies contained in the local development documents.

Where implementation is falling behind schedule or is failing to meet targets reasons have to be given and the need for any update or addition to the local development scheme identified.

Preparation of development plan documents

Development plan documents (i.e. those which the authority intends should form part of the statutory development plan for its area) have to be prepared in four distinct stages:

1   Pre-production: Survey and evidence gathering
2   Production: Preparation of preferred options in consultation with the community, formal participation on these and submission of the document in the light of representations received

3   Examination: An independent examination into the soundness of the plan
4   Adoption: Formal adoption by the authority subject to any changes recommended
      by the Inspector who conducted the examination.

The procedures to be followed in each of these stages are the subject of detailed
Regulations which are explained in PPS12 (ODPM 2004b). The main steps and their
intended timescale are shown in Figure 19.2.

The evidence base provides the information needed to support the authority's
proposals at the examination stage. In two-tier areas county councils are responsible
for supplying general socio-economic data to district councils and particular data
on the transport system, traffic and accessibility by public transport. Views on the
issues which a plan should address and the options available also need to form part
of the evidence base and for this reason the 'front-loading' of public involvement is
encouraged.

Once a preferred option has been identified the authority is required to publish
this together with a sustainability appraisal report and to provide the opportunity for
formal representations to be made within a six-week period. Having considered these
and made any changes which it thinks appropriate the authority then submits the plan
formally for independent examination to the Secretary of State (DCLG).

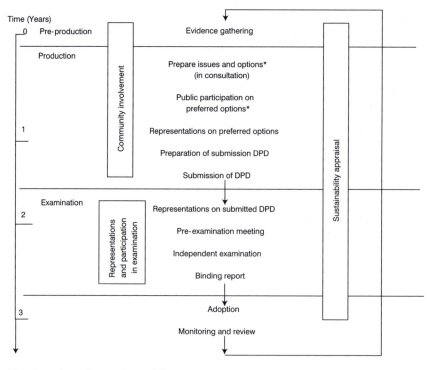

*Note: the requirement for separate consultation
exercises on these two stages has since been
removed – see text.

Figure 19.2 The development plan document (DPD) process (source: PPS12 Figure 4.1)

Experience of the new system in its first three years has led to proposals for a number of detailed changes of the 2004 Regulations on which a consultation paper has been produced (DCLG 2007h). The paper also includes a draft revision of PPS12.

A key procedural change is that the original requirement for two distinct rounds of public consultation (at 'issues and options' and 'preferred option' stages) is being replaced with a single requirement to engage the public and stakeholders, with planning authorities having discretion as to how this is best executed. This provides more flexibility and will help speed cases where a two-stage approach is not necessary. Authorities are also being given the opportunity to amend a submitted plan following receipt of representations on it where these indicate that the plan might otherwise be found unsound and hence risk not being approved (Chapter 22).

19.5 The form and content of development plan documents

The following types of development plan document *have* to be included in the LDF portfolio:

- a *'core strategy'*
- a *site-specific proposals map*
- an *adopted proposals map*.

In addition any number of additional plans of the following types *may* be included:

- *area action plans*
- *other development plan documents* (e.g. dealing in more detail with particular issues, topics or areas).

Core strategy

The core strategy contains the main elements of the planning framework for the area, viz:

- an overall vision which sets out how the district and the places within it should develop
- strategic objectives for the area focusing on the key issues to be addressed
- a delivery strategy for achieving these objectives, setting out what is intended to happen where, when, and by what means it will be delivered
- clear arrangements for managing and monitoring the delivery of the strategy.

Preparation of the core strategy should draw on any strategies of the local authority or other organisation that have implications for the development and use of land – PPS12 refers to the community strategy and the local transport plan as examples. Further advice on the integration of transport and land use policies is given in Annex B – see Box 19.2.

The core strategy has to be kept up to date and all other development plan documents have to be in conformity with it.

Box 19.2 Integration of transport and land use policies

PPS12 2004 Annex B from paras B9–B14

The integration of transport and spatial planning is central to the development and delivery of effective local development frameworks. Local transport policies need to reflect and support the aims of the core strategy development plan document. Land use planning, in turn, needs to take account of the existing transport network and plans for its development.

Local planning authorities have a valuable role to play in improving accessibility as the location of jobs and services have as significant an impact on accessibility as transport provision. Accessibility should be a key consideration when drawing up local development documents. ODPM will issue guidance on accessibility planning on how local planning authorities should be involved in accessibility planning and the importance of directing developments towards sites that are already accessible by public transport.

A key transport-related aspect of a development plan document will be to set out proposed improvements to the transport network in support of the core strategy. These improvements should be included on the adopted proposals map. Local planning authorities, however, need to be realistic about what can be implemented over the plan period, otherwise there is a risk of blight or false expectations. The integration between transport and spatial planning will also be undermined. Scheme proposals should only be included where there is a strong commitment from the relevant delivery agency – for instance, if the local transport authority has included the scheme as a priority in its local transport plan. A clear distinction should also be made between scheme proposals and safeguarding potential transport routes which may not necessarily be taken forward over the plan period.

Site-specific allocations and adopted proposals maps

Each document has to be accompanied by a proposals map which illustrates the spatial extent of the relevant policies. In the case of the core strategy this will normally be in the form of a 'key diagram' covering the whole of an authority's area; other development planning documents will be accompanied by a 'site-specific allocations map'. In addition the authority has to maintain an up-to-date reference map ('the adopted proposals map') showing the areas and sites affected by all extant policies.

Area action plans

In localities where significant change or conservation is needed, an 'area action plan' may be produced. The distinguishing feature of this type of plan is its focus on implementation, with specific site allocations, a timetable for the proposals and identification of the agency responsible. Examples would be plans for growth areas or area-based regeneration.

Guidance on the nature and content of each of the above types of document is given in PPS12. More general guidance on local development planning which has particular relevance to transport is reproduced in Box 19.3.

Box 19.3 Guidance on local development planning relevant to transport

PPS12 2004 Para 27 (iv)–(viii)

In preparing their plans authorities should seek to:
- bring forward sufficient land of a suitable quality in appropriate locations to meet the expected needs for (development) ... taking into account issues such as accessibility and sustainable transport needs (and) the provision of essential infrastructure
- provide improved access for all to jobs, health, education (etc.) by ensuring that new development is located where everyone can access services or facilities on foot, bicycle or public transport rather than having to rely on access by car ...
- focus developments that attract a large number of people ... in existing centres to promote their vitality and viability, social inclusion and more sustainable patterns of development
- reduce the need to travel and encourage accessible public transport provision ... Planning should actively manage patterns of urban growth to make the fullest use of public transport
- promote more efficient use of land through higher density, mixed use development and the use of suitably located previously developed land and buildings.

More detailed guidance on the transport aspects of development planning is given in PPG13 Transport (DETR 2001).

Authorities also have to comply with EU Directive 2001/42/EC which requires formal strategic environmental assessment of plans and programmes which are likely to have significant effects on the environment. This is reflected in the requirement to undertake sustainability appraisal as an integral part of preparing local development documents (21.8). Authorities are advised to integrate sustainability appraisal within a more general monitoring framework which contributes to the evidence base for formulating and reviewing plans (ODPM 2005a).

In the 2007 draft revision of PPS12 greater attention is given to the role of the Core Strategy within the LDF and within this to the delivery strategy:

[The strategy] needs to demonstrate that the agencies/partners necessary for its delivery have been involved in its preparation, and the resources required have been given due consideration and have a realistic prospect of being provided in the life of the strategy. If this is not the case, the strategy will be undeliverable.

(DCLG 2007h para 4.4)

One reason for this emphasis on delivery is the greater pressure that has been brought to bear on the planning system as a mechanism for contributing to the Government's targets for increased numbers of new houses (23.8):

Local planning authorities should set out in Local Development Documents their policies and strategies for delivering the level of housing provision ... that will enable continuous delivery of housing for at least 15 years from the date of [plan]

adoption, taking account of the level of provision set out in the Regional Spatial Strategy.

(DCLG 2006b para 53)

In addition authorities are required to identify specific *sites* where the necessary level of housing can be delivered in the first five years, and to keep the availability of further sites under review so that there is a continuous supply of deliverable sites for a minimum of five years. In areas of major growth this requires not merely the identification of sites and the granting of planning permission to developers who are able to proceed but also securing the timely provision of the associated infrastructure. Transport infrastructure is normally a critical component. If planning authorities fail to maintain a minimum of five years' supply of deliverable sites then, as well as not meeting housing targets, they may be vulnerable to planning applications from developers on non-allocated sites who *are* able to demonstrate the ability to proceed. Typically these non-allocated sites are less desirable in terms of other planning objectives and often involve the development of green-field sites rather than brown-field sites whose assembly and preparation is a more complex task.

19.6 Local development planning in Wales and Scotland

Local development plans in Wales

Local development planning in Wales was reformed under the same 2004 Act as in England but with two main differences:

1   The Welsh Government did not go down the 'portfolio' route with the result that all policies and proposals which are to have statutory status are to be included in a single document – the Local Development Plan (LDP). The required content of these plans is given in section 2 of WAG (2005). Authorities may subsequently prepare non-statutory Supplementary Planning Guidance for particular sites or topics but this must be consistent with the LDP.
2   All authorities in Wales transferred to the system of unitary development plans (UDPs) when its local government was reformed in 1996. However by 2004 the majority of Welsh authorities had not progressed to the point of adopting the new plans so arrangements were made for converting work already undertaken on UDPs into the new LDP format.

Other novel features such as a Delivery Agreement for the production of Plans, a Community Involvement Scheme, Sustainability Appraisal and an Annual Monitoring Report are similar to the English system. The Welsh guidance does however emphasise the goal of completing the process including public examination within four years, subject to any adjustments needed to fit in with programmed reviews of the community strategy.

Local development plans in Scotland

The system of local development planning in Scotland introduced under the Planning etc. (Scotland) Act 2006 has many features in common with those in England and Wales. As in the English shires the previous two-tier system of structure and local plans has been abolished and new Local Development Plans (LDPs) have to be prepared by all local authorities for the whole of their areas. These have to take account of the National Planning Framework and have regard to regional and local transport strategies. In the four city regions of Glasgow, Edinburgh, Dundee and Aberdeen LDPs also have to be consistent with the Strategic Development Plan prepared for these areas and adopt its 'vision' as the basis of their strategy.

The form and content of the Scottish plans represent something of a half-way house between their English and Welsh equivalents. Planning authorities are required to prepare and keep under review *one or more* plans for their area. These may be prepared for different purposes and hence overlap in spatial terms. However, regardless of how many plans cover an authority's area they must all be reviewed every five years (Scottish Executive 2007b).

The Act requires authorities to publish a *monitoring statement* identifying changes in the main characteristics of the area since preparation of the previous plan and the impact of this plan. Outside SDP areas LDPs must contain a *vision statement* indicating how development of the area could and should occur. Each LDP then has to contain a *spatial strategy* (which is defined in traditional terms as a detailed statement of the authority's policies and proposals for the development and use of land) and an *Action Programme* setting out how the authority proposes to implement the plan. Beyond these requirements authorities have discretion on the number and type of plans, details of their form and content and arrangements for public engagement. However each plan has to follow a set procedure of a *Main Issues Report* accompanied by SEA and the opportunity for the public to comment on this and on a subsequent *Proposed or Modified Plan.*

Scottish authorities may also issue Supplementary Guidance with more limited public involvement but, unlike in England and Wales, such guidance will form part of the statutory development plan. The intention is that this enhanced status will enable much material in former structure and local plans to be retained in this form, enabling the new plans to focus on the spatial strategy and on the key policies and proposals.

19.7 Sustainable Community Strategies

The planning reforms introduced throughout Great Britain place increased emphasis on local authorities using plan-making as one of their tools to deliver overall local strategies for economic, social and environmental sustainability. The following (English) example is typical:

> The planning system has been substantially reformed to embed community responsive policy-making at its heart and deliver sustainable development as a new statutory obligation ....
>
> The Government intends that spatial planning objectives for local areas, as set out in the LDF, should be fully aligned not only with national and regional plans, but also with the shared local priorities set out in Sustainable Community Strategies (SCS) where these are consistent with national and regional policy.
>
> (DCLG 2007h Annex 2)

Community strategies are a planning mechanism introduced by the New Labour Government as part of its programme of local authority reform. Under the Local Government Act 2000 all local authorities in England and Wales are required to prepare and keep under review a Community Strategy which gives expression to their statutory duty to promote the economic, social and environmental well-being of their area and to contribute to sustainable development. In doing so they are required to have regard to guidance issued by the Secretary of State (ODPM 2003c; WAG 2008a).

In preparing their strategies authorities are encouraged to form Local Strategic Partnerships (LSPs) with other principal organisations and representatives of stakeholder groups in their area. There is no specified format for the form or functioning of these LSPs – they are 'a voluntary framework for local cooperation'. Ideally an LSP should be developed on the basis of collaborative arrangements already established in an area and the operation of existing partnerships should be brought within the LSP umbrella.

In Scotland a similar system of Community Planning has been established under the Local Government in Scotland Act 2003. It is defined as

> a process ... whereby public services in the area of the local authority are planned and provided after consultation and (on-going) co-operation ... among all public bodies ... and with community bodies.

Community Planning Partnerships have been established in all 32 Scottish local authority areas together with a national Community Planning Network. However unlike England and Wales there is no requirement placed on them to prepare Community Strategies.

For English and Welsh authorities the objectives to be served by a community strategy are as listed in Box 19.4.

The Government's aim is that community strategies should become embedded into partners' managerial cultures, resource planning and budgetary decisions with its long-term vision providing the context in which all other corporate strategies and plans are grounded. (They were re-named 'Sustainable Community Strategies' in 2007.)

The concept of a community strategy is open to criticism as an initiative which is characteristic of New Labour in being strong on aspiration but weak on substance (Sullivan 2004). For practical purposes it is rather woolly and ill-defined and is dependent on 'partnerships' materialising in order to achieve anything. A consultation paper reviewing experience with community strategies and LSPs acknowledged the 'lack of clarity' with which they are perceived (ODPM 2005b) and the Government accepted that productive arrangements would take time to develop.

A community strategy has four main components (ODPM 2003c para 11):

- a **long-term vision** for the area focusing on the outcomes that are to be achieved
- an **action plan** identifying shorter-term priorities and activities that will contribute to the achievement of long-term outcomes
- a **shared commitment to implement** the action plan and proposals for doing so
- arrangements for **monitoring** the implementation of the action plan, for periodically reviewing the community strategy, and for reporting progress to local communities.

As a catalyst for action the Government established a voluntary system of local Public Service Agreements through which councils could obtain additional funding by

---

Box 19.4 Objectives of a Community Strategy

ODPM 2003c para 10

- To allow local communities (based upon geography and/or interest) to articulate their aspirations, needs and priorities
- To co-ordinate the actions of the council, and of the public, private, voluntary and community organisations that operate locally
- To focus and shape existing and future activity of those organisations so that they effectively meet community needs and aspirations, and
- To contribute to the achievement of sustainable development both locally and more widely, with local goals and priorities relating, where appropriate, to regional, national and even global aims.

---

working with partners to secure identified priorities and 'stretched' targets. In addition a system of Local Area Agreements (LAAs) was introduced whereby a local authority, working through an LSP, could negotiate with the Government's Regional Office for the 'pooling' of several funding streams from different Government departments in order to deliver a concerted programme aimed at improving the economic and social welfare of particular local areas.

The central conundrum surrounding community strategies is that decision-making powers and control of mainstream resources remain with the individual agencies. It follows that for any substantive action to occur there has to be agreement between the relevant parties not only to the objectives being pursued but to the particular mix of measures being proposed at a particular time to which they are being asked to contribute. In their defence it might be said that community strategies were not expected initially to deliver more than could be achieved through a series of individual partnerships, but rather that they helped foster them by building trust and collaboration and by highlighting common interests.

The prospects for joint action have been improved with the introduction of a broader system of Local Area Agreements which we discuss in the next section.

19.8 The new local performance framework and Local Area Agreements

In 2006 the Government published a further Local Government White Paper – applicable to England only – which proposed a substantial enhancement of the regime described in the previous section (DCLG 2006c). This was presented as a 'new settlement' between central government, local government and citizens. (Similar arrangements are being developed in Wales through new Local Service Boards and Local Delivery Agreements.)

A key feature of the English reform is the replacement of a very large number of performance indicators used in assessing local authorities in a variety of policy areas (transport being one) by a single national set of 198 indicators. All authorities are to report on these annually for national monitoring purposes. However external assessment of each authority's performance is to be confined to a much smaller sub-set from the national list chosen by the authority as best suited to reflect its particular priorities. This combination of a less intensive performance-monitoring regime coupled with greater discretion over the choice of indicators represents a significant transfer of responsibility to local authorities and a greater emphasis on responsiveness to the needs of local communities.

The manner in which the new performance framework is designed to operate is explained in DCLG (2007a) and illustrated in Figure 19.3.

The changes requiring legislation were enacted in the Local Government and Public Involvement in Health Act 2007 and draft statutory guidance published. In the Foreword to this the Secretary of State (DCLG) Hazel Blears wrote:

> 2008 will be a watershed year for Britain's local democracy. It is the year in which the mature relationship between central and local government, debated for so long and promised in the White Paper *Strong and Prosperous Communities* becomes a reality.
>
> It means greater discretion for councils to put the governing back into local government: not just administering services, but thinking strategically about what local people want and need .... The changes we are introducing offer unprecedented opportunities for local leaders to set out their vision for their communities, while empowering local people to help deliver that vision.
>
> (DCLG 2007a Foreword)

Under the new arrangements responsibility for producing Sustainable Community Strategies is placed with county or unitary councils (including London Boroughs), consulting with district councils where relevant. These councils also have a duty to prepare an authority-wide Local Area Agreement (LAA). Voluntary Local Strategic Partnerships (LSPs) established at county, district or unitary levels continue to provide the forum(s) through which priorities are identified. However all target-setting and consequent financial, contractual or commissioning commitments proposed by LSPs have to be formalised through the relevant local authority or other statutory body which is a member of the LSP.

> Local councils are expected to play a leadership role in these key and over-arching partnerships. It is expected that local government will initiate and maintain momentum in the LSP and ensure appropriate representation across the different sectors including the involvement of local residents where appropriate and scrutiny of the actions of the partner authorities in the LSP.
>
> (ibid. para 2.5)

A number of supporting 'thematic partnerships' (e.g. relating to transport or accessibility) are expected to provide the LSP with the necessary information on which to make decisions, to participate in decision-making and to co-ordinate the delivery of the LSP's priorities.

Under the 2007 Act a new duty is placed on local authorities to 'involve' their local population (to come into force in April 2009). This refers not merely to local residents but to all other parties (e.g. workers, visitors, businesses) who may be affected by a particular function. As a consequence authorities are expected to consider, as a matter of course, the possible information provision, consultation and involvement opportunities they need to provide people across all their functions. In general this duty does not replace existing requirements of this kind (e.g. in

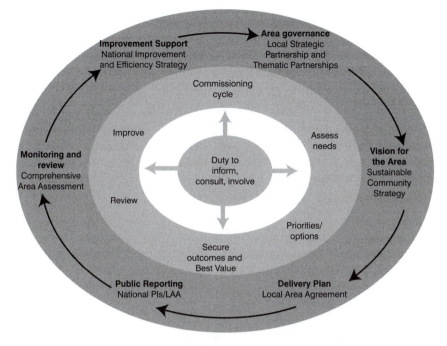

Figure 19.3 The New Local Government Performance Framework (source: DCLG 2007a)

relation to development planning or transport proposals). However authorities do need to consider whether any additional actions are required beyond these specific requirements.

Local Area Agreements (LAAs) are the short-term (three-year) delivery mechanism for delivering improvements in line with the Community Strategy. In defining targets for these improvements the Act lists a number of 'partner authorities' who must be involved. These authorities are placed under a statutory duty to cooperate in the setting of targets and to have regard to agreed targets in the course of their business. They include District Councils, National Park Authorities, the Highways Agency, Passenger Transport Authorities, Transport for London, Regional Development Agencies and NHS Trusts.

These are of course all *public sector* bodies. It is important to note that commercial bus and train companies may be members of LSPs (or more likely a particular thematic partnership) and that individual companies may agree partnership arrangements with transport authorities. However no statutory requirements surround their participation. They are also under no statutory duty to cooperate in the setting of LAA targets or to have regard to them in their day-to-day operations.

An authority may select up to 35 targets framed in terms of the national indicator set. (Transport-related indicators within this set are listed in Table 20.3 in the next chapter.) These targets are negotiated with its partners and the Government (Regional) Office. They are then included in its draft LAA which it has to submit to the Secretary of State to be formally 'designated'. An authority may also identify a number of local improvement targets. These non-designated targets will not be reported on to central government but they will be taken account of as part of a regime of Comprehensive Area Assessment led by the Audit Commission. Authorities are incentivised through payment of a Performance Reward Grant. The overall LAA process is illustrated in Figure 19.4.

In resourcing the delivery of LSP priorities local authorities and other public sector partners may pool their mainstream resources and jointly commission goods and services. To facilitate this, central government has increased local authorities' spending flexibility by moving over £5bn of its grants into non-ring-fenced categories during the three years from April 2008 (i.e. money which authorities are not obliged to use for particular purposes). Of this nearly £1bn is being paid through the general Revenue Support Grant (distributed to all authorities on a formula basis). The majority is being paid through a new Area-Based Grant which is distributed according to specific policy criteria.

From 2008/09 a number of transport-related grants are being included in this pooling arrangement for the first time (Table 19.1) and further grants may be transferred.

Note that as far as items of capital expenditure are concerned, local authorities receive non-ring-fenced grants in the form of a Single Capital Pot. This includes spending on local transport whose planning is explained in the next chapter.

Local authorities may also work jointly with each other in developing Multi-Area Agreements (MAAs) – an innovation promoted by the Sub-National Review (23.7). These derive from the fact that individual authority's boundaries often do not correspond with functional areas:

> Whilst many policies are best dealt with at local authority level, many others, especially those aimed at improving economic development, may be best tackled by local authorities and their partners collaborating at the functional economic area. MAAs provide a means to achieve this and to really drive economic

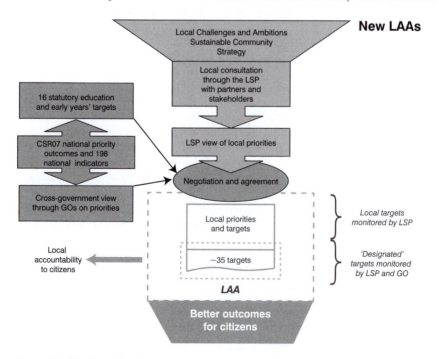

Figure 19.4 New Local Area Agreements (source: ODPM 2007b Ch. 1)

prosperity at the level of the sub-region, focusing on the key policies relating to economic growth such as transport, housing, worklessness and skills.

(DCLG 2007b Chapter 5)

Although MAAs are initially being targeted at economic development innovative approaches on other issues which may be dealt with through an MAA 'will not be ruled out'.

Table 19.1 Former ring-fenced transport-related grants transferred to the single Area-Based Grant from 2008/09

Grant	Central government department*
Detrunking (transferred responsibility for former trunk roads)	DfT
Extended rights to free transport	DCSF
Road safety grant	DfT
Rural bus subsidy	DfT
School travel advisers	DCSF
Sustainable travel general duty	DCSF

*DCSF = Department for Schools, Children and Families

20 Local transport plans

20.1 Introduction

Local Transport Plans (LTPs) prepared by county or unitary councils in England outside London have their origins in TPP documents (Transport Policies and Programmes) which local highway authorities submitted annually to central government (5.6).

The administrative burden represented by the annual cycle of TPPs was intended to be lessened with the shift to the five-yearly cycle of LTPs. In practice this proved questionable as an onerous system of annual progress reporting was maintained. This diversion of professional resources otherwise available for the delivery of services and infrastructure into fulfilling the administrative requirements of the system has been identified as one of its unintended consequences. Against this has to be set the substantial advances made in the scale and quality of local authorities' transport planning activity, which was the prime reason for the Labour Government introducing LTPs as part of its 'New Deal'. Overall the system continues to enjoy considerable professional support:

> ... the strengths of the process are seen as outweighing the weaknesses and many
> of the latter relate to administration, funding and assessment of plan preparation
> and delivery, rather than fundamental principles of the process itself.
> (Atkins Transport Planning 2007a Executive Summary p. xiv)

The above comments derive from an extremely thorough process of independent monitoring of the workings of the new system to which the reader is referred.

In this chapter we note first the intended role of LTPs (20.2), the administrative procedures for their preparation (20.3) and their funding context (20.4). We then consider their overall form and content (20.5) before looking in more detail at three key elements – the setting of objectives and priorities (20.6), performance indicators and targets (20.7) and the treatment of major schemes (20.8). Finally we review the equivalent processes followed in London, Wales and Scotland (20.9).

20.2 The role of Local Transport Plans

DfT and its predecessors have traditionally viewed 'planning' as a relatively narrow and largely technical activity concerned with the way individual investment proposals are generated and assessed for the purposes for allocating grants and approving borrowing. Concerns for a more holistic, spatial approach (even confined to transport alone) have surfaced relatively infrequently – for example the urban land use transport studies of the 1960s and the package approach and multi-modal corridor studies of the mid and late 1990s respectively.

The introduction of Local Transport Plans signified a broader approach to transport planning in several ways. This reflected the 'integration' aims of the *New Deal* White Paper (8.3) for which LTPs were intended as the key delivery mechanism at the local level. As well as replacing the annual TPP system as a means of allocating resources for local transport capital expenditure, their remit was extended to cover all forms of transport and the full range of delivery mechanisms available for pursuing a comprehensive set of objectives.

Initially the Government saw advantages in making LTPs a statutory requirement (as was subsequently enacted in the Transport Act 2000). This was so that they could be linked with legal provisions surrounding road user charging or changes in the regulation of local bus services and allow for stronger linkages with development plans. This highlights the intended role of LTPs in setting the strategic context for local transport generally in an area and not merely being focused on the specific activities for which local highway authorities were responsible. This broader remit required LTPs to be set in the context of wider objectives for the economic, social and environmental well-being of the area and for its proposals to be integrated with policies in these other fields.

However the Guidance produced for the second round of LTPs put a rather different complexion on the role of an LTP by making a distinction between it and the 'local transport strategy':

> All local transport authorities should maintain, review and update an identifiable local transport strategy. *These strategies are not the same as LTPs* – they deal with principles and objectives rather than schemes and targets and should look forward over a longer timescale than the five year LTP period. A local transport strategy need not be a stand-alone strategy, but may be encompassed within other local strategies. The purpose of the LTP is to set out how the local transport strategy translates to a policy implementation programme, and a set of targets and objectives, over a particular period.
>
> There is no requirement to include local transport strategies in full in LTPs. However the Department will, in its LTP quality assessment, look for evidence that a well-considered strategy exists.
>
> (DfT 2004c Part 2 paras 4 and 6; emphasis added)

This is a good example of the 'chopping and changing' which has been a feature of the New Labour era and of the muddle which can result. Clearly there is little point in making the LTP a statutory document so that it can present the strategic context for an area if in fact the strategy is to be found somewhere else! However the Government has offered no guidance on the form and content of such a strategy and its production has certainly not been made a statutory requirement. An even greater anomaly would seem to be that, irrespective of what is contained in an authority's strategy, the substance of its LTP is to be strongly conditioned by what the DfT has determined itself in the way of objectives and targets.

DfT commented that in the first round of LTPs the link between them and the wider planning and policy framework had been identified as a relatively weak area. In LTP2s it would therefore look for evidence that:

- authorities have developed their LTPs through close cooperation with local authority colleagues dealing with spatial planning, local economic development, regeneration, education, health and social services, housing, environmental services, rights of way and tourism/leisure
- these local authority colleagues are therefore fully committed to their part in delivering LTP targets and objectives
- plans, targets, policies and objectives delivered by other areas of local government, including the Community Plans (sic) and Local Development Documents of affected authorities, will in future be drawn up in a way which is broadly consistent with the LTP and its targets and objectives.

(ibid. para 7)

The guidance makes clear the DfT's concern that local transport planning should not be seen simply as a means of overcoming problems generated by other decision-areas as a result of their transport impacts not having been properly considered. On the other hand it does not dwell on the implications of transport planning serving *their* objectives and whether this is consistent with the very specific agenda that the DfT sets for transport authorities themselves.

20.3 Procedures for preparing LTPs

To date LTPs have been prepared for each shire county and unitary authority, except that in the metropolitan areas a single LTP has to be prepared jointly by the constituent metropolitan councils and the Passenger Transport Authority. Administratively the first round of LTPs continued to serve the function of TPPs in providing the basis for central government to assess authorities' capital programmes and determine grant allocation and borrowing approvals. The preparation of Annual Progress Reports (APRs) maintained a formalised cycle for structuring the dialogue between individual authorities and Government Offices which operated (in writing and in person) on an almost continuous basis. An elaborate assessment regime was established (which changed from year to year), the results of which determined the funding each authority received in the following year.

For the LTP2 period the arrangements for progress reporting have been altered radically. However the nature of the LTP documents themselves and the procedures for their preparation followed similar lines in both rounds. The plans were prepared for a five-year period uniformly throughout the country. In the case of LTP2s this had to overlay the annual progress reporting for LTP1s described above – a particularly onerous combination. In place of an annual report for the fifth year a one-off 'Delivery Report' had to be produced reviewing progress over the whole LTP1 period (DfT 2005b). Submission of this was required at the end of July 2006 and its assessment influenced the funding authorities received subsequently during the LTP2 period.

Unlike local development plans there were no requirements for LTPs to publish a timetable for plan preparation or to follow a prescribed process of public consultation. In practice the preparation of LTPs covered a period of two years or so prior to submission. However work on the documents themselves only tended to begin in earnest when the Government published its guidance since, from the local authority's perspective, this identified the hoops through which they were required to jump. These publications tended to be delayed with the result that preparation of the documents was squeezed into an undesirably short time. In the case of LTP2s, final guidance was only published in

December 2004 for plans which had to be submitted formally at the end of the following July (DfT 2004c). Such a timescale pays insufficient regard to the formal consultation and internal approval procedures which authorities need to follow and which themselves can take several months. In the event further delay by the Government in establishing funding guidelines and in making available software for the new element of accessibility planning meant that the versions submitted in July 2005 had to be regarded as 'provisional' with authorities submitting 'final' plans in March 2006.

The uncertainty surrounding the funding to be received in the immediate future as a result of the assessment of LTP material created difficulties for authorities in managing their capital programmes. It also hampered stakeholder involvement at more than a generalised level and the value of LTP documentation as an information source for the general public. This is because the submitted plan is not a 'draft' and the LTP itself is not revised when the Government response is known. In practice however the authority *would* need to review its policies and programmes when it received the DfT's formal response and funding settlement. There were no formalised arrangements for consulting or informing on these changes. Fortunately because of new funding arrangements (below) this shortcoming is now much diminished.

When LTPs were introduced the requirement that they should incorporate public consultation was a notable innovation. The Government stated that it attached a 'high priority' to effective public involvement and that plans should include a section which reported on this in the process of strategy development. In practice this proved problematic:

> Authorities found that the majority of the public were difficult to engage at the strategic level and tended to be interested in their own local issues. They often raised priorities or proposals which conflicted with the Government's national objectives, raising expectations and leading to questions over the validity of consultation .... Consultation exercises often focused on informing the public about proposals, but authorities were less clear about how the results would be fed back into strategy development.
>
> (Atkins Transport Planning 2005 para 3.3.1)

Evidence since suggests that authorities have become more successful in 'managing' the process – principally by adopting a more focused approach and working with stakeholder groups rather than the general public. Whether this fulfils the original aim is doubtful although arguably this was over-ambitious anyway. More disturbing is the idea put forward in the LTP2 guidance that 'involvement' should be justified on the basis of serving the interests of LTP authorities!

> It is in the interests of LTP authorities to involve local people, the local business community, those delivering other public services and other key stakeholders in the development and maintenance of local transport strategies *as this will help maximise local support for LTP proposals*. The Department does not intend to prescribe the nature of partnership or consultation arrangements but invites authorities to describe these arrangements briefly in the LTP.
>
> (DfT 2004c Part 2 para 9; emphasis added)

In practice the volume and complexity of material which LTPs needed to include deterred involvement from all but immediately affected stakeholders and the most hardened transport campaigners. To overcome these difficulties authorities normally produced a summary version of their LTP for consumption by the general public. However this cannot begin to get into the details of the proposed programme (many of which do not appear in the full LTP anyway). Exercises in consultation over particular proposals or particular areas therefore normally proceed as separate exercises from the LTP. Likewise authorities typically establish specialist forums of stakeholders and interest group representatives on particular topics (e.g. cycling or freight) and prepare separate strategies which are subsequently summarised and referred to as ancillary documents in LTPs.

Following the submission of LTP2s a completely different regime was established which reflected the Government's conversion to the principles of reducing the administrative reporting burden on local authorities and to devolving responsibility. In the 2006 settlement Ministers decided to allocate funding for the 'integrated transport' block (programmes of minor capital schemes) for the whole of the period to 2010/11, with no performance assessment or financial adjustment in the intervening years. (Transport indicators continued to be monitored and figure in the Best Value performance assessment of local authorities generally, as with all their other activities.) Ministers also announced that in place of the previous Annual Progress Reports there would be a single mid-term review in 2008 (DfT 2007e).

Lifting the requirement for standardised assessment across authorities and removing the threat (or enticement) of funding adjustments enabled a more constructive approach to be taken to the form of the 2008 Progress Reports (Box 20.1).

These features are elaborated upon in published guidance (DfT 2007d). Annex 1 contains an optional checklist on content whilst Annexes 2 and 3 contain information on authorities' obligation to report in connection with their Network Management Duty (14.4) and Air Quality Management Plans (14.8). The Department 'hoped' that authorities would be able to submit their reports by December 2008.

For the future the Department commissioned Atkins Transport Planning (which had monitored the LTP process thus far) to study options for its development. The consultants concluded:

> The case for change to the LTP model is finely balanced and largely related to the overall objectives which local transport is expected to support. The current process is accepted and supported by a wider range of stakeholders with few calls for a fundamentally different approach. In addition it seems sufficiently flexible to accommodate new policy initiatives and reforms to Local Government. However there is a case for at least some incremental changes to provide solutions to barriers experienced to date, embed local transport within wider corporate and community agendas and reflect emerging opportunities.
>
> (Atkins Transport Planning 2007b Executive Summary)

The Government has responded by proposing governance reforms, particularly in the metropolitan areas and in amending the statutory requirements for LTP preparation. These are now enacted in the Transport Act 2008. Detailed implications for future LTPs are explained in DfT 2008h.

Each local transport authority will be required to develop policies 'for the promotion and encouragement of safe, integrated, efficient and economic transport to, from and within their areas'. An LTP is redefined as one or more documents containing local transport policies plus proposals for implementing these policies. The requirement for a

---

Box 20.1 Features of the 2008 LTP2 Progress Reports

DfT 2007e Local Transport Planning: The Next Steps para 2.6

- Authorities have the flexibility to report on their overall progress in a manner that reflects their individual circumstances and priorities set out in their LTP2 and which builds on their overall reporting processes.
- Unlike the delivery reports produced in 2006 and many of the previous annual progress reports the 2008 progress reports will not be assessed or classified by the Department.
- The reports will provide the opportunity for a dialogue between a local authority (or group of authorities in joint transport planning areas) and its regional Government Office to discuss the progress of its LTP2. This dialogue could provide a forum for constructive challenge and an opportunity to identify good practice and discuss emerging problems. Local authorities should extend the dialogue to encompass local strategic partnerships, public transport operators and other key stakeholders.
- The main aim of the 2008 progress reports will be to assist authorities in reviewing their own progress against the plans set out in their LTP2. Importantly, and in line with the place-shaping policies set out in the Local Government White Paper Strong and Prosperous Communities, the reports will also concentrate on identifying any risks and mitigating actions needed to ensure effective delivery of the LTP2 in its remaining years.

---

separate bus strategy is removed. So too is the obligation to replace the documents every five years; authorities will in future be able to review them as they think appropriate.

20.4 The funding context for LTPs

For LTP1 the possible level of funding which each authority might bid for was speculative. The only guide was its own base level (i.e. the amount it had received in the previous year) plus the amounts for future years which had been identified for local transport expenditure in total in the Government's Comprehensive Spending Review. Since these incorporated large increases authorities were engaging in a very uncertain bidding game. Major schemes were – and continue to be – assessed independently and funded on a year-by-year basis in accordance with progress in implementation and current cost figures.

For LTP2 the DfT retained the formula-based approach for capital spending on road maintenance but decided to alter quite radically both the criteria for assessment and the basis of funding for the 'integrated transport' block, i.e. for all other minor works. The Department came to the view that the system used during the LTP1 period was 'rather opaque and increasingly outdated' and proposed to replace it mainly with a formula approach which it described as a 'transparent alternative'. The composition of this formula was developed through a project group with local authority officers and published in a Consultation Paper in July 2005 (DfT 2005c).

The formula is based on what is presented as the *five* shared priorities for transport, with public transport identified as a separate issue from accessibility. Details are

Table 20.1   The formula-based element of LTP2 funding for 'integrated transport' (source: DfT July 2005c Annex A)

Shared priority	Weight	Indicator(s) used in formula
Public transport	30%	Patronage data for bus and light rail in the LTP area
Road safety	20%	Casualty figures, but using 1994–98 baseline data in order not to penalise authorities who have made good progress since towards the Government's targets
*Congestion and pollution	30%	Resident population and size of urban area, with an adjustment for daytime population (25%); presence of designated Air Quality Management Area (5%)
Accessibility	20%	Resident population, number of non-car-owners and Index of Multiple Deprivation (15%); rural population in settlements < 25,000 (5%)

*Practical data problems prevent the extent of congestion itself being used as an indicator

Note: The DfT claims that about 20% of the funding formula rests on representations of each of the five shared priorities, given that better public transport can contribute to reducing congestion and pollution. The weights for public transport and road safety reflect the proportion of integrated block funding that has been devoted nationwide to these measures in recent years

given in Annex A of the Consultation Paper and are summarised in Table 20.1. The formula is to be supplemented by a limited number of special payments – about £10m in total annually to authorities designated as 'growth areas' within the Sustainable Communities programme and a similar sum to areas with EU Objective One status (Cornwall, Merseyside and South Yorkshire).

Nationally the guideline expenditure in 2010/11 is about 8% higher in cash terms than the average annual indicative allocation during LTP1, but the application of the formula results in major gainers and losers amongst individual local authorities (see Table 20.2). Those which had a high level of funding historically and which did well as a result of the assessments during the first LTP period tend to lose in relative – and sometimes absolute – terms and vice versa. In order to make for a smooth transition the formula approach is therefore being phased in over the five years of the LTP2 period.

The allocations for 2007/08 and remaining years of the LTP2 period deriving from the phased introduction of the formula were added to in certain cases as a result of the Department's assessment of authorities' LTP2s and LTP1 Delivery Reports. (The criteria employed are given in Annex C of DfT 2004c and in 2005b.) Authorities with documents classified as 'excellent' received an uplift of 12.5% in each case. As can be seen in Table 20.2 the combination of the two enabled some authorities (Merseyside and Reading in the examples shown) to avoid – wholly or substantially – the spending reductions they would otherwise have had to contend with. Oxfordshire by comparison was less fortunate.

Notwithstanding transitional difficulties in individual cases the combination of a stable national spending trajectory plus introduction of the formula approach has provided much greater predictability in the amounts authorities can plan to spend. This represents a radical transformation from the very uncertain environment and 'bidding' culture which characterised the early years of LTP1.

Table 20.2 Changes arising from use of the formula approach to integrated block funding (source: From full tables published in LTT 459)

Plan	LTP1 2001/02–2005/06 Avg £m pa	Indicative baseline allocation £m LTP2 final year 2010/2011		Actual allocation** 2007/08 £m	Classification of documents	
		Guideline	Change		LTP2	LTP1 Delivery Report
Conurbation						
Tyne & Wear	15.5	23.0	+48%	17.0	Good	V good
Merseyside	32.2	27.4	−15%	36.5	**Excellent**	**Excellent**
Shire						
East Sussex*	3.3	5.8	+75%	4.1	Good	Good
Oxfordshire	10.2	8.1	−21%	9.2	Good	Good
Urban unitary						
Milton Keynes*	1.5	2.9	+93%	2.0	Fair	Good
Reading	5.5	2.6	−53%	5.2	**Excellent**	**Excellent**

The table shows for each of the three main categories of authority the ones whose guideline funding changed most as a result of introducing the allocation formula.

*Note: Kent and Thurrock received higher proportionate increases but these were influenced by exceptional payments on account of both growth area status and the DfT's decision to continue tolling on the Dartford River Crossing

** Includes the effect of phased introduction of the formula plus 'uplift' payments resulting from the classification of LTP documents – see text

20.5 The form and content of LTPs

For the first round of LTPs the Government asked that five key elements should be included:

- **Objectives** consistent with our integrated transport policy and commanding widespread local support
- An analysis of **problems** and **opportunities**
- A **long-term strategy** to tackle the problems and deliver the objectives. In developing the strategy the range of potential solutions will need to be tested to establish the best combination of measures.
- A costed and affordable 5-year **implementation programme** of schemes and policy measures [with individual schemes costing more than £250,000 separately identified].
- A set of **targets and performance indicators** and other outputs which can be used to assess whether the plan is delivering the stated objectives.

> Each of these should feature as discrete sections or chapters within the LTP.
> (DETR 2000a Part 1 para 29)

However what these represent in practice is highly variable due to the enormous differences in the size of areas for which LTPs are prepared. For example the whole of Rutland's LTP is devoted to addressing issues in an area of just 34,000 population, whereas an equivalent area would barely register in the LTP for Greater Manchester (population 2.1 million)!

Subject to including the above five elements, local authorities had discretion over how they structured their LTPs. Many included separate chapters for particular topics or areas, in part reflecting their particular circumstances. (For example policies for rural areas or for promoting rail use would be much more significant in some areas than others.) However this diversity created difficulties for the Department when seeking to compare LTPs for assessment purposes. It also makes it difficult to form a coherent view of the policies and proposals being put forward for an area covered by two or more LTPs. (Outside the metropolitan areas DfT has tried to encourage the preparation of joint LTPs for closely related areas, but with only limited success – the shift from four plans to one for the so-called 'West of England' (Greater Bristol) area being a notable example.)

For LTP2 the items listed above were retained as the 'basic features' to be contained in a plan. Again DfT did not prescribe any particular format. However a degree of standardisation was implied by asking authorities to present a core of material addressing its priority objectives (explained in the next section).

In contrast to the procedures specified for local development planning there was no requirement for the content of LTPs to be developed through an integral process of sustainability appraisal. (Mention of 'sustainable development', other than as an overarching goal, is conspicuously absent from the LTP2 guidance whereas it occupies a central position throughout the planning guidance issued by ODPM/DCLG.) Only modest encouragement is offered to integrate environmental assessment:

> LTPs should, where possible, include evidence about how the environmental assessment process has improved ... local transport planning. It may also be

helpful for LTPs to include a description of how the role of statutory bodies in environmental assessment and LTP development has improved the LTP, *although this is not a mandatory requirement.*

(DfT 2004c Part 5 para 15; emphasis added)

As far as the substantive content of local transport programmes is concernedp the 'integrated transport' block will include a large number of small-scale schemes. Typically these are developed in a range of programme areas which involve different types of intervention addressing different modes, often utilising particular technical expertise. Examples would be road safety schemes, provision for walking and cycling, environmental improvement, facilities for public transport users, traffic management and minor road or junction improvements and so on. Alternatively programmes may be compiled for particular areas (e.g. sub-divisions of a shire county) and/or in relation to plan objectives.

However programmes are structured, difficulty arises in seeking to identify the overall mix which would best fulfil an authority's aspirations. With larger schemes the detailed impacts of a proposal may be investigated and an economic cost-benefit assessment undertaken which will place different kinds of scheme on a common footing and provide information to help decision-makers choose between them. Usually this is not practicable with small-scale schemes and in any case would not warrant the professional time involved given their relatively low cost.

To overcome this problem and to help manage the reconciliation of claims between different interest groups a systematic process of prioritising schemes is recommended (Atkins Transport Planning 2008). This report reviews a range of approaches to prioritisation adopted by different authorities. However it does not recommend (and the Department has chosen not to specify) a particular methodology. In part this reflects differences in the circumstances of individual authorities and recognition that a 'one size fits all' approach would not be appropriate.

20.6 Objectives and priorities

For LTP1 an authority's objectives had to be consistent with the Government's overarching objectives for transport developed from the 1998 White Paper which formed the basis of the new approach to appraisal (11.4).

For LTP2 a more focused approach was introduced, reflecting the Government's concern to make a more demonstrable impact on improving local services. In 2002 the Government had agreed with the LGA a set of seven 'shared priorities' for local government generally and within this a subset of four priorities for transport:

- tackling congestion
- delivering accessibility
- safer roads
- better air quality.

In its LTP2 Guidance, DfT said that it would look for evidence that 'the aim of delivering the shared priorities is at the heart of all local transport strategies and LTPs' and gave details of how it expected local authorities to plan for each of them. Authorities were recommended to structure their documents so that the contribution of particular modes was reflected in objective-related sections, not in separate modal sections (advice which the DfT conspicuously did not follow in its own 2004 White Paper!).

The focus on congestion was linked to the national objective and target for the issue. The Government intended to take a 'close interest' in the development of local congestion targets and to 'discuss each authority's approach individually through direct engagement'. (The outcome, as far as the ten main urban areas in England are concerned, is reflected in PSA4 reproduced in Box 11.4.) Congestion was recognised as not being a major issue for some authorities and they were therefore not required to generate proposals for it. The same applied to authorities who were not required to pursue mandatory targets for air quality. However this narrow focus presents difficulties for authorities who would otherwise seek to use economic and environmental objectives more generally as the basis on which to justify proposed spending.

The priority of delivering accessibility followed closely the same objective quoted for LTP1, but was developed much more fully as a consequence of a report on the subject by the Social Exclusion Unit (ODPM 2003b). For LTP2 all authorities were expected to use accessibility planning techniques to understand the links between social exclusion and transport in their areas and to develop transport solutions accordingly (DfT 2004d). They were encouraged to develop partnerships with other agencies in fields such as health, education, employment and social services in framing an 'accessibility strategy' and progressively developing 'local accessibility action plans' jointly with other partners to tackle specific problems.

Unfortunately no new funding stream was created to pump-prime collaborative action in this field. As a result it can be difficult for transport authorities to achieve serious engagement of these other bodies and recognition of *their* responsibility for accessibility conditions (in terms of the location of their facilities and the operation of their services in place and time). It is easier for them to follow the traditional path of making their own decisions and to expect any consequential accessibility problems to be addressed through provision of improved transport services. This is a cross-cutting issue of the kind which should benefit from the development of LSPs and Local Area Agreements reported in the previous chapter (Chatterjee et al. 2004).

In addition to the four shared priorities a number of other 'quality of life' issues relating to transport were identified for consideration. These included:

- sustainable communities ('the creation of vibrant and prosperous urban areas')
- the quality of public spaces and landscapes (including the street environment)
- conservation of biodiversity
- community safety
- public health
- noise
- climate change.

The relegation of climate change to the last of a list of 'other issues' is especially remarkable. Although the Guidance quoted the Government's CO_2 reduction targets as set out in the 2003 Energy White Paper, consequential action was confined to a single paragraph including:

> LTPs should take account of the UK's CO_2 targets and should complement the wider aims of Local Agenda 21. The Department is however also keen for

authorities to lead by example and demonstrate through LTPs how wider local transport policies would contribute to the achievement of CO_2 targets.

(DfT 2004c para 95)

The treatment which these and other issues might expect to receive compared with the 'shared priorities' is problematic. The implication seems to be that authorities are at liberty to pursue other objectives as they think appropriate, but that the proposals addressing them should be included in sections focused on the shared priorities. This poses not merely an editorial problem – how for example should schemes be presented which contribute to all the shared priorities, or none? But there is a more substantive problem. It is difficult to take seriously the Department's claim that 'these (other) issues are no less important than the shared priorities' if in fact they have to be justified in sections written to address these priorities!

The result seems likely to be to encourage obfuscation with schemes designed essentially to address other objectives being 'dressed up' so as to appear to make a greater contribution to the shared priorities than is in fact the case. For many types of scheme – often ones which enjoy a large measure of local support – it may prove impossible to present a 'legitimate' case at all. The divergence is particularly evident in the case of schemes linked to spatial planning (including regeneration and new development areas).

20.7 Performance indicators and targets

When LTPs were initiated the idea of developing performance indicators across the range of authorities' activities was in its infancy. In transport even the principle of establishing a 'causal chain' approach to link measures (interventions) with objectives and outputs had only been introduced in 1997. For their first LTPs, authorities were left to determine the precise package of indicators and targets which best reflected local circumstances, subject to including numerical targets in those areas where national targets had been set. In practice the selection of issues and indicators was often strongly conditioned by the availability of local data (or the practicability of generating it). The monitoring of issues, plus evidence on spending and the delivery of programmes, was to be the subject of the subsequent APRs (Annual Progress Reports).

The diversity permitted by this approach presented the Department with difficulties when seeking to compare and aggregate the statistics generated by individual authorities. In the years which followed, the Department therefore sought to tighten up performance monitoring procedures through the guidance it issued for successive APRs. In particular it introduced standardised indicators relating to national transport targets and to services monitored in authorities' Local Performance Plans as part of the national Best Value regime.

The attention given to performance monitoring was arguably the most distinctive feature of the guidance for LTP2. (It occupied only a few paragraphs of the first edition.) The Government's approach to the subject was explained at the beginning of the LTP2 guidance (reproduced in Box 20.2). Its language is very different from the earlier version and nicely captures the 'delivery-speak' characteristic of the middle years of New Labour. It is also notable that the Department claims it does not intend to 'micro-manage' the delivery of authorities' programmes, provided that it is satisfied that its key requirements are met. Aspirations similar to this have been voiced from time to time by central government since the dawn of TPPs. Whether it will ever be

---

Box 20.2 Performance management and direct engagement

From DfT 2004c Full Guidance on LTPs: Second Edition paras 8–9

Consistent with the Prime Minister's principles of public service reform, the Department sees itself as having three main roles in delivering better local transport. Firstly, it must continue to develop the structures of our relationship with local partners, in a way that enables them to innovate and pursue excellence. Secondly, it must provide clear strategic leadership, focused on the real-world results that both central and local government want to deliver. Thirdly, it must provide public investment in a way that delivers the best possible value for money to taxpayers. The Department for Transport intends to develop the LTP system to deliver these objectives, by emphasising its role as a performance management system.

Performance management requires the parties involved to understand what their shared objectives and resources are, to work together to set ambitious but realistic targets for delivering those objectives, and to challenge each other to do better, where possible. The Government therefore intends to engage with all local transport authorities – in groups or individually – as they develop their LTPs, to ensure that those LTPs reflect the principles of effective performance management. The aim of this engagement is not to impose a central strategy on local authorities, but to help authorities develop local transport strategies and plans that are effective and that will deliver real improvements in outcomes, and an appropriate set of targets and objectives against which performance can be tracked.

---

possible for central–local relations to be conducted quite so exclusively within the rather ethereal realms of performance measurement and with so little concern for the actual content of programmes remains to be seen.

For LTP2 authorities were required to set targets for 2010/11 in relation to a number of key outcome or 'mandatory' indicators (shown in Table 20.3). They were also asked to identify intermediate outcomes for these indicators which represented a trajectory of change from the baseline year (2003/04) towards the target against which progress could subsequently be compared. Authorities were at liberty to set additional targets and indicators but were cautioned that too many were likely to prove counter-productive.

For the targets linked to mandatory indicators, authorities were asked to include in their LTPs:

*   evidence that the target was both ambitious and realistic (having regard to likely funding)
*   the key actions of local government and other partners needed to achieve it
*   the principal risks to achievement and how these are to be managed.

From April 2009 specific reporting on the Best Value and LTP2 mandatory indicators is superseded by local authorities' overall reporting on the national indicator set. As shown in Table 20.3 nine of the previous seventeen transport indicators are carried forward into the national set. Of the remaining eight, DfT will continue to produce statistics related to two: total slight casualties and change in area-wide traffic

Table 20.3 Mandatory indicators for LTP2 (to 2008/09) (source: DfT 2004c Full Guidance on LTPs: Second Edition Annex A)

BVPI96	NI 168	Principal Road condition
BVPI97a	NI 169	Non-Principal Classified Road condition
BVPI97b		Unclassified Road condition
BVPI99 (x)	NI 47	Total killed and seriously injured casualties
BVPI99 (y)	NI 48	Child killed and seriously injured casualties
BVPI99 (z)		Total slight casualties
BVPI102	NI 177	Public transport patronage.
BVPI104		Satisfaction with local bus services
BVPI187		Footway condition
LTP1	NI 175	An accessibility target
LTP2		Change in area-wide road traffic mileage
LTP3		Cycling trips (annualised index)
LTP4	NI 198	Mode share of journeys to school
LTP5	NI 178	A bus punctuality indicator
LTP61		Changes in peak period traffic flows to urban centres
LTP71	NI 167	Congestion (vehicle delay)
LTP81		An air quality target

1 Mandatory for only certain authorities.

BVPI = Best Value Performance Indicator, LTP = Local Transport Plan indicator, NI = National Indicator (from 2008/09)
For details and definition of the LTP indicators and the areas to which they apply see Technical guidance on monitoring the LTP2 mandatory indicators DfT December 2004; also Local Accessibility Indicators for LTP2 Letter dated 10 November 2005

mileage. As part of their 2008 review authorities are asked to consider which of the remaining indicators they may wish to continue to monitor.

20.8 The treatment of major schemes

The design and appraisal of local authority major schemes is a protracted business which typically extends over several years. For this reason LTPs do not necessarily include the details of such proposals – rather LTP submission provides the opportunity for authorities to register their *intent* to develop such schemes and the anticipated timescale involved.

To qualify for consideration as a major scheme a proposal has to be seeking funding of more than £5m. It can consist of several components but authorities have to be able to demonstrate that there are additional benefits to be derived from delivering them at one go rather than separately on an incremental basis from the block allocation.

In its LTP2 guidance the DfT noted the increasing pressure on funding of major schemes. This arose from a combination of new demands (e.g. arising from the Multi-Modal Studies programme, the Sustainable Communities Plan and Regional Transport Strategies more generally) plus the 'hangover' effect from a number of approved schemes in the LTP1 period which authorities had taken longer than expected to deliver. The Department was likely to receive many more proposals than it could support. Hence:

> The Department advises local authorities seeking to develop major schemes to concentrate their efforts on major scheme proposals that look likely to offer the best overall value for money according to NATA criteria – especially those that look likely to meet the priorities set out by Regional Planning Bodies in RTSs. Authorities may still decide to include weaker schemes as proposals in their LTPs but the Department recommends strongly that they instead consider carefully how they might deliver the benefits of such schemes through other means – through alternative funding sources, or perhaps through a combination of smaller block-funded schemes and revenue funded programmes.
>
> (DfT 2004c Part 4 para 27)

Because of doubts over funding greater emphasis was placed in the LTP2 guidance compared with the first round in treating major schemes as potential *additions* to the rest of an authority's programme However they were to be summarised in a separate section of the plan, with information showing how the main block-funded programme would be affected if the major scheme were approved and delivered and what additional progress could be expected towards LTP objectives and targets within the four 'shared priority' areas.

Further details on the appraisal and approval processes applied to major schemes are given in Chapters 21 and 22.

20.9 Local Transport Planning in London, Wales and Scotland

London

The local transport planning work undertaken by London Boroughs and the City of London Corporation is similar in kind to unitary councils in the rest of England. However the policy status of the plans they produce is quite different. These councils do not have the same degree of discretion to formulate their own policies within an overarching national and regional framework. Rather their strategic role is to contribute directly to implementing the policies of the London Mayor as set out in his Transport Strategy and in particular to fulfilment of its statutory targets. This difference is reflected in the naming of their plans as Local Implementation Plans (LIP).

The different policy relationship is also evident in the arrangements for progress reporting and funding allocation. London Boroughs do not liaise with the Government Regional Office but with the Mayor and TfL. The total amount of LIP funding likely to be available each year is set out in TfL's five-year Investment Programme. Unlike the rest of England LIP funding includes elements of revenue support although, like LTPs, their main focus is on capital expenditure. Also unlike the rest of England the borough's plans are overlaid by a number of programme areas on which TfL itself takes lead responsibility, e.g. the capital's strategic road network, congestion charging, bus and Underground services and planning for the 2012 Olympic Games.

Until 2006/07 financial assistance was given annually in response to bids made in Borough Spending Plans. Thereafter allocations to each borough were to be determined in response to the LIP and to subsequent Annual Progress Reports. (There are also a number of cross-borough partnerships such as the London Bus Priority Network and the London Cycle Network.) In principle this arrangement would enable boroughs to plan their work programmes and project delivery with more financial certainty and over a longer period than the previous annual cycle. In practice, submission of final LIPs, approved by the Mayor, was not completed for many boroughs by the intended date of July 2006 and a hybrid arrangement therefore had to be adopted for 2007/08.

For 2008/09 to 2010/11 funding applications by boroughs have to meet the following requirements (TfL 2007):

- All proposals seeking funding have to be detailed in forms linked to the LIP process.
- Excluding proposals costing over £1m the total funding sought by individual boroughs for the majority of programme areas must not exceed £7m.
- All proposals must be prioritised in descending order of importance.

Proposals with a total cost of £2m or more have to submit an additional Business Case which is the subject of separate guidance.

Unlike LTPs where central government funding is allocated on the basis of 'blocks' of expenditure covering a number of different programmes, LIP funding is much more disaggregated and tightly controlled by TfL. There are some twenty individual programmes (e.g. walking, school travel plans and controlled parking zones) and applications are evaluated within each of these following criteria set out in Section 7 of the guidance. Overall assessment is undertaken on the basis of the monitoring of outputs (delivery), outcomes and contribution to the Mayor's targets.

TfL is pursuing the following improvements to its planning process:

- development of a common appraisal methodology for LIP proposals
- annual indicative allocations per borough by transport programme
- review of the outcome-monitoring process.

In future, borough LIPs will need to be revised to meet updates of the Mayor's Transport Strategy and London Plan. It is anticipated that revised LIPs will set out how boroughs will meet the new statutory outcome and output targets through the delivery of a five-year programme of transport schemes.

Wales

The introduction of Regional Transport Plans prepared by consortia of local authorities in Wales was explained in the previous chapter. As a result the former requirement for individual authorities to produce LTPs and APRs has been terminated. These authorities will continue to have responsibility for a number of transport-related functions and it remains for them to determine whether formalised programmes will be needed in these areas for their own purposes. Authorities will however continue to undertake survey-based monitoring to meet the requirements of the regional consortia.

Scotland

The institutional environment surrounding the working of local transport authorities in Scotland has changed in much the same way as in Wales with the national executive assuming some additional powers and previously voluntary regional partnerships being placed on a statutory basis. However partly because of differences in timing, the Scottish Executive did not immediately seek to transfer the local transport planning activities of individual authorities to the regional bodies.

Unlike England and Wales LTPs were never legislated for in Scotland. Instead authorities were originally asked to produce a non-statutory local transport strategy focusing on plans for the next three years, in the context of a vision for integrated transport looking 10 or 20 years ahead linked to Development Plan time horizons (Scottish Executive 1999).

Up-dated guidance for these strategies was issued in 2005 in the context of the national and regional changes then in progress:

> While the institutional landscape for transport is changing there will also be continuity. Local authorities and SPT [Strathclyde Passenger Transport – the Passenger Transport Executive for the Greater Glasgow area] will continue to maintain transport infrastructure, plan and deliver services so there is still an important role for local transport strategies.
>
> (Scottish Executive 2005b para 1.15)

Nevertheless authorities were asked to take account of the strategies already produced by the voluntary regional partnerships and SPT whilst their own work would feed into the new statutory regional strategies.

In many respects the nature and preparation of local strategies in Scotland has similarities with the English LTPs. They are expected to follow a systematic process of analysis within the context of national objectives, to engage with stakeholders, link with local development and community plans, employ performance indicators and targets and consider the application of regulations for Strategic Environmental Assessment. A rather stronger role is advocated in the Scottish system of appraisal (STAG) at the strategic level (i.e. in assessing the overall package of measures proposed) and not merely in connection with individual projects. The Guidance states that it expects a local transport strategy to include commentary on alternative strategies considered and why they were not chosen.

The administrative context for the production of Scottish local strategies is however quite different. The guidance is much less prescriptive and the tone in which it is written is more in the nature of constructive advice. There is none of the pre-occupation with specifying 'requirements' relating to the assessment of authorities' documents and delivery that characterised the English LTP2 guidance produced at about the same time. This reflects a key difference between the Scottish and English systems, namely that the Scottish strategies are not linked directly to decisions on annual funding allocation. This in turn permits a more relaxed approach to be taken to production of the strategies themselves:

> We are aware that local authorities are at different stages in the production cycle of local transport strategies and expect most strategies to be completed during the course of 2005/06 although we have deliberately not set a deadline for completion – instead enabling authorities to work to their own timescales.
>
> (Scottish Executive 2005b para 1.17)

Likewise the approach to monitoring embodies a different balance. Authorities are invited to determine the precise package of performance indicators and targets which best reflect their local circumstances and to *include* targets showing the local contribution to national transport-related targets where these have been established – the reverse of the English emphasis on 'mandatory' indicators.

Arguably the weak element in the Scottish system is the limited attention given to delivery. The guidance includes only two paragraphs on 'developing an action plan' which it is suggested should be reviewed annually. In practice the translation of local strategies into deliverable programmes will be the subject of continuing dialogue with the Scottish Executive, particularly as far as decisions on the funding of larger schemes is concerned. Overall it would be an interesting research question as to how far the difference in formal requirements and procedural arrangements in Scotland and England are reflected in differences in local transport delivery.

21 Project appraisal

21.1 Introduction

'Appraisal' is the process of assessing the worth of a course of action. It can be undertaken of individual projects or of plans, programmes or policies. In this chapter we will be exploring the subject in relation to major transport investments (currently defined as schemes with a capital cost of more than £5m) which seek funding from central government.

To students or anyone else who has not experienced the inside world of transport planning, the extent to which the Department of Transport exercises control over the technical procedures followed in the planning and appraisal of projects is likely to come as something of a shock. There are extensive stipulations about the amount and type of information to be supplied, the basis on which this is derived and the format in which it is to be presented. We begin this chapter by explaining the reasoning behind this common appraisal process and noting its implications (21.2).

At the heart of the process is the preparation of a comprehensive statement of impacts relative to a set of objectives drawn from the 1998 White Paper. These are presented in an Appraisal Summary Table (AST) which provides decision-makers with evidence of the diversity of impacts in a manageable form. Because of the importance of this tool we deal with it first (in 21.3) followed by a brief explanation of the forecasting and modelling procedures used to generate the information on which it is based (21.4). From the perspective of cost-effectiveness of public spending the impacts reported in the AST are synthesised in advice to Ministers on 'value for money' (21.5).

There are further technical elements which have come to be recognised as important to appraisal overall. These represent stages in a broader planning process which spans the preparation of the AST. The analysis of objectives and problems takes place previously and is discussed in section 21.6. There are then a number of analyses which are conducted as 'supplementary' to the AST (21.7). Finally in section 21.8 we give a brief description of strategic environmental assessment (SEA) which is a separate requirement under EU legislation.

21.2 The common appraisal process and its significance

Central government has a duty to ensure that the money it disburses for transport and other purposes is spent wisely. In pursuit of this the Treasury has published guidance on appraisal in its 'Green Book' which all departments are required to follow (HM Treasury 2003). This is designed to ensure that spending proposals are assessed in a transparent and consistent manner, that they fulfil objectives most effectively and that they provide 'value for money'. The appraisal methods developed by the Department of Transport previously had much the same purpose and only minor adjustments were needed in order to bring them into line with the Treasury guidelines.

The Department developed its appraisal methods by commissioning research and building up a body of knowledge about what it considers to be best practice. Much of this is now incorporated in a 'virtual' loose-leaf manual of Transport Analysis Guidance (TAG) which is accessible at its own website (www.webtag.org.uk). This is organised at three levels (labelled 'overview', 'project manager' and 'expert') which enable topics to be interrogated at different levels of detail. Readers are encouraged to visit the site and to follow the link from 'Documents' at the top of the home page to 'Guidance Documents' in order to view the table of contents. Each section typically includes directions for further information and a list of specialist references.

Scotland and Wales have their own variants of these procedures known as STAG and WelTAG respectively (Transport Scotland 2008a; Transport Wales 2008).

Use of the term 'guidance' in this context is really a misnomer. It makes the Government's advice appear less overbearing but in fact it represents 'instructions' for its own staff and 'requirements' placed on others. Although there will be scope for discussion in exactly how the guidance is interpreted in individual cases, all applications for major scheme funding have to follow its basic procedures and incorporate its technical methods. Haggling over compliance with the minutiae of these requirements is one of the frustrations which scheme promoters encounter, often believing this to be a delaying tactic. But this should not detract from the value of the DfT's role more generally in promoting high standards of technical competence in professional practice.

The use of a common appraisal process has clear advantages as far as the internal workings of government are concerned. It enables the evidence informing funding decisions to be presented in a standard, consistent manner. It also enables debates to be conducted between professionals about the merits of rival schemes on a basis with which they are all familiar. From a wider perspective however the role of the Department's appraisal process within public decision-making is more problematic. Although its requirements are devised to be as 'fair' and soundly based as possible within their own terms, they nevertheless represent conventions rather than absolute truths. These inevitably cut across different 'views of the world' likely to be held by other groups seeking to influence transport decision-making and impose their own, implicitly superior, legitimacy. In this we are not talking about differences in objective or policy which are acknowledged to reflect value judgements but about the power of technically derived 'evidence' and its presentation being treated as value-free when inevitably it is not.

21.3 The Appraisal Summary Table (AST)

The summary table was the central feature of the new transport appraisal framework (NATA) originally devised for the review of highways schemes inherited by the Labour Government in 1997. It was developed subsequently in the context of the Multi-Modal Studies to enable it to be applied to other types of scheme. This and the guidance prepared for the Studies' overall methodology (known as GOMMMS) have since been incorporated in the DfT's advice. Elements of the advice continue to be updated and added to and further changes are anticipated as a result of a more thoroughgoing review announced in June 2007 (24.8).

The distinctive feature of NATA was and remains the structuring of information in terms of the Government's five main objectives, viz environment, safety, economy, accessibility and integration. Different aspects of performance are assessed for a series of 'sub-objectives' under these headings – so that for example the main objective 'to improve safety' is subdivided into 'to reduce accidents' and 'to improve security' (Table 11.1 previously).

The conclusions are brought together in a single-page 'Appraisal Summary Table' (AST) with each row of the table reporting the impact of the proposal on each sub-objective (TAG unit 2.7.2). The table includes a column for a brief textual description of qualitative impact and a column for quantitative measurement. Depending on the nature of the attribute a final column summarises the assessment in terms of either an impact measurement or score or (where the impact can be assigned a monetary value) a measure of net cost or benefit.

To the uninitiated, there are number of oddities in the appraisal framework, both in the definition of sub-objectives and in the precise way these are interpreted and measured. The explanation of these lies in the compromise made between a desire to present impacts comprehensively and impartially (so that bias is not introduced in the way information is presented to decision-takers), yet at the same time respecting the structure set by the overarching objectives. For example 'Safety' is singled out even though it represents a mix of economic concerns (the costs of damage, healthcare, loss of productive capability etc. associated with accidents) and personal or social concerns – e.g. 'suffering' (which is actually assigned a monetary value) and anxiety over personal security.

The framework's concern for impartiality is reflected in the fact that each sub-objective is presented as of equivalent status. No attempt is made to pre-judge the relative importance of sub-objectives by aggregating individual impacts in any way so as to try and present an overall assessment of the benefit or worth of a scheme. (An important proviso to this surrounds the parallel exercise in determining 'value for money' which we consider below.) However any particular impact is classified, care is taken to ensure that it only appears once in the table (i.e. to avoid 'double-counting').

The precise specification of each sub-objective and the detailed information to be supplied in worksheets accompanying the AST is explained in TAG units 3.3–3.7.

Assessment of the 'Land Use Policy' and 'Other Government Policy' sub-objectives under the 'Integration' heading are different from those in the remainder of the table. They are not concerned with the measurement of substantive impacts and whether these are intrinsically good or bad but rather whether they contribute to or conflict with Government policy in other sectors. (Impacts on individual policies are recorded in accompanying worksheets.) These are aggregated to offer an overall assessment summarised simply as 'neutral', 'beneficial' or 'adverse' in the AST.

Because of the close interaction between transport and land use it can be questioned whether a scheme which conflicts significantly with spatial policies in its area ought to be under consideration at all! This highlights the fact that the relationship with spatial policies should ideally be explored in the genesis of schemes through regional strategies (Chapter 18). It will in any case remain to be tested when planning permission is sought (22.3).

21.4 Forecasts and modelling

The validity of an 'evidence-based' appraisal exercise depends on the ability to estimate future conditions, and how these might be affected by a possible transport intervention at some point. However uncertainty is endemic and even producing a single 'best estimate' of circumstances surrounding an individual scheme is a complex and expensive undertaking. Options are therefore normally assessed in the context of a single 'planning' scenario, although the volume and pattern of travel in each option will be varied to reflect prevailing conditions on the transport network. Rather than explore the full extent of differences which might arise under alternative planning scenarios, more limited investigation can be conducted of the sensitivity of outcomes to changes in the main determining factors. This then provides additional information which can be drawn on in carrying out Risk Assessments (explained in the following section).

The forecasts utilised in appraisal are of two main kinds. The first – sometimes referred to as 'planning data' – relate to exogenous factors, i.e. those which affect travel demand in the study area of the scheme, but which are independent of the transport options being considered. The second relate to the transport networks in the area and the travel patterns which result from the opportunities these offer. It is from these that the estimated impacts on the various sub-objectives within the AST are derived.

Both kinds of data are generated for a single 'forecast year' which may be up to 25 years from the 'base year' on which a particular study is founded. Hence assessments carried out in, say 2008, might be based on initial conditions as they existed in a base year of 2006, with a forecast year of 2026 or 2031. For individual schemes forecasts will also be produced for their opening year in order to identify their initial impact. Estimates of conditions in the years between those for which forecasts are produced are derived by interpolation; for conditions beyond the final forecast year assumptions are applied as appropriate for the remainder of the scheme's economic life.

Planning data consist of Census-based forecasts of population, adjusted locally to reflect future changes in the spatial distribution of development. For the first decade or so these expected changes will normally be embodied in statutory development plans. The advice of professionals within local planning authorities will then be used to extend forecasts beyond the horizon year of these plans. A similar process is followed in producing forecasts for the amount, nature and distribution of employment. Employment is significant not only because of its direct role in the generation of travel (through commuting, business and freight journeys) but as an indicator of non-home-based activity more generally, (e.g. shopping and personal business journeys).

It is important that the planning data used as the basis of different forecasting exercises are consistent with one another and that local policy aspirations (which may involve seeking to promote or resist new development) do not cloud the production of realistic forecasts within a particular study area. For these reasons the DfT requires use of a national set of planning data which it compiles for its own policy analysis work involving the National Transport Model (NTM). Access to this dataset is via a program known as TEMPRO. Individual studies will adopt their own, more disaggregated zoning systems which 'nest' within the NTM zones. The population and employment figures for NTM zones act as control totals for these local studies.

Data relating to current transport networks and travel patterns is assembled from inventories maintained by transport authorities supplemented by field surveys at selected (often most critical) locations. Except for narrowly focused schemes it will be impractical to generate comprehensive travel information for the base year. Instead sample data will be used to 'calibrate' (i.e. adjust on the basis of local evidence) the output of mathematical models built using relationships identified in previous studies. These 'land use–transport models' produce estimates of the volume and patterns of trips given local data on the pattern of land use, the characteristics of transport networks and composition of the population. On the assumption that these relationships hold good through time, the calibrated model is then used in conjunction with forecast planning data to estimate travel patterns in future years. (A full introduction to land use–transport modelling is given in TAG unit 3.1.)

Travel forecasts are produced initially for a hypothetical future situation known as the 'reference case'. This incorporates the effect of exogenous factors, i.e. local changes in land use and the national projections of GDP etc. within TEMPRO, but does not reflect conditions on the local transport network. Implicitly the volume and pattern of demand in the reference case assumes that travel speeds and costs on all parts of the transport network remain the same as in the base year. In practice changes in the exogenous factors alter the volume and distribution of trips as between particular places, modes, routes and times of day. These changes in travel demand alter conditions on the transport network relative to the base year. The changed pattern of opportunities then alters the scale and pattern of demand compared with the reference case, resulting in a new set of transport conditions and so on.

The Department now requires the use of 'variable demand models' to reflect this interaction between demand and supply until an acceptable level of convergence is reached with each option examined (TAG unit 2.9.2). In the simplest case the model will be run to produce a volume and pattern of demand in the forecast year for the 'with scheme' scenario, the impacts of which are then compared against a 'without scheme' scenario. An illustration of variable demand forecasting is given in Figure 21.1. In this example the effect of the scheme is to improve conditions for individual travellers such that an overall increase in trips occurs relative to the without-scheme scenario. However the fact that the total shown remains less than the reference case is not a necessary outcome – in theory it would be possible to improve conditions to the extent that all initially forecast demand was accommodated and additional travel induced beyond this. (Historically this was the case with inter-urban road schemes developed in the era of 'predict and provide', where variable demand modelling was not employed and the 'reference case' forecasts were used as the basis of scheme design.)

The precise form of the mathematical model used will depend on the nature of the intervention being examined. For computational reasons it is not practicable simultaneously to explore interactions within all dimensions of a model if each of these are represented in detail. Where options for individual schemes are being examined the spatial features of demand and supply (i.e. the pattern of zoning and the character of the transport network) have to be represented at a fine level of detail in order that local travel movements can be depicted accurately. The corollary of this is that other dimensions of travel demand (e.g. by person-type or trip purpose) will be represented relatively coarsely and the wider context of transport supply (e.g. the level of parking charges or the availability of public transport) taken as fixed. Conversely if more strategic choices are being examined (e.g. different mixes of public and private transport investment with different regimes of parking or road user charging) then the spatial dimension can be represented more coarsely – possibly in diagrammatic or 'cartoon' form only. The other dimensions can then be disaggregated to enable the

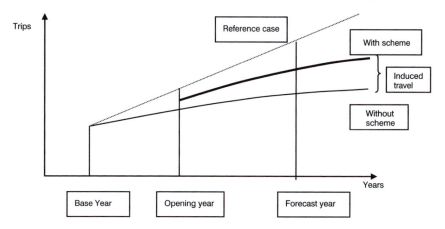

Figure 21.1 Illustration of variable demand forecasting (source: TAG Unit 2.9.2)

response of particular kinds of traveller to particular kinds of change in the transport regime to be represented more accurately.

As demand management assumes more prominence in transport policy, so the technical issue of being able to forecast behavioural responses becomes more significant. Conventional modelling assumes that the response of a particular kind of traveller to a particular type of opportunity will be the same in future as it is today. Hence for example if car drivers in general exhibit a very weak response to current opportunities for cycling or using public transport then they will be forecast to make little use of them in future, even if these modes are improved. In practice this can make it very difficult to demonstrate an economic case for such investments, even though it is a policy aim to do so!

This is a particular example of a more general difficulty with conventional modelling, i.e. of forecasting travel outcomes in situations which are different in kind – not merely quantity – from those prevailing today. For these situations 'stated preference' techniques have been developed. These use evidence from social research in laboratory conditions which elicits from different types of traveller the choices they would make under various hypothetical future conditions. These responses rather than those observed in current 'real-world' situations (where they exist) can be incorporated into the modelling of future behaviour. However such refinements present their own technical difficulties. This highlights the value of various kinds of pilot or demonstration project which enable evidence to be utilised of people's *actual* response to innovations. The question of possible synergy between new types of measure is particularly important – hence interest in the results of the Sustainable Towns Initiative discussed in Chapter 16.

21.5 'Value for money'

As noted earlier the New Approach to Appraisal was originally developed to present information about scheme impacts comprehensively and impartially and to counter a situation in which the results of 'narrow' exercises in cost-benefit analysis were thought to have too dominant an influence on decision-making. However assimilating and weighing the variety of impacts listed in the AST presents a daunting task. From an economic perspective it also raises the opposite danger – that a non-monetised impact recorded in the AST may be seen as reason for 'vetoing' a project otherwise offering a good benefit-cost ratio. This would imply (probably unreasonably) that the sub-objective concerned had some over-riding, potentially limitless value.

To address these difficulties the Department has developed further guidance under the heading of 'value for money' (DfT 2006c). This sets out to standardise the way in which the results of cost-benefit analysis are presented and integrated with a (professional) assessment of non-monetised impacts in the advice given to Ministers. Interestingly such guidance would normally only be known to civil servants (i.e. circulated internally within the DfT). However it was released publicly on the DfT website:

> Our objective in doing so is to encourage and facilitate the assessment of the opportunity cost of different investment choices, by making clear the value for money considerations that will be put to Ministers. We expect this to be of interest not only to scheme promoters and their partners/consultants, but also to those whose role at local and regional level includes advising on choices between projects.
> (ibid.)

Advice on value for money is based on the relationship between three main components:

1   the costs of the scheme to the public sector
2   the value of its monetised impacts
3   judgement as to the net cost or benefits represented by its non-monetised impacts.

The last two in combination represent the overall net benefit of the scheme which is then assessed relative to its cost to arrive at an overall 'value for money' (VfM) categorisation. Each of these is now considered in turn.

Scheme costs

Projects are appraised over the period of their useful life or 60 years (whichever is less). Maintenance and renewal costs anticipated during this period need to be incorporated as well as the initial costs of construction. Account also needs to be taken of any 'residual value' of an asset at the end of its useful life.

The Assessment column in the Public Accounts row of the AST shows the total Net Present Value of all costs and revenues borne by central and local government. (NPV was explained in 12.7.) This figure is derived from the Total figure shown in the accompanying worksheet (Table 21.1).

Achieving accurate estimates of costs is a subject to which the Treasury has devoted much attention in recent years. This has been prompted by experience that the figures presented at the planning stages of a project tend to understate those ultimately incurred by a substantial margin – a feature referred to as 'optimism bias'.

The estimation and treatment of scheme costs is the subject of TAG unit 3.5.9. This identifies three main elements of a scheme cost estimate – a basic cost, a risk adjustment cost and an optimism bias cost. The basic cost is what traditionally would have been regarded as *the* cost estimate. It incorporates promoters' best estimates of the various cost components, necessarily making assumptions about factors beyond its

Table 21.1 The public accounts worksheet (source: TAG unit 3.5.1)

	All modes total	Road infra-structure	Bus and coach	Rail	Other
Central government funding:					
Revenue					
Operating costs					
Investment costs					
Developer and other contributions					
Grant/subsidy payments					
Indirect tax revenues					
Net impact Central Government (A)					
Local government funding:					
[as above excluding indirect tax revenues]					
Net impact Local Government (B)					
TOTAL (A + B)					

Costs and payments are entered as positive numbers; revenues and contributions as negative numbers. All entries are discounted present values in 2002 prices

control. For major schemes the DfT now also requires a Quantified Risk Assessment (QRA) to be undertaken to explore the probability of these assumptions proving wrong, and its implications. The outcome of the QRA is a 'risk-adjusted cost estimate' which is defined as 'the average of all possible outcomes, taking account of the different probabilities of those outcomes occurring'.

As the circumstances of a scheme's implementation are explored in more detail (including possible forms of procurement), so the potential underestimate should fall. This explains why the 'uplift factors' used to calculate the third cost element – the 'optimism bias cost' – are highest when a scheme is initially considered by the DfT, and reduce in subsequent stages (TAG unit 3.5.9 Table 9). The scale of the initial uplift requirement (currently set at 44% for road schemes and 66% for rail schemes) caused squeals of anguish amongst scheme promoters at the time it was introduced, since the economic case for many schemes effectively disappeared overnight. Light rail projects were the most prominent casualties.

Monetised benefits

Monetised items are valued on the basis of market prices (where they exist) and recipients' 'willingness to pay' (which is inferred from other indicators where they do not). Market prices typically incorporate an element of indirect taxes (e.g. fuel duty and VAT) which would traditionally have been excluded from public sector analyses of highway schemes concerned with resource costs only.

The inclusion of 'transfer payments' (taxes, grants and subsidies) does not alter the overall conclusion on economic performance compared with an analysis based on resource costs since a tax 'loss' incurred by a business for example would be offset by a revenue 'gain' by central government. The change was made to accompany the use of CBA in multi-modal and other projects where the private sector is involved so that the financial impacts, as well as overall economic performance, could be identified. These impacts are shown in the worksheet used as the basis of the entries in the 'Economic Efficiency' rows of the AST (Table 21.2).

User benefits are those derived by travellers from undertaking journeys and are calculated on the basis of consumer surplus theory (TAG unit 3.5.3). This holds that the value of a journey – or more usually the activity it makes possible at its destination – is at least equal to the impediments (or 'costs') overcome in making it by the person concerned. There are three main categories of travel cost:

- travel time
- charges met by the user (e.g. fares, parking charges or tolls)
- (for private transport) vehicle operating costs.

The specific values to be used for travel time and operating costs are given in TAG unit 3.5.6.

Operating costs (fuel, maintenance and repair) are mileage related but also include an allowance for vehicle purchase. Separate values of time are used for journeys made during the course of work and for 'non-work' journeys (Table 21.3).

Average values of working time for users of different modes are derived from information obtained in the National Travel Survey. For non-work journeys there is considerable variation between individuals in the value they placed on travel time, and even by the same individual in different circumstances. (These values have been

Table 21.2 The transport economic efficiency worksheet (source: TAG unit 3.5.2)

CONSUMERS	All modes TOTAL	Road Cars and LGVs	Bus/coach Passengers	Rail Passengers	Other
User benefits					
Travel time savings					
Vehicle operating cost savings					
User charges (fares & tolls)					
During construction/maintenance					
NET CONSUMER BENEFITS (A)					

BUSINESS	All modes Total	Road Goods	Cars/LGVs	Bus/coach Passesngers	Rail Freight	Passenger	Other
User benefits							
Travel time savings							
Vehicle operating cost savings*							
User charges (fares & tolls)							
During construction/maintenance							
Sub-total (B)							
Private sector provider impacts							
Revenue							
Operating costs*							
Investment costs*							
Grant/subsidy							
Sub-total (C)							
Other business impacts							
Developer contributions (D)							
NET BUSINESS IMPACT (B + C + D) = (E)							
TOTAL (A + E)							

Benefits (user savings, revenue and grants received by private sector providers) are entered as positive numbers; costs (user charges, costs incurred by private sector providers, and developer contributions) as negative numbers – i.e. the reverse of the Public Accounts Table. All entries are discounted present values in 2002 prices

* Businesses are able to reclaim indirect taxes (excluding fuel duty) and the figures entered are therefore net of these

Table 21.3   Values of time (source: TAG unit 3.5.6 (2006) Tables 1 and 2)

Working time (by mode)	£ per hour (2002 prices)
Car driver	£26.43
Car passenger	£18.94
Goods vehicle driver	£10.18
Rail passenger	£36.96
Bus passenger	£20.22
Taxi passenger	£44.69
Walker	£29.64
Average (all working persons)	£26.73
Non-working time (by purpose)	
Commuting	£5.04
Other	£4.46

identified in studies of situations where individuals choose between slower, cheaper options and quicker, more expensive ones.) Members of higher income groups for example will normally be prepared to pay more for quicker journeys. If this difference were incorporated in the valuation of non-work time it would mean that, all other things being equal, schemes which benefited higher income groups would be shown to offer greater value for money. The distributional implications of this are deemed unacceptable and hence, unusually, they are avoided by adopting overall average (or 'equity') values. This is different from all other elements in appraisal where behavioural values are used and distributional implications are considered in a supplementary analysis.

With all types of journey the relevant unit value of time is applied however large or small the change for individual journeys. Hence the value assigned to 1,000 journeys of a particular kind each saving 1 minute is taken to be the same as 100 journeys saving 10 minutes. A significant proportion of the economic benefits of a scheme may therefore be attributable to time savings which in practice are imperceptible to the individuals concerned! This is a good example of where the conventions embodied in cost-benefit analysis (and resulting conclusions on the merits of a scheme) may be at odds with the 'common sense' perceptions held by groups within the public at large.

By applying the values of time noted above it is possible to aggregate the time and monetary components of a particular journey to produce a representation of its overall cost (i.e. implied value) known as 'generalised cost'. The change in user benefit arising from a scheme is then calculated as the change in generalised cost for each category of journey (from a particular origin to a particular destination, by a particular mode, for a particular purpose), multiplied by the number of travellers involved in each case and summed for all categories. In situations where a change arises in the volume of demand as a result of a scheme (i.e. induced or suppressed trips) then the convention of 'the rule of half' is applied to the trips concerned (TAG unit 3.5.3).

For the future, values of working time are assumed to increase in proportion to changes in income (measured as forecasted GDP per head). The value of non-working time increases at four-fifths of these values.

'Willingness to pay' is not confined to the value placed by travellers on the benefits they receive through transport improvements. It applies also to the valuation of impacts

Table 21.4   VfM categories (source: TAG Unit 3.5.6 (2006) Tables 1 and 2)

BCR	*VfM category*
Less than 1	Poor
Between 1 and 1.5	Low
Between 1.5 and 2	Medium
Over 2	High

experienced by others which are not reflected in costs borne by individual travellers. This can be viewed as the amount these other people would be prepared to pay to avoid the adverse effects of journeys being made. Examples would be the additional amount a household might pay for a property which did not suffer from traffic noise, or a traveller for a journey to avoid the effects of congestion or over-crowding.

Integrating non-monetised impacts into the overall VfM assessment

Although all schemes with a benefit-cost ratio (BCR) greater than 1 might be worth pursuing< financial constraints mean that it is necessary to select between a number of such schemes. It is therefore helpful to try and categorise or prioritise schemes, at the same time taking into account the value attached to non-monetised impacts.

The Department utilises four VfM categories which are labelled as shown in Table 21.4. Non-monetised impacts are then examined to see whether they might alter the categorisation indicated by the BCR. The Department emphasises that impacts need to be significant *relative to costs* in order to change a scheme's categorisation. For example non-monetised benefits would have to be valued at more than 40% of costs in order for an option with a BCR of 1.1 to be raised from the low to medium category.

DfT acknowledges that estimating the implications of non-monetised benefits for VfM is by its nature very difficult. However it goes on to state that:

> In practice they are often comparatively small. In our experience, non-monetised impacts need to be unusually high to move an option two or more 'value for money' categories. Building new infrastructure through an environmentally sensitive area might be an example of the latter. Some road schemes with very high BCRs have been rejected because the negative environmental impacts are so big they end up being 'poor' value for money.
>
> (DfT 2006c para 18)

Submissions to Ministers are expected to contain a section on value for money setting out the BCR, a short commentary on any significant non-monetised impacts and the overall VfM assessment. An illustration of the Department's practice on this subject is given in Box 21.1. This relates to the proposal to improve the western end of the A303 near Ilminster, Somerset via the A30 to Honiton (and thence via an existing improved section of the A30 to the M5 at Exeter). The effect of the scheme would be to complete a near-continuous dual carriageway route from London to South-West England as an alternative to the M4/M5 route via Bristol. This was compared with the option of providing a shorter link from the A303 via the A358 to the M5 at Taunton which avoided the Blackdown Hills Area of Outstanding Natural Beauty (AONB).

Box 21.1 DfT comparison of options for linking the A303 to the M5

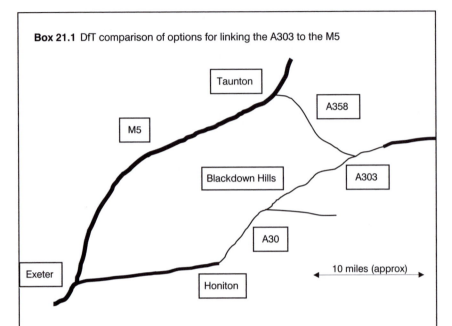

A358 Option (dual carriageway improvement on existing alignment)

BCR is 2.80

The AST identifies a mix of impacts (beneficial, neutral and adverse) on non-monetised issues, but none is described as being 'large'. Overall the value of the adverse impacts is likely to more than outweigh the value of the beneficial impacts, but these are not judged to be quite large enough to justify moving to a medium VfM classification, i.e. they are estimated at being valued as less than 80% of the scheme's costs.
The option is therefore high VfM.

A303/A30 Option (dual carriageway route on new alignment)

BCR is 2.35

The AST identifies a mix of impacts (beneficial, neutral and adverse) on non-monetised issues. However few are assessed as beneficial and of these none is large. On the other hand there are a number of large or moderate adverse impacts with the impacts of landscape and biodiversity being described as 'very large adverse'. This reflects the fact that three-quarters of the route lies within an AONB and that two Sites of Special Scientific Interest are affected together with other considerable cumulative effects on biodiversity.

On balance the non-monetised impacts identified in the AST are likely to be severely negative. This would therefore reduce the VfM of this scheme below that implied by the BCR. If the net cost of all the non-monetised impacts were valued at £160m–£260m the scheme would be low VfM. If the net cost were valued at more than £260m the scheme would be poor VfM.

Local authorities in the South West campaigned unsuccessfully against the A358 option on the basis that the region would remain dependent on a single strategic road link west of Taunton and hence was still vulnerable to being 'cut off' in the event of a traffic accident or similar incident. Although the concept of a 'second strategic route' had strong political appeal the evidence of the appraisal demonstrated that, for the A303/A30 option to be preferred, it would have had to over-ride the combined advantages offered by the A358 option of a lower capital cost, higher BCR, and avoidance of severe adverse effects on landscape and biodiversity.

21.6 The generation of proposals

Choice is exercised most obviously at the point when a decision is being made between rival options or schemes. This explains the enormous amount of attention given to this stage of the planning process in the Department's Transport Analysis Guidance. However this emphasis is misleading in the sense that the output of any appraisal can only be as good as the proposals it is applied to. This begs the question of where proposals come from. Given the almost infinite number of possible schemes – where they are located, the form they take and the purposes they are directed to – it is arguably in the generation of proposals that the greatest amount of choice is exercised. How is this critical element to be handled?

TAG presents this issue in the context of a comprehensive study following the classic 'rational' planning process described earlier (17.2). This process is essentially conducted in a linear sequence of stages (Figure 21.2) although the consideration of options in particular is likely to go through a number of iterations as the evidence from one set of tests is used to refine the possibilities under investigation.

Some general guidance about the initial objectives and problems stages are given in TAG unit 2.2 but this does not really confront the difficulties of theory and practice surrounding the subject. Some of the difficulties of principle were highlighted in Chapter 11.

As far as local and regional objectives are concerned there is no guarantee that these will mesh with those being pursued by DfT, particularly (as is likely) if they are not conceived in purely transport terms. This can lead to a somewhat schizophrenic situation familiar to local government officers in which a locally generated scheme rests upon one set of arguments for local consumption and another for the purposes of presentation to central government! There is no easy technical or political means of reconciling such differences and their separate representation in the regional prioritisation process reflects this (22.6).

Conceptually objectives and problems are linked, in that a problem can be defined as a condition which conflicts with the attainment of an objective. Given a statement of national objectives and targets (11.4 and 11.6) it is comparatively straightforward, though demanding of technical resources, to undertake an analysis of existing and likely future conditions, to identify where problems arise and to focus a study of possible interventions accordingly. This is predominantly the approach followed on the national rail and trunk road networks, partly because these are the responsibility of central government and partly because of the rather unfortunate tradition whereby these have been viewed and managed as 'freestanding' transport arteries operating largely independently of the local areas and communities through which they run.

By contrast local transport networks (which include non-trunk roads of regional importance) are mainly the responsibility of local authorities and their functioning

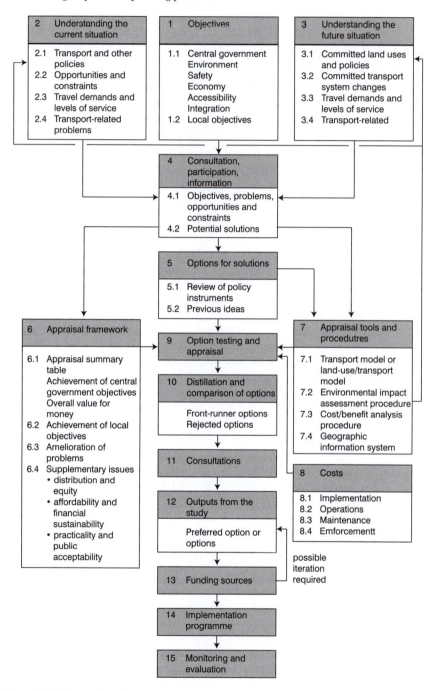

Figure 21.2 The overall study process (source: TAG Unit 2.5)

is more a matter of local concern; it is mostly local people who use them, their performance affects the quality of life of local communities, influences the opportunities and constraints surrounding local developments and so on. In this case it is especially important that the views of local people are incorporated into the planning process. In theory therefore one might proceed by asking local stakeholders (politicians, transport operators, other interest groups and the general public) to identify their objectives and to pursue a similar systematic exercise in problem-identification.

However experience has shown that where local objectives have not already been formulated, attempting to generate them can be difficult, mainly because they are an unfamiliar and abstract concept. Typically it is much easier to canvas opinions on *problems*. These can be input to the planning process directly and/or used collectively to infer a set of underlying objectives which can then be applied to the transport network as a whole. The advantage of the latter approach is that the same objectives can then be applied to forecasted future conditions whereas perceived problems, almost by definition, apply to the existing situation only.

What happens in a particular situation will be strongly influenced by its political setting and by the availability of data and other technical resources. Sometimes a particular 'solution' will have acquired considerable momentum as the result of years of local campaigning. This may mean that it has to be included as one of the options examined without having gone going through the 'ideal' process of being generated systematically from an analysis of objectives and problems. The danger with such long-standing proposals is that they are often the product of past thinking and do not reflect current objectives and circumstances. They may also have been conceived with insufficient regard for cost-effectiveness – particularly if it is central government which is expected to pay for them!

The requirement to undergo rigorous appraisal exposes the limitations of such schemes. The regional prioritisation process also helps demonstrate the *relative* merits of a scheme compared with others competing for funding and may highlight the fact that its high cost and/or low value for money means that it is unlikely to gain approval. Although the politics surrounding long-standing schemes are difficult the advice received from Government Regional Office staff on the evidence supplied can begin the process of engaging in constructive discussion of lower-cost and better-targeted alternatives.

21.7 Supplementary analyses

The work undertaken for GOMMMS identified a number of additional elements which needed to be incorporated in an overall Appraisal Process (TAG unit 2.5). The first three of these can broadly be labelled distributional effects in that they are concerned with the substantive impacts of a scheme (of the kind included in the AST) but not in aggregated form – rather in their incidence relative to various distributional criteria, viz:

- achievement of local and regional objectives
- impact on problems
- distribution and equity.

Local and regional bodies will naturally have their own objectives driving the schemes they promote and will also be concerned about the impact on these objectives of schemes promoted by others. Although the underlying issues may be similar to those represented in NATA, the way they are framed will be different. Typically they prioritise particular localities or social groups, usually as part of broader spatial, economic or social policies. A common example of this is the designation of certain routes within the highway network as being of strategic importance (i.e. a local or regional version of the principle followed nationally with trunk roads). This is accompanied by policies to the effect that investment should be concentrated on these routes – by implication even if better 'value for money' might in theory be obtained from individual schemes elsewhere.

Prioritising problems within a local area can be considered another form of 'pre-determined' distributional assessment – in this case on a subset of situations where conditions have been identified as most in need of improvement. This contrasts with the way in which Government objectives are framed – only identifying *directions* of change. On this basis a certain improvement in conditions for a given expenditure is considered to be of equivalent value irrespective of whether the original condition is relatively good or bad. Clearly this is not how local people tend to view the situation!

DfT advice on this subject is expressed rather tartly:

> Overall, whilst assessment of strategies or plans in relation to solving identified problems is a useful exercise which is important for the decision-making process it is not a substitute for assessing the extent to which strategies or plans offer value for money against objectives.

> (TAG unit 2.5 para 1.4.5)

However without assessment relative to problems there is a danger of improvements being skewed to where they can be obtained most cheaply (because this offers greater value for money) rather than where they are most needed.

As far as distributional effects are concerned, the information presented in the AST is deliberately 'neutral' reflecting the impartiality principle noted earlier. The impacts of schemes are aggregated under the individual sub-objectives irrespective of where they occur and who gains or loses and by how much.

This approach is helpful in the sense that it enables the application of value judgements by decision-takers to be focused on the relative importance of the *overall* outcomes identified under each heading. By itself however this would imply that politicians and others are indifferent to the way these outcomes are experienced by different groups. This is plainly not the case! People *will* be concerned about effects on their own constituencies of interest (e.g. as users of a particular mode or residents of a particular place). They will also have views on how far the issue of 'fairness' should be a factor and whether the impact on disadvantaged groups should be accorded special importance.

To enable these issues to be considered, a supporting analysis of distributional effects is undertaken. Computerised map-based presentations based on outputs from transport models can assist decision-makers considerably in the understanding of spatial distributional effects. The scope of such work will depend on the nature, purpose and circumstances of the scheme in question – information is only required to the extent that it is likely to have significance for the decision being made.

The second set of supporting analyses is concerned with the financial impacts of a proposal and other aspects relevant to its deliverability. These are considered under two headings:

- affordability and financial sustainability
- practicability and public acceptability.

Although the prime criterion in scheme appraisal is value for money, overall judgements must have regard to its financial implications for both the public sector and for private sector interests contributing to the scheme or affected by it. In support of this an Affordability and Financial Sustainability Table has to be produced, as illustrated in Table 21.5.

In relation to practicability and public accountability TAG unit 2.5 offers a checklist which includes the following:

- the technical and legal (procedural) issues which remain to be resolved
- the breadth (scope) and depth (complexity) of the implementation process in terms of the activities and agencies involved

Table 21.5 Outline of affordability and financial sustainability worksheet (source: TAG unit 2.5)

*Public sector**	Total	Breakdown by organisation/budget			
Investment					
Investment costs (listed by year)					
Developer and other contributions					
Grant to/from local government*					
Grant to private sector					
Indirect tax revenues*					
Net total*					
Operations [for years 1, 5, 10 etc,]					
Change in operator costs					
Change in operator revenues					
Net change					
Private sector	Total	Breakdown by route and organisation			
Investment					
Investment costs (listed by year)					
Grant from central and local government					
Net impact					
Operations [for years 1, 5, 10 etc.]					
Change in operator costs					
Change in operator revenues					
Net change					
Subsidy					
Net impact					

Note: All entries in the table show undiscounted £ cash for the year in question

*In the full table there are separate sections for local and central government.
In the case of local government the net total is (investment costs + grant to private sector) – (developer contributions + grant from central governmentt)
In the case of central government the net total is (investment costs + grants to local gov't and private sector) – (developer contributions + indirect tax revenues).

- the scope for partitioning a project: can it be broken down into a series of simpler components which could be progressed separately?
- relationship to other interventions: is it complementary, conflicting or independent?
- the local political context surrounding implementation.

Because of the potential vulnerability of projects during the various procedural stages, DfT emphasises the importance of securing the support of key stakeholders. So important has the demonstration of support become as a factor in winning Government approval that arguably a contrary danger arises – that the genuineness of public consultation and debate is compromised within a broader exercise in public relations designed to deliver the desired 'evidence' of united backing for a scheme.

21.8 Sustainability Appraisal (SEA)

In parallel with the appraisal procedures required by DfT described in this chapter, scheme promoters have to undertake a 'Sustainability Appraisal' in accordance with the EU's Strategic Environmental Assessment Directive (2001/42/EC). (This is commonly referred to as 'an SEA'.) The Directive is in fact applicable to all plans, programmes and projects which have a significant environmental effect or which set the framework for future development consents.

The Directive's definition of 'environment' includes not only the natural and historic environments but also some human effects such as health and material assets. It requires a level of analysis beyond NATA's identification of impacts to include secondary, cumulative and synergistic effects. Unlike NATA's appraisal framework it is centrally concerned with the identification and mitigation of problems. SEA is more integral to the process of scheme development and is a tool for improving the design of proposals, not a presentation of their impact once finalised. Likewise the rationale for SEA is a means of safeguarding sustainable development, not a mechanism for establishing the worth of a proposal.

The significance of the SEA Directive is that it is legally binding and the procedures followed in relation to any particular proposal may therefore be challenged in the courts (unlike NATA which is only an administrative requirement of DfT). Advice on producing an SEA is given in TAG unit 2.11 but the Department notes that this is not definitive and that the responsibility for ensuring compliance with the Directive remains with the scheme or plan promoter. Interestingly it also adds:

> It is important to involve both people who are producing the plan and others, either within the authority or from outside, who can contribute a more detached and independent view to the exercise.
>
> (TAG unit 2.11 para 2.3.2)

Presumably this is so as to strengthen the credibility of the SEA and thus protect the proposal from the possibility of legal challenge. It is notable however that similar attention to 'independence' and 'balance' is not called for in the NATA process itself. This can be a factor which prompts objectors to challenge the evidence base of a scheme at planning application or public inquiry stages.

22 The approval of plans and projects

22.1 Introduction

The appraisal processes described in the previous chapter provide the bulk of the technical evidence used in making judgements about the merits of policies or proposals. This chapter deals with the procedures involved in gaining approval for individual plans and development applications, and with the additional procedures applicable to transport projects which require statutory powers and/or central government funding for their implementation. For promoters of major transport schemes these three processes – planning permission, statutory powers and funding approval – represent key external requirements which have to be satisfied for their scheme to be brought into fruition.

We begin by explaining procedures for the approval of regional strategies and the adoption of local development plans and the significance of these documents to highway authorities and other transport promoters (22.2). We then describe the procedures for determining individual planning applications (22.3) and the holding of public inquiries (22.4). Public inquiries may be held in connection with development applications or with the hearing of objections into applications for statutory powers by transport promoters. In section 22.5 we go on to explain the new arrangements proposed by the Government for considering infrastructure proposals of national importance.

We then turn to the procedures surrounding the funding of major schemes. We deal first with the system of Regional Funding Allocation introduced in the English regions (22.6) and then the procedures followed by central government in its acceptance and programming of individual schemes (22.7). It should be noted that these are *administrative* procedures, unlike the statutory procedures surrounding development plans and applications, public inquiries etc. In the case of statutory procedures the rules to be followed are set in primary legislation or in ministerial regulations made under it. The way in which they are applied to particular cases is open to legal challenge and, in exceptional cases, decisions made by central or local governments may be overturned in the courts. By contrast, subject to an overall 'fiduciary duty' the setting and application of funding procedures is at a government's discretion.

22.2 Regional Spatial Strategies and Development Plan Documents

The inclusion of individual transport proposals within documents forming part of the development plan for an area is not a pre-requisite for them gaining planning approval subsequently. (As with any other form of development, applications may be made at any time and will be assessed against the policies currently in force.) In practice however there are several reasons why highway authorities and other transport promoters are likely to be affected by the provisions of the plan and hence will want to influence its content, particularly as far as major schemes are concerned:

- Transport agencies will want to ensure that the future volume and pattern of travel implied by particular spatial proposals can be accommodated satisfactorily on their networks and is consistent with their own aspirations. (Demonstrating practicability in this respect will in fact be an important part of the testing of the spatial plan.)
- The spatial planning policies establish a context with which individual schemes will need to demonstrate consistency (and preferably offer a positive contribution) as a criterion for gaining planning permission and – in the case of major schemes – central government funding.
- The inclusion of named major schemes in the RTS is an important first step along the way to securing public funding.
- The inclusion of individual transport proposals within development plan documents more generally represents acceptance of their justification in spatial planning terms and (given the principle of the 'plan-led' system) reduces potential uncertainty and delay subsequently in securing their implementation.

Highway authorities are formal consultees in the preparation of plans. They and other interested parties also have the opportunity of making representations on draft strategies/plans and may be invited to participate in the Examination in Public (EIP) to discuss issues raised.

In the case of RSS the EIP Panel is charged with satisfying itself that the strategy is 'sound'. This requires that it is evidence based and internally consistent and fulfils the Government's requirements in both its substance and manner of preparation. The Panel's recommendations for changes in RSS are submitted to the Secretary of State (DCLG) for his or her consideration and possible amendment prior to publication of the final document.

The full list of criteria to be used in assessing RSS are set out in PPS11 (ODPM 2004a) and summarised in Box 22.1. These apply to the RSS as a whole (i.e. including its RTS component) – in this case there is no separate guidance issued for transport policies and proposals.

A similar set of criteria are set out in PPS12 for testing the soundness of local development plan documents (ODPM 2004b para 4.24). A distinctive requirement of DPDs is that they must be in 'general conformity' with the regional spatial strategy (or in London the spatial development strategy). Regional planning bodies and the London Mayor therefore have the opportunity to identify any ways in which they consider this requirement is not met – in which case these must be investigated and adjudicated on by the Inspector. Inconsistency with or omission of individual policies is not itself reason to justify amendment, rather the question is how significant the inconsistency is from the point of view of delivering the strategy.

The issue of consistency is particularly relevant to the integration of land use and transport policies and proposals. For example the content of spatial plans might be examined to determine whether

---

Box 22.1 Tests of soundness applied to Regional Spatial Strategies

The strategy has been prepared

- following the proper procedures
- with satisfactory community involvement and partnership working
- subject to a satisfactory Sustainability Appraisal.

The strategy is a spatial plan which

- meets the objectives set for an RSS (see Chapter 18)
- is consistent with national planning policy (or, if not, an adequate case has been made for the departure)
- is consistent with other relevant strategies for the region and with RSS for neighbouring regions where cross-boundary issues are relevant
- takes into account related regional policies and programmes where these impact directly on the development and use of land and contains policies which will deliver the desired spatial change.

Its policies are

- consistent with one another
- founded on a robust and credible evidence base.

The plan

- is realistic (including availability of resources) and can be implemented without compromising its objectives
- is robust and able to deal with changing circumstances
- contains clear mechanisms for implementation and monitoring.

Source: PPS11 para 2.49

---

a   the policies and proposals for development (in conjunction with existing or proposed transport facilities) satisfy accessibility considerations and are compatible with the characteristics of the transport network
b   the policies and proposals for transport (including any proposals for demand management) support the planned pattern of development, are adequate for its functioning and are consistent with environmental policies and standards.

In practice there is a very wide range of situations which can be deemed consistent. The term can be used to encompass everything from the 'not obviously inconsistent' (such as a new road through an area of designated landscape) through to the fully integrated. Typically the immediate physical interaction between transport and land use is recognised but there is a much poorer appreciation of their dynamic relationship in a more strategic sense over the longer term through changes in the patterning of accessibility.

Procedurally the treatment of DPDs is different from RSS in that the form of the examination can vary from a round-table discussion to a formal hearing where advocates are permitted to be present to test evidence. Individuals or organisations who have made representations seeking a change in the plan have a right to appear at the examination.

(This is because of the site-specific nature of proposals in DPDs.) However if they do not wish to appear then the Inspector may decide to deal with matters solely on a written basis. Normally those supporting the plan will be considered to be represented by the local planning authority, although the inspector may invite others to be present.

After the examination the Inspector produces a report which gives his or her conclusions on the soundness of the plan and makes recommendations for any changes. Unless the Secretary of State intervenes (e.g. because of issues raised of national or regional importance) these changes must be incorporated by the authority without further representation before it adopts the plan.

Essentially the same procedures are followed for the examination of local development plans in Wales (WAG 2005 para 4.32 et seq.). In Scotland too the former inquiry procedure for the hearing of objections into submitted development plans is being replaced by a more flexible and selective examination procedure (Scottish Executive 2007c).

22.3 Individual development proposals

It is a feature of the development planning system in Great Britain that local authorities exercise discretion in considering proposals requiring planning permission and that they do not simply follow the provisions of an adopted plan. However this does not mean that they have free rein – that would invalidate one of the main purposes of preparing a plan in the first place. In fact when assessing applications local planning authorities are statutorily required to determine them in accordance with the development plan unless 'material considerations' indicate otherwise. If an authority decides to refuse permission, or to attach conditions to a development which is permitted then it has to give its reasons for doing so. This is of critical importance because an applicant may choose to lodge an appeal against the decision, in which case the basis of this will be to challenge the reasons quoted.

As explained previously 'development plan' means the regional spatial strategy plus local development documents which have been adopted by the local planning authority as having statutory status. 'Material considerations' means any consideration affecting the use and development of land which has a bearing on the proposal under consideration. In terms of transport-related considerations, examples would be the accessibility of a development site and the design and capacity of provision made for access, movement and parking by the various modes both within the site and in relation to the surrounding networks. As far as transport developments are concerned, examples would be their effect on the natural and built environment and on the functioning of land use activities both in individual properties and across a wider area. (Note however that some developments which consist solely of a transport proposal can be granted deemed planning permission under separate legislation – see following sections.)

National planning policy statements and other guidance notes – even in draft form – provide a mass of relevant material which authorities are required to have regard to in coming to their decision. These generalised statements of policy are particularly important where, as is often the case, adopted planning documents do not provide a sufficiently detailed or up-to-date basis by themselves for determining applications.

Development applications are normally determined by the local planning authority. However the Secretary of State (DCLG) has powers to 'call in' and determine applications herself, although these are only used in exceptional cases. Examples might be where there are significant cross-boundary effects, where the application is especially controversial or where it raises issues of national policy. If either the applicant or local planning authority request it a hearing or public inquiry must be held. To aid the call-in process authorities are required to notify the Secretary of State of any instance where they intend to approve an application which represents a substantial departure from the development plan. The Secretary of State also issues directions requiring notification about particular types of proposal which are of special policy significance. For example, to reinforce the Government's policy over the intensification of urban development in PPS3, authorities within defined growth areas have to notify the Secretary of State before giving planning permission for housing developments at a density of less than 30 dwellings per hectare.

Prior to deciding on a development application a planning authority has to notify various statutory consultees and take account of any representations they may make (Box 22.2).

Planning authorities are set targets for the time period taken to determine applications (eight weeks for minor developments, thirteen weeks for major ones) and their performance in meeting these is included in their Best Value CPA. However authorities will specify the evidence they need to consider different types of application (which in the case of major developments will include a Transport Assessment) and will not accept receipt of an application until this is provided. In practice because of an applicant's interest in maximising the probability of obtaining planning permission there are likely to be extensive pre-application discussions over major proposals before the formal application procedure is set in motion.

A large proportion of applications involve 'householder' or other relatively minor developments which are normally determined by an authority's professional officers under 'delegated powers'. Applications which are considered by elected members have to go before a committee of the authority (i.e. they cannot be decided on by a single executive member). The officer's report on the application, including a summary of the observations made by consultees plus his or her recommendation, is a public

---

Box 22.2 Statutory consultees on development applications

Consultees include

- the Regional Planning Body (on proposals which are of major importance in terms of the implementation of the RSS)
- the Highways Agency, on proposals which affect a trunk road – specifically which

  i) alter access arrangements to an existing trunk road
  ii) are likely to result in a material increase in volume or change in character of traffic on such a road
  iii) are likely to prejudice the improvement or construction of a proposed trunk road
  iv) and in respect of all developments within 67 metres (formerly 220 yards) of an existing trunk road

- (except unitary authorities) the local highway authority (on proposals as (i)–(iii) above which affect a classified road other than a trunk road)

Source: Town & Country Planning (General Development Procedure) Order 1995.

document. This acts as a restraining influence on members not wilfully refusing an application recommended for approval by the officer (since the arguments presented could be utilised by the applicant subsequently on appeal).

Any applicant who has a proposal refused or not decided on within the prescribed period can appeal to the Secretary of State. (The only restraints on making an appeal are the costs and delay incurred.) In practice most appeals are dealt with entirely by Planning Inspectors. Occasionally their reports are referred to senior civil servants for decision, particularly where the interpretation of national policy is involved, and even more rarely to the Secretary of State herself. Most appeals are dealt with by written representations, some by hearings (involving a round-table discussion led by the Inspector) and a very small proportion by public inquiry – the most costly and time consuming method (see next section). On the basis of the evidence presented, the outcome of an appeal may be to confirm, overturn or amend the authority's original decision.

22.4 Public inquiries

Public inquiries are held to enable objections to development applications and scheme orders to be heard by an independent Inspector and for applicants or promoters to put their case and cross-examine objectors. Inspectors write a report of proceedings with recommendations to the relevant Minister (Government department) in whose name the final decision is made to approve, with or without conditions, or to reject.

Historically some of the biggest transport proposals other than roads have been approved by Acts of Parliament – either as local authority or private member's bills or as hybrid bills (where supported by the Government). In these cases assessment is undertaken by select committees in both Houses of Parliament who hear evidence from petitioners requesting changes to the proposal. This procedure was used in connection with the construction of the Channel Tunnel Rail Link. Technically it is still available although in practice it has been superseded by orders made under the Transport and Works Acts as far as light rail and similar local schemes are concerned. In future schemes relating to the national rail network in England will be subject to a new procedure of 'development consent' explained in the next section.

Major infrastructure projects generally are otherwise considered as a development proposal of national or regional significance. Currently these are 'called in' by the Secretary of State (DCLG) or equivalent Ministers in Wales and Scotland rather than determined by the local planning authority and are automatically subject to a public inquiry (ODPM 2005c).

More generally transport proposals which require the granting of statutory orders may be subject to a public inquiry. They include:

* road schemes under the 1980 Highways Act together with orders for the compulsory purchase of land or alterations to existing rights of way
* traffic regulation orders under the Road Traffic Regulation Act 1984
* new rail or light rail schemes under the Transport & Works Act 1992 in England and Wales or Transport and Works (Scotland) Act 2007
* the introduction of road user or workplace parking charges under the Transport Act 2000.

These orders are made by the Secretary of State (DfT) in England and by equivalent Welsh and Scottish Ministers.

Normally an inquiry is held if, following publication of a draft order, formal objections have been received from a 'statutory consultee' or other interested party (e.g. the owner or occupier of an affected property) and these objections cannot be resolved by negotiation or handled through written representations. The procedures applicable to the different types of transport inquiry are explained in DfT 2005g and 2006a. In some cases the granting of orders may be accompanied by 'deemed planning permission' in which case a separate planning application is not needed. In others the order will specify 'reserved matters' which have to be dealt with through the granting of planning permission by the local planning authority.

In the case of local road proposals an order is not needed under the 1980 Highways Act for the scheme itself but the local highway authority has to apply for planning permission (unless as a unitary authority it is also the planning authority). The proposal is then treated as any other development application. If compulsory purchase or side roads orders are needed then these are sent to the Secretary of State (DfT) at the Local Authority Orders Section for confirmation. The highway authority issues a public notice and invites any objections to be sent to the DfT who arranges a public inquiry if this is needed, and appoints an independent Inspector.

Unitary authorities are able to grant themselves planning permission for a local road proposal, subject to consultation and provided they consider that it accords with the development plan. If they consider that the proposal constitutes a departure from the development plan then they have to notify Ministers who can decide whether to follow the call-in procedure. If so an inquiry will be held.

An inquiry is based on initial written 'statements of case' submitted by the scheme promoter and by any objectors or other parties who wish to make representations. These documents and accompanying summaries are placed on deposit for a period before the inquiry commences so that participants can read them and plan any questioning they want to make. If the inquiry is potentially long and complex there is likely to be a pre-meeting for all parties at which the handling of the issues is discussed and a timetable arranged. The inquiry itself normally proceeds by each party, beginning with the promoter, reading out the summary of their case (as contained in written 'proof of evidence') and calling witnesses to speak in support of it. These are open to cross-examination by any of the objectors on the basis of the full evidence submitted. Objectors and others making representations then have the opportunity to present their own case and call their own witnesses and in turn be cross-examined. The promoter has the final right of reply. The Inspector is also likely to make a site visit at which the promoter and other parties can point out any features relevant to their case.

The Inspector may be assisted by a technical Assessor appointed by the Secretary of State whose role is to test and evaluate specialised evidence. An Assessor normally compiles his own written report which is added to the Inspector's own report.

In conducting an inquiry an Inspector should:

- make sure that (it) is open, fair and impartial
- report on objections that are presented at the inquiry
- comment on the arguments for and against the proposals, and
- consider the relevant facts and arrive at conclusions on the matters put to the inquiry and recommend whether or not the proposals should be approved with or without modification or give reasons for not making any recommendation.

(DfT 2005g para 13)

This description is not inaccurate but could be misinterpreted – particularly in the case of trunk road proposals. Here the Inspector is advising the Minister on the *application* of his or her policy in a particular case – the policy itself is not under examination.

> National transport policies are not discussed at an inquiry into a particular scheme. Those policies are a matter for Parliament and the subject of Government White Papers. The Highways Agency's representatives do not have to answer questions about the Government's policy or about the methods, design standards, economic assumptions and forecasts of traffic growth used by the Government. The Highways Agency can and will explain how its proposals fit in with those policies.
>
> (ibid. para 58)

A more general limitation of inquiries as a form of assessment is that what is being adjudicated upon is not strictly the soundness of the proposal or the relative merits of possible alternatives but the validity and significance of the objections which have been made to it. Whilst the Inspector may intervene to seek 'elucidation' on points which do not emerge very clearly from the adversarial exchanges there is a limit (in the interests of fairness between the opposing parties) as to what can be achieved within the constraints of an inquiry format. This is in marked contrast with the more pro-active, inquisitorial role which inspectors are encouraged to take in Examinations in Public.

22.5 The Infrastructure Planning Commission

The appropriateness of the examination procedures surrounding major transport projects was considered as part of the Transport Study conducted by Sir Rod Eddington (Eddington 2006b). Unsurprisingly he came to a similar view as Kate Barker in her review of the planning system, also commissioned by the Treasury and undertaken concurrently (Barker 2006).

> The system has evolved over several decades to the point at which it can impose unacceptable cost, uncertainty and delay on all participants and the UK more broadly.
>
> (Eddington 2006a para 1.174)

Eddington highlighted the complexity of the arrangements facing transport promoters, not merely in gaining planning permission for major projects, but in the number of additional procedures and consents that might be involved in particular cases. (A detailed commentary is given in Chapter 5 of Volume 4 of his Main Report.) Together these create a large measure of unpredictability which he considered wasteful and economically damaging. However the few examples he quotes of major schemes taking as long as three years to examine are untypical – the evidence contained in his report shows that for a cross-section of schemes the time taken to hold a public inquiry, for the inquiry report to be published and for a ministerial decision to be made, ranges between eight months and two and a half years. Interestingly for many of the longer examples the bulk of the time is taken up in the Civil Service's deliberations *after* the Inquiry Report has been published and in agreeing a decision approved by Ministers!

The Treasury view about the desirability of speeding up the planning process is not of course shared by those who see it as a safeguard against unsustainable development:

> The sense of panic whipped up by the Barker Review is quite misplaced. The UK's future is not imperilled by inability to make snap decisions to build runways, motorways, ports, reservoirs, incinerators, power stations and the like in places where nobody had thought of doing so before.
>
> Very few infrastructure projects take significantly longer to get a planning decision than they need to – the same handful of exceptionally complex and contentious cases seem to top all lists. Some of these take a long time only because developers persist despite well-known environmental problems because success against the odds would be so profitable.
>
> (Levett 2007)

Eddington collaborated with Barker in arriving at a set of mutually consistent proposals for reform. His headline recommendations were:

- the primary role of Ministers should be to set national policy statements for major infrastructure development, taking full account of economic, social and environmental considerations, following consultation
- there should be a presumption in favour of development for major infrastructure proposals so long as they are consistent with national policy statements, and compatible with EU law and the European Convention on Human Rights
- an independent commission should be established to manage inquiries and determine individual applications for major schemes in England
- local consultation should be carried out by the applicant at the pre-application stage and inquiries and decisions would have regard to local considerations
- consent regimes should be rationalised to eliminate duplication and overlap, and to treat major projects as a whole, and
- there should be a clear framework for statutory rights to challenge at key stages in the process.

These recommendations were reproduced in the subsequent Government White Paper on the development planning system in England (DCLG 2007g). The proposed legislative changes were included in a Planning Bill introduced into the 2007/08 session of Parliament.

The Bill establishes an Infrastructure Planning Commission (IPC) which will have responsibility for determining 'development consent' in relation to types of development in England classed as nationally significant infrastructure projects. These include:

- the construction or improvement of a highway for which the Secretary of State is or will be the highway authority (i.e. motorways and trunks roads) outside the boundary of an existing highway
- the construction of a railway forming part of the national rail network
- the construction or alteration of an airport which is capable of providing services for at least 10 million passengers a year or 10,000 air cargo movements
- the construction or alteration of a harbour expected to provide a handling capacity of 500,000 TEU (container units) a year, or 5 million tonnes of cargo.

The Secretary of State (DCLG) has an additional power of direction which can bring individual developments within the development consent regime.

The new single consent will remove the need for planning permission and for consents under a number of other Acts including the Highways Act 1980 and the Transport and Works Act 1992. Conversely it will no longer be possible for the Secretary of State (DfT) to make orders permitting works under these Acts in cases where they qualify as nationally significant infrastructure.

Members of the IPC will be appointed by the Secretary of State (DCLG). Applications to the Commission for consent will have to be registered and subject to pre-application requirements concerning publicity, consultation and community involvement. On receipt of an application the Commission will appoint a single Commissioner or a Panel of three or more Commissioners to examine it.

The Commissioner/Panel will make an initial assessment of the issues at stake, hold a preliminary meeting with interested parties and thereafter decide (and inform them) how the application is to be examined. It is intended that greater use is made of written representations than hitherto at public inquiries and restrictions are placed on cross-examination by interested parties at hearings. The Commission has to work within a timeframe of six months to examine each application plus a further three months to take a decision.

The Commission will be responsible for deciding on development consent in situations where there is a relevant designated national policy statement in force. (Otherwise it makes recommendations to the Secretary of State who herself makes the decision.) The Secretary of State may designate an existing policy statement to perform this role or prepare/update a new statement. Before designation the statement must be subject to sustainability appraisal and consultation.

In making its decision the Commission must have regard to any relevant national policy statement. The exact content and degree of specificity embodied in such statements will therefore have a critical bearing on the treatment of any particular proposal since the expression of national policy is not itself open to challenge. (The prospective content of a national policy statement is set out in Box 22.3.)

Nevertheless the Commission is also required to have regard to any other matters which it considers important and relevant to its decision and may decide *not* to determine the application in accordance with the national statement if it is satisfied that 'the adverse impact of the proposed development would outweigh its benefits'.

The proposed IPC prompts concerns on both technical and political grounds. Technically it contravenes the notion of a 'plan-led' system for an area. An application does not need to demonstrate that it is consistent with the spatial strategy for an area (which is in the nature of an optimising trade-off between a *range* of considerations), nor even that it is the best option of its kind; merely that – as a one-off proposal – it conforms with the national policy statement and does not have a net negative outcome. In effect the Bill offers scope to pre-empt or bypass the regional spatial strategy process by the Government declaring in favour of particular types of development at particular locations without their aggregate effect (in combination with all others) having been assessed and consulted upon. Even viewed simply in terms of 'speeding decisions' such attempts at short-cuts are notoriously prone to subsequent reversals.

Politically the arrangement is open to the objection that it removes accountability for strategic decision-making from Ministers. Transferring this responsibility to the Commission will remove the current post-inquiry delays and the opportunity for

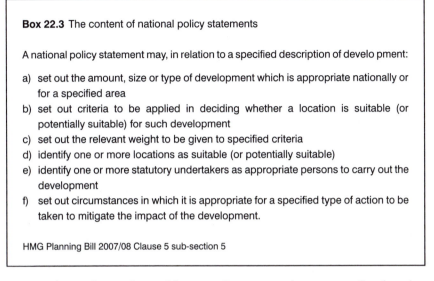

Box 22.3 The content of national policy statements

A national policy statement may, in relation to a specified description of develo pment:

a) set out the amount, size or type of development which is appropriate nationally or for a specified area
b) set out criteria to be applied in deciding whether a location is suitable (or potentially suitable) for such development
c) set out the relevant weight to be given to specified criteria
d) identify one or more locations as suitable (or potentially suitable)
e) identify one or more statutory undertakers as appropriate persons to carry out the development
f) set out circumstances in which it is appropriate for a specified type of action to be taken to mitigate the impact of the development.

HMG Planning Bill 2007/08 Clause 5 sub-section 5

protracted wrangling within and between Government departments. On the other hand with publicly contentious proposals (as many will be) Ministers will appear to be sheltering behind the Commission in making difficult and potentially unpopular decisions, involving trade-offs which should rightly be the focal point of the political process.

22.6 Regional Funding Allocation

As explained in Chapter 18 the list of 'prioritised' transport investments included in an English regional strategy can be viewed as a long-term 'pool' from which schemes will be developed and considered for inclusion in the implementation programmes of local highway authorities and other agencies. In the past this has been a continuing, ad hoc process steered by the Government Regional Office which vets and ultimately approves the funding of schemes in the context of available resources.

In 2004 the Government published a consultation document with proposals for improving this short-term process, linking it more broadly with strategies being pursued in each region and giving regional bodies the opportunity to offer advice (HM Treasury et al. 2004). The Government would give each region a three-year funding allocation (the Regional Funding Allocation or RFA) covering certain items of expenditure in three sectors – transport, housing and economic development – within which advice would be framed. Regional bodies could then comment on the balance of funding between and within the three sectors and propose individual prioritised schemes.

Guidance issued subsequently stated that the purpose of requesting advice was

> to enhance regional input into Government policy development, showing how such priorities relate to each other to form a coherent, credible and strategic vision for improving the economic performance of regions and how these priorities are aligned to resources.
>
> (HM Treasury et al. 2005 para 1.4)

The Guidance gave funding allocations for 2005/06–2007/08 and then projected these annually to 2014/15 on the basis of zero real growth using the Government's inflation target of 2%. This then provided an indicative spending profile over the coming decade. In the transport stream a total of £708m was allocated in the first year, split on a population basis between the individual regions such that the amounts varied between £43m for the North-East to £135m in the South-East. This sum covers the capital funding of local highway authority major schemes together with Highway Agency schemes other than on motorways, and a limited number of trunk roads of national and international importance. The desirability of extending the RFA to embrace other items of centrally funded expenditure was acknowledged and the scope for doing this would be investigated for future spending periods.

The process of preparing advice was to be facilitated by the Government's Regional Office, engaging all relevant interests and concerns, although in practice the RDA and Regional Assembly were the main participants. As well as linking individual proposals to broader objectives the idea of a range of organisations coming together collectively to prioritise schemes within the discipline of a finite budget introduced a new dimension into the regional planning process.

The criteria to be applied to the submitted advice are listed in Box 22.4. A nice ambiguity surrounds the relative importance of national and regional objectives. On the one hand regions were being given the opportunity to advise on priorities from their particular perspective; on the other hand they were counselled that greater weight would be given to advice which demonstrated contribution to national targets!

Schemes proposed for the early years would need to include those already committed or in an advanced stage of preparation. In practice therefore the RFA process was most useful in concentrating minds beyond 2008 in planning affordable programmes and

---

Box 22.4 Criteria for regional funding allocation advice

To maximise influence on decisions taken, the Government would expect the advice from regions to be:

* Evidence based – it is critical that priorities identified from regions are based on robust regional evidence
* Agreed within the region – the Government will take into account the range, depth and quality of the advice and who has signed up within the region. As far as possible advice should represent a regionally-agreed view of priorities
* Realistic – it is important that cost estimates are robust and proposals have been tested for deliverability. Advice that does not reflect the [expenditure] planning assumption will be disregarded
* Consistent – it is important that advice is consistent with wider national policy priorities and takes into account current regional and local strategies except where robust evidence is presented for different priorities

… Regional funding allocations are expected to support transport and housing related PSA objectives and targets. Greater weight will be given to regional advice which demonstrates the contribution to national targets.

Source: DfT 2005q paras 3.6–7

ensuring that the resources required for preparation were being efficiently directed. Nevertheless advantage tended to be held by schemes of a conventional nature and/ or by ones which were of long standing since these implied less risk in being able to achieve implementation within the planned period.

The experience of the first-round RFA process was comprehensively reviewed and commented on (DfT 2006f). The regions themselves had an 'overwhelmingly positive' view:

> All regions felt that the exercise had been very well worth undertaking and that a remarkable amount had been achieved from a standing start and in very difficult circumstances. Whatever their reservations about the size of the funding allocations they recognised that the financial discipline they entailed was crucial to making a reality of infrastructure planning at the regional level and to breaking away from the traditional wish-list mentality. Stakeholders had appreciated that it was crucial for their region not to fall at the first hurdle and had been determined that the exercise should succeed.
>
> The exercise had also demonstrated to promoters that there was no realistic prospect of implementing many of their long-cherished schemes in the foreseeable future. For the most part, that message seemed to have been received and understood; there might even have been an element of relief that some of the more aspirational projects could now be dropped without loss of face.
>
> (ibid. paras 7.1–2)

Items where further guidance from the DfT was requested included:

- The treatment of schemes which, by virtue of their cost, qualify as 'major' (and hence depend on regional prioritisation) but which are primarily of local rather than regional importance; conversely the treatment of very large schemes (typically on trunk roads which are not classed of 'national' significance) and which potentially consume a disproportionate share of a region's overall allocation.
- The balance of 'value for money' and deliverability considerations versus contribution to regional objectives. (Arguably the former are tested in detail by DfT as part of the process of appraising individual schemes leading to potential overlap or duplication in the prioritisation process.)

Regions were also interested in exploring ways of encouraging promoters to bring forward new schemes which would better fit contemporary objectives. The DfT commented that consensus-building in some regions may prove more challenging in future when new schemes will have emerged to compete with long-standing ones and the problems of accommodating very large schemes become more acute.

As anticipated the second round of the RFA process is being broadened to include from 2011-12 the 'integrated block' expenditure of local highway authorities (HM Treasury et al 2008). In addition to continuing to provide advice to Government on the prioritisation of major schemes regional bodies have been invited to comment on the overall balance of expenditure as between these two main categories and on the distribution of integrated block funding between individual authorities (DfT 2008j). Separate guidance (DfT 2008k) has been issued on the linking of this work on RFA advice with regional work on strategic options for the longer term being developed under the Government's TaSTS initiative (24.7).

22.7 Funding approval for major transport schemes

The procedures set by DfT for determining funding approval of major schemes are extremely detailed and protracted. This section describes the process as it applies to highway, public transport or maintenance schemes promoted by local authorities which are to be funded as part of the Regional Funding Allocation. Light rail schemes and schemes forming part of a package to be supported by the Transport Innovation Fund (TIF) are the subject of additional guidance. The criteria for schemes applying to the Community Infrastructure Fund (administered by DCLG) are explained in section 23.8.

An accurate estimate of the public costs of schemes is critical to determining their value for money and to the effective management of RFA programmes. However this information will only become known as a scheme is worked up in progressively greater detail – a process that may take several years. Even if the basic character of a scheme does not change during this period the eventual cost will depend on a greater understanding of the engineering implications, on changes in the level of construction costs and on the particular procurement arrangements secured. Additional uncertainties surround the degree of risk-sharing in any private finance deal, and on the scale of funding contributions from private developers and any public sources other than the RFA budget itself. The significance of these issues has led the DfT to revise the procedure it follows in considering funding approval (DfT 2007c).

The case for an authority's scheme still has to be made in the context of its Local Transport Plan, but procedurally it is now considered separately. A pre-requisite is that it must have been identified as a priority by the relevant region through the RFA process. This has eased the previous situation where individual authorities would 'wait in the wings' for years if not decades, hopeful that their pet scheme would eventually win approval on the 'Buggin's turn' principle. Nevertheless the twists and turns that are forever being made in national and regional policy, technical guidance and prioritisation procedures continue to give hope to many of the 'also-rans'.

To be eligible for major scheme funding the total cost of a scheme (including preparatory costs after Programme Entry) must normally be at least £5m. However for smaller authorities in non-metropolitan areas, schemes will be considered where their cost is

a   at least 75% of the authority's average projected annual indicative allocation for the LTP2 periods (for the integrated transport or maintenance block as appropriate) AND
b   more than 50% of the combined annual indicative allocation.

An initial bid for funding has to be supported by a Major Scheme Business Case which demonstrates the case for the scheme under five heads (Box 22.5). The timing of this work should reflect the period of funding which has been identified for the scheme in the RFA:

> Authorities should also work within the funding envelope assumed in the RFA advice. If the promoter considers that the costs of the required DfT contribution will exceed [this] then further advice should be sought from the region before working up the bid for submission to the Department. The region may wish to consider

---

Box 22.5 Components of a major scheme business case

- Strategic – to demonstrate that the scheme is consistent with and will contribute to local, regional and possibly national objectives in transport and other relevant areas
- Appraisal and value for money – to demonstrate the likely benefits and disbenefits of the scheme against its likely costs
- Delivery – to demonstrate how the promoter will be able to deliver the scheme to time and budget including a clear project plan, governance arrangements, plans for stakeholder involvement and engagement and robust risk management plans
- Financial – to demonstrate that the scheme is based on sound costings, that the promoting local authority is able to meet its own contribution, that any proposed third-party funding is confirmed and that the authority is willing and able to underwrite this element
- Commercial – to demonstrate a sound procurement strategy and a rigorous approach to any private sector involvement.

Source: DfT 2007c Guidance on Major Transport Schemes para 2.7.3

---

whether the scheme remains a priority at the higher cost and what adjustments might need to be made to the RFA programme to accommodate the increase.

(ibid. para 2.3.5)

All submissions should carry at least two options fully through appraisal – the preferred option and a lower cost alternative. In addition light rail schemes should be accompanied by bus-based alternatives and highway schemes by non-road-building options directed at the same objectives, unless these are shown to be impracticable.

The Department's consideration of funding now follows a three-stage process, viz:

- Programme Entry
- Conditional Approval
- Full Approval.

Previously full approval was given before scheme procurement had taken place. This could lead to a situation where the Department found itself committed to the implementation of a scheme before its costs were finalised. Subsequent cost increases would reduce the scheme's value for money and compromise the Department's ability to fund an overall programme as planned.

The approval of a scheme for Programme Entry is not a commitment that funding will be provided either at all, or at a particular time – either of these being subject to further consideration of affordability within the RFA. However Programme Entry status is intended to give the expectation of funding (provided there are no material changes in cost or other features) in order that the promoting authority may apply for any statutory consents required.

Conditional Approval is an intermediate stage after the necessary consents have been obtained but before procurement takes place. It is a firm undertaking by the Department that Final Approval will be forthcoming subject to a limited number of conditions concerning the cost of the scheme (or the Department's contribution), the allocation of risks and a time limit on the application for Full Approval.

Full Approval is given once procurement has taken place and a preferred bidder and final price obtained. This then enables the promoter to commence construction and access grant funds.

Except for schemes procured through PFI (which are negotiated individually) local authorities are expected to contribute at least 10% of a scheme's cost, including 50% of eligible preparatory costs. In the case of light rail schemes however a minimum 25% local contribution is required. The Department maintains that this higher figure 'has not proved a barrier to the development of projects' and will continue. The 10% figure may be relaxed for smaller authorities (where it represents more than the equivalent of 100% of their Integrated Block allocation). Conversely a greater local contribution would be expected where the case for a scheme was made strongly in terms of 'aims other than transport' (e.g. regeneration or economic development).

The scheme cost referred to relates to the Quantified Cost Estimate at Programme Entry stage. The Department will also normally be prepared to pay 50% of any additional costs arising subsequently that fall within the sum originally included as optimism bias. The maximum Departmental contribution, identified at Programme

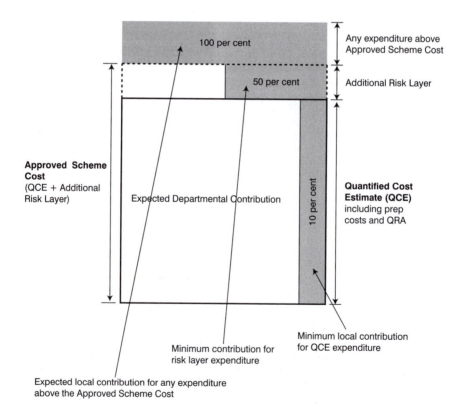

Expected Departmental Contribution = The sum represented by the larger of the white boxes
Maximum Departmental Contribution = The sum represented by the total of the two white boxes

Figure 22.1 DfT contribution to local authority major scheme costs (source: DfT 2007c)

Entry stage, is therefore the sum of the two and is known as the Approved Scheme Cost (ASC).

> If the estimated total cost of the scheme rises above the ASC the Department may require a reappraisal to determine the value for money of the scheme, as well as a consideration of lower cost alternatives. If the Department decides that the scheme can proceed at a higher cost than the original ASC the Department would, in all but exceptional circumstances, expect the local authority to fund 100% of the increase beyond that amount.
>
> (ibid. para 2.7.19)

These provisions are illustrated in Figure 22.1. They represent a significant tightening of previous arrangements and can place a local authority in an extremely difficult position if unexpected cost increases (or a reduction or withdrawal of contributions from other parties) occur at a late stage. It is then faced with either finding 100% of the increase beyond the ASC (or making good shortfalls in other contributions) or abandoning at the final hurdle a scheme which will have been planned for, and resources committed to, over many years.

Part V

The contemporary policy agenda

In this final part of the book we consider the policy agenda as it has evolved since 2004, in effect taking over from the historical account at the end of Part 2. Recent changes in development and local transport planning procedures were generally included in the explanation of these subjects in Part 4. Here the first chapter (Chapter 23) deals with the main substantive changes in transport policy, notably concerning the national roads programme and road user charging plus those arising from the Railways Act 2005 and the Planning and Local Transport Bills progressed in the 2007/08 Parliamentary session.

The period since 2004 has also been notable for the degree of attention given by the Government to preparing for the longer term as seen from the perspective of safeguarding and improving economic performance. This is represented by a series of reports commissioned from the Treasury – from Nicholas Stern (on climate change), from Julia King (on the scope for carbon reductions in transport), from Kate Barker (on housing and planning) and from Rod Eddington (on transport and economic performance). Eddington's report, and the various research exercises contributing to it, has laid the foundation for a review of national strategy to influence programmes after 2014 which the Government is currently undertaking. In Chapter 24 we summarise the findings of these reports and set them in the context of other work on longer term transport scenarios.

The final chapter (Chapter 25) is in the nature of a personal reflection on the strategic issues to be addressed given the need to pursue the overarching goal of sustainable development within a rapidly changing and very uncertain era.

23 The immediate agenda

23.1 Introduction

Since 2004 policy-makers have been occupied with delivering updated versions of the modally specific programmes conceived in the Ten Year Plan and with reforming failed institutional arrangements for the national railways and for transport in major urban areas legislated for in the Transport Act 2000. The main additional – and highly troublesome – item has been the proposal for national road user charging first floated in 2003 and a core feature of the 2004 White Paper.

In this chapter we consider the recent policy initiatives taken in relation to each of the main modes, beginning with the National Roads Programme (23.2), national road user charging (23.3) and the Transport Innovation Fund which promotes local charging schemes (23.4). We then report the structural reform of rail planning introduced by the 2005 Railways Act and the strategy for rail to 2014 announced in the 2007 White Paper (23.5). Proposals for altering the regulation of bus services contained in a 2006 White Paper are described in section 23.6 and then we discuss the additional measures concerning governance in city regions included in the Local Transport Act 2008 (23.7).

An additional dimension to local transport planning in many areas has been the infrastructure requirements arising from the planned large increases in new housing. We report on these in section 23.8 and on utilising the associated new funding streams, including the option of a Community Infrastructure Levy provided for in the Planning Bill published in 2007.

We conclude with the current DfT 'vision' and performance indicators for the Department set by the Treasury (23.9).

23.2 The National Roads Programme

Compared with the controversy generated by the national roads programme in the mid-1990s it has received remarkably little public attention in the years since 2004. However this is not because it has ceased to exist! As a matter of deliberate policy set in the Ten Year Plan the programme now occupies a smaller proportion of total transport expenditure than hitherto (see Figure 12.2 previously). However this should not obscure the fact that investment in these was planned to return to the real terms levels of the mid-1990s and that actual cash spending increased from £1.2bn to £1.9bn in the three years to 2007/08.

The relatively low profile of the programme can be attributed to two main factors – its substance and its presentation.

In substance the programme now consists more of widening existing roads – particularly motorways – and increasing the capacity of junctions which act as bottlenecks. Although the wisdom of this policy can be challenged, it invokes issues of principle and of technical argument rather than the more immediately controversial matter of the local impact of wholly new roads. In addition the Government has been careful to amend or reject proposals for new roads which would have significantly adverse environmental effects. This has avoided creating causes célèbres which might be utilised by campaigners to raise public opposition against 'road-building' more generally.

The low profile is also attributable to the way the programme has been progressed. Since the landmark review conducted at the time of the *New Deal* White Paper there has been no strategic document which has presented the current version of the programme, its rationale and implications, which might have drawn attention to the policy issues at stake. Instead there has been a series of incremental changes including the Government's acceptance of some of the recommendations from the Multi-Modal studies in 2002 and 2003 and subsequent decisions on individual schemes.

In presentational terms it has also been convenient to allow statements made at the time of the 1998 Review to remain 'on the table':

> Ministers still claim publicly that roads are built only as a last resort but privately concede that in many areas there is no other option for coping with rapidly rising traffic.
>
> (*The Times* 22 April 2006, reported in LTT 442)

The Government has also chosen to emphasise its aspirations for better management of the strategic road network at the expense of giving due acknowledgement to the volume of road-building it is still supporting. For example in the chapter on roads in the 2004 White Paper barely a page was given to 'investing in the road network' compared with a dozen on various aspects of management, including the option of charging.

More recently the management of the network and its traffic has come to assume greater significance but for rather different reasons than those originally envisaged. In 2006 following an investigation by the National Audit Office into the escalating cost of road schemes an independent review was commissioned of the Highways Agency's handling of its road programme (Nichols 2007). This recommended that its Targeted Programme of Improvements (TPI) should be replaced by a three-stage process with funding committed incrementally until estimates are judged to be reasonably robust (Box 23.1). A restructuring of the Agency's programme on this basis is reported in LTT 466.

Evidence of cost increases continued to provide embarrassing headlines. The cost of widening sections of the M1 for example was reported to have increased by 38% to £5.1bn. Several Regional Assemblies publicised the fact that, without additional funding from the Agency, they would not be able to continue to prioritise its schemes included in their RFA which had undergone major cost increases. Meanwhile the Public Accounts Committee recommended that large trunk road schemes of regional importance which would otherwise absorb the majority of the regional budget should be taken out of the RFA process and placed within the national programme (LTT 481) – alleviating one problem but aggravating another.

Fortuitously Ministers were presented with a way out of this intractable financial situation by the timely receipt of a report on a pilot study of Active Traffic Management

---

Box 23.1 The Highways Agency's management system replacing the Targeted Programme of Improvements

- Scheme options – delivery of a scheme proposal through investigation of different options, public consultation and a ministerially approved preferred route announcement
- Scheme development – preparation of the detailed scheme, public inquiry process, approval of scheme
- Contractor and financial authorisations for an agreed target cost
- Construction – ministerial approval to construct the scheme.

Source: HA Business Plan 2007/08

(ATM) carried out on the M42 around Birmingham (DfT 2007a). The scheme involved mandatory speed limits varied according to the volume of traffic coupled with use of the hard shoulder as an additional lane during peak periods. Its effects were favourable across a wide range of indicators including reduced and more predictable trip times in peak periods, reduced fuel consumption and emissions and reduced casualty rates. At the launch of this report in November 2007 Secretary of State Ruth Kelly announced that the scheme would be extended across the whole of the Birmingham motorway box and that ATM measures would be investigated on a much wider scale across the strategic road network (LTT 481).

In a remarkably swift follow-up she made a further announcement reporting the results of this investigation in March 2008:

> Our high level analysis indicates that there are a number of sections of the motorway network that would benefit from dynamic use of the hard shoulder at congested times in the short to medium term (initially to 2014) to deliver congestion benefits where they are most urgently needed.
>
> The priority locations we have identified include most sections of the M1, M6 and M62 where there are planned widening schemes but also some locations where there are no planned widening schemes such as the M27 around Southampton, the M4/M5 at Bristol and the radial routes around the M25. Other traffic management interventions without the hard shoulder running facility may also be desirable on other stretches both in traffic terms and in order to create a coherent 'managed network' proposition.
>
> (DfT 2008a)

The immediate effects of this abrupt policy change are reflected in the Highways Agency's Business Plan for 2008/09. This contains only two motorway widening schemes amongst six national road schemes in the 'development' phase. These are both sections of the M25 (M40–A1(M) and M11–Thurrock) where contracts are at such an advanced stage that cancelling them would generate few if any overall cost savings. However for other sections of the M25 and for the locations listed in the Feasibility Study where schemes are still at the 'options' stage, hard-shoulder running is to be studied as an alternative to widening.

The financial attractions of this alternative are clear; ATM measures at around £6m per mile (2006 prices) are less than a third the cost of widening (LTT 489). So too are the political attractions of being able to deliver improvements in traffic conditions on strategic roads more swiftly and more widely than would otherwise be the case. The initiative also appears to be an opportunistic coup in getting the Government out of a hole it had dug for itself on national road user charging (discussed in the next section).

However the strategic implications or even the long-term rationale for this quite dramatic change do not appear (yet) to have been investigated. The RAC Foundation has voiced concerns that the decision to extend hard-shoulder running was taken on the basis of just six months' data – a very short period for such a safety-critical issue (LTT 481). It considered that ATM had a role to play in the short/medium term but could not be regarded as a substitute for a properly planned and funded widening programme. Conversely the Campaign for Better Transport (formerly Transport 2000) thought motorway widening schemes should now be dropped whilst Friends of the Earth regarded hard–shoulder running as motorway widening by stealth and considered the Government should be trialling reduced speed limits without widening in some places.

Once more the future of the strategic road network and its relationship, if any, with national road pricing appears to be up in the air and the policy context set as recently as 2004 has already evaporated. A more strategic reconsideration is desperately needed and hopefully will form a central feature of the White Paper which has been promised during 2008 (since published – see 2008c).

23.3 National road user charging

The Government's 2004 White Paper was notable in bringing the possibility of national road pricing explicitly into the official policy prospectus. It highlighted the 'strategic choice' between continually deteriorating standards of service on the road network and some form of road pricing policy. The expectation was that this would involve distance-based charging utilising global positioning satellite technology which would become standard equipment in cars over the subsequent decade (LTT 426).

As noted previously (15.4) the case had long been made in academic and professional circles for revising the basis on which motorists are charged for road use so that this better reflected environmental and social costs (through congestion etc.). This would enable large-scale benefits to be achieved through more efficient utilisation of the available roadspace.

These arguments were confirmed by further technical work undertaken by DfT as part of the Eddington Study. This indicated that a national scheme could deliver benefits totalling £25bn by 2025, although these would be offset by the costs of the scheme which were as yet unknown. Eddington commented:

> Given the scale of the congestion challenge I believe that there is no attractive alternative to road pricing; without a widespread scheme by 2015 the UK will require very significantly more infrastructure ...
>
> Importantly, given the pace of economic change, pricing also offers considerable flexibility once in place. With pricing it becomes possible to respond to unanticipated change through changing prices much sooner – and a much lower cost – than bringing forward new infrastructure.
>
> (Eddington 2006a paras 1.114 and 1.111)

Closer inspection of the details of such a scheme however reveals some of the difficulties which would arise in gaining public acceptability. Two-thirds of journeys would cost more than the current fuel tax rate of approximately 4p per km. In return most would benefit from improvements in travel times and reliability. However these would be valued most by business users (and high-income private motorists) whilst the burden of increased payments would fall most heavily on car commuters travelling at peak times. This of course includes a large proportion of the voting public! The DfT analysis envisages such people 'changing their behaviour' but of course involuntary change is not an attractive proposition to those affected. Many would say they have no realistic alternative anyway (16.2). More generally research indicates that many people feel they already do everything they can to avoid congestion and believe that improving public transport would be a more effective solution to congestion than road pricing (IPPR 2006).

When the 2004 White Paper was published Alistair Darling had the good fortune of support for the principle of charging from the transport spokesmen of the opposition parties (LTT 397). This appeared to signal a context in which constructive debate on development of the idea could proceed. It is especially regrettable therefore that the Government's handling of the issue since has proved an almost unmitigated disaster.

The first error on such an obviously controversial issue was to publish the results of the Road Pricing Feasibility Study concurrently with the White Paper, thus bringing to public attention an exercise which at that stage should have remained within the confines of technical debate (DfT 2004b). The maximum charge of £1.34 a mile quoted in the study was seized upon to provide headline copy in the popular press, even though only 0.5% of traffic might be charged such a rate (LTT 397). From the very start therefore the Government found itself playing off the back foot.

A second error was not immediately to counter the entirely predictable response that road pricing represented an additional tax on motorists. In fact there is a variety of arguments on either side as to whether the scale and pattern of charges should be devised to be 'revenue neutral', i.e. result in no overall increase in motoring taxation. The main alternative, of the kind considered by Eddington, is to aim for an outcome which is optimal in economic terms, which would imply additional payments, although these could be recycled in the form of investment in transport improvements.

Technically the economic argument is superior in that the present level of motoring taxation is essentially the product of historical accident. However in terms of practical policy-making such a purist approach risks 'the best being the enemy of the good'. The strength of this point is underlined by evidence from the Feasibility Study which showed that almost as much could be achieved in the way of congestion reduction with a revenue neutral scheme as an economically optimal one. The Government could have found a form of words to nullify potential criticism by saying that it had no intention to raise overall taxation on motorists unless subsequent consultation demonstrated that there was support for the additional benefits that it could bring.

The Government's initiative also lost momentum because it did not respond to the recommendation to develop a concrete proposition on which to focus debate. Nor did it set out an indicative timetable for implementing a national scheme as recommended by the Transport Select Committee (House of Commons 2005). This apparent lack of commitment created a vacuum in which crude opposition to the principle of a scheme could flourish culminating in an e-petition from 1.8 million objectors on the Prime Minister's website in early 2006. His reply talked of 'beginning the debate' but this rang very hollow since the political initiative had clearly been lost and DfT statements then and since have all implied a distancing from the concept of a national scheme.

When in March 2008 Ruth Kelly announced the study of Active Traffic Management on motorways she commented that arguments about nationwide road pricing had become 'sterile' and that the action she was proposing would give 'a more immediate and pragmatic focus for the debate' (LTT 489). Much of the press interpreted this gladly as signalling the end of the idea of national pricing (LTT 490). In fact she maintained the mantra that 'it would be unwise to rule out national road pricing in the long term'. However the reality is that the practical and political challenges represented by a national scheme are so great that unless it is deliberately planned for, it is extremely unlikely ever to happen. Her statement can be seen as another example of 'policy layering' whereby an established feature is neither explicitly progressed, amended nor abandoned but is merely overlain (buried?) by a more eye-catching initiative, leaving an overall policy fudge.

A serious consequence of the continued prevarication over national charging is the limbo into which it places planning for the national highway network, since forecast traffic demands (and prospective congestion levels) over the longer term are obviously different with and without charging. We return to this issue in the following chapter.

23.4 The Transport Innovation Fund

Since 2004 the Government has followed the recommendation of the Road Pricing Feasibility Study that, rather than do nothing in advance of a national scheme, local authorities outside London with congested road conditions should be encouraged to introduce local schemes using cordon or area pricing.

The Transport Innovation Fund (TIF) announced in the 2004 Comprehensive Spending Review is intended to support:

- innovative local transport packages that combine demand management measures such as road pricing with measures to encourage modal shift and better bus services
- local mechanisms which raise new funding for transport schemes, and
- regional, inter-regional and local schemes that are beneficial to national productivity.

TIF becomes available from 2008/09 with planned funding increasing from £290m in that year to £2.5bn in 2014/15. (Eligibility for TIF is confined to authorities in England but proportional additional funding has been given to Wales and Scotland.) Schemes are being considered in two categories 'Congestion TIF' and 'Productivity TIF' with priority being given in both cases to proposals which are most effective in securing a financial contribution from significant beneficiaries (DfT 2006k).

Suggestions for the use of Productivity TIF were invited from Regional Development Agencies and consist mainly of rail freight schemes and traffic management on main motorways (DfT 2006j). All proposals in this category are being assessed for their contribution to wider economic benefits and GDP as an additional dimension of the standard economic appraisal (DfT 2006m). About £360m has been allocated to date but uncertainty surrounds possible future rounds (LTT 491).

In relation to Congestion TIF £18m was made available in 2005/06–2007/08 to support preliminary scheme development by local transport authorities.

Table 23.1   Authorities awarded Congestion TIF 'pump-priming' funding

2006	2007
Greater Manchester	Reading
Cambridgeshire	Norfolk (Norwich)
Shropshire (Shrewsbury)	East Midlands (Nottingham/Leicester/Derby)
Tyne and Wear	
West Midlands	
Durham	
Bristol ('West of England')	

> Schemes supported by TIF will need to demonstrate a step change from the [demand management] approaches currently used by bidding local authorities. We are therefore most likely to fund packages involving road pricing although we may, by exception, consider bids involving a Workplace Parking Levy.
>
> (DfT 2006k para 2.5)

Invitations to bid for 'pump-priming' funds were issued in two rounds with the successful authorities listed in Table 23.1. Undoubtedly many of these were motivated to participate less by enthusiasm for the concept of road pricing than by the lure of additional investment paid for by central government, and have since withdrawn their interest because the pricing schemes showed few benefits and/or little public support. Only Cambridgeshire, West of England, Reading and Leeds (which joined later) remain members of the Department's charging partnership. However the whole of the TIF programme has potentially been dealt a fatal blow as a result of the resounding defeat of the proposed scheme for Greater Manchester (notwithstanding inclusion of over £1bn of public transport improvements) in a local referendum at the end of 2008 (LTT510). Meanwhile Nottingham City Council continues to pursue a Workplace Parking Levy scheme for implementation in 2010 outside of the TIF process, designed to provide funding for Phase 2 of the city's Express Transit scheme (LTT 484).

The Department's aim was to have two or three road pricing schemes fully operational by 2013/14. However, mindful of the few schemes coming forward and the time involved in delivery it has announced extension of the funding period to 2018/19 and invited bids for a third round of pump-priming funding (DfT 2008e).

The law surrounding local schemes has also been amended in the Local Transport Act to remove the requirement for the Secretary of State to approve a scheme or to order an inquiry. (These amendments do not apply to Wales so that Welsh Ministers retain these powers under the 2000 Act.) English local authorities also retain powers under the 2000 Act to decide for themselves on consultation or to hold an inquiry.

The introduction of Congestion TIF is recognition of the fact that 'up-front' investment in the improvement of public transport and complementary demand management measures are essential if local road pricing schemes are to be rendered acceptable. Moreover because there is no opportunity to compensate motorists for additional costs through reductions in national taxation these improvements have to be on a large scale for them to be attractive to local politicians and their electorates.

The wisdom as well as the success of the Government's approach to date can be queried. Back in 2005 the Transport Select Committee warned:

> Ultimately it must be up to the judgement of local authorities themselves to decide whether a charging scheme is the best way to tackle their current and

future traffic congestion problems. Local authorities should not be penalised if they decide not to introduce such schemes. Effective public transport services are a good in their own right and should be promoted irrespective of whether a charging scheme is implemented.

(House of Commons 2005t Recommendation 11)

This line of thinking has recently been taken up by the Conservative Party – not without an eye to political opportunism – by stating that, if elected, they would scrap the congestion charging requirement for access to TIF funding and use the money to support 'new green personal travel initiatives' instead (LTT 493). Clearly as the possibility of a Conservative Government in 2010 assumes credibility this will further deter authorities from hazarding their local support on road pricing proposals in the meantime.

A weakness of the Government's current pilot programme is that it does not include any schemes on the strategic highway network – a critical feature of any eventual national scheme. In the past Ministers have said that charges would not be introduced on strategic roads which have not changed. However opportunities to introduce charging on recently widened motorways have been passed by. (The HOV lane previously planned as part of the M1 widening south of Luton has also been abandoned as unworkable.) Nevertheless the possibility was resurrected by Ruth Kelly in her announcement on extending ATM on motorways:

Allowing motorists to enter a reserved lane if they are carrying passengers or willing to pay a toll gives them a real choice without having to change their route. More capacity comes on line, but instead of immediately filling up, we can manage demand over time, adapting to circumstances, maintaining traffic flow and improving the reliability of motorway travel. These are ideas I want to explore further.

(DfT 2008b)

Introducing HOV or tolled lanes in this fashion, coupled with urban charging schemes, could be developed to form a more publicly acceptable (and deliverable) replacement for an all-embracing distance-based national charging scheme (G Emmerson in LTT 485).

23.5 A strategy for National Rail

The Government announced a review of the structure of the rail industry at the time Network Rail was set up to take over the functions of Railtrack. The Government's conclusions were published in a White Paper (DfT 2004e) and its proposals legislated for in the Railways Act 2005. In a move borne of some exasperation the Government proposed to wind up the SRA and to transfer most of its functions 'in-house' within the DfT. New arrangements were put in place with Network Rail to run alongside, and provide the context for, the franchising of passenger services. In an effort to improve operational performance Network Rail was also given overall responsibility for the network and the number of franchises reduced and aligned more closely with its regional structure.

Critically the Government wanted to try and place a ceiling on its financial commitment. (Previously it had found itself at the mercy of the Rail Regulator's review of access charges and the cost of supported services had risen by almost 50% between 2000/01 and 2004/05.) Under new arrangements the Government intended to publish a 'High Level Output Statement' setting out its objectives for the network and the amount it was prepared to pay to fulfil them. Alistair Darling maintained that the Government was not about to mount a programme of line closures to reduce costs. However the fact that clauses were inserted into the Railways Act transferring decisions on closures to the Rail Regulator, and making them subject to assessments of financial costs and benefits only, did nothing to allay fears (Grant 2006). Threatening noises were also made about relatively lightly used rail services in the provincial conurbations with the PTEs being offered the inducement of quality contract powers for bus services to facilitate their replacement.

The Government appears to have undergone a change of heart from the hawkish stance presented in 2005. The first signs were a renegotiation of the Great Western franchise which had originally been invited on the basis of a cost-cutting specification which would have greatly reduced services on the branch lines of Devon and Cornwall (completely at odds with any notion of their retention and development as community rail routes). The strategy later unveiled in the 2007 White Paper (DfT 2007b) also gave unexpected respite by stating that in the period to 2014 there would be no closure of regional or rural lines ('in order to retain flexibility for the future').

More generally the White Paper claims that

> The railway is now in the most stable financial position in 50 years. Growth is delivering significantly enhanced revenues, whilst industry cost control continues to improve.
>
> (ibid. para 12.17)

However this stability has been achieved only through massively expensive Government intervention since 2000 and the large cumulative debt which Network Rail (and hence indirectly customers and Government subsidies) will have to service for many years hence. For the future the White Paper states that the elimination of the renewals backlog and continuing improvements in cost efficiency 'will allow the subsidy requirement to return closer to historic levels'. Essentially this will be achieved by passengers contributing a greater share of total costs. (For an analysis of the Paper's financial component see Ford 2007.)

Between 2009/10 and 2013/14 (known as Control Period 4) passenger revenue is expected to increase at 4.8% a year in real terms with a 50/50 split between increased ridership and higher fares. As a result the proportion of income for passenger services represented by Government support will fall from 32% to 25% and in money terms from £3.2bn to £3.0bn (see Table 23.2). This contribution is now referred to as SoFA (Statement of Funds Available – as required under the 2005 Act). It is divided between franchise payments to operators and grants to Network Rail of the kind made since 2000 (excluding enhancements). The precise split between the two will however depend on the access charges set by the Rail Regulator. The key point with the 2005 Act regime however is that the SoFA figure is fixed. If in CP4 operators are required to pay higher access charges then the amount paid to them by the Government will increase and the amount paid direct to Network Rail will be reduced accordingly. The Government has acted to ensure that it will never again be 'bounced' as it was previously into paying substantially more in total.

Table 23.2 Forecast rail passenger revenue and application of Government funding 2009/10 – 2013/14 (source: CM 7176 Table 12.1)

£bn nominal*	2009/10	2010/11	2011/12	2012/13	2013/14	CP4 total
Passenger revenue	6.7	7.3	7.8	8.4	9.0	39.2
SoFA (Goverment)	3.2	3.0	3.1	3.0	3.0	15.3
of which, e.g.						
Franchise payments	1.6	1.4	1.1	0.9	0.5	5.5
Network grant	1.5	1.6	2.0	2.1	2.4	9.6
Governmentt support	32%	29%	28%	26%	25%	28%

Note: Excludes Government payment for HLOS requirements (see text). Figures assume inflation at 2.75% a year; excluding this (i.e. in real terms). Government support falls by 19% to 2013/14 compared with 2009/10

The growth in use which is the basis of the financial forecasts cannot be accommodated without complementary investment. The High Level Output Specification (HLOS) included in the White Paper specified:

* an increase in capacity to accommodate passenger growth of 22.5% and freight growth of 30% to 2014
* a 3% reduction in the risk of death or injury to passengers or employees
* an increase in reliability from 88% to 92.6% and a 25% reduction in delays of more than 30 minutes.

This is to be achieved by an investment programme during CP4 to which the Government will contribute a total of £8.9bn. Its main components are listed in Box 23.2.

The plans were conceived against the background of forecasts to 2030 but the investment strategy itself did not go beyond 2014. Ruth Kelly commented:

> We are not prepared to commit now to 'all-or-nothing' projects like network-wide electrification or a high-speed line for which the longer term need remains uncertain and which would make little contribution to today's challenges …
> We would end up diverting our resources away from the immediate priorities of passengers.
>
> (reported in *Modern Railways* September 2007)

Nevertheless preparatory work for the longer tem is continuing, including development of the Inter-City Express train – a replacement for the IC125. Further capacity enhancements will be included in the next HLOS to be published in 2012, based on the intermodal analysis of options recommended in the Eddington Study.

As with the Government's current approach to motorways, the 2007 HLOS gives the impression of focusing on immediate problems but otherwise of marking time as far as a longer term national strategy is concerned. Christian Wolmar commented:

> The White Paper contains a short-list of improvements at some of the worst pinchpoints but it was really the least that ministers could offer without admitting they do not give a fig. Ruth Kelly is trying to perpetuate the myth that it is feasible to reduce the subsidy going into railways while simultaneously increasing their

---

Box 23.2 Rail enhancements identified in the High Level Output Specification for Control Period 4 (2009–2014)

- Approval of the Thameslink project (major upgrade of the north–south regional route across London via Blackfriars) – total cost £5.5bn
- Grants of £125m and £425m respectively towards the major redevelopments of Birmingham New Street and Reading stations to eliminate the network's present worst bottlenecks
- £150m grants for improvements at 150 other stations to be identified by Network Rail – typically medium-sized, interchange stations
- 1,300 additional carriages (900 for London and the South-East) as part of a capacity enhancement programme including platform lengthening, power upgrades and additional depot facilities
- £200m to start work on a Strategic Freight Network which will provide routes capable of accommodating European-sized rolling stock and bypass congested (passenger) sections of the network.

Source: DfT 2007b

---

use. As a vision it simply does not add up. While it is commendable that the Government is trying – something which has been sadly lacking in the past – there is no real commitment to growing the railway.

(Christian Wolmar *The Independent* 25 July 2007 quoted in LTT 474)

The White Paper (and Wolmar's comments) were published before a decision on London's CrossRail could be announced. This is in a league of its own as far as expenditure is concerned with an estimated cost of £16bn. Alistair Darling – promoted to Chancellor of the Exchequer following Gordon Brown's succession as Prime Minister – was able announce as part of the 2007 Comprehensive Spending Review a funding package to deliver the scheme (LTT 479). This involves a three-way split between the Government, business contributions and farepayers. The Government grant is sourced from the TIF Productivity fund. The business contributions include direct payments from Canary Wharf, the City of London, BAA (Heathrow Airport) and others, developer contributions secured through planning permissions and the use of a new business rate supplement announced by the Chancellor at the same time (HM Treasury 2007a). The farepayers' contribution will service the debt raised during construction by TfL and Network Rail. Subject to Royal Assent of the CrossRail Bill in summer 2008, construction will begin in 2010 and services could be running from 2017.

23.6 *Putting Passengers First*

Putting Passengers First was the title of a DfT publication at the end of 2006 containing proposals for reform of the bus regulatory framework in England and Wales (DfT 2006e). It followed a review of bus services and meetings with key stakeholders led by the then newly appointed Secretary of State Douglas Alexander. Following further consultation and detailed amendment its proposals were carried forward into the Local Transport Act.

The Government's initiative represents acknowledgement that its previous attempts to improve local bus services through partnership arrangements and legal amendments, plus additional capital and revenue expenditure channelled mainly through local authorities, has not achieved the degree of success which had been hoped for. Its relatively modest objective for growing bus patronage as a whole is in practice being met by a peculiar combination of quite remarkable success in London and a few freestanding towns offset by a general trend of continued decline elsewhere.

> In too many areas, including many of our major cities outside London, partnership is still not working effectively. Bus users and the general public report that many services are not meeting the high standards they expect and in too many places patronage remains on a downward curve. Without further action a vicious spiral of decline is likely to take hold in more of our communities; falling demand and rising unit costs forcing bus operators to raise fares and cut back services, so leading to further reductions in demand or a need for ever-increasing levels of subsidy to maintain services.
>
> (DfT 2006e Executive Summary)

PTEG (the Passenger Transport Executive Group) in particular had been lobbying for years for changes in the regulatory framework beyond those introduced under the 2000 Act. The 'tipping point' in persuading the Government to respond appears to have been its own interest in seeing pilot local road pricing schemes introduced.

> In areas that are developing proposals for such schemes the ability to guarantee tangible improvements in local public transport is expected to be a crucial element of the policy package, so that more people can see a realistic, reliable and cost-effective alternative to the private car.
>
> (ibid.)

Put more bluntly the Government was being told that urban road pricing was undeliverable without a quantum improvement in local bus services and equally that such an improvement was undeliverable within the existing regulatory framework, give that the original Quality Contract procedures were unworkable.

The Government retained the principles of Quality Partnerships and Contracts but sought to amend their terms and procedures to make them a more feasible and attractive proposition (Box 23.3). The Act also strengthens the legal framework surrounding the monitoring of bus punctuality and improves opportunities for the provision of community transport. In all these fields the Traffic Commissioners are to take a more prominent role and in support of this a separate Consultation Paper proposes changes to their organisation (DfT 2007k).

The Act's provisions concerning bus regulation are especially controversial and uncertain in their implications. The Government has published a draft version of guidance (DfT 2007p) which seeks to explain the detailed application of the Act's provisions concerning Voluntary Agreements, Quality Partnership and Quality Contract Schemes plus a section on Competition Guidance provided by the Office of Fair Trading. Notwithstanding 134 pages of guidance the document concludes with the advice that anyone in doubt about how they may be affected by the legislation should consult a lawyer! It is a testament to how complex and bureaucratic the relatively simple business of arranging a bus service has become as the Government struggles

Box 23.3 Changes to bus service regulation

The requirement that Quality Contract schemes may be proposed where they are the 'only practicable way' of implementing an authority's bus strategy is replaced by the following criteria:

- they must contribute to the implementation of 'local transport policies'
- they must offer the benefits of higher quality services and increased use of local buses ('increase' meaning also reducing, arresting or reversing decline)
- the existing requirement that the scheme implements policies in a way that is 'economic, efficient and effective' is complemented by a competition test which requires any adverse effects on competition are proportionate to the public interest benefits.

Approval of a QC scheme requires prior publication of a consultation document demonstrating how the above criteria will be met, plus a statement on funding. In England approvals will be determined by an Approvals Board chaired by a Traffic Commissioner (instead of the Secretary of State) which may hold a public inquiry.

The modified competition test applying to voluntary partnership schemes, ticketing schemes and subsidised local services is extended to multi-lateral agreements and permits inclusion of items relating to minimum frequencies, timings and maximum fares. Operators may also co-ordinate services amongst themselves provided agreements are endorsed by the local transport authority.

Traffic commissioners are empowered to investigate poor punctuality and recommend remedial measures by operators or local traffic authorities.

The powers available to PTEs and other local transport authorities to secure the provision of passenger transport services which would not otherwise be provided are amended to permit the attainment of standards of frequency or timing, or vehicles used (i.e. enabling service enhancements, not merely the replacement of 'gaps' in the network).

The regulations governing community transport are amended so that all section 19 permits (to community groups) are issued by the Traffic Commissioners and allow use of vehicles with fewer than nine seats whilst section 22 permits for the provision of local services allow drivers on these services to be paid and for vehicles with more than 16 seats to be used.

Source: Local Transport Act 2008; NB applies to England outside London and to Wales only

to find a middle way between the competing ideologies of free market and planned provision and the conflicting interests of commercial operators and public authorities.

Included in the guidance is an indication that Ministers are preparing to accept the idea of 'Tendered Network Zones' for co-ordinating bus services in rural areas as proposed by the Association of Transport Coordinating Officers. In areas where the majority of services are tendered this would allow a local authority to specify criteria for local services and to protect a designated network by specifying restrictions on new registrations (LTT 471).

In relation to Quality Contract schemes the Government's intentions could be frustrated by the actions of commercial companies' operators who are opposed to the concept and/or who do not win contracts in an area in which they currently operate.

Delaying tactics could be pursued through legal challenges reinforced by threats to withhold the use of their assets or to deregister services in advance of the contract coming into force, thus leaving an area unserved. (A critical difference compared with the franchising of rail services is that the bulk of existing bus services are not run under contract and that the operator owns the vehicles and garaging facilities used to provide these services.)

The possibility of such tactics has been heightened by the Conservative Party declaring its opposition to the principle of Quality Contracts and by acknowledgement from DfT that even the new procedures could require over two years to deliver such a scheme (LTT 484). During the Bill's second reading the shadow transport secretary Theresa Villiers said that Quality Contracts would:

> prevent free competition between bus operators, undermine service quality for passengers and jeopardise the partnerships between operators and local authorities that have helped to improve service quality.
>
> (reported in LTT 491)

She said that a Conservative Government would 'certainly look to remove Quality Contracts altogether as an option outside London'.

23.7 Transport governance in city regions

Even if the Government's intentions behind the TIF Congestion fund and the legislative changes concerning bus services and local road pricing schemes are realised, in practice it remains doubtful whether the institutional framework in major urban areas is fit for the complex land use/transport planning challenges which they face. Sir Rod Eddington highlighted this concern in his report:

> In the light of the economic importance of the UK's cities and regions and the role that transport can play in supporting that economic success, I believe that effective governance at sub-national level is a crucial issue for the future. Such governance arrangements need to provide for consideration of all relevant modes and all types of policy intervention.
>
> (Eddington 2006a paras 1.154 and 1.157)

The DfT pursued this issue alongside work by other Government departments in connection with the Sub-National Review (DTI 2007) and the Lyons Inquiry into local government (DCLG 2007f).

The recommendations of Sir Michael Lyons concerning place-shaping and the case for greater financial autonomy for local authorities were reflected in the development of Local Area Agreements noted in section 19.8. He also wanted local authorities to create close working alliances with central government, regional and sub-regional partners. However on the basis of past experience he was wary of structural change, preferring authorities to develop 'effective and flexible coalitions that transcend boundaries' (LTT 465). The concept of sub-regional collaboration and multi-area agreements had already been floated in the Local Government White Paper (DCLG 2006c). He proposed a further set of 'tests' including political leadership, accountability and public support which, if fulfilled, would result in the sub-regional collective being provided with funds and powers devolved from

> **Box 23.4** Possible functions for sub-regional alliances
>
> As recommended by Lyons Inquiry (DCLG 2007f)
>
> - Strategic planning powers currently held partly by the individual local authorities and partly by central government
> - Resources and land currently administered or owned by Communities England
> - Powers over some strategic roads currently administered by the Highways Agency
> - Ability to make some adjustments to the quality and frequency of rail services and perhaps to commission or decommission some sub-regional services
> - Allocation of some proportion of regional transport and housing funding
> - Powers and revenues allocated to local authorities in relation to road pricing.

national and regional government. His list of suggestions has particular relevance for transport provision (Box 23.4).

The Local Transport Act contains reforms which may be applied to the governance arrangements of local transport in England outside London. It does not specify the precise nature of these reforms nor the areas to which they should apply. Rather it gives the Secretary of State powers to make orders in response to proposals put forward by local councils, i.e. so that the nature of reforms may be agreed locally and varied from one part of the country to another. The SoS also has reserve powers to require that a review of arrangements is conducted in a particular area and that proposals for reform are submitted.

The basic concept in the Act is of 'Integrated Transport Authorities' (ITAs) which can be regarded, geographically and functionally, as an extension of the existing PTAs. The only necessary changes provided for in the Act are that:

- the six English PTAs will be known in future as ITAs
- their areas will be known as 'integrated transport areas'
- they will have sole responsibility for preparing a Local Transport Plan (previously prepared jointly with the metropolitan district councils)
- they acquire the power, jointly with local traffic authorities, to make road user charging schemes.

However the area, functions and constitution of these bodies may be varied following a review of existing arrangements. In addition proposals for new ITAs may be brought forward elsewhere.

Coupled with the regulatory reform of bus services these changes potentially represent a return towards the more comprehensive transport planning regime previously available to the metropolitan county councils. However reviews in these areas are likely to propose boundary extensions, reflecting the functional expansion of these 'city regions' in the intervening decades. Elsewhere the new regime would be especially valuable in restoring transport integration in similar urbanised areas which were broken up by the creation of unitary councils in 1997. Examples are Greater Bristol ('West of England'), South Hampshire and Teesside where voluntary partnerships have been established in the interim.

Inevitably, given the incremental, bottom-up process being followed, the eventual outcome of governance reform cannot be determined. However it is questionable whether, in the Government's desire to appease local authorities, the degree of flexibility being offered is excessive and whether any coherent overall pattern will emerge, both within and between individual regions. This applies not only to transport in isolation but also to its relationship with other functions meriting multi-authority partnership, notably spatial planning.

Draft guidance published by DfT meanwhile focuses on transport's relationship with economic development:

> All authorities considering governance arrangements ... will want to consider carefully how transport can be planned and managed in a way which best supports their aspirations for sustainable economic growth ...
>
> Local authorities considering changes to transport governance will wish to ensure that there is a read across to any work they may be doing on Multi-Area Agreements and that the transport governance changes are developed in the wider economic development context.
>
> The [Sub-National Review] indicated that the Government would work with interested sub-regions to explore the potential for sub-regional authorities which would enable pooling of responsibilities for economic development ... But the Government does not consider that consideration of broader possibilities should necessarily delay the implementation of improvements in transport.
>
> (DfT 2007q paras 2.6–2.11)

23.8 Growth Points, Eco-towns and the Community Infrastructure Levy

The Government's efforts to increase substantially the rate of new house-building has brought attention to the issue of achieving appropriate infrastructure provision in the places earmarked for growth. This section considers the scale and location of the principal increases, the initiatives which have been taken to facilitate the necessary infrastructure provision and some of the issues arising.

The Sustainable Communities Plan published by ODPM in 2003 proposed increasing the targets for new housing in the four major 'growth areas' in the south-eastern quarter of England to a total of 900,000 by 2031 (8.8). Local authorities and other delivery agencies in these areas were given special 'growth area funding' (GAF) for their additional spending on services and facilities. The Housing Review undertaken by Kate Barker nevertheless concluded that there was a continuing shortfall in supply which needed to be addressed in order to reduce house price inflation, improve the performance of the UK economy via greater labour mobility and ease problems of poor housing (Barker 2004).

In 2007 the Government reported that the housing stock was growing by 185,000 a year against a projected growth in the number of households of 223,000. Accordingly a new national target was set of 240,000 additional homes a year by 2016 and the delivery of 2 million new homes by that date (DCLG 2007e). The components of this total are listed in Box 23.5.

One new element was an additional 100,000 homes to be included in local authority plans within five partnership areas and 22 other 'growth points'. These are

---

Box 23.5 Proposals for delivering 2 million new homes by 2016

- 1.6 million homes already allowed for in existing Regional Spatial Strategies and plans now in place including around 650,000 in Growth Areas supported by the Sustainable Communities Plan
- 150,000–200,000 additional homes in the new round of RSS (or partial reviews) and plans now under consideration
- 100,000 extra homes in 45 towns and cities which comprise the 29 Growth Points
- An additional round of New Growth Points delivering around 50,000 new homes
- Five new eco-town schemes [later increased to ten] providing 25,000–100,000 new homes.

Source: DCLG 2007e Homes for the Future

---

distributed across a number of English regions outside London with the exception of the three most northern regions. This extra provision was secured in response to the offer of additional funding for authorities who were prepared to accept increases over their current plans. (On average the rate of growth at these places is being increased by about a third.)

A revised Growth Fund has been established for the three years 2008/09–2010/11 which will provide £732m of support for mainly capital expenditure to the three newer Growth Areas (i.e. excluding Thames Gateway) and the Growth Points. Instead of funding individual projects the Fund will take the form of a non-ring-fenced grant. For the individual Growth Points this is worth around £10m per 10,000 additional homes provided.

A second, and more radical, element was the announcement of a competition to build a number of new 'eco-towns'.

> Eco-towns are a major opportunity for local authorities, house-builders, developers and registered social landlords to come together to build small new towns .... Uniquely they offer the opportunity to design a whole town – businesses and services as well as homes – to achieve zero carbon development and to use this experience to guide other developments across the country.
>
> (DCLG 2007c)

The competition generated 57 submissions from which 15 have been short-listed. A summary of each bid plus proposals for taking forward the eco-towns initiative were published for consultation in April 2008 and the Government expects to announce up to ten successful projects later in the year (DCLG 2008b).

Although the environmental standards being sought from this initiative are laudable, the forms of 'eco-town' being proposed and the manner in which they are being taken forward outside the 'plan-led' system is controversial. The initiative is really a 'back-door' means of accelerating housing provision still further with the eco-credentials cloaking proposals at locations which in most cases would not normally be favoured for development. In particular the transport implications of relatively small settlements at some distance from main urban areas imply a degree of commuting and other longer-distance travel which appear to be inherently unsustainable.

All types of growth area mentioned so far are also eligible for awards from the Community Infrastructure Fund (CIF). CIF was introduced as part of the 2004 Spending Review and uniquely links the funding of transport infrastructure to the delivery of housing. It is designed to complement mainstream transport funding so as to facilitate or accelerate housing development or to improve the sustainability of main locations of housing growth. The Fund is administered by DCLG but decisions on supported schemes are made jointly by Ministers from DCLG and DfT.

As part of spending plans for 2008/09–2010/11, £300m has been allocated for a second round of CIF. Of this £100m has already been earmarked for 13 local transport schemes in the Thames Gateway, leaving the remaining £200m for schemes in the other Growth Areas, Growth Points and Eco-towns (DCLG 2008a). Unlike Growth Funds CIF2 funding is available only for specific projects (possibly in combination with other funding sources). Schemes must be able to be completed by March 2011 (or have remaining funding secured thereafter).

Funding for transport and other infrastructure associated with new development may of course be derived from section 106 agreements with the developers concerned. However for larger developments in particular there can be a number of difficulties with this as a funding source. For example the scale of funding required for transport infrastructure may be more than the proposed development can support financially, especially if there is already an 'infrastructure deficit' in the locality. If an area is developed in phases it may also be difficult to secure the necessary contributions at each stage which enables the overall infrastructure requirement to be funded and delivered in a manner and at a time which matches the pattern of development.

To address the particular issue of timing, an innovation is being pioneered by the South West region in the form of a Regional Infrastructure Fund as part of its RFA. This enables money to be advanced for the facilities needed to serve major development areas, which is then recouped from s106 contributions as the development proceeds, and 'recycled' to support future development.

Together however these arrangements make for a complex mix as far as the overall planning of development and transport infrastructure is concerned. Funding through CIF is short term and unpredictable whilst developer contributions are uncertain and do not necessarily arise in the places where investment is most needed. (A developer may be able to 'piggy-back' on recent public investment in one part of a town whilst new investment is needed in another part.) Since publication of the Sustainable Communities Plan the Government has acknowledged the need for more fundamental reform.

As part of the current Planning Bill the Government is legislating for powers to enable a local Community Infrastructure Levy to be operated by planning authorities in England and Wales. This follows experience with so-called 'tariff' schemes pioneered by individual authorities under which developers have been charged a standard rate per dwelling or per unit floorspace to pay for ancillary facilities. In areas where such levies are applied, planning obligations are scaled back to 'direct impact mitigation' and affordable housing requirements only. Previously the Government had intended to source more general funding for facilities through imposition of a 'Planning Gain Supplement' (PGS). The Community Infrastructure Levy (CIL) is different in that

a   it is open to individual authorities whether to operate a levy (if they do not then present wholly negotiated arrangements will continue to apply) b   the levy is unrelated to the estimated financial gain derived by individual developers (the stumbling block which defeated the original PGS proposal)

c   the levy *is* related to the additional aggregate costs which an authority expects to incur in an area as a consequence of the planned new development (plus an element for contributing to sub-regional infrastructure).

However CIL is similar to PGS in that the formula for the charge will be pre-determined (DCLG 2008c). As a result delays through negotiating s106 agreements will be reduced and the proportion of 'free-riders' eliminated.

The Government proposes that the policy towards CIL in a particular area will form part of its development plan. This will enhance the planning process by enabling planning authorities' proposals to be examined with greater rigour and certainty as far as the provision of related infrastructure is concerned. It should also enable more appropriately funded and better integrated and managed development programmes to be delivered.

23.9 The DfT's current 'vision' and targets

To conclude this chapter we report on the 'vision' set for the DfT in the Delivery Agreement relating to transport included within the 2007 Comprehensive Spending Review (HM Treasury 2007b). By its nature and relative to the sort of strategic vision one might hope the Department was working towards it is narrowly prescribed and short term, being geared essentially to the three years 2008/09–2010/11. However it encapsulates the present role of the Department as seen within Government and the trajectory within which longer term prospects deserve to be considered. As such it provides a useful bridge into the following chapter.

The basis of the strategy underpinning the PSA is acknowledged to be Eddington's Study of transport's role in sustaining the UK's productivity and competitiveness. It therefore has a somewhat circular, self-fulfilling character – the Treasury sets the brief for the Eddington Study and then uses its recommendations as the basis of steering the Department's work. With the exception of three other PSAs to which transport is recognised to be a significant contributor (see footnote to Box 23.6) other possible perspectives do not get a look in. The PSA is specifically focused on the contribution of transport to economic growth:

> The Government wants a transport system that enables sustained economic prosperity and addresses the needs of the travelling public.
>
> Successful delivery of this PSA will mean, in the context of rising demand for travel, improvements in the reliability and capacity of those parts of the transport system where networks are critical in supporting economic growth and where there are clear signals that these networks are not performing …
>
> The Government's ambition over the 2007 CSR Review period is to minimise congestion and other costs, relative to what would otherwise be expected. The ambition extends beyond more efficient application of existing approaches and includes new ideas and concepts which will maximise the benefits delivered.
>
> (ibid. paras 1.1–1.3)

The overall approach is therefore essentially the one followed by the Government since 2000, but more focused to take account of the particular insights and

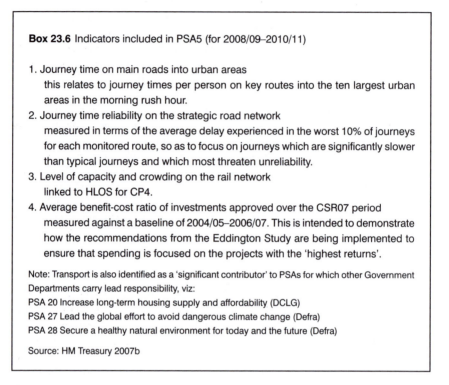

Box 23.6 Indicators included in PSA5 (for 2008/09–2010/11)

1. Journey time on main roads into urban areas
    this relates to journey times per person on key routes into the ten largest urban areas in the morning rush hour.
2. Journey time reliability on the strategic road network
    measured in terms of the average delay experienced in the worst 10% of journeys for each monitored route, so as to focus on journeys which are significantly slower than typical journeys and which most threaten unreliability.
3. Level of capacity and crowding on the rail network
    linked to HLOS for CP4.
4. Average benefit-cost ratio of investments approved over the CSR07 period
    measured against a baseline of 2004/05–2006/07. This is intended to demonstrate how the recommendations from the Eddington Study are being implemented to ensure that spending is focused on the projects with the 'highest returns'.

Note: Transport is also identified as a 'significant contributor' to PSAs for which other Government Departments carry lead responsibility, viz:
PSA 20 Increase long-term housing supply and affordability (DCLG)
PSA 27 Lead the global effort to avoid dangerous climate change (Defra)
PSA 28 Secure a healthy natural environment for today and the future (Defra)

Source: HM Treasury 2007b

recommendations emerging from the Eddington Study. It therefore has the following features which have been noted at various points previously in this book.

- Transport demand is essentially treated as exogenous – the extent to which Government policy, past and present has contributed to the present volume and pattern of demand is not acknowledged.
- Sustained – and sustainable – economic growth is defined by incorporating only certain readily identifiable environmental and social costs as 'boundaries' to the pursuit of GDP growth.
- Because of these assumptions the task facing the Department is phrased in the form of improving conditions 'relative to what they would have been otherwise', not in terms of actual improvements. (Is the ambition for any other field of public policy framed in such a way?)
- The Government remains preoccupied with transport problems as evidenced in the operation of the transport system. Hence the 'needs of the travelling public' signifies 'the interests of people who are currently willing and able to travel'; it does not mean the needs of people who might wish to travel (or travel more or differently) but are currently unable to.

Progress against the overall PSA target 'to deliver reliable and efficient transport networks that support economic growth' is to be measured through four indicators (Box 23.6). The indicator relating to the average benefit-cost ratio of investments approved during the CSR07 period is an innovation. It may help ensure that spending is focused on projects with the highest returns, but it may also handicap the prospects of individual schemes where non-monetised types of benefit, including distributional improvements, are viewed locally as an important part of their justification. Notably none of the indicators (including those to which the DfT is expected to contribute) contain any reference to personal accessibility or social exclusion.

24 Future scenarios and strategic choices

24.1 Introduction

Transport policy and planning in Britain over the last ten years has been a period of intense activity. Many individual changes have been positive but viewed from a broader perspective the improvements delivered have been patchy and strategically it has been ineffective. As we noted in Chapter 3 except for greater use of rail we are as car dependent a nation as we were a decade ago. The overall volume of motorised traffic has increased by a fifth and the volume of CO_2 emissions from surface transport has risen by about 8%.

A great deal of the activity can therefore be likened to rearranging the deckchairs on the doomed ocean liner. Despite the warning signals received during the 1990s (from the New Realism Report, from the anti-roads campaigners, and from the Royal Commission on Environmental Pollution) DfT's overall course has only been marginally adjusted (to plan for somewhat reduced increases in road traffic) rather than fundamentally redirected.

The strategic failure has characterised not only the content of policy but the incoherent manner in which it has been developed and executed overall. We have commented at several points in this book about the practice of policy layering – the frequent superimposition of new policies rather than constructive review of 'old' ones. This creates confusion in both substance and practice as mutually incompatible policies continue to sit alongside (or above and below) one another and as practitioners struggle to catch up with the latest repositioning.

Phil Goodwin – the main protagonist of the New Realism – has made a similar observation. Speaking in March 2008 he said:

> What we've had is a decade of J-turns. A J-turn is an uncompleted U-turn. There is no coherence – there is a series of statements, each of which pleases or displeases one or other group of stakeholders but no feeling that there is an overarching vision in our most senior elected leaders and advisers which is any more profound than anybody in this room and possible a lot less so. And that's uncomfortable.
> (Lecture to Transport Planning Society, reported in LTT 489)

Amidst this vacuum the Treasury has taken the initiative in mounting a series of studies of longer term issues which have effectively set the context within which the Department is now reviewing its own strategy. The introduction of serious analysis is welcome although the limitations of its perspective are disturbing. In this chapter we report the recommendations of the Stern Review on Climate Change (24.3) and the Eddington Study on Transport and the Economy (24.5). (The reports by Kate Barker on Housing Supply and the Planning System were produced in a similar vein and have been noted previously.)

Around these sections we interpose other material relevant to longer term policy options – an initial reflection on 'thinking about the future' (24.2) and examples of scenarios offered by non-Government sources (24.4) and (24.6).

We conclude by noting the DfT's response to the Stern and Eddington reports as contained in its White Paper published towards the end of 2007 and its intended plan of work for a post-2014 strategy including a 'refresh' of NATA (24.7).

24.2 Thinking about the future

Before reporting work on longer term scenarios it is helpful to reflect on the ways in which this is different from the more immediate policy-making and planning which has been the subject of the rest of this book. Instead of considering options for fulfilling a particular specification (e.g. relieving traffic or environmental problems within an area, given forecasts of relevant socio-economic variables) the task is more a matter of identifying what the specification should be, given a high degree of uncertainty about its context.

In one sense this uncertainty represents a positive opportunity since it offers room for manoeuvre to 'shape' the future. (Instead of anticipating what the future *will* be – so that we can plan accordingly – we are more in the position of trying to answer the question of what we would *like* it to be.) In another sense however the uncertainty inhibits strategic decision-making because of fears that it will prove 'wrong', involve wasted expenditure and bequeath to future generations dysfunctional forms of cities and regions which do not fulfil their economic and social needs.

Some of the uncertainty derives from projecting over a relatively long period basic travel parameters which are known to vary over time, but within limited bounds of probability (e.g. population, migration, economic activity, income, car ownership etc.). This can be accommodated by identifying high and low estimates which can be used for robustness testing whilst main strategies are evaluated against mid-range forecasts (Chatterjee and Gordon 2006).

However there are other types of uncertainty which are more problematic, either because they are known about but are inherently less predictable or because they concern some eventuality which literally has not occurred before. Leaving aside the apocalyptic possibilities of war, disease, famine etc. (but not global warming which we consider in the next section) these uncertainties can be divided broadly into the technical and the social.

Technical uncertainty can be subdivided into factors influencing the need or demand for travel on the one hand and factors affecting the nature of the transport options available on the other. Technical innovation can alter the types of activity undertaken but also – through the development of information and communication technology (ICT) – whether it is necessary to travel to participate in them. This applies in fields as various as office work, entertainment, shopping, obtaining information and advice and socialising. (For further discussion of this dimension see Chapter 9 of Banister 2005 and Lyons and Kenyon 2006.)

Technical innovation in transport itself is less a matter of wholly new 'inventions' than the extent to which a combination of economic, institutional and social factors renders development of known products viable and successful at particular points in time. The possibility of developing a replacement for petrol-driven cars is of central importance to the future of transport planning and is a subject we return to later. But there are other more mundane examples. For example 'road-trains' are used very successfully to convey passengers within theme parks and the like but there is not a single town or city centre in Britain which has adopted anything similar. Tow-bars are installed to pull skiers up hills but no-one has done the same for cyclists!

For decades designers have proposed imaginative varieties of city car, electric car or automated personal transit which would transform urban transport (Richards 2001). The difficulty with most of them is the special infrastructure (or adaptation of existing streets) necessary for them to function at all or for their economic and environmental benefits to be fully realised. This means that a threshold of initial investment is required which is almost inevitably prohibitive. In established towns there is the added difficulty of retro-fitting the required facilities within the existing urban fabric and with continuing to provide for traditional modes. Hence the greatest opportunity would appear to lie in their application in new growth areas or 'eco-towns'. At the present time the possibility of a PRT (Personal Rapid Transit) pilot route is being pursued in connection with the development of Daventry – part of the Milton Keynes/South Midlands Growth Area (LTT 492).

Social habits are influenced by technical advances impacting upon mobility at a variety of levels from the global to the personal (Urry 2007). But in the opposite direction social values and practices also act as a dampening mechanism in determining how far and in what ways opportunities that are physically possible are actually engaged in. In relation to ICT it is the extent to which people are willing to alter their *social* habits (going to work, shopping and meeting people etc.) that will have the greatest impact on the extent of travel substitution.

Aside from patterns of activity, social values exert an independent influence on attitudes and travel behaviour. Clearly the extent to which people choose to live independently, buy their own cars, do or don't use bikes, chauffeur children to school, share lifts etc. is influenced by perceived social norms as much as any sober assessment of their cost-effectiveness. Preferences can alter rapidly as the monitoring of social attitudes demonstrates. More generally there are shifts in social values, such as the relative importance of individual versus collective interests, attitudes towards personal security, social equity, health, environment etc. which have an effect on personal activity and travel behaviour and on the perceived merits of planning options. Crucially the achievement of behavioural change in transport is often quoted as a matter of 'winning hearts and minds' – something which public authorities can seek to influence, but which ultimately is dependent on a social revolution of the kind which has taken place in relation to smoking and drink-driving.

Faced with such 'unknowables' the convention in transport planning is to assume that people within defined socio-economic categories will undertake the same pattern of activities in future and respond to travel options in the same way as people in these categories do today. This implicitly assumes that the effect of any one innovation or change in behaviour within a particular social category is marginal and that collectively their impact is randomised (i.e. they do not compound one another). This is in the nature of a working assumption so that, if one or more factors are thought likely to exert a significant effect, this can be investigated separately and the findings applied to overall forecasts. (To date 'behavioural change' and the impact of smarter choice measures has been handled in this way.)

Politically the hazards of uncertainty provide reason for avoiding commitment to any particular long-term strategy. (Individual schemes and developments continue to be approved, but on an incremental basis.) 'Muddling through' enables flexibility to be retained. It also avoids having to present populations (hence voters) with costs or other disbenefits which are designed mainly to safeguard the interests of future generations.

These technical and political stances tend to encourage an approach to planning which is executed through successive 'roll-forwards' of existing programmes, rather than engaging with the more difficult and potentially controversial matter of where these are leading. (In effect the 'where would we like to be?' question posed earlier is never arrived at.) It therefore implies an extremely conservative pattern of change over time. Not only does the pattern tend to follow the same trajectory but the longer it is maintained the more it reinforces and 'legitimises' established and dominant practices. These in turn generate a sense of inevitability about where we are heading. Even if the future consequences of 'business as usual' appear profoundly unattractive we seem to find the possibility of engaging with the changes needed to avoid it even more unpalatable. The prospect of global climate change however places such 'challenges' on to a wholly new plane.

24.3 The Stern Review and the Climate Change Programme

The Review of the Economics of Climate Change conducted by the Treasury's Chief Economist Sir Nicholas Stern was published in October 2006 (HM Treasury 2006). Although the Review says relatively little about transport directly it is nevertheless likely to have profound implications, both through the DfT's own response and because of the high public profile which the Review has brought to an already controversial subject. (Sir Rod Eddington's study overlapped with Stern's and his interpretation of the Review's transport implications formed part of his report which we consider later in this chapter.)

The Stern Review broadly reported the international scientific consensus on global warming and mankind's contribution to it. However its pioneering work lay in estimating the global costs of climate change over the very long term (as far as 2200) and in making an economic case for taking action to abate it in the next few decades. Its immense policy significance lay in its far-reaching implications for all sectors of the economy and government in Britain, coupled with the fact that its central argument was immediately accepted by all three main political parties.

Stern's main conclusion was that if the world follows a 'business as usual' path of greenhouse gas emissions this would result in an average loss of consumption of 5% a year over the next two centuries. This can be presented more graphically as risks of economic and social disruption later in this century and the next on a scale similar to those of the two world wars and the Great Depression in the first half of the 20th century. However much of these costs could be avoided if countries took urgent action to deliver dramatic cuts in carbon emissions. He envisaged that this would cost the equivalent of 1% of global GDP each year. Seen in this light, tackling climate change deserved to be seen as the 'pro-growth strategy' with greater benefits the sooner action was taken.

It is this proposition, rather than the climate change estimates themselves, which generates greater controversy. Stern's analysis acknowledges that the bulk of disbenefits from global warming arise in the 22nd century and that the economic case for early action is based on the application of a discount rate of only 0.1%, i.e. adopting an ethical stance of almost complete inter-generational equity. Some critics query this exceptional assumption and also maintain that the advantages of early action are exaggerated by the 'unreal' supposition in the modelling that nothing would otherwise be done to curb carbon use or counter its adverse effects in the meantime (LTT 456).

Stern proposes three main policy instruments:

1   carbon pricing (through taxation, emissions trading or regulation, or a combination of all three)
2   support for developing a range of low-carbon technologies
3   action to promote behavioural change (through information, promotion and regulation).

On pricing he envisages there being a common global carbon price across all economic sectors over the next 10–20 years, but during the meantime emphasises the importance of governments avoiding becoming locked into high-carbon infrastructure. In fact, as far as transport is concerned, DfT responded immediately by publishing guidance on incorporating the social cost of carbon into scheme appraisal (WebTAG Unit 3.3.5 The Greenhouse Gas sub-objective).

The UK Energy White Paper published at the same time reiterated Stern's observation that transport was likely to be one of the last sectors in which major CO_2 reductions are achieved (DTI 2007). The reason given for this is because the low carbon technologies tend to be expensive and the demand for transport is relatively inelastic so that the welfare costs of reducing it are high.

The White Paper forecasts that CO_2 emissions from domestic transport will continue to rise until about 2015 and decline thereafter because improvements in vehicle efficiency and increased use of biofuels begin to overtake the effect of (reducing) growth in demand. By 2020 transport emissions are expected to have returned to near 2007 levels but, because emissions from other sectors are falling more quickly, transport's share of the national total will be higher than today. The contribution of the individual transport measures included in the Government's Climate Change Programme (CCP) is shown in Table 24.1.

Emissions from all sectors are expected to be cut by 16–22% by 2020 as a result of planned policies. Performance towards the top end of this range would be needed in order to fulfil the 26–32% target relative to a 1990 baseline that the Government included in a draft Climate Change Bill published in 2007. When passed as the Climate Change Act in November 2008, a commitment was given to review this intermediate target given the Government's acceptance of a more demanding long term target of an 80% reduction relative to the 1990 baseline by 2050.

The Act was hailed as the 'the world's first long term legally binding framework to tackle the dangers of climate change'. Its aims are:

•   to improve carbon management and help the transition towards a low carbon economy in the UK
•   to demonstrate strong leadership internationally in the context of developing negotiations on a post-2012 global agreement at Copenhagen in 2009.

In addition to setting legally binding targets the Act introduces a carbon budgeting system which caps emissions over five-year periods for three periods at a time (the first

Table 24.1 Expected carbon savings from transport measures included in the Climate Change Programme [MtC a year against 1990 base] (source: CfIT 2007 Table 3.1 (from Defra and DTI original sources))

	2010	2015	2020
Voluntary Agreements with vehicle manufacturers (including supporting VED and company car tax measures)	2.3	3.1	3.6
Successor to Voluntary Agreements (based on a target of 135g CO_2/km by 2020	0.3	1.1	1.8
Fuel duty escalator (1993–2000)	1.9	1.9	1.9
Renewable Transport Fuels Obligation (based on 5% of fuel sales by 2010)	1.6	1.6	1.6
Sustainable distribution in Scotland	0.1	0.1	0.1
Ten Year Plan (estimated to 2010, assumed constant thereafter)	0.8	0.8	0.8
Smarter Choices (low intensity)	0.2	0.2	0.2
TOTAL	7.3	8.9	10.0

being 2008-2012). These must be set by 1 June 2009 with the Government reporting to Parliament its policies and proposals to meet the budgets as soon as practicable after that. To advise Government on the level of carbon budgets and where cost effective savings can be made, the Act establishes a Committee on Climate Change, a new independent expert body. A Framework Document has been prepared which sets out the role and working practices of the Committee (DECC 2008). The advice from the Committee can be viewed at www.theccc.org.uk.

The planned reductions do not have to be achieved solely by end users in the UK – to do so could be economically damaging as it would imply raising the carbon price of transport and other commodities above prevailing levels in international markets. A proportion is expected to come instead from the EU trading scheme, i.e. through businesses purchasing carbon allowances from other countries or investing in carbon abatement projects in developing countries as is allowed for under the current Kyoto protocol. The Climate Change Committee has a further duty to advise on the appropriate balance between action at UK, European and international levels for each carbon budget. with the Government subsequently introducing secondary legislation which will set a limit on the use of international carbon credits in each period.

24.4 Further scenarios for reducing CO_2 emissions from transport

MARKAL-Macro model

As part of work undertaken for the 2007 Energy White Paper. an economy-wide model ('MARKAL-Macro') was developed to identify how the UK could meet future energy demands at the least cost to society. This work can only be regarded as an illustrative framework since it necessarily relies on a number of assumptions which in practice are

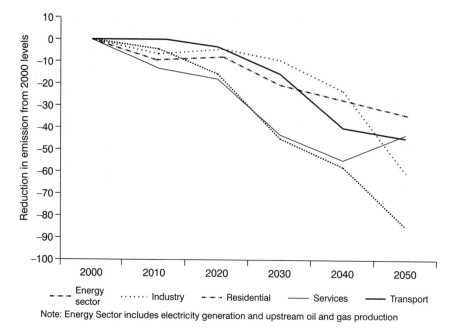

Figure 24.1 UK MARKAL-Macro model emissions reduction pathways by sector achieving a 60%
reduction in total UK emissions by 2050 (source: Energy White Paper 2007)

extremely uncertain. This applies particularly to energy demand, future oil prices and
the availability and cost of new technologies (such as hydrogen and fuel cells) which
are still in their infancy.

The model is limited in that it is focused on the technological possibilities for
reducing emissions. Behavioural change is only represented as a response to costs
(including the implicit carbon price) whereby demand can be reduced or the efficiency
of a given mode improved, e.g. through a switch in fuels. (Modal shift is not allowed for.)
Nevertheless the model suggests that transport could make a significant contribution
towards a cost-effective programme of reducing transport emissions, falling by as much
as 45% against 2000 levels by 2050 (Figure 24.1). Projections are based on an overall
increase of 50% in vehicle distance during this period.

In the base case – where transport is not constrained by carbon-reduction targets
– petrol and diesel hybrid (electric) vehicles are introduced in a range of modes from
2020 and buses, lorries and vans move to hydrogen after 2030. In the 60% carbon-
constrained case the introduction of hybrid vehicles is accelerated in the medium term
and biofuels play a more important role. Use of hydrogen is less prevalent under this
scenario since, unlike the base case where it is derived from fossil fuels, it is more costly
to produce.

CfIT study

CfIT commissioned its own research on this subject and concluded:

> We are concerned that the transport element of the CCP appears to depend
> heavily on relatively expensive measures to deliver emissions savings ....

With 70% of the carbon emissions in the CCP due to be delivered by technology we believe there is a missed opportunity to capture greater cost-effective carbon savings from transport and 'lock in' the positive impacts of technological advances using measures to encourage behavioural change through fiscal and non-fiscal means.

(CfIT 2007 paras 3.41–3.43)

CfIT recommended adoption of an integrated set of cost-effective measures that would increase the CCP savings by 7 MtC – thereby achieving a reduction in transport emissions of 14% against 1990 levels by 2020 instead of stabilising broadly at 2005 levels. Their recommendations were summarised as follows:

1   Adopt a mandatory target for new car sales in the EU to achieve an average of 100g CO_2/km by 2020 complemented by a package of supporting measures incentivising use of low-emission vehicles.
2   Reinforce positive driver behaviour through a combination of measures to sustain fuel prices, encourage eco-driving techniques and promote greater adherence to speed limits.
3   Secure more intensive application of smarter choices to reduce car use, reinforced by improvements to the carbon efficiency of public transport.
4   Secure carbon savings through technological, purchasing and operational changes in the fleets of vans and lorry vehicles.

Details are given in Chapter 4 of the CfIT report.

The VIBAT study

The balancing of technological and other measures in the transport field was explored in a study undertaken as part of the DfT's Transport Horizons Research Programme (Hickman and Banister 2006). In this case however it was the practicability rather than the cost-effectiveness of different measures which was the main focus. In addition a more demanding target was posed of a 60% reduction on 1990 CO_2 levels by 2030 as originally set by the Royal Commission in 1994.

The research used the innovative technique of 'backcasting' from a set of contrasting images of the future (but with the same target CO_2 reduction). Two images were adopted. The first – labelled 'new market economy' – had economic growth as its key driver and a policy emphasis on the contribution of technology. The second – labelled 'smart social policy' – had quality of life as its key driver, assumed slightly lower rates of economic growth and had a policy emphasis on behavioural change.

Over 120 possible individual policy measures were identified – most are well known and many have been implemented on an ad hoc basis in the UK in recent years. Eleven policy packages were then developed by combining individual measures which work well together and concentrating on those likely to create positive synergies. Initial estimates were then produced of their carbon-reduction potential, with a range of values reflecting the intensity of application (Table 24.2).

A key message ... during the policy packaging stage is that the roll-out of many of the measures needs to be prioritised, with a step change in the resources used.

Table 24.2   Potential carbon reduction from policy packages and selected measures (source: VIBAT Study – Hickman and Banister 2006)

	Potential CO₂ reduction MtC (range)	Change in MtC	
		New Market Economy	Smart Social Policy
Population increase		+2.8	+2.8
Average car distance per person		+8.4	−2.4
Increased use of bus and rail		0	+1.1
Policy packages			
PP1 Low-emission vehicles	9.1 – 18.3	−18.3	−9.1
PP2 Alternative fuels	1.8 – 9.1	−3.7	−1.8
PP3 Pricing regimes (inc. env. road pricing)	1.1 – 2.1	−1.1	−2.3
PP4 Liveable cities	0.5 – 2.4	−0.5	−2.4
PP5 ICT	0.3 – 1.8	−1.8	−0.8
PP6 Soft measures	0.9 – 2.4	−0.9	−2.4
PP7 Eco driving (lower speed limits)	2.5 – 4.6	0	−4.6
PP8 Long-distance mode substitution (air → rail etc.)	0.5 – 0.7	0	0.7
PP9 Freight transport (subsidiarity/ dematerialisation)	0.7 – 2.5	0.7	−2.5
PP10 Carbon rationing	Supporting/ enabling other packages		
PP11 Increased oil prices			
Net total reduction		**−15.8**	**−25.9**
Target saving to achieve 60% reduction on 1990		−25.7	−25.7
Shortfall/Surplus		−9.9	+0.2

Tinkering around the edge of the 'business as usual' policy direction will not deliver the ambitious CO_2 reduction target.

(ibid. Executive Summary p. 9)

The final stage in the VIBAT project was to select from and combine the policy packages into 'clusters' – illustrative ways in which the target CO_2 reduction might be pursued consistent with each of the future images. As shown in the table the 'New Market Economy' cluster takes maximum advantage of the potential from technological development to change the composition of the vehicle fleet (and hence is very risky and dependent on consumer choice) but this in turn lessens the potential savings from alternative fuels. Only limited savings are made from other, mostly behavioural change measures as their application is inconsistent with the future scenario. Overall this delivers only 60% of the target CO_2 reduction. A key factor is the extent to which the technological gains are offset by losses due to increased car distance travelled.

The Smart Social Policy cluster is more balanced, relying less on technological improvements but dependent on major behavioural change in a variety of contexts. It allows full achievement of the target CO_2 reduction. (It also has other attributes – no increase in traffic, more liveable cities, better public transport, greater equity and so on, but implies some additional cost and loss of 'freedom' to drive.)

> The overall conclusion reached is that the 60% CO_2 reduction target can be achieved by a combination of strong behavioural change and strong technological innovation. But it is in travel behaviour that the real change must take place ....
>
> We really should see this as a new age for integrated transport and urban planning – a huge opportunity – with the global environmental imperative as the catalyst for a major improvement in the way we live our lives.
>
> (ibid. pp. 18 and 21)

The King Review

In the light of Stern's recommendations about the scale of CO_2 reductions to be aimed for in the UK, the Chancellor set up a review by Professor Julia King 'to examine the vehicle and fuel technologies that, over the next 25 years, could help to decarbonise road transport, particularly cars'. Her report (HM Treasury 2008) concluded that:

> Technology that can reduce CO_2 emissions per car by 30 per cent (on a like for like basis) is already close to market and could be standard within 5–10 years. Despite estimated cost increases of £1,000–£1,500 per new vehicle many of these changes are likely to represent good economic value to the purchaser as a result of their impact on fuel economy ....

> Cars that emit 50% less CO_2 per km than the equivalent current models could be on the road by 2030, subject to advances in hybrid and battery technologies and industry overcoming cost barriers.
>
> Longer term, vehicle technologies to enable a 90% reduction in per km emissions, most likely based on battery-electric propulsion systems are feasible. Achieving this benefit however is dependent on very low CO_2 power generation.
>
> (ibid. Executive Summary paras 14–15)

Given likely constraints on biofuels as a source of supply, carbon-free transport in the long term will be dependent on clean power. As the world moves towards electric vehicles, so countries' road transport CO_2 emissions will increasingly be determined by the composition of their power generation sector. Making progress on decarbonising power generation therefore represents an even more urgent challenge than electric vehicle technologies because of the lead time in implementation.

Significantly King steps outside her remit somewhat to address the issue of consumer behaviour. Her review estimates that savings of around 10–15% could come from this source, much of it in the next few years. In particular four of her recommendations highlight aspects of the 'smarter choices' agenda – reinforcing their complementary potential noted in the CfIT and VIBAT studies above.

King's comments about consumer behaviour invite questions about public awareness of climate change, attitudes towards it and the relationship between

---

Box 24.1 Public attitudes to climate change and transport

There is only a weak link between knowledge and awareness of climate change on the one hand and travel behaviour at the individual level on the other. Raising public awareness of this link is necessary, particularly to galvanise support for carbon abatement policy, but it is not sufficient to change behaviour on its own. In order to effect change many other factors need to be addressed – at the objective and subjective and at the individual and collective levels. These factors will be different for different travel behaviours and different people.

Transport policies can set out to change attitudes directly as a route to behaviour change, or they can be indirect in that they aim to change behaviour first without necessarily changing attitudes. This review concludes that a combination of each of these types of measures is desirable. In addition, any travel behaviour change strategy will be more effective if it targets change at the community level. Community Based Social Marketing offers a strategic framework to transform markets and behaviours.

There is a need to engage the public in issues of transport and climate change using deliberative methodologies to deviate from traditional 'top-down' methods of information provision. New forms of research and communication need to be two-way, explore formats for learning on all sides of the issue, have an iterative and deliberative component and not necessarily strive to reach consensus.

Source: Anable, Lane and Kelay for DfT 2006 Summary Report p. 3

---

attitudes and behaviour. This was the subject of a separate research review commissioned by DfT which encompassed all aspects of travel behaviour, including choice of mode, car purchasing, the frequency and amount of travel and support for transport policies (Anable et al. 2006). Its main findings are summarised in Box 24.1.

24.5 The Eddington Report

In 2005 Sir Rod Eddington, formerly Chief Executive of British Airways, was asked by the then Chancellor Gordon Brown and Transport Secretary Alistair Darling to produce a report on the long-term links between transport and the UK's economy, focusing on the period after 2015. He was provided with a small support team from the two departments and also drew on the expertise of an appointed group of academic 'friends' coincidentally chaired by Sir Nicholas Stern. In addition to his four-volume main report (Eddington 2006b) his main findings and key recommendations were published separately (Eddington 2006a). Summary articles of the main topics covered together with comment and press reaction are included in LTT 458.

Transport can impact on the performance of the economy in two main ways – on GDP and on quality of life (Box 24.2). Eddington's study sought to take account of both sets of factors, and explicitly incorporated Stern's advice on costing emissions consistent with the long-term stabilisation of CO_2 levels. The empirical evidence of the links between transport and GDP are not conclusive (because of doubts about the direction of causality) but Eddington maintains that, by taking a broader view of economic benefit, the value of transport investment is clear.

Box 24.2 The impact of transport on economic performance

1   Impact on Gross Domestic Product (GDP), i.e. the total value of goods and services produced, through:

- increasing the number of inputs used, by stimulating the creation of new firms and growth in employment
- improving the efficiency with which firms use inputs, i.e. increasing productivity, by reducing their transport costs (including through greater reliability), facilitating labour mobility and raising competition
- stimulating innovation through agglomeration economies, trade and foreign direct investment.

2   Impact on quality of life, through:

- increasing benefits to consumers, e.g. the variety of products available and new social and leisure opportunities
- reducing time spent in non-business travel, allowing more time to be spent on other activities
- (positively or negatively) by altering the environment or conditions whilst travelling.

Source: Adapted from Eddington Transport Study Vol 1 Figure 1.1

Eddington studied the connectivity offered by the existing main transport networks in the UK relative to comparable countries in continental Europe and concluded that there was no case for adding to these networks. However much of the network is already congested for the majority of the time in key areas where economic success has concentrated demand, notably in and around urban areas, at international gateways and on busy inter-urban corridors. As Eddington's analysis developed, these came to be identified as the 'priority areas' for future investment.

As a prelude to developing recommendations a wide range of scenarios were tested to reflect uncertainties in both transport demand and supply. One uncertainty was transport policy itself! An initial assumption used as the basis of the 'central forecast' was that government spending would continue in the same pattern as in recent years. This implies an additional 3,500 lane km being added to the motorway and trunk road network during the period 2003–2025. It is important to emphasise therefore that, unlike conventional scheme appraisal, the reference case used to compare scenarios and policy options is not 'do nothing' or 'do minimum', but rather 'business as usual'.

On this basis the National Transport Model (NTM) forecasts that, with an increase of 71% in GDP over the period there would be a 28% increase in car traffic (vehicle km), a 12% increase in HGV traffic and 70% increase in light goods traffic. Passenger travel on inter-urban rail services is forecast to increase by over 35%, bus travel by 21% and walking and cycling by 11%. These increases are driven by:

- rising population
- household incomes rising in real terms
- car ownership continuing to rise (especially in areas other than London which currently have low levels)

- continuation of present trends in migration
- real reductions in the cost of travel (especially car travel).

Despite the volume of road-building assumed, congestion on the highway network (measured as delay relative to free-flow speed) would increase by 30%. Thirteen per cent of traffic would experience very congested conditions by 2025 (compared with 8% in 2003). One-third of London traffic and one-fifth of traffic in other urban areas would experience these conditions. With forecast increases in the length of commuting and business trips, congestion is also expected to spread more widely across the strategic road network, especially in the main inter-urban corridors. Without further action the cost to the economy of lost travel time would be at least £24bn a year, half this being borne by business travellers and freight users. Notwithstanding the increases in traffic volume and congestion, improvements in vehicle efficiency would result in a net 4% reduction in CO_2 emissions from road transport.

Eddington noted that the parts of the network already under pressure were the places which were likely to see the fastest growing demands. Without further action continued economic success is likely to exacerbate problems at these locations under a range of plausible scenarios. By contrast a system of national road user charging would enable these problems to be addressed and would also reduce the case for inter-urban road-building beyond 2015 by some 80% (i.e. to 500–850 lane km in the period to 2025). Without road pricing however there would be an economic case for increasing the rate of road capacity enhancement by over 50% compared with the baseline case.

Eddington's support of road user charging forms part of a general argument advocating the 'better use' of existing networks (Table 24.3):

> Better use options have the potential to contribute significantly to GDP and can have good environmental impacts. Therefore these should always be the first option considered. In some circumstances however making better use can only go so far, prompting the need to consider the costs and benefits of additional infrastructure.
>
> (Eddington Main report para 4.1)

Table 24.3 Better use measures (source: adapted from Eddington Main Report Figure 2.1)

	Measure	*Impact on the network*
Supply-side measures	Traffic management	Active management of traffic throughput to increase flow
	Incident management	Improved traffic throughput by making the network more resilient to disruptions
	Reallocation of capacity	Reallocate infrastructure capacity between modes to increase overall benefit and/or support wider strategy
	Maintenance	Regular maintenance regimes prevent future disruption and extend asset life
Demand-side measures	Pricing	Better pricing can spread demand and, if well targeted, allow the network to be used more effectively
	Soft measures	Increasing public awareness of travel options and reducing demand for car travel by taking small practical steps to making alternatives 'easier'
	Regulation	Improving transport performance (including impact on externalities) by specifying minimum service levels

An earlier report by SACTRA (1999) had concluded that, because of less than optimal pricing, the form of analysis undertaken to date might not reflect the full extent of economic benefits. DfT's initial response was to extend the appraisal framework to include local economic effects in regeneration areas. Research was also commissioned to explore the issue more generally (DfT 2005k). A key factor identified was the higher productivity which firms enjoyed where they were clustered spatially (so-called 'agglomeration economies') and the contribution which transport improvements made in such areas ,not merely to firms who benefited directly but by all others who benefited from increased agglomeration.

Eddington's study took account of these agglomeration effects and also explored the implications of incorporating estimates of the monetised value of impacts such as journey time reliability and carbon emissions which had not been possible before. By analysing a sample of nearly 200 projects covering a wide range by size, location and mode he was able to conclude that overall benefits would increase by up to 50% in individual cases.

Eddington did not set out to propose a particular investment programme or to adjudicate on particular schemes – rather to establish the principles which should govern such work. He was particularly concerned that assessments should be cross-modal, consider urban and inter-urban schemes on a like basis and take account of the contribution of small as well as large-scale interventions. Nevertheless his overall message was that there was a strong case for targeted new infrastructure:

> Government should therefore continue to deliver, together with the private sector, sustained transport investment. There are good returns across the priority areas, but smaller projects which unlock pinch-points, variable infrastructure schemes to support public transport in urban areas and international gateway surface access projects are likely to offer the very highest returns, sometimes higher than £10 for every pound spent. However large projects, with speculative benefits, and relying on untested technology, are unlikely to generate attractive returns.
>
> (Eddington 2006a para 12)

However, as with cost-benefit analysis generally, it is important to note that Eddington's findings do not explicitly consider impacts upon problems or other distributional effects (by time, place or social group). Neither do they include second-order effects (other than the particular issue of economic productivity) nor impact upon spatial or other policies. His focus upon priority areas and accent on 'economic return' as the basis of decision-making begs questions about the prospects for less cost-effective transport improvements in other areas and consequential implications for their local economies. To what extent should potential 'gains' from investment in the priority areas be forgone in the interests of maintaining the welfare of other areas, on the basis of both equity and of sustainability (i.e. avoiding greater dependence on opportunities further afield)? Eddington does not enter this important field but a national strategy would not be worth the name if it followed suit.

24.6 *Roads and Reality*

Roads and Reality is a report published by the RAC Foundation which usefully extends aspects of the analysis undertaken as part of the Eddington study (Banks et al. 2007).

However it cannot claim to be disinterested and its focus (on the future of the inter-urban road network) as it is deliberately focused.

> The main road network is a highly valuable asset. Its value is being undermined by failure to develop it effectively to deal with growing demand. The Royal Automobile Club Foundation has been concerned that the importance of its future has been understated by governments, politicians, some transport experts, and indeed the population at large.
>
> We felt that the Eddington Study was a positive report which started to address some of these issues and recognised the economic importance of the network. However we also felt that the report did not look far enough ahead and we were encouraged by Sir Rod Eddington to initiate our own study to look beyond 2025.
>
> (ibid. Foreword)

The RAC Study used much the same source data as Eddington and the same or similar assumptions, forecasts and appraisal conventions. However it differed by using a longer timeframe – up to 2041 – and by making several detailed but important adjustments. These included using regional variations in the value of time and separating the benefits and costs to the economy and individuals from those accruing to the Treasury through changes in taxes and charges. The authors maintain that their method gives a clearer picture of the real implications for the economy and people and asserts that how the Treasury raises the money it needs in the longer term is a separate issue. The RAC Study does not include the 'wider economic benefits' assessed by Eddington.

The key choices for the inter-urban and strategic road network are presented as:

- to do nothing and let **congestion** and wasted time match demand to the supply of road space
- to build or widen **more roads** without pricing
- to introduce some form of **road pricing without additional road building** and use the price mechanism to determine who should use the roads where there is insufficient capacity
- to employ a **combination of road building and road pricing** – the building to provide for growing demand for travel and the pricing to ensure efficient use of road space.

Like Eddington the RAC Study came to the conclusion that both road investment and road pricing are necessary but makes a different and higher assessment of the level of road building that would be economically justified.

The RAC Study begins by using official sources to generate the basic socio-economic inputs. By 2041 the population of Great Britain is expected to be 11% higher than in 2005 with average incomes 70% higher in 2030, over twice as high in 2040 and perhaps 2.5 times higher by 2050. An increase of 12% in total trips by all modes including walking and cycling is predicted with an average weekday growth of 24% in car trips and 37% in car miles. However there are important regional variations, mainly arising from differential rates of population growth. Car traffic in the West Midlands, Wales, North-West and North-East England and Scotland would increase between 23% and 33%; elsewhere the increase would be 39–46%. Across Britain HGV traffic would increase by an average of 27% and van traffic by 73%. These increases, it should be emphasised, do not incorporate any deterrent effects of potentially greater congestion. In effect they represent levels of demand assuming the conditions for travel remain the same as today. (In practice they could therefore be more or less depending on the policy response.)

Road users already adapt their behaviour in response to traffic conditions. This has resulted in the progressive spreading of peak periods such that the scope for further adaptation is becoming more limited. The authors acknowledge the variety of measures which can be introduced to reduce car use, including conventional demand management, improvement of public transport, and the range of 'smarter choices':

> All have potential for reducing road use cost-effectively in suitable locations and circumstances but the actual reduction is small in relation to total road use. Suitable locations for many of these measures tend to be in urban areas and on local roads so that they do not greatly affect traffic on the main road network.
> (ibid. Chapter 4)

Likewise there is a range of measures available for managing traffic on main roads, especially motorways but again the authors claim that their impact on the overall situation is small:

> Traffic engaged in longer distance trips relies to a large extent on the motorways and trunk roads which have become progressively more crowded. Here additional capacity generally offers the best means of improvement. As current opportunities for widening and junction improvements are implemented the potential for increasing the capacity of existing strategic roads will diminish and consequently the case for building more new roads will strengthen.

The Study tested options for inter-urban road building, with and without pricing, against a base scenario which assumed completion of the Highways Agency's Targeted Programme of Improvements projected to 2015 (an extra 1,594 lane km in England), no increase in road capacity after that and no pricing.

Scenarios for the period 2010–41 consisted of additional capacity at the rates of 200, 400, 600 and 800 lane kilometres per annum (Lkmpa) with junctions improved to match the capacity of links. The capacity is allocated approximately 60:40 between motorways and trunks roads and 30:70 between conurbations and other areas, but varied between regions. In the 800 Lkmpa scenario the extra 200 Lkmpa is confined to the fastest growing regions only.

The pricing scenario applied a national charging scheme with rates reflecting the 'marginal cost to society', i.e.

- a rate per vehicle km for the cost of providing and maintaining the roads and for environmental and safety impacts which vary by vehicle type, road type and degree of urbanisation, and
- a rate for congestion which varies with traffic conditions, time of day and day of the week to reflect the additional delay imposed on other roads users and carbon emissions (zero in uncongested situations).

The results of these scenarios in terms of their effect on flows and speeds in 2041 relative to the base case are shown in Figure 24.2. Without a national charging scheme,

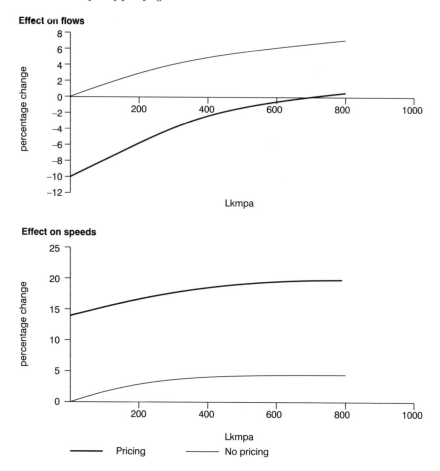

Figure 24.2 Effects of additional capacity and pricing on flows and speeds on the strategic network in 2041 relative to the base scenario (source: Banks et al. 2007 for RAC Foundation Figure 5.1)

flows would increase by up to 7% and speeds by 5% if the largest road-building option were adopted. With charging, flows would be reduced by 10% in the base case and rise to their 2015 levels by 2041 in this same scenario; speeds would increase by 14–20%. In both cases the rate of improvement diminishes with increments of road-building. This is reflected in the economic assessment which shows a BCR of 5:1 for introducing pricing in the base case and the marginal BCR for additional road-building reducing from 4.0:1 with the 200 Lkmpa option to 1.9:1 with the 800 Lkmpa option. Without pricing, the marginal BCR for successive increments of road-building is somewhat higher, reducing from 5:1 to 2.7:1.

Without charging, road-building would increase fuel consumption by up to 5% compared with the base scenario. With charging, consumption would be reduced by 15% in the base scenario, but with lower reductions as additional road-building was introduced. However the authors noted that reducing CO_2 would largely come about from more advanced vehicle design together with improvements in fuels cutting emissions. They concluded:

The Study shows that there is a strong economic case for more strategic road building at an annual rate of around 600 lane kilometres, irrespective of whether road pricing is introduced. However road-building combined with efficient pricing would result in a much higher economic return because mobility would be enhanced as well as congestion reduced.

(ibid. Conclusions)

The rate of road-building proposed equates with that undertaken during the decade from 1990, but is some five times greater than the Highways Agency's programme for 2003–15.

24.7 *Towards a Sustainable Transport System*

'Towards a Sustainable Transport Systsem' (commonly abbreviated to TaSTS) is the title of a White Paper published in October 2007 which represents the Government's formal response to the Stern and Eddington reports and considers their implications for work on the planning of transport in 2014/15 and beyond (DfT 2007s):

Our aim is not just to set out how the Government sees the Eddington and Stern Review being implemented, but to start a process of engaging with stakeholders in a way that has not always underpinned previous Government-level transport planning.

(ibid. para 1.24)

This work takes place in the context of an extension of the long-term funding guideline for transport spending announced in the 2007 CSR which grows at 2.25% per annum in real terms to 2018/19. In this section we report on the procedures that Government intends to follow whilst in the following section we note the indications it gives for the 'goals' to be pursued and the 'challenges' to be addressed.

Eddington had concluded that transport planning was conducted in a way which often focused too early on developing a specific scheme or solution. These were conceived within institutional arrangements which structured work around particular modes or types of intervention. Planning should be more inter-modal and look at a wide range of possible actions. In addition, to ensure that the best long-term outcomes were secured, he recommended a three-level decision-making cycle based on a 20–30 year outlook, a 10–20 year medium-term strategy and short-term plans looking 5–10 years ahead (Figure 24.3).

To overcome the tendency to develop solutions – especially grandiose ones – in search of a problem he also recommended a rigorous objectives-led approach to planning (Box 24.3).

The Government accepted both these recommendations and DfT has therefore begun to explore ways in which current decision-making processes might be reformed so as to:

- allow choices to be made across the different modes
- provide clarity on the expected availability of funding
- ensure that larger schemes are not allowed to swallow up all the funding available just because they are planned further ahead than smaller interventions
- provide enough flexibility to be able to deal with future uncertainties.

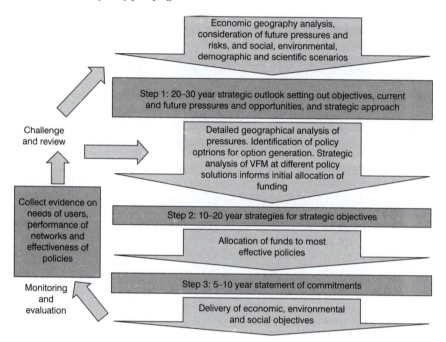

Figure 24.3 Eddington's suggested long-term decision-making cycle (source: Eddington Transport Study Vol 4 Figure 1.3)

Box 24.3 Eddington's recommended objectives-led approach to planning

- Start by being clear on the policy goals and desired outcomes.
- Identify the key transport challenges drawing on detailed geographical analysis of pressures, and the improvements in performance sought, focusing on the 'whole journey' rather than particular stages or modes in a journey.
- Consider the full range of possible actions for meeting the challenges and delivering the improvements, including different modal options, and policies for making more efficient use of existing capacity as well as small and larger scale capacity enhancements and packages of policy measures.
- Prioritise limited public resources on those policies which most cost-effectively deliver Government's objectives, taking account of the full social, environmental and economic costs and benefits ('listen to the numbers').

Source: DfT 2007s para 4.8

The first step in creating a new approach is to establish an appropriate multimodal planning cycle. The most convenient way of doing this is to build on the five-year cycles already in place for the national railway. In practice this would mean aligning planning work on other modes with the one already established for rail, i.e. with the plan – in rail's case the High Level Output Specification – being published in 2012 for the period 2014–19. Special arrangements would need to be made for

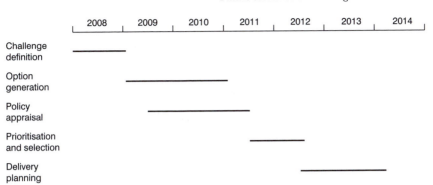

Figure 24.4 Indicative timetable for preparation of 2012 forward transport plans (source: DfT 2007 Figure 4.3)

investments which require commitments over an even longer timescale (e.g. the programme to replace the HST train fleet) whilst ensuring that sufficient unallocated funding remained for genuinely cross-modal decisions to be taken within each five-year period.

The aim is to arrive at a *programme* of schemes which has been systematically prepared for each period, thereby overcoming some of the problems which arise at present as successive proposals are examined individually. The budget certainty provided by the extension of the long-term funding guideline plus the improved strategic planning process envisaged will also provide an attractive environment for harnessing private sector support in the financing of public investments.

In preparing this programme the Department comments that its capability in using analytical evidence is acknowledged but that external parties have remarked on the need for dialogue at a much earlier stage and throughout the policy formulation process. In response the Department has set out an indicative timetable for the preparation of 2012 forward plans (Figure 24.4) and the arrangements it is making for stakeholder involvement during this period.

Following an initial informal dialogue with transport interest groups and public bodies a further document titled *Delivering a Sustainable Transport System (DaSTS)* was published in November 2008 intended to 'continue the debate with you on the fundamentals of our long-term planning system' (DfT 2008g). Its most notable feature is the decision to focus national planning on fourteen 'strategic national corridors' which collectively link the country's main ports and airports, the ten largest conurbations and other areas (such as the Thames Valley and South Cambridgeshire) with strong economic growth (Figure 24.5).

These corridors will replace the current 'national' category of Highway Agency roads from 2014 onwards (LTT508). Although the DfT claims that focusing on these corridors 'does not mean that we are ignoring other areas of the country', the economic implications for cities such as Plymouth and Norwich which lie well beyond them, plus the regional funding of other areas currently served by HA routes which will lose their national designation, will undoubtedly be a source of controversy.

The Department's plans for the nation's core transport infrastructure are being progressed by a new cross-modal National Network Strategy Group headed by the junior minister Lord Adonis with 'senior partners from the Highways Agency, Network Rail, HM Treasury and other Government departments as required'. The Group will consider how best to make use of existing networks (for example by the selective

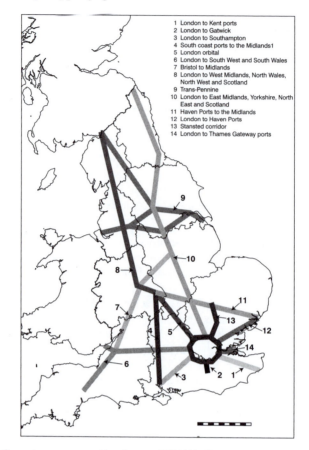

1 London to Kent ports
2 London to Gatwick
3 London to Southampton
4 South coast ports to the Midlands1
5 London orbital
6 London to South West and South Wales
7 Bristol to Midlands
8 London to West Midlands, North Wales,
    North West and Scotland
9 Trans-Pennine
10 London to East Midlands, Yorkshire, North
    East and Scotland
11 Haven Ports to the Midlands
12 London to Haven Ports
13 Stansted corridor
14 London to Thames Gateway ports

Figure 24.5 Strategic transport corridors (source: DfT 2008g Figure 4.1)

extension of rail electrification of the wider implementation of hard-shoulder running on motorways) as well as longer term solutions for the strategic transport corridors (including possible wholly new rail lines). To pilot the approach to be followed an initial case study has been undertaken into the London to the North-West corridor which is reported in Annex 1 of *DaSTS*.

24.8 Goals, challenges and the NATA refresh

Following the Stern Review the substance of the 2007 *TaSTS* White Paper is notable for being the first policy document published by DfT to make 'sustainability' (in the sense of CO_2 emissions) a key feature. (This is a mere 14 years after publication of the UK's Sustainable Development Strategy!) However the true character of the Paper is better encapsulated in its sub-title 'Supporting Economic Growth in a Low Carbon World' and in the Ministerial Foreword:

> Transport has a vital role to play in supporting sustainable economic growth, but I am clear that it must *also* play its part in the overall framework for reducing carbon emissions.

(DfT 2007s, emphasis added)

The objective of supporting economic growth, and its relationship to CO_2 reduction, has taken on a radically different complexion following the global financial crisis in the latter half of 2008 and the prospect of an economic recession deeper than any experienced previously since the Second World War. As far as transport is concerned the Government's initial response was reflected in the Ministerial Foreword by Geoff Hoon in the *DaSTS* document published towards the end of the year:

> When *TaSTS* was published economic prospects were good. Today the global economy is in trouble. Government, companies and households across the world have to think harder about their priorities. In the UK we need to support people and businesses through the downturn and help them emerge stronger on the other side[1]. We have thought hard about transport's contribution to this.
>
> The Government remains committed to investment and to tackling problems of congestion and crowding.... If we don't tackle them they will become a brake on economic growth and employment.
>
> We still want to cut transport's carbon footprint. It is wrong to think that, in a time of economic difficulty, we can put the climate change agenda on the back burner. ... Stern stresses the importance of tackling climate change in the most economically efficient manner. That means preserving freedom of choice, facing people with the true carbon cost of those choices, forcing the pace of technological change, and helping people reduce their need to travel or switch to lower-carbon modes. It does not mean rationing transport demand by constraining the capacity of our transport networks.
>
> (DfT 2008g)

In line with Eddington's recommendation about the importance of clarifying goals the 2007 Paper includes a chapter on the subject as the basis of discussion. The list offered (Box 24.4) is essentially a revamp of the five over-arching objectives included in the *New Deal* White Paper (Environment, Safety, Economy, Accessibility and Integration) and which have been used as the basis of the NATA appraisal framework in the decade since (Table 11.1).

Since the Paper does not refer directly to its predecessor it is not clear what policy significance should be attached to the changes proposed, or whether it is more a 'tidying-up' exercise. For example incorporating safety within a broader health and life-expectancy goal seems a matter of more logical structuring. On the other hand singling out CO_2 reduction as a separate goal, rather than retaining it as a sub-objective within the Environment group is said to signify the greater importance now to be attached to the subject. A consequence of this particular change is that most other issues within the former Environment objective are subsumed within a new 'quality of life' goal. This rather imprecise term is expressed in terms of improvements for transport users and non-users which rather implies that the protection of the natural environment exists only for the enjoyment of passing humans! (This idiosyncracy has been rectified in the revised wording adopted for the five goals included in *DaSTS*, also shown in Box 24.4).

---

1 As part of a Government-wide initiative to offset the effects of the impending recession the DfT in December 2008 accelerated £1bn of transport investment, including dualling of the A46 in Nottinghamshire, introducing more ATM schemes on the motorway network and an extra 200 train carriages plus a number of smaller projects serving ports and airports(*LTT 508*)]

The former Economy objective is redefined more specifically in terms of contributing to GDP growth whilst the accessibility objective is redefined in terms of 'greater equality of transport opportunity'. The Integration objective is dropped altogether. Taken together at face value these have rather peculiar implications. The comfort and convenience of people making ordinary journeys (previously incorporated as an element of economic efficiency) does not figure explicitly, but may come to be addressed as part of the 'quality of life' goal. Isolating equality of opportunity (= tackling social disadvantage) as a goal without reference to the desirability of improving accessibility (opportunities) for the population as a whole appears as an omission which may or may not be intended. It also severs the link with land use policies previously recognised under the Integration objective.

Some of these apparent anomalies may come to be rectified as part of the 'refresh' of the full NATA framework. This is an exercise which is being undertaken in parallel and includes further work on the measurement and valuation of particular types of impact following Eddington's recommendation that the scope of the monetised elements of the Department's 'Value for Money' assessments should be extended where practicable.

A consultation paper on the NATA Refresh (DfT 2007r) highlighted five areas in which the framework needed to be developed so that:

- more strategic analysis across modes could be undertaken at various levels in decision-making

---

Box 24.4 Future policy goals

Consultation version TaSTS (DfT 2007s)	Revised version DaSTS (DfT 2008g)
Maximising the overall competitiveness and productivity of the national economy, so as to achieve a sustained high level of GDP growth.	To support economic competitiveness and growth by delivering reliable and efficient transport networks.
Reducing transport's emissions of CO_2 and other greenhouse gases, with the desired outcome of avoiding dangerous climate change.	To reduce transport's emissions of carbon dioxide and other greenhouse gases, with the desired outcome of tackling climate change.
Contributing to better health and longer life-expectancy through reducing the risk of death, injury or illness arising from transport, and promoting travel modes that are beneficial to health.	To contribute to better safety, security and health and longer life-expectancy by reducing the risk of death, injury or illness arising from transport and by promoting travel modes that are beneficial to health.
Improving quality of life for transport users and non-transport users, including through a healthy natural environment, with the desired outcome of improved well-being for all.	To promote greater equality of opportunity for all citizens, with the desired outcome of achieving a fairer society.
Promoting greater equality of transport opportunity for all citizens, with the desired outcome of achieving a fairer society.	To improve quality of life for transport users and non-transport users, and to promote a healthy natural environment.

- 'better use' measures could be included within the options considered by promoters
- small-scale projects could be appraised proportionately
- levels of appraisal were identified appropriate to successive stages in the development of schemes
- guidance on some individual aspects, e.g. environmental impacts and reliability, could be strengthened.

The consultation paper referred to the Scottish Transport Appraisal Guidance, STAG, which distinguishes between a simpler, strategic level of analysis used at an initial stage and subsequent more detailed assessment of individual schemes (Transport Scotland 2008a). This minimises wasted time by the preliminary testing of potential solutions – a process which is also more accessible to non-experts and therefore facilitates public involvement. A further interesting example of such preliminary testing, using multi-criteria analysis (scoring of weighted objectives) has been applied in an exploratory study testing a wide range of intervention options to a controversial bypass scheme at Wing in Buckinghamshire (see Steer Davies Gleave 2007 and LTT 486).

The Refresh also provides the opportunity to remedy the present sprawling nature of the WebTAG guidance (Chapter 21 earlier) with clearer direction on its application to different levels of decision-making and distinguishing between mandatory and advisory elements. Other common criticisms to be investigated include the treatment of time savings which represent the aggregation of a large number of very small savings to individuals and the perceived bias against schemes which involve a loss of revenue to the Exchequer (notably fuel duty in the case of schemes which reduce car use). However more fundamental critiques have been submitted in response to the consultation (see Buchan and Goodwin in LTT 492). (An official summary of all responses has since been published – see DfT 2008f.) Whatever words are included in Government policy documents the power exerted by the appraisal system is such that the outcome of the Refresh exercise – and particularly the extent to which these more fundamental criticisms are addressed – will have a profound influence on future transport policy as it is actually executed.

The next stage in the Government's strategic planning process is to promote discussion on the main 'challenges' (problems and opportunities) to achieving its suggested goals. In support of this the 2007 White Paper includes an 'initial assessment' which is structured by the five goals and the four spatial levels at which they are to be addressed within the Department's cross-modal organisation (Figure 24.6). The international level is excluded here. This form of presentation has the disadvantage that individual types of intervention are linked with individual goals whereas several – e.g. the promotion of walking and cycling – contribute to some or all of them. Nevertheless the figure is reproduced here as the most recent indication of the issues on which options for the post-2014 plans are likely to focus.

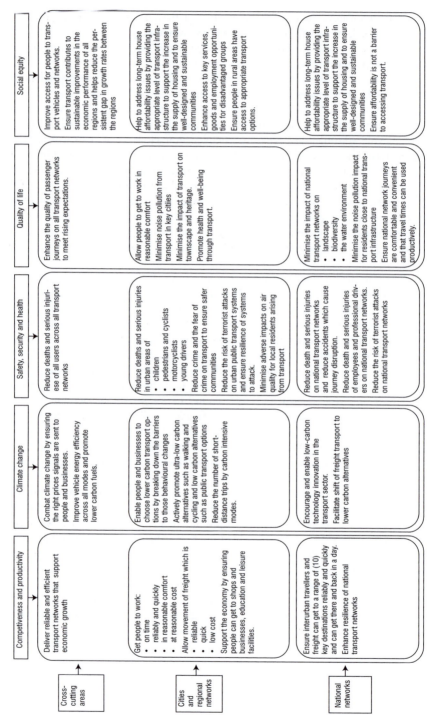

Figure 24.6 Initial assessment of challenges underlying transport goals (source: from DfT 2007's Figure 2.5)

25 Postscript

Thinking afresh

We really need to start working differently in the transport sector – we can't solve problems using the same thinking we used when we created them.

(Hickman and Banister 2006)

25.1 Introduction

This final chapter is different from the remainder in being a personal reflection – mainly on the strategic choices reported in the preceding chapter. The comments offered are not the product of a formal research exercise but are in the nature of 'conclusions' developed during the course of writing this book.

The historical, social and spatial planning perspectives which have been applied to transport policy at various points re-emerge here in the way its future is considered. Hopefully the reader will find the material an interesting counterpoint to the themes of conventional wisdom which have been reported thus far. Of course other authors have offered their own divergent views which perhaps warrant synthesis into an 'alternative' text (e.g. Whitelegg, Hillman and Plowden to name three of the most enduring) – but that would be a project in itself. However it is worth singling out the work by David Banister on the prospects for sustainable transport in an international context and his conclusions on the need for more imaginative thinking about the future (Banister 2005 Chapter 11). These set the context within which the more specific comments are made here about strategic policy in Great Britain.

We begin by arguing that behavioural change should be the basis on which future forecasts are generated, not as a means of tweaking the outcomes of a business-as-usual scenario (25.2). This requires that reducing traffic growth and protecting accessibility are viewed as priority objectives (25.3). An urban strategy is proposed based on lessening individual car ownership as this opens up the possibility of more discriminating travel choices (25.4). We then explore the need to rethink inter-urban travel as the erstwhile 'no go' area for reducing car use (25.5) and propose two policy initiatives to bring about better use of inter-urban roads and counter car dependence (25.6).

With the exception of halting inter-urban road-building these suggestions can be used to enhance the current trajectory of official policy. They are believed to be key steps which would enable transport to play its part in contributing to genuinely sustainable development.

25.2 A holistic view: behavioural change not business as usual

At present the strategic debate on transport tends to be dominated by the climate change agenda and the extent to which we in Great Britain could or should develop policies to reduce our reliance on fossil fuels and cut transport's contribution to CO_2 emissions. This is a rather precarious basis on which to conceive a long-term strategy because the costs and timescales involved in moving to widely available alternative technologies are very uncertain. As far as regulation and consumer behaviour is concerned the issue is also clouded by uncertainty over whether there will be political support for measures which appear to run counter to our short-term interests, individually and collectively. This is especially so if, as seems probable, there is a lack of global agreement to cut emissions with the result that we are faced with making 'sacrifices' unilaterally.

Arguably even more significant is the uncertainty which surrounds the availability and price of oil over the medium term. The fact that work undertaken using the National Transport Model for the 2004 White Paper adopted fuel costs of $16 a barrel for the 2030 reference case and that within only four years market prices had risen to $120 ought of itself to inject a much greater sense of precaution into strategic planning! Even if over the longer term technological and behavioural changes globally were to reduce demand for oil such that its price abated there is clearly a very uncertain and prolonged interim period. During this time the vulnerability of the British economy and individual lifestyles to the effects of intermediate shortages – possibly occasioned by international political upheaval – is very unsettling. In this context, to construct any strategy (as do the Eddington and the RAC Foundation reports) on the assumption of greatly increased vehicle use, and investing billions in road-building accordingly, appears reckless in the extreme.

The bizarre feature of the risks involved in these strategies is that planning for such increases is both unnecessary and undesirable. Considering sustainability more broadly than simply CO_2 emissions and energy sources there are a host of good reasons for pursuing a strategy based on less intensive car use:

> Transport policies that are the best to tackle it [global climate change] are, on the whole, the policies we ought to be pursuing for other reasons, even if the carbon problem were solved by a wonderful new chemistry tomorrow. It is a hugely fortunate irony. The reason why the transport sector may well be able to make a decisive contribution to carbon reduction is because there are other, less important, reasons for doing so.
>
> (P Goodwin in LTT 494)

The 'less important' reasons have to be put in the context of possible global catastrophe – not because they are unimportant by any ordinary standards. For example the long-term future of the nation's cities and countryside is at stake (see below) whilst inactive travel behaviour is a contributory factor threatening severe medical problems amongst a predominantly obese population by 2050 (DIUS 2007).

Goodwin points out that, even if nobody else did the same, we would not damage ourselves by choosing the low carbon route:

> Quite the reverse. Just imagine what would happen to fossil fuel prices if the world as a whole does not limit its dependence. In that case the minority of countries

that have re-engineered their whole structure of economic and leisure activities away from such an increasingly unobtainable or unaffordable commodity will have an efficiency premium of self-sufficiency and welfare.

(ibid.)

In any case it is quite wrong, as do Eddington and the RAC Foundation, to contemplate the future of transport without considering the spatial development context within which it will be operating and indeed whose objectives it should be serving. We have for the last 10–15 years begun to reverse the long-term trends of counter-urbanisation and to pursue policies of regeneration and urban renaissance. The economic, social and cultural capital of large towns and cities is being put to good use.

This is 'sustainable development' in its wider sense (ODPM 2005d) and includes reducing the need to travel, retaining local facilities, encouraging the use of non-car modes and maintaining opportunities for people without use of a car – a combination which offers economic, environmental, social and health benefits. The corollary of this strategy is to restrict significant development in rural areas, thereby enabling the protection of the countryside and its ecology and retaining it as a resource for local agricultural production, recreation and tranquility.

Proposals for major road investment around or between cities run completely counter to such a strategy by delivering a relative accessibility advantage to peri-urban areas and sites near junctions along the inter-urban corridors. This inevitably results in the dispersal of land use activity, in longer, mostly car-based trips and pressures for development in 'unsustainable' locations. We are currently living with the consequences of the 'first generation' of motorways and trunk roads in this respect and self-evidently do not need a second generation of this kind.

It is also amazing that the RAC Foundation imagines that an additional 'super-network' of inter-urban roads might ever gain political acceptance; if the first generation ground to a halt in the face of fierce public opposition in the 1990s a second is hardly likely to be welcomed in today's more sensitive environmental climate. If there is to be major new inter-urban infrastructure then this must surely take the form of rail lines which can operate with electric traction from the outset and which deliver accessibility advantages to urban centres and key regeneration and growth locations in the manner of the first high speed route to the Channel Tunnel.

It is just possible that, several decades hence, having completed the transition to low or zero carbon motoring, and with a continuing population increase, the case for additional capacity on main inter-urban roads may deserve to be reviewed. However, by that time this would almost certainly consist of more efficient utilisation of existing infrastructure (i.e. bringing individual vehicles under some degree of automated control to permit closer headways) rather than the primitive device of building new swathes of concrete across the countryside.

A further reason for needing to link the planning of inter-urban transport with the spatial development context is to consider the 'whole journey' of trips which are expected to constitute the additional demand on inter-urban roads. In a 'business as usual' scenario some of this growth in vehicle mileage would result from continued increases in trip length but most of it would be the product of population growth and of increases in car ownership. However this is to ignore the changing conditions which will characterise travel within towns and cities from where the bulk of trips will continue to start and finish.

The extent to which such growth will be physically possible varies from place to place. However with the increasing population size and density of urban areas it is inevitable that, because of greater congestion, or because of pricing or other measures taken to combat it, there will be pressures to substitute or shorten trips and to transfer to non-car modes. As is already evident in Inner London this could feed through into a slowing or decline in car ownership. A situation in which people come under increasing restraint on car use in towns but are expected to continue to utilise cars at will for travel between them is not only functionally inconsistent, it is also culturally incoherent. Prolonged exposure to higher oil prices and higher motoring taxes for larger cars will reinforce this. As now there will be sections of the population who prefer a car-dependent lifestyle and who – if they can afford it – will choose to live and work in places where they can maintain this, but as a proportion of the total they will reduce over time.

Such changes expose the fallibility of adopting a 'business as usual' scenario as the basis of strategic transport planning. The models which the Eddington and RAC Foundation studies adopt to produce their reference case forecasts are predicated on the absence of behavioural change. And yet, in the context just described, behavioural change is bound to be a major feature – more so if public policy is deliberately orientated to promote it. However the forecasts do have value in demonstrating what 'business as usual' would imply and hence in drawing attention to the extent of policy change which is needed if their predicted outcomes are not to materialise (if only as self-fulfilling prophesies). As Susan Owens observed more than a decade ago we need to move from thinking in terms of 'predict and provide' to 'predict and prevent' (Owens 1995).

As Hickman and Banister noted in the quotation heading this chapter it is not possible to change direction by taking as given those practices which have put us along our present path. We need to identify features of our present institutional and policy environment which were conceived at a time when circumstances were different and when the adverse consequences (as we now see them) were not or could not be appreciated. How might things have been done differently if we'd had the benefit of foresight and what opportunities are there to 'retro-fit' the necessary changes now?

There is potentially a very long list, but the focus here is on measures which

- could make a big difference
- if not wholly original, are outside current mainstream thinking
- should be politically deliverable.

By nature the measures are designed to release the potential for behavioural change, i.e. where there is good reason for believing there is suppressed demand, rather than seeking to bring about enforced change. That said, some complementary action would be logical and indeed all the measures are seen as proceeding in parallel with current best practice in sustainable transport. By strategic planning standards relatively modest expenditure would be involved, achieved mainly by reorientating the development programme of the Highways Agency. Continued – preferably enhanced – programmes of investment in rail and urban transit, local transport and road pricing are envisaged although the latter could well take the more selective and 'lower-tech' forms which Eddington acknowledged merited consideration (Eddington 2006b para 3.87).

25.3 Priority objectives: reducing traffic growth and protecting accessibility

Before exploring the measures which could contribute to large-scale behavioural change we need to reflect on the criteria which would be used to assess them. Clearly little progress would be made if, as now, business-as-usual criteria are used to assess policies which are aimed at something completely different! Hopefully the NATA refresh exercise will result in some changes being made in this direction, but probably not on a sufficiently radical scale.

The central problem with current planning and appraisal methods is that every potential intervention is viewed incrementally so that increases in car travel are judged to be benefits even though, in aggregate – over the longer term and taking account of second-order effects on land use activity – they ultimately make conditions worse. Accessibility may be maintained or even improved in the interim (for people with use of a car) but only through greater mobility and car dependence which cannot be sustained.

Our perception of what constitutes an 'improvement' would be fundamentally different if we were to adopt accessibility rather than mobility as our goal and to revise planning and appraisal procedures accordingly. The overall objective would then be to maintain or improve accessibility (opportunities) whilst minimising the costs involved in utilising them, i.e. by reducing the volume of travel and the share made in the form of single-occupancy vehicles. This has two further important corollaries:

1 'Transport planning' would be removed from its preoccupation with catering for movement and would embrace other means of promoting or safeguarding opportunities. These include use of ICT, home or local deliveries, land use planning and the management of public facilities. Conversely planning in other sectors should be required to account for (and minimise) its transport consequences. It is bizarre that, at present, the 'non-transport' arms of Government propose closures of post offices, GP surgeries, cottage hospitals, magistrates courts and the like in order to make financial savings whilst the transport arm proposes expenditure to cope with the increasing volume of travel and then uses time-savings as its principal justification!

2 'Accessibility planning' (in the sense in which it is employed in LTPs, i.e. to counter social exclusion) would become part of mainstream transport planning and not, as at present, treated as a form of residual damage limitation exercise, whilst the main investment strategies focus on catering for increased mobility. Critically, if increasing demands are met instead with measures to improve accessibility by modes other than the car, the *whole* population benefits and the growing polarisation in opportunities available to people with and without use of a car is avoided.

The idea that we should set out to reduce or limit traffic volumes as a central objective of national and local policies – and hence that we might adopt 'traffic reduction targets' – has been fiercely resisted by DfT (DETR 2000d). This is on the basis that traffic growth is not itself a problem but that traffic-related problems are (congestion, CO_2, pollution, safety etc.). Hence it is argued we should focus attention on – and set targets for – dealing with these problems as and where they occur and can be dealt with most cost-effectively.

There are two fundamental flaws with this argument:

1   The (growing) volume of traffic is a central factor in *all* the types of problem listed. Addressing them individually does not generate the synergy obtainable from overall traffic reduction. It is also in the nature of a 'sticking plaster' solution since one of their principal causes is unaddressed, and traffic growth will require continuing expenditure simply to prevent congestion and other problems from getting worse.
2   By confining action to particular types of problem at particular locations, conditions on the road network as a whole are unaffected. This accounts for the phenomenon (evident in LTP Delivery Reports) that, despite many individual 'improvements', overall conditions typically get worse. Without concerted action to reduce traffic in general it is inevitable that the present 'drop in the ocean' approach will at best achieve localised success, offset – or overwhelmed – by general failure.

Discussing traffic-related problems without addressing the issue of traffic growth is to ignore the elephant in the room. It means in effect that professional effort is channelled into types of action which in an immediate sense are less politically contentious, but which are ultimately ineffective. Practitioners' views on the need to register an unmistakeable paradigm shift were well demonstrated at a national conference on climate change in October 2007 supported by the TPS and RTPI where a succession of votes showed overwhelming support for both a national road traffic reduction target and a national target for reducing CO_2 emissions from transport (LTT 479).

25.4 Lessening individual car ownership

As Sir Colin Buchanan observed a half a century ago the motor-car is a 'mixed blessing' (Buchanan 1957). Since then both its advantages and disadvantages have become much more pronounced. It is strange therefore that public policy has not been directed more towards trying to ensure that the use of cars is concentrated on the types of journey for which it offers unique advantages. Clearly traffic congestion and parking difficulties prompt motorists to exercise greater discretion themselves on when and where they drive. (Road pricing would extend this further.) But set against this the continuing pattern of private car *ownership* has the perverse incentive of encouraging people to drive wherever possible in order to spread the unavoidable fixed costs (the financing of car purchase, depreciation, tax and insurance) over as many journeys as possible.

The growth of individual car ownership is a classic example of the 'tragedy of the commons'. At any point in time there is advantage to any one person in acquiring a car even though the additional mobility it brings is enjoyed at the expense of disadvantage incurred by everyone else. Not only is the efficient use of roadspace diminished but since the new car owner is not required to continue paying for the public transport services he or she used previously these become less economic and a downward spiral is created whereby progressively fewer and poorer people are left to pay for them. (Only residual 'socially necessary' services are funded from the public purse.) Left to run its course – as is already the case in many lower density suburban and dormitory areas – the eventual outcome is an unholy combination of excessive traffic on the one hand and minimal public transport on the other.

As we noted earlier (1.5) the distinctive feature of the last 30 years is that growth in car ownership has mostly taken the form of additional households with two or more cars. In other words we have moved from a situation in which the car was a household commodity to one in which it is increasingly the province of individual adults. It has also been an era characterised by counter-urbanisation and more suburban lifestyles so that for most people acquisition of a car has not been constrained by the availability of a parking space at either home or workplace. Car running costs have been relatively low so that little disadvantage has been incurred by households owning larger cars which are used to capacity on only rare occasions, or indeed from having a second car which is only used on odd days.

This situation is changing and will change a great deal further in the coming decades in the main urban areas where the bulk of additional population will live. The cumulative effect of development densification and restrictive parking provision will place a premium on available space at both home and workplace to be allocated through some combination of rationing or pricing. The areas over which comprehensive on-street parking control will apply will extend ever outwards from urban centres. Both national taxation and local charging can be expected to apply a greater differential according to vehicle size (strictly vehicle emissions) whilst the average cost of new cars within a particular class will rise in order to fulfil more stringent emissions standards. Higher car purchasing and/or running costs, coupled with more widespread traffic congestion and improved opportunities for travel by non-car modes on segregated or prioritised routes will result in motorists reviewing their options for individual journeys and whether to renew their vehicle ownership – and, if so, in what form.

Because car use is so strongly linked with levels of car ownership (2.9) it should be a central feature of public policy in urban areas to create the conditions in which it is attractive for their residents to reduce average car ownership levels over time. This can be done through three types of inter-linked measure (additional to 'conventional' demand management strategies):

1   through policies adopted in new residential developments
2   through improving and promoting opportunities for non-car travel for work and school journeys (i.e. those which are made daily)
3   through extending the spread and scope of personalised travel planning.

1) Policies in new residential developments

The more people's home circumstances are car-oriented the less likely they will choose modes other than a car for any particular journey. Attempts by public authorities to achieve modal shift on individual types of journey are therefore faced with an ever-bigger handicap to overcome. It is a travesty therefore that present national planning policy in England makes no reference to the desirability of designing and managing new housing developments in ways which will encourage reduced car ownership and use (PPS3 para 51). There is no requirement to prepare and maintain a residential travel plan for larger developments and no reference even to the Good Practice Guidelines on this subject which have been published by the Department of Transport (DfT 2005f). It should be axiomatic that all such developments have their own car clubs, car-hire and lift-share schemes or provide residents with links into schemes operating locally. In favourable situations the option of 'car-free' development should be examined (Morris 2005).

The provision of facilities offering the choice of car *use* for particular journeys (plus of course for walking, cycling and public transport as appropriate to the location) provides the context in which it is possible to encourage lower levels of private car *ownership* amongst residents. For those who do not need a car on a day-to-day basis there is the advantage of only paying for one when it is needed and being able to select a type of vehicle which is best suited to the journey being made. Further incentive can be introduced by requiring that a maximum of one private parking space is provided within the curtilage of each dwelling and that a minimum (possibly 50%) of the total residents' parking is provided in the form of separately rented spaces. The aim of this is to ensure that most households have to make a deliberate decision as to whether to utilise one or more additional rented spaces (and incur an on-going payment) and, of course, whether to own and run the private car(s) associated with them.

Whatever amount of residents' parking is provided within a development as a whole this arrangement ensures that the allocation between individual dwellings is not pre-determined. Hence the parking space actually used in relation to a particular dwelling can vary from one set of occupants to the next and a given household may vary its requirement during its stay according to changing circumstances. If for example one member did not need a car regularly for a period there would be an incentive for them to give up their vehicle and space during this time and to consciously rethink their options when their circumstances changed again.

2) *Improving and promoting opportunities for non-car travel for journeys to work, college and school*

Current local policies typically aim at 'modal shift' for work and education-related journeys in order to reduce the traffic-related problems at peak times and to complement restrictive parking policies at the destinations concerned. However such policies imply leaving household cars at home instead which are then available for travel at all other times.

Increasing opportunities for non-car travel to work etc. should not merely be to improve traffic conditions at peak times but be designed to remove the need for private car ownership in order to fulfil these daily travel needs. This then creates a situation in which the option of people using a mix of rented or shared cars plus other modes for remaining journeys (as suggested above) becomes attractive, and *overall* car mileage per household is reduced. It also opens the way for reduced parking provision and more efficient space utilisation within residential developments.

Two types of action are suggested to support this, both of which seek to redress historical anomalies. The first is to secure business support for non-car alternatives; the second is to improve the context for promoting walking and cycling.

As noted previously the growth in private car ownership has not been accompanied by any obligation on firms or households to contribute to maintaining the general standards of public transport service and accessibility. The ensuing spirals result in more congested traffic and parking conditions on the one hand and fewer, more expensive bus services on the other. Some firms have responded by moving to peripheral locations. This may ease conditions for access by car but at the price of almost complete car dependence and of effectively precluding people without a car from being employed if they live more than a short distance away. Current best practice concerning development location, workplace travel plans and developer contributions helps counter such trends in respect of new developments but leaves the bulk of (existing) workplaces untouched.

In theory Workplace Charging Levy powers could be used by local authorities as a means of generating funds from businesses in an area to support public transport improvements with the charging itself having a complementary role in discouraging employee parking provision. However, except where major city-wide investment is planned (as currently in Nottingham) a statutory approach on this scale seems unnecessarily heavy handed and should perhaps be regarded as a fall-back option in the event of lighter-touch partnership arrangements failing to materialise.

In the context of appropriate policies set out in an LTP, local authorities could work with groups of employers (e.g. in relation to a town centre or a suburban business park) with a view to declaring a number of 'business travel zones'. (Provision might be made for these to be registered statutorily, rather like Quality Bus Partnerships, to prevent 'free-riders'.) An independent travel management organisation would be established for each zone with income and expenditures entirely channelled through it, although with public funding to help kick-start schemes.

In these zones the proliferation of travel plans for individual organisations – whether devised voluntarily or as a condition of planning permission – could be avoided with firms becoming partners within the zonal body instead. Unlike the current situation with development-related travel plans, the zonal arrangements and firms' contributions would operate in perpetuity.

The activities of the travel organisation would be similar to those operating on behalf of individual firms, but on a much larger scale and with many economies derived from collective provision. Examples would be dedicated bus services to/from a nearby rail station, town centre or park-and-ride car park, employees' car-share schemes, facilities for cyclists, travelcard discounts and possibly on-site parking management arrangements. An advice service on accessibility and travel options could be offered to new staff when appointed and to existing staff when moving house. A valuable additional social dimension would be the right for any current or prospective employee living within the relevant Travel to Work Area to ask for special transport arrangements to be brokered where access by ordinary public transport was impracticable.

As far as journeys to school are concerned there is clearly major scope for increasing the proportion of children walking and cycling, possibly in organised groups, and reducing the number of parents for whom 'the school run' is a major factor in their consideration of car ownership. There are a host of conventional measures which could be applied in a more intensive form to achieve this (Sloman 2003), particularly through promotional programmes with schoolchildren and their parents. However these are always 'swimming against the tide' if they have to be deployed in areas where the presumption prevails that motorised traffic has priority.

At present the introduction of traffic calming and a speed limit below 30 mph has to be justified on an 'exceptions' basis. It is worth recalling that when the present standardised limit was set in built-up areas (in 1930) there were less than 4% of present vehicle numbers, and 'traffic' on residential streets (in the sense of continuous flows) was non-existent. Even by the indulgent standards of the time it is doubtful whether the present life-threatening conditions in residential streets would have been legislated for. Today a paradigmatic shift reasserting the safety and liveability of streets could be signalled by the Government adopting 20 mph as the default speed limit on unclassified roads within built-up areas (a change which would add barely a minute to each end of most car journeys) – and by publicising this to redress the climate of fear surrounding serious injury to pedestrians and cyclists. Additional home zones could be designated in which these modes were accorded automatic priority.

3) Extending the spread and scope of personalised travel planning

At present personalised travel planning is still in its infancy although, following experience in the 'Sustainable Towns' (16.6), similar programmes should become commonplace across the country during the coming decade. To date however the individual marketing and associated smarter choice measures have been presented in terms of the options available for different types of *journey*.

Within the strategic context being advanced here however the scope of these programmes should be extended to address more explicitly the options for reducing private car *ownership* and thus raising the potential for reduced car use on to an altogether higher plane – in effect 'demarketing' the private car (Wright and Egan 2000). This requires the pattern of trip making and vehicle ownership by households to be considered more holistically. Where the daily use of a car is not essential and where reduced car use is acknowledged to be desirable, different mixes of vehicle choice (car ownership, car club and car hire) should be explored *in conjunction with* different mode choices for regularly made journeys. Amongst many multi-person households retention of a 'family car' is likely to be seen as desirable but from a public perspective reducing the proportion of such households owning two or more cars (and thereby breaking the tendency to wholesale car dependence) would be an immensely valuable achievement.

With increasing complexity surrounding the capital, and running costs of cars of different efficiency ratings under different fuel price scenarios, independent advice should also be offered on the options available when the vehicles currently owned are replaced. The sort of change in purchasing behaviour being promoted by national policy on VED differentials would be enhanced if local authorities followed suit in residents' parking schemes.

On a more radical level there is scope for encouraging significantly smaller-sized vehicles (for ownership or rent) thus achieving further economies in fuel consumption and parking space requirements. Examples are the Smart car already in widespread use plus wholly new concepts such as city versions of golf buggies (Wright and Curtis 2005)! Like all 'new' modes their take-up is inhibited by existing infrastructure being designed around conventional cars. However pilot schemes could be invited from local authorities, promoters of eco-towns etc. in which, in conjunction with personalised marketing programmes, parking bays on street, in car parks and within residential developments would be allocated for car club and city cars at reduced rates.

This change in car purchasing behaviour would be best promoted in places where there were already good opportunities for making non-local trips by modes other than the car or where strategies are in place to bring this about. We explore this inter-urban dimension in the next two sections.

25.5 Rethinking inter-urban travel

Although 'traffic in towns' has traditionally been regarded as problematic it is in fact inter-urban travel which is the Achilles' heel of transport policy in the 21st century. Because urban trips are relatively short distance with a range of modes available it is possible to conceive of future 'solutions' following practices of demand management, targeted investment and smarter choices that are already well known – even though, as suggested in the previous section, they will need to be pursued more intensively. An enhanced version of 'business as usual', following the established policy trajectory and progressively extending best practice to all areas, is therefore plausible.

No such future beckons with inter-urban travel. As we have already demonstrated, business-as-usual scenarios which seek to accommodate prospective traffic demand over the long term are extremely risky, expensive and environmentally harmful. They also conflict with, rather than complement, the land use/transport strategies which will have to be followed in urban areas if sustainable development is to be secured overall. Even national road pricing, were it ever to materialise, would only diminish and not remove the problem. If one accepts that nothing new can be done to change inter-urban travel behaviour then indeed the various combinations of congestion, pricing and road-building presented in the RAC Foundation Study (24.6) are logically the only choices available. None of these are attractive propositions. Hence something new needs to be done and, as we will go on to argue here, can be done.

Currently 60% of car traffic occurs outside urban areas and 47% on motorways and A roads. As Stephen Potter pointed out from his analysis of NTS data in the 1990s only 1 in 7 trips is longer than 10 miles (and therefore likely to include an inter-urban component) but they account for nearly *two-thirds* of the overall distance travelled (Potter 1995). The proportion of medium and longer distance trips is increasing over time with trips in the 5–10 and 10–25 mile bands showing the greatest growth in volume and also the highest car mode share.

Even if the fuel requirement and emissions problems associated with this category of travel were magicked away tomorrow, the problem of how to accommodate the traffic physically (and reconcile it with restraint policies within urban areas) would remain.

The remarkable feature about the dominance of the car for medium and longer distance trips is that, even from an individual's perspective, it holds no clear advantages (other than privacy and carriage of bulky goods) over equivalent legs by coach or train for the main inter-urban part of the journey. In fact for car drivers it has the pronounced disadvantage that time and energy has to be spent driving rather than working, reading, relaxing or whatever. This 'truth' is reflected in the common practice of people using cars as a feeder mode to rail, even in situations where there is no prohibitive parking regime at the destination. However outside London, it is only on a handful of rail corridors that average train speeds and frequencies are high enough to attract people with the option of car use.

If incomes continue to rise, train services improve and inter-urban traffic congestion worsens then, as has occurred over the last decade (and as DfT modelling indicates) train use will rise, subject to capacity constraints. However even if the growth in inter-urban rail use was double that projected it would barely dent the forecast increase in road traffic.

The primary attraction of cars for medium and longer distance trips is the way that a single vehicle combines the very different functions of urban access and egress (requiring individualised routeing and slow speed) with the main inter-urban function (common routeing and high speed). In doing so it cuts out the inconvenience, uncertainty and time losses involved in interchange. Intriguingly this 'dual-mode' function is something of a historical accident with motor vehicles originally being developed to supersede horse-drawn ones on local roads. Their longer distance potential was only realised over subsequent decades through technical development and the building of purpose-built motorways etc.

If 'high speed' cars, like trains, had been confined to purpose-built roads from the outset then we might have conceived their 'interchanges' with local roads differently. Like railway journeys we would expect to use a variety of modes appropriate to urban use for the feeder/distribution function at either end, switching to a different type of vehicle geared to continuous high speed for the main inter-urban leg. As with early developments on the railways the original idea of people maintaining their own vehicle for use on the network would rapidly diminish in the face of the economies obtainable from utilising collective vehicles. (Only the Queen maintains the practice of her own train for personal use!)

During the 21st century it is very possible that the concept of an all-purpose motor vehicle will increasingly come to be seen as inefficient and inappropriate for fulfilling the overall mix of travel requirements. Because of the distinctive considerations surrounding feeder and line haul functions separate 'modes' for each will be developed instead, e.g. with motorways offering the facility for electronically coupled 'trains' of individual vehicles. With this futuristic scenario in mind we can move to explore the opportunities available in the shorter term to reduce the amount of car traffic between towns, complementing the more sustainable living patterns being advocated within them.

25.6 Better use of inter-urban roads

This section proposes two distinct but complementary initiatives designed to reduce the amount of car traffic associated with volume of inter-urban travel – the first on motorways, the second on other inter-town routes, mainly within more urbanised regions. Aside from their own merits these form part of the overall strategy being presented here to reduce cases where private car ownership is 'necessary' and thereby counter the growth of car dependence.

1) *Promoting choices for motorway journeys*

As we saw in Chapter 23 the Government has embarked on a programme investigating Active Traffic Management, including possible use of hard-shoulder running, as an alternative to widening some of the most congested sections of motorway. These schemes may include provision for one or more lanes to be reserved for particular classes of user – e.g. multi-occupied vehicles (MOV) or other vehicles paying a distance-related charge. This approach could be developed further to explore the potential which exists

- to increase the density of people travelling within a given traffic flow (hence permitting a greater passenger throughput)
- to offer additional travel choices for people making inter-urban journeys
- to link the development and management of motorways more closely with that of the main urban areas they serve.

Increasing passenger throughput without adding to vehicle numbers could be achieved by promoting MOV use and by greatly increasing the opportunities for coach travel. MOV use can be arranged informally (e.g. between friends or work-mates or through liftshare.com), encouraged by cost-savings and by preferential facilities such as reserved lanes and priorities at access points and junctions. The Highways Agency itself could foster more spontaneous lift-giving by arranging pick-up and set-down bays at service stations and other main interchange points, with signing (like bus stops) indicating the main destinations. This is a formalised version of hitch-hiking with the important difference that provision would be made for access to and from the pick-up points via the local road network, including by car with free parking for those taking lifts. (The Agency's views on extending the functions of MSAs are set out in a recent consultation document – see Highways Agency 2007.)

The same arrangements could also be used for people to access motorway coach services. (Coaches would also benefit from MOV lanes etc. introduced on the motorways themselves.) A major opportunity missed at the time motorways were built was to make provision for coach use for intermediate journeys. As a result frequent services are currently only available for journeys between the main cities (e.g. London–Birmingham or London–Bristol) where the 'end to end' demand justifies it. Even relatively large towns in between such as Coventry, Northampton or Swindon have much poorer levels of service because of their lower 'end to end' demand and/or because of the time losses incurred in deviating from the relevant motorway to access the central bus or coach station at more than one point along the route. These slow, infrequent but cheap and convenient through services cater for distinctive sections of the overall travel market (principally as an alternative to rail) but have little to offer would-be car drivers, particularly those whose trip origins or destinations lie in outer suburban, dormitory or rural areas.

Ironically it is precisely the development of motorways and the inter-urban road network generally which has encouraged the shift of households and businesses to these peripheral areas, but without any measures to facilitate public transport use for journeys between them. As a result inter-urban public transport (road and rail) is caught in something of a time-warp, catering best for those journeys between the main centres of population which were dominant two generations ago.

With strategic planning now focusing on urban regeneration the significance of these traditional patterns is recovering, but there remains a major part of the contemporary travel market which is inextricably linked with places where using the inter-urban road network is the obvious choice. Even in main corridors where frequent inter-urban rail services operate, car owners in these places are likely to find road use preferable for journeys up to 100 miles or so (other than to Central London) because of the time losses otherwise incurred in gaining access to and from the rail network. It is to this market that a new breed of motorway coach services should be aimed, at the same time providing much-improved travel opportunities for people without the use of a car living in outer suburban and peri-urban areas.

The Highways Agency should be empowered to contract these corridor services (in a similar fashion to franchised rail services) with open access provision for other services to utilise passenger facilities at the interchange points. Real-time information would be an essential feature. The DfT is in a position to adopt a strategic planning role in the integrated management and development of transport infrastructure and passenger services (road and rail) in the nation's principal corridors.

Although the concept of interchange points has been introduced here in the context of managing travel demand on motorways it is also significant in terms of urban transport planning. (It is essential therefore that their planning should proceed in partnership with local transport authorities.) The possibility of people travelling 'outwards' from urban areas on to motorways, changing modes at the interchange points is matched by the possibility – desirability in fact – of motorway users changing modes when travelling 'inbound'. In effect the interchange points become two-way

Table 25.1 Promoting travel choices for motorway journeys utilising new interchanges

	Access mode to motorway	Mode on motorway	Egress mode from motorway
Current options	Private car	Private car	Private car
	Hired car	Hired car	Hired car
	Coach	Coach	Coach
	Lift	Lift	Lift
Additional options	Private car	Private car	Urban mode*
		Coach	Urban mode*
			Hired car
		Lift	Urban mode*
			Hired car
	Urban mode*	Hired car	Urban mode*
			Hired car
		Coach	Urban mode*
			Hired car
		Lift	Urban mode*
			Hired car

*Urban mode = walk, cycle, public transport, taxi, city car, rented club car; or car passenger (lift)

Park and Ride sites as far as motorists are concerned. However the interchanges could be developed to cater for many more modal combinations than the present P&R sites, particularly if patterns of private vehicle ownership evolve in the manner suggested earlier. For example an urban resident might use a bus, bike, taxi, city car or a rented club car to access the motorway and then switch to a coach service, lift or conventional hired car depending on the nature of their journey. In the opposite direction someone arriving by car or coach would have option of switching to one of the urban modes, or of being picked up by a relative or work colleague as happens now at rail stations.

An illustration of the range of options envisaged is given in Table 25.1. They would offer much greater travel choice for individuals and contribute to reduced car use – hence congestion and emissions – both on motorways and in towns. They should eliminate the need for any additional inter-urban road-building. However the over-riding advantage of the package suggested is that, by moving away from wholesale car dependence, it would retain flexibility over the longer term in how the strategic road network was managed in the face of uncertain futures surrounding traffic growth, fuel prices, technological developments, and carbon-reduction targets.

2) Inter-town express services

A second example of where public transport is stuck in something of a time-warp concerns inter-town services in the south-eastern quarter of England and other urbanised regions. (The term 'inter-town' is used specifically to describe links between adjacent medium and large towns rather than the longer distances incorporated within 'inter-urban' journeys.) These links are important in the context of the growth of journeys in the 5–25 mile range mentioned earlier and the extent to which these are currently dominated by car use.

Orbital journeys between the main suburban centres (formerly separate towns) within Greater London and the other conurbations are a distinctive sub-set within this general category. As with the main inter-urban motorways the M25 around London and the equivalent orbital routes in the West Midlands and Greater Manchester have been built without any attempt to incorporate provision for public transport.

In the areas beyond the conurbations some of the inter-town links are catered for well by rail services which, in the main, radiate from London and from other regional and sub-regional centres. But many others either lost their rail services in the Beeching era or – more likely – were never rail connected. The pattern of bus services linking these towns typically reflects the era when each of them functioned as discrete markets for employment and other services. Although individual routes may run from town A to town B they have traditionally operated primarily to connect rural settlements in between with their respective 'market towns'.

Since the 1960s public authorities have intervened financially to support rural bus services, with enhancements funded by the Rural Service Bus Grant at the end of the 1990s. But the focus of public concern, and particularly of local elected members, has been with protecting accessibility and countering social exclusion within the smaller settlements. As a result services are often slow and meandering and their use for 'end to end' journeys is inevitably confined to people without the option of car use.

Over the last decade some commercial operators have recognised the opportunities which exist to make more attractive provision for the inter-town market, and major changes have been made in particular cases, e.g. to serve airports, out-of-town retail centres, hospitals and the like where there are concentrations of demand. But the traditional pattern is still strongly in evidence and even where inter-town improvements have been made, services are still relatively infrequent as operators are working from a very low patronage base. Planned interchanges with the rail network are rare and there is no comprehensive marketing of these services as a distinctive product.

This pattern has to be set in the context of substantial population growth in the Outer South-East in particular and of the transition in functional terms from 'freestanding towns' to urbanised sub-regions. Planning restrictions in these areas coupled with the workings of employment and housing markets typically results, in substantial 'enforced' commuting and other trip-making between separate towns for which there is no reasonable alternative for would-be car users. This is most strongly evident in the major growth areas of Milton Keynes/South Midlands and the Thames Gateway – areas which are ostensibly being developed as 'sustainable communities'!

Although local authorities are now empowered to pay for enhancements to commercial bus services the intervention required to bring service levels 'within scope' for people with the option of car use is completely beyond their means, even if they were minded to do so. In any case to make serious inroads into the present pattern of car-dominated behaviour would require a comprehensive strategy involving a network of services across local authority boundaries, with funding support and extensive marketing, plus complementary investment in passenger facilities and high quality vehicles. The institutional inability to fund such a strategy contrasts starkly with the hundreds of millions of pounds spent by the Government on supporting local rail services which – albeit patchily – deliver a similar function.

Given an overall policy context which, nominally at least, is founded on the principle of offering sustainable travel choices, the need to remedy this deficiency is glaring. Not doing so – and hence not being able to tackle car dependence in the areas referred to – is also extremely risky over the longer term as we are literally building new city regions without being able to guarantee the transport wherewithal to sustain them. Logically the development of integrated inter-town public transport networks needs to be planned and funded at the regional or sub-regional levels and would best accompany a devolution from Central Government of funding support for local rail services. This is a prospect which is emerging in Scotland and Wales but as yet can scarcely be glimpsed in the English regions.

25.7 Conclusion

This final chapter has focused on transport and the future of urban areas in Britain over the longer term bearing in mind the demands of a larger and wealthier population coupled with the need for sustainable development and the wisdom of adopting the precautionary principle.

It has been argued that a solution can be found by taking a holistic view, linking reduced car use on peak-time journeys with a broader strategy of lessening individual car ownership. This in turn provides scope for personalised marketing and sustainable transport programmes aimed at breaking the habit of people using their own cars as an all-purpose 'mode of first resort' for the very different requirements of urban and inter-urban journeys and for different journey purposes. Lessening the stock of conventional cars privately owned would have major benefits in more efficient and more attractive urban development.

The particular prescription offered here challenging conventional wisdom and the prolongation of 'business as usual' represents a personal view. There will be many other ideas and perspectives to be heard if in fact the official straitjacket is removed sufficiently to allow useful debate to take place.

Much of this book has concentrated on the means available for delivering prevailing policy objectives – since that inevitably is where the bulk of professional activity lies. But this should not obscure the more fundamental rationale of planning, which is to assert our collective ability to influence the future for the better and to illuminate the choices available as to what that future might be.

Bibliography

Publications of Government departments are listed separately. Note that, unless otherwise stated, the reports listed here prepared for DfT or other Government departments over the last decade are generally available via the relevant departmental website.

Addison L (2006) 'Securing residential travel plans through the development control process: a wasted opportunity?' in Marsden G (ed) *Wasted Miles, Wasted Money?* Cambridge, CICC

Aldous E (2000) 'Household expenditure on transport' in *Transport Trends (2000) Edition* London, TSO

Anable J (2005) 'Complacent Car Addicts' versus 'Aspiring Environmentalists'? Identifying travel behaviour segments using attitude theory' *Transport Policy* **12** 65–78

Anable J, Lane B and Kelay T (2006) *Review of Public Attitudes to Climate Change and Transport* Report for DfT

Atkins Transport Planning (2005) *Long Term Process and Impact Evaluation of the LTP Policy* Interim Report for DfT

Atkins Transport Planning (2007a) *Long Term Process and Impact Evaluation of the LTP Policy* Final Report for DfT

Atkins Transport Planning (2007b) *Review of Future Options for Local Transport Planning in England* Report for DfT

Atkins Transport Planning (2008) *Advice on the Prioritisation of Smaller Transport Schemes* Report for DfT

Bagwell P and Lyth P (2002) *Transport in Britain* London, Hambledon and London

Banister D (ed) (1998) *Transport Policy and the Environment* London, E&FN Spon

Banister D (2001) *Transport Planning* 2nd edition London, Spon

Banister D (2005) *Unsustainable Transport: City Transport in the New Century* London and New York, Routledge

Banister D and Berechman J (2000) *Transport Investment and Economic Development* London, UCL Press

Banks N, Bayliss D and Glaister S (2007) *Roads and Reality* London, RAC Foundation for Motoring

Barker K (2004) *Barker Review of Housing Supply* Report to HM Treasury and ODPM London, TSO

Barker K (2006) *Barker Review of Land Use Planning* Report to HM Treasury and DCLG London, TSO

Barker T (ed) (1987) *The Economic and Social Effects of the Spread of Motor Vehicles* London, Macmillan

Barker T and Savage C (2005) *An Economic History of Transport in Britain* Abingdon, Routledge (first published by Hutchinson, 1959)

Beesley M (1964) 'Urban form, car ownership and public policy – an appraisal of traffic in towns' *Urban Studies* **1**(2) Oliver & Boyd

Begg D (2003) Foreword in Docherty I and Shaw J (eds) *A New Deal for Transport?: The UK's Struggle with the Sustainable Transport Agenda* Oxford, Blackwell Publishing

Bendixson T (1974) *Instead of Cars* London, Temple Smith

Bonsall P and Milne D (2003) 'Urban road user charging and workplace parking levies' in Hine J and Preston J (eds) (2003) *Integrated Futures and Transport Choices* Aldershot, Ashgate

Bradshaw R et al. (2000) *The Family and the School-Run* Report by Transport Studies Group, University of Westminster for AA Foundation for Road Safety Research

Breheny M (1995) 'Counter-urbanisation and sustainable urban forms' in Brotchie J, Batty M, Blakely E, Hall P and Newton P (eds) *Cities in Competition* Melbourne, Longman Australia

Breheny M, Gent I and Lock D (1993) *Alternative Development Patterns: New Settlements* Report for DOE London, HMSO

Brindley T, Rydin Y and Stoker G (1989) *Remaking Planning: The Politics of Urban Change in the Thatcher Years* London, Unwin Hyman

Briscoe B (2007) 'Shaping places' *Town and Country Planning* **76**(5) London, TCPA

Brog W (2003) 'Reducing car use ? – just do it!' in Roberts S (ed) *Sharing in Success: Good news in Passenger Transport* Cambridge, CICC

Buchanan C (1957) *Mixed Blessing: The motor car in Britain* Leonard Hill

Bus and Coach Council (1991) *Buses Mean Business*

Button K (1993) *Transport Economics* 2nd edn Aldershot, Edward Elgar

Cairns S, Sloman L, Newson C, Anable J, Kirkbride A and Goodwin P (2004) *Smarter Choices: Changing the Way We Travel* Report for DfT

CBI (1989) *The Capital at Risk* and *Trade Routes to Europe* London

CfIT (1999) *National Traffic Reduction Targets*

CfIT (2002a) *Paying for Road Use*

CfIT (2002b) *Public Subsidy for the Bus Industry* Report by LEK Consulting

CfIT (2003) *10 Year Transport Plan – second assessment report*

CfIT (2006) *Are We There Yet? – a comparison of transport in Europe*

CfIT (2007) *Transport and Climate Change*

Champion T and Dorling D (1994) 'Population change for Britain's functional regions 1951–91' *Population Trends* no 77 pp14–23

Chatterjee K and Gordon A (2006) 'Planning for an unpredictable future: transport in Great Britain' *Transport Policy* **13** 254–264

Chatterjee K, Harman R and Lyons G (2004) *Local Strategic Partnerships, Transport & Accessibility* Report by University of West of England for DfT

Cheek C (2008) 'Does the UK bus industry have a platform for growth or is it doomed to decline?' *Local Transport Today* 485

Cherry G (1972) *Urban Change and Planning* Henley on Thames, Foulis

Coburn T, Beesley M and Reynolds D (1960) *The London–Birmingham Motorway: Traffic and Economics* Technical Paper 46 Crowthorne, Road Research Laboratory

Cole S (2003) 'Changing organisational frameworks and patterns of governance' in Hine J and Preston J (eds) (2003) *Integrated Futures and Transport Choices* Aldershot, Ashgate

Countryside Agency (2000) *Great Ways to Go: Good Practice in Rural Transport*

CPRE (2006) *Saving Tranquil Places* London

Cullinane S and Stokes G (1998) *Rural Transport Policy* Oxford, Pergamon

Cullingworth B and Nadin V (2006) *Town and Country Planning in the UK* 14th edn Abingdon, Routledge

Curtis C and Headicar P (1997) 'Targeting public awareness campaigns: Which indiviudals are more likely to switch from cars to other forms of transport for the journey to work?' *Transport Policy* **4**(1) 57–65.

Dearlove J and Saunders P (2000) *Introduction to British Politics* 3rd edn Cambridge, Polity

Dickson M (2000) 'Characteristics of the escort education journey' in *Transport Trends (2000) Edition* London, TSO

Docherty I and Shaw J (eds) (2003) *A New Deal for Transport?: Struggle with the Sustainable Transport Agenda* Oxford, Blackwell Publishing

Docherty I and Shaw J (eds) (2008) *Traffic Jam: Ten Years of 'Sustainable' Transport in the UK* Bristol, Policy Press

Dorling D and Thomas B (2004) *People and Places* Bristol, Policy Press

Dunleavy P and O'Leary B (1987) *Theories of the State: The Politics of Liberal Democracy* Basingstoke, Macmillan

ECOTEC Research and Consulting Ltd (1993) *Reducing Transport Emissions Through Planning* (report for DOE and DTp) London, HMSO

Eddington R (2006a) *The Case for Action: Sir Rod Eddington's Advice to Government* Report to HM Treasury and DfT London, TSO

Eddington R (2006b) *The Eddington Transport Study: Transport's Role in Sustaining the UK's Productivity and Competitiveness Main Report* Report to HM Treasury and DfT London, TSO

Elson M (1986) *Green Belts: Conflict Mediation in the Urban Fringe* London, William Heinemann

Evans P (ed) (1992) *Where Motor Car is Master* London, CPRE

Faludi A (1989) *A Decision-Centred View of Environmental Planning* Oxford, Pergamon

Farthing S, Winter J and Coombes T (1996) 'Travel behaviour and local accessibility to services and facilities' in Jenks M, Burton E and Williams K (eds) *The Compact City : A Sustainable Urban Form?* London, E&FN Spon

Ford R (2007) 'Informed sources' *Modern Railways* September

Foster C (2005) *British Government in Crisis* Oxford, Hart Publishing

GfK Consumer Services (2008) *Public Attitudes to Transport: DfT's On-line Citizen's Panel 'Wave 1'* Report to Department for Transport.

Giddens A (1998) *The Third Way: The Remaking of Local Democracy* Cambridge, Polity Press

Gillespie A (1999) 'The changing employment geography of Britain' in Breheny M (ed) *The People – Where Will They Work?* London, Town and Country Planning Association

Gillespie A, Healey P and Robins K (1998) 'Movement and mobility in the post-Fordist city' in Banister D (ed) (1998) *Transport Policy and the Environment* London, E&FN Spon

Glaister S, Burnham J, Stevens H and Travers T (2006) *Transport Policy in Britain* 2nd edn Basingstoke Palgrave Macmillan (1st edn 1998)

Glasson J and Marshall T (2007) *Regional Planning* London, Routledge

Goodwin P (2003) 'Towards a genuinely sustainable transport agenda for the United Kingdom' in I. Docherty and J Shaw (eds) *A New Deal for Transport?: The UK's Struggle with the Sustainable Transport Agenda* Oxford, Blackwell Publishing

Goodwin P, Hallett S, Kenny F and Stokes G (1991) *Transport: The New Realism* Report for Rees Jeffreys Road Fund by Transport Studies Unit, Oxford University

Goodwin P et al. (1995) *Car Dependence* Report by ESRC Transport Studies Unit, Oxford University for RAC Foundation for Motoring and the Environment, London

Grant S (2006) 'The (2007) Beeching Report – a preview' *Modern Railways* July

Haigh N and Lanigan C (1995) 'Impact of the EU on UK environmental policy-making' in Gray T (ed.) *UK Environmental Policy in the 1990s* Basingstoke, MacMillan

Halcrow Group (2007) *Assessment of Network Management Duties within Local Transport Plans* Report for DfT

Hall P (1980) *Great Planning Disasters London,* Weidenfeld & Nicholson

Hall P et al. (1973) *The Containment of Urban England* London, Allen & Unwin

Hamilton K and Potter S (1985) *Losing Track* London, Routledge and Kegan Paul in association with Channel 4

Hanley F and Spash C (1993) *Cost-Benefit Analysis and the Environment* Aldershot, Elgar

Headicar P (1996) 'The local development effects of major new roads: M40 case study' *Transportation* **23** 55–69

Headicar P (2000) 'The exploding city region: can it – should it – be reversed?' in Williams K, Burton E and Jenks M (eds) (2000) *Achieving Sustainable Urban Form* London, E&FN Spon

Headicar P (2003) 'Land use planning and the management of transport demand' in Hine J and Preston J (eds) (2003) *Integrated Futures and Transport Choices* Aldershot, Ashgate

Headicar P (2004) *Planning for a Step Change in Rural Passenger Transport* Report for Kennet Passengers; accessible at http://www.kennetandbeyond.co.uk/news_reports.shtml

Headicar P (2008) 'Trends in car ownership, use and dependence: their implications for a sustainable transport agenda' in M. Higgitt (ed) *Transport Policy in Transition* Cambridge, CICC

Headicar P and Curtis C (1996) *The Influence of Previous Experience on Current Travel Behaviour and Attitudes* Report for ESRC School of Planning, Oxford Brookes University

Headicar P and Curtis C (1998) 'The location of new residential development – its influence on car-based travel' in Banister D (ed) (1998) *Transport Policy and the Environment* London, E&FN Spon

Healey P (1997) *Collaborative Planning: Shaping Places in Fragmented Societies* Basingstoke, Macmillan

Hickman R and Banister D (2006) *Looking Over the Horizon: Visioning and Backcasting for UK Transport Policy (VIBAT)* Bartlett School of Planning and Halcrow Group Ltd

Higgitt M (2007) 'Smarter choices: its future application' in Whyte D (ed) *Transport Challenges Facing the UK: Major Scheme Funding and the Environment* Cambridge, CICC

Highways Agency (2007) *Roadside Facilities Policy Review* Public consultation

Hill M (2005) *The Public Policy Process* 4th edn Harlow, Pearson Education

Hillman M (1973) (with Henderson I and Whalley A) *Personal Mobility and Transport Policy* PEP Broadsheet 542 London, Policy Studies Institute

Hillman M and Whalley A (1980) *The Social Consequences of Rail Closures* London, Policy Studies Institute

Hillman M, Adams J and Whitelegg J (1990) *One False Move? – A Study of Children's Independent Mobility* PSI Report 707, London, Policy Studies Institute

Hills P (1974) 'Transport and communications' in Cherry G (ed) *Urban Planning Problems* Leighton Buzzard, Leonard Hill Books

Hine J and Preston J (eds) (2003) *Integrated Futures and Transport Choices* Aldershot, Ashgate

House of Commons (1973) *Urban Transport Planning*, 2nd report from the Expenditure Committee session 1972/73

House of Commons (2002) *The Ten Year Plan for Transport* 8th report of the Select Committee on Transport, Local Government and the Regions

House of Commons (2005) *Road Pricing: The Next Steps* 7th report of the Transport Committee

House of Commons (2006a) *How Fair Are the Fares? Train Fares and Ticketing* Government Response to the Transport Committee's Sixth Report of Session 2005–06 Thirteenth Special Report 2006

House of Commons (2006b) *Reducing Carbon Emissions from Transport* 9th Report of the Environmental Audit Committee

IHT (1997) *Transport in the Urban Environment*

IHT (1999) *Rural Safety Management Guidelines*

IHT (2003) *Urban Safety Management Guidelines*

IHT (2005) *Parking Strategies and Management*

IPPR (2006) *Steering Through Change: Winning the Debate on Road pPicing*

ITP Ltd (2005) *Making Car Sharing and Car Clubs Work* Report for DfT

Jain J and Lyons G (2008) 'The gift of travel time' *Journal of Transport Geography* **16** 81–89

Jones M (2007) *Upstairs Downstairs: The Impact of Vehicle Type on Bus Passengers' Perception of Personal Security* Unpublished MSc dissertation, Department of Planning, Oxford Brookes University

Jones P et al. (1983) *Understanding Travel Behaviour* Aldershot, Gower

Jones P et al. (1996) *Public Attitudes to Transport Policy and the Environment* Report by Transport Studies Group, University of Westminster to Department of Transport

Jones P, Boujenko N and Marshall S (2007) *Link and Place: A Guide to Street Planning and Design* London, Local Transport Today

Leibling D (2007) *Trends in Modal Shift: An Analysis of the British Social Attitudes Survey* Report for RAC Foundation for Motoring

Levett R (2007) 'Misconstrued problems; misconceived solutions' *Town & Country Planning* **76**(9)

Llewelyn Davies and JMP Consultants (1998) 'Parking Standards in the South-East' Report for DETR

Lloyd M and Peel D (2007) 'Strategic planning in Scotland' *Town Planning Review* **78**(3)

Lyons G and Kenyon S (2006) *INTERNET: Investigating New Technologies Evolving Role, Nature and Effects for Transport* Research report for EPSRC accessible at www.transport.uwe.ac.uk/research/projects

Lyons G et al. (2007) *Strategic Review of Travel Information Research* Report to DfT

Mackett R (2001) 'Policies to attract drivers out of their cars for short trips' *Transport Policy* **8** 295–306

Mackie P (1998) 'The UK Transport Policy White Paper' *Journal of Transport Economics and Policy* **32** 399–404

MacKinnon D, Shaw J and Docherty I (2008) *Diverging Mobilities?: Devolution, Transport and Policy Innovation* Oxford and Amsterdam, Elsevier

Maddison D and Pearce D (1995) 'The UK and Global Warming Policy' in Gray T (ed) *UK Environmental Policy in the 1990s* Basingstoke, MacMillan

Mann E (2005) 'Personal choices in transport' in Hills V (ed) *Transport Excellence Through Practical Delivery* Cambridge, CICC

Marsden G (2006) 'The evidence base for parking policies – a review' *Transport Policy* **13** 447–457

Marsden G and Bonsall P (2006) 'Performance targets in transport policy' *Transport Policy* **13** 191–203

Marshall T (2004) 'Regional planning in England' *Town Planning Review* **75**(4)

May A (1991) 'Integrated transport strategies: a new approach to urban transport policy formulation in the UK' *Transport Reviews* **11**(2)

May A, Kelley C and Shepherd S (2006) 'The principles of integration in urban transport strategies' *Transport Policy* **13** 319–327

McKinnon A (2003) 'Sustainable freight distribution' in Hine J and Preston J (eds) (2003) *Integrated Futures and Transport Choices* Aldershot, Ashgate

Metz D (2008) 'The myth of travel time saving' *Transport Reviews* **28** 321–336

Mitchell C (2000) 'Transport in an ageing society' in *Transport Trends (2000) Edition* London, The Stationery Office

MORI (Market & Opinion Research International) (2001) *Public Attitudes to Transport in England* London, Commission for Integrated Transport

Morphet J (2007) 'A meta-narrative of planning reform' *Town Planning Review* **78**(2)

Morris D (2005) 'Car-free development: the potential for community travel plans' *Proceedings of UTSG Conference, Bristol*

Moseley M, Harman R, Coles O and Spencer M (1977) *Rural Transport and Accessibility* Report by the University of East Anglia to the Department of the Environment

MVA (2004) *Integration of Regional Transport Strategies with Spatial Planning Policies* Report to DfT

MVA Consultancy (1995) *The London Congestion Charging Research Programme – Principal Findings and Final Report* London, HMSO

Nairn I (1957) *Counter-attack Against Subtopia* London, Architectural Press

Nash C (2003) 'Rail regulation and competition – developments since 1997' in Hine J and Preston J (eds) (2003) *Integrated Futures and Transport Choices* Aldershot, Ashgate

National Audit Office (1999) *Examining the Value for Money of Deals under the Private Finance Initiative*

Newbery D (1994) 'The case for a public road authority' *Journal of Transport Economics and Policy* **28** 325–354

Nichols M (2007) *Review of the Highways Agency's Major Roads Programme* Report to DfT

Noble B (2000) 'The travel behaviour of older people' in *Transport Trends* (2000 edition)

Nutley S (1990) *Unconventional and Community Transport in the United Kingdom* New York, Gordon and Breach

O'Connell S (1998) *The Car in British Society: Class, Gender and Motoring 1896–1939* Manchester University Press

O'Riordan T and Cameron J (1995) *Interpreting the Precautionary Principle* London, Earthscan Publications

Operational Research Unit (2005) *Personalised Travel Planning: Evaluation of 14 Pilots Part Funded by DfT* Report to DfT

Ove Arup and Partners (1997) *Planning Policy Guidance on Transport (PPG13): Implementation 1994–1996* Report to DETR

Owens S (1995) 'Predict and provide or predict and prevent?: pricing and planning in transport policy' *Transport Policy* **2** 43–49

Pearce D, Markandya A and Barbier E (1989) *Blueprint for a Green Economy* Report to the UK Department of the Environment London, Earthscan Publications

Plowden S (1972) *Towns Against Traffic* London, Andre Deutsch

Plowden W (1971) *The Motor Car and Politics in Britain* London, Bodley Head

Potter S (1993) 'Transport, environment and fiscal policies: on the road to change?' *Policy Studies* **14** (2)

Potter S (1995) 'The trip length surge' in *Transportation Planning Systems* **3** (1) London, Landor

Potter S, Enoch M and Rye T (2003) 'Economic instruments and traffic restraint' in Hine J and Preston J (eds) (2003) *Integrated Futures and Transport Choices* Aldershot, Ashgate

Preston J (2003) 'A thoroughbred in the making? – the bus industry under Labour' in Docherty I and Shaw J (eds) (2003) *A New Deal for Transport?: Struggle with the Sustainable Transport Agenda* Oxford, Blackwell Publishing

Quinet and Vickerman R (2004) *Principles of Transport Economics* Cheltenham, Edward Elgar

Rawls J (1999) *A Theory of Justice* Oxford, Oxford University Press

RCEP (1994) *Transport and the Environment* 18th report London, HMSO

RCEP (1997) *Transport and the Environment: Developments Since (1994)* 20th report London, TSO

Richards B (1966) *New Movement in Cities* London and New York, Studio Vista/Reinhold

Richards B (2001) *Future Transport in Cities* London, Spon Press

SACTRA (1980) *Trunk Road Proposals: A comprehensive framework for appraisal* London, HMSO

SACTRA (1992) *Assessing the Environmental Impact of Road Schemes* London, HMSO

SACTRA (1994) *Trunk Roads and the Generation of Traffic* London, HMSO

SACTRA (1999) *Transport and the Economy* London, TSO

Shaw J and Farrington J (2003) 'A railway renaissance?' in Docherty I and Shaw J (eds) (2003) *A New Deal for Transport?: Struggle with the Sustainable Transport Agenda* Oxford, Blackwell Publishing.

Simmonds D and Coombe D (2000) 'The transport implications of alternative urban forms' in Williams K, Burton E and Jenks M (eds) (2000) *Achieving Sustainable Urban Form* London, E&FN Spon

Sissons Joshi M and Maclean M (1995) 'Parental attitudes to children's journey to school' *World Transport Policy and Practice* **1** (4)

Sloman L (2003a) *Less Traffic Where People Live* Machynlleth, Transport for Quality of Life

Sloman L (2003b) *Rural Transport Futures* London, Transport 2000

Smyth A (2003) 'Devolution and sustainable transport' in Docherty I and Shaw J (eds) (2003) *A New Deal for Transport?: Struggle with the Sustainable Transport Agenda* Oxford, Blackwell Publishing.

Social Exclusion Unit (2003) *Making the Connections: Final Report on Transport and Social Exclusion* London, TSO

Starkie D (1982) *The Motorway Age: Road and Traffic Policies in Post-war Britain* Oxford, Pergamon

Stead D (2001) 'Relationships between land use, socio-economic factors and travel patterns in Britain' *Environment and Planning B* **26** 499–528

Steer Davies Gleave (2007) *Alternatives to the A418 Improvements* Report for Friends of the Earth and Buckinghamshire County Council accessible at www.wingbypass.info/

Stoker G and Wilson D (2004) *British Local Government into the 21st Century* Basingstoke, Palgrave Macmillan

Stradling S (2003) 'Reducing car dependence' in Hine J and Preston J (eds) (2003) *Integrated Futures and Transport Choices* Aldershot, Ashgate

Sullivan H (2004) 'Community governance and local government' in Stoker G and Wilson D (2004) *British Local Government into the 21st Century* Basingstoke, Palgrave Macmillan

Sutton Trust (2006) *No More School Run*

TAS Partnership (2007) *Park and Ride in Great Britain*

Taylor B and Brooke L (1998) 'Public attitudes to transport issues: findings from the British Social Attitude Surveys' in Banister D (ed) (1998) *Transport Policy and the Environment* London, E&FN Spon

Tetlow J and Goss A (1965) *Homes, Towns and Traffic* London, Faber and Faber

TfL (2006) *Central London Congestion Charging Impacts Monitoring: Fourth Annual Report*

TfL (2007) *LIP Annual Progress Report Guidance 2008/09–2010/11*

Thomson M (1969) *Motorways in London* London, Gerald Duckworth

TRL (2006) *Development of a Speed Limit Strategy for the Highways Agency*

Tyme J (1978) *Motorways versus Democracy: Public Inquiries into Road Proposals and their Political Significance* London, MacMillan

Urry J (2007) *Mobilities* Cambridge, Polity Press

Verplanken B, Aarts H, van Kippenberg A and Knippenberg C (1994) 'Attitudes versus general habit: antecedents of travel mode choice' *Journal of Applied Psychology* 24 285–300

Vigar G (2002) *The Politics of Mobility* London, Spon Press

Vigar G, Healey P, Hull A and Davoudi S (2000) *Planning, Governance and Spatial Strategy in Britain* Basingstoke, Macmillan

Walton W (2003) 'Roads and traffic congestion policies' in Docherty I and Shaw J (eds) (2003) *A New Deal for Transport?: Struggle with the Sustainable Transport Agenda* Oxford, Blackwell Publishing

Ward S (1994) *Planning and Urban Change* London, Paul Chapman Publishing

White B (2006) *Residential Parking in the Real World* Kent Highway Services

White P (2009) *Public Transport: Its Planning, Management and Operation* 5th edn London, Routledge

Whitelegg J *Critical Mass: Transport, Environment and Society in the 21st Century* London, Pluto

Williams K, Burton E and Jenks M (eds) (2000) *Achieving Sustainable Urban Form* London, E&FN Spon

Wolmar C (2001) *Broken Rails* London, Aurum Press

Wood C (2007) 'Changes to development plans: how good? how radical?' *Town Planning Review* 78(2)

Wright C and Curtis B (2005) 'Reshaping the motor car' *Transport Policy* 12 11–22

Wright C and Egan J (2000) 'Demarketing the car' *Transport Policy* 7 287–294

WS Atkins (1999) *Assessing the Effect of Transport White Paper Policies on National Traffic* Report for DETR

WSP and Arup (2005) *Impacts of Land Use Planning Policy on Transport Demand and Congestion* (Research report for DfT) Cambridge, WSP Policy and Research accessible at http://www.wspgroup.com/upload/documents/PDF/news%20attachments/PPG13_Final_Report.pdf

WSP Ltd (2007) *Residential Car Parking* Research Report to DCLG

Government publications

[Published in London by TSO (The Stationery Office) – formerly HMSO. Most publications since1997 are also available on the relevant departmental website.]

Ministry of Transport (MOT) to 1970
Ministry of Housing and Local Government (MHLG) to 1970

MOT (1946) *The Design and Layout of Roads in Built Up Areas*
—— (1961) *Rural Bus Services* (Report of the Jack Committee)
—— (1963) *The Reshaping of British Railways* (The Beeching Report)
MOT and MHLG (1963) *Traffic in Towns: A Study of the Long Term Problems of Traffic in Urban Areas* (The Buchanan Report)
—— (1964) *Traffic in Towns* Circular 1/64
MOT (1964) *Road Pricing: The Economic and Technical Possibilities* (The Smead Report)
—— (1965) *The Development of the Major Trunk Routes*
MHLG and MOT (1965) *The Future of Development Plans* Report of the Planning Advisory Group
MHLG (1965) *Parking in Town Centres* Planning Bulletin 7
MOT (1966) *Transport Policy* Cmnd 3057
—— (1967a) *Better Use of Town Roads*
—— (1967b) *Cars for Cities* Report of a Working Group led by J Garlick
—— (1967c) *Public Transport and Traffic* Cmnd 3481
—— (1968) *Traffic and Transport Plans* Circular 1/68
—— (1969) *Roads for the Future: A New Inter-Urban Plan* Consultation Paper
—— (1970) *Roads for the Future: A New Inter-Urban Plan* Cmnd 4369

Department of the Environment (DOE) 1970–97
Department of Transport (DTp) 1977–97

DOE (1972a) *New Roads in Towns* Report of the Urban Motorways Project Team
—— (1972b) *Roads in England 1971*
—— (1973) *Local Transport Grants* Circular 104/73
—— (1976) *Transport Policy: A Consultation Document*
—— (1983) *Streamlining the Cities: Government Proposals for Reorganising Local Government in Greater London* Cmnd 9063
—— (1985) *Lifting the Burden* Cmnd 9571
—— (1993) *PPG6 Planning for Town Centres* [Revised as PPS 6 2005]
DOE et al. (1990) *This Common Inheritance: Britain's Environmental Strategy* Cm 1200
DOE and DTp (1994) *PPG13 Transport*
DOE et al. (1994) *Sustainable Development: The UK Strategy* Cm 2426

DTp (1977) *Transport Policy* Cmnd 6836
—— (1978a) *Policy for Roads, England 1978* Cmnd 7132
—— (1978b) *Report of the Advisory Committee on Trunk Road Assessment* (chaired by G Leitch)
—— (1978c) *Review of Highway Inquiry Procedures* Cmnd 7133
—— (1983a) Manual of Environmental Appraisal
—— (1983b) *Railway Finances* Report of a Committee chaired by Sir David Serpell
—— (1984) *Buses* Cmnd 9300
—— (1989a) *Funding of Light Rail Schemes* Circular 3/79
—— (1989b) *National Road Traffic Forecasts (Great Britain)* HMSO
—— (1989c) *New Roads by New Means – Bringing in Private Finance* Cm 698
—— (1989d) *Roads for Prosperity* Cmnd 693
—— (1990) *Trunk Roads England: Into the 1990s*
—— (1993) *Paying for Better Motorways* Cm 2200
—— (1995a) *Better Places Through Bypasses: Report of the Bypass Demonstration Project*
—— (1995b) *Decriminalised Parking Enforcement Outside London* Local Authority Circular 1/95
—— (1995c) *The Way Ahead* Speeches by Dr B MacWhinney, SoS for Transport, launching the 'Great Debate'
—— (1995d) *Trunk Roads in England: 1995 Review*
—— (1996a) *The National Cycling Strategy*
—— (1996b) *Transport: The Way Forward* Cmnd 3234

Department of Environment, Transport and the Regions (DETR) 1997–2001
Department of Transport, Local Government and the Regions (DTLR) 2001–02

DETR (1998a) *A New Deal for Transport: Better for Everyone* Cm 3950
—— (1998b) *A New Deal for Trunk Roads in England*
—— (1998c) *Breaking the Logjam: The Government's Consultation Paper on Fighting Traffic Congestion and Pollution through Road User and Workplace Parking Charges*
—— (1998d) *Modern Local Government; In Touch with the People* Cm 4310
—— (1999a *20mph Speed Limits and Zones* Traffic Advisory Leaflet 09/99
—— (1999b) *From Workhorse to Thoroughbred: A Better Role for Bus Travel*
—— (1999c) *Towards an Urban Renaissance* (Final report of the Urban Task Force chaired by Lord Rogers of Riverside)
—— (2000a) *Guidance on Full Local Transport Plans* (LTP1)
—— (2000b) *PPG3 Housing* [Revised as PPS3 2006]
—— (2000c) *PPG11 Regional Planning* [Revised as PPS11 2004]
—— (2000d) *Tackling Congestion and Pollution: The Government's First Report Under the Road Traffic Reduction (National Targets) Act 1998*
—— (2000e) *Tomorrow's Roads – Safer for Everyone: The Government's Road Safety Strategy and Casualty Reduction Targets for 2010*
—— (2000f) *Transport 2010: The 10 Year Plan*
—— (2001) *PPG 13: Transport*
DTLR (2001) *Planning: Delivering a Fundamental Change* (Green Paper)

Department for Transport (DfT) since 2002

DfT (2002a) *Delivering Better Transport: Progress Report*
—— (2002b) *Powering Future Vehicles Strategy*
—— (2002c) *Flexible Transport Services*
—— (2003a) *Managing Our Roads*
—— (2003b) *The Future of Air Transport* Cm 6046

—— (2004a) *Evaluation of Rural Bus Subsidy Grant and Rural Bus Challenge*
—— (2004b) *Feasibility Study of Road Pricing in the UK*
—— (2004c) *Full Guidance on Local Transport Plans*; Second Edition
—— (2004d) *Technical Guidance on Accessibility Planning in Local Transport Plans*
—— (2004e) *The Future of Rail* Cm 6233
—— (2004f) *The Future of Transport: A network for 2030* Cm 6234
—— (2004g) *The National Safety Camera Programme – Three Year Evaluation*
—— (2004h) *Walking and Cycling: An Action Plan*
—— (2005a) *Concessionary Fares Schemes: Explanatory Notes on the Provisions of the Transport Act 1985*
—— (2005b) *Final Guidance on LTP1 Delivery Reports (2006)*
—— (2005c) *Financial Planning Guidelines for LTP2*
—— (2005d) *Kickstart Bus Funding: Guidance on the 2005 Competition*
—— (2005e) *Making Campaigning for Smarter Choices Work: Guidelines for Local Authorities*
—— (2005f) *Making Residential Travel Plans Work: Good Practice Guidelines for New Development*
—— (2005g) *Public Local Inquiries into Road Proposals*
—— (2005h) *Public Service Vehicles Accessibility Regulations 2000: Guidance*
—— (2005j) *The Government's Motorcycling Strategy*
—— (2005k) *Transport, Wider Economic Benefits and Impacts on GDP*
—— (2005m) *Travelling to School Initiative: Findings of the Initial Evaluation*
—— (2005n) *Using the Planning Process to Secure Travel Plans*
—— (2005p) *Technical Guidance on Accessibility Planning in Local Transport Plans*
—— (2005q) *Regional Funding Allocations: Guidance on Preparing Advice*
—— (2006a) *A Guide to Transport and Works Act Procedures*
—— (2006b) *Guidance on Agreements with the Secretary of State under s278 of the Highways Act 1980*
—— (2006c) *Guidance on Value for Money*
—— (2006d) *High Occupancy Vehicle Lanes* Traffic Advisory Leaflet 3/06
—— (2006e) *Putting Passengers First: The Government's Proposals for a Modernised National Framework for Bus Services*
—— (2006f) *Region's Advice on Transport Regional Funding Allocations – The First Round*
—— (2006g) *Regional Spatial Strategies: Guide to Producing Regional Transport Strategies*
—— (2006h) *Setting Local Speed Limits* Circular 01/2006
—— (2006j) *Transport Innovation Fund (Productivity)*
—— (2006k) *Transport Innovation Fund; Guidance January 2006*
—— (2006m) *Transport, Wider Economic Benefits and Impacts on GDP*
—— (2007a) *ATM Monitoring and Evaluation* [results of 6 months trial; superceded by report with same title on 12-month trial published in July 2008]
—— (2007b) *Delivering a Sustainable Railway* Cm 7176
—— (2007c) *Guidance for Local Authorities Seeking Funding for Major Transport Schemes*
—— (2007d) *Guidance on Second Local Transport Plan (LTP) Progress Reports 2008*
—— (2007e) *Local Transport Planning: The Next Steps*
—— (2007f) *Low Carbon Transport Innovation Strategy*
—— (2007g) *Manual for Streets* London, Thomas Telford
—— (2007h) *Planning and the Strategic Road Network* Circular 2/07
—— (2007j) *Review of the Community Rail Development Strategy*
—— (2007k) *Second Review of the Government's Road Safety Strategy*
—— (2007m) *Strengthening Local Delivery – Modernising the Traffic Commissioner System*
—— (2007n) *The Essential Guide to Travel Planning.*
—— (2007p) *The Local Transport Bill: Improving Local Bus Services Draft Guidance*
—— (2007q) *The Local Transport Bill: Outline Guidance on Governance Reviews and Publication of Governance Schemes*
—— (2007r) *The NATA Refresh: Reviewing the New Approach to Appraisal*
—— (2007s) *Towards a Sustainable Transport System* Cm 7266

—— (2008a) *Advanced Motorway Signalling and Traffic Management Feasibility Study*
—— (2008b) *Delivering Choice and Reliability* Speech by Ruth Kelly 4 March
—— (2008c) *Local Bus Service Support – Options for Reform* Consultation Paper
—— (2008d) *Roads – Delivering Choice and Reliability* Cm 7445
—— (2008e) *Supporting the Development of TIF Packages*
—— (2008f) *The NATA Refresh Summary of Responses*
—— (2008g) *Delivering a Sustainable Transport System*
—— (2008h) *Consultation on Local Transport Plan 3 Guidance*
—— (2008j) *RFA Transport Advice : Supplementary Note*
—— (2008k) *Draft guidance to regions on delivering a sustainable transport system*

Office of Deputy Prime Minister (ODPM) 2002–06
Department of Communities and Local Government (DCLG) since 2006

ODPM (2003a) *Making It Happen: Thames Gateway and the Growth Areas*
—— (2003b) *Making the Connections* Report by the Social Exclusion Unit
—— (2003c) *Preparing Community Strategies: Government Guidance to Local Authorities*
—— (2003d) *Sustainable Communities: Building for the Future*
—— (2004a) *PPS11: Regional Spatial Strategies*
—— (2004b) *PPS12: Local Development Frameworks*
—— (2005a) *Local Development Framework Monitoring: A Good Practice Guide*
—— (2005b) *Local Strategic Partnerships: Shaping their Future*
—— (2005c) *Planning Inquiries into Major Infrastructure Projects: Procedures* Circular 07/2005
—— (2005d) *PPS1: Delivering Sustainable Development*
DCLG (2006a) *Guidance on Changes to the Development Control System* Circular 01/2006
—— (2006b) *PPS3: Housing*
—— (2006c) *Strong and Prosperous Communities: Local Government White Paper* Cm 6939
—— (2007a) *Creating Strong, Safe and Prosperous Communities Statutory Guidance: Draft for Consultation*
—— (2007b) *Development of the New LAA Framework: Operational Guidance*
—— (2007c) *Eco-towns Prospectus*
—— (2007d) *Guidance on Transport Assessment*
—— (2007e) *Homes for the Future*
—— (2007f) *Lyons Inquiry into Local Government: Place Shaping – A Shared Ambition for Local Government*
—— (2007g) *Planning for a Sustainable Future* Cm 7120
—— (2007h) *Streamlining Local Development Frameworks: Consultation* (includes draft revised PPS 12)
—— (2008a) *Community Infrastructure Fund: Round 2 Bidding Guidance*
—— (2008b) *Eco-towns – Living a Greener Future*
—— (2008c) *The Community Infrastructure Levy*
—— (2008d) *Regional Spatial Strategy and Local Development Framework: Core Output Indicators – Update 2/2008*

Other Government Departments

Cabinet Office (2001) *Your Region Your Choice* Cm 5511
HM Treasury (2003) *Appraisal and Evaluation in Central Government*
DfES and DfT (2003a) *Travelling to School: An Action Plan*
DfES and DfT (2003b) *Travelling to School: A Good Practice Guide*
OFT (2003) *Guidance on the Competition Test (Bus Service Regulation)*
HM Treasury et al. (2004) *Devolving Decision-making: A Consultation on Regional Funding Allocations*

Defra et al. (2005) *Securing the Future: UK Government Sustainable Development Strategy*
HM Treasury et al. (2005) *Regional Funding Allocations: Guidance on Preparing Advice*
HM Treasury (2006) *The Stern Review: The Economics of Climate Change*
Defra (2007) *The Air Quality Strategy for England, Scotland, Wales and Northern Ireland*
DfES (2007) *Home to School Travel and Transport Guidance*
DIUS (2007) *Tackling Obesities: Future Choices* Project Report by Government Office for Science
DTI (2007) *Meeting the Energy Challenge: A White Paper on Energy* Cm 7124
DTI et al. (2007) *Review of Sub-national Economic Development and Regeneration*
HM Treasury (2007a) *Business Rate Supplements: A White Paper* Cm 7230
HM Treasury (2007b) *PSA Delivery Agreement 5*
BERR and DCLG. (2008a) *Prosperous Places: Taking Forward the Review of Sub-national Economic Development and Regeneration*
BERR and DCLG (2008b) *Prosperous Places: The Governement Response to Public Consultation*
HM Treasury (2008) *The King Review of Low Carbon Cars, Part II: Recommendations for Action*
HM Treasury et al (2008) *Regional funding advice : guidance on preparing advice*

Welsh Assembly Government (WAG) and Transport Wales

WAG [Documents accessible at http://new.wales.gov.uk]
—— (2001a) *Plan for Wales*
—— (2001b) *The Transport Framework for Wales*
—— (2002) *Planning Policy Wales*
—— (2004) *People, Places, Futures; The Wales Spatial Plan*
—— (2005) *Local Development Plans Wales*
—— (2006) *Connecting Wales* (Consultation document on Wales Transport Strategy)
—— (2007a) *Guidance on Regional Transport Plans*
—— (2007b) *Transport* Technical Advice Note 18
—— (2008a) *Local Vision: Statutory Guidance on Developing and Delivering Community Strategies*
—— (2008b) *One Wales: Connecting the Nation – the Wales Transport Strategy*
Transport Wales (2008) *Welsh Transport Planning and Appraisal Guidance* (WelTAG); accessible at http://new.wales.gov.uk/topics/transport/publications/weltag?lang=en

Scottish Office, Scottish Executive and Transport Scotland

Scottish Office (1998) *Travel Choices for Scotland* Edinburgh, TSO
—— (1999) NPPG17 *Transport and Planning*
Scottish Executive [Documents accessible at http://www.scotland.gov.uk]
—— (1999) *Guidance on Local Transport Strategies and Road Traffic Reduction Reports*
—— (2002) *Scotland's Transport; Delivering Improvements*
—— (2003) SPP17 *Transport and Planning: Maximum Parking Standards, Addendum to NPPG17*
—— (2004a) *National Planning Framework for Scotland*
—— (2004b) *Scotland's Transport Future* (White Paper)
—— (2005a) *Modernising the Planning System* (White Paper)
—— (2005b) *Scotland's Transport Future: Guidance on Local Transport Strategies*
—— (2006a) *Scotland's National Strategy – a Consultation*
—— (2006b) *Scotland's National Transport Strategy*
—— (2006c) *Scotland's Transport Future: Guidance on Regional Transport Strategies*
—— (2007a) *Draft Regulations on the Planning Hierarchy*
—— (2007b) *Draft Regulations on Development Planning: Consultation Paper*
—— (2007c) *Draft Regulations on Development Plan Examinations*
Transport Scotland (2008a) *Scotland Transport Appraisal Guidance* (STAG); accessible at http://www.transportscotland.gov.uk/node/3171
—— (2008b) *Strategic Transport Projects Review*

Index

A303/A358 assessment of options 360–1
access charges (rail) 132–3, 395
accessibility: role in future planning 437;
    significance of land use pattern 33, 35; to
    bus stops/services 15, 255; to facilities 35,
    181, 185; to motorway network 19; to
    rail stations 15; see also rural accessibility
accessibility (personal) 184–5, 407, 430
accessibility planning 340
accidents (road), see road safety
accountability 144–5, 170–1, 376
active traffic management 225, 388–90
Adonis, Lord 427
affordability 365
age: structure 26–8; relationship to travel
    42–3
agenda-setting 176, 182
agglomeration effects, see wider benefits
air quality 55–6, 60, 180, 235–7
Air Quality Action Plans 236–7;
    Management Areas 56, 236; Strategy
    235
aircraft noise 54
Alexander, Douglas 159, 397
Annual Progress Reports, see Local
    Transport Plans
appeals 372
appraisal 82, 194, 204, 348–65; criticisms of
    current approach 431, 437
Appraisal Summary Table (AST) 349–50
Area Action Plans 320
Area-Based Grant 328–9
arterial roads 75, 91
assessment (eg of road schemes), see
    appraisal; environmental assessment
Association of Commuter Transport 261
Association of Transport Coordinating
    Officers (ATCO) 92, 220, 399
attitudes (public) 59–63, 259–61, 418
Audit Commission 327; National Audit
    Office 129, 388

backcasting 415
Banister, David 433
Barker Review (housing: 2004) 402;
    (planning: 2006) 374–5
Barnes, Alfred 80
Beeching Report (1963) 83–4
Beeching, Dr Richard 82–3
Begg, David 127, 138
behavioural change measures 258–73, 410,
    417; future importance 434–6
BERR 163, 302
Best Value, see performance assessment
better use measures (roads) 420, 431
Better Use of Town Roads (1967) 93
bio-fuels 412, 414, 417
Blair, Tony 123, 129, 135, 162
Blears, Hazel 162, 326
British Railways Board 81–2, 168
British Road Services 77
British Transport Commission 76, 82–3
brokerage, see community transport
Brown, Gordon 132, 162, 197, 244, 418
brownfield sites 136
Brundtland Report (1987) 133
Buchanan, Sir Colin 87, 438
Buchanan Report (1963) 87–9, 91, 93, 224,
    247
Bus and Coach Council 122
bus industry 74, 166, 211–12
bus lanes, see bus priority
Bus Partnership Forum 219
bus priority 216, 224, 227, 229
bus rapid transit 104
Bus Service Operators Grant, see fuel duty
    rebate
Bus Strategy (LTP) 217
bus use: targets 189–90; trends 21, 39–41, 47
buses: fares 214–6, 252; Kickstart funding
    253; London 216, 252; quality
    partnerships/contracts 127, 216–17, 395,
    398–400; registered services 214–16, 218,

221; regulation/deregulation 99–100, 214–16, 218, 397–9; service levels 16, 18, 20–1; tendered (subsidised) services 213, 216, 219, 252, 256

Buses (White Paper) 1984 99–100, 211, 216

business rates 98, 150, 199, 397

business travel zones 441

Byers, Stephen 133, 159

by-passes 86, 111, 118, 180

Cabinet 144

Campaign for Better Transport 390

canals 69, 76, 83

Canary Wharf (London) 106

capital receipts 199

car availability 24–5, 29, 44

car clubs 231, 264, 270–1, 442

car dependency 259

car occupancy 46

car ownership 22–5, 28, 259, 270; case for lessening individual ownership 438–9; de-marketing the private car 442; *see also* company cars

car use: effect of car ownership/availability 44, 259, 440; trends 39

carbon pricing/trading, *see* Stern Review

car-free developments 271, 439

Castle, Barbara 84

catalytic converters 55, 208

Channel Tunnel 102, 151, 193

Channel Tunnel Rail Link (CTRL) 102–3

Cheap Trains Act (1883) 71

children: freedom to cross roads 52; travel to school 38, 43–4, 269; trip-making 42, 53, 259; *see also* personal security

choice (in decision-making) 361; (travel) 116, 184, 259–60, 440

churn 263

city cars 442

Civil Service 144, 157, 163

Clarke, Kenneth 115

Cleaner Vehicles Task Force 127

clearways 87, 230

climate change 114, 183, 340, 411, 434; public attitudes 417–8

Climate Change Act (2008)/Programme 412–3; Committee 413

CO_2 emissions 58–9, 61, 155, 188, 428–9; potential reductions 414; projections 412; targets 190, 340, 438; *see also* global warming

coach services 20, 97, 212; scope for development 444–5

Commission for Integrated Transport (CfIT) 127, 137–8, 168–9, 188, 414–5

Common Inheritance (White Paper) 1990 113–15

community charge (poll tax) 98

Community Infrastructure Fund 404

Community Infrastructure Levy 403–4

community involvement, *see* Community Strategies, public consultation

Community Planning Partnerships (Scotland) 324

Community Rail Partnerships 250

Community Strategies 129, 281, 323–6

community transport 181, 221–2

company cars 22, 44, 245

compensation principle 204

competition 151, 210–13

Competition Act (1998) 211

Competition Commission 163, 211

comprehensive (re)development 78, 90–1

Comprehensive Area Assessment, *see* performance assessment

Comprehensive Spending Review: (2000) 130; (2004) 138–9, 202, 392, 404 (2007) 397, 405, 425

Concessionary Bus Travel Act (2007) 254

concessionary (bus) fares 92, 127, 154, 165, 180, 253–6

Confederation of British Industry 107, 132, 197

congestion *see* traffic; targets 177, 189–91

congestion charging scheme: Central London 135, 248; Greater Manchester 393; (*see also* road user charging

Conservative Party 394, 400

Controlled Parking Zone (CPZ) 230, 246; *see also* parking on-street

Core Strategy (in LDF) 319, 321

corridor assessment (of road proposals) 117–18; *see also* Multi-modal studies

cost-benefit analysis 80–2, 195–6, 202–5, 339, 354–60, 421, 430; *see also* appraisal; wider economic benefits

costing of schemes 354–6, 380

counter-urbanisation 27–8, 33–4

county councils 174

County Surveyors Society 80

CPRE 77

Crosland, Tony 93

CrossRail (London) 103, 397

cycling: casualty rates 51; historical development 71, 73; National Cycling Strategy 119; policy 95, 273; to school 44; tracks/segregated paths 53; trends in use 39–41, 47

Darling, Alisdair 133, 138, 159, 162, 244, 248, 391, 397, 418

DCLG 159
de minimis (tendered bus services) 219
DECC 163
decision-making 276–7; *see also* planning; planning process
decriminalised parking 231, 246
DEFRA 159
Delivering a Sustainable Railway (White Paper) 2007 395
Delivering a Sustainable Transport System (2008) 427–9
demand management 112, 115, 122, 184, 223, 245, 393
demand responsive services/transport 220
density: of development 33, 136; of settlements, *see* population
DETR 123, 159
de-registration, *see* buses: registered services
Design and Access Statement 238
de-trunking (roads) 125
developer contributions 121, 199, *see also* Section 106 agreements
development (statutory definition) 312–3
development control 77–8, 237–8; application for planning permission 370–3
Development Plan Scheme 317
development planning (Scotland and Wales) 322
development plans/planning 78, 89, 104–5, 120–1, 137, 238, 280, 303, 312–23, 405, *see also* spatial planning
devolution 128, 164–6, 168, 280, 282, 293
DfT 203–5, 262, 330, 349; current 'vision' 405–7; organisation structure 163–4
dial a ride, *see* demand-responsive transport
Disability Discrimination Act (1995) 209, 249
disabled people 154, *see also* concessionary fares
discount rate 205
discrimination (anti-) 154
distribution (of welfare) 151–2, 180–1,196, 204, 242
distributional effects 364
distributor roads 88
Docklands Light Railway 15, 103, 106
DOE 81
Dorling, D and Thomas, B 32
driver licensing 209
driving test 209
DTLR 159
DVLA 208

economic activity 30–2
economic development 196–7, 199, 402, 405
economic efficiency 147, 180, 203–4

economic recession (2008) 429
eco-towns 403
Eddington Study (2006) 374–5, 390–1, 400, 405, 418–21; Government response 425
Education Act (1944) 256, (1980) 256
Education and Inspections Act (2006) 257
efficiency (of travel) 179
elections 145
employment, *see* economic activity
employment location 34
energy conservation 95
enforcement 177, 225, 231, 268; *see also* speed cameras
enterprise zones 106
Environment Act (1995) 119, 235
environmental areas/capacity/traffic management 88, 234
environmental assessment 110, 117, 321, 338, 366
environmental issues 180, 366
equity 151, 204, 242; equality of opportunity 430
European Union 177, 199, 321
Eurostar, *see* CTRL
Examination in Public (in RSS) 368–9
executive agencies 168–9
external effects ('externalities') 148–9

fares, *see* buses, railways
fiduciary duty 98, 367
forecasting 351–3
forecasts (traffic) 419, 422
freedom to travel 146, 154, 181
freight transport (trends) 11–12, 47–8
Freight Transport Association 132
Freightliner 84
Friends of the Earth 119, 390
fuel consumption 58, 208
fuel duty 243–4, effect of 2000 changes 137; escalator 115, 127, 132, 162, 243; protests 132; RCEP recommendations 114; resource conservation 155
Fuel Duty Rebate (buses) 127, 251–2
functional areas/regions 27, 174–5
funding: growth areas 403–4; local transport plans 334–7, 340; major schemes 343, 380–3, *see also* RFA
Future of Air Transport (White Paper) 2003 138
Future of Rail (White Paper) 2004 394
Future of Transport (White Paper) 2004 138–9, 186, 189–90, 197, 283, 390–1

goals, *see* objectives
goods vehicles, *see* freight transport
Goodwin, Phil 125, 408, 434

grants for transport investment 89–90, 98, 328–9
Great Debate (1995) 118–9
Greater London Authority (GLA) 171
Greater London Authority Act (1999) 304
Greater London Council (GLC) 89, 90–1, 98–9
Greater London Development Plan (GLDP) 89, 91
green belts 85
growth areas, *see* Sustainable Communities Plan
growth points, *see* Homes for the Future
Gummer, John 115–16, 118

hard shoulder running, *see* active traffic management
Hatfield rail crash 133
health/fitness 184–5 *see also* obesity
Heathrow Express 103
Heseltine, Michael 103, 105
Hickman and Banister 415, 433, 436
High Level Output Specification (rail) 396–7, 426
Highway Code 225
Highways Act (1980) 238, 372–3, 376
Highways Agency 119, 168, 228–9, 231, 388–9; consultation on development applications 237, 239; position at public inquiries 374; scope for developing services 445
HM Treasury 162, 167, 348, 408
Home Office 163
home shopping 264–5
home zones 181, 234
Homes and Communities Agency 294
Homes for the Future (2007) 402–3
Hoon, Geoff 162, 429
House of Commons: Environmental Audit Committee 244; Transport Select Committee 131, 169, 250, 391, 393
households: car ownership 22–5; income 23, 30, 39; size, composition 29, 32
housing (new), *see* Homes for the Future
HOV lanes 227, 394
Human Rights Act (1998) 154
Humber Bridge 179

ICT, *see* telecommunication
ideology 96, 177
indicators, *see* monitoring
individualised travel marketing, *see* personalised travel planning
induced traffic, 118
information (to consumers) 149, 271–2
infrastructure (to serve development) 403–4

Infrastructure Planning Commission 375–7
inner cities 105
Integrated Regional Strategy 303
Integrated Transport Authorities 401
integrated transport block, *see* LTP funding
integrated transport studies 121–2
integration (land use and transport) 125, 139, 183–5, 320–1, 350, 368, 400, 430, 435; *see also* PPG13
integration (political) 177
integration (transport administration) 401
interchanges (urban periphery), *see* park and ride
InterConnect (Lincolnshire) 219
inter-generational equity 205
inter-urban roads: impact on development location 435
inter-urban travel: need to confront 'business as usual' 443
investment 192–202; future national investment 427, 429; large investments 151; *see also* programmes, railways, roads
issues 176–81, 183–5; contemporary Government focus 431–2

journey times, *see* travel
journey to school, *see* school transport; travel plans (school); scope to promote non-car use 440
Jubilee Line (London) 106

Kelly, Ruth 159, 389, 392, 394, 396
Kickstart, *see* buses
King Review (2008) 417
Kyoto Protocol 58–9

Land Compensation Act (1973) 91, 153
land use 33–5, 48
land use/transportation studies 87, 89, 121
land use planning 135, 284; *see also* town planning; spatial planning; PPG13
Levett, Roger 375
licence holding (driving licence) 24
licensing: of vehicles 208, drivers 209, operators 210
lift-giving (longer distance journeys) 444–5
Lifting the Burden (White Paper) 1985 105
Light rail 104, 137, 166; ownership 167; targets for use 189–90
Light vans: trends in use 47
Livingstone, Ken 98, 135, 248
Local Area Agreements 325–8
Local Development Framework 316–22
local government: past reorganisation 89, 92, 99; present pattern 170–5; current reform 400–2; sub-regional collaboration 400–1

Local Government Act (2000) 129, 323
Local Government and Public Involvement in Health Act (2007) 326
Local Government in Scotland Act (2003) 324
Local Government, Planning & Land Act (1980) 106
London Amenity and Transport Association 91
London Mayor 128, 135, 165, 171, 305
London Passenger Transport Act (1933) 75
London Traffic Management Unit 86
London Transport 75, 83, 98–9, 135, 216; *see also* Transport for London
lorries: charging scheme 132; size and weight 208
Low Carbon Vehicle Partnership 208
Low Emission Zone 237
low-carbon technology 412, 414, 417
Lyons Inquiry (2007) 400–1

M1 80, 107, 394
M25 106–7, 110–11, 194, 229
M42 (Birmingham) 81, 389
Macdonald, Lord 'Gus' 130–1
MacWhinney, Brian 118
major schemes 343, 368
Major, John 109, 117
Managing Our Roads (Green Paper) 2003 138, 194, 228
MARKAL-Macro model 413–4
market failure 147
marketing 271–3
markets 146–7
Marples, Ernest 80, 83, 86
Meeting the Energy Challenge (White Paper) 2007 412–4
Merron, Gillian 273
metro systems, *see* light rail, Underground
Metrolink (Manchester) 104, 166
metropolitan areas 170, 175
Metropolitan County Councils 90, 98–9
Midlands Expressway (M6 toll) 168, 194
Midland Metro 104
Miliband, Ed 163
Milton Keynes/South Midlands 174, 410, 447
minibus permit, *see* community transport
minicabs, *see* taxis
Ministry of Transport 75, 79, 81
mobility 179; personal 24–5, 28, 43, 181
mode share, *see* travel
modelling, *see* forecasting
monetised impacts, *see* cost-benefit analysis
monitoring 187–8, 298, 315, 323, 341–3
monopolies: natural 151, 193; territorial 211–12

motorcycling 209–10; casualty rates 51–2; trends in use 40–1
motoring costs, *see* transport costs
motoring taxation 243–5
Motorists Forum 169
motorways: casualty rates 51; development of network 13, 80–1, 94, 107–8, 154, 177; impact on employment location 34; scope for increasing passenger throughput with less traffic 444–5; share of road traffic 48–9; widening 388–9, 394
Multi-Area Agreements 328–9, 402
multi-criteria analysis 431
Multi-Modal Studies 125, 137–8, 263, 388

NATA 184, 203, 205, 349–50; Refresh 430–1
National Bus Company 100, 168
National Cycling Network (NCN) 119, 127, 273
National Cycling Strategy 119, 127
National Freight Corporation 84
National Network Strategy Group 427–8
national planning 281–2
National Planning Framework (Scotland) 288
National policy statements, *see* Planning Act 2008
National Road Traffic Forecasts (NRTF) 107, 110
National Transport Model (NTM) 263, 351, 419, 434
nationalisation 166–7
needs assessment 98
network management 228
Network Rail 133, 167, 198, 213, 394–5
New Deal for Transport (White Paper) 1998 123–7, 132, 135, 139, 183–4, 189, 254, 283
New Labour 124, 165, 189, 198, 324, 331, 341
New Realism (1991) 112–13
new settlements 105, *see also* eco-towns
New Towns 34, 84–5
Newbury By-pass 110, 118
NIMBYism 105, 110
noise (from traffic) 53–5, 60, 180; mitigation 91
Non-Departmental Public Bodies 168–9
non-metropolitan areas 170, 175
Nottingham Express Transit 246

obesity 177, 181, 269, 273, 434
objectives 182–6, 300, 361; current Government proposals 429–30; in LTPs 339–41
Office of Fair Trading 163, 211–12
ODPM 136, 159

oil prices 95, 132, 244, 434; *see also* transport costs
older people 42–3; *see also* concessionary fares, personal security
one-way (traffic) systems 227
opportunities, *see* accessibility; choice
OPRAF 101
optimism bias, *see* costing of schemes
out-of-town development 105–6
outputs/outcomes 187
Overground (London) 249

package approach 122
parish/town councils 170
park and ride 246; case for development 445–6
parking (on-street) 87, 93, 224, 229–31, 245
parking charges 245
parking standards (in new development) 239–41, 246, 440
Parkinson, Cecil 114
particulate traps 208
partnerships (public/private) 151, 167, 198
Passenger Transport Authority (PTA)/ Executive (PTE) 15, 89–90, 99–100, 166, 171, 217, 249, 395, 401
Patten, Chris 110
peak hours (travel) 36–7
pedestrianised areas 52, 86, 226, 234
pedestrians, *see* walking
Pedestrians Association 73
performance assessment (of local authorities) 129, 187–9, 325–7, 334, 341–2
performance indicators, *see* monitoring; targets
personal security 53, 188
personalised travel planning, *see* travel plans; case for extending scope 442
place-shaping 281, 314; *see also* spatial planning
planning: for longer term 409–48; nature of 276–82; see also development planning, spatial planning, national planning
Planning & Compensation Act (1991) 120
Planning and Compulsory Purchase Act (2004) 137, 286, 299, 313, 322
Planning Bill (2007)/Act (2008) 375–7, 404
planning data, *see* forecasting
Planning etc (Scotland) Act 2006 288, 322
Planning for a Sustainable Future (White Paper) 2007 375
planning gain, *see* developer contributions
Planning Gain Supplement, *see* Community Infrastructure Levy
planning obligations, *see* section 106 agreements

planning permission, *see* development control; Infrastructure Planning Commission
Planning Policy Guidance/Statements 284; PPG13 (Transport) 115–17, 136, 239, 270, 284; PPG/PPS3 (Housing) 115, 135, 240–1, 270; PPG/PPS6 (Retail and Town Centres) 115; PPS11 (Regional Planning) 294, 300, 368 PPS12 (Local Development Frameworks) 318–9, 321, 368
planning/study process 277–8, 361–2, 425–7
PNR (private non-residential) parking, *see* parking standards
police, *see* enforcement
policy layering 130, 139, 392, 408
Policy Unit (Prime Minister's Office) 125
'polluter pays' principle 149
pollution, *see* air quality
population 26–9, 33
precautionary principle 155
precincts, *see* pedestrianised areas
predatory practice (bus industry) 212
'predict and provide' 109
Prescott, John 123–4,128–9, 134, 136, 159
pressure groups 176
Prevention of Ribbon Development Act 1935 77
prioritisation (of schemes): in LTPs 339; regional 363, 377–8; use of CBA 359
private bill procedure 372
private finance 150, 197–9
private hire vehicles, *see* taxis
privatisation 97–8, 166, 177, 280
problems 361–3
programmes 279, 283, 301, 307, 323, 339
PRT (personal rapid transit) 410
PTEG 398
public consultation/participation 89, 299, 317–9, 326, 332–4, 363, 366, 431; *see also* Infrastructure Planning Commission
public expenditure 93–100, 111, 130, 165, 177, 187, 197, 200, 251; *see also* Comprehensive Spending Reviews
public goods 150
public inquiries 81–3, 372–4
public opinion 145, *see also* attitudes
public ownership 157, 167, *see also* nationalisation
Public Sector Borrowing Requirement (PSBR) 97, 197
Public Service Agreements 189, 324–5, 405; PSA5 (2008–11) 405–7
public transport: attitudes towards 61; information 148; trends in use 40; use by age and gender 42–3
punctuality, *see* reliability

Putting Passengers First (2006) 397

quality of life 114, 130, 418, 429–30
quality partnerships/contracts, *see* buses
quantified risk assessment 356
quiet lanes, *see* rural roads

RAC Foundation 390, 421–5
Rail Regulator 126, 212–13, 394–5
rail use: targets 189–90; trends in passenger
    use 16, 22, 40–1; trends in rail freight
    47–8
RailTrack 100–101, 132–3, 166
railways: accessibility to rail stations 15;
    business sectors ('sectorisation') 97;
    changes in service levels 20; closures
    83–4, 97, 395; development of network
    15–16, 19, 69–71, 73; fares 61,214,
    249–51; franchising of services 101,
    151, 211–15, 395; High Level Output
    Specification 396–7, 426; investment
    137, 201–2, 396, 427; Modernisation
    Plan (1955) 83; nationalisation 76; open
    access 102, 151, 212; overcrowding
    61; privatisation 100–101, 213; Public
    Service Obligation grant 92; safety 50,
    133; station (re-)opening 15; subsidies
    89, 151–2, 249, 395–6; *see also* reliability,
    Beeching and Serpell Reports
Railways Act (1993) 101, 213; (2005) 394–5
ramp metering 229
real-time information 148, 216
Red Flag Act (1865) 71
red routes 230
Rees Jeffreys Road Fund 111
reference case, *see* forecasting
regional assemblies 128, 165–6, 293–7, 303
regional development agencies 128, 165–6,
    199, 293–4, 303
regional economic strategy (RES) 296
regional funding allocation (RFA) 377–9,
    388
regional infrastructure fund (South-West
    region)
regional offices (of Government) 164,
    293–4, 299, 317, 325, 377–8
regional planning body (RPB) 299–301, 303
regional planning guidance (RPG) 120, 136,
    293
regional spatial strategy (RSS) 137, 293–300
regional sustainable development framework
    296
regional transport consortia (Wales) 306–8
regional transport partnerships (Scotland)
    308
regional transport plans (Wales) 306–7

regional transport strategies (RTS) (England
    outside London) 136, 293, 300
regional transport strategies (Scotland) 308
regions (England) 164
registered services *see* buses
reliability and punctuality 21, 61, 190
residential development: design, road layout
    52, 57; scope to reduce car ownership
    and use 439–40; *see also* travel plans
    (residential)
residents' parking schemes 230
resource conservation 155, 180
retail development (location) 35
revenue support payments 89, 92, 94, 98, 253
ribbon development, *see* suburban
    development
Ridley, Nicholas 105
right of way 154
rights 153–4
ringways (London), *see* urban motorways
Rio Summit 114
Ripa di Meana, Carlo 117
road classification 75
road haulage licensing 76–7, 84
road hauliers' blockade (2000) 132, 177
Road Improvement Asociation 72–3
Road Improvement Fund 72, 75, 243
road pricing, *see* road user charging
Road Pricing Feasibility Study (2004) 138–9,
    248, 391
road safety: targets 187–8, 190; trends in
    casualties 49–52, 233
Road Safety Strategy 231
road service licence (buses and coaches) 74,
    76, 100, 214
Road Traffic Act (1930) 74; (1991) 231
Road Traffic Reduction Act (1997) 119;
    (National Targets) Act (1998) 130, 188
road user charging: local 127, 134–5, 247,
    436; national 138, 390–2, 420, 423–4
roads: development of national network
    13–14, 19, 68–9, 71; environmental
    impact /objections 57, 81–2, 110, 159;
    future road-building 423–5, 433–5;
    inter-urban roads programme 75, 80–2,
    94, 106–7, 111–12, 387–390; public
    attitudes towards new road-building 60;
    road hierarchy 49, 86, 88, 224; *see also*
    motorways
Roads and Reality (2007) 421–5
Roads for the Future (White Paper) 1969 80
Roads for Prosperity (White Paper) 1989
    106–8, 114
roadspace reallocation, *see* street
    management
Rogers, Lord Richard 135

rolling stock (rail) 197–8
route utilisation studies (rail) 194, 214
Royal Automobile Club 72
Royal Commission on Environmental
    Pollution 114, 116, 119–20
rural accessibility/transport 13, 15, 16, 23, 32,
    92, 179, 220–2
rural bus services: subsidies 153, 219; Rural
    Bus Challenge 221, 252; Rural Bus Fund
    127; Rural Bus Services Grant 252
rural railways 249–50
rural roads and traffic 48–9, 55, 60, 224,
    232–4; quiet lanes 234

SACTRA reports: induced traffic 118;
    strategic environmental assessment 117;
    transport and the economy 421
safety 149–50 *see also* railways, roads
scenarios 415–7, 420, 423–4; *see also* planning
school transport 256–7 ; scope for promoting
    increased non-car use 440; *see also* travel
    plans;
school-run 36, 269
Scotland planning 281–2
Scotland's Transport Future (White Paper)
    2004 287
Scotlands' National Transport Strategy (2006)
    287
Scottish Office 164
Scottish Parliament 128, 165, 254
SEA directive, *see* sustainability appraisal
Secretary of State 158, 162
section 106 agreements 237–8, 268, 404;*see
    also* developer contributions
section 278 agreements 238
security (national) 177
segmentation (of travel market) 261, 272
Serpell Report (1982) 97
SERPLAN 120
settlement pattern 27: *see also* counter-
    urbanisation, population, land use
settlement size: relationship with travel and
    car use 42
severance 52, 57, 61, 180, 182
shared priorities, *see* objectives (LTP)
signs (roads) 223, 225, 231
Single Capital Pot 327
Single Outcome Agreement (Scotland) 310
Smarter Choices (2004) 263–271, *see also*
    behavioural change
social car schemes, *see* community transport
social contract 151
social enterprise 222
social exclusion/inclusion 30, 125, 139, 181,
    185
Social Exclusion Unit 125, 159, 253

socially necessary services 92, 181, 216, 218,
    220–1
soft measures *see* behavioural change
spatial planning 280–1, 314–5: England
    284–5: Wales 286; Scotland 288–9
Special Roads Act (1949) 80, 154
speed cameras 232–3
speed limits 71–3, 231–3, 441; *see also* active
    traffic management
STAG 346, 349, 431
stakeholders, *see* public consultation
standards 153, 180
State: nature 144–6; role 146–57
stated preference techniques 353
Statement of Community Involvement (SCI)
    317
statistical sources 6
Stern Review (2006) 411–12; Government
    response 425
Stonehenge (A303) 13, 155
Strategic Development Plan (Scotland) 323
strategic national corridors 427–8
strategic planning 94, 293–310; English
    regions 293, 303; London 304
Strategic Rail Authority (SRA) 125, 213, 394
street management 234–5
Strong and Prosperous Communities (White
    Paper) 2006 325
structural maintenance 193, 199–200
students and young adults 23, 31, 37, 42, 52
sub-national planning 289–91
Sub-National Review 302, 400, 402
subsidiarity 280
suburban development 73, 77
Supertram (Sheffield) 104, 167
sustainability appraisal 366
Sustainable Communities Plan (2003) 136–7,
    402
Sustainable Community Strategies; *see*
    Community Strategies
sustainable development 113–15, 125, 139,
    155, 213, 302, 314, 366, 435
Sustainable Development Strategy (UK)
    115–16, 189
Sustainable Travel Demonstration Towns
    272–3
Sustrans 119

TAG (transport analysis guidance) 349,
    361–2, 431; supplementary analyses
    363–66; worksheets 354–7
targets 186–91, 297, 327; in LTPs 340–2
taxis: origins 70, 73; licensing 220; trends in
    use 41; use of bus lanes 227
telecommunication 36, 179, 410
teleworking/conferencing 264–5, 267

Ten Year Transport Plan (White Paper) 2000 130–1, 137, 189, 199–201, 283; 2004 Review 139

tendered network zones 220, 399; *see also* rural bus services

tests of soundness (development plan documents) 368–9

Thames Gateway 103, 304, 447; *see also* growth areas

Thameslink 2000 103

Thatcher, Margaret 95, 98, 102, 105, 109, 113, 134

tolled lanes (on motorways) 394, 444–5

tolls 150, 194

Towards a Sustainable Transport System (White Paper) 2007 425–8

Town and Country Planning Act (1947) 77; (1968) 104; (1990) 226, 238

town planning *see* development planning, spatial planning

traffic (road): distribution between classes of road 48–9; noise 53–5; perceived danger 52, 181, 188; trends in volume and composition 46–9; speeds (journey times) 21; *see also* congestion, road safety, rural roads and traffic, speed limits

traffic calming 233–5

Traffic Commissioners 74, 92, 210, 214–16, 221–2

Traffic in Towns (1963) *see* Buchanan Report

traffic management 86–7, 89, 93, 224–6; *see also* network management; demand management

Traffic Management Act (2004) 228; Traffic Manager/Director 228

traffic reduction 262–3, 423, 437–8; targets (national) 114, 119, 139. 188

traffic regulation order 225–6

traffic signals *see* traffic management

traffic wardens 87

Tramlink (Croydon) 104

trams (historical development) 73–4, *see also* light rail

tranquil areas 55, 57

transfer payments (cost-benefit analysis) 356

transport: effect on land use pattern 10, 13, 48; link with economic development 9–12, 48, 418–9; technical innovation 409–10

Transport (Scotland) Act (2000) 165; (2001) 287; (2005) 287, 308–10

Transport (Wales) Act (2006) 285, 306

Transport Act (1947) 76; (1953) 77; (1962) 83; (1968) 84, 89, 92–3; (1980) 97, 99, 214; (1985) 100, 214, 220, 253; (2000) 134, 137, 154, 217–18, 234, 253, 271, 331, 372

Transport and Climate Change 2007 414–5

Transport and Works (Scotland) Act (2007) 372

Transport and Works Act (1992) 372, 376

transport assessment (of development proposals) 239–40

transport costs: of supply 133, 137, 249, 252, 388; to users 11, 18–22,

Transport Direct 127, 271–2

Transport for London (TfL) 167, 171

Transport Innovation Fund (TIF) 202, 392–4

transport planning: England (exc London) 282–3; London 305; Scotland 287–8; Wales 285–6

Transport Policies and Programmes (TPP) 90, 121, 126

Transport Policy (Consultation Paper) 1976 94; (White Paper) 1977 94

Transport Scotland 168, 287

Transport Supplementary Grant (TSG) *see* grants

Transport Wales 168, 285

travel: 'decoupling' from economic growth 12; effect of economic development 10–11

travel behaviour (trip-making): actual 36–44; prospective 410; mode share 39–44; relationship to income and car availability 44; trip duration/journey times 38, 63, 179; trip length 11, 34, 41, 42; trip purpose 37–8, 41

travel: plans 239, 264–72; personalised 272; residential 270, 439; school 264–5,269–70; workplace 267–8, 441

travel substitution (prospective) 410

Travelwise 261

trial areas *see* Transport Act 1980

trunk roads: origins 75; proposed redefinition of national roads 427; transfer to local authorities 111

Trunk Roads Act (1936) 75

Trunk Roads Reviews: (1994 and 1995) 111; (1998) 125

turnpike trusts 69, 71

Twyford Down (M3) 13, 110, 117

Tyne & Wear Metro 94

uncertainty 155, 186, 351, 380, 409–11, 419, 434

Underground (London) 166–7, 188, 198

unitary councils 171, 174–5

urban containment 33–3, *see also* green belts

Urban Development Corporations 106, 136

urban motorways 87, 90–1

urban rail schemes 94
urban regeneration 121; renaissance 135; renewal 79, 86, 90
Urban Task Force 135
urban traffic control (UTC) 224
urban transport planning 88–92

value for money 203, 248, 353–60
value of time 358
VAT 243–4
Vehicle and Operator Services Agency 210
Vehicle Excise Duty (VED) 127, 133, 208, 243–4
VIBAT Study (2006) 415–7
Vigar, Geoff 119
Villiers, Theresa 400
visual intrusion 57

Wales planning 281–2
Wales Spatial Plan 286
Walker, Peter 81

walking: casualty rates 51; freedom of movement/severance by traffic 52; mobility difficulties 43; perceived danger from traffic 52–4; policy 95, 127, 273; trends in use 40
Way Forward (Green Paper) 1996 119
Welsh Assembly 128, 165, 254, 285
Welsh Office 164
Welsh Transport Forum 285
WelTAG 349
Westway (London) 91
wider economic benefits 392, 421–2
Wing Bypass (Bucks) 118, 431
Wolmar, Christian 133, 396–7
women: economic activity 31; escorting children 38; licence-holding 24; *see also* personal security
Workplace Parking Levy 127, 134, 246, 393, 441

yellow (school) buses 257